ANANDAMURTI

The Jamalpur Years

BY THE SAME AUTHOR

Felicitavia
When the Time Comes
The Ashram
Devi

ANANDAMURTI

The Jamalpur Years

Devashish

InnerWorld Publications
San Germán, Puerto Rico
www.innerworldpublications.com

Copyrigh 2010 by Devashish Donald Acosta

All rights reserved under International and Pan-American Copyright Conventions. Published in the United States by InnerWorld Publications, PO Box 1613, San Germán, Puerto Rico, 00683.

Library of Congress Control Number: 2010906904

Cover Design © Lourdes Sánchez (Mukti)

No part of this book may be reproduced or transmitted in any form or by any means, electronic or mechanical, including photocopying, recording, or by any information storage or retrieval system, without permission in writing from the publisher, except for the inclusion of brief quotations in a review.

ISBN 9781881717102

Barackpur, December 1960

Contents

Preface   ix

Part One

I. An Old Soul   1
II. School Days   7
III. Kalikananda   17
IV. Accounts Department: 1941–1947   23

Part Two

V. The Early Disciples   41
VI. The Death of Stalin   57
VII. The First Gathering   61
VIII. Death Demonstration   65
IX. Now Many People Will Come   72
X. Bindeshvari's new lease on life   78
XI. A Philosophy Takes Shape   84
XII. Samkalpa   90
XIII. Prachar   97
XIV. The Circle Widens   106
XV. Demonstration Year   122
XVI. Divine Madness   131
XVII. Problem of the Day   138
XVIII. Tantric Guru   147
XIX. A Place of Awakening   164
XX. A Civil Ceremony   172
XXI. For the Welfare and Happiness of All   179
XXII. To The Patriots   187
XXIII. A Family Relationship   193
XXIV. The Tiger's Grave   214
XXV. Personal Contact   230

Part Three

XXVI. Revolutionary Marriage	243
XXVII. A Monastic Order Begins	258
XXVIII. The Search for the City of Bliss	277
XXIX. Education, Relief, and Welfare	288
XXX. Past Lives	303
XXXI. In The Office	322
XXXII. Last Years In Jamalpur	339
XXXIII. Departure	361
Epilogue	365
Selected Bibliography	373
Glossary	374
Notes	377

Preface

ONE DAY IN 1969, a small group of disciples got together with the idea of writing a biography of their guru, Shrii Shrii Anandamurti, whom they affectionately called Baba.[1] When they sat down and started writing, however, they realized how little they really knew about his life. So they decided to approach him and request him to write his autobiography. At first Baba refused, protesting that he had no time for such things. But after repeated supplications, he finally acquiesced to their pleas. The next day, at the regular Sunday gathering, the same disciples were surprised when Baba announced that he had finished his autobiography. "Do you want to see it?" he asked. His curious devotees looked at one another, wondering how he could have possibly finished it so quickly, even at the tremendous speed with which the master customarily worked. Baba called them over to his cot and handed them a sheet of paper. On it they found a single sentence written out in longhand: "I was a mystery, I am a mystery, and I shall always remain a mystery."

This was typical of Anandamurti, who throughout his life insisted on staying out of the public eye so that he could concentrate on his work—the establishment of a global mission for spiritual elevation and social change. In his earlier years, he would often say that he did not want a cult of personality but rather a cult of ideology; true to his word, he took great pains to deflect the attention of his followers from the guru worship that had become so deeply rooted over more than seventy centuries of Indian cultural history. Indeed, he was a spiritual master unlike any who had gone before him on the Indian subcontinent, as much a social revolutionary as a spiritual guru. He did not allow his disciples to simply enjoy his company while they practiced meditation in a search for spiritual enlightenment. He entrusted to them a social mission, and he would not allow anything to distract them from that mission, not even their understandable fascination with his own person.

How then does one begin to reveal the mystery of who he was, when he went to such pains to conceal himself? The obvious answer is that one does not. Anandamurti left no testament of his inner experience, no hints at what lay behind the gaze that so enchanted his disciples, no real way of knowing who he was, other than through discovering who we ourselves truly are. What he did leave, however, was his imprint on the lives of so many thousands of people, the impact of which still continues to reverberate throughout our planet. This biography, then, is the story of Anandamurti as seen through the eyes of those who knew him—his disciples, family, friends, and colleagues—in the hope that through that open window the reader may be able to catch a glimpse of the man standing behind it.

In one of his messages to his disciples, Anandamurti said, "I have merged myself in my mission; if you wish to know me, then serve my mission." Indeed, it is in many ways impossible to separate Anandamurti from his missionary endeavors and the ideology he left behind. His life was a reflection of his ideology, and there is no better teaching of the ideological principles meant to guide human beings in their lives than the life of the spiritual master who embodied those principles. I would go so far as to claim that the inverse of his oft-repeated message is equally true: If you want to know the mission, then try to know the life of the master who embodied its spirit with every breath he took.

A note of thanks:

The information contained in this book was primarily drawn from the oral histories of Anandamurti's colleagues, friends, family, and disciples, as well as from various written sources published during and after his lifetime. Most of it has been recast in narrative form, interspersed here and there with passages quoted directly from the interviews. I would like to thank all of the several thousand people, too numerous to thank individually, who sat patiently for these interviews and shared their reminiscences. Some of what they shared was personal and for that reason was kept out of this book. Other material was left out for lack of space, but all of it has been faithfully preserved for future generations. I hope they are aware of the incalculable value of their contribution and how much it is appreciated.

PART ONE

1

An Old Soul

The future of humanity is not dark. I have this faith. Human beings will seek and one day realize that inextinguishable flame that remains ever-burning behind the veil of darkness.[1]

> I am in my mother's womb. From there itself I can see my mother; I recognize her so well. I see my father, my sister, and my other relations. How well I know them; I know their names also.
> I am born. Normally children weep at birth. I don't. I am all smiles. In fact, I am happy to be born. I want to address the people around me by their names because I know them so well. But alas, how incapacitated I am! My vocal cords do not permit me to speak yet. They want to feed me. They have put a piece of cotton in a cup containing milk. Drop by drop, they drop milk from the cotton into my mouth. How silly of these people! Am I a child, to be fed in this manner? I shall drink from the cup, not the cotton. I protest and raise my hand to hold the cup. They are taken aback at what I have done. I realize that I have done much to perplex them, and I return to being a newborn child.
>
> —Anandamurti's earliest memories, as recounted to Amitananda in the winter of 1969 in Ranchi.

OUTSIDE THE HOUSE of Lakshmi Narayana Sarkar and his wife, Abharani Devi, the small town of Jamalpur was springing to life at the beginning of a hot summer day—May 11, 1922.[2] Temperatures were expected to reach forty degrees Celsius in the shade; hence, most of the town's inhabitants were already busy, taking advantage of the cool morning air to accomplish as much as they could before walking through the dry, scorching streets became a chore best avoided. Here and there, the town's few Buddhists were busy with their worship on this, the most important day of their year, the full moon in the month of Vaishak,[3] commemorating the birth of the Buddha. A few hundred kilometers away in the town of Bodh Gaya, site of the Buddha's enlightenment, pilgrims from around the world were burning incense and chanting mantras to celebrate the birth of the enlightened one with the rising of the sun.

Inside the modest three-room house, tucked into a small plot on a side street off the main Keshavpur road, the family of Bengali immigrants, together with visiting relatives, had been busy for hours, preparing for the birth of the couple's fourth child. They were all hoping for a son, most of all Lakshmi Narayana. Several days earlier, he had had a vision that his wife would finally give birth to the male heir he had long hoped for, so important in the Hindu tradition, and he was sure that his vision had been a true foretelling. His family had already endured its share of sorrowful births. His second daughter had died when she was two and a half. His third child, a boy, had died in childbirth. Only his oldest daughter, Hiraprabha, had survived, a gentle, quick-witted seven-year-old who was already showing the talent for music that would give her parents many hours of happiness in the years to come. This birth, the vision had promised, would be different. He would have a son who would survive him and make him proud, and he was eager to see his wish come true.

Abharani Devi's contractions had begun late in the evening, light but steady. As the first rays of dawn began to appear through the open windows, the female members of the family gathered around her bed in anticipation, just as thousands of pilgrims in distant Bodh Gaya began to blow on conch shells and place offerings before images of the Buddha. At seven minutes past six, with the two elderly matriarchs of the family assisting, the grandmothers Indumati Mitra and Vinapani Sarkar, a ruddy-cheeked infant boy was born, the scarlet rays of the rising sun reflecting on his body through the open windows. In keeping with the family tradition, Indumati held a silver cup with fresh milk. She dipped some cotton into it and began to feed the baby drop by drop. To the surprise of everyone, the newborn infant reached out his hand and grabbed the cup, as if trying to drink directly from it. Vinapani gasped and exclaimed, "He's not a baby, he's a *burha*, an old soul." From then on, whenever she saw her favorite grandchild, she would call him "Burha," fondly recalling that unusual moment.

Later that morning, Lakshmi Narayana, a devout Hindu who would frequently host religious discussions in his house with the local pundits and visiting holy men, invited some astrologers to his home to prepare the boy's horoscope. By common consent, they named the child Prabhat Rainjan,[4] after the rising sun with which he was born and in keeping with the horoscope, which foretold an illustrious future for the newborn infant. The reading they gave for the family members, however, was contradictory and puzzling. The chart foretold that the boy's name would become known throughout the world, bringing great fame to his father and family, but it also showed that he would have little to do with them. He would have the qualities of a king, but he would pass his life like a sadhu, a spiritual renunciant, spending all his time with monks and yogis.

The astrologers' reading greatly disturbed Lakshmi Narayana. There was a troubling history in his father's family of male members renouncing the world to become wandering ascetics, and he did not wish to see his eldest son and heir become a monk. After due thought, he decided to burn the horoscope. He banned any discussion of it among his family and friends, despite the fact that he could read the portents in the boy's chart almost as ably as the astrologers could and had always trusted the accuracy of this ancient Hindu art. Still, he would not fan the flames of an unwelcome future if he could help it. The family would heed his wishes until well after his death, when it became clear that the astrologers had correctly foretold the boy's future. The incident with the cup, however, passed into family lore. The elders of the family never tired of recalling how the infant Prabhat had tried to drink directly from the cup only moments after his birth.

Other unusual experiences would soon be added to the list of favorite family stories. During his first year, Prabhat was painfully conscious of not being able to walk, his unresponsive body forcing him to crawl in order to move around, his elbows and knees full of aches and pains. Yet, whenever he became dejected, wondering how much longer he would be forced to suffer such indignities, he would hear a voice speaking clearly into his ears, consoling him, "Some days more, just a few days more; I know you are in trouble, but just a few days more." He would look around, wondering who was talking to him, but there was never anyone to be seen. As he learned to walk and became more comfortable with his body, the voice became less frequent and finally disappeared, but he never forgot the comfort it gave him.

Late one night, when the two-year-old Prabhat was sleeping by his mother's side, he woke up to find the space around him filled with a sweet and soothing effulgence. A sense of rapture carried him away until he lost all sense of where he was. A few nights later, he woke up again and saw a multitude of different creatures streaming out of his left ear. The fascinated boy sat up on the bed and watched as they danced about the room. But when they crowded next to his other ear and started entering back in, it seemed so fearsome that he gave a shout and grabbed hold of his mother. As she rubbed her confused and sleepy eyes, he began describing the host of creatures he had witnessed coming out of his ear: reptiles, mammals, birds, insects, human beings. Abharani consoled him that it was only a dream and told him to go back to sleep. But the same dream repeated itself over and over again in the days and weeks that followed. Sometimes the boy would wake his mother up and warn her to beware of the creatures, as if he were still seeing them dancing around him in the room.

Abharani marveled at the scope of her son's overactive imagination. She wondered if the child might have seen pictures of those creatures, though there was no such book in the house. At other times, he would see stars, planets, and galaxies streaming out of his ear instead of living creatures. As the dreams continued, they gave her cause for concern. Sometimes she would complain to her husband and other relatives and friends that her boy was a weakling who was frightened by nightmares; at other times, she would joke with them that it seemed like the whole universe was coming out of one ear and into the other. But as time went on, she started searching for other explanations. She even took him to several Tantrics to see if they could use their occult arts to tell her what was going on with her son, but none of their explanations were enough to satisfy her.

Other strange dreams followed. One morning, Prabhat told his mother that during the night he had seen a far-off village on fire and a group of sannyasis running away from it. When the news reached her of the fire and the sannyasis a couple of days later, she realized that what her son had seen had not been a mere dream but a vision. This helped to fuel her growing conviction that the boy she had given birth to was no ordinary child.

One day she got in an argument with her mother-in-law, Vinapani Sarkar, over something that had happened a few years earlier. The argument stalled briefly while both of them struggled to recall exactly what had taken place that day. Prabhat helped to jog their memory. "I remember that incident," he told them matter-of-factly. He then reminded them of the details they had forgotten.

"How do you know that?" his astonished grandmother asked him. "You were not even born then."

"I know, that's all," was his laconic reply.

Abharani simply smiled. In the years to come, whenever one of her other children would ask her a question she could not answer, she would say, "Ask Bubu.[5] He knows everything. Whatever I don't know, he knows."

By this time, Prabhat was already becoming quite independent, despite his tender age. As a toddler he had been rather mischievous, sometimes exasperating his mother to the point that she would run after him, intent on spanking him to teach him a lesson. The light-footed Prabhat invariably scampered away and stayed out of his somewhat portly mother's reach until she calmed down. Then he would snuggle up to her and she would take him on her lap, all forgiven. But as he grew older, his restless nature gradually settled. He began to spend most of his time outside, exploring the neighborhood or playing with friends. He had, by then, developed an attraction for the stories of Shiva, father of the yogis, that he would hear from his parents and relatives. He especially loved the colorful descriptions of the great god's magnanimity and detachment. Though he knew little of religion and rituals, he obtained a Shiva lingam, and each morning before breakfast he would bathe it while reciting whatever mantras he had heard his elders using and then place it on a brass plate.[6] Once he got the lingam straight, he would consider it a sign that Shiva had accepted his worship.

From time to time, Prabhat would sit and watch a group of mendicants who gathered regularly on a nearby hillock to chant devotional hymns in a circle around a holy fire. Many townspeople, with the natural reverence for wandering monks that was common in those days, would also join in the chanting.

While Prabhat enjoyed listening to the mendicant's hymns in praise of Shiva, he found the mendicants themselves less than appealing. He disliked their habit of smoking hemp in pipes. With the quick eyes of a child, he noticed how their minds seemed to be more on the delicious foods the pious townsfolk would bring for them than on their meditation. One day, to test them, he stole up to the edge of their circle while they were meditating and silently snatched some sweets that an old woman had left for them. Several of them jumped up from their meditation and started to give chase, but Prabhat had already mapped out his escape: up a nearby alley and down behind some public latrines where he knew the caste-conscious monks would never follow. After that, he lost whatever illusions about the monks he might have had and would annoy them whenever he had a chance.

Around this time, another recurring dream began. One night he dreamt that he was in the midst of a powerful storm. The storm lifted him up and carried him through the air until it dropped him rudely on a wide sandbank by the edge of the river Ganges, filling his eyes and mouth with sand. He wiped the sand out of his eyes, and when he opened them, he saw a mendicant standing in front of him with a trident in his hand. The mendicant began reciting a long mantra; then he asked Prabhat to repeat the mantra after him.

"No!" Prabhat shouted.

"Recite it, my son," the mendicant insisted. "It will be good for you."

"No, under no circumstances shall I recite it."

The mendicant lifted his trident. "You will have to recite it."

"No, never! I will never recite it!"

At that moment the storm arose again and lifted him up into the air. It carried him away and dropped him back onto his own bed, at which point he awoke. He realized then that it had been just a dream, but the incident remained fresh in his mind for the rest of the morning.

For twenty consecutive nights Prabhat had the same dream; soon he had memorized the mantra, not because he had made any effort to do so but simply because he had heard it so often. In the meantime, however, the boy began to feel a sense of desperation. He considered it a matter of disgrace that every night the mendicant scared him by menacing him with his trident, and yet he had done nothing about it. Finally, he resolved that if he had the same dream again that night, he would put an end to the charade. The dream unfolded again, exactly as it had the previous twenty nights, but this time, when the mendicant brandished his trident and warned the boy that he would have to recite the mantra, Prabhat snatched the trident and threw it at him. He heard a loud thwack. When he looked, the mendicant was gone; in his place stood a stone statue of Shiva. The sound he had heard had been the sound of the trident rebounding off the statue. There was a smile etched on the statue's face and Prabhat felt that Shiva was smiling joyfully at him. At that moment the dream broke and Prabhat found himself in his bed, perspiring. The dream did not return again.

Prabhat told the story to his sister, who as usual was fascinated by her brother's colorful dreams. By this time, it was only a few days until Shiva Chaturdasi, the foremost Shiva festival in the Hindu calendar. Unmarried Hindu girls traditionally fast on this day, in the hope that their fast will induce Shiva to find them a noble bridegroom. Hiraprabha, by then nearly twelve, also decided to fast in keeping with the tradition. Remembering her brother's dream, she suggested that he fast as well, and he happily agreed. That evening the family visited the nearby Shiva temple to perform their traditional worship. When it was Prabhat's turn, he stood in front of the idol and poured water over the Shiva lingam as prescribed in the ritual. As he did, he started reciting loudly the mantra he had heard in his dream.

Dhyáyennityam mahesham rajatagirinibham cárucandrávatamsam
Ratnákalpojjvalámgam parashu-mrga-varábhiitihastam prasannam
Padmásiinam semantic stutamamaraganaervyághrakttim asana
Vishvádyam vishvabiijam nikhilabhayaharam paincavaktram trinetram[7]

One should meditate constantly on Maheshvara, radiant like a silver mountain adorned with the lovely moon/Whose limbs are bright like the splendor of jewels, axe in hand, protector of animals, bestower of boons, the ever-blissful one/Seated in lotus posture, wearing a tiger skin, worshipped by the gods/The seed and cause of the universe, who removes the boundless fears, the one with five faces and three eyes.

The local priest was astonished. He went up to Lakshmi Narayana and congratulated him enthusiastically. "You must be commended for teaching your son such a difficult and important mantra. I could scarcely believe my ears to hear such a young child reciting the *dhyana* mantra of Shiva."[8] An equally surprised Lakshmi Narayana had to profess ignorance. It was only when he asked Prabhat about it that he discovered how he had learned the mantra. Due to this incident, Prabhat's parents became convinced that there was a special bond between their boy and the god Shiva. For the next few years, they made sure that Prabhat observed the traditional Shivaratri worship, including the recitation of the sacred mantra that he had learned in his dream. The story of Prabhat reciting that difficult and little-known mantra as a child was another that would pass into family lore, often repeated by his neighbors during the coming years whenever anyone would ask them about the Sarkars' unusual son.

II

School Days

You must have a flaming moral purpose so that greed, oppression and exploitation shrivel before the fire in you.[1]

BY THE TIME Prabhat turned five, he'd begun his lifelong practice of sitting for meditation early in the morning and again in the evening. No one in the family knew when he had started this practice or how he had learned it, nor would he say, but by then the family had learned to leave the independent-minded young boy alone about such matters.

Nearly as unusual was his refusal to eat any non-vegetarian food, despite the fact that his family was not strictly vegetarian. Like most Bengali families, the Sarkars ate fish and on infrequent occasions other non-vegetarian items. When Prabhat was still a toddler, he used to weep quietly whenever his grandmother brought live fish from the market and began preparing it. When they first noticed this, they thought something was wrong with the boy, but when they saw that he only reacted this way when they brought live fish to the kitchen, they stopped doing so.

The Sarkar family followed the Indian tradition of feeding their children a vegetarian diet until they reach the age of four or five, in accordance with the popular belief that the delicate digestive system of a young child is not ready for meat, fish, or eggs. When Prabhat reached the socially approved age for eating non-vegetarian food, they attempted to feed him fish but he refused to eat it. His parents didn't mind all that much. A large section of the society was vegetarian, for both religious and health reasons, and as good Hindus they conceded the value of a vegetarian diet. Indeed, his mother rarely ate any non-vegetarian food.

Prabhat's grandmother, however, had quite a different reaction. For centuries, people in Bengal have believed that fish promotes the growth of the brain and stimulates intelligence, a tradition that Bengali grandmothers have carried on proudly through the ages. Vinapani grew increasingly exasperated with her favorite grandchild, who refused to eat what he was served. She tried cajoling the boy, telling him how important fish was for the brain. "You don't want to grow up to be stupid, do you, just because you won't eat fish?" None of her entreaties, however, were able to move her intransigent grandson. Finally one day at dinner, fed up with Prabhat's stubbornness, Vinapani forcibly shoved a piece of fish into his mouth. Prabhat spit it out on the dining table. "You foolish boy!" his grandmother said. "Do you want to be a dolt all your life?" Prabhat got up from his chair and told his grandmother that if she or anyone else ever tried to force him to eat non-vegetarian food again, it would be the last time he would sit at the family table for a meal. Then he turned around and went to his room, shutting the door behind him. Neither his grandmother nor his mother ever brought up the subject again. Prabhat would live the rest of his life without ever once swallowing a morsel of non-vegetarian food.

It was at this age that Prabhat started attending the Bengali primary school, where he soon earned the nickname "encyclopedia" for his prodigious memory and his seeming ability to answer any question the other boys put to him. During the four years he spent there, his personality underwent a slow, almost imperceptible metamorphosis from a gifted, fun-loving child into a quiet, far-seeing youth whose hidden depths set him apart from the rest of the boys in ways that often took more than a second glance to notice. Bihar in those days was the most caste-conscious state in India, a place where going against the deeply ingrained mores and behavioral rites of Hindu society was practically unthinkable, especially in a small town such as Jamalpur where failure to observe caste proscriptions was certain to bring immediate reprobation. Prabhat's family followed the orthodox practices, just as every Hindu family did, but Prabhat in his quiet way gradually made it clear that he shared none of their caste consciousness.

One day he invited a scheduled-caste boy to his room and they sat together on his bed. Abharani didn't say anything while the boy was there, but once he left, she rebuked her son and complained to him that she would have to wash the bedsheet and pillowcase as enjoined by the scriptures, since they were now polluted. Prabhat listened to her without saying a word. After she had removed the sheet and the pillowcase, he grabbed the mattress and the pillow, took them outside to the washbasin, and started immersing them in water.

"What on earth are you doing?" Abharani shouted.

"Since you say that everything is polluted," Prabhat replied, "then these are also polluted. I am washing them as well."

His exasperated mother tried to make him understand his foolishness. "That is not necessary," she told him. "We have to wash the pillowcase and the bedsheet because the boy touched them, but we only need to sprinkle some Ganges water on the mattress and the pillow."

"No," Prabhat replied, continuing to wash the mattress and pillow, "if you say that the bedsheet and the pillowcase are polluted, then everything is polluted."

His mother tried to argue with him, but she had no success. Finally she threw up her hands and exclaimed, "It is very difficult to convince you of anything!"

On another occasion, Prabhat was sitting on the porch in front of his house. There was an empty platform across the road where people from the neighborhood would often gather to chat or play cards. A member of the so-called untouchable class, who was walking along the road, stopped and asked Prabhat if he had seen a certain person or knew where he might find him. He addressed Prabhat as "Khokha Babu," (little gentleman). Prabhat was surprised to see that the man stood on one leg while he asked his question and remained in that posture while he waited for his reply.

"I know who he is," Prabhat said, "but I don't know where he might be at this moment. Please come and sit on the bench. You can wait for him here if you like."

"Khokha Babu," the man replied, "I cannot do that. There is a rule that a low-caste person has to remain in this position whenever he goes to a big man's house."

Prabhat requested him several times, but the man would not sit or put down his leg. The injustice of the custom angered Prabhat, but he knew the futility of saying anything more at that moment, so he held his tongue. When the man left, however, he swore to himself that he would fight this ugly tradition and help to put an end to it one day.

Throughout Prabhat's childhood, the family paid frequent visits to Lakshmi Narayana's native village of Bamunpara, especially during the hot summer vacation when the abundant vegetation and open spaces provided a cooling respite from the unremitting heat of Jamalpur. Summer was mango season and Bamunpara was full of mango trees, as well as papaya, banana, jackfruit, guava, and many other delights that made the Sarkar children look forward all year long to their Bamunpara vacation. Like most Indian children, they adored sitting in the cool canopied shade of those huge arching trees, sipping the sweet, juicy flesh of its tree-ripened fruit. Afterwards, they would run off to play with the village children and roam the fields that ringed the village. Prabhat also loved mangos, but while his siblings were playing, he would often seek out the shade of those same trees for long sessions of silent meditation or go for long, solitary walks through the fields or to the neighboring villages.

At other times, he would spend hours reclining on a cot with his eyes open, staring off into space. On one of those visits, his sister Hiraprabha, then fourteen and a sensible young woman, asked her seven-year-old brother what he was doing lying down all day. "I'm reviewing the history of the universe," Prabhat told her, an answer that did little to please his sister. The next day she asked him again. This time he replied, "I am watching what is going to happen on this planet after a thousand years." Finally, Hiraprabha got fed up with her lazy younger brother. She started taunting him for his idleness. "There you are, wasting your time doing nothing; you still haven't even learned how to write your own name in your mother tongue." Prabhat looked at her for a few moments with his typical silent smile. Then he went to a drawer, pulled out a piece of paper and a pen, and wrote out his name in ten different scripts, including English, Arabic, and a number of different Indian scripts. His sister was so startled when she saw this that she flew away like a frightened bird and avoided her brother for the remainder of their vacation.

Years later, while giving dictation to one of his disciples, Vijayananda, Prabhat reminisced about that vacation in Bamunpara. He told him that while he was lying on his cot, supposedly idling away his hours, he was busy planning out his life's work, which would include his fight against the caste system and other social evils. It was during that vacation, Prabhat said, that he devised the coming structure of Ananda Marga, the socio-spiritual organization that he would found in 1955, more than twenty-five years later. Then he went to his desk and pulled from a drawer a yellowed piece of paper that he smoothed out on the desktop in front of his disciple. The faded writing, still clearly visible, contained an outline of the organization he would later create.

In 1930, Prabhat was admitted into the East India Railway High School, where he would continue his studies through matriculation. The boy that entered the railway high school was now very different than the boy who had entered primary school a few years earlier. While the rest of the boys were, on the whole, boisterous and restless, Prabhat's quiet demeanor and thoughtful way of speaking set him apart. When one word would do, he would never use two. He was friendly with everyone but did not take part in the typical merriment during free time and recess. He kept to himself, either sitting under the large pipal tree in the courtyard with a book or on the veranda, although whenever any skirmishes broke out or the boys used uncouth language, he was quick to get up and intervene. From time to time, other boys would approach him to discuss one topic or another, often concerning problems they were having with their schoolwork, but mostly they respected his love of solitude.

Prabhat's reputation for being able to answer anyone's questions followed him from primary school; here also, it became a common practice among the other students to send him anyone who had questions no one else could answer. One afternoon, he and his classmates were sitting around a table during recess looking at a new geography book that had just arrived. Prabhat flipped through the pages along with everyone else. Then he closed the book and challenged them to ask him any question from any page. The other boys jumped to the challenge. They opened the book so that he couldn't see it and started asking questions. One by one, he answered them all correctly. They were impressed but they had seen this before. Vimalendu Chatterjee, however, who had recently moved to Jamalpur from a small village in the Silhet district of East Bengal, had not. When he expressed his surprise, Prabhat asked him the name of his village and then proceeded to describe it in minute detail, right down to the division of the rice fields and the placement of the wells. The more Prabhat went on, the more astonished Vimalendu became. Everything was exactly as Prabhat described it. "But how can you know all that?" he finally burst out. Prabhat gave a little grunt, as if in disgust. "You people don't study," he said. "That's why you don't know these things." It was only some years later that Vimalendu realized that the information Prabhat had described so accurately wasn't found in any book.

After school, Prabhat would accompany the other boys to the fields outside of town, but instead of participating in their games, he would disappear into the nearby hills, generally reappearing before dusk to accompany his classmates back to town. In those days, the Kharagpur Hills were the gateway to a wilderness that few townspeople dared enter. It was two miles from the edge of town to the beginning of the stony ascent into the chiseled granite hills that had served for centuries as the natural southern defense for Monghyr, seven kilometers to the north, the ancient capital of the kingdom of Anga. Between the town and the hills lay many acres of spacious meadows and shady trees, as well as a natural reservoir that ran along the foot of the hills for several kilometers. Adults would go there to walk and children to play, except for the expansive areas to the east that belonged to the Railway Institute, off-limits to Indians in those days.

Beyond the reservoir, a long, narrow valley jutted into the mountain range, a forested area named Death Valley by local inhabitants in memory of a fierce battle fought centuries before in which over a thousand warriors had died and been left as carrion for the many wild animals that lived there. In those days, Death Valley and the Kharagpur Hills were a subject for whispered conversations. Wild animals lived there, tigers had been spotted, and, according to some, the ghosts of the dead warriors still roamed the woods, unable to find peace and haunting the footsteps of anyone who dared enter their forbidden domain. On the opposite side of the reservoir from Death Valley, hundreds of stone steps had been carved into the mountainside. At the top of the twenty-minute ascent, in the shadow of the forest, stood two old temples: a Kali temple, from which the hill got its name of Kalipahar; and a Shiva temple, a couple of hundred meters further on, beyond which nobody dared go. The ascent to the Kali temple was breathtaking. Halfway up, one could see all of Jamalpur. From the top, on a clear day, it was possible to see past Monghyr, on the banks of the Ganges, to the Gangetic plains beyond. On weekends and religious holidays, pious pilgrims from Jamalpur and Monghyr would climb to the Kali temple to worship before the image of the Divine Mother and tie ribbons on the branches of the ancient, gnarled bel tree behind the temple. It was said that Mother Kali would grant the wishes of those who left ribbons for her on her favorite tree, and every pious-hearted mother of Jamalpur had a son or a daughter who needed the Divine Mother's favor. But once the sun started dipping towards the tree line in late afternoon, Kalipahar would become deserted, for it was well known that Kali would not promise safe passage out of that wilderness to anyone foolish enough to remain there once dusk set in.

Kalipahar, Death Valley, and the Kharagpur Hills became young Prabhat's private retreat, a vast wilderness that he had practically all to himself. He would sometimes be seen climbing into the hills at the same time that the last of the pilgrims were coming down from the temples. On more than one occasion, well-wishing neighbors who recognized the boy let his father know that they had seen his son wandering in those dangerous hills at an hour when no right-minded person would dare think of going there. When his father questioned him about it, however, Prabhat assured him that the neighbors were exaggerating. He simply liked to walk where it was quiet, so he could think. It was more or less the same answer he gave the other boys when they asked him what he did when he went there, though by then many of them were aware of his habit of searching out solitary places to meditate. Sometimes he would bring a bamboo flute with him and spend hours sitting in the hills exploring the different scales and variations of Indian music. Sometimes it was a friend's esraj. On the rare occasions that a friend or two accompanied him on his walks, he would talk of God and ask them to sit and sing the praises of the Divine. One of his friends told him once, "If you keep this up, Prabhat, you're going to become a sannyasi." Many of those who knew him assumed he would.

One afternoon, when Prabhat was eleven, Sachindranath Marik, who lived a few houses away from him and was two years his junior, could no longer contain his curiosity. Together with a couple of friends, Sachin decided to follow Prabhat into the hills. Excited by the prospect of spying on their mysterious elder classmate, the three boys were careful to stay out of sight as they followed Prabhat up a rarely used path that wound precariously up the hill and into the forest. Young boys as they were, they soon became scared, having heard stories about the tigers and other wild animals that supposedly roamed those forested slopes. At the top of the ascent, the path dipped again and disappeared into the trees. No longer able to see or hear Prabhat, none of them dared go any further; they decided to wait for him to come back. Some forty minutes passed. Then Sachin saw something that made him shake his head and stare. He shouted to his two companions and pointed: Downwards from where they were standing, in a clearing among the trees, they saw Prabhat riding at a gentle pace on the back of a tiger. They watched dumbfounded as he got down from the tiger's back, patted it a few times, and watched it stroll off and disappear into the woods.

When Prabhat made it back to where they were waiting, the three of them accosted him at once with questions about the amazing sight they had witnessed. Prabhat immediately denied it. "Are you mad?" he said. "Me, riding a tiger? Nonsense! You had better not repeat such a thing."

Sachin refused to pay heed to Prabhat's adamant denials. When Prabhat still would not admit it, he threatened to tell his mother, a threat that only made Prabhat laugh. "Do you honestly think anyone will believe you?" he said. Sachin didn't listen. When he got back to town, he told both his own mother and Prabhat's mother what he had seen. Naturally, neither of them believed him. Abharani did take the trouble to question her son about it, but Prabhat's indignant reply satisfied her. "Please, mother, do you honestly think I can ride a tiger? They are just making up stories." Sachindranath and his friends were scolded for lying. When Prabhat saw them the next day in school, he rebuked them for telling tall tales. "Whatever scolding you received, you deserved it." After that he avoided them. When they got a chance to ask him why he was avoiding them, Prabhat rebuked them for spreading gossip. "If you talk like that, what will people think of me? Am I an animal that I ride on a tiger's back? As long as you go around saying things like this, I will have nothing to do with you." From then on, they said nothing more about this or any of the other unusual things they noticed about Prabhat, and he gradually resumed his easy friendship with them.

A few years later Sachindranath heard a story about a lady Tantric said to be living in the forest of the Kharagpur Hills. People claimed that she had caught and tamed a tiger with her occult powers. He remembered the incident with Prabhat and realized that he might have been going to the forest to visit her.

Despite Prabhat's denials, his careful reserve, and his marked dislike of drawing any attention to himself, his reputation in Jamalpur, especially among his fellow students, grew steadily. In the winter, when temperatures could drop to three or four degrees Celsius once the sun went down, Prabhat continued to wear shorts and a light shirt, while the rest of the boys wore woolen clothes. When they asked him if he felt the cold, he said, "No. You wrap your bodies with warm clothes, but what about your mind? Do you also cover your mind?"

"But we don't feel cold in our mind."

"Well, the mind is made of the same material as the body. That's the reason I don't feel cold."

Some of the younger boys started following Prabhat around after school hours, accompanying him to the fields and waiting for him to return from the hills so they could walk with him back to town. The parents of one boy, annoyed because their child was coming home late each evening, scolded him for following Prabhat around and asked him to stop. When he complained, they demanded to know what the attraction was.

"I feel good whenever I am near him." he said. "Once, when I saw Prabhat stop on the road, I saw that he was surrounded by a brilliant aura. Anyone who is surrounded by an aura like that cannot be an ordinary human being, can he?"

His parents had no reply to this. After that they made no further objections.

Manoranjan Banerjee, who was several years junior to Prabhat, had often seen him sitting for long hours in the Shiva temple in Keshavpur with his eyes closed, a sight that never ceased to impress him. One day he saw something that amazed him even more:

> One day, when I was studying in class six, a group of four or five bulls started chasing me down a narrow lane. I dropped my books and ran for my life. As I was running, I saw Bubu-da standing at the end of the street. When I reached him, he shielded me from the bulls. Just before they reached him, they suddenly stopped and became as still as statues. I was amazed. Then he asked me to go and pick up my schoolbooks. I was frightened to do so, because in order to reach the books, I had to cross where the bulls were standing. But Bubu-da repeatedly assured me that I had nothing to worry about. They would not harm me. I hesitated, but finally I walked past them and picked up my books. Then I went back to Bubu-da. The bulls didn't move an inch the entire time. After I came back with the books, Bubu-da waved his hand in the direction of the bulls. Only then did they move; they turned around and walked away. This incident made me realize that Bubu-da had some special powers.

Incidents like this and Prabhat's obvious spiritual inclinations lent to his growing reputation among his peers and neighbors as a spiritually elevated young man doted with unusual powers. In the West, people might not have known what to make of him. Most people would have distrusted the stories they heard. But in India, with its long history of yogis and saints, Prabhat was looked upon as another spiritually minded youth following in the footsteps of his illustrious forefathers. His family and most other families in the neighborhood were aware that he was not an ordinary boy. His mother would later say that she secretly considered her young son to be a spiritual genius, but she never brought up the subject, nor did anyone else in the neighborhood. For thousands of years their culture had taught them to respect the privacy of those whose minds were turned towards God, and in a small town in Bihar during the 1930s that tradition was still very much alive.

It was while he was attending the railway high school, that Prabhat had the definitive spiritual experience of his boyhood. He described it for Amitananda years later on that unusual winter evening in Ranchi.

> I have gone to the Jamalpur hills to do meditation. I am sitting at a particular place when I hear a voice whisper in my ear, "Come with me. I will show you a better place to meditate. Follow me." I see no one, but I follow the voice whose presence I feel so clearly. The voice leads me to a particular spot and asks me to meditate. I begin

to meditate. After a while I hear it say, "Are you mad? How long do you want to remain under the spell of maya? Who do you think you are—P. R. Sarkar? Look, see who you are!" In that moment a reel of my past lives flashes before my eyes and I realize who I am.

In the afternoon of January 15, 1934, a terrible earthquake struck Northern India with its epicenter on the border between Nepal and Bihar, some three hundred kilometers from Jamalpur. It measured 8.1 on the Richter scale and left thirty thousand people dead. Monghyr was practically reduced to rubble; Jamalpur, though not nearly as badly affected, suffered extensive damage. The Sarkar house partially collapsed. On the morning of the earthquake, Lakshmi Narayana had left for Calcutta to fix the date of Hiraprabha's upcoming marriage. When he returned the next morning at five o'clock, the entire family was waiting for him in the train station, wrapped in blankets after a night when the temperature had reached a record low. That day he took his eldest boys around with him to survey the devastation. What he saw left him shocked. Despite the damage to his own house, he plunged immediately into full-scale relief efforts, taking leave from his job as an accountant in the Jamalpur railway workshop to treat patients and collect and distribute relief materials.

Prabhat's father was an accomplished homeopathic doctor who for years had spent weekends and holidays in his dispensary attending to long lines of patients—British as well as Indian—many of them dependent on him to keep their families healthy when they could not afford the expensive Western medicines that were slowly replacing traditional Indian healing practices. Now his skill as a doctor was put to the test, with the numbers of sick and injured far too much for the local medical community to handle. Not only did he treat patients, he also collected food, blankets, clothing, and medicine for distribution. Prabhat organized a group of his friends and joined in by his father's side. What was left of the Sarkar house became a storage center for relief materials. In the weeks that followed, the entire family assisted Lakshmi Narayana in his efforts to relieve the tremendous suffering that surrounded them. In recognition of his efforts, the Bihar Government soon put Prabhat's father in charge of the distribution of relief materials for Monghyr District.

After this period of arduous work and little sleep, Lakshmi Narayana's health gradually began to deteriorate. No one was able to diagnose the exact malady, and a trail of different doctors and different medicines began that met with little success. He passed away on February 12, 1936. Prabhat was studying in class nine when his father died, the oldest son but still too young to support the family. His mother received her husband's provident fund from the railways to go along with their savings,[2] but there was no pension for Indian employees at that time and the change in their financial fortunes was drastic. Until then they had been relatively well off by Indian standards. None of them had ever faced any financial hardship, least of all Prabhat's mother, Abharani, who had grown up as the daughter of a well-to-do doctor from the Hooghly district of Bengal and then married into a middle-class family. Once the period of mourning was over, however, she took stock of the situation and instituted the necessary changes in the household so that the family could survive on its drastically curtailed income. The generous spending to which they were accustomed was no longer possible, but she made sure that the children did not want for any of the necessities of life. Neighbors who had been the recipients of Lakshmi Narayana's generosity and kindness came forward to help. His brother, Nirmal Chandra, visited every Sunday to make sure Abharani had what she needed to keep the family going. When Prabhat graduated from high school, he tried to convince his mother to let him find a job, but Abharani would not hear of it. It had been her dream to see Prabhat go to college, and nothing he could say or do could convince her otherwise. Thus it was that in the fall of 1939 the family put Prabhat on a train to Calcutta, where he had been admitted into Vidyasagar College.

III

Kalikananda

Krishna has rightly said: "If even a diehard criminal comes under my shelter, I will save him or her from all sins; I will see to it that the person attains liberation or salvation. Hence no one, no spiritual aspirant—however black or despicable one's past life might be—should be worried about anything."[1]

WHEN PRABHAT ARRIVED in Calcutta at the house of his maternal uncle, Sarat Chandra Bose, to take up his studies in the summer of 1939, the former capital of India was alive with the fervor of independence and the uncertainty of war. Student activism was at its apogee, with most students favoring the radical freedom-at-all-costs stance of Subhash Chandra Bose, President of the Congress Party, while others sided with Gandhi and Nehru's policy of wartime cooperation with the British. Wherever one's sympathies lay, the talk of independence and war was impossible to escape, whether in the classroom, the dining room, or on the street.

Around the time Prabhat arrived in the turbulent metropolis, he began corresponding with various revolutionary leaders in Bengal, such as the radical humanist, M. N. Roy; Shyama Prasad Mukherjee, founder of India's first Hindu nationalist party; Arun Chandra Guha, General Secretary of the Bengal Congress; and Subhash Chandra Bose, who was a distant relative on his mother's side. Prabhat's letters attracted their attention due to his astute analysis of the political situation and the provocative suggestions he made regarding what actions would best serve the nation's interests at that time. When they discovered that P. R. Sarkar was a seventeen-year-old student, some of them were taken aback, but Prabhat was soon invited to closed sessions at M. N. Roy's house with him and other revolutionaries of the time who would help decide the fortunes of the soon-to-be-born nation.[2]

Despite Prabhat's involvement with some of India's radical revolutionary leaders, he did not join any political party or student organization. As in high school, he mostly kept to himself, spending his time outside the classroom either alone or in the company of a few close companions, to whom he made no mention of his relationship with Subhash, M. N. Roy, and others. Among these were his cousin Ajit Biswas, the future actor Rabin Mazumdar, and the future football standout Anil Kumar Dey. Apart from his letters to political leaders, Prabhat wrote articles, poetry, and short fiction under various pen names and saw them published in different newspapers and magazines,[3] such as the *Statesman* and the *Searchlight*. His articles dealt primarily with social issues such as the caste system, capitalism, and the dowry system, and contained many of the radical ideas that would later appear in his Prout philosophy. He enjoyed the affection of his unmarried uncle, a disciplined Tantric, and used to pay regular visits to his aunt in north Calcutta who later became famous as Lady Goranga, a Vaeshnava saint. He also worked part time as a sub-editor in a Calcutta newspaper and tutored students to meet his expenses. Above all, he continued searching out solitary places to pursue his meditation.

In Calcutta, Prabhat kept up his habit of taking long evening walks. He often walked by the banks of the river Ganges, a route that took him through an area dotted with burning ghats, some still smoldering with the remains of cremated bodies. It was a solitary area that the townspeople avoided, rumored to be unsafe after dark. On the evening of the full moon in August, shortly after his arrival in Calcutta, Prabhat's evening walk took him through the Kashimitra burning ghat. The bright moon of Shravan cast enough light to illumine his path through the cremation ground.[4] He stopped at one point and found a place to sit near the riverbank. A short while later, he heard footsteps behind him. Without bothering to turn around, he asked his unknown visitor to sit down. Rather than sit, the burly, imposing man who appeared by his side whipped out a large dagger and demanded that Prabhat hand over his money and his valuables; otherwise, he would not hesitate to take his life.

"Are you short of money?" Prabhat asked, seemingly unaware of the dagger glistening in the moonlight, a few inches from his face. When his surprised assailant repeated his threat, Prabhat answered him in the same fearless tone of voice. "So, have you made it a habit then of robbing people, even poor, defenseless students like myself?" Again the thief tried to frighten the young man, but Prabhat answered in the same unperturbed manner. "I will give you my money, don't worry, but I have something much more valuable than money. Would you not like to know what that is?"

The thief began to feel unnerved by the eerie calm and strange smile of the slightly built teenager sitting in front of him. After a moment's hesitation, he asked Prabhat what he meant.

"First, tell me one thing," Prabhat said. "If your material requirements were fulfilled, would you keep on stealing?"

The thief, whose name was Kalicharan Bannerjee, hesitated again, and then told him that if it were possible to quit, he would.

"Good," Prabhat said. "Now if you wish to have what I can give you, throw away your knife. Go to the river and take a bath. When you are done, come back and sit here. I will wait."

Kalicharan suddenly felt humbled in front of the boy that he had pulled a dagger on only a scant minute or two before. Tears appeared in his eyes. He walked down to the edge of the river, threw the dagger into the water, and immersed himself. When he returned, the water still dripping from his bare shoulders, Prabhat initiated him into Tantric meditation and in the process accepted Kalicharan as his first disciple. Kalicharan could barely contain his tears. He agreed to give up his life of crime and listened carefully to Prabhat's instructions about how to conduct his life. When he expressed his remorse and tried to explain what had led him to such a path, Prabhat told him to forget his past. "From today you begin a new life. The old Kalicharan no longer exists."

Afterwards, Kalicharan insisted on walking Prabhat back home. "The city is full of cutthroats," he said, "who won't hesitate to murder someone over a few coins." When they reached his uncle's house, Prabhat gave him some final instructions and told him when to come back and see him.

When Kalicharan returned to the house a few days later, Prabhat was practicing meditation. Kalicharan waited outside the door until Prabhat was finished. When Prabhat opened the door, he stretched out a hand to his new disciple and handed him his watch and a one-anna coin. "Had you robbed me, this is all you would have gotten," he said. When Kalicharan began to weep, Prabhat extracted from him a promise to take the same energy he had dedicated to robbery and to use it to serve the creation.

Later, Kalicharan would take *kapalik* initiation from Prabhat and receive the monastic name Kalikananda.

In late April 1940, Prabhat caught a night train to a village in Bankura District, some two hundred kilometers from Calcutta, to attend the wedding of a friend. As the sun was going down, he set out with the groom and several friends for the bride's house, but since the astrologically ordained time for solemnizing the marriage was late in the night, he decided to go for a long walk in the surrounding countryside. After several kilometers, he came to a vast, uneven stretch of land dotted by thickets, far from the nearest habitation. It was exactly the kind of place Prabhat favored for his evening walks. Here and there, he noticed a few jackals roaming about. He could hear the call of the bhutum owl among the trees, punctuating the silence. The only light came from the vast panorama of stars and the occasional beam of his flashlight. Soon he came to an area that seemed to be both a cremation ground and a dumping ground for animal carcasses. He could see several skulls strewn around and other bones that had been picked bare by carrion eaters. Attracted by the poignant beauty, he located a clear, clean place with his flashlight and sat down to relax and practice his meditation.

After a short while, he noticed a shadowy figure coming slowly in his direction. He greeted him from a distance, but instead of answering him, the man took up the following refrain in a melodious voice: "The play of life has ended, brother; the festival of the world has disbanded. Return, O man of this world, return."

When the man drew closer, Prabhat asked him who he was and where he was from.

"Babu," the man said, "the road is my home." Then he added the refrain of another song: "Traveler I am, dwelling on the path; going is as coming to me, coming is as going.

"Well, Babu," he continued, "I don't want to put on airs, so when I have to introduce myself, I tell people I'm from the Candil area."

"What's your name, my friend?"

"Now you want to know my name also? People say that my name is Kamalakanta Mahapatra."

"Well, Kamalakanta, please sit. Sing me another song."

Kamalakanta sang several mystical songs, each one more beautiful than the one before it. Then he asked Prabhat where he was coming from and Prabhat told him.

"That's quite a distance," he said. "You must be dead tired. Why don't you lie down for a bit and let me massage your feet a little. After all, you still have to walk back."

"You must be just as tired as I am," Prabhat protested.

"No, Babu, I don't feel any discomfort. I told you, the path is my home. Lie down; you're just a young boy."

"However tired I may be, I don't think it appropriate for an older person to massage my feet."

"Then put your head on my lap and lie down and stretch your legs."

Prabhat soon fell asleep in the heart of the cremation ground with his head in the stranger's lap. When he woke up, it was the early hours of the morning. He felt a sharp pain in his feet and opened his eyes to find Kamalakanta clutching them with both hands. His head was no longer in Kamalakanta's lap. Instead, Kamalakanta had placed three human skulls under his head to serve as a pillow.

Prabhat called out to Kamalakanta, but the man gave no reply. He sat up and pushed him. A little shove was all it took for Kamalakanta's body to fall over. Prabhat felt for the man's wrist and found no signs of life. His body was already growing cold. The man whose home was the path had moved on to an unknown destination.

Prabhat got up and started back. Dawn was breaking when he reached the wedding place, where his anxious friends had been waiting for it to grow light so they could go out and search for him. He told them what had happened and asked them to accompany him back to the cremation ground to complete Kamalakanta's last rites. But when they reached the spot, Kamalakanta's body was nowhere to be seen, though the skulls that had served as Prabhat's pillow were still there where he had left them. "Are you sure you weren't drinking bhang?"⁵ his friends chided him good-naturedly, but Prabhat shook his head. "The man was a great yogi," he told them. "He chose that time to leave his body. There is a mystery here, but my imagination has nothing to do with it."

Prabhat continued to initiate a few select disciples, all of them in secret. Apart from a couple of exceptions, however, these early initiates were not known to his later disciples.

In the summer of 1940, Prabhat returned to Jamalpur for summer vacation. Both M. N. Roy and Subhash Bose came to see him there, and he took them for a late night walk to the fields near Kalipahar. They stopped at the tiger's grave, a local landmark that would later become Prabhat's favorite halting place during his evening walks. A heated discussion ensued. Subhash argued the cause of political freedom at all costs. Roy insisted that India should first pursue economic freedom and only later focus on political freedom. Though the details of that conversation are not known, we do know that Prabhat agreed in principle with M. N. Roy. History, however, tells us that it was an argument Subhash won, with unfortunate consequences for the nation. That night, Prabhat taught both Roy and Subhash Tantric meditation. On July 3, Subhash was arrested by the British in an effort to halt the rapidly growing influence of his newly formed Forward Bloc, the radical opposition to the Gandhi wing, feared by the British for the open ultimatum it had delivered to them to quit India. The revolutionary leader used his time in jail to practice meditation, which would ultimately have a profound effect on the man whose charismatic personality would play a decisive role in the events leading up to India's independence.

Prabhat returned again to Jamalpur for the winter vacation. One day, he was sitting on the veranda warming himself in the midday sun. A couple of women from the neighborhood approached and left a plate of sweets for him. They retreated back into the street and stood there watching. Prabhat called them to come back but they hesitated. He continued to insist and finally they approached. "Young master," they told him, "we belong to a low caste. How can we come near you?"

Prabhat caught their hands and made them sit next to him on the veranda. He took the plate and ate the sweets, which made them visibly happy. After inquiring about their health and their family, he said, "Ladies, the caste system is evil. You should never think of yourself as inferior to anyone. If you ever need any financial help for the education of your children, do not hesitate to come to me. I will help you."

In the meantime, his mother stepped out onto the veranda and saw him talking to the two women, who were well known to her. She went back into the house without saying anything, but when they were gone, she grabbed Prabhat by the ear and pulled him into the bathroom. There she filled a bucket with water and added to it a bottle of Ganges water. She insisted that Prabhat wash himself with the so-called sacred water and then went out to the veranda to purify the place where they had sat by cleaning it with cow dung. Prabhat silently obeyed his mother but when she called him for lunch he refused to eat. When his mother asked him why, he expressed his dislike of her caste prejudice. After some discussion, he told her of his intention to do all he could to remove casteism from the society.

"That is impossible," Abharani protested. "The caste system is an injunction from God. Many great people have come to this earth and none of them were able to remove the caste system."

"The caste system has been created by men. It is a social evil, and sooner or later it will disappear. You will see."

Years later, the family priest's son, who by tradition was supposed to be Prabhat's priest, took initiation from Prabhat; instead of becoming his priest, he became his disciple. One day, the young man requested Prabhat to allow him to eat the food left over on his plate, which he considered prasad, food made holy by the touch of the guru. When Prabhat pointed out afterward to his mother with a smile that a high-caste Brahmin had eaten food from his plate, a blasphemy in traditional Hinduism, he asked her if she remembered their discussion many years earlier.

His mother smiled. "Yes, Bubu, I remember. You were right about the caste system; it's on its way out."

After completing the spring semester in 1941 and passing his ISc examination with honors,[6] Prabhat returned home once again for the summer vacation. The family's financial difficulties by then had grown quite serious. Despite the urging of his mother to continue his studies, Prabhat decided that the time had come for him, as the eldest son, to shoulder the family's financial burdens. He submitted his application for employment to the accounts department of the railway workshop. His application was accepted. In August of that year, he began work as an accounts clerk in the same office where his father had worked.

IV

Accounts Department: 1941–1947

The entire humanity of this universe constitutes one singular people. All humanity is bound together in fraternity: those who remain oblivious to this very simple truth, those who distort it, are the deadliest enemies of humanity. Today's humanity should identify these foes and build a healthy human society overcoming all obstacles and difficulties. It must be borne in mind that as long as a magnificent, healthy and universalistic human society is not well established, humanity's entire culture and civilization, its sacrifice, service and spiritual endeavor, will not be of any worth whatsoever.[1]

IN 1862 THE British established India's first railway workshop in Jamalpur. By the turn of the century it had become Asia's largest, home to the subcontinent's principal training facility for railway engineers, later known as the Indian Railways Institute of Mechanical and Electrical Engineering. With the growth of the workshop, Jamalpur soon became famous for its comfortable Anglo-Indian social life and its relaxed, small-town ambiance. At the time of Prabhat's birth, it employed more than twelve thousand people. About one thousand of these were British and Anglo-Indians who enjoyed a social life that rivaled that of Calcutta and other urban centers in the Empire but in a far more appealing setting: several thousand sprawling acres of wide, tree-lined boulevards and spacious meadows that reached to the edge of the Kharkhanian Hills. Railway employees could take long, picturesque walks and enjoy the charms of nature, or else entertain themselves with a full schedule of social pastimes. The Institute had its own movie theatre, a six-lane swimming pool, four tennis courts, two billiard rooms, and a bowling lawn. Its dances were renowned, so much so that railway personnel and their families came from all over Eastern India to attend. There was little more that an Indian railway employee could ask for—that is, as long as he was British. As with most of British India, the posh residential suburbs and recreational facilities were off-limits to Indians. They were literally on the other side of the tracks, the railway lines neatly dividing the township from the institute. Indians comprised over ninety percent of the workforce, but they enjoyed little of the privileges that made Jamalpur such a desirable appointment for railway personnel. Still,

Prabhat would say years later that when he was young it was the best town in all India.

Lakshmi Narayana had joined the railway accounts department as a clerk in 1911, having emigrated from his native Bengal following the death of his father at the age of forty-four (a fate that he would also share). His son was nineteen when he began working in the same office, which consisted of a suite of spacious halls filled with bare-topped desks in the British bureaucratic style. Here employees would spend their days poring over paperwork and penning entries into the hundreds of ledgers that piled up on shelves and in cabinets and in some cases directly on the floor beside their desks. Prabhat signed on as a lower-division clerk with a salary of thirty-three rupees per month, a slightly built teenager with thick black glasses whose short stature and quiet, sober demeanor would not ordinarily attract a second glance. Most of the men he was now working with had worked with his father; many of them had been beneficiaries of Lakshmi Narayana's homeopathic remedies, and they were happy to welcome the son who showed many of the same traits that had endeared them to the father. Like his father, Prabhat was methodical in his work habits, visibly sincere, and uncommonly punctual. He would enter the office exactly on the hour each morning, generally finishing the work assigned to him ahead of time, and leave exactly at five each afternoon.

When Prabhat joined his office service, World War II was in full swing. Despite its distance from the principal battlefields, India was feeling the effects. Prices skyrocketed on everything from rice to clothes. Many items became nearly impossible to obtain. Blackouts and curfews were instituted as fears rose over a possible Japanese invasion, and these fears were confirmed when the Japanese advanced on Burma in January of 1942. In February, Singapore fell. By mid-summer Japanese troops were nearing India's eastern border. Soon afterwards, the first air attacks on Calcutta by Japanese bombers began and the city underwent a massive evacuation. In Jamalpur, only 280 kilometers from Calcutta and home to the empire's largest railway workshop, tensions were high. A curfew was instituted. At night people were afraid to light a fire for fear of showing Japanese bombers the way to their town. Though the rapid entrance of the Americans into the Pacific after Pearl Harbor would help to divert Japanese attention away from India, tensions over a possible invasion would continue until the war neared its close.

As might be expected, the war was foremost on everybody's mind. During lunch hour and break time, employees would gather together to discuss the progress of the conflict, catching up on the latest news from the battlefront and wondering aloud how the war would impact India's future. When Prabhat joined the conversation, his colleagues noticed that he would often narrate recent events from the battlefield or the political front in vivid detail, almost as if he had witnessed those scenes with his own eyes. News of these events would not appear in the local papers or on the radio until several days afterward due to a three-day news blackout on war-related incidents. When they asked him how he had come by news that had proven to be up-to-the-minute, he would simply smile or change the subject.

Prabhat's astute analysis of the political ramifications of the war and his extensive knowledge about military procedure, strategy, and history seemed incongruent with his tender age and apparent lack of worldly experience. He was never at a want for answers to the questions they put to him, and oftentimes he would steer the conversation into realms his other colleagues rarely visited—classical literature, linguistics, applied sciences, mysticism, philosophy—often by asking them questions that he would then answer. Soon his desk became a meeting point during the lunch hour and break time. Prabhat never left the office to eat in the workshop canteen. He brought a light meal with him from home in an aluminum tiffin carrier and would nibble at his food and talk with his colleagues until it was time to go back to work.

During the course of these discussions, his colleagues discovered that Prabhat was an accomplished palmist.[2] In fact, they found that he was well versed in all aspects of Hindu astrology, of which palmistry is a part. With the natural regard they felt for practitioners of this ancient Hindu art, they began seeking his advice from time to time. Impressed by the accuracy of his readings, they also began bringing their friends.

Jiten Mandal had a friend, Vishvakarma, who was growing desperate because he had been unable to find a job. One day Jiten asked him to come to the office to see Prabhat during the lunch hour. When Vishvakarma asked Prabhat if he would be willing to look at his palm to see when he might find a job, Prabhat told him that he did not need to see his palm. All he needed to see were the lines on his forehead. Prabhat looked at him fixedly for a few moments. Then he told Vishvakarma that he would find employment on such and such a date. Vishvakarma forgot about the forecast. But when he received his appointment on the exact date that Prabhat had foretold, he remembered the prediction and rushed to Jiten to inform him that it had proved true.

On another occasion, one of Prabhat's colleagues told a friend of his, Mritunjay Sanyal, about Prabhat's prowess in the astrological arts. He assured him that if anyone could help him it would be Prabhat. Mritunjay, a head clerk in a different department, was nearing retirement age. Despite his best efforts, he had not been able to find a husband for one of his daughters, and he had grown deeply worried about it. He was a Barendra Brahmin and proud of his caste, but in his desperation he agreed to humble himself and ask for Prabhat's help. Prabhat's reply was short and to the point. "This is a simple matter," he said. "The groom is sitting just in front of you in this office." Prabhat pointed to a young clerk, Maitra Babu, who was sitting at a desk in a different part of the room, attending to his work. "Approach his guardian and your desire will be fulfilled." Mritunjay did as Prabhat suggested. He found that the family was of the same caste and had just begun searching for a bride. The negotiations presented no difficulty and the marriage was soon solemnized.

As time passed, the scope of Prabhat's counseling activities increased. One day, on his way into the office, he noticed that a coolie was sitting idle with a pained expression on his face. Prabhat asked him if he were not feeling well. "I want to work, sir," the coolie told him, "but I can't. I think I need to go home and get some treatment, or else, if you have something you can give me for the pain, I would be obliged."

"I am not a doctor," Prabhat said, but when the coolie repeated his request, he went and plucked a plant from the workshop grounds and instructed him how to make a simple medicinal preparation from its leaves. The next day the coolie was back at work, fully recovered. He told his fellow laborers that Prabhat knew many medicines. After that, other coolies started seeking Prabhat's help when they fell sick. Though Prabhat was not a homeopath like his father, his office colleagues also started seeking his advice for their medical problems, and he often prescribed herbal or naturopathic treatments as part of that advice.

One of Prabhat's colleagues was Gunadhar Patra, who was also a practicing homeopath and a student of natural remedies. He took advantage of his close proximity to Prabhat in the office to question him about the remedies to different diseases, many of which he began using in his own practice.[3] One day he asked Prabhat to take him into the hills near the Kali temple to show him some of the medicinal plants that he recommended. As they were walking back, they passed a crowd of women gathered outside a house.

> He asked me why those people were gathered there, so I went and inquired. They told me that a boy of that house was sick. He was fainting and vomiting and having fits that they were worried might be epilepsy. When I went back and told him, he said he wanted to see the boy. He went into the house and asked the family to describe the boy's symptoms to him in detail. He listened to what they had to say and then waved his hand over the boy's body. Then he told everyone that they could leave. He assured them that the boy would be all right. I was a doctor and I was thinking, How was it possible that the boy could be cured without any medicine or treatment? The next morning I went again to that area. I used to go to the spring near there to collect drinking water. I went to that house and inquired how the boy was. The family told me that he was fine. They said that a man with glasses had gone there the previous day and waved his hand over the boy and after that he was cured. I suspected he must have used some kind of mantra to cure the boy and I wanted to learn, so I went and asked him how he had done it. He appeared surprised at my question and didn't seem to remember the incident. Then I reminded him that it was when we

were coming down from the Kali hills. He remembered and told me that there was no mantra, nothing like that. These things can be done by touch also, he said. I had trouble believing it, but he assured me it was true. I was a doctor, he said, and I would also be able to cure patients by touch. Then I requested him to let me take the dust of his feet.

On another occasion, one of Prabhat's colleagues was deeply worried about his wife, who had fallen seriously ill and failed to respond to any of the medicines that the doctors had prescribed. He approached Prabhat and asked for his help. Prabhat closed his eyes for a few moments. Then he told him to bring him a certain red flower. The man brought the flower, but instead of prescribing some medicine to be made from its petals, as he had assumed he would do, Prabhat intoned some mantras and told him to keep the flower by his wife's bed. He promised that she would recover within forty-eight hours. When his wife recovered as Prabhat had predicted, his colleague spread the story around the office, adding to Prabhat's growing reputation.

Such incidents inspired confidence in his colleagues. They even began to approach Prabhat for advice about matters that required little or no knowledge of astrology or palmistry. Mr. Jha, for instance, was unable to afford the costly funeral rites for his father, who had recently died. As per Hindu tradition, a Brahmin priest was needed to conduct the necessary rituals to send his father's soul to heaven. Unfortunately, the priest was charging fifty gold sovereigns for his services, far beyond Mr. Jha's means, and his mother and other family members were putting tremendous pressure on him to pay it.

"Even if you spend a hundred times that amount," Prabhat told him, "it still wouldn't do any good. You still won't be able to send your father's soul to heaven because heaven and hell don't exist, other than the heaven and hell we create for ourselves in this world through the consequences of our good or bad actions. Heaven and hell are just dogmas created by certain religious people to exploit the gullible and play upon their fears."

"But Prabhat-da," Jha said, "even if it is just a dogma, I won't be able to convince my mother or my relatives of that. They'll never give me any peace if I don't perform the rites according to the scriptures."

Prabhat nodded. "Of course. I understand. But do one thing. Ask the priest how far he can send your father's soul if he reduces his fee."

The next day Jha told Prabhat that the priest had agreed to reduce his fee to thirty gold sovereigns. For that sum, he could take his father up to the gates of heaven. But he would have to open the heavy gates himself to be able to go in.

"I see," Prabhat said, smiling. "Go back to the priest and ask him how far he can bring your father if you pay him in silver."

The next day Jha told Prabhat that the priest had made a lengthy recalculation.

For one hundred silver coins he could take his father to the steps of heaven. From there he would have to climb the long, winding steps himself to reach the gate.

"Can you afford one hundred silver coins?" Prabhat asked.

"No, Prabhat-da. I have a very large family. I don't want them to suffer unnecessarily."

"How much can you afford then?"

"I suppose I could afford thirty silver coins," Jha said.

"Very well. Go back and talk to the priest. Ask him how far he can bring your father for thirty silver coins."

The next day Jha showed up at the office in a happy mood. When he had a chance to talk with Prabhat, he told him that at first the priest had been quite annoyed. Finally though, he had made a long calculation and told him that for that sum he could send his father three miles from heaven.

Prabhat laughed. "Very good. Tell the priest that your father was a healthy man who used to walk four or five miles every morning. If the priest can send him three miles from heaven, then he can cover the rest of the distance during his morning walk."

The office was not the only place where people came to Prabhat for advice or to have their palms read. People from the neighborhood would occasionally stop by the Sarkar house to seek his help with one difficulty or another. Sometimes the advice he gave was purely practical. One time a distraught young woman from the neighborhood approached Prabhat's mother and asked Abharani if she might be willing to ask her son's advice for a problem that she was having with her mother-in-law. That evening, when Prabhat came home from work, his mother explained to him the difficulty that the young woman was facing: She was new to the neighborhood, having married a local boy, and her mother-in-law was making her life miserable, a common complaint in traditional Indian society. As in most Indian households where the daughter goes to live with the son's family, she was expected to do the bulk of the cooking and cleaning. The mother-in-law would wait till the girl had finished cooking the noon meal. Then she would lock the kitchen with a padlock and go out to visit friends where she would generally take tea and snacks. The famished girl would have to wait for hours, until the mother-in-law returned, before she could eat. Prabhat counseled the girl to put her own padlock on the door after the mother-in-law went out and then make sure she was not there when the mother-in-law returned. She should only unlock the kitchen if the mother-in-law promised never to lock it again, no matter what threats the mother-in-law might make. A couple of days later the girl returned to offer her heartfelt thanks. Her mother-in-law had agreed not to lock the kitchen anymore.

On occasion, Prabhat's help took a more supernatural bent. Once a rumor went around the neighborhood that Prabhat had a magic mirror in which he could show the souls of the deceased and what people in distant places were doing. In actuality, it was not a mirror but a pane of glass that Prabhat had asked his brother Manas to paint black on one side, giving it a reflective quality. It was Manas's duty to fetch the mirror and set it up whenever Prabhat needed to use it.

One day the wife of Pundit Ramchandra Jha, Prabhat's high school Sanskrit teacher, came to visit Abharani. Mrs. Jha had not been present at her mother's death and had come to share the sorrow she was feeling. Prabhat overheard the conversation and later told his mother that if the old lady wished he could show her her deceased mother, as long as she promised not to be afraid and not to tell anyone about the incident. Mrs. Jha agreed. She came over a couple of days later. Manas set up the glass and set a candle burning before it. Prabhat instructed her to concentrate on the candle. The old lady quickly slipped into a semi trance state. While in that state, she saw her mother sitting in a boat. Afterwards, she thanked Prabhat and told him that now she could rest easy, knowing that her mother was safe and continuing on her journey.

On another occasion, another old lady from the neighborhood was worried about her son and came to Prabhat to ask for his help. Her son had gone abroad, and she had not received a letter from him for some weeks. Prabhat agreed to help and asked Manas to bring the glass and light a candle. The lady slipped into a trance and had a vision of her son going into a shop to buy food in the country he was visiting. The vision was enough to allay her fears.

After a few months, Abharani became worried that such séances would affect her son's health, and, in fact, he did fall sick after one such session. Prabhat, who always showed the utmost respect and consideration for his mother, retired the glass and never used it again.

This was typical of the relationship he had with Abharani. Each evening before bed, he would massage his mother's feet. Whenever he wanted to go anywhere, he would ask her permission, even in later years when he became preceptor to a multitude of disciples. Each month he handed his salary over to her; she would then give him a small allowance for his personal expenses. Abharani was a devout woman who kept a small altar in her house where she would perform her daily Hindu worship in front of a small image of Krishna. Prabhat made it a regular habit to bring her flowers for her worship. Once, for a stretch of several days, whenever she placed a garland around the image of Krishna, she saw an image of her son sitting there in place of the idol. She rubbed her eyes and started her worship again, but it kept happening. Finally, she went to her son and complained that he was bothering her worship. "It is because you love me so much," Prabhat told her, "that you keep seeing me."

The rest of the family was well aware of Prabhat's unusual abilities, but for his younger siblings it was simply a normal part of their lives. One day the Sarkar children were gathered at the dining table. Prabhat was eating his morning meal before leaving for the office. Suddenly the family cat jumped on the table. "Do you want to see some magic?" Prabhat asked his younger brothers and younger sister. He made a small motion with his hand and the cat froze, as if it had been turned into a living statue. The children crowded forward to have a closer look. They touched it, oohing and ahing. At that moment, Prabhat's mother came into the room; when she saw what was happening, she rebuked her son. "Leave the cat alone, Prabhat, otherwise it might die." Prabhat made another small motion with his hand, and the cat started breathing again. It jumped off the table and ran away. His mother returned to her morning chores, mildly annoyed, but otherwise going about her day as if nothing out of the ordinary had happened.

The other children were convinced that their elder brother knew everything, as their mother often told them. One day in early 1948, Himanshu broached the subject. "Dada, you know everything.[4] Can you teach me how you do it? I would love to be able to know everything also." Prabhat frowned. "It is not good to know everything," he said, "not good at all. You would not like it. There is a reason why Providence does not allow this."

A couple of days later, Prabhat was sitting at the dining table with his cousin Ajit Biswas, who was spending the holidays at the Sarkar house. While Prabhat's younger sister, Bijli Prabha, was serving them a snack, Abharani began scolding her for her lack of skill in household matters. "You are going to be married soon and you still haven't learned how to serve a table properly, what to speak of cooking! What will your husband think?" Prabhat started defending Bijli Prabha, until Abharani fell quiet and left her daughter in peace.

"There is no need for her to master such domestic chores," Prabhat told Ajit, once they were alone again at the table. "The marriage that my mother is busy arranging for my sister will never take place."

"Prabhat, it must be wonderful to be able to know what is going to happen in the future," Ajit exclaimed, shaking his head and marveling at his cousin's unique abilities.

"Not at all," Prabhat told him. "It is not a blessing; if anything, it is a curse. You see, my sister is destined for a short life. She will not live to see her marriage day. That is why I wish that she be left in peace, so that she does not face any unnecessary troubles in her final days. Think about it. Whenever I see her, I am reminded that her death is fast approaching. You see a healthy young woman; I see her death. Just imagine how difficult it would be for someone to act naturally or be at ease with their friends or family if they knew that someone close to them was about to die. There is good reason why Providence has arranged that human beings should not know what is to happen in the future."

The next day, Prabhat asked Himanshu to accompany him to Calcutta for a few days. When the two brothers arrived back in Jamalpur some four or five days later, they found the family in a state of mourning. Their carefree sister

Bijli Prabha had died the previous day of black fever, a disease that had shown no signs of its immanent arrival when they had set off for Calcutta a few days earlier.

Prabhat's family continued to pay visits to Bamunpara, where everyone still called him by his nickname, Bubu. Anil Ghosh recalled what those visits were like:

> Even though Bubu was a younger relative, I still showed him much deference. We would visit him as soon as we heard of his arrival. One day we saw that Bubu was doing something inside his room. His grandmother was my sister-in-law. On inquiry, she replied, "Bubu is sitting in meditation. He practices meditation and contemplation for long periods. The last time when he was here and was meditating for a long time, I curiously peeped inside the room through the window. I saw him levitating. His body was floating a little above the ground. I got frightened and closed the window. It is better not to disturb him while he is practicing meditation. But now it has already been some time and he is about to get up." Sure enough, after a while Bubu came out. Seeing me, he happily embraced me. Bubu always was an effusive person and had a pure nature. He would mix freely with us all.
>
> It is difficult to describe the joy he gave us by raising various topics for discussion. At that time in our village, there were two very educated gentlemen: Sachidulal Mitra and Gopikrishna Mitra, who was a chartered accountant. Both were older than Bubu. It was fascinating to watch them in any discussion or argument, be it deep philosophy, literature, ethics, sociology, or other topics. Bubu's knowledge of so many different subjects churned everyone's mind. He would lucidly explain any subject by quoting various Sanskrit verses to support his contentions. It appeared as if he had crammed all the Vedas, Vedanta, the social codes, Puranas, and Tantras into his brain. Whatever subject others asked him about, Bubu gave clear, precise replies with the requisite illustrations from various sources. Everyone would be completely satisfied with his replies.

Naresh Ghosh, who was five years younger than Prabhat, had formed a habit during his childhood of following him around whenever he got the chance. He also recalled those visits:

> When he came to Bamunpara, Bubu-da would speak elaborately on various subjects, including linguistics, history, Bengali literature, philosophy, and spirituality. I noticed that Bubu-da spoke effortlessly

on the gradual development of Bengali literature. I most enjoyed his descriptions of the step-by-step evolution of the various Prakrita languages derived from Sanskrit. I particularly enjoyed listening about how original Sanskrit words became transformed over the ages and how they have come into modern Bengali. He could speak many languages fluently. He would explain various philosophical topics, quoting profusely from the Vedas and Upanishads. We were delighted to watch his extraordinary memory in action and his deep knowledge on different subjects. Occasionally, he spoke on different schools of philosophy, like Shaiva, Shakta, Vaeshnava, Saora, and Ganapatya. He would speak on so many things at a time that we would simply lose the trail.

People said Bubu-da could read palms very well. I say that he never read a palm. I have watched him; he would ask the person to stand erect and simply look sharply at him from head to foot. It was as if he were taking an X-ray. Then he would speak rapidly without any hesitation about the person. It is difficult for me to understand how he could enter a person's body and mind.

Once, my elder brother, Narayana, developed a brain disorder. The family decided to commit him to a mental hospital. My father wrote to Bubu-da, seeking his advice before taking any action. Bubu-da respected my father very much. In reply, Bubu-da advised against sending my brother to the hospital. He prescribed some medicines, asked that he practice some yoga asanas, and gave dietary instructions. Because of that letter, there was no need to send my brother to the hospital.

Naresh's brother Suresh also recalled his impressions of Prabhat at that time:

> When I was studying in college, we often discussed Bubu-da among ourselves. One day, I plucked up my courage and said to Bubu-da, "Why don't you read my palm?" Though he loved us all very much, we were in some ways afraid of him.
>
> He said, "Tell me what you want to know."
> "Up to what level will I study?"
> "How far do you want to study?" he asked.
> "Up to MA."
> "Of course," he said, "you will pass your MA, but it won't be easy and you will have to struggle hard. You won't pass it at one go."
> I then wanted to know about my future financial situation. After thinking a while, he said, "Money will come to you, but from early on you will be burdened with debts." Then I wanted to know about my future reputation. Bubu-da said, "Well, you will have a good

reputation, but your unpopularity will be no less. And the most interesting thing will be that friends unrelated to you will praise you, whereas your own people will criticize you."

"What about my longevity?"

"You will live a long life, but you will have several accidents." Then Bubu consoled me. "Whatever be your fate, an invisible power will follow you like a shadow and help you whenever necessary."

Suresh then detailed how each of Prabhat's prophecies came true: the eighteen years it took him to pass his MA, and the eighteen accidents, one of which left him in a coma for seven days. "If I go on telling," he said, "how many times and in how many ways Bubu-da saved me and my family from difficulties and catastrophes, it would become an epic. The grace and blessings of Bubu-da have always shielded me."

On one of these visits to Bamunpara, Prabhat was sitting with Gopi Babu, when Gopi started telling him about a yogi named Bamakhyapa from the Birbhum district of West Bengal; Gopi was convinced that he had great spiritual powers.

"Once the ticket collector put him off the train because he didn't have a ticket. As soon as he was off the train, the whistle blew and the driver started the engine, but the train wouldn't move. One of the passengers told the guard that the person they had taken off the train was a great yogi. The train would not move until he was allowed back on. They tested this by allowing him back on the train. As soon as they did so, the train started moving."

"One needs some kind of spiritual power to do this, no doubt," Prabhat said, "but it is not a very high class of spiritual power. This, by itself, doesn't mean he is a great yogi."

Gopi Babu raised a suspicious eyebrow. "Could you do it?" he asked.

Rather than answer him, Prabhat smiled and changed the subject. "When are you going back to Kolkata?"

"I'm going back tomorrow," Gopi said.

"Good. I am also going tomorrow. We can go together."

The next day Gopi Babu stopped at the Sarkar house on his way to the station.

"I'm not quite ready yet," Prabhat said when he saw him. "Anyhow we have time. There's no hurry."

"Prabhat-da, I have urgent work in Kolkata. I can't afford to miss the train."

"Then you go ahead. I will be along presently."

Gopi Babu hurried to the station and proceeded to the platform after buying his ticket. The train was standing on the platform and the passengers had already boarded. Then Gopi saw Prabhat in the distance, approaching the station at a leisurely pace. He shouted for him to hurry, the train was about to leave, but Prabhat didn't quicken his pace. The train blew its whistle, but

Prabhat continued to stroll calmly towards the station, as if he had all the time in the world. Finally, he entered the station and went up to the counter to buy his ticket. The whistle blew again but the train still failed to move. Only when Prabhat got into the train and took his seat next to Gopi Babu did it start to move. Gopi looked at him distrustfully but didn't say anything. When the train arrived at Bandel, where it was scheduled for a long stoppage, Gopi got up with the other passengers and started towards the platform to take a cup of tea.

"Better not get out of the train," Prabhat said. "Today it will only stop here for a couple of minutes."

"Nonsense," Gopi said. "It always stops in Bandel for at least twenty minutes."

Gopi had barely ordered his tea when the signal sounded and the train started to move. He rushed back to his compartment and asked Prabhat in a vexed tone of voice how it was that he knew the train would only stop there for a couple of minutes.

Prabhat smiled. "The train is late; it was delayed in Shaktigarh. Now it is making up the gap."

Soon after Prabhat joined the office, the British government announced the creation of the Indian Engineers Force, a voluntary adjunct to the Indian Territorial Army,[5] designed to train young Indian engineers to assist in the defense of their country. Those who enlisted would be required to devote a certain number of hours on weekends and after work. They would also be sent for periodic short training stints to different parts of India, including West Bengal, Assam, and the North-West Frontier Province. In return, they would be paid a stipend of eight annas per day.[6] With his family in need of the money, Prabhat added his name to the list. He was quickly promoted to corporal and put in charge of a small platoon of Indian cadets who soon developed a strong sense of loyalty for their young Bengali platoon leader. On one training excursion, a British officer came for inspection while Prabhat was absent; he went ahead with the inspection without waiting for Prabhat to return. When Prabhat returned, he rebuked the officer for having conducted the inspection in his absence. One of Prabhat's men heard the altercation from the barracks and came out with a loaded gun. He saluted Prabhat and asked him in which direction he wanted him to shoot. The officer beat an immediate retreat.

On another occasion, several of Prabhat's men complained to him about one of their comrades who kept a locked chest under his cot with biscuits and other delicacies that he never shared with his fellow cadets. Prabhat listened to their complaints and promised to deal with it.

"Let us do one thing. I will get him out of the tent tonight on some excuse. When I give the signal, sneak into the tent from the back and make some sounds like an animal might make. Leave when I give the signal again."

That night, Prabhat invited the greedy cadet to go for a walk. As they were walking he gave the signal, a loud cough. Within moments, they heard strange sounds coming from the empty tent.

His companion halted suddenly. "Prabhat-da, did you hear that?"

"Yes. It sounds like a wild animal has gotten into the tent. It must be sniffing around. Do you keep any food in your tent, biscuits or any such thing?"

"Well, yes . . ."

"That is the problem then. It must be trying to get at the food."

Baba coughed again and the sounds ceased. "I don't hear anything now," he said. "Let's go take a look.

Cautiously the two men entered the tent. They saw signs of a disturbance around the cot.

"Just as I feared," Prabhat said. "It was trying to get into your chest."

"Oh no, what'll I do? What happens if it comes back while I'm sleeping?"

"I suggest you leave some of your food outside at night for the animal. He'll eat it and go away. Otherwise, who knows what might happen."

The cadet followed Prabhat's advice and that evening his comrades were able to enjoy his unplanned generosity.

It is not known to what extent Prabhat continued initiating disciples during the years leading up to Independence, but he would occasionally be seen in the company of wandering mendicants, such as were seen from time to time in any Indian town. Townspeople would sometimes spot him in their company during his evening walks in the solitary areas near Kalipahar and Death Valley.

One afternoon in 1944, Rameshvar Baita, a neighbor and a classmate of Manas Sarkar, was passing by the Sarkar house in Keshavpur along with his friend Ganesh. He noticed Prabhat sitting on the porch reading his newspaper, as Prabhat often did after arriving home from work. On the small platform across the street, a group of men from the neighborhood were playing cards, a common sight there in the afternoons. A man dressed in tattered clothes was sitting on one side of the platform, laughing to himself and speaking to no one in particular. Obviously some kind of a madman, Rameshvar thought. It was nothing new. He had often seen beggars and crazy-looking people sitting there in the late afternoons and early evenings—he had always assumed it was a good place to beg—and he had seen this particular fellow there for the past several days. This time, Ganesh wanted to stop and watch the card game. Rameshvar told him that he was in a hurry to get home, but he obliged his insistent friend for a few minutes.

As they were standing there, they heard the madman laugh and exclaim, "They call me mad. The Lord of the Universe has come to Jamalpur and is working in the railway workshop, and still they sit around and waste their lives playing cards. Fools! And they call *me* mad?"

The men playing cards winked at the two boys and shook their heads, laughing uproariously. "Sure thing, *pagal* (madman), the Lord of the Universe is in Jamalpur." They added a few more derisive comments before returning to their game.

Rameshvar and Ganesh joined in their laughter and then continued on their way. Rameshvar thought nothing more of it until years later when he took initiation and started hearing stories about Prabhat's earliest disciples. Then he remembered how Prabhat would sit out on the veranda for a short time after work to read the paper or enjoy the cool evening air. Rameshvar would often say hello to him as he accompanied Prabhat's brother Manas in or out of the house. From time to time, he would notice strange people sitting on the platform whom he mistook for beggars or crazy people. Later, it dawned on him that they had actually been mendicants and yogis who would sit there to catch a glimpse of the master.

Prabhat continued to write letters to Indian politicians. As the date for independence approached, he corresponded with Shyamaprasad Mukherjee, president of the Hindu Mahasabha, in regards to the demarcation of the borders between the future states of Pakistan and independent India.[7] The British representative responsible for border demarcation was Sir Ratcliff, who was working together with two Indian ICS officers: Chaudhuri Mahomed Ali, representing the future Pakistan; and H. M. Patel, representing India. Patel was not so familiar with the Punjab and Bengal, the two large Indian states that were being carved up in the formation of East and West Pakistan; as a result, areas were being awarded to Pakistan that would severely compromise India's access to Kashmir and the northeast areas of Assam and Tripura, as well as contributing to various other problems. Shyamaprasad raised these points on the floor of the provisional Indian Parliament. When Nehru and Vallabhai Patel questioned him as to where he had come by this information, he told them that it had come from one P. R. Sarkar, an employee of the Jamalpur railway workshop. This was the first time that the name P. R. Sarkar came to the attention of Nehru.[8]

After independence, Nehru, now Prime Minister of the world's newest and largest democracy, kept a secret but watchful eye on the man who had been the source behind Shyamaprasad's provocative comments on the floor of parliament. Years later, after Nehru had died and his daughter, Indira Gandhi, had turned the Prime Ministership into a dictatorship, Nehru's chief of intelligence, B. N. Mullick, confided that after independence Nehru had asked him to keep an eye on two organizations—the radical RSS and the Muslim League—and one man, P. R. Sarkar. By this time the watchful and secret eye of Nehru had morphed into a very public distrust and antagonism on the part of his daughter towards the former railway employee, who was by then the guru of India's largest and most controversial spiritual movement.[9]

Some of Prabhat's suggestions were acted upon and some were not, but by the time of the partition much harm had already been committed that could not be undone. Later on, those political leaders involved in the partition would receive caustic criticism from Prabhat in his analysis of the events that led to the dismemberment of the country and the genocide it occasioned, criticism that would not endear him to Indira, whose father had been one of the principle architects of independence.

According to Prabhat, in the 1930s the British government had begun implementing a systematic program to encourage communal divisions, such as religious and caste differences, in order to undermine the cause of Indian independence. The principle failure of India's leaders at the time, he pointed out, was their failure to adequately combat these divisions. Some political parties were openly based on communal sentiments; they gave their support to the British policies in exchange for favorable considerations from the outgoing rulers. Other unscrupulous leaders took advantage of the scope afforded by The Government of India Act to secure ministerships for themselves and provincial autonomy for their regions, to the detriment of the nation. They committed severe blunders, practiced appeasement in the face of communal demands, and turned a blind eye to political errors for which the nation would later suffer. In Prabhat's opinion, the reforms introduced by the British in the 1930s and 1940s, such as the Montague-Chelmsford Report, the Communal Award of Ramsay Macdonald, and the Government of India Act 1935, did incalculable damage to the unity of the nation and led directly to the partition of the country.

As Prabhat later explained to his disciples:

> Factually, as per the Government of India Plan at the time, India was trifurcated while Bengal, the Punjab, and Assam were bifurcated. Sindhu and the North-West Frontier Provinces went out of India. This was the result of the Communal Award, and unfortunately, the great patriots of India supported the Communal Award. They failed to learn the lessons of history ... At that time there was no mutual faith; there was want of mutual understanding. That is why the country was divided. Otherwise, the British could not have divided the country. There was both physical disintegration and psychic, or rather psychosocial disintegration for want of proper political education.[10]

On the morning of August 15, 1947, following the stroke of midnight, India attained its independence. In the weeks that immediately preceded and followed, an estimated half million people were slaughtered by communal death squads while trying to cross the borders into India or Pakistan, one of the greatest genocides in modern history and a direct result of the willingness of India's leaders to allow the division of their country. For better or for worse, the bloodshed that accompanied India's independence and the creation of West and East Pakistan (later Bangladesh) ushered in a new era for the subcontinent, home to the planet's oldest civilization and its newest democracy. It also marked the end of one era in Prabhat's life and the beginning of another. The quiet, mysterious youth, who had steadfastly kept his spiritual depths hidden from the eyes of all but a few, was about to begin the concrete materialization of his life's work: a mission that would leave a mark not only on India but on the entire world in a way that the politicians who read his letters and either accepted or spurned his advice in the years leading up to independence could never have foreseen.

PART TWO

V

The Early Disciples

Churn your mind through spiritual practice and God will appear like butter from cream. He is like a subterranean river in you. Remove the sands of the mind and you will find the clear, cool waters within.[1]

PRANAY KUMAR CHATTERJEE was a short, slender, highly intelligent twenty-two-year-old when he joined the Jamalpur railway workshop accounts department on June 2, 1947, two months and thirteen days before India attained its independence from Britain. He was also a confirmed skeptic who put his faith in science, rather than in what he viewed as the religious "superstitions" of his culture. That morning his supervisor introduced him to the people he would be working with, including Prabhat, whose desk was directly opposite his. At eleven thirty, Pranay broke for lunch, along with the rest of his new colleagues. As he started opening his tiffin box, he noticed the crowd gathering around Prabhat's desk. Curious, he turned to the person beside him and asked him what was going on.

"Don't you know?" his co-worker replied in a hushed tone, "Prabhat-da is a great scholar. He can read your palm and tell your future."

True to his nature, Pranay's initial reaction was one of outright skepticism. What would a great scholar be doing working as an accounts clerk in Jamalpur for forty-odd rupees a month? As he ate the rice and curried vegetables that his mother had packed for him, he watched the scene with interest. He noticed the deference with which the other office workers treated Prabhat. Finally his curiosity got the better of him. When he was done eating, he crept up to the edge of the crowd. He watched Prabhat examine the palm of one of his colleagues and listened to the advice he gave. He found it fascinating, but at the same time he felt uncomfortable with the whole idea of fortune-telling, especially in the workplace. It seemed indicative to him of what he vaguely felt was holding his country back. On the other hand, he thought, it couldn't hurt to give it a try.

A few minutes later he got his opportunity. Pranay approached Prabhat and asked him if he would read his palm also. Prabhat looked at him momentarily, a slight smile on his lips, and then motioned wordlessly for Pranay to hold out his hand. The moment Prabhat touched his hand, Pranay was startled to feel a pleasant sensation pass through his body, almost like a mild electric shock. But just as suddenly, Prabhat closed Pranay's hand and turned to speak with someone else. How rude of him, Pranay thought, to turn away like that without even having the courtesy to say so much as a single word! He went back to his desk, mildly irritated, and resolved to have nothing more to do with Prabhat, whom he suspected of being some kind of a charlatan.

Over the next couple of days, however, Pranay grew more and more preoccupied. Both his parents and grandparents were devout Hindus—his father, in fact, was a Brahmin priest from Bengal—and despite his youthful reaction to what he considered their blind faith and dogmatic beliefs, he was not entirely able to escape the effects of his upbringing. What had Prabhat seen in his hand that he refused to divulge? What if there were some disaster looming up ahead? Though Pranay prided himself on his rational approach to life, he was unable to dismiss these nagging worries from his mind.

A couple of days later, Pranay saw Prabhat standing alone in a secluded corner of the office veranda. Taking advantage of the opportunity, he reminded his colleague that he had shown him his palm a couple of days earlier.

"Was there something you saw in my hand that you didn't want to tell me?" he asked.

Prabhat's mood turned grave. "Do you really want to know?"

"Yes, please."

"As you wish. Meet me at the reading room about seven thirty. We can talk then."

When Pranay entered the railway library reading room that evening, he saw Prabhat sitting at a table, flipping rapidly through the pages of the English newspaper. The Hindi and Bengali papers were lying open in front of him. They greeted each other and Prabhat asked him if he would like to go for a walk. On their way out, Pranay asked Prabhat if he had been looking at the headlines.

Prabhat smiled. "No, I read the articles. You can ask me about them, if you like."

Pranay thought he detected a subtle challenge. He remembered a couple of articles he had read earlier in the day and formulated several questions. To his surprise, Prabhat answered them with such precision that it appeared as if he were quoting verbatim from the articles.

The two men headed up the spacious boulevard that ran alongside the rear wall of the railway compound. From there, they turned onto another boulevard that led to the fields outside of town. It was a clear, late-summer night with enough of a breeze to dispel the last of the daytime heat. As they walked, Prabhat began narrating the history of Pranay's birthplace, Bhagalpur. The conversation moved on to different subjects—geography, language, culture, botany, astronomy—flowing effortlessly from one to another like water around a bend. The more Pranay listened, the more the depth of Prabhat's knowledge amazed him. It was no wonder that his colleague had called him a great scholar, he thought. He seemed more widely read than any person he had ever met. The one subject, however, that Prabhat did not touch upon was his palm. Pranay was too polite to interrupt, but as the evening wore on and the two men went further and further afield, he began to lose patience. They had been walking for well over an hour when he finally blurted out that this was all well and good but he had come there to find out what Prabhat had seen in his palm.

Prabhat halted and fixed his gaze on Pranay, who immediately felt disconcerted.

"Do you really want to know?" Prabhat asked, after several moments pause.

"Of course. That's why I am here."

"Very well then." Prabhat resumed walking. "Tell me, what is the aim of your life?"

"Be happy," Pranay said. "Laugh and make merry."

Prabhat laughed out loud. "Your thinking is defective, Pranay. I can see that you are headed towards a great abyss. If you continue on this path, you are going to fall."

Pranay shuddered. He reminded himself that he didn't believe in fortune-tellers, but he couldn't help but feel apprehensive.

"Is there anything I can do to prevent it?" he asked.

"I feel pity for you, Pranay. Let me think over the matter. Why don't you meet me again tomorrow evening at the same time?"

The twenty-four hours leading up to their next walk did little to lessen Pranay's anxiety. Again they met at the reading room and headed towards the fields. Again Prabhat talked without making any mention of Pranay's future. But this time, when they reached the tiger's grave, Prabhat stopped and sat down. He pulled a piece of paper from his pocket and handed it to Pranay. "This is the *dhyana* mantra of Shiva. Practice it faithfully each morning according to my instructions and you'll escape the calamity that is waiting for you."

Pranay looked at the mantra with the aid of his flashlight and tried to hide his disappointment as he listened to Prabhat's instructions. He disliked anything to do with the Hindu gods and goddesses. The last thing he wanted was to practice a Hindu ritual with a mantra to the god Shiva. But rather than be impolite, he thanked Prabhat for his help and promised to practice it.

Over the next couple of days, he made a few half-hearted attempts to use the mantra as Prabhat had taught him, but he couldn't bring himself to put any faith into his practice. On the third day, when he went to work, he found Prabhat waiting for him outside the office entrance.

"Scoundrel! Worthless chap! Disrespecting a sacred mantra after you had promised to practice it sincerely! If you are not going to practice it properly, then give me back the mantra."

Pranay was taken aback by Prabhat's harsh tone and even harsher words. He apologized and asked Prabhat how he had known.

"A sadhu with matted locks and a long beard told me."[2]

Prabhat's remark puzzled him, but he felt a sense of relief. At least he wouldn't have to practice the mantra any longer. He asked Prabhat what he meant by returning the mantra.

"Take the piece of paper I gave you and immerse it in water, either in a pond or in a river."

Pranay did as he was told. That evening he dropped the slip of paper with the mantra into a small pond near his quarters. He was glad to see it go, but his sense of relief did not last long. Soon he found himself listening to Prabhat's lunch-hour conversations with avid interest, his earlier resolution to avoid him forgotten. He remembered fondly how much he had enjoyed the conversation of his enigmatic colleague during their two evening walks. One day, Pranay approached Prabhat during work and asked him if it would be possible to accompany him on his walk some evening. Prabhat readily agreed and the invitation soon turned into a regular custom. Prabhat would leave his house around seven thirty each evening, after completing his spiritual practices, and would return around ten or ten thirty. Pranay accompanied him whenever he could. As time passed, he grew more and more attached to Prabhat's company. No matter what the subject, the depth of Prabhat's knowledge seemed fathomless. Soon Pranay began seeking Prabhat's advice for personal matters, just as his co-workers did, although he never again showed him his palm. He became so charmed by his eloquent companion that those evening walks soon became the main attraction of his life in Jamalpur.

There was no branch of human knowledge outside the scope of Prabhat's interest, but the one subject he returned to more than any other was spirituality, and it was this subject that Pranay liked the least. He listened patiently, sometimes even with interest, but he felt uncomfortable talking about things he did not feel and could not see. From time to time, Pranay would reiterate that the object of his life was to enjoy like the people of America and England. "This is just the umbra and penumbra of enjoyment," Prabhat would say, "like a dog whose mouth bleeds when it chews on a dry bone and thinks that it's enjoying a tasty delicacy, when in fact it is its own blood that it is tasting." Pranay argued with him, but as time passed, the questions Prabhat posed, the riddles to the mystery of human life, sunk into his psyche and began to demand more and more of his attention.

Nineteen forty-eight gave way to 1949. India attained its freedom. The work of building the new Indian republic got under way. Everything seemed possible in the afterglow of independence, but despite the general optimism in the air, Pranay became more and more aware of a growing emptiness within him. One morning in early August, while he was seated at his desk, he felt his despair overcome him. He sat there despondently, without attending to his work, absorbed in his thoughts. After some time, Prabhat got up from his desk and walked over to him.

"What's the matter with you?" he asked.

"Oh, nothing," Pranay replied, jolted from his thoughts.

Prabhat's next words were in Sanskrit.

"Please, Prabhat-da," Pranay said, "I don't understand what you're saying."

Prabhat reached out and tapped Pranay between the eyebrows, at the *trikuti*.[3] Startled, Pranay looked at Prabhat and saw light flash from his eyes, like a sudden bolt of lightning. An electric current passed through his body, like a shock from a high voltage wire, followed by a wave of bliss. Prabhat turned around and walked back to his desk, returning to his paperwork as if nothing had happened.

Pranay's heart began to palpitate. For a few moments, he felt as if he might be going mad. As he stared across the room at Prabhat, he felt his long resistance give way. There must be some spiritual truth that I cannot perceive, he thought, tears welling in his eyes. I am just groping in the dark. Unless I can reach that light, my life has no meaning. I must have the shelter of some great man who can guide me. His decision made, he got up and went over to Prabhat's desk, where he bent down to touch his friend's feet. "I surrender, Prabhat-da. Please guide me. Accept me as your disciple."

Prabhat smiled and said softly, "Very well, then. Come to the field tonight. We'll talk there."

That evening Prabhat took Pranay directly to the tiger's grave and initiated him into the practice of Tantric meditation. He also gave him some yoga postures and dietary restrictions. During his initiation, Pranay felt a powerful, indescribable vibration that he was unable to comprehend, even stronger than what he had felt in the office. When he returned home that night, he couldn't sleep. He kept reliving the day's events over and over again: the mysterious flash of light, his surrender to Prabhat, his initiation in the field and the vibration he felt there. He kept asking himself what manner of man this was who could do such things, but he was unable to find an answer.

When he arrived at the office the next morning, Prabhat asked him to come to the field again that night. He had something more to teach him.

That night, when the two men reached the lamppost by the culvert at the edge of the field, Prabhat stopped and took a piece of paper from his pocket. He handed it to Pranay.

"This is *yama* and *niyama*,[4] the ten principles of yoga ethics. As a spiritual practitioner, you will have to follow yama and niyama very strictly."

Pranay read what Prabhat had written. "Prabhat, these rules are for sadhus in the forest," he objected. "It is not possible to follow all of them in modern society."

"What are you saying!" Prabhat raised his finger and said in a commanding voice, "You will have to follow them, you will have to follow them!"

Suddenly, Pranay found himself encircled by numerous images of Prabhat, each of them admonishing him with the same upraised finger. The sound of "you will have to follow them, you will have to follow them!" reverberated in his ears like a series of echoes. He threw up his hands. "Okay, Prabhat-da, okay! I promise. I will do as you say." As he said this, the multiple images of Prabhat vanished.

Prabhat's voice softened. "Come, let us walk." They walked to the tiger's grave, where Prabhat gave Pranay his second lesson, the guru mantra.[5] It was shortly after eight when they finished.

"Pranay, it seems that you didn't sleep last night. You look tired."

"You are right, Prabhat-da. I couldn't sleep at all."

"Come, put your head in my lap and rest for a while."

Pranay lay down on the grave with his head in Prabhat's lap and quickly fell asleep. It was after midnight when he woke up to the sound of Prabhat's voice.

"Hey, wake up! This is no time to be sleeping! We have to work tomorrow."

They walked back to town in silence. Pranay hastened to keep up with Prabhat's rapid pace, feeling as if he were following, in his own words, "the monarch of the universe." Years afterwards, as an old man, he would claim that never in his long life had he enjoyed such a restful sleep as he had that evening on the tiger's grave with his head in the master's lap.

Since Prabhat never allowed any contact between his later disciples and those he had initiated during the previous decade, Pranay would become Prabhat's first publicly recognized disciple, the first among those who would take active part in the spiritual organization he would later found. For the time being, however, a veil of secrecy was still in place. Prabhat gave Pranay strict instructions not to disclose his identity to anyone. As a result, Pranay could not know for sure who his fellow disciples were, or if he even had any. The thought that he might be the only disciple made him uneasy, so he started watching out for signs that someone else might be following his secretive master. In time, he noticed distinct changes in behavior in certain colleagues: an irreverent or coarse nature turning courteous and thoughtful; lifelong carnivores inexplicably giving up meat; rumors of co-workers locking themselves in their rooms at home for some secret practice. He would think, Ah, another one has fallen into the trap, but he couldn't ask them to confirm his suspicions without violating his guru's command.

The next person whom Prabhat initiated appears to have been Haraprasad Haldar, another young Bengali, a few years older than Pranay, who worked as a draftsman in the mechanical section. One day, Haraprasad stopped by the accounts department to talk with a friend who worked there. Prabhat called him over to his desk to inquire about an accounts clerk living in Haraprasad's boarding house who was absent from work that day. Haraprasad knew who Prabhat was, though he had never spoken to him. While Prabhat was inquiring about his roommate, Haraprasad noticed that he was staring intently at his forehead. Aware of Prabhat's reputation, he asked him what he was looking at.

The Early Disciples

"It's nothing," Prabhat said. "Anyhow, whatever is past is past. Better not to think about it."

Haraprasad suddenly felt queasy. "No, please, tell me."

"You are preoccupied with three things in your life. I will tell you the first two, but the third I'll only disclose at a later date."

Prabhat described with uncanny accuracy two of Haraprasad's three main concerns in life. Then he shocked him by declaring that Haraprasad was destined to have a short life span, and that the date marked for his death was fast approaching. Haraprasad was too unnerved to say anything in reply.

"Don't worry about it," Prabhat continued, as if what he was saying were the most natural thing in the world. "Now that you have come in my contact this can be changed. I will take care of it. You will meet me at the tiger's grave one month from today, in the evening around eight. We will talk then."

Haraprasad was badly shaken by this encounter, but he did his best not to let it affect him. He was aware of Prabhat's reputed ability to foretell the future. Though he did not trust what he had said, he told himself that should this be his fate, he was ready to face it. Nor did he believe for a moment that Prabhat had the power to alter his destiny, whatever it might be. But despite his best efforts to dismiss what Prabhat had told him, the specter of his possible death continued to plague his mind. He wrote a letter to a close friend, Sukhen Naik, in his hometown of Krishnagar, disclosing Prabhat's prophecy. When Sukhen showed the letter to Haraprasad's father, his father sent Sukhen and Haraprasad's cousin to Jamalpur to console him and keep him away from Prabhat. "The man is undoubtedly a Tantric," his cousin told him when they arrived. "Stay away from him and everything will be okay."

Haraprasad took their counsel to heart but destiny had other plans for him. On May 18, 1950, exactly one month after Prabhat had told him that he would meet him at the tiger's grave, he went to the railway library in the evening. As he entered the reading room, he saw Prabhat sitting at a table reading the newspaper; the sight stirred up the fears of death he had done his best to put out of his mind. Anxious to avoid another encounter with the man who was the source of his anxiety, he left hurriedly, hoping that Prabhat had not noticed him. Preoccupied, he walked for some time without paying attention to where he was going. A short while later, he was startled by a voice calling him by name from the tiger's grave, where he had unwittingly wandered. The voice belonged to Prabhat, who wasted no time in reminding him of what he had forgotten: he had told him one month before that they would meet again on this night, at this time and in this place.

Uneasy, but resigned to the encounter, Haraprasad allowed Prabhat to lead him to a grassy area near the tiger's grave where three palm trees formed an equilateral triangle. Prabhat removed his shoes before entering. Haraprasad followed suit, and the two men sat down on the grass facing each other. On a later occasion, Prabhat would explain to him the significance of that spot, a spiritually charged site known as a *tantra pitha* where the Nath yogi,[6] Prabhirnath, had achieved enlightenment, and where many other saints had come to do their spiritual practices.

"Now tell me, Haraprasad, why do you have such a strong desire to follow the spiritual path?"

It was the third thing that had been dominating his thoughts for the past couple of years, something he had not shared with anyone. He had, in fact, secretly begun practicing certain yogic techniques that he had learned from a book. To his astonishment, Prabhat mentioned the practices he was doing and cautioned him that they should not be done without a proper guide. Prabhat went on to explain the inner significance of the Bhagavad Gita, the classic Hindu scripture that is revered in India as a seminal yogic text. Prabhat's explanation cleared many of Haraprasad's doubts about the Gita. When Prabhat was done, Haraprasad finally gathered the courage to ask him about his death.

"That is your destiny but your destiny can be changed."

"How?" he implored. "What can I do? Please, help me." He reached down and grabbed hold of Prabhat's feet in the traditional Indian gesture of respect for one's elders and teachers.

"You will have to practice the meditation I teach you, do asanas according to my instructions and not out of a book, and you will have to give up non-vegetarian food."

Haraprasad readily agreed.

"First of all," Prabhat continued, "you have to give up any caste feeling you might have. God has no caste. We are all children of the Supreme Father. If you accept the Lord as your Supreme Father and the goal of your meditation, then you must accept that all creatures are his children with equal rights to his blessings. There can be no caste distinction between them. Now sit in lotus posture and remove your sacred thread."[7]

Haraprasad's misgivings mounted. Here I am, he thought, in this lonely place with a Tantric. As long as I am wearing my sacred thread, he can't harm me. But if I remove it I'll be at his mercy. "I give you my word," he said. "I will take it off, but not here, not now."

Prabhat tried to reason with him, but Haraprasad continued to resist. An edge came into Prabhat's voice. "What nonsense you are thinking!" Prabhat reached out and touched him on his forehead. Haraprasad felt an electric current pass through his body and in its wake a feeling of intense bliss. All his doubts and suspicions vanished. Without any hesitation, he took off his sacred thread and placed it in Prabhat's hands. Prabhat chanted some mantras and threw it away. Then he initiated him into meditation and asked Haraprasad to practice the technique in front of him. Within a few minutes, Haraprasad entered into such a state of bliss that he lost all sense of time and place. After he came out of his meditation, he remained in an intoxicated state. As they walked back to town, everything around him—the fields, the trees, the nearby hills, the distant lights from town—appeared to him as an expression of God, and he himself was also God.

Prabhat accompanied him to his boarding house where his roommates were asleep. They had left some dinner for him but Haraprasad had no appetite. After he said goodbye to Prabhat, he went up to the roof and remained there for the rest of the night, sometimes meditating, sometimes pacing back and forth in his God-intoxicated state.

In the morning, Haraprasad seemed to be lost in a daze, unable to talk, unable or unwilling to touch any food. His roommates didn't know what to make of his strange condition; they were afraid that he might have contracted some unknown illness. They counseled him to take rest in the hope that after a day or two he would come back to his senses. But as the days passed, his condition showed little sign of abating. That weekend, a neighbor invited the residents of the boarding house to a Satyanarayana worship. They tried to convince Haraprasad to accompany them, but he told them that he himself was Lord Narayana—he would accept their worship from the boarding house.

While they were out, Prabhat dropped by to check on his new disciple. They went up to the roof to talk and Prabhat asked him if he were undergoing any difficulties.

"No, no difficulties, only bliss. The only problem I have is people coming and disturbing me."

"Don't worry. As long as I am here we won't be disturbed."

Prabhat touched him on the forehead, and Haraprasad felt the same electric current and intense bliss that he had experienced during his initiation. When he came back to his normal senses, Prabhat gave him his second lesson and then left.

When his roommates came back, they found that Haraprasad's condition had worsened. They asked the cook if anything had happened while they had been gone. The cook told them that a man had stopped by and talked with Haraprasad on the roof for quite some time. This fired their suspicions but they could not be sure of the man's identity. Not knowing what else to do, they contacted Haraprasad's family, who came and brought him back to Krishnagar. He remained there for one month on leave, during which time he gradually came back to normalcy, though the blissful sense of God's presence continued.

After Haraprasad returned to Jamalpur, his roommates discovered that he was spending time with Prabhat, sometimes walking alone with him at night in the field. They became convinced that Prabhat had put some sort of Tantric spell on their companion and suspected that he was teaching him strange occult practices. After some discussion, they decided to teach Prabhat a lesson. One of them, Sadhan Dey, had earned a reputation as a tough character that no one wanted to tangle with. Sadhan vowed to catch Prabhat alone and frighten him to the point that he would never bother Haraprasad again.

Sadhan made some discrete inquiries about Prabhat's nighttime walks.

One evening, he slipped a dagger into his pocket and waited for Prabhat near Jubilee Well, knowing that he would pass there on his way to the field. Sadhan's plan was to follow a safe distance behind and then catch him alone when he reached the solitary areas outside of town. But to his surprise, Prabhat called out his name as he passed by the well and went up to him like he was greeting an old friend, though the two had never formally met. Prabhat invited Sadhan to accompany him on his walk. Unsure what to do, Sadhan agreed. As they headed for the field, Prabhat inquired about each of his family members by name, back to his great grandparents. Prabhat asked about his native village in East Bengal and chatted about the dialect prevalent there and other familiar matters with such disarming charm that Sadhan found himself falling under the spell of Prabhat's personality. As they walked, he became uncomfortably aware of the dagger in his pocket. Every time Prabhat drew close to him, he fidgeted nervously, afraid that Prabhat might accidentally brush up against him and become aware of the hidden knife. Several times Prabhat smiled and asked him why he was fidgeting, which only made him more nervous.

When they reached the tiger's grave Prabhat suggested they sit.

"Sadhan," he said, "why don't you take that dagger out of your pocket."

Sadhan's face became flushed. "What are you talking about?"

"Take the dagger out of your pocket. Now!"

Sadhan's bravado failed him. He hesitated a moment longer and then took out the dagger.

"Put it down on the grave."

Sadhan obeyed and laid it on the grave beside him. Prabhat's tone softened.

"Sadhan, you and your fellows are laboring under a misconception. There is nothing the matter with Haraprasad. I have taught him yogic meditation. That's all. You would do well to practice it yourself."

Prabhat explained to him the benefits of yogic practice and cleared up his misunderstandings.

Finally, Sadhan agreed to learn meditation. After receiving initiation, he meditated for a few minutes in front of Prabhat. He too felt something of the intoxication that Haraprasad had felt. When he reached his boarding house, his companions, who had been waiting anxiously for his return, found him radically changed. Afterwards, Sadhan and Haraprasad started practicing meditation together. They accompanied Prabhat on his evening walks whenever they got his permission. Thereafter, their roommates gave up their efforts and abandoned Haraprasad and Sadhan to their strange new life.

One by one, Prabhat quietly initiated new disciples among his fellow railway employees, always maintaining the strict code of secrecy that prevented them from knowing who their fellow disciples were. But soon a chain of initiations began that would extend Prabhat's circle of initiates outside of Jamalpur. It began with a childhood friend, Shiva Shankar Bannerjee, who had grown up in the same neighborhood in Keshavpur. Sometime in 1951, Shiva Shankar came back to Jamalpur to visit his family, taking a couple of weeks leave from his post as a sub-inspector of police. At the time, he was suffering from severe respiratory problems. He had seen a number of different doctors and tried different remedies but could not get any relief from his ailment. As a result, he had become severely depressed. Shortly after he arrived in Jamalpur, he saw his childhood friend walking in the street in front of his house. The two men greeted each other and started catching up on old times. When Prabhat inquired about his health, Shiva Shankar related his problems and expressed his despair of ever finding a cure.

"I know how to cure your illness," Prabhat said. "There is a practice I can teach you. But I can only teach you if you agree to certain conditions. I'm not sure you'll like them."

"You have to tell me," Shiva Shankar replied, suddenly hopeful. "This is ruining my life. I'm ready to try anything, anything at all, as long as it works."

"I'll teach you," Prabhat said, "but you'll have to accept me as your guru. Are you willing to do that?"

Shiva Shankar was surprised to hear that his friend had become a guru. But he was desperate to find some kind of relief from his condition.

"If it works, then I'm ready," he said.

"It will work."

Prabhat brought him to his room, where he taught him meditation and a specific *pranayama* technique, as well as some yoga postures.[8] He prescribed a change in diet and a medicine made from dissolving the leaves of a certain plant in unboiled milk. Shiva Shankar practiced the techniques faithfully and took the medicine. By the end of his leave, he was thrilled to find that his chronic and hitherto incurable condition had seemingly disappeared. Before returning to his post, he thanked Prabhat for what he considered a miracle cure and told him that he was ready to look upon him as his guru. Prabhat gave him his second lesson and detailed instructions regarding his conduct and practices.

When Shiva Shankar left Jamalpur and returned to his post in Sahebganj, he brought Prabhat's teachings with him, including strict adherence to the yogic code of ethics, yama and niyama. But as he settled back into his life as a policeman, he found it increasingly difficult to follow his guru's instructions. Corruption was endemic at his post, as it was in almost all areas of public service at that time. When it became clear to his colleagues that he was no longer willing to accept bribes or look the other way in the face of his fellow officers' improprieties, he began facing strong opposition and veiled threats. Determined to follow Prabhat's instructions, he applied for a transfer to a small outpost in the Bihar Military Police (BMP) in the hope that in a small and unenviable outpost he would be free to lead a principled life.[9] His request for a transfer was granted in late 1952, and he soon found himself in Dumka under the command of a thirty-five-year-old sergeant-major, Chandranath Kumar.

When Chandranath received the news that a sub-inspector from a prominent station in the Sahebganj colliery belt had requested and received a transfer to Dumka, the sergeant-major became suspicious. Generous monthly bribes were counted on as a regular addition to one's salary in the colliery belt; hence such a transfer was unheard of. Chandranath was one of those rare officers in the BMP who followed a strict code of ethics and paid scrupulous attention to his duties. Tall, lean, and athletic, with an acute sense of honor, he had been raised in the countryside by a disciplinarian father who had taught him to appreciate the value of a simple and straightforward life. When the new officer arrived, he kept alert for any signs of dereliction of duty, bad character, or other shortcomings that might have forced him to request the transfer. What he found instead was a man of exemplary conduct who impressed him in every aspect of his professional and personal life. Intrigued, he finally asked him why he put in a request for a transfer.

When he heard Shiva Shankar's story, Chandranath felt a surge of inspiration. He had been in search of a spiritual master himself for several years. During that time, he had met a number of gurus without feeling drawn to any of them, until he finally met a saint in his own native village of Gaddopur who greatly impressed him. But when he requested initiation, the saint refused. Instead, he assured Chandranath, "You will get it when the time comes." Now, a year later, Chandranath had a sudden premonition that his time had come. He told Shiva Shankar that he wanted to meet the man responsible for such a transformation, but he was disappointed to hear that Shiva Shankar's guru did not allow his identity or whereabouts to be disclosed. The best Shiva Shankar could do would be to present his request at the next opportunity and await his master's response. Chandranath wasted no time. He granted his subordinate immediate leave to visit his master and waited impatiently until his return two days later. His request was granted and the date and time fixed for him to come to Jamalpur.

When Chandranath arrived at Prabhat's house, Manas was seated on the porch. Manas ushered him into the front room and then went through a curtained doorway to inform his brother that someone had come to meet him. From the other side of the curtain, Chandranath heard a voice say, "Has the time come?" echoing precisely the words of the saint from his village. A few seconds later, Prabhat passed through the doorway and pulled up a chair for Chandranath next to the wooden cot where he normally sat when he received guests. After Chandranath introduced himself, Prabhat told him politely that he could ask whatever questions he wished. He would do his best to answer them.

"I haven't come with any questions," Chandranath said. "I have come for spiritual initiation."

"Are you sure?" Prabhat asked.

"Yes, I have been searching for a spiritual master. I feel like I've come to the right place."

Prabhat's mood changed suddenly. In a commanding tone of voice, he instructed Chandranath to sit in front of him on the cot with his legs crossed in meditation posture. Then he proceeded to initiate him. When the initiation was completed, Prabhat took a piece of paper and wrote down the ten principles of yama and niyama with brief explanations. He made sure that his new disciple understood them and then told him, "Follow yama and niyama very strictly. Let there be nothing in your conduct that can embarrass me. It is through the conduct of the disciple that one knows the guru. Let your face always be illumined with spiritual light."

After a brief conversation during which Prabhat explained various aspects of spiritual practice and spiritual life, he asked Chandranath the following questions: "Where does the soul come from? In what does it merge? Where does it remain when immersed in forgetfulness?" When Chandranath could not answer the questions, Prabhat supplied the answers: "The soul comes from the unqualified Brahma,[10] gets involved in the qualified Brahma, and gets attached to the body when it becomes lost in maya."[11]

When Chandranath was getting ready to leave, Prabhat added a few final words: "Do as much spiritual practice as you can and serve all creatures of this world. Search for opportunities to serve the people. And remember the words of Tulsi Das: 'When you came into the world, you were crying and the world was laughing; live your life in such a way that when you leave this world, the world is weeping and you are laughing.'"

Chandranath took Prabhat's words to heart. He began practicing his meditation with the utmost sincerity. Later that spring, Nagina Prasad Sinha, a distant cousin of the same age who worked for the Central Excise Department in Bhagalpur, came to pay him a visit. When dinner was served, Nagina was surprised to see that while his close friend had served him his usual non-vegetarian fare, he himself was eating a vegetarian meal. When Nagina asked why, Chandranath explained to him that he was now practicing meditation and yoga. Yogis recommended a vegetarian diet for those who wished to advance in the path of spirituality since meat and other non-vegetarian foods dulled the mind and incited the baser propensities. Chandranath had also given up smoking for the same reason. Nagina took this as a veiled reproach. He was a robust man, a former wrestler on his high school team who enjoyed drinking, smoking, and the best European cuisine with the relish of a gourmet. Over the following months, he made a good-natured attempt to convince Chandranath to give up this new fad, but he was unable to exert any influence over his resolute companion.

In October, Chandranath came to Bhagalpur and spent the night in Nagina's quarters. In the evening, Nagina took advantage of his cousin's visit to unburden himself. For the past several months, his boss had been doing his best to make his life miserable. Just that day the situation had gotten to the point where Nagina wasn't sure if he could tolerate it any longer. Chandranath listened patiently and consoled his friend. Finally he told him, "Nagina, I defy anyone to try and harm me. Even if God himself wanted to, he would have to think carefully about it." Then Chandranath excused himself; it was time for his evening meditation. He left his friend to ponder his words while he shut himself in Nagina's drawing room to meditate.

While Chandranath was meditating, Nagina lay down on a cot in the next room and wondered what kind of force Chandranath had acquired that could make him feel ready to challenge even God. He knew very well that his lifelong friend was far too humble to exaggerate his own strength or utter even a single word of self-praise. As he was contemplating Chandranath's words, he began to see the image of a man gazing at him from within his mind. The man was short in stature, light-skinned, with his hair combed back. He wore black eyeglasses and the traditional white cotton *dhoti* and *kurta*, and his face glowed with a divine luster.[12] Nagina soon found himself absorbed in the blissful vision. It was only when he heard his servant calling him that the spell was broken and the image dissolved. He was surprised to hear his servant say that dinner was served; Chandranath had been waiting for him for some time. He looked at his watch and was startled to see that two hours had passed.

When the two men sat down to eat, Nagina started plying his companion with questions about his yogic practice, but Chandranath was less than forthcoming with his answers. When Nagina asked him if he had a guru, Chandranath told him that he had a master but he was not permitted to say anything about him. Realizing that he would not get anything more from his friend, Nagina tried a different tack. He told Chandranath that he was going to describe someone and he wanted to see if Chandranath could tell who it was. Nagina then gave a detailed description of the man in his vision.

Chandranath stared at him. A hint of annoyance crept into his voice. "Why are you bothering me with so many questions about someone you obviously know so well?"

Nagina was surprised to see his suspicions confirmed. He went on to recount what had happened to him while Chandranath was meditating. Then he begged his friend to arrange for him to meet his master.

"I will do my best," Chandranath said. "If the mere thought of a great man can provoke such changes in you, then once you receive his blessings and are under his protection, you will be capable of defying even God."

When Nagina discovered that the master lived in Jamalpur, a scant two hours away by train, he insisted they leave immediately for the station to catch the night train. They could return in the morning after Nagina had gotten initiation and the master's blessings.

The Early Disciples

"That won't be possible, Nagina," Chandranath told him. No one is allowed to know who the master is without his prior permission, or where he lives.

"Then please, go and request permission for me."

"You are my friend and my relative. I know that you're going through difficult times, so I'll go to Jamalpur and present your petition, but I can't assure you that you'll get a favorable reply. Some people wait for months, even years, to get his permission, and you want it right away—and his blessings as well!"

Nagina passed an anxious day at the office before Chandranath arrived back in Bhagalpur the next evening and telephoned him from the station with the news that the master had given him permission to come for initiation. He had also sent him a message to face boldly whatever situations might arise; everything would turn out well. That night, Chandranath nearly took Nagina's breath away when he told him that before he had even had an opportunity to present his petition, the master had said, "So, you've come to talk about your friend Nagina."

It was November 3 when Nagina reached Prabhat's house. Stepping into the drawing room, he was overwhelmed when he saw the same effulgent face that he had seen in his vision. Prabhat asked him to sit in front of him in lotus posture and then initiated him. By the time the initiation was finished, Nagina was experiencing back pain. He began to slump.

"Can't you sit straight?" Prabhat asked.

"I've been having back problems for a long time now. It's difficult for me to sit in this posture."

Prabhat closed his eyes for a moment. When he opened them he said, "Drink hot water and your pain will go away."

After his initiation, Nagina wanted to know if it were necessary to be vegetarian to practice meditation and yoga. "I don't know if I could live without eating meat," he said.

Prabhat smiled. "It is better to be vegetarian. In fact, it is also better to give up onions and garlic. They have even more static properties than meat."

"But how can I give up eating meat? I just can't."

Prabhat laughed. "Up until now, you have only thought about the best way to prepare meat. Perhaps you've never even thought about the possibility that you could give it up. Just think about it and see whether or not you can.

"The path and process that I've shown you are very rational and logical," Prabhat continued. "Understand them properly and practice accordingly. *Sadhana*,[13] spiritual practice, is a must for human existence. But put it to the test; question why you do it. If you understand the rationale behind it, you'll be more motivated and you'll enjoy it more."

After Nagina returned to Bhagalpur, he disregarded Prabhat's instructions to drink hot water. Instead, he continued taking the medicines prescribed by his doctors, but his condition continued to deteriorate. Soon he was having difficulty breathing and had to take to his bed; he was unable to sit or walk without support. His bewildered doctors recommended that he go to Patna, the state capital, to take x-rays. Two weeks after his initiation, on a Saturday, Chandranath dropped by to see if he wanted to accompany him to Jamalpur for the Sunday program. Nagina was in no condition to go. He asked Chandranath to carry his salutations to the master and convey the message that since his initiation he had not been able to sit down and do meditation properly due to the pain. Chandranath returned the next evening and wasted no time in confronting Nagina.

"Gurudeva told you to take hot water, but instead of following his instructions you are taking all these medicines! That is going to end now."

Chandranath gathered up the medicines that were lying on the night table beside the bed. He threw out those that had been opened and asked Nagina's domestic servant to return the rest to the shop the following day. He then gave strict instructions to the servant and Nagina's wife that Nagina should only be served hot water. From that moment on, they gave him nothing but hot water to drink. When Nagina woke up the following morning, most of his pain was gone. Within a few days it completely disappeared.

With Nagina's initiation, the circle of disciples spread into the Central Excise Department. Though Prabhat did not allow his disciples to disclose his identity without his permission, he told them that if anyone approached them with a sincere desire to learn spiritual practice they could forward their names to him. If Prabhat approved, then they could give the person his name and address along with a time to come for initiation. Just as Shiva Shankar had brought Chandranath, Nagina now began bringing colleagues and friends of his.

Shortly after Nagina's initiation, Chandranath was transferred to the BMP training center in Nathnagar, a suburb of Bhagalpur. His presence there had such an impact that soon the number of disciples in the BMP would be second only to those in the Jamalpur railway workshop. A few years later Prabhat would say, only half in jest, that his favorite means of spreading his teachings was to get his disciples transferred.

VI

The Death of Stalin

In communist countries there is no sanctity in moral life—society is devoid of moral principles. In the name of this defective theory one of the leaders of the Soviet Union killed more than 500,000 people and sent many more to labor camps in Siberia. Among all the anti-human and homicidal theories that have been created in this world, communism is the most barbarous . . . All human society will have to undergo atonement for the sins committed by communism—not even the innocent will be spared. This dangerous theory has committed many atrocities against society, and it will continue to do so until it is finished in name as well as in theory.[1]

FOR NEARLY THREE years after Pranay's initiation, he continued to address Prabhat as he would a friend or a colleague, calling him Dada or Prabhat-da, though he had now begun to revere him as his guru. One day, while walking in the field, Prabhat told him that this form of address was not proper between guru and disciple. He should not call him "Dada," except in the office or in public, but rather "Baba." From then on Pranay followed this traditional form of address whenever they were alone. Prabhat instructed the other disciples to do the same. Soon everyone was calling the master "Baba," even though some of them, such as Chandranath and Nagina, were older than he was.

The number of disciples continued to mount, but, with few exceptions, individual disciples did not know who the others were, other than the person who had brought them and the persons they had brought. Baba had made it a rule that if they saw him with somebody else, whether at home or in the field, they should turn back and come to see him at a different time. These measures allowed Baba to maintain his anonymity. Not every disciple, however, was quite so strict. One day in 1952, Subodh Chatterjee, a childhood acquaintance who had taken initiation the previous year, was chatting with Dr. Sachinandan Mandal, who had also grown up with Baba. While they were talking, Subodh saw Baba pass by on the street. After pointing him out, he confided to Sachinandan that Baba had become a great yogi with supernatural powers and his own philosophy. Every evening, different people went with him to the field to listen to his spiritual wisdom, take his blessings, and witness his miraculous powers. When he heard this, Sachinandan remembered a couple of incidents that had given him pause. Recently another mutual friend, Gopi Kishore, had related to him that he had once gone to Baba for advice and discovered that his knowledge was so vast that not even professionals in their field could come close to matching him. On another occasion, Sachinandan had been coming down the stairs from his second-floor office after examining a patient; Baba had been going up the stairs at the same time. As they passed, Baba asked him if his patient was suffering from pain on both sides. Surprised at the question, Sachinandan thought for a moment that Baba might have seen him through the window checking the patient on both sides with his stethoscope, until he realized that it would have been physically impossible given the height of the window.

After listening to Subodh, Sachinandan decided to seek out his old classmate and learn from him. But when he met Baba and told him that he had heard of his greatness and that he too wanted to learn, Baba rebuffed him. "Nonsense," Baba said. "These people are making up stories. I don't know anything." Sachinandan was not so easily deterred. He continued to pester Baba whenever he saw him. Eventually Baba told him that if he were really interested he could give him the address of a Tantric in Nathnagar who could teach him. But Sachinandan was adamant. He insisted that he would only learn from him. Baba told him to first read the books of Ramakrishna; then he would see. A couple of months later, he handed Sachinandan a handwritten piece of paper with the ten principles of yama and niyama written out and told him to start practicing them. A few days later Baba called him to his house for initiation.

In the first week of February 1953, Sachinandan had the opportunity to go for an evening walk with Baba. They were accompanied by Sadhan Dey, who, unbeknownst to him, was also an initiate. When they reached the tiger's grave, they sat down and began conversing, a ritual that Baba observed every evening, regardless of who was accompanying him. At one point, Baba looked up at the sky and began to talk about astronomy. After a few minutes on this subject, he fell silent. He broke the silence by asking Sadhan to close his eyes and concentrate his mind at his sixth chakra.[2] Sachinandan, only recently initiated, watched with increasing fascination as Sadhan seemed to enter into a state of trance. Baba then ordered him to take his mind to the Kremlin and see what Stalin was doing. Absorbed in his trance, Sadhan replied that he was sitting alone and thinking. "Enter into his mind and see what he is thinking," Baba commanded. Sadhan replied that Stalin was brooding over how to spread communism around the world; he was formulating a plan to attack neighboring countries, especially India. "Tell Stalin to desist from any such plans," Baba said in a steely tone of voice, "otherwise it will mean disaster for him." Then Baba brought him out of his trance and began speaking about the history of Birbhum District, Sachinandan's native place.

Three weeks later, on March 1 or 2, Baba was seated on the tiger's grave with Haraprasad and Shiva Shankar Bannerjee. In the middle of their discussion, Baba suddenly asked Haraprasad if he would like to experience death.[3] Haraprasad, understandably uneasy at the prospect, respectfully declined. Baba repeated his request. He told him that he had nothing to fear, he would bring him back to life, but Haraprasad would not be convinced. At that moment, a man wearing the Territorial Army uniform was passing near the tiger's grave. Baba called out to him in Bhojpuri and asked him to come over and sit down for a moment. They exchanged a few pleasantries and then Baba made a special gesture with his hands.[4] The soldier collapsed. Baba asked Haraprasad to check his pulse, but he couldn't find any. The soldier did indeed appear dead, a discovery that provoked the immediate anxiety of both disciples.

"Don't worry," Baba told them. "I will bring him back, but first I'm going to bring a bodiless mind into his body."[5]

They watched dumbfounded as Baba reached out his foot and touched his big toe between the eyebrows of the soldier. The soldier's body stirred but his eyes did not open.

"Go to the Kremlin," Baba said, "and tell me what you see."

The prostrate soldier answered the question without opening his eyes. "Stalin is in a conference room with the officers of his military command. He is explaining something to them in Russian and pointing to a map."

"Enter into Stalin's mind and discover what his plans are."

"He is making plans to invade India."

"Tell him to stop immediately, otherwise it will mean disaster for him."

"I have told him."

"And what was his reaction?"

"Some fear has arisen in his mind. He has left the conference room and gone into his private chambers."

"Very well then." Baba turned his attention back to his disciples and began conversing on other subjects, while the soldier's body lay inert beside them on the grave.

Half an hour passed. Baba again turned towards the soldier and ordered the bodiless mind to return to the Kremlin and see what Stalin was doing.

"He has overcome his fear and is preparing to issue final orders to his officers."

Baba's mood darkened. "Stalin has failed to learn his lesson; now his time has come." Baba raised his right index finger in the air and made a cutting motion with his hand; at the same moment he said in a commanding voice, "Stalin, *nipat jao* (Stalin, be destroyed)."

Moments later, Baba ordered the bodiless mind to leave and the soldier's body became lifeless. He then ordered the soldier's mind to return. A few moments later the soldier began to breathe again; his body moved slightly. A few minutes later he opened his eyes and sat up, too tired to speak. Baba asked his disciples to massage him; a little while later the soldier was able to get up and walk away.

On March 5, Haraprasad had another chance to go on the evening walk with Baba. On his way home, after accompanying Baba to his residence, he saw a crowd gathered around a radio in a sweetshop. He stopped to find out what was going on and was stunned to hear the news that Stalin's death had just been announced.

Some years later, in 1970, Baba was walking with a South Indian disciple, Bhaktavatsalam. During their conversation, Baba told him that while Stalin's death had been announced on March 5, he had actually died a few days earlier. The Kremlin had kept the news secret because of a power struggle between Baria and Khrushchev over who would succeed the Russian leader.

"I was sitting on the tiger's grave one evening," Baba told him, "when a little boy from the Himalayas sent me a telepathic message: 'Baba, Stalin is planning to attack India. Please do something.' Stalin was given a warning. Three weeks later, I was sitting at the tiger's grave and that same little boy sent me another telepathic message: 'Baba, Stalin is about to declare war; he's planning on destroying India. Please do something.' You know, Bhaktavatsalam, Stalin died a short while later."

Later in that same year, Baba was giving a talk in Ranchi. During the talk he told his disciples that everything occurs due to the wish of the Supreme Consciousness; nothing can function without his wish. He then asked Vinayananda to stand up and give a speech about Ananda Marga. In the middle of Vinayananda's speech, Baba made a motion with his hand. Suddenly Vinayananda was unable to utter a single word. As he stood there, mute, Baba smiled and explained that he had withdrawn his power to speak; without his permission he would be unable to say anything. Then Baba gave him back his power to speak, and with a touch to his forehead, he put him into a spiritual trance. Baba got up as if to leave the room, but then he sat back down again and said, "The power by which Vinayananda's ability to speak was cut off is called the 'cosmic scissor.' By using the cosmic scissor, Paramapurusha, the Supreme Consciousness, can stop the functioning of anything in the universe. In the *Markendeya Purana* this power is called *chandika shakti*." He paused for a few moments and then added, "At the time of Stalin's death, the artery supplying blood to the brain was cut off by use of the cosmic scissor and he died immediately."

After saying this, Baba got up and left the room.

VII

The First Gathering

When a knower of truth merges in the Supreme Being, his petty sense of existence loses itself, and attaining unity with the Supreme Entity, he becomes Supreme himself. Spiritual practice is the means for expansion of the soul, not for its annihilation; so samadhi [spiritual trance] does not mean suicide but self-transcendence. One who has known the Supreme Consciousness becomes Supreme himself, for the individual entity takes on the very form of his object of ideation.[1]

As the decade of the fifties progressed, India struggled with innumerable demands on its new nationhood, but in the small town of Jamalpur, far from the great metropolises of Delhi and Calcutta, life continued at a more leisurely pace. Baba became a supervisor of the inspection section of the accounts department, and his reputation as a palmist, healer, and counselor continued to spread, even outside Jamalpur to places such as Sahebganj, some four hours away by rail. In 1951, Baba's brother Himanshu was transferred to Sahebganj by the East India Railways. Shortly after his transfer, the widowed mother of a colleague, Ram Rainjit Bhattacharya, came to him with a request. She was worried about the future of her second son, Bubai, who was doing poorly in his studies. She hoped that Himanshu could speak to his brother about him.

During his next weekend visit to Jamalpur, Himanshu communicated her request. The family had just finished lunch and Baba was lying down. He closed his eyes once Himanshu finished speaking and started describing the boy in great detail: the color of his skin, the shape of his eyes, his bone structure, and so on. When Himanshu confirmed that the description tallied, Baba told him to get a piece of paper and a pen and began dictating the boy's future. He instructed Himanshu to put a mark next to those areas where the boy would face difficulty. "Don't reveal these points to the boy's mother," Baba told him, "otherwise her worries will increase." When he finished, he told Himanshu to note down the time. "When you reach Sahebganj ask the boy exactly what he was doing at this hour."

A couple of days later, Himanshu visited the family. In answer to his question, the boy told him that something very strange had happened at that hour. He had been reading in the study at precisely a quarter to three when somehow he had lost consciousness for exactly twenty minutes. One moment it was 2:45. A moment later it was 3:05. Yet he was quite sure that he had not fallen asleep. He simply had no explanation for what had happened. Later that evening, Himanshu showed Baba's predictions to the boy's mother. She felt a great sense of relief. The next time Baba came to visit his brother in Sahebganj, she brought him sweets and other delicacies as a token of her appreciation.

Baba continued to select people for initiation as his disciples brought him the names of candidates who had expressed a strong interest in learning. Among them was Bindeshvari Singh, a contractor from Jamalpur who was Nagina's cousin. Bindeshvari had been greatly impressed by the changes he had seen in Nagina and had pestered him over a period of months to arrange a meeting with his guru. But when Nagina brought his petition to Baba, the master dismissed it. To Nagina's dismay, he informed him that Bindeshvari would not live for much longer. "What can he do in such a short period of time?" Baba said. Knowing that Bindeshvari suffered from periodic chest pains, Nagina sadly resigned himself to his cousin's fate. But Bindeshvari continued to insist with greater and greater urgency. Finally, Nagina returned to Baba and pleaded with him to give Bindeshvari a chance to learn spiritual sadhana. "However long he may have," Nagina said, "you could still give him a chance for salvation if you wanted to. If you wished, you could even extend his life."

Baba eventually relented. In June of 1954, Nagina brought Bindeshvari to Baba's quarters for initiation. When Bindeshvari came out of Baba's room, he staggered up to Nagina, put his hands on his cousin's shoulders, and said, "Do you know who is sitting in that room?"

"Yes, of course," Nagina replied. "It's Prabhat Rainjan Sarkar."

"No," Bindeshvari answered, barely able to contain his emotions. "He who came as Shiva, he who came as Krishna, is sitting in that room."

For the next month, Bindeshvari remained in such a God-intoxicated state that he was not able to work. In fact, he was barely able to take care of himself. He would lie on his bed for hours muttering "Baba, Baba, Baba" over and over again, or else pace up and down in his room crying for his guru. Nagina was forced to take time off work to assist him. Eventually, Bindeshvari was able to go back to work, but he never completely recovered his former state of mind. For the rest of his life, he would remain absorbed in the thought of his beloved master. At times he would become so absorbed that he would start speaking and gesturing exactly as Baba did, sometimes even asking the other disciples to do prostration in front of him. When they later complained to Baba about it, he excused Bindeshvari, explaining to them that he was in a state of *bhava*,[2] so absorbed in his devotional ideation in those moments that he fully identified himself with his guru.

Incidents like this helped to widen the circle of admirers who looked to Baba

The First Gathering

for guidance and inspiration. Most of them, however, had no idea that Baba was quietly gathering around him a group of disciples to whom he was teaching Tantric and yogic techniques as well as the beginnings of the philosophy that they would one day disseminate around the globe. In late October 1954, Baba sent an invitation to each of his disciples to attend a spiritual gathering on Sunday, November 7, at the railway quarters allotted to his brother Sudanshu at 339 E-F, Rampur Colony.[3] Sudanshu had given the quarters to Baba to use as he wished; Baba had in turn given them to Pranay to use for his spiritual practices after Pranay's grandfather, a staunch Hindu, had objected to Pranay doing his practices at home. Baba used the quarters on occasion to meet his disciples or initiate new ones. Now they would serve as the meeting place for the first gathering.

In the early evening, several disciples went to Baba's house to wait for him. When he came out, they accompanied him on the ten-to-fifteen minute walk from his Keshavpur home to the Rampur Colony quarters, where the rest of the disciples were waiting. When they arrived, Baba introduced everybody to one another. Many, especially those from Jamalpur, were surprised to see friends, colleagues, and acquaintances gathered there, often people they had known for years without having any idea that they were disciples of the same guru. After the introductions were made, Baba took his seat in the front room on a small wooden cot covered by a simple cotton sheet. The disciples came up one by one and did *sastaunga pranam*, the traditional full prostration before the guru. Then he started to talk about the goal of spiritual practice, the attainment of God, and the various stages of *samadhi*, or spiritual trance, wherein the spiritual aspirant attains temporary unification with the Divine, the final stage in the eight-fold path of yoga.[4] Then he called Pranay and asked him to sit in front of the cot in full-lotus posture.

Speaking in Bengali, Baba said, "Close your eyes and concentrate your mind at *ista* chakra,"[5] O Kulakundalini,[6] I, Yogeshvar Anandamurti, order you to leave the *muladhara* chakra and rise up to *svadhisthana*."

Pranay's body began to tremble.

"O Kulakundalini, I, Yogeshvar Anandamurti, order you to leave the *svadhisthana* chakra and rise up to *manipura*."

A violent tremor shook Pranay and then gradually subsided. His spine became rigidly erect and his head arched backwards.

"O Kulakundalini, I, Yogeshvar Anandamurti, order you to leave the *manipura* chakra and rise up to *anahata*."

Pranay fell backwards, his legs still bound in the full-lotus posture. He started making a loud, guttural "hum, hum" sound, one of the common symptoms that occur when a yogi goes into trance.

Baba then ordered the kundalini to rise to the *vishuddha* chakra; Pranay became absolutely still. His face shone with a glow of immense peace. Again Baba ordered the kundalini to rise, this time to the *ajina* chakra;[7] Pranay's face became even more resplendent.

While Pranay remained absorbed in this state of ecstasy, Baba smiled and looked towards his awestruck disciples. "This is the much-coveted state of *savikalpa* samadhi in which the unit mind merges into the Cosmic Mind.[8] The permanent establishment of a spiritual aspirant in this state is known as *mukti*, or liberation. By the regular practice of sadhana, with diligence, determination, and intense concentration, you too will be able to attain this state."

Baba continued describing the various stages of samadhi and the process by which a yogi achieves such exalted heights. Then he turned towards his oblivious disciple and ordered the kundalini to return to the *vishuddha* chakra. Pranay started weeping copiously, as if he were suffering an intense sorrow. "Okay, let him enjoy that state a little while longer," Baba said. He chatted with the other disciples about spirituality for a few minutes more. Then he turned back to Pranay and ordered the kundalini to descend, chakra by chakra, back to *muladhara*. Pranay wept loudly. When he opened his eyes again and sat up, still crying, Baba called him over and placed his head in his lap. He caressed the back of his head tenderly like a doting father and promised his tearful disciple that he would soon have another opportunity to enjoy what Baba had given and then taken away.

After the program was over, Pranay and a few others accompanied Baba to his house. The other disciples dispersed singly or in groups of twos and threes. As they left, they talked amongst themselves about what they had witnessed that evening, most of them still in awe over the demonstration. Some of them openly wondered what manner of guru could order the kundalini of his disciple to rise on his command and who used the epithet Yogeshvar, Lord of the Yogis, a title attributed to both Shiva and Krishna in a past so distant that it had crossed into the shadowed hinterland of myth and legend.

VIII

Death Demonstration

What happens when spiritual aspirants succeed in their quest to know Purushottama [Supreme Consciousness] and attain union with him? All bondages are snapped. When one loses all attachment for pettiness, the bondages which create pettiness also perish. With the dissolution of the unit-mind, that is, with the attainment of mental expansion, suffering also gradually wanes. Even the bondage of life and death is broken, for life and death belong to the finite, and so does the fear of them. The Great Brahma is beyond the scope of life and death, and so the one who becomes completely identified with him also remains unassailed by their ceaseless play.[1]

THE FOLLOWING SUNDAY, the disciples gathered once again at the Rampur Colony quarters for Baba's *darshan*.[2] Baba gave a spiritual talk and demonstrated another type of samadhi through the medium of Pranay. A strong sense of camaraderie began to spring up among the disciples as they became acquainted with one another and shared their devotion for their guru, the profound, life-altering sentiments that only their fellow disciples could understand. A community was in the process of being born, and those who were present during those initial gatherings could feel it right from the outset, the ties of spiritual brotherhood that would bind them more closely to each other than to their own families.

The word spread quickly among the initiates about the demonstrations. The following Sunday, November 21, saw an even greater influx of disciples eager to witness what Baba would do next. That morning Virendra Kumar Asthana, who had been unable to attend the previous two Sundays, arrived in Jamalpur from his home in Bhagalpur and went straight to Baba's house. About a year earlier he had been transferred to Nagina's office as the Assistant Collector of Central Excise and Customs, replacing the man who had earlier given Nagina so much trouble. Impressed by what he saw in Nagina, he had expressed his desire to meet his guru and take initiation. Despite being turned down by Baba several times, he had kept on trying and had finally gotten permission a couple of months earlier.

Asthana arrived at Baba's house shortly after breakfast and was fortunate enough to find the master alone. Together they sat and talked about spirituality. Baba patiently answered his disciple's questions and instructed him in the finer points of meditation. While they were talking, a young man appeared in the doorway. The moment Baba saw him he started scolding him. "Scoundrel! Good-for-nothing chap! How dare you show your face here! Go away! I don't want to see you anymore." Asthana was greatly surprised. Never had he seen Baba in such a mood. The master had always seemed to him the image of serenity, love, and wisdom.

The young man, however, didn't heed Baba's words. He caught hold of Baba's feet and started pleading with him. "Forgive me, Baba, I couldn't help it. Please forgive me."

Baba's tone softened. "You have committed a grave error. Are you ready to accept punishment for what you've done?"

"Yes Baba, whatever you decide," the man replied, relief showing through his tears.

"Virendra, go get one of your shoes and bring it here."

A bewildered Asthana jumped up to fetch the shoe and brought it to Baba. Baba then ordered the man to lick the sole of the shoe, an act of extreme humiliation in Indian culture. Asthana sat and watched, too shocked for words. As soon as the man began to lick the shoe, Baba stopped him and gave him his blessing. He told him he could go but that he should come to the Rampur Colony quarters that evening for the program. Once he had left, Baba told Asthana that the man had committed a great sin but he had forgiven him. Then he picked up the conversation where they had left off, nothing in his voice or facial expression giving any indication that something out of the ordinary had happened. What kind of guru do I have? Asthana thought, as they continued the conversation, unable to reconcile the fierce disciplinarian he had just witnessed with the magical figure who had begun to inundate his life with bliss.

By late afternoon the Rampur Colony quarters was teeming with disciples. When Baba arrived, the small front room was so tightly packed that the spectators were scarcely able to move. Baba made his way to the empty cot and sat down. He smiled and greeted everyone and chatted with those sitting closest to him. One of the disciples sang a devotional song. Then he began his talk.

He started by explaining life from the yogic point of view, emphasizing that life requires a parallelism between the body, the mind, and the vital energy. When this parallelism is lost due to changes in the physical wave, such as those brought about by illness or injury, or due to changes in the psychic wave, then the mind separates from the body.

"Most people are afraid of death," Baba said, "but no one need be. Death is a natural process, as natural as life itself. People commonly think that dying is painful. They see the stages that a dying person goes through and think that the person must be suffering greatly, but generally this is not the case. In most cases the experience of dying is not much different than that of falling asleep. From the outside the person may appear restless. They may appear to be suffering, but their inner experience is quite different."

From there, he went on to explain in detail the yogic conception of the body's vital energy. "The human body," he said, "has ten *vayus* or vital airs, five internal and five external. Of the five internal vayus, *prana* governs the area from the navel point to the throat; *apana*, the area below the navel; *saman*, located at the navel point, maintains the balance between apana and prana; *udana* governs the throat area; and *vyana* is distributed throughout the body. Each is responsible for the bodily functions in their respective areas. For example, prana controls respiration." After elucidating in detail each of the internal vayus, he explained the external vayus in the same manner, and then went on to explain what happens to the vayus during death. "In the human body the navel point is the point of balance between the upper and lower portions. When saman fails to maintain the balance between prana and apana, then prana becomes dislocated, which gives rise to navel breathing. These three vayus, failing to maintain their individual integrity, merge together and strike at the udana. When udana also loses its individual integrity, the four vayus merge with vyana and look to escape the body."

At this point Baba asked the disciples if they would like to see a demonstration on the subject. "Will you be afraid?" he asked them. When they assured him they would not, he called Krishna Chandra Pal—or Kestopal, as he was commonly called—to the front of the room and asked him to sit in lotus posture and close his eyes. Asthana recognized him as the young man whom Baba had disciplined so sternly that morning.

"Take your mind to ista chakra and concentrate it there," Baba said in a firm and solemn tone of voice. Kestopal began concentrating as instructed. "Prana vayu, leave your position and strike at saman vayu," Baba continued.

Kestopal's breathing became deeper. When Baba asked what he was feeling, he replied that he was feeling very relaxed and that he was losing the feeling in his hands and feet.

"Prana and saman, merge together and strike at the apana vayu."

Kestopal's breathing became heavy; he started gasping for air. Murmurs of concern went through the assembly, but when Baba asked him if he were feeling any discomfort, he shook his head.

"Prana and saman, merge with apana and strike at the udana vayu."

Kestopal fell over on his back. Several of the onlookers gasped. A rattling sound came from his throat and saliva foamed on his lips.

"Now, prana, saman, apana and udana, merge with vyana vayu."

All movement in Kestopal's body ceased. His head tilted slightly to one side.

Baba asked Dr. Sachinandan Mandal to come forward and examine him. "Is he dead or alive?" Baba asked in a calm, seemingly unconcerned tone of voice. The doctor examined him for a minute or two as the tension in the room increased.

"Baba, I can't find any vital signs; he has no heartbeat, no pulse."

Baba looked around the room for a few moments. Signs of apprehension were visible in the faces of nearly everyone present. "Clinically, he is dead," Baba said. He paused for a dramatic moment or two. "But actually he is not dead. Prana vayu is still present in the spinal column in a suspended state. Now it so happens that in certain rare cases, before the vayus completely escape and merge into the universal prana,[3] they remain suspended in the spinal column. This can happen in the case of certain accidents, snakebites, and occasionally with cholera victims. In such cases the person has no vital signs. He appears to be dead but actually he is not. In those countries where burial is the custom, it is possible that a person may revive after he has been buried. There have been cases noted in these countries where a coffin has been disinterred and scratch marks have been found on the inside of the lid. Or the skeleton may have shifted position. Sometimes people attribute this to ghosts. For this reason, in ancient India the bodies of people who had died from cholera or snakebite were traditionally floated downriver on a raft in the hope that they might revive. This is one of the reasons why I support cremation. Should a person's life force be suspended and this not be discovered by the doctors, then there is no chance of their awakening inside the coffin and dying a second, horrible death."

Baba raised his finger and ordered prana vayu to leave the body. Kestopal's head tilted even farther and his mouth opened slightly. "Now he is dead," Baba said with an air of finality. "As I was saying, I support cremation for reasons I have already explained. You can now make arrangements for the disposal of the body."

Murmurs of alarm passed like a contagion among the disciples. Several of them importuned Baba to bring Kestopal back to life. "What can I possibly do now?" he replied. "I have no such capacity." Some became worried about what would happen to them when the police found out. Others were wondering what manner of miracle maker Baba was to be able to do such a thing. A few were quietly enjoying the drama, their faith in the master holding firm. Rasamay was terrified. Kestopal had gotten married only a few days before and he and his new bride were staying with him while they were in Jamalpur. How could he tell her that she was a widow, that Kestopal's guru had taken his life?

Baba smiled. "Don't worry," he said. "Remember, you promised you would not be afraid. I am going into the next room for a short while. In the meantime, keep watch over Kestopal's body and make sure that no insects are allowed to enter through any orifice."

Baba asked Nagina and Pranay to accompany him into the next room, where he gave them instructions to massage his feet and hands while he sat for meditation. They spread a blanket on the floor for Baba to sit and massaged him for some fifteen to twenty minutes while Baba remained in a state of trance.

Finally Baba opened his eyes and returned to the room where Kestopal was lying inert among an anxious group of disciples.

Baba sat down near Kestopal's head. He reached out his right foot and touched the big toe to the crown of his disciple's head. Almost immediately Kestopal stirred. A collective gasp of relief passed through the crowd.

"Open your eyes," Baba said. Kestopal opened his eyes.

"Who are you?" Baba asked. To everyone's surprise he gave a completely different name.[4]

"Why are you here?" Baba asked.

"Because you asked me to come and protect this body."

"Very well. Then as long as you are here you should do some work. Take your mind to the moon."

"I am there."

"What do you see?"

"Arid plains and mountains."

"Is there any sign of life?"

"No. There is no oxygen."

"Go below the surface of the planet. What do you see?"

"Baba, I see vast deposits of gold and silver."

"Now take your mind to Mars. Is there any sign of life?"

"Yes."

"What kind of life?"

"Microbial life."

"Now take your mind to a planet of the star Ashvin. Does life exist there?"

"Yes."

"What kind of life?"

"Human life."

"Does this human life bear any resemblance to human life on earth?"

"No, Baba. They have a different physical structure."

"What is the spiritual standard of that civilization?"

"They are far more advanced than human beings of Earth. Their young children are initiated into advanced processes of meditation."

"I see. Now take your mind to Tibet." Baba gave him instructions to go to a certain cave in the Himalayas near Limpopo. "What do you see there?"

"Baba, there is a yogi with long hair meditating in the cave."

"Can you recognize him?"

"Yes, Baba; it is Subhash Chandra Bose."

"Ask him if he wants to come back to India."

"He is shaking his head no."

"Very well. Now take your mind to the Kremlin. What do you see?"

"I see Malenkov meeting with members of his cabinet."

Baba's voice suddenly hardened. "Tell Malenkov that if he does anything to disturb the cause of world peace, he will meet the same fate that Stalin met."

Baba gave permission for that mind to leave, after which the body remained lifeless. He looked around the room and told everyone that he would now bring Kestopal's mind back to his body, but before doing so, everyone had to promise that they would not tell Kestopal what had happened.

"As I explained earlier, the experience of dying is not much different than that of falling asleep. When Kestopal regains consciousness, he will assume that he was asleep. However, he will feel very tired and disoriented, much more than usual, due to his body having been uninhabited for some time, during which the circulation of the blood was stopped. I will ask someone to massage him. This will help him to recuperate faster."

Baba raised one hand and began tracing small circles with an outstretched finger. "Wherever you might be in the great void, come now to Earth. Come down to India. Come to the state of Bihar. Come to the city of Jamalpur. Enter into the quarters number 339 EF, Rampur Colony. Enter into this body."

One by one, Baba ordered the vayus back into the body. As everyone watched in suspense, they saw a little movement in Kestopal's hands. Then his feet stirred slightly. Finally after a couple of minutes he opened his eyes again. Baba chanted some mantras in Sanskrit; moments later Kestopal was able to sit up.

"Kestopal," he said, "you look out of sorts. What happened?"

"I am sorry, Baba. I must have fallen asleep. I feel so tired."

Baba instructed two disciples to give him a massage and told another to prepare a cup of hot milk for him.

Asthana was as amazed as everyone else by the events of that day, but a burning curiosity remained in his mind. Why had Baba scolded Kestopal so mercilessly that morning? The next time he had a chance to be alone with the master, he took advantage of the opportunity to pose this question.

"That rascal. When I initiated him I forbade him to marry, knowing he had a samskara for a short life. You know very well what the position of widows is in this country.[5] It is pitiful. They are expected to never remarry and to retire from society and go into seclusion, even if they are very young. The deceased husband's family often mistreats them. If Kesto got married, then an innocent girl would soon be widowed and forced to undergo needless suffering. I didn't want to see that happen. But the scoundrel went ahead and disobeyed my orders. What could I do? He is my disciple. He had a samskara to die at a young age and that samskara had to be exhausted. So I did the death demonstration. Now that samskara has been satisfied and he can live a long life."

The disciples could not hold their tongues for long. Eventually one and then another approached Kestopal and asked him if he knew what had happened to him that evening?

"Sure. I fell asleep while I was supposed to be meditating."

"No, Baba demonstrated death on you! You were dead! We all saw it."

Once the vow of secrecy was broken, Asthana asked Kestopal about that day, after relating what Baba had told him.

"Yes, it's very true," Kestopal said. "The previous week I had gone to my native village on vacation to visit my parents. Unbeknownst to me, they had made preparations for my marriage. They had chosen a bride from a neighboring village, fixed the date, and invited the guests. I tried to protest and tell them that my guru had forbidden me to marry, but it didn't do any good. The pressure from the family was so intense that in the end I caved in. When I arrived back in Jamalpur, I left my wife in the station and went straightaway to Baba to apologize and explain what had happened. But as you saw, there was no need. He already knew. He knows everything."

Nagina also questioned Baba about the incident and asked him why he had requested them to massage him when he went into the other room. "My mind was withdrawing into the state of nirvikalpa samadhi," Baba explained. "If I had allowed that to happen, it would have taken me some time to come back to a state of normal consciousness and his body would have begun to decompose, making it difficult or impossible to bring back his mind. For that reason, I did not want to go into samadhi. I asked you to massage me so that my mind would remain conscious of the body. In spite of taking these precautions, I still went into samadhi for a short time."

Kestopal would indeed live a long life. He died in August of 2008, during the preparation of this manuscript.

IX

Now Many People Will Come

Despite its advent onto this earth many thousands of years ago, humanity has not yet been capable of building a well-integrated and universal society. This is in no way indicative of the glory of human intellect and erudition. You, who have understood the predicament, realized the urgency, seen the naked dance of evil and heard the hypocritical and raucous laughter of the divisive forces, should throw yourself into this noble task without further delay. When the ends are just and noble, success is inevitable.[1]

Though no one had any inkling yet of the vast extent of the philosophy that Baba would soon be unveiling, he made the basic tenets of his teachings clear to everyone right from the beginning. Baba required all his disciples who wore the sacred thread to remove it before he would initiate them. He spoke out openly against all kinds of religious dogma, including the idol worship and the caste system so fundamental to orthodox Hinduism. He urged them to openly oppose all sorts of social injustice. The only "ism" he supported was universalism, emphasizing time and again that all human beings belonged to one cosmic brotherhood with equal rights to the gifts of Providence. It was a fundamental part of their practice, he explained, to treat everything, animate or inanimate, as varied expressions of one Divine Consciousness. This implied a spirit of service to the creation, a willingness to work not only for the welfare of human beings but of all living beings and even inanimate objects.

These and the other ideals he preached became the basis of the message he asked them to spread: a rational, scientific spirituality that immediately started to attract the progressive minded in Jamalpur and nearby towns and would soon begin drawing the ire of the orthodox Hindu community. Even the so-called miracles they had witnessed had a scientific explanation, and Baba went to great lengths to elucidate the subtle mechanisms behind them, though his explanations were sometimes too complex or too subtle for them to follow. "There is nothing supernatural in this universe," he told them. "Everything is natural. It is only that some things are comparatively rare so we take them to have some supernatural origin." Despite the demonstrations and other manifestations of his spiritual power, he constantly reminded them that he wanted them to propagate his ideals and not his personality. "Look to the teachings," he would say, "not to this body; after some time this body will be gone but the teachings will remain." In the coming years, Baba would continually remind them that he wanted a cult of ideology, not a cult of personality.

In the middle of December, Baba was walking with Chandranath, Pranay, and a few others in the field, when he turned to them and said, "Now many people will start to come. You will need an organization to receive them." In previous years he had on occasion mentioned to his brothers Himanshu and Manas that he intended to start an organization one day through which he would open service projects, such as schools, orphanages, medical clinics, tribal welfare centers, and so on. This, however, was the first time that any of his disciples learned of his plans. A few days later he mentioned the same thing to another group of disciples. The idea jelled and it was decided, on Baba's suggestion, to officially found the organization "on the first day of the international calendar." In the meantime, Baba suggested they hold a meeting in order to draft a constitution and a set of by-laws, required to legally register the organization. It was decided to use the Christmas holiday for this purpose.

On Christmas morning, a group of disciples led by Pranay met at the Rampur Colony quarters to draft the constitution. Unaware of the meeting, Nagina also arrived in Jamalpur that morning along with Dr. Vishvanath, a childhood friend and veterinarian whom he had brought to Baba for initiation earlier that year, and Dipnarayan, a young clerk who worked under him in the Central Excise Department.

Dipnarayan had been initiated two weeks earlier under rather unusual circumstances. Within minutes of being ushered into Baba's room, he had lost consciousness and had to be carried out.

> I remember I entered the room and sat down in front of Baba, who was sitting on a cot. Then his grace entered me and I went into a state of samadhi. When I began to recover my consciousness I was lying in a corner of the next room. I heard Baba tell Sukumar to give me a cup of hot milk. I tried to get up but I couldn't. I was a champion weightlifter in college but I couldn't even stand up properly. My body was as cold as ice. The other people there helped me to get up. Then gradually it came back to me that Baba had given me a mantra that I was supposed to repeat. That was all I could remember from the initiation. The next day Baba revised my meditation.

Three days later, while Dipnarayan was in the bathroom, it occurred to him that it would not be proper to recite a sacred mantra in such a dirty place. He stopped his internal recitation and waited until he was out of the bathroom before he began again. That evening Baba came to the ashram and gave a short talk in which he explained that the mantra should be recited silently, everywhere and anywhere, even on the toilet. "Do you understand, Dipnarayan?" Baba said. Afterwards, Dipnarayan had to explain to the curious disciples why Baba had singled him out.

Now, ten days later, Dipnarayan, Nagina, and Vishvanath were heading towards Baba's house in high spirits to spend Christmas day with the master. Before they reached the house, they saw Baba walking in their direction. They rushed up to him and bowed down to touch his feet in the traditional show of respect for one's elders and one's guru known as *pranam*.[2] Baba informed them of the meeting and suggested they go to the ashram to help the others with what was certain to be a long day's work. On their way to the ashram, they stopped at Bindeshvari's house to eat an early lunch. Nagina, an inveterate smoker, was about to leave his cigarettes at the house, as he normally did, but Vishvanath convinced him to bring them along. It was going to be a long afternoon, he reasoned; Nagina would be hard-pressed to go that long without a smoke.

When they arrived at the ashram, Nagina left his cigarettes outside on a window ledge before joining the others, who were sitting in a circle in front of a wooden cot. A batik cotton sheet covered the cot and on it was a framed photo of Baba in *varabhaya mudra*.[3] Pranay asked Nagina to take dictation and he immediately set to work. Late in the afternoon, with the greater portion of the constitution completed, Nagina excused himself to go outside and have a smoke. The other disciples, however, wanted to press on. Someone suggested that Nagina fetch his cigarettes and smoke while they continued working. All eyes turned to Pranay who had been designated as the ashram manager. Pranay thought about it for a moment and then hit upon a compromise. "Shishir, take Baba's photo into the next room and leave it there until Nagina is done smoking. That way we won't be disrespecting the guru." When the photo was removed, Pranay made a makeshift ashtray for Nagina. Though Nagina felt uneasy about it, he lit a cigarette and went back to work. After a couple of puffs the cigarette went out and he was unable to light it again before he ran out of matches. He shrugged his shoulders, left the cigarette in the ashtray, and continued writing.

A couple of hours later the group finished their work. Some of them, including Nagina, left to meet Baba at his house. The rest decided to remain in the ashram and relax until Baba arrived. As Nagina and the others were walking down the road towards Baba's house, they saw him heading towards the ashram at a furious pace. When Baba drew near, they realized that his mood was even more furious than his gait. Turning to accompany him, they struggled to keep pace, disconcerted by the stormy look on the master's face. Finally someone timidly asked him what the matter was. "My whole body is burning," Baba shouted. After that no one dared say anything. When they reached the ashram, Baba strode directly to his chair and called for a piece of paper, a pen, and someone to take dictation.

"Punishment order number one," Baba said, once Nagina was ready with a pen. "Nagina will not touch my feet until further notice,[4] and he will not participate in *gurupuja*."[5] A distraught Nagina tried to keep his hand from trembling as he noted down his punishment. "Punishment order number two: Dipnarayan will not touch my feet for a period of four days. Punishment order number three: Pranay Kumar and Shishir will not touch my feet for a period of three days." Unable to control himself, Nagina started weeping while everyone else trembled in the face of Baba's ire.

"Do you think that if you remove my photo to the other room I won't be able to see what is going on here? My whole body was burning from the smoke."

That night during field walk, Baba again scolded Pranay for not preserving the sanctity of the ashram. He rebuked Nagina for disobeying his instructions to avoid smoke, which he had given Nagina when he had taught him pranayama. Nagina, who had not realized that avoiding smoke also meant he should stop smoking himself, vowed to quit, and indeed that would be the last cigarette he would ever smoke.

When Nagina returned home, he found that he had been demoted from his position of Superintendent, Central Excise, effective December 25, the same date as Baba's punishment. He was so upset by the incident that he was afraid to even touch Baba's feet mentally without permission, so he wrote a letter to Baba and asked whether or not it was permitted. Baba wrote back that it was allowed and also explained to him in a second letter that he should not allow the sanctity of the ashram to be violated under any circumstances. A week later, Dipnarayan brought Nagina a third letter from Baba lifting his punishment along with advice on how to get his demotion overturned. Nagina followed Baba's instructions and was eventually restored to his previous post.

The next meeting was held on Saturday, the first of January, in Baba's presence. Baba began by telling the disciples that he was thinking of calling the new organization "Ananda Marga." "*Ananda*," he said, "is the Sanskrit word for infinite happiness or bliss, the goal of every living being. *Marga* is the path that leads to that goal. Thus Ananda Marga is 'the path of bliss.'" He asked everyone what they thought of the name; when they voiced their approval, he suggested the name "Ananda Marga Pracaraka Samgha," the society for the propagation of Ananda Marga, as the official name of the new organization. Their school of philosophy, he explained, would also be called "Ananda Marga." The process of sadhana would be called *sahaj* yoga, "easy" yoga, though as Nagina remarked to Baba a few days later, there was nothing easy about it. Baba was chosen president at everyone's insistence and over his own objections. He then selected the various officers: Pranay was appointed the general secretary and Shishir the treasurer.

Baba gave the disciples some simple guidelines for the organization. He told them they should get together in their respective communities every week and hold a collective meditation, preferably on Sunday. This collective meditation would be called "Dharmachakra," the circle of spirituality. He taught them some Sanskrit chants to begin and end the meditation. He suggested that district committees be formed in the different cities to organize activities. He also made it official that the name and address of the guru should not be disclosed. Pranay drew up a document to that effect that Baba signed as president. At one point Baba pointed to himself and said, "Now many people will start to come and it will not be possible for me with one physical body to initiate them all. Some of you will have to act as my representatives and undergo training as acharyas."[6] A few days later Baba would start training Pranay to be the first acharya, followed in February by a group of five more. Finally, Baba declared that on the following Sunday they would hold a large spiritual conference with a collective meal afterwards, and thereafter at periodic intervals. In the future, such collective spiritual gatherings would be called "Dharmamahachakra," the great circle of spirituality.

Later that evening Baba sat and gave a formal discourse. Several disciples took notes in longhand, trying to preserve the contents of his speech as best they could. The subject of the discourse was "The Gradual Evolution of Society." For the first time, Baba used the name "Ananda Marga" to refer to the new philosophy and spiritual movement. ". . . During the introversal phase of the Cosmic mind," he began, "when the quinquelemental creation came in touch with the divine powers of Purushottama,[7] the Supreme All-knowing Entity, it developed the vibrations of life, and the more this vital energy received Brahma's brilliance, the more enlightened it grew, and this glow led it forward on the path of self-realization." From there, he traced the evolution of consciousness as it manifested in the evolution of society, from its inception until the present age, ending with a concise description of the disastrous state of contemporary human affairs. He then pointed out the need for change in words shorn of any ambiguity. "This state of affairs cannot be allowed to continue. This structure of inequality and injustice must be destroyed and powdered down for the collective interest of human beings. Then and then alone may man be able to lead society on the path of virtue." Finally Baba exhorted his disciples, and indeed the entire human race, to accept responsibility for creating a blissful society:

> O man, frame the social structure having regard to the needs of man. Do not perpetrate any o achievements actuated with limited motives, destitute of cosmic feelings, cannot last. The cruel touch of time will annihilate them into an oblivion which nobody can comprehend. It is not necessary to study books for the purpose of knowing how to work, how to act, how to retain and how to renounce. The need is to look upon every living being of the universe with sincere feelings of love and sympathy, and then and then alone, you will realize that whatever you make, retain, or break is generated and controlled by

the Universal Cosmic Bliss. With this devotion, and actions guided by knowledge, you will be able to explore the very soul of souls, the Supreme object within you whom you had concealed unknowingly within the precious treasures of your heart.[8]

In a single discourse Baba summed up the spirit of Ananda Marga, laying the foundation for the ideology he would now begin openly disseminating, and letting his disciples know that his teachings and his life would not be confined to the spiritual elevation of a select group of individuals. Unlike other spiritual movements, his disciples would have to accept the demanding work of social change as their direct responsibility, something very different than they were used to seeing in Indian gurus. He made it clear to them that he would be content with nothing less than the transformation of an entire planet for the welfare of every living being that inhabited it. This was his mission. By accepting him as their guru, it would also become theirs.

X

Bindeshvari's New Lease on Life

For those who are established in introspective trance, the objects that are visualized internally appear to be indistinguishable from their own ego. Onlookers cannot comprehend such a state as this. Some ridicule such sádhakas [spiritual aspirants]; some call them crazy or mad. They do not know that to become like them requires the merit of several births and demands a concentrated yearning to attain the One to the exclusion of all. It is only these "lunatics" that can lead the collective mind forward . . .[1]

WHEN NAGINA ARRIVED at the ashram on Sunday, January 9, the first thing he noticed was a "No Smoking" sign by the door. Alongside it was a second sign with a Sanskrit couplet from the *Guru Gita: shive ruste gurustrata/gurau ruste na kaschana*—if God is angry with you the guru will protect you, but if the guru is angry with you then no one can protect you. Nagina could not help but flash a wry smile as he entered the premises.

Inside the compound, preparations were underway for the evening Dharmamahachakra, or DMC as Baba referred to it. A few disciples were busy preparing a small raised platform on the veranda for Baba to sit on while he delivered his discourse. Others were in the kitchen preparing food for the collective meal. By the time Baba arrived, between sixty and seventy disciples had gathered to attend. Though Ananda Marga was only nine days old, they had already begun referring to themselves as "Ananda Margis," or simply "Margis."

Baba's talk that evening was the first in a long series of discourses delivered over several years that together would contain a systematic exposition of the spiritual philosophy of Ananda Marga. He began at the beginning, with an explanation of yogic cosmology and the interplay of forces that govern the expressed universe, paying special attention to the influence of these forces on the human mind.[2] His scientific approach to spirituality made it clear that he was reinterpreting ancient mystical teachings in a language adapted to the needs of the modern human being and the generations to come. He also took advantage of the philosophical platform to show how caste consciousness degrades the human mind. "The followers of Ananda Marga have no caste," he told his disciples. "They do not acknowledge the baneful and delusory manmade classifications."³

Finally, Baba explained the significance of the sound om, symbol for the cosmic sonic vibration that accompanies the creation of the universe. He explained how advanced yogis are able to perceive that sound in their meditation and follow it to its source, the infinite Supreme Consciousness. Then he instructed the disciples to sit in meditation posture and concentrate their minds.

"Everyone will now hear this sound," Baba said, "in accordance with the stage of sadhana they have attained." Within a few minutes everyone started hearing the om sound, some very faintly, like the distant hum of crickets, others so clearly that they quickly became absorbed in the sound and entered into trance with cries of "hum" and "Baba." After ten minutes or so, Baba ended their meditation by intoning a Sanskrit chant. When everyone's eyes were open again, he explained the theory of kundalini and the various symptoms that a yogi experiences as the kundalini rises through the chakras. Then he called Shiva Shankar Bannerjee to the front and asked him to close his eyes and begin meditating. As on previous occasions, Baba commanded his disciple's kundalini to rise through the chakras, one by one. Shiva Shankar's body began to writhe like a snake. As the kundalini moved upwards, he exhibited the various symptoms that Baba had just described. When the kundalini reached the seventh chakra, he fell backwards in trance and remained motionless while Baba explained the subtle nuances of the samadhi that he was experiencing. Finally, Baba ordered him to "be normal"; gradually he regained his normal consciousness.

When the demonstration was over, the disciples performed gurupuja collectively for the first time. A couple of the newer initiates had brought fruit and flowers to offer to the guru, as was tradition in the Hindu community, but the other disciples explained to them that Baba did not approve of physical offerings. They instructed them to offer mental flowers instead, symbolic of their attachments and desires. While offering a mental lotus in whatever color most attracted their mind, they were to ask God or the guru to free them from those desires and attachments that hindered their spiritual progress.

A few months earlier, Nagina had questioned Baba about this injunction. "Baba, it is our tradition that one does not go empty-handed before one's guru or one's king. If nothing else, one should take green leaves, fruits, flowers, or even fresh water as an offering."

"Nagina, it is true that in olden days the guru wanted the disciple to offer him fruit. But which fruit? The fruit of his actions. In time, the spirit of this was lost and gurus started accepting sweet fruits instead of the karma of their disciples. Now this has become a custom. You are free to offer the fruits of your actions whenever you like but not actual fruits. Furthermore, if I accepted fruits from you then your poorer brothers would also do the same. This would put them into financial difficulties. If I accepted those fruits, knowing full well the economic difficulties involved, it would not be ethical on my part. Do you want Baba to discriminate among his disciples? Rather, the disciple should only ask that the guru's desires be fulfilled."

"Baba, sometimes when I see something nice I feel a desire to bring it for you. What should I do in such situations?"

"In that case, you should offer it to me mentally then and there. I will receive it and then you can take it as *prasad*."[4]

After the program, the Margis dispersed, except for Pranay and Haragovind Mandal who remained with Baba in his room. Baba was talking to them about the future of Ananda Marga and the profound impact that it would have on human society when he suddenly said, "Now that I have started Ananda Marga, my mission on this earth is complete. You people will get the work done. Now allow me to leave my physical body." At first they couldn't quite believe what they were hearing. But when Baba lay down and asked them to chant *hari bol, hari bol*,[5] his voice grew weaker and weaker. It dawned on them that he might be serious. Overcome by emotion, they grabbed Baba's feet and implored him to stay. Their voices quavered and tears wet their cheeks but Baba remained silent, seemingly too weak to reply. After repeated entreaties, however, he finally acquiesced. "Help me to sit up," he said in a whisper. "My whole body is in pain." The two disciples started massaging his arms and legs. Gradually Baba's physical strength returned. Finally, he promised that he would stay and help them complete the mission of Ananda Marga. After they had left the master at his house, Pranay and Haragovind walked together for some time discussing the strange event they had witnessed; neither of them knew quite what to make of it.

The following week, Baba suggested that DMC be held each month on the Sunday closest to the full moon. The Margis met together and decided that the next DMC would be held in Bhagalpur, since Bhagalpur had the greatest number of disciples outside Jamalpur. In the meantime, Baba completed Pranay's acharya training and authorized him to start giving initiations. He also started training five more acharyas: Chandranath Kumar, Shiva Shankar Bannerjee, Sukumar Bose, Shishir Dutta, and Chandranath's wife, Ram Pari Devi. When their training was completed in March, Baba stopped personally initiating disciples.

On the morning of February 6, Baba arrived with Pranay at Chandranath's sergeant-major's quarters in Bhagalpur for the second official DMC. The first thing he did after his arrival was to ask Chandranath to bring him everyone in the family who was not initiated. One by one, Chandranath brought his three children (the fourth was a baby at that time), his cook Makhan, and his eighty-year-old aunt to Baba's room. When his aunt, a devout Hindu, entered the room, she said, "Guruji,[6] what can I do at this old age? My body has become weak and infirm." Baba smiled and said, "Ma, do what you can. I will do the rest."

By noon, some thirty-five disciples had gathered in the living room. Baba gave a discourse entitled "Karma and Karmaphala," actions and their reactions, in which he continued his delineation of the interplay of forces that gives rise to the universe, and detailed the theory of cause and effect, action and reaction, both on the macrocosmic and microcosmic levels. He ended the discourse with an explanation of the yogic practice of *madhuvidya*, the technique whereby a yogi learns to act without creating new reactions, or *samskaras*,[7] thus paving the way for liberation.

During his discourse, Bindeshvari was seated just to the left of Baba's cot. Midway through the talk, Bindeshvari's breathing started to become labored. Moments later he cried out, "No, no." Baba paused and looked at him. Some of the other disciples who knew of his heart condition became afraid that he might be having a heart attack. Suddenly, without getting up or uncrossing his legs, Bindeshvari started crawling towards Baba, until he collapsed with his head on Baba's lap. Baba put one hand on his head and said, "Be calm, there is no need to worry. I am always with you." With his other hand, Baba signaled for Nagina to remove Bindeshvari from the room. Helped by another disciple, Nagina carried him to the drawing room while Baba continued with his discourse. They laid him on a sofa where he continued to mutter "no, no" and other words that no one could understand.

At the end of the discourse, Baba called Dipnarayan to the front and demonstrated a specific form of samadhi on him. Dipnarayan later recounted that during the demonstration he felt an electric current surging up and down his body and sparks of something akin to electricity jumping from chakra to chakra, until he finally lost consciousness, overwhelmed by a tidal wave of bliss. When he recovered his senses, the DMC was over and he was alone in the room.

After the program, Baba went to his room and called for Nagina. "Nagina," he said, "Bindeshvari was supposed to have died today. It was his time. But since he was in DMC, I gave him another lease on life. I gave him a little bit of my own prana and my own mind, enough to keep him alive. However, he's going to start to act very strangely now. Though he's a grown-up, he's going to start acting like a little child. You'll have to take care of him. One more thing: Whatever you do, don't tell him that he was supposed to have died today, or that I have deferred his death."

Nagina went into the next room to check on his cousin. He found him surrounded by a small group of disciples. He was alternately laughing and crying, repeating over and over again that Baba had saved him from the jaws of death.

"What are you talking about?" Nagina asked.

Bindeshvari reached out and tearfully grabbed his cousin's hands. "My heart began to palpitate, and I became overpowered by fear, so I crawled into Baba's lap, sure that I was about to die. As soon as I reached Baba's lap, my life force left my body and I became dead. But then I felt a force injected into me. I regained consciousness and felt myself being thrust back into my body."

Again Bindeshvari started crying loudly, telling everyone that Baba had saved him from the jaws of death. When he calmed down a bit, he turned again to Nagina and said, "It's thanks to you also that I'm alive. If you had not forced me to come to DMC, I would have certainly died at that moment."

When Nagina informed Baba that Bindeshvari was telling everyone that he had given him new life, Baba closed his eyes for a moment. When he opened them again, he said, "Since I gave him a small bit of my own prana and mind when he was dying, he knows what is in my mind. Anyhow, let him say whatever he wants. Just tell him forcefully that he is speaking nonsense. Be very cautious in this regard."

Bindeshvari remained in an abnormal state for a period of several weeks. One moment he would laugh and the next moment he would cry. Sometimes he would start trembling, his face would turn red, and he would fall silent, completely absorbed in his ideation, except for an occasional exclamation of "Baba, Baba." At other times, he would declare that he was Baba and ask people to prostrate in front of him. Nagina took a leave of absence to remain in Jamalpur and take care of him. During the day, Bindeshvari would often climb onto his lap like a young child. At night he insisted on sleeping with Nagina in the same bed. This alarmed Bindeshvari's family; they began to blame Nagina for his madness. Finally Nagina went to Baba for help. Baba told him to bring Bindeshvari to see him.

As soon as he entered Baba's presence, Bindeshvari became completely abnormal. Baba scolded him and threatened to suspend the ecstasy he had given him if he continued to act that way. This helped him to calm down. Baba then gave Nagina instructions to keep Bindeshvari away from him for some time, since being in his presence would only exacerbate his condition. Whenever he began to become abnormal at home, he should remind him that Baba would be angry with him if he found out that he was acting that way. The recipe worked and Bindeshvari gradually regained his normal consciousness— normal, that is, for Bindeshvari. For the rest of his life, Bindeshvari would enjoy a well-deserved reputation for spiritual intoxication. As the years went by, he would become known for being able to see other people's thoughts, effecting miraculous cures, and putting people into states of trance by touching them between the eyebrows. Baba made it clear that he disapproved of such things, but when other disciples would complain about it, Baba would smile and tell them to let Bindeshvari be.

After the DMC, Chandranath's elderly aunt practiced her meditation as sincerely as possible. She quickly began to share the faith in Baba that she had seen blossoming in her nephew and his wife. In October of that year, Ram Pari Devi went to Jamalpur for Baba's darshan. "Now your aunt's time on this earth is drawing to a close," Baba told her. "Be ready."

She went back to Bhagalpur and informed her husband. The whole family was put on alert. A couple of days later the old lady, who had been growing weaker by the hour, finally collapsed. Makhan carried her to her bed, while Ram Pari Devi sent a messenger to bring Chandranath from the office. By the time Chandranath arrived, her breathing had become very faint but she was still conscious. He brought a picture of Baba in *varabhaya mudra* and held it in front of her eyes. "Picture Baba's image in your mind," he told her. The old lady's eyes closed. "Do you remember your ista mantra?" he asked. She nodded. Moments later, her head fell to one side and she breathed her last.

A few days later, Chandranath went to Jamalpur to inform Baba of her death. While they were walking, the master listened silently as Chandranath described her final moments. "Don't worry," Baba said. "She is with me now. She achieved her goal with her final breath."[8]

XI

A Philosophy Takes Shape

*From the inanimate to the animate goes the process of evolution. Consider a piece of stone, for instance. It has neither the power of action nor the sensation of mind. What is the reason? It is because hitherto there has been no manifestation of mind in the stone at all. Consider the trees and plants that are more animate than the stone. There is activity in them. They grow, draw vital juice from the earth, maintain their species by creating seeds in their own bodies, and enjoy, and suffer pleasure and pain when taken care of or hurt. We see in them the manifestation of consciousness, for mind has awakened in them. Thus progressing on the path of mental development, we see in humanity its greatest manifestation. Just as evolution takes place from the subtle to the crude, similarly the unit entity reverts step by step from the crude to the subtle, towards the same Absolute Consciousness whence it came. It is just like the waves of the sea, rippling back whence they have come.*¹

WITH THE FOUNDING of the organization, Baba began the concrete materialization of his life's work, putting into effect the ambitious plans he had chalked out during his childhood years. He had by now created a small base of dedicated disciples, but up until this point he had given them no more than vague hints of what was in his mind. One day in early spring, while walking with Chandranath, Baba turned and said, "When your ideology goes outside India it will spread very rapidly." Chandranath was surprised. Here we are, he thought, a handful of disciples in a small town in India and already Baba is talking of spreading to foreign countries. When Baba went on to say that one day they would be holding Dharmachakra in New York, Rome, and Moscow, Chandranath objected.

"How is this possible Baba? Westerners are *tamaguni*.² They are not spiritually minded like Indians."

"No, you are wrong," Baba replied. "The majority of Westerners are *rajaguni*. What are the signs and symptoms of *rajaguna*? Courage, confidence, agility, an active and energetic nature, the power of persuasion. Look at Western society and you will see that those qualities stand out. And *rajaguna* is very close to *sattvaguna*. When they take up spirituality they will make rapid progress."

When Baba said in December that many people would now be coming and that they would need an organization to receive them, Chandranath had thought he had meant a few hundred disciples, maybe one day a few thousand. The idea that Ananda Marga would spread outside India was hard to imagine. But the speed with which the mission would grow would soon catch them all by surprise.

After the first DMC, Baba started giving a series of informal talks on philosophy at the tiger's grave during his evening walks. He asked Shiva Shankar Bannerjee to take notes. Each night after arriving home, Shiva Shankar would organize his notes and add whatever he had failed to write down. Then he would bring them to Baba to review. By the end of February, a manuscript was ready in Bengali. Baba gave it the title *Ananda Marga Elementary Philosophy*. Pranay arranged contributions from different disciples and in early March the first edition came back from the press. By then Chandranath was already nearing completion of the Hindi translation.

The terms that Baba used in his discussions were drawn principally from Sankhya,[3] the first of the six recognized systems of Indian philosophy, and the world's oldest. These terms, however, took on a new life in *Elementary Philosophy*, which, despite its title, was anything but elementary.

Baba began his exposition with a deceptively simple opening in a chapter entitled "What is Dharma?"[4]

> Man is the highest evolved being. He possesses a clearly reflected consciousness and that makes him superior to animals. No other being has such a clear reflection of consciousness.[5]

He then showed how man's clearly reflected consciousness leads him on a quest for happiness, first through material enjoyments—possessions, power, position—then towards subtler and subtler pursuits as his consciousness becomes aware of the temporary and thus ultimately unsatisfactory nature of such enjoyments, until the mind gradually intuits that only an infinite being can satisfy its infinite thirst.

> The nature of consciousness is to seek for the Infinite or Brahma . . . And so man derives real happiness only when he can obtain Brahma or enter into the process of obtaining it. The conclusion we thus arrive at is that the universal religion or dharma of man is to realize the Infinite or Brahma. It is only by means of this dharma that he can enjoy eternal happiness and bliss.[6]

Baba then posed the first in a series of epistemological questions—"It is therefore necessary to see whether Brahma exists or not"—thus embarking on the first of the great philosophical queries: Can the existence of God be substantiated? For Baba, it was not simply a matter of faith but rather of both perception and philosophical logic. In order to answer his query, he led the reader through an intricate analysis of the process of perception, beginning with the functioning of the sensory organs, and continuing inwards through the different functional layers of the mind, until he was able to demonstrate that our feeling of existence can only be substantiated by the presence of a witnessing consciousness.

> The existence of 'I' in my mind only proves that there is another real master which is beyond the mind and which is aware of the mind's existence. This 'I', which is the witnessing entity and witnesses the existence of mind and therein the existence of *Buddhitattva* or feeling of 'I', is called *Atman* or unit consciousness. Thus by introspection and concentrated thinking it is observed that Atman and mind, i.e., unit consciousness and mind, are two separate entities.[7]

After elucidating this subtle and fundamental point in greater detail, he explored the relationship between unit consciousness and the different layers of the mind, showing not only how they interact but how the presence of one substantiates the existence of the other, a purely philosophical understanding that could nonetheless be confirmed through deep introspection. He then showed how each successive layer arises out of the previous one in order of subtlety as a result of the qualifying power inherent in consciousness, until he arrived at the universal character of this witnessing consciousness, the Universal Soul or God, thus establishing a philosophical and perceptual proof of the existence of the Supreme Being.

It was not an easy argument to follow, but Baba took the time to make sure his disciples understood each subtle nuance of his argument. When necessary, he made them sit for meditation in his presence until they could perceive for themselves what he was formulating in the language of philosophical logic.

Using his substantiation of the existence of a Universal Consciousness as a starting point, Baba examined in detail, chapter by chapter, the major philosophical questions facing mankind—What is the nature of God? What is the nature of the universe? What is the nature of the human being? What is the nature of the human being's relationship with God and the universe? How should human beings live their lives? What is the aim of life?—until he arrived at the need for intuitional practices, their modus operandi, and the reasons why human beings fail to do such practices. It was a seamless, logical progression that began with a detailed exploration of yogic cosmology—the involution of consciousness into matter and the evolution of consciousness out of matter—and ended with an exploration of how the human being completes the cycle of creation by attaining the state of spiritual perfection through intuitional practices. Thus his treatise served not only as a basis for a philosophical understanding of existence but also as an exhortation to human beings to participate in their own evolution in an intelligent, enlightened manner. Baba also took advantage of the opportunity to point out the drawbacks of certain religious credences and practices that were not consonant with a rational, scientific understanding of spiritual endeavor, such as ritual sacrifice, neutralizing the influence of the stars, different forms of ritualistic prayer and worship, and so on. In regards to the form of prayer most common in traditional religion, he stated:

> . . . asking for favors from God is only pointing out to the Sole Giver his mistakes in the distribution of his favors . . . One who performs actions shall also bear the consequences, and blaming God for it as his partiality is not going to save one from bearing those consequences. A hand plunged in fire will surely get burnt. No amount of praying is going to save it . . . In God's creation there is no flaw, only because all things, small or big follow their own nature (dharma). Otherwise there would have been disorder at every step.[8]

Though Ananda Marga was only a few months old, Baba's candidness about the shortcomings of traditional religion and his rational analysis of certain superstitions and dogmas prevalent in society would soon generate opposition to Ananda Marga in orthodox religious circles, an opposition that would later spread to the government when Baba began to propound his social philosophy. Ram Avatar Sharma, owner of the Navajivan Press and editor of a local magazine, expressed his opinion of Ananda Marga in an editorial: "Ananda Marga is the child of a poisonous snake; if it is not killed now, in the future Ananda Marga will swallow the entire world."

Baba devoted the last chapter of *Elementary Philosophy* to the various fears and misconceptions that keep people from taking up spiritual meditation. In answer to those who believed that it was necessary to renounce worldly life in order to achieve illumination, Baba pointed out that avoiding worldly life deprived a person of the opportunity to do social service, which he considered an essential part of the spiritual path. He coined a phrase in Sanskrit to serve as the motto of the new organization: *atma mokshartham, jagat hitayaca*, self-realization and service to the creation. He told his disciples unequivocally that a spiritual aspirant could not have one without the other. It was the first time that a prominent Indian spiritual teacher had ever declared that selfless service was an essential prerequisite for achieving spiritual illumination.

In a subsequent DMC, Baba gave a long discourse on the different types of service in which he explored this teaching in greater detail:

> The principal cause for the bondage of the fruits of action is ego . . .
> But when you perform an action while imposing the idea of Narayana

on the person served, there can be no possibility of any ego or yearning for fame growing in your mind. Then you will realize that it is through the grace of Narayana that you have the opportunity of serving Narayana. Our hands and feet are not ours; they are his and by serving himself with those hands and feet, he sports with himself. Such an action alone is action without attachment. Through this alone can a person attain salvation from the bondage of karma. You must feel that the person served is Brahma. The persons served are his finite manifestation. Never, even by mistake, take the object of service to be a man or a living being ... By working with feelings of Brahma, you will gradually be able to perceive Brahma in everything.[9]

Early in 1955, the disciples opened their first service project, a food co-op in Jamalpur that lasted a couple of years before their lack of expertise rendered it unviable. Soon after the co-op opened, Margis from Bhagalpur opened a free medical clinic. They called it Abha Seva Sadan in honor of Baba's mother. Shortly thereafter they opened a second Abha Seva Sadan in Jamalpur. They also began a program for feeding the poor in Jamalpur and Bhagalpur called Narayana Seva that was soon replicated in other cities as well. As the number of disciples increased, so did the number of service projects, despite an acute lack of funds, and as the years went by, Baba would gradually place increasing pressure on the disciples to expand the scope of their service activities.

Shortly after *Elementary Philosophy* returned from the printers, Baba asked Pranay to begin taking dictation for a second book, *Ananda Marga Caryacarya*, the do's and don'ts of Ananda Marga. While *Elementary Philosophy* was designed to serve as an introductory text to the spiritual philosophy of Ananda Marga, *Caryacarya* would serve as its social code. Two thousand years earlier, the sage Manu had written the *Manu Samhita*, a set of rules and practices that would thereafter serve as the Hindu social code. The *Manu Samhita* included everything from the daily observances of Hindus to the wedding ceremony. It was through the *Manu Samhita* that the caste system became solidified, cementing itself in Hindu life as social law. *Ananda Marga Caryacarya* also contained the daily observances for Ananda Margis, such as twice-daily meditation and the various other yogic practices, as well as a list of prescriptions and proscriptions for spiritual aspirants in the different arenas of life. The new book included a compendium of social ceremonies, such as the Ananda Marga wedding ceremony, funeral rites, baby-naming ceremony, housewarming and tree planting ceremonies, a list of Ananda Marga festivals, and so on. It also contained a detailed outline of the organizational structure, from local and district boards and secretaries to their global counterparts, as well as an economic policy and a system of punishment for social transgressions.

Though most of the disciples were well aware that by accepting Baba's teachings they were parting ways with their Hindu upbringing, few of them had suspected how deep the breach would become. With the publication of *Caryacarya*, Baba served notice that Ananda Marga was not only a spiritual philosophy and a system of spiritual practices; it was also a socio-spiritual movement capable of governing itself and regulating all aspects of its social life.[10] *Caryacarya* gave a structural framework to the growing sense among the disciples that they were now engaged in the work of building a spiritual community. In keeping with Baba's philosophy, that work would have to include all aspects of human life, from professional and family responsibilities to the effort to attain the Supreme. Ananda Marga was barely a few months old, but already Baba was making his long-term intentions clear: the creation of a movement that would one day encompass the globe and be capable of meeting all human needs, from the mundane to the spiritual.

XII

Samkalpa

God is a master magician who, by his magic spell, has created all and has hidden himself inside his creation. If at all you want to know the creation, the trick of the magician, it can only be done when you join him and his party.[1]

On March 22, Nagina, who had taken four months leave of absence, went to Baba's house about seven in the evening to accompany him on field walk. While he waited outside on the veranda for Baba to finish his sadhana, he could hear someone inside singing "Hari, Hari" in a melodious voice. He assumed it was Baba's younger brother Manas, but when the door opened moments later he realized that it had been Baba whom he had heard. Nagina did sastaunga pranam. Instead of leaving immediately for the field, as was his custom, Baba called him inside and asked him to sit on the chair opposite his. After they were seated, Baba closed his eyes. A few minutes later his head drooped to his chest. Afraid that Baba's glasses would fall off, Nagina jumped up from his seat and cradled his hands under Baba's chin. Baba opened his eyes and asked who was there.

"It's Nagina, Baba."

"Ah, when did you come?"

"A few minutes ago, Baba," Nagina answered, surprised at the question. "I did pranam and you asked me to sit."

"Well, well then."

Baba fell silent. Nagina assumed that he was experiencing the aftereffects of samadhi. Again Baba closed his eyes and once again his head drooped to his chest. Nagina cradled Baba's chin in his hands a second time. Baba opened his eyes and stared at him as if he had been startled from sleep.

"Baba, your glasses will fall off." Gently, Nagina took off Baba's glasses and placed them on the small table between them. Baba motioned for him to sit on the floor in front of him. Nagina sat on the floor and started massaging Baba's feet. A few minutes later, he heard a knock at the door and Baba motioned for him to open it. Pranay walked in and did pranam. Then he pulled up a chair and began fanning himself with his handkerchief, sweat beading on his brow from the sultry heat of late March. After a few moments, Baba signaled for him to sit on the floor as well, where he joined Nagina in massaging Baba's feet.

Samkalpa

As the two disciples silently continued their massage, they noticed that Baba's feet were gradually growing colder and colder. They exchanged worried glances. Then Baba broke the silence in a voice that was barely a whisper.

"Today my dear acharya and my dear disciple are with me at the very moment that my samskaras are becoming exhausted. What better opportunity could there be than this?"

Pranay began to weep. "Baba what are you saying? You have just created Ananda Marga. It cannot survive without you and now you are thinking of leaving your body? What will become of us? What will become of the mission?"

Nagina began to weep as well, as the import of Pranay's words dawned on him. The two men grabbed Baba's feet and started imploring him not to leave.

"Let me go," Baba said, "let me go."

The two disciples clung even tighter. "No, Baba. We won't."

"Take whatever you want—savikalpa samadhi, nirvikalpa samadhi, anything—but let me leave."

"No, Baba," they cried in unison, "we won't let you go."

Baba's voice grew weaker and weaker until they could no longer hear what he was saying. He reached down and tried to forcefully remove their hands from his feet but they refused to let go. Finally Baba shoved them so hard they both fell backwards, but they jumped up immediately and grabbed his feet again.

"Baba, no matter what you do, we won't let you go."

"Okay, okay. *Shanti, shanti.*[2] I will take a *samkalpa*, a resolution."[3]

"Do you promise?" Pranay asked, letting go of Baba's feet.

"Yes, I am taking a samkalpa. Help me to sit in lotus posture."

While Pranay helped Baba to bind his legs in lotus position, Nagina asked him to take a samkalpa for a long life. Baba agreed and closed his eyes for several minutes. When he opened them again, he got up and the three of them left for their evening walk.

As they passed Rampur Colony, Pranay left to go to the ashram. Soon afterwards, Baba started humming "Hari, Hari" in a soft voice. Still feeling uneasy, Nagina asked him why he was singing this mantra.

"Hari is my ista mantra.[4] I left my last three bodies singing this mantra. I haven't given this mantra to any disciple because if someone practiced it with deep concentration I would feel like abandoning my body."

Nagina stiffened. "Then stop singing this mantra, Baba. You took a samkalpa to live a long life."

"Don't worry, Nagina. It's all right."

When they reached the far side of the bridge, Baba turned to Nagina and said, "You can go back now. I have an appointment with some people in the field."

"Baba, I don't want to leave you alone today, especially since you are chanting Hari, Hari."

"There is nothing to be afraid of. You can set your mind at rest. I've taken a samkalpa. Now go."

Nagina reluctantly turned back, but along the way he met a young disciple, Harisadhan. "Baba is on his way to the field," he told him. "Go and see if he will let you walk with him to the tiger's grave. If he does, don't let him chant Hari, Hari."

"Why?"

"I'll tell you later. I'll wait for you in the ashram."

Harisadhan arrived back at the ashram around half past ten. Nagina eagerly asked him for a report.

"Yes, he was chanting Hari, Hari. I requested him to stop, like you said, but I really started enjoying it, so I just listened."

"What! Why didn't you follow my instructions? I asked you not to let him repeat that mantra. How can you expect anyone to depend on you?"

When Nagina calmed down, he explained what had happened earlier that evening. Harisadhan assured him that he had seen Baba safely to his house, but that did little to allay Nagina's worries. In the morning he returned to the ashram to talk to Pranay. Pranay also assured him that there was nothing to worry about. He had seen Baba that morning and everything was normal. But Nagina was still not convinced.

On the twenty-fifth, Baba left for his evening walk with Nagina and Bindeshvari, but he turned back midway and headed for the ashram. There they found a number of senior disciples, both acharyas and acharya trainees: Pranay, Shiva Shankar Bannerjee, Chandranath, Shishir Dutta, and six or seven others. Baba called his senior disciples into his room and asked them to shut the door. Nagina and Bindeshvari remained outside on the veranda. After a while they got up to leave, assuming that Baba would be occupied for the rest of the evening giving acharya classes, as he had been doing for the past month. As they were walking out of the courtyard, however, they heard someone calling them. Baba had sent a message that they should wait. While they were waiting, Nagina overheard the sound of Hari, Hari coming through the crack in the door, which had been left ajar. He peeked through and saw Baba lying on the cot, encircled by his disciples; he was chanting Hari, Hari, Hari in a soft voice. He rushed in and grabbed hold of Baba's feet.

"Baba, it was only three days ago that you took a samkalpa to live a long life and now you are doing the same thing again. I beg of you, please stop repeating this mantra!"

Looking around the room, he said, "Baba is trying to leave his body. He did the same thing a few days ago but Pranay and I were able to stop him. If we all massage him then he won't be able to leave."

He was met with a number of skeptical looks but at his urging they started massaging Baba's legs and arms, except for Bindeshvari, who slumped down in a corner, overcome by his emotion.

"Baba, you cheated us," Nagina continued. "You told us that you were going to take a samkalpa for a long life, but you only took a samkalpa for three days. How can you leave us alone like this?"

Baba stared off into space and said, "Kishun, your work is done." When Nagina cried out that Kishun was not there, Baba's only response was "Hari, Hari."

After a few moments, Baba turned his face towards Vishvanath. "What do you desire?" he asked.

"Baba, I wish to have you always in front of me," Vishvanath replied.

"*Shubhamastu*," Baba said. So be it.[5]

Over and over again the disciples implored him not to leave. Finally he agreed. "Okay. Help me sit up. I will take another samkalpa."

After Baba sat up, he asked them all to leave the room.

""No, Baba, please," Nagina said. "Why can't we stay?"

"It is necessary. Don't worry. I said I would take a samkalpa and I will."

The disciples passed a few anxious minutes outside Baba's door. Then one of them called out, "Can we come in now?"

"Don't distract me," Baba said from behind the door. "I am taking a long samkalpa."

More anxious minutes passed until Baba called them inside again. "It is done," he told them. Then he began talking of spiritual matters as if nothing had happened. When he left for his house in the company of Pranay, several others followed behind at a distance, just in case. They noticed that Baba was walking markedly slower than he normally did. Afterwards they discussed the situation amongst themselves. Pranay was of the opinion that Baba was still undecided whether or not he wanted to retain his body. Though he had assured them that he had taken a samkalpa for a long life, he had said the same thing three days earlier. Who knew how long the samkalpa was for this time? They decided that they would take turns watching Baba as closely as possible and hope for the best.

For the next few days everything appeared normal, but several incidents made it clear that Baba was still undecided. One evening, while crossing the bridge, he turned to Nagina and said, "Nagina, if I do not keep my body, please see to it that *Ananda Marga Elementary Philosophy* is translated into Maithili by a native speaker of the language."[6] One or two evenings later at the tiger's grave, Baba said abruptly, "Now my mind no longer feels at home on this planet. There is no longer anyone here who is *nirman chitta*."

One of the disciples asked him what he meant by *nirman chitta*.

"After intense meditation, when a spiritual aspirant exhausts all his samskaras and attains the goal of spiritual perfection, he may continue living in this world with the same body, or he may choose to take a new body in order to serve the creation. The samkalpa he takes to serve the creation for a fixed period of time becomes a new samskara for him. He remains on the planet for that length of time and then he departs. Such perfected beings are called *nirman chitta*. They do not need to do sadhana, but they do so for two reasons: to enjoy the bliss it brings and to set an example for their disciples that one should do sadhana no matter what the circumstance."

On the evening of April 1, Nagina and Shishir were waiting on Baba's veranda for evening field walk along with a young disciple from Monghyr, Harivansha Jha, who had brought with him the proofs of the Hindi translation of *Ananda Marga Elementary Philosophy*. The door opened and Baba called Nagina inside. Nagina mentioned that the proofs had arrived but Baba dismissed this with a wave of his hand.

Once they were inside, Baba said, "Nagina, those rascals in your office have harassed you unjustly. Today is your chance to rectify the situation. Give me their names and I will see to it that they are punished by nature."

Nagina, who suspected that it was a test, kept silent.

"Nagina, I am short of time. This is your last chance. Tell me the names of those whom you want punished."

"Baba, I don't want anyone punished. If someone has to be punished, then please punish me."

"Don't talk of ideals at this moment. Be practical."

"Baba, I don't want anyone punished."

In an effort to change the subject, Nagina asked Baba if he could do sastaunga pranam. When Baba assented, he prostrated and then started massaging Baba's feet. Baba's feet were unusually cold and as he massaged them he noticed them growing colder. Alarmed, he mentioned it to Baba.

"Yes," Baba said. "Now I will not retain this body."

Nagina started weeping. He clung to Baba's feet just as he had done ten days earlier in that same room.

"Nagina, you had a strong desire to be promoted to Assistant Collector. I will make you Assistant Collector here and now. Just let me go."

"No, Baba, I won't," Nagina said through his tears.

"Whatever you want, be it spiritual or material, ask and it is yours. But let me go."

"No, Baba, never."

A couple of minutes later Baba relented. "Okay, okay, do not insist any further. Let us go to the field."

Nagina released Baba's feet and then heard Baba order himself in a commanding tone of voice, "Prabhat Rainjan Sarkar, be well for some time. You have to go to the field." Baba stood up and started for the door. As Nagina followed behind, he caught a glimpse of Baba's mother peeking in through the curtained doorway to the next room. It occurred to him that Baba might have relented because of her presence.

The three disciples accompanied Baba to the field. At the first opportunity, Nagina alerted his two companions to the seriousness of the situation. As they walked, they noticed that Baba's arms were hanging limply by his side, rather than swinging as they normally would. Along the way, they were joined by Harisadhan. When they reached the tiger's grave, they found Kishun there waiting for them. Once they were all seated, the disciples jointly repeated their request for Baba not to leave his body.

"That would be contrary to the laws of nature," Baba said. "It would be wrong to go against the laws of nature."

"The rules of nature are for those who are within the bondage of the world," Nagina replied, "but you are the master of nature. Please don't try to fool us like this. Have pity on us."

"This is my decision. Now allow me to leave my body. You all sit for meditation now."

The disciples refused. Following Nagina's example, they grabbed hold of Baba's feet and arms.

"Let me be. My time here is finished."

The disciples clung even more tightly, each of them imploring him to stay. Baba gave them a shove with his feet and hands. Despite being bigger than Baba, all five were thrown back onto the ground in front of the grave. They jumped up again and grabbed his legs and arms. Nagina buried his head in Baba's chest and wrapped his arms around him.

"My physical presence is no longer necessary here," Baba said. "Once I took the decision to leave my body, I released my spiritual vibration through the medium of my *janusparsha* and *varabhaya mudras*.[7] With the help of these vibrations, you people will progress and help guide the world towards the Supreme Beatitude. In the future, *sadhakas* will be able to catch my vibration by concentrating on those mudras.[8] They will receive my guidance just as they had through the medium of my physical body.

"Now listen to me. Before the guru leaves his body, he becomes Kalpataru, the wish-fulfilling tree. If he so desires, he can grant his disciples anything they wish, be it spiritual or material. I am now assuming the form of Kalpataru. Ask for whatever you desire and it will be granted."

One by one, Baba asked his five disciples what they wanted, but no one answered, except for Nagina.

"Baba, I don't want anything from the Kalpataru."

"Nagina, this is not the way to speak to the Kalpataru. You must ask for something. Otherwise it will be an insult."

"If this is an insult then I have one request. My wish is to celebrate the Kalpataru day before your living body every year for the next fifty years."

"You cannot make that request," Baba said in an angry tone of voice. "You're trying to trick me. Ask for something else."

"No," Nagina replied. "I won't take back this wish." He would later say that Baba sounded so fierce at that moment that had he not had his face buried in Baba's chest he doubted that he would have had the courage to hold firm.

"I will give you one more chance," Baba said. "You should not make a wish that is contrary to the laws of the creation. Change your wish, otherwise you will soil the spotless reputation of the Kalpataru."

"My wish is immutable," Nagina replied. "Let it be a test of the Kalpataru to see if he fulfills it or not."

Baba continued to argue with his disciple but Nagina held firm. "So be it," he said at last. He laid his hand on Nagina's head. "Okay, help me to sit in lotus posture. I will take one final samkalpa."[9]

When he finished, the disciples began massaging his legs and arms. After a few minutes Baba said, "I have removed seven-eighths of the prana from my body, so my body has become quite weak." They continued the massage for another twenty minutes. Then Baba asked for water. "If you cannot bring me water soon, it will be difficult for me to keep my body despite the samkalpa."

Hurriedly, Nagina sent Harivansha running in the direction of the nearest house. While he was gone, Baba repeated his request; his voice made a rasping sound as he spoke. Nagina then told Harisadhan to run to the sweet shop at the crossing for water. As the minutes passed, Baba became increasingly restless; he continued to ask for water. Then Nagina remembered that Baba had once mentioned that thirst could be controlled by means of a special mantra.

"I already used it," Baba told him when he asked about it. "I can't use it anymore. If someone else applies it then it may help."

"Then teach me."

Baba taught Nagina the mantra and the repetition seemed to help, but Baba warned them that the mantra could only help him retain his body for another half hour. If he did not get water by then, it would be too late. The disciples passed some anxious minutes before Harivansha returned with a glass of water in his hand. In his haste he had spilt half of it, but what was left seemed to help considerably. A few minutes later Harisadhan returned with a full pitcher. Baba drank a portion of it and seemed completely restored. But still he could not walk. "I withdrew most of my prana for a significant period of time," he said. "The joints will need some time before they function normally again."

"Baba, I have my car at Bindeshvari's house," Nagina said. "I can go and bring it."

"No, the best remedies for this are walking and nirvikalpa Samadhi. But if I go into nirvikalpa samadhi I won't want to come back. So I will have to walk."

They continued their massage. Finally, Baba extended his feet over the side of the tomb and put them on the ground. He recited a long blessing in Sanskrit while his disciples were touching his feet and applied another mantra to the different joints of his body. Then he stood up and began walking home, while his bewildered disciples struggled to make sense of what had just happened.

When Nagina told the story to Pranay the next day, Pranay was happy but skeptical. "You have asked Baba to stay for a very long time. I wonder if he will be able or willing to stay that long." News of the incident quickly spread among the other disciples, and in the years to come, Baba would sometimes joke that Nagina's victory and his defeat had given the devotees Ananda Marga.

XIII

Prachar

The fact that the fortune of every individual, not only of this earth, but of the entire cosmos, has been wreathed together, will have to be admitted one day by humanity. Spiritual aspirants have to fetch that auspicious moment sooner by their pauseless effort, service and propagation of the great ideology. This alone is the supreme task for the present humanity.[1]

WITH THE ESTABLISHMENT of the new organization, Baba began encouraging his disciples to actively propagate his teachings. He had named the organization Ananda Marga Pracaraka Samgha, or AMPS, the society for the propagation of Ananda Marga, using the Sanskrit word *prachar*.[2] As the name of the organization implied, prachar quickly became its main activity. The one restriction was that the master's name or whereabouts could not be disclosed to new initiates until they were given permission to meet him for the first time. The disciples quickly printed up a couple of small pamphlets to help them with their prachar efforts. One contained the ten principles of yama and niyama; the other introduced the organization and some of its basic tenets. An excerpt from the text of the second leaflet shows their enthusiastic acceptance of Baba's early teachings:

> We are against man-made, divisive tendencies of all sorts. We firmly believe that all living beings are the children of the Supreme Lord. No one is superior or inferior to anyone else. We belong to one human family irrespective of our country, religion, color and community. All are brothers and sisters and there is one dharma for all human beings. We are against religious hypocrisy and religious exploitation of all types. We have no faith in so-called "guru-dom," "Christ-dom," or the philosophy of divine incarnation. We are against religious dogmas such as animals slaughtered in the name of religion, tyranny over innocents, idol worship, and hereditary authority in religion.
>
> We are dead against social, psychic and religious superstitions and dogmas of all types. To strengthen the foundation of unity we have to bring humans closer together. We support widow remarriage, inter-

caste, interstate and international marriages. We consider wrongs done to widows, child-marriage and the dowry system as heinous social injustices. We believe that ghosts, spiritism and possession by gods and goddesses are psychic superstitions.

In April, Baba asked Chandranath to go to his native village of Gaddopur, some sixty kilometers north of Patna, to arrange a *tattvasabha*.

Chandranath replied without any hesitation. "Certainly, Baba. I just have one question. What is a tattvasabha?"

Baba laughed. "A tattvasabha is a public meeting or debate on spiritual philosophy.[3] Organize an open discussion with the local pundits and debate the merits of Ananda Marga philosophy versus traditional Hindu ideas. Ask Shiva Shankar, Harisadhan, and Ram Tanuk to go with you, plus your wife and Ram Tanuk's wife. Once everything is organized, come and see me and I will prepare you for the debate."

The day before they left, the five acharyas met Baba at his house in Keshavpur. Harisadhan and Shiva Shankar were deputed to give the opening lectures. Baba dictated the subject matter, which they hastily scribbled down as best they could. He asked Chandranath to answer the pundit's questions and then dictated a list of the questions they would ask along with his answers. The list included: Why do you oppose idol worship? Why don't you accept caste differences? Why do you insist on giving up the sacred thread and the *shikha*,[4] or topknot? He also supplied him with scriptural references to support his answers. The two female acharyas were given the duty to go door to door and talk to the village women, vitally important in an era of strict separation between men and women in traditional village life.

On the day of the tattvasabha, the entire village, young and old, gathered in a mango grove in front of a twelfth-century temple. The pundits sat separately, formally dressed in turbans, dhotis, and kurtas. Among them were several Sanskrit scholars with somber faces who were capable of speaking and lecturing in Sanskrit. Harisadhan and Shiva Shankar gave their opening talks. Then Chandranath opened the floor to questions. The most imposing of the pundits, who had been given the title "Suvakta" (well-spoken) for his scriptural prowess, stood up as their representative. One by one, he asked each of the questions Baba had dictated on the previous day. As Chandranath gave his well-rehearsed answers, the pundit gradually lost his patience, especially when his adversary adroitly quoted passages from the Vedas to support his answers. His final question was, Why do you teach yoga sadhana to family people when it is only for renunciants? Chandranath's answer brought a round of applause from the audience that so incensed the pundit that he started verbally abusing the Margis. He accused them of being atheists and going against the Vedas. One of the most respected elders of the village, Janaka Kumar, a retired schoolteacher, stood up and confronted the pundit.

"Punditji, that is enough. We have been listening to you people since our childhood and you just keep parroting the same thing over and over again like a bullock going round an oil mill.⁵ We're tired of it. We want to listen to what these young men have to say. It's logical and rational. Stop disturbing them."

That night the five acharyas stayed up late giving initiations. When they were finished, several of the older members of the village came to Chandranath and politely asked him if he would explain to them about *satripu* and *ashtapasha*,⁶ the six enemies and the eight fetters. This was a question for which he was unprepared. It was after midnight, so Chandranath asked them if they could come back in the morning. Once they were gone, he lay down and tried to remember what Baba had said about the subject, but he wasn't able to recall much before he fell asleep. While he was sleeping, he had a dream in which Baba appeared and gave him a detailed explanation of each of the fourteen *ashtapasha* and *satripu*, along with the means a spiritual aspirant can adopt to overcome them. In the morning, Chandranath received his guests and repeated what Baba had said in his dream. His visitors went away satisfied. When the five acharyas returned to Jamalpur, Baba's first question for Chandranath was, "So, what about *ashtapasha* and *satripu*?"

After this, the acharyas started organizing regular tattvasabhas in villages and towns near Jamalpur, as well as simple conferences and lectures. On one of these occasions, a weekend lecture was set up at Monghyr High School, but when the scheduled day arrived, it was discovered that all the available acharyas were busy elsewhere with other programs. Baba was in the ashram when he was informed of the situation. Sitting next to him was Baban Tiwari, a young police constable. Baba turned to Baban and told him that he would have to give the lecture.

"Baba, not me, please," Baban said nervously. "I've never given a talk before, much less in front of a crowd. I'd be terrified. I only have an eighth grade education. I don't even know the philosophy. I'm just a devotee."

"Baban, no one else is there. You have to go."

"But Baba—"

"This is an order, Baban. Repeat your guru mantra and I will take care of the rest."

When Baban arrived at the high school auditorium and saw the size of the crowd, his first thought was to slip out the back door and go straight back to Jamalpur. But he found the thought of displeasing Baba even more terrifying than the prospect of facing the waiting audience. Better to embarrass myself, he thought, than to face Baba's anger. He had no idea what he would say when he walked up to the podium, but after a few anxious moments the words started tumbling out. He was surprised to hear that he was actually making sense. His talk received an enthusiastic round of applause and many people stayed afterwards to ask questions about spiritual philosophy and yogic practices.

At the same time that Baban was giving his talk, Baba was sitting in the ashram with a couple of disciples. "Do you know what our Baban is doing now?" he asked. When Baba told them that he was giving a public lecture in Monghyr, they found it hard to imagine. Not our Baban, they thought, as they looked at one another, careful not to voice their disbelief. But when Baba proceeded to narrate Baban's talk for them, an erudite, lucid explanation of the fundamental principles of Baba's philosophy, they immediately suspected that Baba was playing a game with them. When Baban came to the ashram the next day they approached him casually.

"By the way, Baban, we heard that you gave a talk last night at Monghyr High School?"

"Yes, I did, in fact."

"Would it, by any chance, have gone anything like this? . . ." They then repeated what they remembered of Baba's narration.

Baban stared at them in surprise. "I didn't see you there. How do you know what I said? Who told you?"

When they told him that Baba had narrated his talk at the same time that he had been giving it, Baban nodded as if he had just had a revelation. "I see. I had been wondering where all those words came from."

After this Baban started giving talks on a regular basis. Once he became an acharya, he began having great success initiating people after his talks. One day he met Baba on the road. After accepting Baban's salutations, Baba asked him to address another public conference. Baban arranged the meeting and a good-sized crowd came to hear him speak, but for the first time no one took initiation. Afterwards he went to see Baba. "Is your vanity now broken?" Baba asked him, as soon as he had finished his pranam.

"Yes, Baba," he replied, carefully examining the floor. "But your work is undone."

"It was necessary. When you went there, you went with the ideation that you are a very wise person and a great spiritual aspirant. Had I allowed you to continue thinking in this way, it would have been your undoing. Such thoughts are not a sign of intelligence but rather of foolishness. They are harmful. That's why I had to break your vanity."

While the acharyas started organizing regular lectures and conferences, most of the prachar was simple word-of-mouth among the Margis' friends and relatives. Such was the case with Nityananda Mandal, a tall, athletic young foreman in the brass-finishing shop. Nityananda had been living in Haraprasad Haldar's boarding house for the previous couple of years, along with his cousin Jiten Mandal. Inspired by Haraprasad's colorful stories, Jiten had taken initiation late the previous year, followed soon afterwards by two other housemates, Haragovind and Birunda Bohari. The four of them used to pester Nityananda about the importance of yogic sadhana.

"Nityananda," they would say, "what are you waiting for? The goal of human life is to realize one's spiritual nature and meditation is the key. Only by meditation can you know your true self. Be careful. Life is short. Are you just going to let your life pass you by?" Then they would invariably tell him some fantastic story about their omniscient guru and his miraculous powers, or wax enthusiastic over some blissful or mystical experience of their own.

"Okay, if he's really as great as you say he is, then take me to meet him."

"No, no, you know we can't do that. First you have to take initiation and practice meditation for some time. Then we'll take you to meet him. Anyhow, he's from South India.[7] He only comes to Jamalpur from time to time to give darshan to the initiated disciples."

And there the conversation would invariably bog down. Nityananda actually had an avid interest in yoga and meditation, but what he did not tell them was that at the age of five Krishna had appeared to him in a dream in the form of spiritual effulgence and told him, "Nothing in this illusory relative world can give you lasting shelter. Surrender to me, the absolute and immutable Divine Consciousness, and I will guide you across the ocean of *samsara* to your spiritual goal."[8] Since that moment, he had accepted Krishna as his *ista devata* and vowed that he would not bow down before any worldly guru, only before Krishna himself.[9] Whenever he would meditate on Krishna, he would start weeping with longing, torn by his desire to see Krishna physically and the knowledge that this was impossible.

One morning in late April, Nityananda was approaching gate number six of the railway workshop when he noticed a handsome, regal-looking gentleman entering the gate with a tiffin box in one hand and an umbrella in the other. He stopped and stared as the man walked towards the accounts office, marveling at the graceful step and solemn gravity of this unknown figure. Only when the man disappeared through the office door was the spell broken. Just then he noticed his cousin Jiten passing by on his way to work.

"Jiten," he said, rushing up to his cousin, "Did you see that man who just went into the accounts office, the one holding a tiffin box and an umbrella?"

Jiten smiled and nodded. "Of course. That's Prabhat Rainjan Sarkar, the president of Ananda Marga. He enters this gate every day at exactly this time."

The next morning, Nityananda arrived early at the gate and waited until he saw Baba passing through. Again he experienced the same sense of fascination. Again he felt unnerved by the extraordinary serenity that seemed to envelop Baba as he walked. As Baba passed Nityananda, he turned his head and looked him directly in the eyes. The young foreman suddenly felt completely unmasked, as if his personal vanity and mental complexes had been laid bare by that one glance. Nityananda lowered his eyes, unable to sustain Baba's gaze.

The next day he returned again to the gate and watched Baba pass. That night he went to Haraprasad and asked him to arrange for his initiation. If the president of Ananda Marga is so attractive, he thought, such an obviously elevated soul, then this Anandamurti must truly be an extraordinary personality. Come what may, I have to meet him.

Haraprasad arranged for him to take initiation the next day from Arun Mazumdar, who worked in the same office with Baba. A few days later, they informed him that Anandamurti himself would be visiting Jamalpur on May 6 to conduct a special spiritual program called Dharmamahachakra.

By this time, over a thousand people had been initiated, an exponential leap from the seventy or so disciples that Baba had personally initiated in the six years prior to the founding of Ananda Marga, and several hundred disciples were expected to attend the program. The site arranged for the DMC was the palace of a local raja, situated on the bank of the Ganges in Monghyr. Flyers were sent out announcing the program as the Ananda Purnima DMC, in celebration of the guru's birthday.

Baba arrived at the palace just before noon; he was brought directly to his room by a private entrance so that he would not have to pass in front of the thronging disciples. In the meantime, the hundred or so new initiates who were taking part, those who had not yet had their first darshan, were instructed to line up in front of the door to Baba's room for a personal contact with the master. There they waited in anxious anticipation, enduring the sweltering May heat, their imagination stoked by the wondrous stories they had heard from the older disciples. Perhaps no one was more anxious than Nityananda, who could not wait for his first darshan of the master of Prabhat Rainjan Sarkar, his heart dancing with the thought that he might be about to meet the Lord of his many past lives.

Once Baba was settled in his room, the word passed like a brushfire through the line that Anandamurti had arrived. Several senior disciples walked up and down the line instructing the newcomers in the proper protocol. Each disciple was instructed to prostrate in front of the master upon entering, to answer any questions he might ask but to refrain from asking any questions of his own, and then to exit by the side door so the next disciple could enter. Chandranath took up his position by the door and opened it to let the new disciples in, one by one. Shiva Shankar Bannerjee stood next to Baba's cot, fanning the master vigorously with a bamboo fan. As the new initiates entered, Baba asked them their name, gave them his blessing, and added a word or two of advice or encouragement. The whole process took no more than a minute or so for each disciple.

When it came Nityananda's turn to enter, he was shocked to see that the man sitting on the cot being fanned by his disciple was the same Prabhat Sarkar. As he stood there, momentarily paralyzed by the realization that he had been deceived, Baba ordered Shiva Shankar and Chandranath to close the doors and windows and remain outside. Before Nityananda could recover from his shock, he found himself alone in the room with Baba.

"Come here, come here, come closer," Baba said, beckoning him with his hand.

Suddenly Nityananda felt afraid. He stood as stiff as a stone idol, his eyes fixed on the floor, wild thoughts racing through his head. Why had he ordered them to close the doors and windows and leave? What does he want with me?

Again Baba called him closer. Not knowing what else to do, Nityananda approached the cot, telling himself that he would not prostrate before this man. He would not accept him as his guru.

When he drew close, Baba reached out and gave him an affectionate hug. Nityananda started crying profusely. Tears rolled down his cheeks, though he could not understand why.

"When you were a child, you used to cry for me very often," Baba said. "Do you remember? I've been waiting for you. You are going to do great and auspicious work in this world. Be ready." Baba laid his hand on his head. "*Shubhamastu*," he said. "May the blessings of the Lord be with you. Now go. We will talk again soon."

Baba called for Chandranath and Shiva Shankar. Before Nityananda realized what was happening, he was out on the lawn with the other disciples. Lunch was about to be served but he was in no mood to eat. The encounter had left him shaken, but his anger over the deception quickly returned. Who are these people? he asked himself. How could they do such a thing? His first impulse was to leave, but his cousin and Haraprasad caught up with him before he could do so. While he fumed and expressed his frustration, they did their best to justify why they had purposely misled him, patiently trying to convince him to remain for the rest of the program. Finally he agreed to stay.

In the early evening, there was devotional singing and a collective meditation. At seven o'clock, Baba entered the main hall to give his DMC discourse, a long, philosophical dissertation on the different levels of existence of both the microcosm and the Macrocosm, from matter to the pure, undifferentiated Universal Consciousness. The last part of his discourse was devoted to the difference between relative truth and supreme truth.

> Suppose the light-waves of the Mahabharata age take another eight hundred years to reach a certain star.[10] At this time, if one, with the help of a telescope, observes the earth, what will he see? He will see that the Mahabharata has not yet been fought here. For him, it will happen after eight hundred years; after this period of time he will see the war of the Mahabharata being waged. What is past for one is present for another and future for the third. All these are relative truths.[11]

After exhorting his disciples to realize the absolute truth beyond all relativities, he called Kestopal forward and directed him to sit in full lotus and close his eyes. Baba then ordered Kestopal's kundalini to rise one by one through the different chakras. When it reached the seventh chakra, Kestopal fell backwards, absorbed in the trance of nirvikalpa samadhi. Baba pressed his toe to Kestopal's navel point and started asking him questions.

"There is a lot of propaganda nowadays about Tansen and Hillary's ascent of Mount Everest. What do you have to say about it? Has Mount Everest been conquered?"

Prostrate in his trance, his body stiff, his eyes shut tight, Kestopal answered. "The earth's highest peak is an intractable region. It has not been conquered."

"Go back in time. See the condition of the earth 3500 *crore* years ago."[12]

"It was extremely hot and inhospitable."

"Now come forward to 3500 years ago. What era is in progress?"

"It is the Dvapar Yuga,[13] the age of Shri Krishna."

"What is Krishna doing?"

"He is walking along the banks of the river Yamuna with a flute in his hand."

"Is there any similarity between his physical body and his appearance as he is depicted in modern paintings?"

"No."

"Describe his appearance."

Kestopal described his appearance and then recited a Sanskrit verse in a voice so feeble that only the people sitting near him could hear.

> *Naviinameghsannibham sunnilakomalacchavim*
> *Suhásarainjitádharam Manama krishnasundaram*
> *Yashodánandanandanam surendrapádavandanam*
> *Suvarnaratnamanianam Manama krishnasundaram*
> *Bhavábdhikarnadhárakam bhayárttinásharakam*
> *Mumukshumuktidáyakam Manama krishnasundaram*

> Salutations to Krishna the beautiful, who was an object of delight to Mother Yashoda, whose lotus feet are worshipped by the gods, and whose body is adorned with precious gems. Salutations to Krishna the beautiful, the most reliable helmsman on the ocean of this universe, who removes the fear of annihilation, who grants salvation to aspiring souls.

Upon hearing this, Baba entered into samadhi and fell back on his cot. Nityananda, who had been sitting nearby, climbed up onto the dais and helped Pranay, who was sitting to Baba's right, to adjust Baba's body into a more comfortable position. The moment Nityananda touched Baba, he felt an electric current pass through him, accompanied by a wave of bliss. He saw bright effulgence emanating from Baba's body, an experience shared by many others in the audience, and he smelled the sweet fragrance of flowers. For several minutes he became abnormal. When he came back to his senses, all his hesitation had vanished.

He now felt that there was no difference between the Krishna he had adored since childhood and his newfound guru.

After some thirty minutes or so, Baba opened his eyes briefly and then shut them again. This happened a couple of more times. Then Baba gestured for them to help him sit up.

"Can someone bring me a cup of hot milk?" he asked.

One of the disciples ran to the kitchen and returned a couple of minutes later with a glass of hot milk. Baba drank it and then touched his toe again to Kestopal's navel. "*Manusya bhava,*" he intoned—be a human being. Kestopal opened his eyes; within a few minutes he was able to sit up. Baba asked someone to massage him; he also sent someone to bring Kestopal a cup of hot milk. Finally, Baba left the stage and walked slowly to a car that was waiting to bring him back to Jamalpur. Nityananda ran alongside him, shouting *Parama Pita Baba ki jai,* "victory to Baba, the Supreme Father," swept away by the same spiritual wave that had carried off his cousin and Haraprasad a few years earlier.

XIV

The Circle Widens

Whenever the devotees of Hari assemble together they do not like to gossip, but prefer to do Hari kirtan,[1] and nothing else. Whoever comes within the circumference of that spiritual gathering will certainly feel an irresistible desire to participate in that spiritual dance. The sweet spiritual environment created by the kirtan is called Hariparimaṅdala in the scriptures . . . Whenever Hariparimaṅdala is created, be it for five minutes, three hours or twenty-four hours, due to the intense collective devotion, the environment becomes so sweet and blissful that it becomes highly congenial for spiritual ideation (dhyana). At that time Hari moves His nucleus there and becomes the focal point of dhyana, the object of ideation.[2]

ONE DAY IN late July, Ram Khilavan, a well-to-do Jamalpur businessman, was lying on a cot in front of his house in the Olipur neighborhood reading the Bhagavad Gita. How nice it would be, he thought, if I could spend my whole life like this, repeating the name of the Lord and reading books about God. The chapter he was reading, however, bothered him. He didn't like it when Krishna equated himself with the greatest of everything, such as the Ganges among rivers. If God is in everything, then why does he have to praise himself by comparing himself to the greatest and most important things on this earth, and thus try to set himself apart?

At that moment, a passerby wearing a white dhoti and kurta stopped and asked him what he was reading. When Ram Khilavan told him, the stranger sat down without introducing himself and asked if he could have a look.

"Ah yes, chapter ten," the man said, fingering the pages. "How do you like this chapter?"

"I love the book but I have a problem with this chapter. I don't see why Krishna should have to praise himself like this. 'I am the Ganges of the rivers; I am the Meru of the mountains; I am the sacred banyan of all the trees.' He seems to be beating his own drum."

"No, no, you shouldn't think like this," the man replied calmly. "Though God is present in everything, the Gita expresses it in this way so as to arouse devotion, to show that in everything the Lord is the highest expression. That's all it is doing. Well, I must be on my way. Enjoy your reading."

The man saluted Ram Khilavan and continued down the road towards Rampur colony. When Ram Khilavan returned to his reading he discovered that his feeling towards that passage had changed. Well, maybe Krishna is right after all, he thought.

A few days later his close friend, Dasarath Singh, a bifocaled, forty-four-year-old soft-spoken headmaster of a nearby school, came to his house brimming over with excitement. "Ram Khilavan," he said, clasping his friend's hands, "do you remember a few weeks ago, when we were talking about finding a spiritual master, you told me that I shouldn't settle for any ordinary guru, that I should only accept the best, a perfect master? Well, I found him, and I didn't even have to leave Jamalpur. Can you imagine?"

Ram Khilavan's heart began to beat faster. "Is it really true? You've found a perfect master? In Jamalpur itself?"

"Yes. I am so fortunate; I can't tell you how grateful I feel. The gods have smiled on me, my friend."

"If that's so, then you must take me straight away to meet him. You know how long I've been waiting to find a spiritual master."

Dasarath hesitated. "It's not that easy. He doesn't allow us to disclose his name or his address without prior permission. First we have to give him the name of anyone who's interested. Then he closes his eyes and reviews their samskaras, both this life and the past ones. Then he decides if the person is fit for initiation or not. His disciples say that he only accepts persons who were already practicing sadhana in their previous lifetimes."

"Well, if this is the case, then please put my petition before your master at the first possible opportunity. I will wait."

Ram Khilavan was so impressed with the sense of gratitude and good fortune expressed by his friend, whom he knew to be the soberest and most unassuming of men, that that night, as he lay on his bed, he mentally addressed Dasarath's new master. "I don't know if you will consider me fit or not, whether you will give me permission or not, but I want to tell you that from this moment onward I accept you as my master. Even if you do not give me permission to take initiation, I will continue to consider you my master, and no other."

A couple of days later, Dasarath was sitting in the ashram with Baba and some fellow disciples. Baba turned to him and said, "A person close to you has made a direct approach to me. Tell him that he should go through proper channels, as per system."

Dasarath was surprised. "Who was it?" he asked.

"You name the persons close to you and I will tell you which one it was."

One by one, Dasarath named his relatives and close friends. After each one Baba shook his head no. Running out of names, he finally mentioned Ram Khilavan, though he was sure that it could not be him. To his surprise, Baba said, "Yes, that is his name. He should go through proper channels. Anyhow, you may tell him that he has permission to contact an acharya and take initiation."

The next evening Dasarath went to Ram Khilavan's house, feeling miffed at his friend. "Ram Khilavan, I told you I would put your petition before the master. Why did you make a direct approach to Baba without waiting?"

"What are you talking about? I made no such contact with your Baba. How could I? You didn't even tell me his name or where he lives. What exactly did he say?"

When Dasarath recounted his conversation with Baba, Ram Khilavan remembered his fervent prayer from two days earlier and told his friend what had happened. "Now, explain to me the proper system."

When Ram Khilavan met Baba for the first time some days later, he recognized him as the man who had stopped and changed his mind about the Gita. His wife and four young daughters would take initiation shortly afterward, and all of them would soon be counted amongst the most ardent of Baba's followers.

Gradually the circle widened. More and more newcomers were drawn by the devotional fervor that was rapidly blossoming among the disciples. In March 1956, Chandranath brought his nineteen-year-old cousin Harinder, whom he had initiated a few weeks before, to his first darshan. Harinder described his reaction when he saw Baba for the first time, a reaction typical of many new disciples during those first years of Ananda Marga:

> I was sent into Baba's room by Shiva Shankar-da and immediately did sastaunga pranam. My first thought when I got up was that he had sent me into the wrong room because the person I saw in front of me was wearing very ordinary dress—dhoti, kurta, and spectacles—an ordinary gentleman, whereas I had been expecting a holy man with orange robes and flowing hair.
>
> After I came out, Pranay-da told me to take a seat in the hall with the others. Bindeshvari was singing a song about Baba. He was laughing one moment and crying the next. I thought he must be a serious mental patient and had come to Baba to get cured. Pranay-da asked some of the others to remove him from the hall; as they were taking him out, he cried, "You can throw me out of the hall but you can't throw me out of Baba's heart." Then another person started singing a Bengali song: "I don't know anything Baba, and you are the knower of all. There is nothing to say about me; your glory is on everyone's lips." Then this person also became abnormal and they also carried him out.
>
> Baba came out and took his seat on a cot. There were no decorations, just an incense stick burning and a single tube light for illumination. As soon as Baba came out, many people started acting abnormal: weeping, laughing, falling on the floor, dancing. I was convinced that my cousin had brought me to a place full of madmen, a kind of

lunatic asylum. Then Baba gave a long discourse. I didn't pay much attention—I was watching the people—but I remember he talked about surrender.

After the talk was over and Baba had left, we went out to the compound of the school. Pranay told the new people that the DMC was over, that we should each go into Baba's room and do pranam and then we were free to go. I went and stood in line. When my turn came, I prostrated before Baba and immediately lost consciousness, I don't know for how long. The next thing I remembered was hearing Baba's voice telling me, "Harinder get up." When I got up, I found that I was wrapped in a black blanket; I was crying. When I tried to understand why I was crying, the tears started flowing even more profusely. I thought I had become one of the madmen. Pranay-da said, "Listen, you have to see that others also get time. So don't take the time of others."

I went out and sat in the compound, but I felt an irresistible attraction pulling me toward Baba, a tremendous urge to go and sit near him. My entire body was very, very light. I felt very healthy and energetic. Since my childhood I had never had such a feeling. After that, a couple of other devotees accompanied me to the railway station. When I got there I could feel my mind pulling me back again to Baba. It was almost impossible to resist. At that moment I realized that the love I had been missing since the death of my parents had returned to me manyfold. I had finally found the one I had been searching for so many years.

The person who sang the Bengali song was Gopen, an official in the Central Excise Department posted under Nagina. He would often go into samadhi when he sang devotional songs for Baba at the beginning of the DMC or darshan program. At times other devotees would also become affected when they tried to bring him back to normal consciousness; the mere touch of his body somehow communicated his intoxicated state. In fact, Gopen would usually become abnormal whenever he saw Baba, sometimes dancing on one leg, at other times weeping and calling out Baba's name as he entered into various states of ecstatic trance. Several devotees recall entering Baba's room and finding Gopen lying there in a state of samadhi. One time in Ranchi, Gopen went into samadhi just as he was about to initiate someone. As might be expected, the prospective initiate immediately ran away. On another occasion, after Baba had left the DMC dais, Gopen became so absorbed in his ideation that he sat down on the empty dais, opened his hands into *varabhaya mudra*, and began repeating over and over, "I am Anandamurti; I am Anandamurti."

It was soon rumored that Baba had given Gopen the power to see the past, present, and future. One Sunday, while waiting for Baba to arrive at the ashram,

Nityananda decided to test him. "I have some urgent work with Baba," he told him. "Do you know if he is already on his way to the ashram, or if he is still at his house?" Gopen raised his eyebrows, clearly annoyed by the question, and looked away. But Nityananda continued to insist. Finally Gopen smiled and closed his eyes. "Baba is on his way now to the ashram," he said, his eyes still closed. "At this moment he is walking down the market lane on his way toward Rampur Colony." Nityananda jumped up and hurried out the door to his bicycle. He pedaled as fast as he could toward the market lane, knowing just where he would intercept Baba if what Gopen had said were true. Sure enough, Baba was exactly where Gopen had indicated he would be. The enigmatic Gopen, along with Bindeshvari and others like them, were an integral part of the intense devotional climate that surrounded Baba, an environment so unusual to the uninitiated that it made Harinder wonder if his cousin had brought him to a lunatic asylum.

Baba's evening field walk was another opportunity for the disciples to enjoy the master's company and bask in the glow of his multifaceted personality. No topic was outside Baba's range of interest. On any given night the discussion could segue from politics to astronomy to natural history to anthropology to art, all enriched with a never-ending series of illustrative stories and quotations from poets, writers, and philosophers, sometimes in languages they had never heard before, which he would then translate.

Once Ram Tanuk and several other disciples were accompanying Baba on field walk near Ranchi. After a long explanation of how the caste system had developed during the Buddhist era, Baba launched into a discussion of the difference in psychology between the people of Magadha in Southern Bihar and those of Mithila in Northern Bihar, pointing out how the domestic cows of those areas also shared some of these same psychological differences. He stopped and asked them why there was so much dust there. Everyone remained quiet.

"You will find that Southern Bihar is very dusty while Patna is not," Baba said. "The weather in Patna is sultrier and the soil becomes quite sticky during the rainy season, whereas in Southern Bihar it becomes very dusty once the rain stops. Can anyone tell me why that is?" Baba paused but no one ventured an answer. "It is because the soil here is newly formed by comparison, whereas the soil of Patna is quite old and therefore has more elasticity. Newly formed soil turns to dust very easily. If you walk in Patna after a rainfall, it becomes difficult to take a second step because the soil clumps to your feet."

Sometimes Baba would turn the spotlight on the disciple's personal history, recalling incidents from their past that they themselves had forgotten, as if he had been there to witness them. Harinder recalled a few such incidents from his early field walks that were typical of the intimate and informal nature of Baba's relationship with his disciples at this time:

Once I was sitting with Baba on the tiger's grave when he asked me what my father's last words were when he was on his deathbed. That was in 1947. I told Baba I couldn't remember but he asked me repeatedly to keep trying. I tried as hard as I could, but all I could remember about the scene was that there were tears in his eyes. Three of my uncles were present there and also one elderly man of the village, a servant, two sister-in-laws, and myself. That much I remembered, but not what he said. Then Baba touched me on the back of my spine. Immediately the scene flashed in my mind and I remembered. As I spoke the words, Baba also spoke them along with me. "Harinder, I am sorry I could not do anything for you. You should maintain good relations with all. You should work hard and remain in the company of good people." Baba and I repeated the same words together at the same time.

Another time, when I was sitting with him on the grave, he started telling me that there used to be two women in my village who were both called Radhiya. They were mother and daughter, and both were widows. They were also great devotees of God and sincere spiritual aspirants. He said that they used to take bath regularly in the rivulet in front of my house. I told Baba that the water was unfit for bathing because drainage water is funneled into it, but Baba told me that it had been a flowing river at that time and even boats used to ply it. He said that there had been a ghat in front of my house where they used to take bath. Then I remembered that when they were digging a well in that area the people had found some broken remnants of a boat. The next time I went to my village, I inquired about the two women but nobody seemed to know anything about them. There was one very old man there who was well over a hundred. He had been a good hunter in his younger days and was very sturdy. I went to visit him and started to talk about this and that. In the end, I asked him whether at anytime there had been two women in the village named Radhiya and Radhiya, mother and daughter. He remembered right away that when he was very young he had seen them regularly taking bath in the river in front of my house. After that they would spend hours worshiping God. They were both widows and did not have any descendents. He asked me how I had learned about them. I said that I had heard about them from a saint.

Another day at the tiger's grave Baba was talking to me about the need for keeping good company. He reminded me of an incident from when I had been a student of class eight. One day, the public relations department from Muzaffarpur showed a documentary film in our village high school. I went to see the documentary but I arrived very late. It was already over. While I was returning home, a big storm arose, which is common in summer. On the way, one boy told me about a particular mango grove where lots of mangoes were sure to have fallen to the ground in the storm. He said they were very sweet and he tried to convince me to go there with him. Actually he had something against the owner of that grove. When we got there, we found that a few mangoes had fallen. But the boy climbed a tree and started vigorously shaking the branches. A lot of mangoes fell to the ground. I knew that if the owner came to know about it, he would complain to my family that I was stealing mangoes from his grove in the dark. I could well imagine the consequences. I was very frightened and ran home; I spent the whole night shaking with fear. I was also angry with that boy for taking me there under false pretences. This incident disturbed me for many days. Baba reminded me about the incident and he told the name of the owner of the grove—Rudar Singh—and the name of the boy who took me there—Raghunandan Paswan. It felt strange to hear Baba recount the whole incident in such detail, including their names, since I had completely forgotten about it. I told Baba that the boy had deceived me and that I had run away when I realized that he was trying to use me. "Yes," Baba said, "that is why I say that it is essential to always keep good company."

There were two things that all the disciples who accompanied him on these walks agreed upon: Baba was a superb storyteller and he was extremely humorous. One day Baba was sitting on the grave talking about the relationship between adult children and their elderly parents. He told a story to illustrate his point. As always, he accompanied his story with the gestures and shifts in tone of voice of an accomplished actor, eliciting loud laughter from the disciples in the process.

"Once there was an old man who lived with his son and his daughter-in-law. One day a friend of his dropped by for a visit and asked him how he was doing. 'Don't ask!' the old man said, 'I don't even get proper food these days.'

"His friend thought about it for a moment. Then he handed him a silver coin. 'Here, take this coin. Each night, when your son and his wife go to bed, take the coin and drop it against the bedstead two hundred times.'

" 'Why? What good would that do?'

" 'Just trust me,' the friend told him. 'I'll come back after a week or so and see how it's going.'

"The old man did exactly as his friend asked. Each night his son and daughter-in-law heard the sound of the coin clinking against the bedstead. They became convinced that the old man had a secret stash of money that he was counting each night. One day, while the old man was out, they searched his room. They didn't find anything but that only convinced them that he was hiding it really well. They didn't want to take a chance of losing the money when he died, so they started treating him better. When his friend came back, the old man said, 'My friend, this coin has changed my life.'

"When the old man finally died, his son and his daughter-in-law searched his room but all they found was a single silver coin lying near his pillow. Only then did they realize that the old man had been cleverer than they had given him credit for."

Though Baba was rarely quiet on field walk, there was one week in 1956 when he made an exception. On Sunday he made an announcement: "During the coming week I am going to maintain a strict watch on all my disciples to see how sincerely they are following the principles of yama and niyama. At the end of the week I will hand out punishment for any deviations, though I won't disclose the actual faults in public. All conversation at the tiger's grave is forbidden during this time. No one should ask any questions. I will be watching my disciples wherever they might be and I don't want to be disturbed."

Naturally the disciples were determined to be on their best behavior. One evening, a few days later, Nityananda was standing in the courtyard of the ashram with Goba and Dwarikanath when his desire got the better of him.

"Dwarikanath, give me the snuffbox."

"What! You promised you wouldn't take snuff this week. You know Baba is watching."

"Just hand it over, Dwarikanath. It's been long enough."

Dwarikanath reluctantly handed him the snuffbox. Just as Nityananda was about to take a pinch, Dwarikanath started scolding him, his tone of voice and mannerisms suddenly identical to Baba's.

"What do you think you are doing, Nityananda? Do you think you can hide your actions from me? I told you I would be watching. If required, I appear in physical form also. Nobody can perform any secret action without my knowledge. Do you understand?"

Goba's eyes went wide in surprise. "Dwarikanath has become Baba!" he exclaimed. He ran into the ashram shouting over and over again, "Dwarikanath has become Baba, Dwarikanath has become Baba, come and see." Then he ran back to where Nityananda and Dwarikanath were standing and did sastaunga pranam in front of Dwarikanath. Several Margis were trailing behind him, eager to see what was happening. In the meantime Nityananda became frightened. He hurriedly put the snuffbox back in Dwarikanath's pocket while Dwarikanath stood there with his hands on his hips and a stern expression on his face, continuing to chide him for failing to observe proper discipline. After a few minutes, Dwarikanath reverted back to his normal self.

"What happened to you?" Nityananda asked. "Why were you acting like that?"

"I don't know," Dwarikanath replied with a confused look on his face. "I don't know what happened. It was like I wasn't there at all."

The curious Margis spent the next few minutes discussing amongst themselves, finally coming to the conclusion that Baba had somehow borrowed Dwarikanath's body for those few minutes in order to reprimand Nityananda. Nityananda, however, had his doubts. Perhaps because we were talking about Baba, he mused, the thought of Baba came into his subconscious mind and that influenced his conscious mind. When everyone else had left, he invited Dwarikanath to accompany him to his quarters, with the intention of testing him when no one else was around. When they arrived, Nityananda asked once again for the snuffbox. As soon as Dwarikanath handed it over, his voice and mannerisms changed.

"Nityananda," he said, "are you trying to test me? Don't you know that I am always with you, watching your every action, every moment of the day? If necessary, I will even appear physically in front of you. You cannot hide anything from me, neither your actions nor your thoughts."

Startled, Nityananda threw the snuffbox out the window. Moments later Dwarikanath reverted to his normal self. When Nityananda questioned him, he was unaware of what had happened. It was as if those few minutes had not registered at all on his consciousness.

On Sunday the Margis assembled in the ashram for Baba's darshan. A blackboard was brought and Baba started to write down the names of various disciples. Beside each name he wrote out their respective punishments. After writing Nityananda's name and his punishment, he drew a line through it. Then he turned to the disciples and said, "Nityananda was about to commit a mistake; in fact, he had already committed that mistake mentally. But since he didn't actually do it, the punishment is hereby struck off." When one Margi asked for clarification, Baba said. "He was about to take snuff, a punishable offence, when an unseen force prevented him from committing that mistake. Because of the warning from this unseen force, he was able to restrain himself. For that reason I have forgiven him."

Ram Naresh Pandey, an officer in the BMP, was posted in Jamalpur from 1955 to 1957. During that time he availed of every possible opportunity to accompany the master on evening walk. Ram Naresh was an excellent singer. Whenever he was present at the tiger's grave, Baba would request him to sing a devotional song or two, generally in Bhojpuri, Ram Naresh's mother tongue and Baba's favorite childhood language.

One night Ram Naresh was delayed by his official duties. By the time he reached the field, it was nearly ten o'clock. He went straight to the tiger's grave, hoping fervently that Baba might still be there. Finding the grave deserted, he started searching the other places where the master would occasionally stop but to no avail. Unhappy that he had missed out on Baba's darshan for the night, he went back to the grave and sat down. While he was sitting there, storm clouds gathered with the startling rapidity so common in the rainy season in Northern India. It quickly became so dark that he couldn't see more than a few feet in front of him. Then the heavens opened and a sudden heavy downpour left him shivering and drenched to the bone. Refusing to accept his defeat, he got up and started walking back toward the ashram, singing a Bhojpuri song with his arms upraised and his eyes half-closed, buoyed by the conviction that he could call Baba to him with his song. "O Baba," he sang, "I have developed such an intense love for you; it is the love of eons." He sang the same lines over and over again with his eyes half-closed as he made the long, soggy journey through the fields to the outskirts of town. When he reached the wooden footbridge that crossed the railroad tracks to the east of the station, he felt someone reach out and catch his arm. Turning, he saw Chandranath looming out of the darkness.

"Ram Naresh," Chandranath said, "you have done something wondrous, but why didn't you come to the ashram with the weather so bad? Baba was giving us some important dictation there. Suddenly he stopped and told us that we needed to go to the grave. 'Ram Naresh is waiting for me there,' he said, 'crying and getting totally wet.'"

"Where is Baba now?" Ram Naresh asked, tears forming in his eyes.

"He's right here." Chandranath turned and shone his flashlight on Baba, who was standing a few feet away in the pitch dark.

"My son," Baba said, "today I have given you much pain. It is my mistake."

Ram Naresh fell at his feet weeping, despite the soggy conditions. "No, Baba, when I came out of my house the weather was fine but then the storm sprang up."

Yes, I know. You have followed my order but I didn't follow it."

"Please, Baba, don't say that."

"Okay. Come, let us move."

Throughout the walk back to Baba's house, Ram Naresh had to struggle to fight back his tears, overcome by his love for the master, a love so powerful it had drawn Baba to him in the rain.

Ram Naresh was not the only singer of devotional songs who was able to command Baba's presence by his longing. On another occasion, Mashin Bahadur was meditating in Baba's room in the ashram when Ananda Kishore arrived with his eleven-year-old daughter. Ananda Kishore asked his daughter to wait for him in the front room and then joined Mashin for meditation. While the two men were meditating, his daughter started singing a devotional song, dancing and crying as she sang. Soon both men found themselves crying as well. They lost consciousness of the passage of time, half listening to the song, half meditating. Suddenly they heard Bindeshvari shouting, "Who is there?" When the two men opened their eyes, they found Baba sitting beside them, his eyes half-closed, listening in rapture to the girl's song. Bindeshvari was with him and looking very upset.

"Just look at Baba's feet!" Bindeshvari shouted. "See how red they are!" The men were startled to see the condition of Baba's feet, but still they didn't understand what was going on. "You brought him here on a hot summer afternoon. What were you thinking? See, he didn't even take time to put on his shoes."

Both Mashin and Ananda Kishore started to cry. They began massaging Baba's feet, while the master remained in rapture, seemingly oblivious to their presence. Slowly Baba returned to his normal consciousness and they were able to accompany him to his house. After they had left Baba at his door, Bindeshvari told them what had happened.

"I was lying on a bench on my veranda, trying to get some relief from the heat, when I saw someone in a dhoti and an undershirt walking barefoot down the road. I was startled to see someone walking barefoot in this hot sun, but it took a minute or two before I realized that it was Baba. I couldn't believe it. So I ran and brought Baba inside the house. While he was sitting down, I brought a pair of shoes and a shirt for him. When I asked him what he was doing out walking barefoot in the hot sun like that, he told me that his devotee was in the ashram calling him. He couldn't bear to stay away."

Every devotee had a story to tell about their relationship with the master, a relationship so deep that whenever they faced any serious problem, be it physical, mental, or spiritual, they put their faith in him to rescue them from their predicament. One of these was Jitendra Tyagi, a wealthy, hard-drinking businessman and a close friend of Asthana who had taken initiation from Baba in October 1954 after his family, concerned by his heavy drinking, had urged him to adopt some spiritual path. Soon after his initiation, Baba sent Shiva Shankar Bannerjee to Bhagalpur with a message that Tyagi was suffering from an advanced case of tuberculosis in both lungs. If he wanted to live, he would have to give up drinking immediately. Tyagi was shaken by the message, but the idea of giving up alcohol was unthinkable. Plagued by a chronic cough for the last few months, he had been able to control his problem with regular doses of whiskey, the same miracle drink, he liked to brag to his friends, that had enabled him to spend his winter vacation in the mountain resort of Darjeeling without having to wear anything more than a light shirt. He would consider seeing a doctor, but giving up alcohol was simply out of the question.

Within a week Tyagi was running a temperature. Soon he became so weak that he found it difficult to get out of bed. Asthana, worried that his friend was not following Baba's instructions, urged him to stop drinking and do his meditation and yoga postures as strictly as possible.

"How can you expect me to meditate when I find it difficult to even sit up?" Tyagi told him. "Are you trying to kill me with this meditation? My problem only became worse after I got initiated."

But Asthana continued to insist, and a few days later, when Tyagi began to cough up blood, he finally made good on his promise to see a doctor. He left the next day for Calcutta, where he stayed in the house of Raghuvir Prasad, Collector of Customs and one of his closest friends as well as Asthana's boss. There he was examined by an eminent specialist, Dr. Bidhan Chandra Roy, who confirmed the contents of Baba's message.[3] He was diagnosed with an advanced case of acute tuberculosis in both lungs and put on a long-term program of daily injections and strict bed rest. But eventually, after he failed to respond to the treatment, the doctor broke the sad news that there was not much more he could do. "Pray to God," Dr. Roy advised him. "At this point he is your best hope."

The next morning, while lying in his bed, Tyagi heard a voice inside him say, "Once you have surrendered to me, you cannot surrender to the doctors and their medicines." As the day advanced, the voice grew stronger, and by evening he had made up his mind. Though he was barely able to walk, he got up from his bed. Over the worried objections of his host, he somehow made his way to the train station, where he boarded the overnight train for Bhagalpur. Once he arrived in Bhagalpur, he phoned Asthana and requested him to take him to Jamalpur by car. "I have thrown my medicines away," he said. "I will put my life in Baba's hands. If he cannot save me, then I will go home to Delhi and die there, but I will not take any more medicines or see any more doctors."

The two men arrived in Jamalpur in the evening and proceeded directly to the railway quarters ashram, where a small group of disciples had gathered to wait for Baba. While Tyagi sat quietly in one corner, Asthana told the disciples about Tyagi's condition. Collectively they discussed how best to approach Baba. While they were conversing, they heard a knock at the door. Everyone fell quiet. Pranay rushed to the door to open it, and in stepped Baba with his characteristic energy. He strode up to the cot and sat down while the disciples gathered round him. He gave a short talk and conversed directly with several disciples, but he didn't say anything to Tyagi and no one dared bring the matter up directly. Then Baba surprised them by saying that he had some important work and needed to be left alone. Everyone spilled out into the courtyard and began discussing what to do, but a minute or two later a shout went up. "Tyagi sahib, Tyagi sahib, Baba is calling you."

Tyagi rushed to Baba's room and prostrated in front of the master.

"Where are you running away to?" Baba asked him.

Tyagi had no idea what Baba was referring to. Not knowing what to say, he kept quiet.

"Are you ill?" Baba asked.

"Yes, Baba," Tyagi replied, bowing his head. Baba closed his eyes for a few moments; then he reached out his left foot and touched his toe to Tyagi's chest.

"Go, eat and be merry."

Tyagi did pranam and left the room. As soon as he was back in the courtyard, Asthana was stunned to see him looking younger and stronger, as if he had instantly put on weight. "What happened?" he asked, but the only thing Tyagi could say was that he was starving. They accompanied Bindeshvari to Bindeshvari's house where Tyagi ate a huge meal, the first good meal he had eaten in several months. It was only after he had eaten that he was able to explain what had transpired while he was alone with Baba.

"What did you feel exactly?" they asked, after he completed his story. "Did you feel an electric current pass through you when Baba touched you?"

"No, nothing. I just felt ravenously hungry."

A few days later, Tyagi returned to Calcutta and told Raghuvir that his guru had cured him. Raghuvir accompanied him to Dr. Roy's for a fresh examination. The doctor was pleasantly shocked to find that all traces of his tuberculosis had disappeared.

"Your x-ray is that of a patient who has had TB in the past and recovered. Who treated you? How were you cured?"

"No one treated me," Tyagi replied. "I just prayed to God as you advised me."

The next day Raghuvir Prasad phoned Asthana and insisted that he arrange for his immediate initiation. The Collector of Customs would soon become one of Baba's most fervent disciples.[4] Now that he had recovered, Tyagi felt the urge to drink return, but when he went to a liquor shop to buy a bottle of whiskey, he discovered that he no longer wanted it. He never drank again.

When Asthana communicated Raghuvir's request to Baba, the master told him that he was going to Bhagalpur the following week and that Raghuvir should meet him at a particular spot on the bank of the Ganges at sunset. Immediately after his initiation, Raghuvir was filled with self-doubt, convinced that it would be difficult for him to atone for all his sins in one life, but Baba told him, "God has given you eyes in the front of your head and not in the back. Look forward and not backward. A cursory look back might be necessary once in a while to remind oneself that one never wants to go back there again, but that is all. I have cleansed you of your past today. From now on you are a new man."

Tyagi was not the only person with TB to seek a cure from Baba, quite understandable considering the widespread prevalence of the disease at that time. It is estimated that in 1955 there were fourteen million cases of tuberculosis in India. Even today, it remains the country's number one cause of infectious disease mortality with a half million deaths in two million reported cases, thirty percent of the worldwide total.

Later in the same year, Dr. Vishvanath found out that his brother-in-law was suffering from an advanced case of tuberculosis. He took him to a renowned specialist, Dr. Matsu, who had had great success treating tuberculosis, but after examining the patient the doctor told him that the disease was at such an advanced stage that he could do nothing for him. When the family learned that the disease was incurable, they became desperate. Having heard the miraculous stories that Vishvanath would often tell, they started pressing him to ask his guru to intercede. Vishvanath was reluctant to do so. He explained to them that Baba did not meet people who were not initiated; moreover, the patient would almost certainly have to travel to Jamalpur, something he did not appear to be in a condition to do. The family, however, was insistent. They agreed to take initiation and to travel together with the patient. Vishvanath acceded and traveled with them to Jamalpur, where he arranged for their initiation without disclosing the purpose of their visit. Once they were initiated he went to see Baba. Before he could get up from sastaunga pranam, Baba started scolding him.

"Why are you turning me into an asylum, Vishvanath? The only reason you brought your relatives here was to try and cure your brother-in-law's disease. None of them took initiation due to spiritual motivation."

Vishvanath hung his head, unable to look Baba in the eyes.

"You know the philosophy of samskara. Your brother-in-law is suffering from this disease as a result of his previous actions. As per the law of Prakriti, he has to undergo this suffering in order to expiate the reactions of his evil deeds from the past. Do you want me to violate the laws of Prakriti?"

Again Vishvanath kept silent. He folded his hands to his chest and mentally told Baba that he would accept whatever he thought best.

"Very well," Baba said. "Do one thing. Take the patient to the well and give him a bath with forty buckets of cold water. Then bring him to see me. And don't worry. There is no question of his dying."

Vishvanath was ashamed that he had bothered his guru with such a request, but he was confident that whatever Baba prescribed was sure to work. He went back to his sister's family and conveyed Baba's instructions. At first they were frightened, especially the patient, who was afraid that he might die there and then from such a bath. But Vishvanath would not take no for an answer. "This is the guru's command. You go against it at your peril." The thinly veiled warning was enough. Vishvanath gave the patient the bath as Baba had instructed and then took him to meet the master. Baba gave the brother-in-law his blessing and told Vishvanath to take him for a walk to the tiger's grave by Baba's normal route and back again without stopping. Despite the fact that the patient was feeling extremely weak and had been prescribed total bed rest by his doctors, he was willing to follow Baba's instructions. By the time they completed the nearly two-hour circuit, he was feeling better than he had in months. The family was astonished to see the change. The patient was so happy that instead of returning home with the rest of the family, he stayed on for another month in Jamalpur to have Baba's daily darshan.

Not long afterward, Vishvanath came down with severe throat pain, so severe that he had difficulty drinking water. He saw a doctor but the treatment didn't help. Still, he declined to tell Baba about it, preferring to undergo the samskara and let the disease run its course, Baba's lesson now firmly implanted in his mind. After three days, a person whom he had never seen before knocked at his door and handed him a package. "Baba sent me to deliver this to you. He said it is a medicine for your throat." Vishvanath folded his palms to his chest, sending his silent pranam to Baba. He took a dose and within a few hours the pain subsided. The next day, his throat now completely healed, he went to Baba and asked him for the formula, inspired by the thought that he could help a lot of people if he knew how to prepare the remedy. Baba smiled and said, "Ah, Vishvanath, do you want to earn money with this remedy?"

Baba declined to tell him the formula.

As time went on, Baba would get more and more strict with his disciples about not projecting him as a miracle worker, especially when it came to curing people of their diseases. Virendra Asthana remembered Baba's attitude at the time in one of his interviews:

> In 1956 or 1957, the wife of one of the senior officers of the Indian Civil Service, Saroj Lal, came down with cancer. I think it was 1957. I got a trunk call from the Chief Minister's office informing me of her situation. I had no courage to ask anything more about her because she was not even initiated. They requested me to at least ask Baba. I told them that since she was passing through the last stages of the cancer, there was no question of even asking. It was too late for that. Still, when I went to Jamalpur, I told Baba that such a call had come to me from the phone of the Chief Minister. Baba asked me what I had told them in reply. I told him that I had said it was too late, that if they had asked earlier then she could have learned sadhana and then there would have been a chance of a cure. Baba told me, "Look, I don't want to be projected as a doctor. I don't want to be projected as a Christ. This practice people have of talking about these things should be stopped. Baba didn't come to this earth to show miracles. These are not my miracles. It is due to people's surrender that such things happen. Why should I be advertised as a doctor or a miracle worker?" That was his attitude in 1957. I said, "How can I prevent it?" Baba said, "Why not? You are in contact with many people. People are moving here and there and talking about these things. I don't want any of my disciples talking about these things to other people."
>
> Anyhow, there was a customs officer, Omprakash Setty, who worked in the customs office in Allahabad. He was from Lucknow. He took initiation, as almost everyone in the customs department had done. There were about a thousand or two thousand people who had taken initiation in that department. Before initiation he used to smoke a lot, but after initiation he gave up the habit. Then one day another person in the Allahabad customs office who had also taken initiation

came to me and said, "Sir, my friend Setty is in trouble." I asked him what the trouble was; he told me that Setty had gone to Lucknow for a health examination and the doctors there had told him that he had lung cancer. If it had been tuberculosis, then it might have been curable, but since it was cancer it was not curable at that time. He came back to Allahabad and his wife was weeping. She came to our house crying and pleaded with me to do something. I listened, but kept quiet. I didn't say anything or promise anything. Then she went to my wife and insisted that Baba could do something. At that time her husband was thirty-two and she was about twenty-nine. My wife came to me and told me that they were so young, I must talk to Baba about the matter, but I was reluctant to do so, knowing how Baba felt about these things.

Then we went to Jamalpur and went on field walk. My wife went with us to the tiger's grave. She told Baba about Omprakash Setty's cancer and what the doctors had said. Baba said, "What can I do? It is due to his samskara." She told Baba that he should do something because his wife was so young and they had a new baby. She kept insisting that Baba should cure him. Finally Baba said, "All right, you ask Virendra what should be done. Don't worry, everything will be all right." Now, I did not know anything about yogic *cikitsa* at that time.[5] Baba's book had not come out yet. I just told him to do sadhana properly. Within one fortnight his cancer disappeared. Probably Baba wanted to rectify his sadhana. Later, he became an acharya and his elder brother's daughter became an *avadhutika* (female monastic disciple).

XV

Demonstration Year

The seed of omniscience lies inherent in the human mind itself, but due to utter ignorance, the human mind has forgotten its inherent nature and capacity.[1]

DESPITE THE GROWTH of Ananda Marga, Baba's private life continued to be as simple as ever. As Dilip Bose, an acharya who was related to Baba by marriage, noted, "Baba was one person with his disciples and a completely different person in his family life. He was so completely normal in his family life and other social situations that no one would think he was anything other than an ordinary man." At home, Baba lived the life of a dutiful son and a good neighbor in a lower-middle-class family that could not afford undue luxuries. The room he shared with his brother Sudanshu had a wooden bed, a small bench that doubled as a table, a small bookshelf, and a few hangers for their clothes, nothing more. He wore his shoes until a hole appeared in the sole and then he would take them to a cobbler to get them resoled, rather than buy new ones.[2] Instead of throwing away his soap bar when it became too small to grasp, he would paste it to the new soap. Unlike traditional Indian gurus, he would not accept gifts from his disciples, neither food nor clothes nor even flowers. In fact, he permitted himself no unnecessary extravagance, following his own teaching that true wealth is mental and spiritual, and that attachment to physical possessions more often than not proves harmful to the elevation of the human spirit.[3]

Baba's efforts to keep his identity as the guru of Ananda Marga a secret were so successful that for a long time most of his neighbors and even his family members were not sure exactly what his connection to Ananda Marga was. Many assumed that he was a member of the new organization; some knew that he was the president. Lakshmi, Baba's next-door neighbor, suspected the truth, but he was too polite to ask Baba directly. Instead, he pestered his old schoolmate Rameshvar Baita about the matter, having seen Rameshvar on occasion accompanying Baba to the field. Whenever he asked him if Prabhat-da was the propounder of Ananda Marga, Rameshvar would either change the subject or be as evasive as possible with his answer. One day, while Rameshvar was walking with Baba in the field, they stopped at a natural spring. While

Baba was squatting down to drink, Rameshvar asked him if it were proper for a disciple to evade the truth by subterfuge.

Baba looked up at him. "No, of course not. Why are you asking me this?"

"Baba, my conscience is bothering me. Almost every day Lakshmi asks me if you are the guru of Ananda Marga, and I always have to do my best to evade a direct answer."

"Rameshvar, this is not a selfish action on your part. You are doing it for my sake. I have a lot of work to do. I have to go to the office, to the ashram, to the market. If everyone comes to know that I am the guru, it will create problems for me. Not only for me, but for my neighbors, my colleagues, and my relatives as well. It is a matter of courtesy."

As late as 1963, a man from Jamalpur came to Anandanagar to admit his son into the Ananda Marga primary school. When he arrived, he told the disciples that he was an acquaintance of Prabhat-da. "He is a very good devotee of Ananda Marga," he told them. "He attends every Ananda Marga meeting. He is a very knowledgeable person also. He cannot be defeated in debate." The disciples smiled and nodded but did not mention to him that his Prabhat-da was actually the guru of Ananda Marga.

Since the inception of his work as a spiritual teacher, Baba had been conducting demonstrations for the benefit of his disciples, practical illustrations of the spiritual teachings and fascinating looks at aspects of incarnate life that were normally beyond the purview of human perception. In 1956 such spiritual demonstrations became a regular occurrence, prompting some of the senior disciples to speculate that Baba was using them to accelerate the growth of the organization and deepen the understanding and commitment of the many newcomers. Although the nature of the demonstrations varied greatly, many of them were variations on common themes. Demonstrations of samadhi were frequent, along with looks at the various symptoms associated with the awakening of the kundalini. There were numerous demonstrations showing the subtle mechanisms underlying the functioning of the universe, many of them centuries away from being discovered by modern science. The death demonstration would be repeated on a number of occasions over the coming years. But perhaps no demonstrations were more popular than those that showed the process of reincarnation and the effect of our past actions on our present lives.

In the beginning, different disciples served as Baba's subject for these demonstrations. But as time went on, Dasarath gradually became his principle medium, the quiet high school headmaster whom everyone respected for his honesty, simplicity, and rapidly developing aura of saintliness. The first time he met Baba, Baba told him that he would be a sadhu on the inside and a gentleman on the outside. He soon became a dedicated spiritual practitioner who rose each morning at three thirty to sit for three hours of meditation before beginning the day's activities, a practice he would maintain for the rest of his life.[4] Yet, much the same as his master, he would play the roles of family man and educator to perfection, always keeping his life as a yogi a private matter.

Baba would usually touch Dasarath on the back of his head at the level of the medulla oblongata and ask him to look into the mind of a nearby disciple and describe what he saw. As Dasarath's own practice progressed, however, Baba dispensed with touching him and simply asked him to concentrate his mind and look. Suddenly, upon Baba's command, the fog in his mind would clear and he would start seeing images appear, as if he were inside a cinema hall watching a motion picture. Then he would describe what he saw, well aware that he was only a medium. As time passed, Dasarath began to develop the ability to see the mental plates of others even in Baba's absence, an ability he would not find as agreeable as one might think.

In one interview, Dasarath described his experience:

> At times, Baba used to select me to see spiritual vibrations. On one such occasion, I was shown the different kinds of waves radiated by the persons present in Baba's room at the Jamalpur jagriti. These waves were radiating from the heads of the persons there. The waves were of different colors. One of these persons, an intellectual, had greenish waves around his head. Baba told us that greenish waves represent intellect.
>
> On another occasion, I saw a person with a curious kind of wave. I had never seen such a phenomenon. Black waves were coming from the right side of his head and face and white ones from the left side. I was stupefied and could not speak for quite some time. Baba understood my perplexity and said, "Yes, the man is very good within but his exterior is rough. The white waves show his inner, sentient nature, and the black ones his superficial states."
>
> On yet another occasion, I saw the waves of a young boy before his personal contact with Baba and then again after it. Before meeting Baba, the waves were quite black. After the personal contact, the blackness of the waves was greatly reduced and they were mixed with streaks of white.
>
> Then I developed a habit of seeing others' waves. It gave me much pleasure, and so, even without his permission, I continued my curious vision. One time I noticed white waves around the heads of two persons standing on the veranda of the Jamalpur jagriti. I happened to meet one of them later when he had almost left the Marga. The waves around him had become dark and distressing.
>
> I told Baba that I was seeing people's waves even without his orders. Baba asked me not to do so, as it was a path fraught with the possibility of downfall. I have since given up this kind of thing.

Dasarath recounted in another interview that it was as if he were seeing people's auras and thoughts with his open eyes in the same way that he saw their clothes, except in this case he was using his inner eye and there was no way to close it. He discovered that it was all too often a disagreeable experience. Too many people had dark colors swirling in their auras, a reflection of their negatives states of mind and unsavory character, and hearing their thoughts was sometimes like listening to a madman speak. Finally, Dasarath went to Baba and complained, and Baba mercifully withdrew the ability.

As the demonstrations increased in frequency, Dasarath gradually acquired such a reputation that newcomers would sometimes be afraid of him, worried that he might be able to see their private thoughts. His notoriety grew to the point that once in the early sixties a college student named Amit came to Jamalpur to see Dasarath after having heard that he could see people's past and future.[5] It was only after he went on his first field walk that he realized that Dasarath was only a medium, and that the real power resided in Baba.

Among the demonstrations that were often repeated were ones in which Baba showed that the revolutionary hero Subhash Chandra Bose was still alive, despite official reports of his death. In one such demonstration, Dasarath was seated in the ashram with the other Margis for Sunday darshan. "Concentrate your mind," Baba told him, "and start moving toward the eastern horizon. Describe what you see."

"Baba, I see a succession of forested hills and open plains."

Baba continued to guide him as if he were an air traffic controller, asking him to change directions several times. Under Baba's guidance, Dasarath started east and then turned in a more northerly direction until he reached the Himalayas, describing the scenery as he went. Baba led him through the foothills to the higher ranges of the Tibetan plateau.

"Stop there," Baba told him. "Where are you now?"

"A remote mountain, Baba, near Limpopo in Tibet."

"Now descend and look for a cave in the mountainside."

"I can see a cave set into the mountainside, below an outcropping."

"Enter the cave and describe what you see."

"It is quite dark inside. I can see the figure of a yogi sitting on an animal skin, performing meditation. His upper body is naked, he has long hair, and there are some cooking utensils nearby."

"Do you recognize the yogi?"

"No, Baba."

"Look closer and see if you can recognize him."

Dasarath hesitated for a few moments. "Baba, it looks like Subhash Chandra Bose."

"Yes, that is correct. Ask him if he would like to come back to India."

Dasarath remained silent for some moments before answering, perfectly motionless in lotus posture with his eyes firmly shut, as was the yogi in the cave that he was witnessing with his inner vision. "No, Baba. He has no wish to come back to India. His only wish now is to dedicate his life to spiritual practices."

"Leave him in peace then. He has done enough service for the society. Now he has reached a stage in his life when he should concentrate on sadhana."

On another occasion, Baba summoned a *dakshini*, a type of luminous body, or *devayoni*,[6] and told Dasarath to ask her if Subhash was still alive and then look closely at her forehead. If he saw a star then he was alive; if he saw a cross then he was dead. He saw a star. Baba would do numerous demonstrations over a period of years showing Subhash living the life of a yogi hermit.

Demonstrations about the mysteries of reincarnation were common. Once a female disciple, who used to visit Jamalpur regularly, lost her young son to a fatal childhood disease. One day in the jagriti, overcome by her lingering sadness, she requested Baba to tell her how her dead son was doing. Baba consoled her for a few minutes and then turned to Dasarath and told him to see if her son had already been reborn. Dasarath concentrated his mind and began narrating that he had taken birth in a well-to-do family of Gowahati in Assam. He was about to say the name of the family when Baba stopped him.

"It will create too much tension in her mind," Baba said, "if she thinks that she can locate her son. Now enter the baby's mind and see whether there is any awareness or anguish over his separation from his previous mother."

"No, Baba," Dasarath replied. "The baby is very happy in its new family. He is receiving a lot of love and affection."

"Now look into the baby's future. What do you see?"

"Baba, the baby's future is very bright."

"Good. Now go deep into the baby's mind and see whether or not he would like to go back to his previous mother, were it somehow possible."

"Baba, the baby does not want to be disturbed. He is happy where he is and does not want to leave."

When the demonstration was finished, the woman discovered that the anguish she had been harboring for so long had dissipated. In fact, she felt relieved to hear that her son had gotten a happy birth in which he could continue his spiritual journey. Baba went on to explain the karmic reasons why her son had come to her for such a short time, the samskaras that he had needed to exhaust through the medium of his early death. He concluded by saying, "Human relationships with those who are close to us only last for a certain period of time. Family life can be compared to a railway journey. At every station new passengers board the train and some of the old ones get off. It is natural that we befriend the ones that get on and develop a sense of warmth and affection for them. But do we shed tears when they get down at their respective destinations? No, not at all. The same applies to all family relationships. As long as we are together, we should love each other and honor our duties toward each other. But once the tie is broken, we should not give way to grief and despair. All such relationships are temporary. The only lasting relationship is with Paramapurusha, the Supreme Lord."

On another occasion, a young man from a well-to-do family came to Jamalpur for his first darshan. While the Margis were seated with Baba in the jagriti, Baba asked Dasarath to see the young man's past life.

"Baba, I see a dense forest. In the middle of the forest there is a sadhu sitting and performing meditation."

"Now move ahead a few years. What do you see?"

"I see a dead body covered by a white cloth."

"Yes, this boy was a spiritual ascetic in his previous life. He was a good sadhaka, but he harbored an attraction toward material enjoyments. At times, he would hope that he could be born into a rich family in his next life. Since he was a spiritual aspirant and regularly repeated God's name, a snake bit him in order to fulfill his latent desire. For this reason he was born in a merchant's family."

Baba turned his attention to the boy. "Are you afraid of snakes?"

"Yes, Baba. I've had a terrible fear of snakes ever since I was a child. Even now I can't abide the thought of them."

"Do your sadhana sincerely. Gradually that fear will vanish."

Demonstrations where Baba showed the past lives of different disciples became so commonplace that many of them became overly curious to know who they had been, although few had the temerity to ask Baba directly. An intellectually minded disciple from Calcutta, Manohar Lal Gupta, used to visit Jamalpur whenever he got the chance. He too became curious about his past lives and soon convinced himself that he must have been a very advanced yogi in his previous life to merit such a powerful guru in this one. On one such occasion, Manohar attended the darshan with a group of friends whom he had recently inspired to take initiation. During the darshan, his mind wandered while Baba was giving his discourse, musing once again about his hidden past. He was jolted back to the present by the sound of Baba calling his name. Manohar made his way to the front of the room and sat down next to Dasarath, excited by the thought that Baba might be about to show him his past life. Sure enough, Baba asked Dasarath to peer into his mind and see who he had been in his previous life.

"Baba, I see a pond outside a small village in what appears to be rural India. A sadhu is approaching the pond and preparing to take bath. He is taking off his shirt and his *lungi*,[7] leaving only his loincloth. Now he is wading into the water and chanting *Rama, Rama* in praise of the Lord."

Manohar felt a sense of anticipation, wondering if Dasarath or Baba would name the saint or tell in what era he lived and how elevated a soul he had been.

"Baba," Dasarath continued, "he is swishing his hands in the water while he remains absorbed in ideation."

"Yes, what more?"

"I see an old fish approaching the saint. The fish seems to be dying. He is barely able to move. He is just to the side of the sadhu." Dasarath remained quiet for a few moments. "Ah, the sadhu's hand touched the fish; immediately afterward the fish rolled over and went still, floating up to the surface of the pond."

"Okay. Now, tell me, who was this boy in his past life?"

"He was that fish, Baba."

"Yes," Baba drawled in his slow, gravelly voice, while the blood rushed to Manohar's face. "He was a fish in his past life. At the very moment that the fish died, its body came in contact with the hand of that saint. Because the saint was absorbed in cosmic ideation, the spiritual vibration emanating from him caused the fish to undergo *ulambhan*, a leap in evolution."

Manohar returned to his friends, unable to hide his embarrassment. But after a few years had passed, he would enjoy telling the story and making fun of his earlier arrogance.[8]

In one interview, Chandra Shekar, now a retired engineer, described a similar demonstration during his student days:

> A feeling came in my mind at that time that I must have been either a great person or a king in my previous life. Due to this, some ego arose in my mind. It was probably the third time I saw Baba. I was sitting near him, and although I had a feeling of surrender, I also had some ego. A clash was going on between my feeling of surrender and that ego, and the ego was not letting my feeling of surrender grow. There was a discussion. Baba's mood became grave; suddenly he said, "He is full of ego." Everyone looked around to see whom Baba was speaking about. He was looking at me. Baba's mood had completely changed. I felt that I had allowed a crude mentality to come into my mind. Baba asked me to stand up in front of everyone and then he asked Dasarath to see my past lives. Dasarath started to stare at me and I was also looking at him. Then Dasarath said that he was seeing the flesh in my body without the skin over it. Then he said that the flesh had fallen away and he was only seeing a skeleton standing there. While he was saying those things, I was also feeling that I was a person without skin, and then without flesh, just a skeleton. These feelings came into my mind, one by one.
>
> Dasarath was having some difficulty seeing, so Baba helped him. Then Dasarath said that he saw a large meadow. In the meadow there was a tree, and under the tree someone was sitting. Again he had trouble seeing and Baba helped him. Then Dasarath said that

he could see an eagle flying in the sky. Baba asked him whether or not there was something in the eagle's claws. Dasarath said that the eagle was indeed carrying something in its claws.

Then Baba told us that I had been an eagle in my last life in some jungle of Brazil. He began telling us that one survey party had gone there and one engineer had become separated from the survey team. He got lost and became very hungry. He was sitting under a tree, counting the last breaths of his life, thinking that he was going to starve to death. It so happened that the eagle was carrying a piece of meat in its claws. As it flew over the tree, it dropped the piece of meat, which landed in front of that man. When he saw the piece of meat, he became overjoyed. He immediately thought that the food had appeared through the grace of God. When he looked up, he saw the eagle, so he prayed to God to do something good for that eagle. He was a very pious person; due to his blessing that eagle became Chandra Shekar in this life through *ulambhan*. Baba mentioned that much.

And so all my vanity and ego got powdered down before him. Then Baba told me to proceed further with my sadhana and try to become great. He told me not to think about my last life, because such thoughts would make me regress. I should look forward and continue moving further and further toward my goal.

Baba often used similar demonstrations to show the intricacies of the law of action and reaction, cause and effect, and how it impacts the long journey of the living being across lifetimes. In his philosophy, he made it clear that a person's destiny depends on the nature of their thoughts and actions and the resulting samskaras. Continued indulgence in crude thinking can, he pointed out, cause the mind to degenerate to such a point where it is forced to adopt an animal body in the next life in order to satisfy its acquired samskara.

Once Baba was walking toward the ashram with Dasarath. As they passed in front of one house, they saw a large crowd gathered together. The atmosphere was grave and solemn. Baba asked Dasarath to go and see what was happening. After making a brief inquiry, Dasarath returned and explained that the head of that family had died a few hours earlier. Family and friends were gathered in mourning as they prepared the body for its final journey to the cremation ground.

Baba listened quietly and then resumed walking. "Dasarath," he said, "look carefully and see if you can trace the future path of progress for this disembodied mind."

Dasarath concentrated for a few moments and then said, "Baba this mind has regressed. It will take the body of a dog in its next life."

"Yes, that is correct. Though this man was a prominent member of the

Brahmin community, he was not a pious man as befits a Brahmin. In fact, he was a sinful and greedy man who never reflected on his misdeeds or repented for them. He was full of caste vanity and arrogance. Throughout his life he treated the lower castes with scorn. What will be his reward for his pride and vanity? He will be reborn as a dog. If he wanders into a gathering of Brahmins, will they not treat him as an untouchable and drive him away, just as he did to others in this life?"

Though the demonstrations were often humorous and always instructive, there were times when Baba used them to impart a stern and sobering lesson to some wayward aspirant. On one such occasion, a new disciple from Hazaribagh, Kamalesh, was participating in his first field walk. As they were walking toward the tiger's grave, Baba turned to Dasarath and asked, "Now, tell me, what life will this little boy get if he dies at this time?" A look of shock appeared on Kamalesh's face. "Don't worry," Baba said. "I am not saying that you are going to die now. I am only asking Dasarath to see what type of body you would take if you were to die now."

Dasarath looked at the boy for a few moments and said, "Baba, if he died now he would take the body of a scorpion."

Baba turned to Kamalesh with a grave look on his face. "What sort of activities are you involved in that would make you develop the reactive momenta of a scorpion?[9] Tell me."

Kamalesh kept silent. When he didn't answer, Baba changed the subject and began conversing with the other disciples who were accompanying him.

The next day before General Darshan,[10] Baba asked some disciples to call the boy who had come from Hazaribagh and bring him to his room. After a few minutes, everyone could hear Kamalesh weeping inside Baba's room. When the door opened nearly an hour later and he and Baba came out, Baba asked him, "Do you understand why your mentality became like that of a scorpion?"

"Yes, Baba."

"Then don't worry about what you have done any more. Those reactive momenta are finished. Forget your past and look to the future. From this moment forward, live your life like a true human being."

Though 1956 would be looked back upon as demonstration year, such demonstrations would remain an integral part of Baba's teaching style throughout his lifetime. Though the disciples would sometimes share these stories with non-Margi relatives and friends, they were aware of how fantastic they sounded. As one disciple remarked, "Sometimes we wanted to run out into the street and shout to everyone to tell them what was going on inside that room, but of course we couldn't. Nobody would have believed us. Sometimes we had a tough time believing it ourselves and we were right there watching it happen."

XVI

Divine Madness

When devotion (bhakti) touches the spiritual wave of pure Consciousness, which is beyond the three principles, it can no longer be called sentient or qualified, but can legitimately be called kevalá. In kevalá bhakti there remains no bondage of limitation. One who reaches the stage of kevalá bhakti forgets all protocol, and dances, sings, cries, and laughs in supreme joy. It is only at this height of spiritual elevation that worldly bondages, ripus, pashas and social restraints cease to exist.[1]

EARLY IN 1957, Baba called several senior disciples to his room and told them that he was thinking of forming prachar groups and sending them to different areas for intensive prachar programs. When they endorsed the idea, Baba asked Pranay to start informing the Margis of the program by letter.

Rameshvar Baita, Tarkeshvar, Mahadeva, and Chandradeva were assigned to Gaya, one of the major centers of Hindu pilgrimage. After fixing the dates for their tour and arranging leave from work, they came to Jamalpur to have Baba's darshan before proceeding on to Gaya. Baba called the four of them into his room and gave them a short talk about the importance of the work they were about to do. Then he assigned each of them a different topic on which to address the public.

"Baba," Rameshvar said, "I don't feel confident speaking in public."

Baba's demeanor underwent a sudden shift. "Who has to speak? Is it you or is it I?"

"You, Baba."

"Then why are you telling me that you can't talk on this subject? You simply stand there; I will talk."

Rameshvar bowed his head and nodded. Baba called the four of them closer to him. One by one, he touched them between the eyebrows at the site of their sixth chakra. All four entered into a state of trance. When they regained their normal consciousness, Baba was smiling.

"Now are you ready to go and give your talks?" he asked.

"Yes, Baba," they answered, still feeling the spiritual energy coursing in their spinal columns.

"Good. Now your time is up; go and catch your train."

They reached Gaya at midnight and passed the night in the station. In the morning they went to the house of a relative of Mahadeva to wash up and prepare for their work. Within a few hours, they were able to arrange a lecture hall and a microphone for the following day at six. Following Baba's instructions, they dispersed to different street corners to talk to the passersby about the philosophy and hand out invitations. By the time the program began, the hall was full. Each of them spoke on the subject Baba had assigned him. After Mahadeva gave the final speech, he asked the audience who was interested in initiation. Nearly everyone raised his hand and the four of them remained there until dawn teaching meditation.

From Gaya, they started moving in the direction of Jahannabad, village by village, following the sequence Baba had given them. In each village they went to the village chief, explained the purpose of their visit, and asked him to help them arrange a place for the meeting and inform the villagers of the program. After their talks and subsequent initiations, they would catch a bus or a train for the next village. When they finally reached Jahannabad, they boarded the train for Jamalpur and went straight to Pranay, the general secretary, to report on their efforts. Pranay informed them that Baba was sick and asked them to go immediately to Baba's quarters to offer him their pranam.

When they arrived at Baba's house, they found him lying on a cot outside his room with a fever of 102 degrees. Baba sat up and greeted them with a wide smile and a namaskar. Despite the fever, he insisted on hearing a detailed account of their trip. When they finished, he excused himself and went inside to take a cold bath. When he returned, Rameshvar asked him, "Baba, why did you take a cold bath? Shouldn't one avoid taking a cold bath when one has a fever?"

"Don't worry," Baba said, "nothing will happen to me. You had to walk in the sun, and it is because of the sun that blue fever is spreading. If you fell sick who could do my work? Shiva Shankar is in Assam; everyone else is out on tour. Now that you are back, I'll be fine."

The next day all signs of Baba's fever were gone. When Rameshvar saw this, he started weeping, sure that Baba had prevented them from falling sick by taking their samskaras on himself.[2] Over the next few months, prachar groups went to places as distant as Assam and the interior areas of West Bengal. They met with great success and further extended the reach of the organization.

In February, Dr. Sachinandan organized a DMC in his native village of Indas in the Birbhum district of West Bengal, about forty kilometers from Shantiniketan, the international educational and cultural center founded by Rabindranath Tagore. A few months prior to this, on Baba's instructions, Sachinandan had moved his dispensary from Jamalpur to Indas, an act of sacrifice that endeared him greatly to the local people. He started doing active prachar in the nearby villages, a practice that would lead his father to disown him for going against orthodox Hinduism. By the time of the DMC, Ananda Marga had become an established presence in the district. More than four hundred initiates were waiting for Baba when he arrived on the fifteenth at the nearest railway station, Maheshpur. More than half of them were from the local area. Baba traveled the three kilometers from the station to the village by bullock cart, still a common means of conveyance in rural areas at that time. As the entourage approached the village, the men started jumping and singing and blowing on conch shells, while the women started making the *ulu-ulu* sound, a loud, high-pitched, undulating peal made by moving the tongue against the inner lips, considered auspicious in Bengali culture.

During the day, the Margis took Baba for field walk to a place called Milanpur, where the Bakreshwar and Kopai rivers met. There he pointed out an ideal spot for a dam and gave them detailed instructions how to improve the economic situation in that area, including what crops to plant and where, how to open up small mills for those crops, and a plan for producer and consumer cooperatives for the end products. He also gave a long talk about the history of Birbhum, starting with a little-known story of how the name "Birbhum" came into existence. He related the history of the founding of Indas and some of the nearby villages and indicated where they could find the archeological ruins of the original settlement.

By evening, the devotional fervor had become so intense that when the DMC concluded the devotees were rolling on the ground and crying; many did not even notice when Baba left the dais. One of the Margis who remained unaffected by the fervor described his experience:

> In the morning we were given puffed rice and fried black chili and molasses for breakfast. In the meanwhile, Haraprasad Haldar came and he started to eat from our plates. He wouldn't eat from some people's plates; he said they had not repeated their second lesson mantra before eating. When we asked them about it afterward, they said it was true, they had not taken their second lesson before their meal. A little while later, Haldar ordered a dog to place its feet on the head of one advocate and the dog obeyed his command. It was so surprising. It stood up on its hind legs and placed its front paws on the sahasrara chakra of the advocate.
>
> At least fifty people in that place became abnormal. When the villagers saw all these things, they became convinced that there must be something very powerful in Ananda Marga. Many of them came forward and took initiation. There was a Dr. Chakraborty there and he also exhibited the same symptoms of madness. I was sleeping next to him after the DMC. He wrapped his arms around me in the night while he was in some kind of trance. I became afraid when that happened, so I went to Baba and told him that such and such things

were going on, that people had gone crazy and Dr. Chakraborty from Ranchi was doing such and such. Baba listened to everything I said. Then he told me that everything would be all right in the morning once he left. In the morning it was peaceful again, though some people still had some symptoms of the madness in them.

In those early days of Ananda Marga, the devotional relationship between Baba and his disciples often resembled a kind of madness in which the devotees danced and sang as the spirit moved them. One example of this was Vijay Ray, an advocate from Krishnagar who had taken initiation from Haraprasad during one of Haraprasad's prachar visits to his native city. He had then received further lessons from Sukhen, a local acharya whom Haraprasad had initiated and sent to Jamalpur for training, the same Sukhen whom Haraprasad's father had sent to Jamalpur to succor his son just after Haraprasad's initiation. Vijay soon began experiencing such intoxication in his meditation that he would often dance and sing in his room, especially at night, giving full vent to the joy he felt. His wife and other family members became convinced that the advocate had gone mad. The situation became so bad that neighbors would drop by to gawk at the astonishing sight of a lawyer dancing and singing like a madman with no thought or care for what people might think. Naturally, they laid the blame at the feet of Ananda Marga and the yogic practices he was now performing.

One night, around two in the morning, a loud knocking awoke Sukhen from a sound slumber. Groggy from sleep, he opened the front door to find a local Margi who informed him that Vijay was causing a terrible commotion. He had better come quickly. Sukhen hurried to Vijay's house and found him sitting in lotus posture with his eyes shut tight, swaying back and forth and conversing with Baba as if Baba were physically present. His wife was close to hysterics. Sukhen started massaging him. When Vijay opened his eyes, Sukhen explained to him that he was upsetting his family and that he needed to come out of his trance and act normally. Gradually he succeeded in coaxing Vijay back to some semblance of normalcy. The advocate ate something and was able to calm the fears of his family, but the next night and the night after that the same scene repeated itself. The following morning, Sukhen received a letter from Pranay with a message from Baba telling him not to worry: Vijay was not mad but rather undergoing certain spiritual symptoms resulting from the movement of the kundalini that was causing him to dance and sing. "Don't worry about the accusations or abuse of others," Baba advised in the letter. "Move ahead; I am always with you. In the meantime, take him to court with you. He will gradually come back to normalcy."

Sukhen did as Baba instructed, but after a few days Vijay's family locked him in a room and brought in a Muslim fakir who forced him to eat some medicinal roots that he claimed would remove Vijay's madness. The result was the exact opposite. Vijay had a violent reaction to the medicine, and the family ended up admitting him into a psychiatric ward. Though he was quickly released, they decided to file a case against Sukhen and Ananda Marga for bringing on Vijay's madness. Another letter arrived from Jamalpur telling Sukhen and the other Margis not to worry; no one had the power to harm them. Sukhen sent for Haraprasad, who went with him to meet the family and the authorities. The family accused the Margis of stealing their son's soul. Haraprasad countered by saying that Vijay's entire family should be locked up for insanity for making such an accusation. The case was thrown out, and after some heated discussion, Sukhen convinced the family to allow them to take Vijay to his guru by promising them a cure for his "disease."

A DMC had been scheduled for March of 1958 in Amra, Nityananda's native village, also located in Birbhum District. Sukhen, Haraprasad, and another dozen or so Margis from Krishnagar brought Vijay with them to the DMC. They arrived one day early with the intention of requesting Baba for a cure. As soon as Baba arrived, Sukhen was ushered into his room by Pranay. "So, what is the news from Krishnagar?" Baba asked. When Sukhen hesitated to answer, Baba turned to Pranay and began describing how one Margi from Muzaffarpur was dancing and singing, how it was good prachar for Ananda Marga, and how the same thing was happening in another place with the same results. "So, Sukhen," Baba continued, "what is happening with you?" Sukhen carefully recounted the problems Vijay was causing in Krishnagar. Baba offered the same council he had sent by letter. "What is happening with Vijay is a good sign, Sukhen. He is experiencing the reactive momenta from his previous life. Give him time. He will gradually become normal. In the meantime, go with him to court and help him to adjust with his daily duties."

When Sukhen left Baba's room, Nityananda caught him and asked him to help him initiate some local villagers who were waiting in a house about a half a mile away. The rest of the Margis from Krishnagar now got permission to enter Baba's room. They pleaded with Baba to return Vijay to normalcy. Baba listened patiently and then sent Partha to bring Vijay. Once Vijay arrived, Baba instructed everyone to sit in meditation posture. "Those who have dhyana, practice dhyana," he said. "Those who only have *ishvara pranidhana*, practice ishvara pranidhana."[3] Within moments everyone started experiencing various states of ecstasy. Some began to sway back and forth and moan; others got up and started dancing and singing with their eyes closed. Half a mile away Sukhen was giving initiation. Suddenly he felt as if he were being lifted from the earth and then dropped from the sky. Having just given his new initiate his mantra, he opened his mouth to further explain the meditation process but no words came out. The intoxication was so powerful he felt as if he might be going mad. He staggered out of the room and found Nityananda in the same state. Unable to understand what was happening to them, they walked back to Baba's quarters to ask the master what was going on. Just outside Baba's quarters they met Haraprasad, who had just come out of Baba's room. Tears were streaming down his face. "My body is burning," he told them, "the joy is so intense." The other devotees from Krishnagar poured out of Baba's room behind him. Among them, the only one who was in a normal state was Vijay, who was, unhappily for him, completely "cured."

While the other Margi's intoxication gradually subsided, Haraprasad's persisted unabated. As he walked through the streets of Amra, dancing and laughing, the world around him appeared to him like a shimmering tapestry of light—translucent images in a 360° panorama. As he walked past the trees and other plants, he narrated their secret thoughts and emotions for the Margis who accompanied him and tried to explain to them how to understand the thoughts of other living beings. Some fanatic Margis had uprooted some basil plants in the village, since the Hindus worshipped it as a goddess. Haraprasad shamed them when he translated for them the tales of woe these same plants had told him. The village goats, sheep, and oxen followed them as they walked. Some tried to approach Haraprasad and lick him and rub against him. One unruly ox approached them threateningly. The other Margis backed away but Haraprasad grabbed its tail and stroked it; the animal became completely docile. Haraprasad told them that the oxen in the village were being mistreated. They had complained to him that after a lifetime of toil their Muslim owners would butcher them. He called the owners and scolded them for mistreating their animals. Several people whom Haraprasad touched found his state of intoxication contagious. They too started dancing and singing. A newcomer, an attorney from Bankura, had been impervious to the general devotional mood until Haraprasad touched him in the main hall, where he had been lying with a shawl over his head. Instantly he got up, lifted his arms, and started dancing and singing with the others.

Although the DMC area had been roped off and limited to Margis only, loudspeakers had been set up outside for the villagers; most of them came to sit and listen to Baba's discourses. When the program was over, the Margis formed a large procession to accompany Baba across the Mayurakshi River to the train station. A large crowd of villagers came to see them off, some of them more interested in Haraprasad than in Baba, drawn by the rumors of his divine intoxication. After Baba's departure, the Margis queued up with the other passengers to buy their tickets. An elderly Brahmin was standing in the queue. When Haraprasad saw him, he instructed the Margis to tell him that there was no need for him to buy a ticket. "Tell him that he should go home and take rest." Sukhen and some others conveyed the message. With great difficulty they were finally able to convince the thoroughly annoyed Brahmin to cancel his trip and go back home. Once he'd left, Haraprasad told the Margis that he would die within a few hours. "It is better he die in his own bed," he said. The next day they got the news that the man had indeed died, as Haraprasad had predicted.

Before Haraprasad boarded the train, a large group of villagers crowded round him and asked him for some spiritual instruction. He asked one acharya traveling with him to conduct a mass initiation. Then they boarded the train. After a few stations, a couple of sannyasis entered their compartment and began doing *harinam* kirtan. Sukhen and one other Margi offered their seats to the monks, who sat down beside Haraprasad. Within a few minutes the monks started trembling. They left their seats and sat on the floor in front of him. Despite his protests, they began massaging his feet and crying out to him to save them. Haraprasad repeatedly requested them to take their seats but they continued to insist. Finally, he told them that they should learn meditation and instructed Sukhen to initiate them.

Haraprasad's intoxication continued unabated even after they reached Krishnagar. Sukhen soon became so concerned that he traveled to Jamalpur to inform Baba. Baba told him to instruct Haraprasad to meditate properly and assured him that he would soon be okay. Gradually, over the next few weeks, Haraprasad returned to normalcy. Both he and Vijay were sorry to see their madness go, but the rest of the Margis were glad it was over.

XVII

Problem of the Day

The accumulated distortions of many lifetimes cannot be removed in the twinkling of an eye. The removal of these distortions requires the prolonged cultivation of knowledge, selfless devotion and untiring action. The world expects tremendous work from you, so you must not sit idle like a frog in a well under the spell of inertia. Therefore, arise and awake.[1]

ON A CHILLY Saturday evening, January 26, 1958, between five and six hundred disciples gathered together in the spacious courtyard of Narasingh's manor house in Trimohan to watch the drama that was about to take place on the makeshift stage at the back of the compound. This was the first two-day DMC program, and Shiva Shankar Bannerjee, Bhagalpur's senior-most acharya, had suggested that some form of entertainment be included in the festivities. A couple of local Margis wrote up a rough script dealing with problems in the institution of marriage, a topic very much in the public eye at the time, and other members of the local unit bravely volunteered to act it out in front of the DMC crowd. Despite not having had time to rehearse, they took the stage and performed a satire on widow remarriage and the dowry system that left the audience shaking with laughter, while Baba looked on from the window of his second-floor room.

Baba's youngest brother, Manas, was in the audience, eagerly awaiting his first darshan of the master. He had been initiated eighteen months earlier by Pranay and had been carefully kept in the dark as to the identity of the guru—though he did have his suspicions. The evening after his initiation, he approached his brother while Baba was massaging his mother's feet and told him that he had taken initiation into Ananda Marga, expecting him to be happy at the news. "What!" Baba replied, to his surprise. "Who told you to do that? Why Ananda Marga?"

Why is Prabhat-da angry? Manas thought. I must have made a mistake. I don't know if he is the guru or not, but I know that he can answer any question that anyone puts to him. Even if he is not the guru, he knows everything, so I must have committed a mistake by taking initiation into Ananda Marga.

A couple of days later, Baba approached him and said in a conciliatory tone of voice, "After further reflection, I think it's okay. Go ahead and try to practice. It's not bad." Manas felt relieved. As he remarked years later, "at least I had done something that was 'not bad.'"

After the drama concluded, Baba came out of his room and descended the stairs. Shouts of *Parama Pita Baba ki jai*, victory to the Supreme Father, rang through the courtyard. When Manas saw his brother making his way toward the stage, he turned to the Margi next to him and asked, "Where is Baba? I don't see him." The Margi pointed to his brother and said, "What do you mean, you don't see him? That's Baba." Manas gave a shout, overjoyed to discover that his brother was indeed the guru of Ananda Marga. A transport of ecstasy swept over him, and a couple of concerned acharyas, who had been secretly deputed to look after him, worriedly sent word to Baba onstage that his brother had become abnormal. Baba sent back a message that they were not to worry. Manas recovered after a few hours, but by his own admission he would remain somewhat abnormal for the next few months.

After Baba took his seat on the dais and listened to a couple of devotional songs, he delivered a lengthy discourse that was unlike any he had given before. He entitled it "Problem of the Day" and began with the idea of the creation as a common patrimony:

> Paramapurusha is my father and Parama Prakriti is my mother. The universe is my home and all of us are citizens of this cosmos. This universe is the imagination of the Macrocosmic Mind, and all entities are being created, preserved and destroyed in the extroversive and introversive phases of the cosmic imaginative flow. In a personal way, when a person imagines something in their mind, for that moment that person is the owner of the thing and no one else. When a thought-born human being roams about in an imaginary cornfield, the imaginary person is not the owner of that field, rather the one who is imagining it is. This universe is created in the imagination of Brahma, the Supreme Entity, so the ownership of this universe lies with Brahma and not with the microcosms created out of Brahma's imagination. None of the property of this earth, movable or immovable, belongs to any particular individual; everything is the common patrimony of all.[2]

After developing the idea of human society as a joint family, pointing out that "nature has not assigned any portion of this property to any particular individual," and drawing parallels to the traditional property rights of joint families in ancient India, Baba launched into a scathing indictment of capitalism, making no effort to mince his words.

The capitalists of this modern world are anti-dharma, anti-social creatures. To accumulate their massive wealth, they reduce others to skin and bones, forcing them to die of starvation; to dazzle people with the glamour of their garments, they compel others to wear rags; to increase their own vital strength, they suck dry the vital juice of others ... A member of a joint family cannot be considered a social being if he or she does not possess the feeling of oneness with the other members of that family, or if he or she does not want to accept the lofty ideal of joint rights and the principle of rationality.[3]

The analysis of capitalism that followed led Baba to a conclusion that would soon see him branded in India as a social revolutionary:

When the entire property of the universe is the common inheritance of all its creatures, how can there be any justification for a system in which some are rolling in the lap of luxury while others are dying for want of a handful of grain? ... Considering the collective interests of all living beings, it is essential that capitalism be eradicated.[4]

It was Baba's contention that the capitalist mentality—or as he put it, "the ambition to become rich by exploiting others"—was a psychic disease.

If the longing of the human mind does not find the proper path leading to psychic and spiritual fulfillment, it becomes engaged in accumulating excessive physical wealth by depriving others ... When capitalists declare, "we have amassed wealth by our talent and labor; if others have the capacity and diligence, let them also do the same; nobody is preventing them," they do not care to realize that the volume of commodities on the earth is limited, whereas the requirement is common to all. Excessive individual affluence, in most cases, deprives others of the minimum requirements of life.[5]

Baba went on to discuss what methods should be adopted to put an end to capitalism. While he emphasized that "nothing would be better, if it were possible, than the eradication of capitalism by friendly persuasion and humanistic appeals," he made it clear that the untold millions who were suffering could not wait indefinitely "for good sense to prevail among the exploiters."[6] His argument flew directly in the face of the Gandhian ideal of non-violence, an ideal that was, as Baba would later explain, a distortion of the ancient yogic principle of ahimsa, non-injury to other living beings.

Though the humanistic approach works in some cases, in most instances it does not produce any result; and even where it does work, it takes a very long time. So, wherever necessary, capitalism must be

forced to abandon its ferocious hunger by taking strong measures
... Tremendous circumstantial pressure will have to be created. To
create this circumstantial pressure, the application of force is absolutely necessary. Those who believe that the non-application of force
alone is ahimsa are bound to fail.[7] No problem in this world can be
solved by adopting this kind of ahimsa.[8]

Later in the discourse, Baba again returned to the subject of non-violence while discussing the peace movement and the difference between sentient and static peace:

If any country perpetrates atrocities on its minorities or attacks
any weak neighbor, then the other neighbors should take up arms;
by mobilizing the required force they should restrain the tyrant in
order to establish sentient peace. This is why people who want to
restore sentient peace will have to make continual efforts to acquire
strength. It is impossible for goats to establish sentient peace in the
society of tigers. Sadly, those who hold the view that non-violence
is non-use of force can neither establish sentient peace nor can they
defend hard-earned freedom.[9]

In a country where the Gandhian ideal of non-violence was revered by public and politicians alike, it was an argument that would not only place Baba firmly on the side of the more radical social revolutionaries but which would eventually earn him a reputation among governmental authorities as a "dangerous" figure in Indian society.

After establishing that it was in the best interests of human beings that capitalism be eradicated, Baba continued with a discussion of how to reorganize society. This begins, he asserted, with economic decentralization; the creation of self-sufficient economic regions; and the management of industry, agriculture, trade, and commerce through cooperative organizations. In his view, only those enterprises that are either too small or too large and complex to be successfully managed as cooperatives, such as very small businesses or large-scale industries like energy and steel, should be managed either by individuals or by state or local governments.

As the discussion unfolded, Baba touched on a number of different social ills, such as the caste system, discrimination against women, provincialism and communalism, the misuse of science, and so on. He offered solutions in each of these areas, and this led him to the question of politics.

The colors of casteism, provincialism, communalism and nationalism
keep fading with the progress of time. The human beings of today
must understand that in the near future they will have to accept

universalism. Those who seek to promote social welfare will have to mobilize all their vitality and intellect in the endeavor to establish a world government, abandoning all plans to form communal or national organizations.[10]

While addressing the various obstacles standing in the way of the formation of a world government, Baba suggested that the biggest hurdle was local leaders' fear of losing their power and influence within their respective communities. In order to circumvent these obstacles, he proposed a gradual transition to a world government, beginning with its introduction as a law-framing body, with the administrative power remaining temporarily in the hands of the different countries, and then proceeding step by step to an eventual ceding of that power to the global body. "As [the local government] will not have any power to enact laws arbitrarily, it will not be easy for any government to inflict atrocities on its linguistic, religious, or political minorities according to the whims of the governing majority."[11]

While addressing the ills of party politics, calling it "a malady more dangerous than germs," he suggested that a future world government would be established by those working outside the ambit of political conflicts.

> The greatest social welfare for the human race will be accomplished if those who aspire to establish a world government, or Ananda Parivara,[12] engage themselves only in constructive activities and selfless service, instead of wasting their vital energy in the vortex of politics, or in political conflicts... Those states which cooperate with such missionaries in their social service activities will be considered to be desirous of establishing the world government, or Ananda Parivara. The common people of those states which do not cooperate will become agitated, and those agitated people will form the world government, or Ananda Parivara, through revolution.[13]

In his political analysis, Baba did not hesitate to point out the defects inherent in democracy.[14] He emphasized that "as a system of government, democracy cannot be accepted as the highest and best. Among all the systems human beings have been able to devise so far, democracy can be considered to be the best of a bad lot."[15] After discussing some of these defects, he gave his disciples the first glimpse of the principles of governance that would become a cornerstone of his social philosophy. Leadership, he suggested, can only be entrusted to those who have attained a high measure of ethical, mental, and spiritual perfection through rigorous training. Such people he called *sadvipras*; to them he assigned the responsibility of guiding society. Having already asserted that a classless society is a utopian and impractical ideal, Baba offered an analysis of the cyclical movement of society as a movement from the dominance of one psychic class to another, with human society being composed of four predominant mentalities: the *shudra*, or working class mentality; the *kshattriya*, or warrior mentality; the *vipra*, or intellectual mentality; and the *vaeshya*, or capitalist mentality. At any one time, one of these four classes dominates. The social cycle moves from shudra to kshattriya to vipra to vaeshya, most advanced countries at present being in the midst of the first vaeshyan age, with either revolution or evolution effecting the transition from one age to another. In the past, he reasoned, the ruling class has always exploited the masses. Hence, the leadership of society must be entrusted to sadvipras, who imbibe the best qualities of all four classes and who hold as their firm ideal the welfare of each and every member of society. "Only they," he said, "can represent human beings selflessly."[16]

Baba ended his discourse with an ancient Sanskrit verse from the Rig-Veda, humanity's oldest surviving literature. He called it the chorus of the sadvipras:

> *Samgacchadvam samvadadhvam salvo manásijánatám*
> *Devábhagam yathá purve samjánáná upásate*
> *Saman van acute samánáh hrdáyáni van*
> *Samánámáastuvo mynah yathá van susahásati*

> Let us move together, let us sing together, let us come to know our minds together. Let us share like sages of the past so that all people together may enjoy the universe. Unite our intentions. Let our hearts be inseparable. Let our minds be as one mind, as we, to truly know one another, become one.[17]

The next morning, Baba announced the formation of the first subsidiary wing of Ananda Marga: Renaissance Universal. The purpose of RU, as Baba began referring to it, was to provide a platform for intellectuals and artists to discuss the burning issues of the day and through these conferences and discussions to disseminate progressive ideas among the intelligentsia, students, and interested members of the general populace. He called his senior disciples together for a meeting and asked them to start forming RU clubs in their respective towns and cities. The first program of the RU club would be to host public discussions on important current issues and invite prominent and progressive speakers to address the audience and mediate the subsequent discussion. He also announced that from then on he would give an RU discourse on the evening before his DMC discourse. "Problem of the Day," he said, should be considered his inaugural RU discourse.

Although not everyone was paying close attention to Baba's talk—many devotees were content simply to watch Baba and immerse themselves in the devotional mood—the discourse struck a powerful chord among many of them, especially among the numerous students who had begun taking initiation in increasing numbers as the family acharyas concentrated more of their prachar efforts in the schools and colleges of Bihar. A little more than a decade had passed since India had attained its independence, and the large student population of the day who had grown into adulthood in a free and independent India had become increasingly frustrated with the lack of progress they perceived in their country's struggle to rise out of the quagmire of poverty and join the community of developing nations. The high hopes that had accompanied the struggle for India's freedom had mostly faded, as idealistic students and intelligentsia became aware, in Baba's words, that they "had traded the white exploiters for brown exploiters." Frustration continued to mount when it became clear that the capitalist machinery and endemic political corruption had not left with the British but had simply changed its colors.

Even some who ostensibly supported the government were able to recognize the warning signs. In early 1958, Rajagopalachari, writer, statesman, and India's first Governor-General, wrote: "Political emancipation and democracy, instead of cultivating a sense of humanity and responsibility, have been allowed to intoxicate majority caste groups with a thirst for power and tyranny and electoral corruption of the unprivileged classes." A few weeks later, the economist John Mathai, India's first Railway Minister, wrote: "The momentum created in the earlier years of independence is subsiding and giving way to a spirit of passive acceptance of the inevitable. We seem to be at the beginning of a period of mental stagnation and lack of purposeful activity. Respect for law is gradually diminishing, and the sense of unity which filled us in the first flush of fulfilled nationalism is disappearing." For many Indians, only a few years removed from decades of the struggle for freedom, whose greatest heroes remained the revolutionary figures of those days, such as Subhash Bose, Aurobindo, and Gandhi, it was a difficult reality to accommodate. The Margis, especially the younger ones, were not immune from such feelings.

In the days and weeks that followed, the excitement amongst the younger and more revolutionary-minded disciples mushroomed rapidly as news of Baba's discourse circulated among those who had not been present. Baba had hinted at his view of capitalism in a brief paragraph in *Caryacarya* on economic policy where he first mentioned the idea of the joint family,[18] but none of them were prepared for "Problem of the Day." For many who hungered for change, it was a revelation to discover that Baba was a more radical social thinker than they had imagined. His words gave shape to their inarticulate desires for a better and more just world. While some of the older Margis wondered if it were not a utopian dream, most took it as a promise that the ideal society they longed for was an inevitable part of humanity's future.

The discourse was soon published in booklet form, for which Baba wrote the following dedication: "To the great hero, Subhash Chandra Bose, whom I did love, and whom I do love even now." It was not only a reference to the various demonstrations in which Baba had shown that the revolutionary hero was still alive but, even more so, a signal that it was time for a revolutionary consciousness to take birth among his disciples.

Unbeknownst to the disciples, Baba had begun dictating a book on social philosophy during his lunch break at the office a couple of months before delivering his "Problem of the Day" discourse. These noontime dictation sessions had long since become a regular part of his office life. In the previous few years he had used them to re-dictate his DMC discourses, which were collected into the series entitled *Subhasita Samgraha*. His regular stenographer was Sushil Dhar, a co-worker and initiate from a different department. Several Margis were deputed to take notes during the DMC talks, but these notes ended up being more of a synopsis of Baba's discourse, since none of them were trained in shorthand and Baba spoke quicker than anyone could write. At a later date, Sushil would bring these notes with him to the office. Baba would ask him to read out the first couple of lines and thereafter he would begin dictating the original discourse over again in his mother tongue, Bengali,[19] often expanding on a topic that had been limited by the time constraints of a spoken lecture.

The new book, a separate work rather than the redictation of an earlier talk, was entitled *Human Society, Part I*. Consisting of five chapters, it began with a chapter on ethics wherein Baba laid out the true foundation of his social philosophy, the premise that an ideal human society can only be achieved when that society is founded on a universal code of ethics derived from a universal spiritual outlook. By extension, the leaders of that society must be those who have most perfected themselves in the practice of that code of ethics. His analysis of human ethics contained a sharp look at the divisive role that the different world religions have played in human history, and the prevalence of dogmatic thinking and intolerance in those institutions. The chapter concluded with his summation of the meaning of the concepts "society" and "social progress":

> When morality leads human beings to the fullest expression of their finer human qualities, then alone is its practical value fully realized. The concerted effort to bridge the gap between the first expression of morality and establishment in universal humanism is called "social progress." And the collective body of those who are engaged in the concerted effort to conquer this gap, I call "society."[20]

In the remaining chapters Baba discussed education, social justice, the judicial system, and the role of different professions. He analyzed the impact of these areas of human life on human society, the problems facing humanity at this juncture in our evolution, and the role that each area needs to play in the formation of an ideal society.

With the appearance of *Problem of the Day* and *Human Society, Part I*, the disciples now had a social philosophy to go along with their already extensive spiritual philosophy. The spirit of that social philosophy had been summed up in Baba's very first DMC discourse, "The Gradual Evolution of Society," back on New Year's Day 1955, but what had been a distant image on the horizon would now become a part of their daily reality. From this point forward, Baba would begin laying even stronger emphasis on his "mission," exhorting his disciples not only to spread the ideals of spirituality and do social service but to work toward the formation of an ideal human society, asking them to shoulder nothing less than full responsibility for the transformation of a planet. The Margis were aware that they were few in number, and that the ideal that Baba held out before them was seemingly beyond their reach, or at best distantly remote. But Baba would not accept any faintheartedness from them, and they were able to understand what he repeatedly reminded them: if they wanted to be great themselves, they would have to adopt a great ideal and keep that ideal always in front of them. What ideal could be greater than this, they asked, to work toward the creation of an ideal society while they walked the path to spiritual illumination?

XVIII

Tantric Guru

It is impossible to conquer a crude idea and to replace it by a subtle idea without a fight . . . Hence, Tantra is not only a fight, it is an all-round fight. It is not only an external or internal fight, it is both . . . The practice for raising the kulakundalini is the internal sadhana of Tantra, while shattering the bondages of hatred, suspicion, fear, shyness, etc., by direct action is the external sadhana. When those who have little knowledge of sadhana see the style of this external fight, they think that the Tantrics moving in the cremation ground are a sort of unnatural creature. Actually the general public has no understanding of these Tantrics.[1]

WHEN JATASHANKAR ARRIVED in Amra for his first DMC in April 1958, he found it all very strange. He could not understand why these people were dancing and singing all the time. He was not aware, perhaps, that the Margis from his hometown of Madhepura also found him rather strange due to his rough speech, his undisciplined and often odd behavior, and his habit of wearing the orange robes, rudraksha beads, and long hair of a wandering ascetic, despite not being a monk at all. A few hours before delivering his DMC discourse, Baba called Jatashankar into his room and told him to sit in meditation posture. He looked at him intensely for several moments and then informed him that he had been a great worshipper of Kali in his previous life. "Are you ready to learn Tantra sadhana again in this lifetime?" Baba asked. When the curious Jatashankar answered yes, Baba raised his hand and Jatashankar saw lightning explode from his guru's forehead. "Are you sure?" Baba asked. "Will you be able to meditate on a dead body, or will you run in fear?" Trembling at this display of Baba's supernatural power, but excited at the prospect of becoming a real Tantric, Jatashankar assured Baba that he was ready. "Very well then," Baba said. "Come to Jamalpur next month on the day of the new moon and I will initiate you there."

A few weeks later, Jatashankar arrived in Jamalpur accompanied by his friend Harivallab, who was also a new Margi. When they reached the jagriti, Kedarnath Sharma, a hard-nosed policeman and senior acharya, scolded him for bringing Harivallab and suggested forcibly that both of them return home.

Angered by this rude reception, Jatashankar went to the station to buy their return tickets, but in the early evening he went to Baba's house in Rampur Colony and planted himself in front of the veranda in protest. When Baba opened the door to leave for field walk, he greeted Jatashankar and Harivallab affably and invited them to accompany him to the field. Before Jatashankar had a chance to voice his protest, Baba added, "And don't mind Kedarnath. He is very strict, but he is also a great devotee."

Baba led them to the *tantra pitha* formed by the three palm trees. While Harivallab waited at the tiger's grave, Baba initiated Jatashankar into the first of four lessons of *kapalik* meditation.[2] Then he initiated Harivallab, who would later become the first known Margi to receive all four lessons. When the initiations were complete, Baba gave them some further guidelines for their practice. The meditation was to be done either in a cremation ground or a graveyard between the hours of twelve midnight and three in the morning. They were to practice every night until the next new moon; this was to be known as the "compulsory period." Thereafter, they were only required to practice on the night of the new moon, the darkest night of the month, though they had the option of doing the meditation on other nights as well during the stipulated hours. He explained to them that the main purpose of this sadhana was to overcome the fear complex.[3] If practiced properly, at least fifty percent of their fear complex would disappear within a short period and the rest gradually over time. One side effect of the practice, he warned, was the possible development of occult powers; they were, however, expressly forbidden to ever use such powers should they develop them. Then Baba touched each of them on the forehead and put them into a state of trance. Though most kapaliks would practice once a month on the new moon night once their compulsory period was over, Jatashankar would maintain his nightly practice for a number of years.

News of Jatashankar and Harivallab's initiation into Tantra sadhana spread quickly among the disciples. Many of them soon approached Baba with requests for initiation, despite the widespread public misapprehensions concerning Tantra. Although it was accepted everywhere in India that Shiva, India's most popular spiritual figure, was the father of Tantra as well as the father of yoga, Tantric yogis were reputed to be mysterious and dangerous figures. They were generally believed to frequent the forests and cremation grounds, possess strange supernatural powers, and practice occult rites that included dead bodies and skulls, bearing many similarities to what is known in the West as black magic. A good example of these public fears can be seen in the story of Aniruddha's initiation into Ananda Marga.

Aniruddha was a successful contractor in Bhagalpur who, by his own admission, drank several bottles of wine per day and only ate vegetables once or twice a year. When he went to Jamalpur in late 1955 to see Baba for the first time, Baba recited a detailed list of his bad habits and told him that he should give them up immediately. Aniruddha was worried that Baba might hypnotize him, but he could not stop himself from visiting Baba, and within a month he had given up meat and alcohol and going to bars, seemingly against his own volition. His wife, who was shocked by this radical change in habits, asked his friends to take him to their regular haunts and try to persuade him to go back to his old ways. They obliged her, even offering him a large building contract if he would give up his new life, but Aniruddha held firm. He soon brought his brother, Harinder,[4] to Ananda Marga, and afterward his father, Narasingh, at whose place Baba would later give *Problem of the Day*. At the beginning, Aniruddha was terrified of Baba. He considered him a mighty Tantric, though that didn't stop him from visiting him. In an interview, he described the following incident from his first field walk:

> Baba asked me if I wanted to see something. I told him, "If you want to show me, then show me." He asked me again. When I agreed, he told me to close my eyes and not open them till he said it was okay. Then he lit his flashlight and told me to open my eyes.
> "What do you see?" he asked.
> There was a person standing there about seven feet tall. Baba revolved his flashlight and the person started growing until he was thirty feet tall, as high as a palm tree. I bent down and caught Baba's feet, terrified. I offered him one hundred thousand rupees to spare me. "Will you make me a palm tree also?" I asked.
> Baba said, "Don't worry, I won't kill you or make you a palm tree. Just hold on to my feet." Then Baba made the person shrink to six feet and called him to come over. That fellow had laughed like a giant when he heard me offer Baba money to spare me. Both were smiling and I thought both were great Tantrics and that he might be a ghost whom Baba had summoned to kill me. "Don't worry," Baba said, "he is Kalikananda." He told him to go and the fellow disappeared suddenly. Then Baba said, "It has become late; we must return now, otherwise you will miss your train."
> "Then I will miss my train," I said. "I am feeling extremely hungry. Ordinarily I would have eaten two meals in this time."
> Baba said, "I know. In this span of time you would have eaten kebab, chicken, eggs, and liver." I was thinking that Chandranath must have told him this. He looked at me and laughed. "No, no. No one has told me."
> "So you want me to believe that you are a God," I said, "that no one has told you these things, that you knew my name and place without anyone telling you. No, no. Don't think for a moment that I will believe you." Baba just laughed and told me to catch my train.
> "I am feeling too hungry to catch my train," I said.

"Then go and eat. The train won't leave the station until you've finished."

I just laughed and said, "Anything you say. If you say the train won't leave, then it won't leave."

We walked back and the Margi who had met me in the station was waiting on the bridge. Baba told him to take me to a restaurant first and then bring me to the station. Then Baba told me to come tomorrow.

"No, I won't come," I said.

"You must."

I said, "How much will it take to get you to leave me alone?"

"I don't want any money."

"Then why do you want me to come back?"

Baba just smiled. The Margi took me to a pure veggie restaurant. I said, "What is this place? I don't eat this kind of food."

He said, "All the Margis eat here."

I said, "I am not a Margi. I don't eat this grass and stuff."

He ordered some pakhoras and other spicy things. The manager came up and said, "Don't worry, you have time, the train is an hour late." I gave that person money to purchase a first class ticket. He told me that Margis travel by third class. I told him the Margis could go to hell.

Much of the public reticence toward Tantra was due to the branch of Tantra known as *avidya*.[5] For several millennia in India, avidya Tantrics had been cultivating secret practices, often for the express purpose of developing occult powers. In many cases, they would use these powers for personal gain, or even to do harm to their enemies. Baba had talked about avidya practices on occasion with the disciples; it was commonly assumed among them that he was a master of avidya as well as *vidya* Tantra, though he would not teach it to them, his rationale being that avidya Tantrics did not practice their arts in order to attain God. He did, however, teach them how to deal with avidya Tantrics, should they come face to face with one. First of all, they were to use their guru mantra. He assured them that the avidya Tantric's powers would have no effect over them if they did. "Many avidya Tantrics," he said, "try to frighten people by using their mental powers to drop stones or other objects on a house, or move things within that house, thus frightening the people who live there. In such cases, you will find the avidya Tantric hiding somewhere nearby, since such powers do not work at a long distance. You should look for him, catch him, and shake him to break his concentration. Once their concentration is broken, their powers cease to function. But don't forget that this is also an art. Do not interfere with it unnecessarily; otherwise, this art will disappear."

There were a number of incidents where Margis came under attack from avidya Tantrics and defended themselves as Baba had instructed. One such attack even led to an unexpected initiation. A disciple from Dumka, Vasant, was one of the first to learn kapalik meditation from Baba. Soon after he returned home from Jamalpur, he started hearing stories from the neighbors about strange sounds coming from a cremation ground at night: babies crying, strange animal cries, and other unusual and frightening sounds. Vasant decided to start going to that cremation ground to practice his kapalik sadhana in the hope that it might be the work of some avidya Tantric, taking it both as a challenge and an adventure. Sure enough, Vasant's suspicions proved to be well-founded. A powerful local avidya Tantric by the name of Sudanshu had been using that cremation ground for his nightly practice. When he noticed that Vasant had begun meditating there as well, he began using his avidya techniques to frighten him away. Vasant, however, continued steadfast in his meditation, protected by the ritual barrier that encircled him, part of the first lesson of kapalik. When the terrifying noises and flying objects did not have any effect, the avidya Tantric finally resorted to *mantraghat*, a direct attack with special mantras designed to inflict harm on a person through the concentrated application of psychic force. Vasant repelled the attack with his guru mantra, causing a boomerang effect that knocked Sudanshu to the ground, after which Sudanshu fled.

The next day, Sudanshu showed up at Vasant's house, intent on learning the name of the guru of this man who was able to repel with ease his most ferocious attack. After hearing about Baba, Sudanshu became eager to take initiation. Vasant made the arrangements and brought him to Jamalpur. When Sudanshu was ushered into Baba's room for personal contact, Baba grabbed him by the ear and started scolding him for misusing his avidya powers and attacking one of his disciples. After extracting a promise from him to stop his avidya practice, Baba informed Sudanshu that he was withdrawing the powers he had attained through avidya sadhana. "You will no longer need them," he said. "From now on you will be a practitioner of vidya sadhana."

The mystery and the aura of the supernatural that surrounded such practices made it natural for common people to be afraid of Tantrics, and just as natural for the Margis, especially the younger ones, to be interested in kapalik initiation. After Harinder and Sudhir, both in their early twenties, learned kapalik, they asked Baba if it would give them occult powers. Baba replied, "After doing anything you gain something, either good or bad. You will also gain something by doing kapalik, but I will seize whatever powers you gain. When the time comes for you to utilize those powers for social service, I will release them, but not until then. They should only be utilized for service."

Although the lessons would remain confidential, Baba would soon demystify Tantric practices through a series of discourses in which he showed that Tantra was the philosophy of the indigenous peoples of India and the original source of all yogic practices. In his second RU discourse, entitled "Tantra and the Indo-Aryan Civilization," delivered just before he began teaching kapalik sadhana, Baba stated:

> The greatest difference between the Aryans and the non-Aryans was in their outlook. The Aryans wanted to establish themselves on the basis of their racial superiority, whereas the non-Aryans, following the precepts of Tantra, did not recognize any distinctions between one person and another. Everyone was a human being. All belonged to the same family, the family of Shiva . . . Here it is necessary to remember that Tantra is not a religion. It is a way of life, a system of sadhana. The fundamental goal of this sadhana is to awaken the quiescent spiritual force of the individual, the *kulakundalini*, and direct it upwards, stage by stage, until it merges in *Brahmabháva* or Cosmic Consciousness. Tantra is a science of spiritual meditation or sadhana, which is equally applicable to anyone no matter what their religious affiliation. Tantra is certainly older than the Vedas.[6]

Despite Baba's efforts to demystify Tantra, the aura of mystery remained, fed by the many unusual experiences that the disciples shared with one another as they made their way deeper into the Tantric tradition.

One night, Pashupati, an acharya from Bhagalpur, went to the cremation ground in Trimohan to practice his kapalik sadhana. As he was beginning his meditation, he saw a light approaching. He thought at first that it might be a policeman, an obstacle that kapaliks would have to learn to avoid when they went to the burial grounds or cremation grounds at night. But when the light reached him, it passed by and vanished. No one was there. A few days later, he went to Jamalpur and mentioned the incident to Baba. "It was a *devayoni*, a luminous body," Baba told him. "Normally, you can't see them because they lack the solid and liquid factors. But sometimes sadhakas can see them if their minds are subtle enough, especially on very dark nights. It was not unusual, what you saw. They are often attracted to kapaliks when they go for meditation. The spiritual vibration attracts them. They can even help sadhakas at times."

Other kapaliks soon reported incidents where they were helped at the time of kapalik by strange lights. One group of three acharyas had to cross a stream on the night after a heavy rain in order to reach the cremation ground, but they had trouble locating a spot shallow enough to cross. Suddenly a strange light appeared and hovered over the stream. As they stared at it, unable to find an explanation for what they were seeing, the light began to move downstream. At a certain point it stopped and hovered there. They remembered what Baba had said about *devayoni*s and tried to cross. To their surprise, they found that the stream was only knee deep at that spot. As soon as they reached the other side the light disappeared into the distance. They reached the cremation ground and completed their sadhana. When they started walking back, the light returned and guided them back to the same spot.

On another occasion, Pashupati was trying to cross the river Gerua but was unable to find the crossing. After trying for half an hour, he was startled to see the whole area suddenly illuminated by a soft effulgence, as if it were a moonlit night with the moon only shining on that particular area. With this help of this light, he was able to find the path of stones that he was looking for. When he reported the incident to Baba some days later, Baba told him that there had been a number of murders on that riverbank, hence some *siddhas*, a type of *devayoni*, were keeping watch there to help any kapaliks who might need their guidance.

Kshitij, the acharya who along with Kedarnath Sharma started Ananda Marga in Ranchi, recounted the following experience:

> I used to travel from Ranchi to Dhanbad every Friday night. I would stay in the waiting hall at the station and then take the four a.m. train to Sindri, which arrived about five. Then I would give initiations and lessons to the students in the Sindri hostel till seven thirty. The Margis there would make all the arrangements during the week. One night in the waiting hall, I dreamed that there was a Tantric of fair complexion residing below the hall who had killed a child. The child's mother came to me to ask for my help, knowing that I was also a Tantric. I agreed to help her. I approached that Tantric and told him that since he had not given life to the child, he had no right to take it. He replied that he wanted two bodies and that my body would be the second. "Go ahead and try," I said. "I am the son of Anandamurti." I started doing meditation. Baba appeared in my meditation and taught me a two-word mantra. He told me that if I would touch the Tantric on his *ajina* chakra and say the mantra, it would put an end to him. I did so and the Tantric died. Then the police got annoyed with the two deaths. I decided to run away. I grabbed my luggage and ran down the stairs and caught a taxi. Then I woke up.
>
> What a funny dream, I thought. While returning from Sindri, I met Baburam Singh in the station. I didn't like him, so I used to avoid him whenever possible. When he saw me, he said in a sarcastic tone, "How are you, *adrajji*?"[7]
>
> "I am fine," I said, ignoring the insult. "I am going to the office now. I don't have time for you."
>
> He said, "How is your Anandamurgi?"[8]
>
> I got wildly angry. "The person whom I respect, you are insulting? You will realize him when you are bedridden. Never say this again." He said it again. I was beside myself with anger. I remembered the mantra

I had received in the dream and used it on him. Then I went home and fought with my wife, with my son, and later on at work with my boss. When I returned home that evening, I knew I had to meditate properly to get my composure back, but I could not concentrate. I berated myself for having lost my temper, knowing that it was the cause of my troubles, and resolved to go out and do some prachar. At that moment, Baburam knocked on my door. When I opened it, he was irate. He asked me if I honestly thought I could make him a Margi by force. "I've had a 104 degree fever ever since I met you this morning," he said. Then he stormed off in a rickshaw.

I realized my mistake and decided to go to Jamalpur. When I got there I met Pranay. He told me to stand by the side of the step when Baba came out for his walk. I waited there until Baba came out and then did namaskar. He accepted my namaskar and asked me how I was doing. Then Baba said that today only those who were kapalik could go with him on his walk. Ram Tanuk, Lalan, and I went with Baba. When we reached the field, Baba started lecturing me. He said that those who practice kapalik grow very strong mentally and physically. Their mental power lies at *ajina* chakra and their physical power at *anahata* chakra. When these powers get concentrated, a kapalik gets the strength to kill three persons, physically or mentally. "You must never misuse this power," he said.

I caught Baba's feet and begged him to forgive me. "I have committed a great mistake," I told him. "I was unable to tolerate what that man said."

"Give me back the mantra I gave you in your dream," Baba said. I offered it that night in gurupuja. Afterward I had a very good meditation. The next day I was mentally and physically sound again. When I got back to Ranchi, I went to meet Baburam and apologize. He had also recovered, and I was surprised to hear that he wanted to take initiation. A few days later, Baba came to Kedar's place. I asked Baburam if he would like to meet Baba. At first he declined, but Kedarnath was able to convince him to go. I took him and sat him close to Baba. Baba came and gave a talk. Baburam was not looking at him or even lifting his head. I thought I had made a mistake by bringing him. Baba had said in the past that the guru cannot tolerate anybody's ego. If he shows ego the guru neglects him. But when Baburam raised his head, I could see the tears falling like a shower. Afterward, he kept begging me to take him to Baba; he was crying continuously. After that, he became a strong Margi and a staunch follower of yama and niyama.

In the Tantric tradition the guru often tests the disciples, using these tests to help them overcome their various mental weaknesses. While most of Baba's tests fell well within the range of the disciples' normal experience, he sometimes used avidya techniques to add to these challenges. Dilip Bose, who was twenty when he took initiation at the end of 1954, recalled some of the tests Baba had put him through when he was barely out of his teens:

> Once Baba asked me to meet him at the tiger's grave late at night. I went there but there was no trace of Baba. It was about eleven thirty or twelve. Then Baba arrived from somewhere and begged my pardon for having come so late. He told me he had forgotten something and asked me whether or not I could fetch it for him. I told him I would do my level best. He said that he had left a box of matches near the door of the Kali temple at the top of Kalipahar. It didn't even occur to me that he didn't smoke. Why should he be carrying a box of matches? Now you can imagine having to climb Kalipahar at that time of night in the pitch black without a torch. It took me about one hour but I did it. I came to know later that these were his tests. That was the test of fear.
>
> He also took a test of shame. That also took place at night when we went for field walk. There was a tea stall near the railway line; the shop belonged to someone named Hira. He asked me if I could bring him a cup of tea and I said that I could. But he put a condition: I had to go totally naked. I hesitated at first. Then I thought that there was no question of disobeying him since I considered him the polestar of my life. But it was the strangest thing. I passed many people on the way and none of them even gave me a second glance. I went to Hira's shop, bought the tea, and brought it for him. Neither Hira nor anyone else said anything or looked at me in any unusual way. It was as if no one could see that I was naked.
>
> Another time, in the middle of 1955, he asked me to make a circuit of the field with his shoes in my mouth. I did it without any hesitation. When I returned to the grave, he told me that he had kept some good food for me. When I looked at where he was pointing, I saw a dead body in an advanced state of decomposition lying on the ground in front of the grave. He scooped out some flesh from its belly and asked me to eat it. That time I really felt that I would not be able to do it. Then he told me that I would have to give up all feelings of revulsion. He asked me to close my eyes and take his name and eat it. I did it and it tasted very sweet. When I opened my eyes, the dead body was gone.
>
> He took many such tests. He showed me many strange apparitions that appeared in front of us and then touched his feet. These things took place in front of my eyes.

Once Baba explained to Kishun that avidya gurus use such methods to help their disciples overcome propensities such as hatred and revulsion, propensities that are very strong and difficult to overcome.[9] "I don't ask people to do this anymore," Baba told him, "but I used to carry some sugar candy with me and sometimes with the help of maya I would make it look like a human corpse and ask them to eat its flesh. This was to destroy the bondages of *satripu* and *ashtapasha* in their minds. Afterward, I would ask them how it tasted and they would tell me it was sweet."

When a teenage Rameshananda first asked Baba for kapalik initiation, Baba told him he was too young. Rameshananda kept pestering him. One evening, while sitting on the tiger's grave, Baba told him that he would grant his request, but first he had to pass a little test.

> Baba said, "Go to that tree over there. Under it you will find a dead body. Eat a little of its flesh and then come back." The tree was about two hundred meters from the grave. It was pitch dark at the time. Being very young, I was a little afraid of the dark. I started walking toward the tree, but as I did, I felt overcome by fear. I battled it as best I could and kept walking until I reached the tree. I couldn't see any dead body but there was a strong odor of decaying flesh, so I was sure it was there. I got down on the ground and groped around with my hands until I found it. It was so decomposed that I was able to grab some flesh with only a little pressure. The smell was so bad that it took an enormous effort to put it in my mouth, but as soon as it touched my tongue I found it very sweet. I had never eaten anything so delicious in my life. The smell also disappeared and at that moment my fear evaporated. When I came back to the tiger's grave, Baba was laughing loudly. I asked him to initiate me, but he told me that first I had to start a school in a certain part of Bihar. I went there and was able to open a school without too much difficulty. Two months later, on May 4, he initiated me into kapalik.

One day Haraprasad Haldar passed by Baba's office looking very distraught. When Baba asked him what the matter was, he explained that his cousin Santu had died and that the two of them had been very close. He had returned home for the cremation but had not been able to see his cousin's body before it was cremated. This was also weighing on his mind. He regretted the fact that he had not been able to see him one last time, even dead.

Baba paused for a moment and then asked, "Do you want to see him?"
"Is that possible?"
"It is possible. Come to the field with me tonight."
When they reached the field that evening, Baba sat down on the Englishman's

grave and told Haraprasad to get ready. He was going to show him his dead cousin. He asked him to remove his clothes. Haraprasad stripped down to his loincloth.

"Remove your loincloth as well."

Haraprasad reluctantly obeyed. Baba taught him a mantra and asked him to repeat it while he walked toward the tiger's grave, a distance of about twenty meters. He warned him that when he saw his cousin, he must not touch him under any circumstances, otherwise he would be in danger. Haraprasad took a few steps toward the grave but he became so afraid that he forgot the mantra. He came back and informed Baba that he had forgotten it. Baba reminded him and told him again to move toward the tiger's grave. Haraprasad took a few steps in that direction but again he forgot the mantra. This time Baba started scolding him. "Fool, if you cannot remember this mantra, how will you work in the organization? Put your sandal in your mouth and rub your nose on the ground."

Haraprasad did as he was ordered. On the third try, he was able to keep chanting the mantra as he walked toward the grave. When he got within a few steps, he suddenly stopped and blanched, feeling as if someone had thrown a bucket of cold water over him. Standing in front of the grave he saw his cousin Santu. The two cousins looked at each other for a minute or two without speaking. Haraprasad began to sob. Then he returned to the Englishman's grave. Baba ordered him to do sastaunga pranam and put back on his clothes.

"Now tell me, Haraprasad. What did I teach you today?" When Haraprasad could not answer, Baba said, "I taught you to overcome shyness, repulsion, and fear. You overcame shyness when you removed your dress. You overcame repulsion when you took your shoe in your mouth. And you overcame fear when you met your dead cousin Santu."

Surendra received his kapalik initiation a few days after the new moon in January 1960. His compulsory period lasted twenty-four nights, during which time he had difficulty putting up with the frigid temperatures. On the final night he went to the cremation ground with Harinder of Trimohan. When the two young men had finished and were heading back, Surendra exclaimed, "Thank God that hell is over; now I only have to practice this sadhana once a month. What a trial I have been through!"

Harinder was quick to warn his friend. "Be careful what you say, Surendra. If Baba comes to know about it, he will be upset with you."

"Don't worry, Harinder. I won't repeat it to anyone. Anyhow, Baba is in Jamalpur; he is probably sleeping right now."

A few days later, Baba left Jamalpur to conduct a DMC. Along the way, his train stopped in Ekchari Station, near Trimohan. Surendra and Harinder were among the huge crowd that gathered in the station to have Baba's darshan. A few minutes after the train pulled in, they were called to Baba's compartment.

After asking how they were, Baba said, "You know, a few days back on the new moon night, I happened to be sleeping when a gentle breeze reached me from Trimohan carrying with it the conversation of two acharyas." Baba repeated word for word their conversation and then said, "Surendra is an assiduous sadhaka and very regular in his kapalik sadhana. How could he speak such contemptuous words? I began to doubt the message I received from that breeze. That is why I called you both, to assure myself that Surendra never spoke such words."

Surendra begged Baba's forgiveness and received his guru's smile in return.

The disciples had known that Baba was a Tantric guru long before he began teaching kapalik sadhana. As Asthana had discovered, somewhat shockingly, on the morning of the death demonstration, Baba was not only a loving master, a devotional figure, and a constant source of inspiration; he was also a stern taskmaster and a fierce disciplinarian who would not hesitate to punish his disciples when they deviated from the proper path. This side of the Tantric guru, traditionally absent in the ordinary yogic or Vedic guru, has been an essential part of the Tantric tradition for millennia, perhaps most famously embodied in the story of Milarepa and his guru, Marpa.[10] Rather than simply teaching their disciples the spiritual practices and encouraging them to move forward on the path, Tantric gurus, as Baba explained in a 1960 DMC discourse, "take meticulous care to ensure that their disciples follow their teachings. If they discover that their disciples are negligent in any way, they compel them to practice more painstakingly by applying circumstantial pressure . . . the preceptor must also be *nigraha* (capable of inflicting punishment) and *anugraha* (capable of bestowing grace). One who punishes only or who bestows grace only is not an ideal preceptor."[11]

While Baba had always been prompt to use whatever means necessary to ensure that his disciples followed the correct path, this side of his personality started coming even more to the fore about the time he began teaching kapalik sadhana. Sometime in 1958, he started openly calling attention to his disciple's mistakes in General Darshan, something he had refrained from doing until that point. Several of the senior disciples had already been forewarned of the changes. "Many of the devotees who come here to join in the devotional singing and meditation are not following yama and niyama strictly," he had told them. "From now on I am going to become more strict in this regard. Otherwise, when the crowds become very large, it will be difficult to control them. The work of the guru is not only to give blessings but also to give punishment for the welfare of the disciples. Without punishment one cannot follow the spiritual path properly." Baba started implementing the new policy the very next Sunday.

During one of these Sunday darshans, Baba asked a young student from Muzaffarpur to approach his cot. After asking him a question or two about his studies, Baba said, "Now tell me, at night you go into your cupboard and take out a bottle. After you've had a drink, you hide it in the cupboard again, and then you feel drowsy and neglect your studies. Just what is in that bottle that you are drinking from every night?" The boy hung his head, unable or unwilling to look at Baba. "Tell me, tell," Baba said, but still the boy didn't answer. Then Baba started scolding him openly. "This boy secretly keeps wine in his hostel cupboard and drinks it at night when he thinks no one is looking. Boy, your secret is out! Whenever you do any action, my two eyes are watching you. Do you think that what you are doing is right? You are falling behind in your studies and misusing and abusing your parent's money. What will happen if some other boy sees you and starts copying your bad behavior? Is this how you follow yama and niyama?"

Baba leaned forward and touched him between the eyebrows. The boy fell senseless to the ground. "By stimulating the *ajina* chakra," Baba told the disciples, "there has been some hormonal secretion from his pineal gland. Due to this the boy has gone into samadhi. This hormonal secretion of the pineal gland is described as *amrita rasa*, nectarean hormone. It is a divine intoxication. After some minutes he will return to his senses. When he returns from samadhi, you people will see that his eyes are red, as if he were drunk, but this has nothing to do with wine; it is a divine intoxication."

After fifteen to twenty minutes, the boy came out of his trance. His eyes were swollen and reddish. "How did you enjoy this kind of intoxication?" Baba asked. "Which do you find more enjoyable, this or drinking wine?"

"Baba," the boy replied, "this is a thousand times better than wine."

"Yes, when a person drinks wine he loses his sense; his mind becomes crudified, it becomes blind. But when a person goes into samadhi, he becomes refreshed; his consciousness is illuminated." After the boy had promised not to drink again, Baba told him, "Do more sadhana and you will be able to enjoy samadhi and the hormone secretion from the pineal gland. It will give you more concentration of mind, which will help you with your studies. Don't waste any more of your father's money purchasing wine. Remember, for samadhi you don't have to spend a single paisa."

In another General Darshan, Baba asked a police officer to stand up. Baba started explaining to everyone that this disciple had heard that Baba went to sleep at twelve and got up again at four, so he had started drinking during those hours, thinking that Baba wouldn't know. "Do you think Paramapurusha sleeps at this time?" Baba asked him. "Do you think you can hide from him? Water, earth, fire, this whole planet—everything is an agent of Paramapurusha. You cannot hide from him no matter what you do, so it is better you admit your fault and take punishment." The policeman admitted that he had been drinking secretly at that hour. Baba ordered him to rub his nose on the ground and made him promise that he would never drink again.

On another occasion, a government officer was singing a devotional song at the beginning of General Darshan. He had a beautiful voice and the song brought tears to the eyes of many of the devotees. When he was finished singing, Baba said, "You see, he is singing a devotional song and bringing tears to everyone's eyes, yet in the office he is accepting bribes. What kind of hypocrisy is this?" Baba turned his attention to the officer. "Is it not true that you accept bribes?" Reduced to tears, though not of devotion, the officer admitted that he had been accepting bribes in exchange for government favors.

In yet another darshan, Baba scolded a different police officer so severely for victimizing an innocent person that the officer started shaking visibly for all to see. "If you act like an animal, then perhaps I should give you the body of an animal!" Afterward, a number of disciples became scared that Baba might actually transform them into an animal.

Word spread quickly that Baba had begun exposing the disciples' wrongdoings in public. As a result, attendance at General Darshan dropped precipitously. Over the next several months, the disciples became extremely conscious of their behavior, not wanting to give Baba any pretext to expose them in front of their fellow devotees; many of those who were not following the precepts of yama and niyama thought it more prudent to stay away. One day, Acharya Chandradeva went into Baba's room to confess a mistake he had made and ask for punishment, thinking it wiser than to wait for Baba to point it out in front of everyone; however, Baba chose not to punish him. When Chandradeva asked why, Baba said, "Everyone makes mistakes, Chandradeva. To err is human, but some of these people are criminals. They require harsh measures; otherwise they won't change. At any rate, I am thinking that from now on I will start calling people for private sessions and scold them and punish them at that time." A few days later, Baba announced the system of Personal Contact. Every disciple, he explained, would have the right to one private personal contact with the guru. What Baba didn't announce, but what everybody knew, was that nothing remained hidden from the master. Whoever wanted to have personal contact had best come prepared.

One evening, Acharya Raghunath and some other Margis were sitting with Baba on the tiger's grave when a strange man approached in the garb of a forest ascetic. Baba motioned for the Margis to make room for him, but instead of sitting on the grave, he sat on the ground directly in front of Baba. For several minutes the man stared silently at Baba. The Margis remained silent as well, until the man closed his eyes and entered into a state of trance. Then they asked Baba about him. Baba told them that he was their brother disciple and then changed the subject. Nearly two hours passed before the yogi came out of his trance. When he did, he prostrated in front of Baba and left.

A few weeks later, Raghunath was again walking in the field with Baba and two other Margis. Baba suddenly stopped and brought his folded hands to his heart, just as he normally did when responding to someone's namaskar. His mood turned grave and he resumed walking slowly and silently. After a few minutes, he turned to Raghunath and said, "Do you remember that night when a man came to meet me at the grave and went into deep samadhi for a long time? You were very curious to know who he was."

"I remember, Baba."

"He is free from all mundane and supramundane bondages now. He left his physical body a few minutes ago. When he came to see me that day, he had come to seek permission to leave his body." After pausing for a few moments, visibly moved, Baba said, "He was a great yogi and a Tantric; he had experienced many kinds of samadhi."

It was not uncommon in those days for unknown yogis and Tantrics to visit Baba. From time to time, the Margis would see one of them waiting for Baba in the field. On such occasions, Baba would generally ask the Margis to wait for him and then disappear with that person in the direction of Death Valley or Kalipahar. When the disciples asked him about it, he explained that he had other initiates who were not members of Ananda Marga. "They have other work to do outside the organization," he told them, but no other information was forthcoming, and Baba never let the Margis meet any of these unknown ascetics.

One evening, Nagina, Lalan, and Vindhyachal Pandey were accompanying Baba on field walk. As they passed the culvert leading to the field, they saw an unknown man standing there with white, tangled hair, a long white beard, and ragged clothes. He approached Baba with his hands raised and cried out, "*Jai Shiva Shankar*. O Lord, many days have passed in anxious waiting."

Baba signaled for the old man to follow them. He continued talking to his three disciples in a light mood, keeping up the conversation until they reached the tiger's grave. Once at the grave, Baba's mood turned serious. "Look, you all get to see me whenever you want, but this poor man has been waiting for many days without having had an opportunity to talk to me. He has something very urgent to discuss with me. You should all return back now so he and I can talk. There is no sense in wasting your time here."

The three disciples were disappointed, but they had no choice. As they began walking back toward town, they discussed the strange sadhu. Before they had gone more than a few hundred meters, they decided that this would be a perfect opportunity to catch one of these strange visitors and find out what his relationship was with the master. They doubled back and hid themselves at three different spots spaced far enough apart that the stranger would have to pass one of them on his way out of the field. Once he had finished his conversation with Baba, they would catch up with him and satisfy their curiosity.

It was just after eight when they took up their posts. Baba normally remained at the tiger's grave until ten or ten thirty. Ten o'clock passed, then eleven, and soon it was getting near midnight and there was no sign of either Baba or the mysterious stranger. Finally, one of the three spies lost patience and started walking toward the grave. He found it empty. Baffled, he informed his two fellow disciples and they returned to town.

A couple of days later, Nagina again had a chance to go on field walk with Baba. As they were walking, Baba turned to Nagina and asked, "Nagina, if I am not mistaken, after you left the other night, the three of you made plans to catch the sadhu who came to talk to me. Were you able to meet him? Did you find out what you wanted to know?"

"No, Baba," Nagina said softly, "we kept watch until midnight, but somehow he slipped by us."

Baba smiled. "There were only three of you. Had you been three hundred and all on horseback, you still would not have been able to catch him—not unless he wanted you to. He was that elevated a soul."

Nagina begged Baba to tell him who the man was, and after a minute or two Baba acquiesced.

"That old man is a very advanced sadhaka. He has been practicing sadhana very diligently for many years. He is a resident of Viratnagar in Nepal. His spiritual practice is almost complete and now he wishes to leave his physical body. He came here to ask me for permission."

"But why does he need permission?"

"That is the rule. If any sadhaka wishes to leave their physical body they must seek permission from *sadguru*."[12]

"Did you give him permission?"

"No, I did not. He has a duty to perform. Only after he completes the assigned duty will I allow him to leave his body."

"What duty is that?"

"I have made a new rule. Before any sadhaka can give up their body, they must render social service, no matter how great a spiritualist they may be. They must return the debt they owe society. He had not yet fulfilled that condition, so I told him he would have to do rigorous social service for three months."

"And he agreed?"

"You see, Nagina, when someone exhausts their samskaras, they find it painful to remain in their body. He begged me to reduce the time, so I reduced it to one month. Still he wouldn't accept it. So I reduced it to two weeks, but even that was too much. So I reduced it to five days. But still he appealed for mercy. So I made one final concession. I reduced the term to three days."

"What service does he have to do?"

"That I cannot reveal."

The next day the news came that the body of an old sadhu had been found near the tunnel that runs between Jamalpur and Bhagalpur. Some days later, Haragovind, who had heard the story from Nagina, asked Baba if the old sadhu who had been found near the railway tunnel was the same person who had come to see him three nights before.

"Yes, he was that sadhaka from Viratnagar. He has fulfilled all his duties in this life and merged with the Supreme Consciousness."

As time went on, some of the Margis took to calling these unknown disciples the "Brahma Avadhutas." Stories of their sightings were passed around, but no one ever got a chance to talk to one of them face to face. In a DMC held at Monghyr in May of 1957, Gayatri, one of Ram Khilavan's four daughters, arrived early and took a seat near the front. She noticed a group of twenty or so ascetic monks seated in front of the dais with their hands upraised. They had tangled locks and wore either robes or animal skins around their waist. Their *kamadal* pots were on the ground by their feet.[13] She watched them curiously for five or ten minutes and then turned her attention elsewhere. When she looked back a few minutes later, she was surprised to find that they were gone. Gayatri didn't think much more of it until fifteen years later when Bindeshvari stopped by her house to pay a visit. In the course of their conversation, he mentioned the Brahma Avadhutas. When she heard his description, she recalled this incident. Bindeshvari told her that the monks Baba had initiated before creating Ananda Marga used to do pranam by raising their hands. They would occasionally attend DMC, but they had the power to remain unnoticed. It was Baba's grace, he told her, that she was able to see them.

Gayatri's glimpse of these unknown disciples was about as close as any of the Margis ever came to meeting them.

XIX

A Place of Awakening

The spiritual aspirant is engaged in fight. It is for the brave, it is for courageous people ... He who wants to keep himself away from fight is unknowingly committing suicide, mental and spiritual suicide. Each and every person should be ready for fight—fight in the mental stratum, fight in the family stratum, fight in each and every stratum of life. This is Tantra.[1]

In 1957, the Bhagalpur Margis joined together to buy some land and commenced construction of the Bhagalpur *jagriti*, a word that Baba had used in *Caryacarya* to refer to Ananda Marga centers instead of the more common word "ashram." They completed construction in the summer of 1958. In August, Baba came to inaugurate the building and give his monthly DMC. During the inauguration, Baba explained that the word *jagriti* in Sanskrit meant "a place for spiritual awakening." It was the first property owned by Ananda Marga and its first jagriti. He also inaugurated the medical clinic, Abha Seva Sadan, which was already up and running with its own doctor and free medical treatment for the public, as well as a library of spiritual books housed in a separate room, which the disciples named Prabhat Granthagar.

In the meantime, Baba and his family had to move out of their rented house in Keshavpur, as the owners had put it up for sale. Out of necessity, they moved to the Rampur Colony quarters that up until then had served as a jagriti. Deprived of their center, the Margis had no alternative but to shift their weekly activities from one Margi's quarters to another until they were able to rent a small place in the market area. With the limited funds at their disposal, however, it was barely adequate at best, and nobody was happy about the situation.

As soon as Baba returned from Bhagalpur, he told Pranay that Ananda Marga needed a jagriti of its own in Jamalpur and that he should arrange for it without delay. Just how they would be able to do this, Pranay didn't know, since the organization had little or no funds, but he didn't dare express that to Baba. He knew that any faintheartedness on his part or attempts at making excuses would bring a stern reprimand or worse from the Tantric guru. Accordingly, Pranay passed the word among the Margis to start looking for land and informed them that it would have to be as cheap as possible.

A few days later, Baba asked Pranay for a progress report. When Pranay informed him that they had not found anything yet, Baba told him that they would find their land at Olipur, the neighborhood where Ram Khilavan lived. Pranay communicated this to Ram Khilavan, and after some inquiries Ram Khilavan learned of a plot for sale. There was just one problem: the land was under dispute. A day laborer in the Jamalpur workshop, Bacchu Mandal, who had earned a well-deserved reputation as a local thug, had taken a loan to buy the plot. When he had been unable to repay the loan, the court had deeded it to the lender as repayment. After the court's decision, Bacchu Mandal let it be known that he was not about to give up his land. If the owner, or anyone he might sell it to, dared set one foot on the property, he and his sons would kill them. The moneylender, a local businessman, had taken Bacchu at his word and was prepared to let it go quite cheaply to anyone who was willing to take the risk.

By the time Ram Khilavan finished his story, Pranay was sure that this was the land Baba had alluded to. It was exactly the kind of challenge he would want for his disciples. Despite the risks involved, he contacted the owner and settled on a bargain price. After collecting donations from the Margis, he signed the deed and began the process of registering the property. Shortly thereafter, Ram Khilavan brought news that the adjoining plot had been abandoned by a Muslim family during the partition of India and was still unoccupied. Pranay, who had remained unsatisfied with the size of their original purchase, made further inquiries and learned that the land was due to come up for auction. He then went to the land office in Patna along with Dasarath, Vaedyanath Ray, and Sijanath. There they explained to the authorities that they wanted the land in order to build a spiritual ashram. The officer-in-charge agreed to give it to them for fifteen hundred rupees, significantly less than it would have brought on open auction.

While Pranay was busy purchasing the two plots in Olipur, Baba conducted DMCs in Ramnagar and Krishnagar in September and October.[2] One of the organizers of the Krishnagar DMC was Manoranjan Sen, the local Unit Secretary. Manoranjan had been initiated the previous year. He was a friend of Acharya Sukhen and had long resisted Sukhen's efforts to convince him to take initiation. But early in 1957, he underwent a severe bout of sciatica. When three months of bed rest and medical treatment did not alleviate his pain, his resistance gave way and he requested Sukhen to cure him with his "mantra and Tantra." Sukhen gave him initiation, and he and Haraprasad assisted Manoranjan in performing certain asanas along with his meditation. In a week, he had recovered enough to be able to walk without excessive pain. They took him to Jamalpur where he had his first field walk. As they set out, Baba was walking at his normal rapid pace and Manoranjan struggled to keep up. By the time they reached the tiger's grave and sat down, his previous pain had returned.

When they got up from the grave, Manoranjan could not stand. Frustrated, he complained to Sukhen, "Why did you bother curing me if you were going to finish me off like this!" When Baba heard this, he turned and shouted for the two of them to come over. Sukhen helped his friend approach Baba who said, "Tonight Haraprasad will give you a massage; after that you will be okay. Now, come along." Haraprasad gave him a massage that night according to Baba's instructions and Manoranjan's pain disappeared, never to return.

Krishnagar was the birthplace of Chaitanya Mahaprabhu, the great fifteenth-century Vaeshnava saint who popularized the practice of kirtan.[3] Krishnagar had risen to prominence as one of the most important spiritual and cultural centers in Bengal at a time when Calcutta was still a small fishing village, and it was still extremely influential in her cultural life.

Over two months earlier, Baba had hinted to some of the Margis in Bihar that the Krishnagar DMC would be a special one. The word spread and more than a thousand Margis attended, coming from as far away as Bombay. It was the first all-India and the first three-day DMC. Baba was scheduled to arrive from Calcutta on the noon train, but due to a last minute change of plans, he arrived an hour earlier by car and went straight to the house arranged for his stay. In the meantime, the Margis were waiting in the station for the train to arrive. The municipal commissioner, Mohan Kali Biswas, went to the station to receive Baba on behalf of the city, but before the train arrived Bindeshvari caught him and touched him between the eyebrows. An electric current passed through his body. Overcome by the experience, he sat down on the platform and started crying. He was still crying when the train pulled in.

While the Margis were searching the train for Baba, Manoranjan reached the station with the news that Baba had already arrived by car and had sent instructions for the Margis to hold a kirtan-bhajan procession from the station to the town hall,[4] site of the DMC, along a specific six-kilometer route. Manoranjan assembled everyone in rows and nearly a thousand Margis started marching through the streets of Krishnagar, chanting a devotional refrain. After the procession advanced a short distance, one devotee started leading *harinam* kirtan, the same kirtan introduced by Chaitanya Mahaprabhu. Soon everyone was dancing and crying, overcome by feelings of spiritual intoxication, including many members of the public who had thronged the roadside to watch and then joined in at the rear of the procession. When they reached the town hall, the local acharyas opened its doors and conducted a public Tattvasabha on Ananda Marga philosophy in front of a capacity crowd.

In the evening, more than five thousand townspeople gathered in the square outside the hall, eager to attend the discourse of this saint whose devotees had vibrated the city that afternoon with their kirtan. The streets leading up to the hall were so crowded that Baba's car was unable to pass. Sukhen had to take him by rickshaw to the back entrance. In the meantime, a commotion arose when the public was informed that only Margis with signed gate passes from their acharya would be allowed into the hall, which was barely big enough to accommodate the Margis. Once Baba was inside, the doors and windows were shut. A huge clamor went up outside. After Kamalesh finished singing a devotional song, Baba called Shiva Shankar and asked him what the uproar was about. When Shiva Shankar explained, Baba asked him to open all the doors and windows and place loudspeakers out in the square so that everyone could hear. The volunteers did so as quickly as possible. Those townspeople who could somehow squeeze into the hall did so, while the rest sat outside and tried to catch a glimpse of Baba through the open doors and windows. The devotional songs, dancing, and crying continued for some time, but once Baba began his talk there was pin-drop silence, both inside and outside. Sukhen remembered his surprise at the time:

> I was moving around outside, directing the volunteers and making sure everything was under control. I was astonished to see respectable lawyers and doctors sitting outside on the grass and listening to Baba's talk. I overheard them saying that they had never seen anyone like Baba, nor had they ever heard anyone speak such a pure and refined Bengali. I couldn't listen much to Baba's talk, but afterward he raised his hands and everyone in the hall started to dance and sing. Outside in the field, Margis and general people were dancing and singing together and shouting *Anandamurtiji ki jai* and *Chaitanya Mahaprabhu ki jai*.[5] After the talk, I went on field walk with Baba to the riverbank with seven or eight other Margis, to the site of our present Ananda Marga ashram. Baba was very happy. He was extolling the greatness of the people of Krishnagar and telling many stories about the city and Chaitanya Mahaprabhu.

On DMC night the same scene repeated itself. When the DMC was over and Baba left the hall around eleven, the Margis returned to their lodgings at the high school. After dinner, the kirtans and bhajans started up again. Gopen was standing in one corner with his eyes closed. Suddenly, he raised his arms and started dancing and singing *harinam* kirtan. After a few minutes he fell to the ground in a spiritual trance. One by one, everyone started dancing and singing. Many of them joined Gopen in a state of trance. The ecstatic mood continued all night and into the morning. In the morning, Nityananda told Baba what had happened and remarked that it seemed as if Baba were making the devotees dance to the beat of the cosmic rhythm in *harinam* kirtan. Baba smiled and said, "Do you know, the great devotee Shiromani Narada asked God a question about *harinam* kirtan. 'O God, where do you live?' In reply, God said, 'I do not live in heaven or in the hearts of yogis, Narada. I live where my devotees sing.'"

Some of the Margis recalled that the ecstasy they experienced during the

Krishnagar DMC lasted for months afterward. Many of the townspeople who participated claimed that Krishnagar had not seen anything like it since the times of Chaitanya Mahaprabhu. For many Margis it would remain their favorite DMC of all time.

By the time of the Krishnagar DMC, the two plots of land had been purchased and registered. Pranay now faced the problem of how to evict Bacchu Mandal. Baba continued to ask for progress reports, and as the days passed he started to ratchet up the pressure. Pranay was unsure what to do. As usual, he was facing an acute shortage of funds, especially after raising the money to buy the land, and he was unsure how to deal with Bacchu. With the help of Vaedyanath, a practicing advocate, he filed legal eviction proceedings, but such proceedings could easily drag on for a year or more and Pranay was well aware that Baba would not put up with much more delay.

In the meantime, Baba told Dasarath to inform Bacchu Mandal on behalf of the new owners that the construction would begin on such and such a day and that Baba wanted Bacchu to lay the foundation stone. The mild-mannered schoolteacher did as Baba requested. Bacchu and his sons became so infuriated when they heard that Bacchu had been asked to lay the foundation stone for his own eviction that his eldest son, Tara Mandal, grabbed a *bujali* and attacked Dasarath.[6] Dasarath raised his umbrella to defend himself and closed his eyes, remembering Baba, sure that he was about to meet his death. But the attempted blow never materialized. When nothing happened, Dasarath opened his eyes and saw Tara Mandal red with anger, his hand still upraised, unable to move it and unable to understand the cause of his paralysis. Dasarath left and went to the rented jagriti to inform Baba of what had happened.

As soon as Dasarath entered Baba's room, Baba said in Angika, " The Master Sahib's head would have been split into two today had I not applied *stamban kriya*.[7] You had a narrow escape, did you not?"

A tearful Dasarath replied in the same language, "Oh Baba, this was your magic; otherwise Tara Mandal surely would have killed me. But he became paralyzed. If not for your magic, I would have died."

A few days later, Dasarath learned that Bacchu Mandal had erected a makeshift temple on the land with some clay idols and pictures of gods and goddesses and was performing a simple worship in the evenings. Dasarath rushed to Pranay and told him that all was lost. Once the court found out that the land was the site of a functioning temple, they would never give a verdict for eviction. When they conveyed the news to Baba, he said, "Then you will have to fight. Pranay, go there in force and throw Bacchu and his goons off the land for good." Pranay, a slightly built man who had never been in any kind of physical altercation in his life, began to tremble when he heard Baba's order. Still, he gathered his courage and a group of seven or eight Margis, including Asthana, Tyagi, Sakaldev, and Devi Chand. They went to the land and confronted Bacchu and his gang who attacked them with lathis. Pranay and one or two others sustained a few hard blows before the unarmed Margis ran away.

When they got back to the jagriti, none of them wanted to tell Baba what had happened, but they finally agreed that they had no choice. As expected, Baba was quick to show his anger. "What! Are you such weak cowards that you turn your tail and run? You should have given up your life rather than run away in shame. I don't want to see your faces! One hit and you run away? Maybe you should be wearing bangles and saris! What work can you accomplish in your life if you act like this? I don't want to hear such things. If you can't do anything then I will go there myself."

Baba got up from his cot and started moving toward the door. The Margis began crying and pleading with him. "No, Baba, no. We promise. We'll throw them off the land."

Baba sat back down and softened his tone. "In the future you should always take lathis with you in such situations. It is foolish to enter a battle without preparing yourself properly. Now inform Kedarnath, Chandranath, and the other members of the BMP. They will know what to do. I want the boundary wall constructed immediately."

Pranay sent urgent telegrams to Kedarnath Sharma in Ranchi, Chandranath in Bhagalpur, and several others. Kedarnath sent back a prompt reply telling him not to worry. He would make sure that the boundary wall was completed as Baba had instructed. He alone would be enough to take possession of the land, he wrote, but he would not come alone. Early the next morning, a Sunday, a truck arrived in Jamalpur filled with Margis from the BMP garrisons of Kedarnath, Chandranath, Kishun, and Kuldip. When they arrived at the land, Bacchu Mandal and his small gang put up a short-lived resistance and then fled. He and his sons were never seen again in the Olipur area.

The Margis immediately set to work building the boundary wall with materials that Kedarnath had ordered the previous day. Scores of Margis continued to arrive from different towns during the course of the morning to join in; by midnight the boundary wall was completed. When Baba was informed, he was pleased with the news but he did not let up on the pressure. "I want the jagriti building completed within twenty-one days," he said, "on which day I will hold DMC there. If the building is completed by this time, then we will face no more problems with the land, but if it is not, we will continue to face severe problems in the future."

The construction of the building began the following morning. Numerous Margis took leave from their jobs and went to work full-time on the construction, which went on unabated, day and night. Some of them even slept on site. Those Margis who could not get leave spent all their free hours pitching in. Advocates, professors, and government officials worked alongside coolies, students, housewives, and children. Margis from different towns pitched in to send materials and food. Others brought musical instruments, and many of the disciples danced and sang devotional songs as they worked. Baba paid regular visits to the site, one of which Baban Tiwari described in an interview:

> We were all very busy with the work, day and night, but the Lord was never out of our minds. Once it was raining very heavily; for that reason Baba could not come to visit us. My mind became restless while I worked, due to Baba's absence. I was humming to myself, "O Baba, you did not come today. What is the matter? How can I stay here without you?" All I could think about was the Lord and how much I missed him. Suddenly I saw Baba approaching. He was holding an umbrella over his head with one hand and lifting his dhoti up with the other to keep it clear of the water and mud flowing down the street due to the torrential rains. I ran up to him and asked him why he had taken so much trouble to come in this rainy weather.
>
> "You called me, so I came," Baba said.
>
> "Oh no, Baba," I told him. "It was just idle thinking. I didn't actually mean that I wanted you to come physically in such rough conditions. I wasn't complaining so that you would hear me and come. How could you walk all this way down these muddy, dirty streets in this terrible rain?"
>
> "How can I think to stay away when my devotee is demanding my presence?" he said. "It is just not possible."

Chandranath's nephew Ramakanta was one of those who often slept at the site, working on the construction full-time until it was finished. One night Kuldip, who had taken one month's leave to help with the work, went on field walk with Baba to the tiger's grave and took advantage of the opportunity to sing the young man's praises. "Baba, I have never seen such a hardworking young man. He works day and night without stopping, but it is a shame he doesn't get to do much meditation." Baba smiled and continued walking. When Kuldip returned to the rented jagriti that evening, he found Ramakanta lying in Baba's room in trance. When he asked the other Margis what had happened, they told him that he had come there to do his evening meditation at about eight o'clock and had gone into Samadhi—the same time that Kuldip had been talking to Baba about him. His trance lasted for three hours; in the morning Ramakanta was back at work.

The building was finished on December 27, one day ahead of schedule. The Margis set up a large tent in front of the new jagriti, and the next evening Baba inaugurated the building and held a DMC. The title of his discourse was "Energy and its Expression." While Baba was in the middle of his talk, the District Magistrate arrived to investigate charges filed by Bacchu Mandal against the Margis for destroying a temple. When he saw the building, the boundary wall, and the hundreds of devotees listening in perfect silence to

Baba's lecture, he realized that he was wasting his time. He asked Vaedyanath and Akhori Himachal Prasad a couple of quick questions and then went back to Monghyr with a couple of Baba's books under his arms that the two Margis had gifted him. The following day he dismissed the case. The Margis finally had a place of their own.

XX

A Civil Ceremony

Preceptors must be more than intelligent, they must be super-intelligent. They must also be married, for, according to Tantric injunction, only a married person can be the guru of married people.[1]

In late March 1959, a DMC program was held in the Bihar village of Arraha, home to acharyas Dipnarayan and Natkat Kedar. Baba arrived on the morning of the twenty-seventh at Mithai Station in Saharsa. The Margis received him with ringing blasts from conch shells and a raucous kirtan backed by a flute and drum ensemble while a host of curious onlookers crowded the platform. Outside the station, a parade of elephants was waiting. Baba and Pranay mounted the lead elephant with the help of a bamboo staircase, and a huge procession set out for Arraha, four kilometers distant. Bindeshvari, Nagina, and others from Baba's party rode the remaining elephants; the rest of the Margis traveled by bullock cart or jeep, or else ran and danced alongside the lumbering beasts. The band followed and the Margis continued singing at the top of their lungs the entire way. Cows, goats, and other animals joined in. At one point, Bindeshvari went into trance and would have fallen off his elephant had Nagina not caught him. The route was lined with villagers who could hear the procession approaching well before they caught sight of it. A number of them, assuming they were watching a marriage procession,[2] commented on how handsome the groom looked.

When the procession arrived in Arraha, Natkat Kedar led Baba's elephant up to the newly constructed jagriti, a traditional village structure with earthen walls and a thatch roof. Baba climbed down the bamboo staircase, and as he walked up to the veranda, the women threw parched rice on the path in front of him, waved lamps, and sang devotional songs, all in keeping with the local tradition. Baba cut the long ribbon of mango leaves that ran across the entrance and stepped onto the veranda where Dipnarayan's wife, Jivaccha Devi, was waiting to perform the traditional *arati*.[3] She lifted a silver plate laden with burning camphor and incense and began tracing slow, solemn circles in front of Baba while everyone chanted in unison the arati verse. Then Baba entered the jagriti, which had been prepared as his residence for the three-day program.

That afternoon, a commotion arose in a large tent that had been set up a couple of days earlier near the jagriti. Members of the Ramnath Society, a fundamentalist Hindu group, started shouting anti-Ananda Marga slogans through a cheap loudspeaker. They hurled insults at Baba and the Margis, alleging that Ananda Marga violated the Hindu scriptures because it asked Brahmins to remove their sacred thread, spoke out against idol worship, and allowed women to attend programs alongside men. They were led by a renowned Hindu scholar from Benares, Bhayankar Acharya Shastri. When Baba heard the commotion, he came out of his room and asked the Margis what was going on. When they told him, he smiled and nodded his head. "Don't worry," he said, "the more they shout 'Ananda Marga,' the more they do publicity for us."

The next morning, Bhayankar Acharya issued a written statement challenging Anandamurti to a scriptural debate. A group of Margis brought the challenge to Baba. Many of them were angry at the ongoing insults coming from the Ramnath tent and were restless to take some kind of action. Baba listened and said, "This kind of debate is for followers of the same scripture. Since we do not accept the Vedas or the Gita as proof,[4] there is no question of a scriptural debate; but since they have invited us, we can extend them the courtesy of attending. Indradev Gupta and Chandranath will be our representatives."

"Baba," Indradev said, "Bhayankar is insisting that the debate be conducted in Sanskrit. Chandranath and I are both very weak in Sanskrit. What should we do?"

"Don't worry," Baba replied. "Tell him it should be in French, and then scold him in French for two minutes." Then Baba reached out and touched Indradev at his trikuti.

The debate was fixed for midday. By the time the noon hour struck, more than a thousand people were sitting on the grass in front of the Ramnath tent. Baba was watching from the window of his room in the jagriti. The four local pundits who had been selected to serve as judges sat on chairs to one side; Bhayankar Acharya, Indradev, and Chandranath stood and faced the audience. As expected, Bhayankar opened by insisting that the debate be held in Sanskrit, the language of religious scholarship. Indradev immediately held up his hand.

"I object. The debate should rightly be in Hindi; otherwise, no one in the audience will understand. Only the judges and one or two others will be able to follow the discussion."

"If you don't know Sanskrit, then why do you have Sanskrit verses in your books!" Bhayankar shouted. "Remove them from your books or else debate in Sanskrit."

Indradev looked back at Baba, who nodded from his window. Then he turned his attention back to Bhayankar. "You want the debate to be in Sanskrit so you can befool the people. It might as well be in French then."

Indradev followed with a long string of epithets in French. Though no one could understand what he was saying, everyone in the audience laughed, even the pundits. When the laughter died down, however, the pundits agreed with Bhayankar that the debate should be held in Sanskrit.

Bhayankar began the debate. He put a question to Indradev that concerned grammar and its role in the establishment of a proof. Though Indradev's Sanskrit was rather sketchy, he understood the question. Fortunately, it was a subject with which he was familiar. After pointing out that the question had nothing to do with the topic of the debate, he answered it in Sanskrit in half the allotted ten minutes and then used the remaining five minutes to repeat the same thing in Hindi. He not only gave the correct answer but also pointed out several grammatical errors in Bhayankar's framing of the question. The crowd applauded and the smiles on many of their faces gave Indradev the confidence that he would be able to win them over to his side. When the applause died down, one of the judges announced that the debate would now continue in Hindi. They had only wanted to make sure that Indradev knew Sanskrit.

As the debate progressed, Bhayankar raised questions about the sacred thread, the caste system, and the equal rights of women to perform spiritual practices. Indradev, with Chandranath's help, answered each question with patience and logic. As he continued to win over the crowd, his opponent began losing his patience, often interrupting the Margis while they were speaking. At four thirty, Bhayankar insisted that it was too late to continue. Indradev and Chandranath were declared the winners by the judges, to the enthusiastic applause of the audience. Afterward, many of the villagers stayed behind to congratulate the speakers. They would remember Indradev, especially, with respect for years to come. When the crowd finally dispersed, Indradev and Chandranath went to Baba for his blessing.

Baba put his hand on Indradev's shoulder and said, "Indradev, very good, very good. I didn't know you spoke Sanskrit so well."

Indradev laughed. "Neither did I, Baba. That was only your grace."

"You see, Indradev? They wanted to debate me, but my disciple defeated them. It was a good lesson for them."

Late that night, Bhayankar Acharya sought out Indradev and congratulated him for how well he spoke Sanskrit. He apologized for any inconvenience he might have caused. "I have no fight with you or the Margis," he said. "The Ramnath Society paid me five hundred rupees to come here and oppose Ananda Marga. It was just a job. Now that it's over, I'll be leaving in the morning."

After that, the only commotion in the village was the devotional exuberance of the Margis. The next morning, at the Margis request, Baba visited each of their houses while the rest of the devotees followed behind. In each house, he sampled something from the plates of food the Margi women brought out for him, and as he walked through the village the non-Margi women also came out from their homes with plates of dried fruit and nuts to offer him. At the house of Natkat Kedar, Natkat's wife became so lost in her devotional feelings that she washed Baba's feet in milk without realizing it, instead of the sandal water that she had prepared. The morning after the DMC, the Margis took Baba back to Mithai Station by car. The entire village lined both sides of the street to wish Baba farewell. Many of them accompanied the Margis to the station, singing and dancing as they went.

In the meanwhile, unbeknownst to the Margis, Baba's family was busy making arrangements for Baba's marriage. Baba's mother had decided that her son's marriage was long overdue. Now that she was getting on in years, preparing to turn sixty without another female in the house, she needed a daughter-in-law to help her with her domestic responsibilities. Baba had shown no interest in the idea whatsoever, but over time Abharani gradually increased the pressure on her son and eventually he agreed. She deputed Hiraprabha, then raising her children as a widow in Chinchura, to search for a suitable bride. Early in the year, Hiraprabha entered into negotiations with the family of a postal department superintendent from the city of Bandel, forty-eight kilometers to the north of Calcutta, who had been searching for a husband for their twenty-year-old daughter, Uma Devi Dutta.

Shortly after the Arraha DMC, an agreement was reached between the two families, typical in traditional Indian society at that time where arranged marriages were still the norm. Hiraprabha explained to them that her brother would not accept a religious ceremony or any of the pomp and circumstance generally associated with an Indian marriage. A simple civil ceremony would have to do, and the family agreed.

While the negotiations were going on, Baba said nothing to the Margis—or practically nothing. One day, Pranay was reviewing organizational matters with Baba when Baba said, "Pranay, your mother wants to meet me." Pranay was confused; his mother, an initiated Margi, lived with him and got to see Baba on a regular basis. He wondered if there was some obscure spiritual significance to Baba's comment, but he didn't ask. A couple of days later Vaedyanath Rai told Pranay that he had a stunning secret to divulge. Baba was going to get married! The family of the bride had made discreet inquiries in the workshop about the groom's character, salary, and so forth, standard in an Indian marriage negotiation, and the inquiries had come to his department. In fact, he had learned that Baba was scheduled to catch the overnight train to Howrah that very night.

Pranay was stunned, but then he remembered Baba's earlier comment. What had been an incomprehensible remark suddenly made sense. Pranay told Vaedyanath that he knew nothing about it, but he intended to find out. Without wasting any time, he went directly to Baba's house and entered straight into Baba's room without requesting permission, as he was wont to do at times. He found Baba packing his suitcase. Baba informed him nonchalantly that he was going to Chinchura for a few days. Pranay made a pretext of discussing some organizational matter. While Baba's back was turned, he took a quick look in the suitcase. He saw some silken shirts, a bottle of aftershave, and a red card that looked suspiciously like a marriage invitation. There was nothing in Baba's behavior that indicated anything out of the ordinary, nor did Pranay ask, but he had his confirmation. As soon as he left Baba's house, he started passing the word among the Margis that Gurudeva was getting married.

The news sent shock waves through the Margi community in Jamalpur and beyond, as the Margis there started sending the news to Margis in other places. Many did not believe it could be true. They had always assumed that Baba would remain unmarried, a sannyasi in spirit if not in dress, as was the practice with the vast majority of spiritual gurus in India. For some, it was a blow to their faith. How could their spiritual master be married or have family relations with a woman? Some of them came to Pranay to express their disbelief and confusion. Even Dasarath felt some reaction. He considered it strange indeed that Gurudeva would give his consent to such an arrangement. But Pranay scolded him and the others who came to see him. "What of it?" he said. "Marriage is a perfectly natural affair. Sooner or later everyone gets married. Why should Gurudeva not lead a natural life?" He called their attention to the first edition of *Caryacarya* in which Baba had written: "Marriage is not a hindrance to Dharma Sadhana; marriage is a Dharmika ceremony ... No disciple should harbor any inferiority complex about being married, and for this purpose every disciple should consider that the guru of the Marga is married." Baba had always emphasized this to his married disciples, Pranay pointed out, so why should they feel strange now when he was about to turn his teaching into a concrete reality?

Baba would later point out in a discourse on Tantra that one of the characteristics of the Tantric guru is that he must be married in order to set a proper example for his householder disciples that illumination is equally accessible to all, regardless of whether one is a monk or married.

When Baba arrived in Chinchura he met his first cousin Ajit Biswas who accompanied him to the bride's house and then on to the civil register for the marriage ceremony, along with Hiraprabha's family and the family of the bride. Hiraprabha's brother-in-law served as the best man. It was the first time the bride and groom had met.

After the wedding, Ajit informed Baba that the family had scheduled a traditional ceremony for the next day, one in which Baba would have to dress up in the traditional groom's costume, somewhat similar to a prince's garb from ancient times. Baba objected. He pointed out that he had insisted on an unostentatious, non-religious ceremony. Ajit laughed. "Bubu-da, you are caught by your own words. This is a purely social ceremony; it has no religious background." Baba gave in, and the bride's family was happy to have a little pomp and circumstance after the rapid and rather austere ceremony at the register's office.

Back in Jamalpur, Pranay was able to find out which train Baba was returning by, an easy matter for a railway workshop employee. He, Chandranath,

A Civil Ceremony

Ramasvarath, and some fifty other Margis met the train in Bhagalpur. Pranay, Chandranath, and a few of the senior-most disciples made their way to Baba's compartment to pay their respects and salute the marriage party. In the compartment they saw a young woman sitting opposite Baba, her head and face veiled by the fold of her sari. As they paid their respects to their guru, it was clear to them that Uma Devi found it all very strange and very unexpected. In fact, she had no idea that she had married a spiritual guru. All she knew about Baba was that he was an accounts clerk in the Jamalpur workshop and very well behaved.

Ramasvarath was standing just outside the compartment. He had taken initiation about a year earlier from Acharya Sarangi, his supervisor in the Varishvar Block Development office. Still beset by doubts about his guru getting married, Ramasvarath wondered, as he looked at Baba, if Baba might perhaps now lose his spiritual powers. Suddenly he felt a powerful vibration running through his spinal column. A wave of ecstasy overcame him that would take many days to abate. His body shook and Chandranath had to physically hold him up to keep him from falling. All his doubts vanished.

After Baba and his new bride arrived in Jamalpur, Pranay requested and received permission from Baba to hold a wedding reception for the Margis; a separate reception was held for family members. He asked Baba how his wife should be addressed, and Baba told him that she should be called "Marga Mata."[5] Pranay prepared an invitation card in the name of Marga Gurudeva and Marga Mata and sent it out to all the Margis. Baba acted as host during the reception, which was held in the courtyard of the jagriti. Some of the Margis straightaway accepted Uma Devi as one with the master, following a centuries-old custom, and did sastaunga pranam before her at the beginning of the reception. Others, less sure how she should be treated, simply did namaskar and took their seats. Baba sat on a specially decorated dais alongside Uma Devi while people took photos. Both he and Uma Devi gave short talks. Then Baba listened while his wife, who was a skilled instrumentalist, gave a sitar recital. Afterward, he walked around and made sure that everyone was satisfied with the food, asking the guests one by one if they needed anything.

After the reception, life returned to normal in the Sarkar house. There were now five adults in the small, two-bedroom quarters where Baba lived with his mother and his younger brothers, Sudanshu and Manas—a rather congested living arrangement for a man who by this time had thousands of disciples but entirely characteristic of Baba with his love of simplicity, especially in the world's second-most-populous country where such an arrangement might be considered comfortable. Uma Devi took over most of the domestic chores and was not seen much by the Margis, at least in the beginning. Sudanshu, with the lifelong devotion he showed his brother, now took on the added responsibility of looking after Uma Devi's material needs. He brought home Baba's monthly pay and gave it to his mother along with his own. Abharani in turn gave Baba five rupees a month for pocket expenses, as she had been doing, and two rupees to Uma Devi. Baba's brother Himanshu, who would visit on weekends and holidays, later wrote that while for the rest of the family there was a noticeable change after Uma Devi came to live with them, they could see no change whatsoever in Baba. He followed the exact same routine as before: leaving and returning from the office with such punctuality that you could set your watch by it; going for field walk, darshan and DMC; and maintaining his personal time for sadhana. He offered no outward hint that anything had changed in his life.

There was one point, however, concerning his wife, in which Baba left no ambiguity. Not long after the marriage, some of the Margis went to Pranay and asked him to convey their request to Baba that Marga Mata share the stage with him during DMC. For them it was a matter of showing the ultimate respect to the guru's wife, in keeping with traditions passed down from their forefathers. Baba's reply was short and sharp. "In DMC Anandamurti is a singular entity; there is no place for any second entity." The matter was never brought up again. Baba did give permission for her to address the Margis when he was not present on the stage. After that, from time to time, Pranay would arrange for Uma Devi to give a short talk at some point during the DMC program. He remembered her as being a quiet, simple Bengali housewife at the time, somewhat overwhelmed by the turn of events that saw her married to an increasingly popular and controversial spiritual master. In fact, the first few times he asked her to give a talk, he had to coach her beforehand on what to say. The time would come, however, when Uma Devi would feel ready to give spiritual talks of her own, with consequences that none of the Margis at that time could possibly foresee.

XXI

For the Welfare and Happiness of All

Spirituality is not a utopian ideal but a practical philosophy, which can be practiced and realized in day-to-day life, however mundane it be. Spirituality stands for evolution and elevation, and not for superstition in action or pessimism. All fissiparous tendencies, and group or clan philosophies that tend to create the shackles of narrow-mindedness, are in no way connected with spirituality and should be discouraged. That which leads to broadness of vision alone should be accepted.[1]

Late in 1957, Baba was walking in the field with a few Margis, one of whom was Shashi Rainjan, a distinguished MP (member of parliament) with a gift for oratory and a pure-minded devotee who found no conflict between his educated upbringing and his single-minded faith in his guru. His devotion for Baba was so strong that he could not refrain from telling whoever would listen that God had taken birth once again in the great land of India, as he had done in ages past in the forms of Shiva, Krishna, Buddha, and other great masters.[2] Often people would reply to him that if God were walking the earth again, then why was he not able to remove the poverty and suffering of the people? What was the use of a God who didn't think about his suffering children? Shashi Rainjan, in his simple, straightforward manner, told Baba what people were saying and asked him what reply he should give them. Baba told him to wait for some time. The answer was coming, but only at the proper moment.

In late May 1959, Baba started giving a series of evening classes for acharyas on the veranda of the Jamalpur jagriti. Normally, Baba's classes would range over a wide variety of subjects, anything from ancient history to applied science or agriculture, with philology being one of his favorite topics. Two days after the inauguration of the Jamalpur jagriti, for example, he gave a class on the origins and development of different major languages that lasted nearly two hours. As usual, he sat on a wooden cot with a blackboard and a piece of chalk. Some twenty-five Margis sat in front of him and watched as he traced the development of Sanskrit, Chinese, Russian, and other classical languages through a period of several millennia, translating sentences from one language to another on the chalkboard and showing the links between related languages.

On another occasion, he gave a long discourse on the mechanisms whereby different animals and insects protect themselves by emitting foul odors, the relationship between those emissions and their hormonal secretions, and how a human being's thoughts and emotions affect his body's odor by stimulating certain specific hormonal secretions, depending on the nature of those thoughts and emotions.

These classes, however, were different. Baba asked the Margis to take careful notes and informed them that these notes would be compiled into a textbook of Ananda Marga philosophy to which he would give the name *Idea and Ideology*. The classes lasted from May 27 to June 5. They were conducted primarily in English with occasional explanations in Hindi. Ram Tanuk Singh, acknowledged as the fastest writer among them, took notes along with several others. After each lecture they compared their notes, edited them, and presented them to Baba for additions and corrections.

Five years of DMC discourses and eight volumes of *Subhasita Samgraha* had already provided an extensive textual base for the spiritual philosophy of Ananda Marga. But Baba had yet to dictate a manuscript that contained all the fundamental tenets of that philosophy in one concise and definitive text, as had been tradition throughout the five-thousand-year existence of Indian philosophical systems. *Idea and Ideology* would serve as that text, eighty-two densely packed pages in which Baba would explain in a precisely honed philosophical language everything from the creation of the universe to the origin of life. As with *Elementary Philosophy*, many of the terms and ideas were similar to those of the dominant schools of Indian thought, especially Kapil's Sankhya and Patanjali's Yoga Darshan, but as usual Baba reinvented those terms and ideas in a way that gave birth to an entirely new understanding, an interpretation of life and the universe so modern, so rational and scientific in character, that it became obvious that among his goals was the creation of a text that would project spiritual philosophy into the future while at the same time preserving its link to the past and the birth of human spirituality on the Indian subcontinent. The title of the book came from the chapter entitled "Psycho-spiritual parallelism," and his explanation of the two words "idea" and "ideology" summed up the underlying spirit of the text:

> In the end, when [the mind's] wavelength will, as well, become infinite, and those waves will also flow in a straight line, the mind will get transformed into the *átman* [consciousness or soul]. This state is called samadhi. Here the psychic waves have attained a parallelism with the spiritual waves of the átman. This psycho-spiritual parallelism is known as "idea" or *bháva*. When this *bháva* or idea is conceived on the psychic level, it is "ideology." Ideology, therefore, is the conception of idea and nothing else. Hence when we call some materialistic or political principles of a person, party, nation

or federation an "ideology," it is a wrong use of the term. "Ideology" involves in it a spiritual sense; it is an inspiration which has a parallelism with the Spiritual Entity.[3]

As Baba generally did when he was teaching class, he gave frequent demonstrations to illustrate his points. In one of the afternoon sessions, after explaining the workings of the crude, subtle, and causal minds,[4] and what happens to the mind after death, he called Dasarath to the front. Baba reached out with his stick and touched him between the eyebrows at the seat of the *ajina* chakra. Then he asked him what he saw. Dasarath replied that he was seeing many small balls of light of different colors. They were blinking and moving around and congregating near different people. Baba explained that these small balls of light were bodiless minds.

"After death the unit mind moves around searching for a congenial environment until it encounters a proper body where it can take rebirth. If your vision were subtle enough, you would see that there are actually thousands of unit minds moving nearby. If you are happy, then those unit minds whose fundamental nature or characteristic wavelength reflects happiness will gravitate toward you. That will increase your feelings of happiness. If you are in a sad mood, then those unit minds that are sad by nature will be drawn toward you, and they will make you sadder. If you are in a negative frame of mind, then the negative minds will come near you and reinforce your negativity. If you are positive, then positive minds will gravitate toward you and reinforce your positivity. It depends on your mind, on your own nature."

Some of the philosophical concepts presented in *Idea and Ideology* were modern redefinitions of ideas first presented thousands of years ago, such as the interplay between the three fundamental causal forces: *sattva*, the sentient force, *rajas*, the mutative force, and *tamas*, the static force. Others were making their first appearance on the stage of Indian philosophy. Among these was Baba's explanation of the origin of life, an explanation that had long been the pursuit of both science and philosophy. After showing in intricate detail how pure consciousness passes through a process of involution, transforming itself into mind and from mind into matter, resulting in the creation of structural bodies whose integrity is maintained through a balance between the resultant interial and exterial forces, he showed how this process of involution reaches a zenith point wherein its very momentum, by reaching its apex, pulverizes portions of the material body. In this process of pulverization, those portions are transformed back into the crudest form of ectoplasm,[5] thus initiating the process of evolution in which mind, already inherent in matter, begins the journey of returning to its original state—pure consciousness.

> Here is the specialty of the philosophy of Ananda Marga over other philosophies, explaining by a logical and analytical theory that mind

is a creation of matter. This view is also supported by the materialistic schools of thought. But materialist philosophers fail to explain further, as they fail in explaining the rudimental cause of matter. Ananda Marga philosophy penetrates deeper into the ultimate cause of all the manifested effects and enunciates that matter is the metamorphosed form of Purushottama—the Nucleus Consciousness existing as the noumenal cause. Thus, as a result of clash within the material structure, a subtle base is created and this in turn gives rise to the formation of crude mind or unit citta, which has neither the ego ("I do" or second mental subjectivity) nor the first mental subjectivity ("I am").[6]

Also presented for the first time in Indian philosophy was Baba's explanation of how the seed of creation sprouts due to an imbalance in the three forces of Prakriti surging within the non-manifest, infinite consciousness. During the discussion of this elusive topic, Baba mentioned that sadhakas reach a stage where they feel that the entire creation emanates from them and is absorbed back into them again. They feel "I alone exist." When Baba finished his explanation, Acharya Indradev Gupta complained that such ideas were very difficult to follow. "It would help if you could give a practical demonstration," he said. Suddenly Baba's face began to change. It shone brighter and brighter until some of the disciples felt as if they were gazing at the sun. Everyone began experiencing a mental change; a feeling of immense joy swept over them like a tidal wave until everyone felt that they alone existed, that the entire universe existed within them, billowing forth in an eternal cycle of creation and dissolution. Then Baba opened his hands into *varabhaya mudra*. While the disciples remained absorbed in trance, Baba slipped on his shoes and walked back home. No one offered him his shoes, as was the custom, or accompanied him to his house. When the disciples finally recovered their normal consciousness, they were surprised to see the empty cot in front of them.

The final classes that Baba gave were on social philosophy, the final two of eleven chapters. Just as the nine chapters on spiritual philosophy began with the cycle of creation, the *brahma chakra*, the chapters on social philosophy began with the social cycle, or *samaj chakra*, expanding upon a theory he had introduced in his first official discourse, "The Gradual Evolution of Society." In his explanation of the social cycle, Baba traced the development of human society through the evolution of four dominant psychological classes.[7] The first of these, which he refers to as the *shudra* class, were those who survived through manual labor, characteristic of the first primitive societies. He pointed out that neither the sense of acquisition nor intellectual exploitation existed in that age. "Though life was brute, it was not brutal."[8]

Gradually the leadership of those formative societies passed into the hands of those who excelled through physical strength and personal valor. He referred to them as *kshattriyas*, or the warrior class. With the rise of the kshattriyas, the importance of the family developed and leadership tended to become hereditary.

As society developed further, the role of the intellect became more and more prominent. "A reference to the mythology of any ancient culture reveals numberless instances where the hero of the day had to acquire specific knowledge from teachers. Subsequently this learning was not confined to the use of arms only, but extended to other spheres, such as battle-craft, medicine and forms of organization and administration, so essential for ruling any society. Thus the dependence on superior intellect increased day by day, and in the course of time real power passed into the hands of such intellectuals."[9] These intellectuals he referred to as *vipras*, and their age of dominance, the *vipran* age. Here a hereditary superiority became difficult to maintain and so the vipras, in order to maintain their power, "actively tried and prevented others from acquiring the use of the intellect by imposing superstitions and rituals, faiths and beliefs, and even introducing irrational ideas (the caste system of Hindu society is an example) through an appeal to the sentiments of the mass. This was the phase of human society in the Middle Ages in the greater part of the world."[10]

This continued exploitation, and the necessity for the collection and transfer of goods in a more complex society, led to the rise of a fourth psychological class, the *vaeshyas*, loosely translated as capitalists, i.e. those who control the means of production and distribution. It was in this era, Baba said, that human exploitation reached its zenith. The psychology of acquisition stimulated the development of a psychology of exploitation and reduced a majority of the society to shudras, whatever might be their actual psychology.

After discussing the rotation of this cycle from one class to another through the processes of evolution and revolution, counter-evolution and counter-revolution, Baba called for the rise of a class of sadvipras,[11] those spiritually and ethically perfected persons who, he foresaw, would one day assume responsibility for guiding the *samaj chakra* through successive cycles without allowing the exploitation of the dominant class to crystallize. When necessary, these sadvipras would apply force—intellectual, political, or physical, depending on the class in power—to ensure that the greater mass of human beings would not suffer the pervasive social exploitation that has been their lot throughout the course of recorded history. In short, he proposed that the best and the wisest among us guide society, rather than allowing it to be bent to the will of vested interests.

In the final chapter, "The Cosmic Brotherhood," Baba reiterated that human society is one family and must be treated as such. He followed this with a detailed discussion of four objective goals that must be attained in order for this sentiment to take root: A common philosophy of life, a single constitutional structure, a common penal code, and the availability (production, supply, and purchasing capacity) of the minimum essentials of life for all. Baba was careful to differentiate his approach from unsuccessful theories of the past, such as Marxism, which failed to properly account for human psychology.

> Every human being has certain minimum requirements, which he or she must be guaranteed. Guaranteed availability of food, clothing, medical assistance and housing should be arranged, so that human beings may be able to utilize their surplus energy (energy until now engaged in procuring the essentialities of life) in subtler pursuits. Side by side, there should be sufficient scope for providing other amenities of the progressive age. To fulfill the above responsibilities, enough purchasing capacity should be created. If the supply of requirements be guaranteed without any condition of personal skill and labor, the individual may develop the psychology of idleness. The minimum requirements of every person are the same but diversity is also the nature of creation. Special amenities should therefore be provided so that the diversity in skill and intelligence is fully utilized and talent is encouraged to contribute its best toward human development.[12]

Such a guarantee presupposed the necessity of a ceiling on the acquisition and accumulation of wealth.

> But the supply in the physical sphere is limited and hence any effort for disproportionate or unrestricted acquisition of physical objects has every possibility of creating a vast majority of 'have not's,' thus hampering the spiritual, mental and physical growth of the larger majority. So while dealing with the problem of individual liberty in the physical sphere, it must not be allowed to cross a limit whereby it is instrumental in hampering the development of the complete personality of human beings; and, at the same time is not so drastically curtailed that the spiritual, mental and physical growth of human beings is hampered.[13]

Baba summed up the chapter in these words: "Thus, the social philosophy of Ananda Marga advocates the development of the integrated personality of the individual, and also the establishment of a world fraternity, inculcating in human psychology a cosmic sentiment."[14] He then gave a name to the new philosophy: Prout, the Progressive Utilization Theory. Those who advocated this theory, he said, would be called "Proutists."

When Baba finished his final lecture, he instructed Pranay to send a message to Shashi Rainjan that the time had finally arrived for him to answer the question that Shashi had posed two years earlier. The Margis then set to work preparing the manuscript. One evening on his way to the tiger's grave, a few days after the completed manuscript had been sent to the United Press in

Bhagalpur, Baba stopped at the railway crossing and asked a disciple to run back to the jagriti to fetch some paper, a pencil, candles, and matches. When the disciple returned and met the group at the tiger's grave, Baba dictated the five fundamental principles of Prout.[15] He told the Margis present that these principles would in the future serve as the basis for the creation of a sadvipra society. Then he sent Vaedyanath to Bhagalpur by the night train with instructions to bring those pages to the press first thing in the morning and add them to the end of *Idea and Ideology*.

In September, Baba went to Motihari and gave a seminar on Prout philosophy for students. Sujit Kumar and Ram Tanuk took notes and presented those notes to Baba for correction. During the seminar, Sujit asked Baba if these ideas would be confined only to books.
"Why are you asking?"
"Because I am frustrated with the present situation in society."
"Just wait," Baba said. "You will find everything you desire in Ananda Marga."
When the seminar was finished, Baba conducted DMC and then requested Indradev Gupta to form a students group, the first official organ of Prout, to which he gave the name Universal Proutist Students Federation, or UPSF. The following month, Baba held the First Conference of Proutists in Jamalpur, further expanding Prout philosophy in another series of lectures that he asked the Margis to note down and prepare for publication. The notes from these seminars were published as *Discourses on Prout*, with the exception of a long, elaborate discussion on the seven stages of revolution. This discussion contained Baba's most radical ideas to date, a succinct manual on revolutions and how to conduct them, from the role of intellectuals and artists to the mobilization of mass sentiment. The Margis printed up the condensed notes as a separate booklet entitled *A Discussion*, but Baba eventually banned the book and ordered existing copies to be burned. Acharya Dhruvadeva Narayana was carrying Baba's umbrella on their way to Baba's quarters when Baba explained the reasons for his decision.
"People kill snakes because their bite might prove fatal. But what about snake eggs? They cannot harm anyone. Why do people destroy them then? Because it is from the egg that the snake emerges. So those who recognize snake eggs destroy them as soon as they see them. Similarly, your organization is in the form of an egg, and those who recognize it for what it is will try to smash it and destroy it. You must exercise extreme caution in this regard."
The students who attended these seminars went back to their respective universities and began organizing UPSF chapters. With the fervor of youth, they started preaching the new philosophy on campuses all over Bihar, and afterward into U.P. and West Bengal. By the middle of 1960, they had begun the publication of two monthly journals, which they sold on campuses throughout

Northern India: one in English, entitled *Education and Culture*, and one in Hindi, entitled *Yuga ki Pukar* (The Call of the Age). For the first time, they had a concrete social platform through which to channelize their energies, and thereafter, whenever they came to Jamalpur, Baba encouraged them to work for Prout. The dreams they harbored of changing society now seemed to be within their grasp with the birth of Prout, propagated, as Baba wrote, "for the happiness and welfare of all."

XXII

To The Patriots

A sadhaka is verily a soldier. The pricks of thorns on the difficult path signify one's progress. The collective welfare of the universe is the crown of laurels of one's victory.[1]

In October 1959, during the Durga Puja holidays, Baba conducted a DMC in Kirnahar, a large village in Birbhum District, a few kilometers from Indas where Sachinandan had organized a DMC two years earlier. The DMC was held in the local high school. As he had done the previous year in Amra, Baba asked the Margis to stage a Kabigan performance during the first night. In the afternoon, he called a group of Margi artists together and explained to them why Kabigan was such an ideal vehicle for prachar in the village life of Bengal. Then he coached them on how to present the ideology within the context of the art form. About nine o'clock, the musicians gathered outside and began beating the drums, a signal to all the villages within earshot that a Kabigan was about to take place. The villagers, who by then had finished their dinners, followed the drums to the open area chosen for the performance. The artists split into two parties and began staging a musical debate, firing improvised questions and answers back and forth at one another in the form of traditional melodic stanzas, each party with their own instrumentalists supporting the singing debaters. One party represented Ananda Marga ideology; the other represented the old rituals. Over five thousand people from the surrounding villages turned up for the performance, which lasted until well after dawn. As in Amra the year before, the local villagers would continue to talk about it for months afterward, often singing the songs they heard that night as they worked in the fields.

During the DMC program, the high school grounds were roped off and only Margis were allowed to enter, but loudspeakers were placed outside so that interested villagers could listen to Baba's discourses. This created a reaction in the large zamindar family that owned vast tracts of land in the area and controlled most village affairs,[2] especially when they insisted on speaking to Baba but were not allowed. On the evening of the second day, while Baba was doing sadhana before his discourse, some smoke bombs exploded in his room. When the disciples burst through Baba's door immediately afterward, they found him standing on his cot, engulfed by the smoke that filled the room. Baba assured them that he was not hurt and indicated that the bombs had been thrown in through the open window. The organizers held a hurried meeting, and while Baba gave his discourse they conducted a rapid investigation. All evidence pointed toward several younger members of the zamindar family. When they reported this to Baba after his discourse, he explained to the angry Margis that this was the zamindar family's reaction after being excluded from the DMC. "We have a system," Baba told them, "and we cannot go against this system, but we can invite some representatives to come and meet me." When Kshitij and others objected, Baba said, "There are good people among them, and when we do prachar here in the future some of them will come forward."

The next day, some of the elder members of that family came to apologize for the incident, and the invitation was extended to them. A short while later, they were ushered into Baba's room where some blankets had been spread for them to sit on. Baba politely requested them to ask him whatever they wished but no one said anything. "Whatever you would like to know, I would be happy to tell you," Baba continued, but no one uttered even a single word. "Well then, if you have any questions in the future, there are very knowledgeable acharyas in this area who will be more than happy to answer them." Afterward, when the other members of their family and prominent members of the village questioned them, all they would say was, "He is a good man; we should leave him alone and not disturb him."

The next morning Baba announced unexpectedly that he would give his DMC talk at ten a.m. instead of at night as originally scheduled. All Margis, without exception, were to leave by the afternoon train. Rushed preparations were made for Baba's discourse and after lunch the Margis left as instructed.

After their return to Jamalpur, a group of senior disciples held a meeting to discuss matters of Baba's security. The incident in Kirnahar was relatively minor, but with Baba's emerging reputation as a social activist, it was evident they could not go any longer without making some arrangements for his protection. They decided to organize a group of volunteers to act as bodyguards during field walks and DMCs. In addition, the volunteers could also provide security for the Margis during collective functions—as the number of people attending programs continued to increase, so did the possibility of unforeseen disturbances. They brought the proposal to Baba, who told them that the Margi's decision would be his decision. They named the new group VSS, Vishva Shanti Sena, the universal peace force; Baba soon amended it to Volunteer Social Service, preserving the same initials. He also gave instructions that the volunteers should be given training in disaster relief and other types of social service activities, in addition to security training. Nityananda was elected commander-in-chief, and a training camp was planned for December in Ranchi before the scheduled DMC, during which the new wing would be officially inaugurated.

In the meantime, a DMC was held in Gorakhpur in November. Afterward Baba was invited by the Allahabad University Department of Philosophy to give a lecture for faculty and graduate students. It was the only time in Baba's life that he would give such a public lecture. The topic was "Mind and Vital Energy." The head of the department, R. N. Kaul, was so impressed by the talk that after Baba left the stage he told the audience that in his opinion Anandamurti was one of the three greatest personalities to ever walk the soil of India.

In early December, the volunteers met in Bhagalpur for a training session with Margi members of the Bihar Military Police, including Chandranath, who was superintendent of the BMP training center in nearby Nathnagar. Baba arrived in Bhagalpur one evening during the training. The next morning Chandranath brought him to the parade grounds shortly before sunrise. As the sun inched toward the horizon, the new volunteers marched in front of Baba in the chill air. He took their salute from the dais, then came down the steps and inspected them from one end to the other. When he was finished with the inspection, he gave a short talk, offering some words of encouragement and telling them that they should use their life to do service to others. For this, they should keep their bodies healthy, eat well, and stay physically fit.

A few weeks later, a seven-day VSS camp began in Ranchi with approximately fifty volunteers attending from different parts of India. A strict routine was instituted for the camp with set times for collective meditation, ideology classes, and training sessions. Collectively, they drew up a code of discipline for the volunteers, a list of duties, and worked on a design for the VSS uniform and the VSS flag. Baba visited the camp on the opening day and gave an informal talk. As one Margi who attended recounted, "It seemed as if a lion was roaring when he spoke. The wave that passed through us made us feel that we could have jumped from the tallest tree had Baba wanted. It was *vira bhava*.[3] He told us that we would be benefitted by the battle for dharma, no matter what happened. If we died, then we would get liberation, and if we survived, then we would enjoy the victory of dharma. The next day we went to the Ranchi field and Baba took our salute beneath the flag."

After leaving the camp, Baba stopped in Barhi for lunch where he met Ram Bahadur. Ram Bahadur was on his way to the camp and requested Baba to send a message for the volunteers. The message Baba wrote out would, for many of his disciples, embody the spirit of VSS:

> As a soldier you must not search for worldly pleasure or comfort. Be ready for all sorts of sufferings. Let suffering be your asset. Suffering will help you in establishing the sadvipra samaj. You must not argue, you must not think twice. You should do or die. I do not want to see the face of my defeated sons and daughters in flesh and blood.
>
> Yours affectionately,
> Baba

From then on, at least one volunteer would always be present with Baba during larger programs, such as DMC. The free access that the Margis had had to Baba, especially in Jamalpur, was slowly becoming a thing of the past. Not all of the disciples liked it, but everyone understood its necessity. As the new decade was ushered in, so was a new stage in the development of Ananda Marga, as Baba prepared his disciples to step more and more into the public eye.

Before the VSS camp, Baba visited Ranchi for a few days and gave General Darshan for the Margis in Birla Boarding. The program began with Natkat Kedar performing arati and singing a devotional song to welcome Baba.

> Baba, come into the temple of my heart and unveil to me your face
> If you go from here it will become a lonely wasteland
> Our relationship is just like that of spark and fire
> It is you who are burning in this body like a flame
> Come, come into my heart.

The Margis began weeping and the devotional fervor continued unabated for the next four days. In the meantime, a large tent was erected on the grounds of the Ranchi jagriti, which was by then nearing completion. Baba inspected the construction and conducted DMC under the tent. After the DMC, Akhori brought his car to take Baba back to Jamalpur. Kshitij sang a song about the loneliness of Braj after Krishna's departure, and the Margis began crying so bitterly that they lay down in front of Baba's car and refused to let him leave. Baba himself started weeping softly and had to wipe the tears with his handkerchief. He requested Kshitij not to sing any more; otherwise, he said, he would not be able to control himself. "Don't cry," he told everyone. "I will be back soon. In the meantime, work sincerely for the mission."

Eventually the new volunteers were able to convince the Margis to clear the road so Baba could leave, but the weeping continued even after Baba's car had disappeared from sight. A few days later, Baba informed Pranay that the Margis in Ranchi were still in an abnormal state, crying and unwilling to eat. He asked him to go there for a week to console them, which he did, but only with partial success. In early February, Baba returned to Ranchi. Only then did the Margis return to normal.

On the first of January, Baba gave his bi-annual RU address, this time as part of the Progressive Writer's Conference, which was organized at Jamalpur under the aegis of RU. It was entitled "To the Patriots" and was published shortly thereafter as a separate book, as had been the case with *Problem of the Day*. The discourse began with a historical analysis of the factors that gave rise to the nation state. It focused primarily on the long history of the Indian subcontinent and the rise and fall of different nations within the subcontinent over the course of various millennia. After showing that the first true expression of pan-Indian nationalism arose due to the creation of anti-British exploitation sentiment, Baba analyzed the fundamental mistakes made by Indian leaders during the decades of the freedom movement and the years immediately following independence.

> When, as a result of anti-British sentiment, the Indian nation was formed in the nineteenth century, the then leaders of India should have started a struggle for economic independence instead of launching a political movement. All Indians could have fought together unitedly, there being no Hindu, Muslim, Punjabi, or Marathi feelings in this economic struggle, and as a result an anti-exploitation sentiment could have been developed in India. This sentiment could have made Indians stronger. If there had been no fight for political independence, the fear that Muslims would have to remain under the suzerainty of the Hindus after the independence of India could not have crept into their minds. In the absence of Hindu phobia, there would have been no demand for the homeland of the Muslim nation, and when India would have gained economic independence, Hindus and Muslims would have lived together as brothers and sisters in an undivided India. The fight for economic independence would have brought political independence also. There might have been some delay in it, but political independence would have surely come.[4]

Baba then accused the leaders of that time of purposely avoiding the struggle for economic independence for several reasons, one being that they themselves were members of the bourgeois class and had a vested interest in keeping capitalism alive. He analyzed the mistakes they committed during the formation of the new nation and made a sobering prediction: "The little bond of unity which existed in Indian society is going to be spoilt by the unwise actions of these leaders. The three great lapses which are going to destroy the unity of India are the effort to demarcate provincial boundaries on a linguistic basis; the question of national language; and the use of local languages as the medium of instruction in higher education."[5] After analyzing in detail the problems inherent in the governmental policies taken by the new nation in these three areas, Baba proposed his solutions for the creation of a strong and exploitation-free India. As usual, the spotlight shone on the question of economic liberation. "Most of the people in India are poverty-stricken. They want to be free from exploitation. Political independence has no value for them if it cannot give them economic independence."[6]

After pointing out that anti-exploitation sentiment cannot be sustained forever, Baba ended his talk on a spiritual note, reflective of the spiritual basis of his social philosophy: "One Cosmic Ideology will have to be propagated and that ideology is that one Supreme Entity—the Cosmic Entity—is the goal of all living beings. This spiritual sentiment will keep human beings united for all time to come. No other theory can save the human race."[7]

Not long after this discourse, Baba launched a new movement aimed at addressing some of the problems he had pointed out in his discourse and in Prout classes, especially one that he felt quite strongly about—the partition of Bengal. One day he called Nityananda and asked him to begin setting up a new organization that would have no link with Ananda Marga. He gave it the name *Amra Bengali*, "We are Bengalis," and explained that it would focus on combating the various types of exploitation affecting the Bengali people. Its long-term goal would be the reunification of the sundered Bengal (now West Bengal and Bangladesh) into a politically and economically independent region. He told Nityananda and Balai-da, who agreed to be its first secretary, that one day East and West Bengal would be reunited, and that Amra Bengali would play a critical role in that process. Though the progress of Amra Bengali would be slow during the first years of its existence, it would gradually gather steam and become a well-known and influential movement in Bengal in the years to come.

Baba's frank undressing of the mistakes made by Indian leaders in the recent past, many of them still in power at the time, and his unforgiving analysis of the present government's policies, served not only as an added chapter to his newly disseminated Prout teachings but also as a reminder to the Margis why the creation of VSS and the new security measures surrounding Baba were an idea whose time had come. While the rest of *To the Patriots* was dedicated to Baba's proposals for rectifying the problems engendered by the ill-conceived policies of India's leaders, the sting of his criticisms was not easily overlooked, nor did it pass unnoticed by the young Proutists who were looking to Baba for guidance on the path of social reform. Throughout its history, India had shown itself to be all-embracing in its acceptance of spiritual teachers, but much less welcoming when it came to social revolutionaries. The combination of the two had never been seen before to any appreciable extent, and already some of the more farsighted disciples were beginning to grow concerned over what the future might bring.

XXIII

A Family Relationship

While doing as per his desire, one should always remember: that Supreme Entity is not the boss; that Supreme Entity is the loving Father. The relationship is not official; the relationship is purely personal.[1]

As THE NEW decade began, the spiritual lives of most disciples still revolved around seeing Baba in the jagriti, going on field walk, and attending DMC programs whenever they got the chance. When they would see other Margis in the street, they would often embrace each other and shed tears. One day, Baba was talking with Kshitij when he warned him that this devotional phase would not last much longer.

"You will all be sad to see it pass," Baba said.

"But Baba," Kshitij asked, unable to hide his disappointment, "why does this have to happen?"

Baba remained impassive. "After the devotional phase comes the intellectual phase. Without an intellectual revolution, an ideology cannot be established."

Around the same time, Baba made an unannounced trip to Calcutta and stayed with his brother Himanshu in Narkeldanga, close to where Haraprasad was living at the time. In the evening, Baba walked over to Haraprasad's house, knocked on the door, and invited his startled disciple to go for a walk. They walked out to Beliagata Lake and remained there until ten thirty. Before heading back, Baba told Haraprasad, "Now you people have me very close to you, but after a few years you will have to look through binoculars to see me." Haraprasad was shocked to hear this, but he quickly forgot about it. His sentiment echoed that of most Margis at the time. There was no sense worrying about the future when the present was enough to last a lifetime.

The routine in the Olipur jagriti continued much the same as it had been in Rampur Colony. Of the two rooms in the initial construction, one was reserved for Baba. The only piece of furniture it contained was a wooden cot, which was covered with a cotton bed sheet and a pillow. The Margis cleaned the room each day with meticulous care and brought fresh flowers and kept them in a vase near the cot. These daily duties were considered a privilege for some fortunate disciple. A picture of Baba was kept on the cot whenever he was not there, and whatever Margis were present would sit in front of it during the morning and evening hours to sing devotional songs and practice their meditation. On Sundays and holidays, Baba gave General Darshan, and occasionally on weekday evenings if the weather did not permit him to go to the field. From time to time, he gave evening classes there for acharyas and Margis. On rare occasions, he also stopped by in the morning to take care of organizational work before continuing on to the office, a practice that grew more and more frequent as the sixties wore on and the organization continued to grow.

On days that Baba was expected for General Darshan, the Margis would arrive early and sing devotional songs in front of his cot until he arrived. Then either Pranay or Dasarath, or whoever was serving as his personal assistant at the moment, would direct the Margis out of the room. Baba would sit on his cot and complete whatever organizational work was pending. If he wanted to see anyone privately, he would call him. Then his attendants would open the doors and the Margis would file in. Baba would usually chat with them informally for some time and then give a discourse, often accompanied by a demonstration. Afterward the Margis would do pranam, one by one, and Baba would leave for home in the company of a few selected disciples, a number that was soon limited to five. No one else was allowed outside the jagriti gate until well after Baba had left. This rule had been instituted because the Margis had developed the habit of running after Baba into the street, weeping and crying, giving vent to devotional feelings that the neighbors were unable to understand. This created a strange scene that the senior disciples felt was best avoided. Considering Ananda Marga's reputation in Jamalpur at the time, it is easy to understand their concern. Ramchandra, who later took initiation and became an ardent disciple, remembered his impressions of Ananda Marga when he was growing up in Jamalpur:

> I used to fear the name of Ananda Marga when I was young. We used to pass by the Ananda Marga ashram on our way to school. My schoolmates used to say that Ananda Marga was a place of great magic; it was protected by a magic boundary wall and it was dangerous to talk when you were near it. So we used to remain silent whenever we passed by that compound. The word had spread all through Jamalpur that Baba was a great magician. I used to think that if I saw Baba, he could do something to me. So I always tried to avoid seeing him or letting him see me.

During the fifties and early sixties there was no system of recording Baba's General Darshan talks or taking notes, nor did Baba re-dictate them afterward, as he did with his DMC and RU talks. Occasionally, some interested devotee would take notes of his own volition, but the vast majority of those discourses have been lost.[2] In March 1963, one devotee took notes during a General Darshan. The following excerpts show the informal nature of Baba's General Darshan talks at that time. In the preface to his notes, this disciple explained that while it was too difficult to preserve Baba's exact words, the spirit of what Baba said was faithfully reproduced.

> As Baba took his seat, he said, "In the Mahabharata period we find two persons coming quite close to Shrii Krishna—Arjuna and Sudama. Both were greatly devoted to him. Now tell me, which of the two is the greater devotee of Shrii Krishna, and whom would you choose as the ideal of your life?" One by one, the persons present there expressed their views . . . when all had expressed themselves, Baba said, "Devotion means unconditional self-surrender. One who has more of it is a greater devotee than one who has less. Arjuna and Sudama were both great devotees, but while comparing their devotion by this yardstick we have to say that Sudama was a greater devotee . . . Arjuna refused to fight when Shrii Krishna asked him to do so. This shows that Arjuna did not have full faith in, and complete surrender to, Shrii Krishna . . . On the other hand we notice a complete surrender by Sudama. He never desired anything from Krishna, his friend who could have given him anything and everything . . . Even when his wife forced him to go to Shrii Krishna to request him to remove his poverty, he went to him but didn't ask for a thing . . . Now whom should you take as your ideal? Neither of the two, neither Arjuna nor Sudama. Neither of the two is perfect, so how can you take anything imperfect as the ideal of your life? Your ideal is to be perfect, so your ideal should be the Lord and the Lord alone. No one else should be your ideal.
>
> "And if he finds that you have the potential to do his work, but you are lacking in self-surrender and you have not foregone your ego, then in such a case he will first create circumstances in which your ego will be forced to yield and surrender. Only after this will the Lord choose you to be the medium for his work. This was the case with Arjuna. Arjuna had the potential, but he also had some ego left in him. Shrii Krishna first made him surrender by showing him his cosmic form, and then alone was Arjuna chosen to be his medium."

In one of these General Darshans, Baba asked everyone if they wanted to hear the cosmic sound.[3] Their response was an enthusiastic yes. Baba asked for the doors and windows to be closed. He had the women sit on one side and the men on the other. Then he asked everyone to begin meditating. "Those who do not hear the sound," he said, "should raise their hands but remain silent." A few disciples raised their hands but put them down again a few moments later.

Sakaldev, a lawyer from Muzaffarpur, started hearing the beautiful sound of a flute. The longer he meditated, the more it grew in intensity. But at one point he felt a sudden urge to open his eyes. When he did, he was surprised to see Baba leaving. The rest of the Margis were deep in their meditation. Some had already fallen into trance. Afraid that he might never hear that sound again, he ran after Baba and caught up with him just outside the gate. When he reached down to touch Baba's feet, Baba said, "Sakaldev, what do you want? *Mukti? Moksha?*"

"Baba, I just want to be with you."

"*Tatastu*," Baba replied. So be it.

On another occasion, Pashupati was massaging Baba in his room while the other Margis sat on the floor around his cot. Baba's mood turned serious. He asked everyone if they wanted to witness divine effulgence. Naturally, everyone was eager to. "Okay," Baba continued, "I will show you one percent. You will not be able to stand more than that." Suddenly the room was filled with a sweet, bright white light; the joy they felt was so intense that everyone was forced to close their eyes. After a few moments the light disappeared. "You see?" Baba said. "And this is only one percent."

Though not even one percent of the devotees' experiences with Baba in those early days has been preserved in writing, that which has is enough to dazzle the eyes of anyone who tries to look back at that period and imagine what it was like to be around Baba in the days prior to the "intellectual phase," before the organization grew to become a global mission with hundreds of thousands of disciples. The Jamalpur jagriti was the scene of many of those experiences, the one place perhaps, along with the tiger's grave, that best evokes the aura of that period. What follows now are a few incidents that took place in the jagriti around the beginning of the decade.

Madhan was a high school student in Bhagalpur at that time. His family disapproved of Ananda Marga and didn't allow him to go to Jamalpur to see Baba, so he used to sneak out whenever he could and make the trip without permission. Late one afternoon, he slipped out of the house unnoticed and went to the station to board an express train to Jamalpur, a journey of an hour and a half. When he arrived at the jagriti, he requested Pranay for permission to go on field walk but the list was already full. Bitterly disappointed by his ill fortune, he went into Baba's room and sat for meditation. Instead of meditating, however, he began praying to Baba to make it rain, knowing that if it rained, Baba and the disciples would have to come back to the ashram. In the next room there was an axe on the wall. When he remembered this, Madhan mentally threatened Baba that he would kill himself with the axe if Baba didn't come to see him. Then he started fighting directly with Prakriti, insisting that she make it rain so that Baba would come back.

After an hour of this supposed meditation, it started to rain. A short while later, Madhan heard a commotion at the gate signaling Baba's arrival. Rather than run to meet Baba, as most of the Margis normally did, he kept "meditating," thinking, If Baba really loves me he will come and look for me rather than making me search for him. A few moments later, he heard Baba asking, "Where is Madhan?" Madhan felt a thrill. He got up from his meditation. The first thing Baba said when he saw him was, "What do you think you are doing! You earn fifty paisa and you go ahead and spend one rupee. Do you understand?"

"No, Baba."

"Whatever you achieve in spiritual practice, you should not spend it. If you waste your power fighting Prakriti, or demanding something that you should not be asking for, then you are sure to meet your downfall. Do you want to leave Ananda Marga? Do you want to deviate from the spiritual path?"

"No, Baba."

"I don't want that either. So from now on, do not utilize your spiritual power in such a foolish way. Do you understand?"

"Yes, Baba, but I have to face so many problems to be able to come and see you. My family won't give me permission to come, and then I get here and Pranay-da won't let me go on field walk."

Baba held up his hand. "Okay, okay, but promise me you won't do this anymore."

Baba inquired politely about Madhan's family and the local Margis. Finally he asked him if he had money to get back home. He didn't. Baba reached into his pocket and handed him a two-rupee note.

One day Gwarda was visiting his maternal uncle's brother Ratu, and the talk turned to Ananda Marga. Gwarda tried to convince his relative of his guru's greatness, but Ratu was less than receptive. "Look," Ratu said, "there is one sure sign that all great spiritual gurus have. The big toe of their right foot is abnormally large. Does your guru have this?" Gwarda didn't know what to say, so he remained silent. "Well then," Ratu continued, "unless he has an abnormally large big toe, I can't accept him as a spiritual guru."

A few days later, Gwarda was sitting in the jagriti with several Margi friends, chatting about Indian cinema, when Baba showed up unexpectedly. After everyone did pranam, Baba asked the boys what they were gossiping about. No one said anything; they were reluctant to admit that they had been discussing films in the sanctified environment of the jagriti.

"I think you were gossiping about the cinema," Baba said with a smile on his face. "Is it not?" He turned and addressed Gwarda directly. "Okay, then tell me the name of the film in which this song is sung." Baba sang the first lines from a popular song, but neither Gwarda nor any of the other boys could remember the film. "What?" Baba said. "You all are experts in Hindi cinema. I don't see a single film. Try another one." Baba sang a few lines from another song, but again no one could guess what film it was from. Then Baba turned again to Gwarda.

"I can see that the name of the film is coming to you, but you can't quite catch it. Do one thing. Catch the big toe of my right foot and see if that helps."

Baba stuck out his right foot and Gwarda caught hold of the big toe. As soon as he did, he forgot all about the film. All he could remember was his relative's challenge. He was startled to see that Baba's big toe appeared to be abnormally large.[4] The other Margi boys asked him if he remembered the name of the film. "Yes, yes, I remember," he said, but he was so engrossed in Baba's toe that he didn't say anything else. After Baba left, he ran straight to Ratu's house to tell him that he was right; Baba's big toe was just as he said it should be.

Even after Pratibha took initiation, she continued to perform her traditional Hindu rituals at home, but instead of worshipping Krishna, she replaced her old idols with a photo of Baba. Each day she would do her traditional arati, waving her tray with its lamp and its incense before the altar with Baba's picture. Once, after returning from the jagriti, she scolded her daughters for not lighting the lamps on the altar, but this time her daughters refused to indulge her. "Now that you've joined Ananda Marga, you shouldn't do this any more," they told her. "This is not what Baba teaches. It seems your bad samskaras are not over with yet."

Pratibha became annoyed. "Just because I've joined Ananda Marga doesn't mean I have to give up my old ways. I can still do arati if I like. And to think, I have to hear this from my own daughters. Well, that is just too much."

Pratibha lit the lamps herself and began her arati. The next day she returned to the ashram to attend the Sunday darshan. Baba's talk was entitled "Worship, Ritual and Praise." During the discourse, he began talking about arati. While he was looking toward the women, he said, "Just imagine if you were a god and someone started waving a lighted lamp in front of your face; how would you feel? Wouldn't you feel uncomfortable and ask them to stop? Wouldn't you tell them that your face is burning? Imagine if someone waves incense sticks in front of you; wouldn't you feel suffocated from the smoke? Is it not so? Now imagine how the deity feels."

At that moment, Pratibha turned to the woman next to her and whispered that she had been performing arati just one day earlier in front of Baba's picture. Baba interrupted her whispered conversation. "Yes, Pratibha. I am talking to you. Why are you doing such a thing?"

Pratibha stood up and folded her hands to her chest. "Baba, I won't do it again." She grabbed her ears and started doing tic-tics as punishment,[5] without being told to do so.

Ramtanuka, the wife of Ram Khilavan, used to treat Baba as her son, in the manner of a traditional Hindu mother. She reserved the right to quarrel with Baba whenever he did something that incurred her displeasure, a sense of intimacy that she would pass on to her four daughters, all of whom became ardent devotees. One day she came to Nityananda's quarters for darshan—this was before they had purchased the land for the Jamalpur jagriti. Baba was sitting in the back room with Dasarath and Pranay when she arrived. The rest of the Margis were in the front room, waiting for Baba to come out for darshan. After a short while, Pranay came out and announced that Baba had decided he would not give darshan anymore until the Margis solved the jagriti situation. The Margis were saddened but resigned; they resolved to do something about it as soon as possible. Not so Ramtanuka. When Baba came out of the room and began receiving the pranams of the Margis before heading for home, she rebuked him loudly.

"I have been doing idol worship since I was ten, but I gave it up for your sake when I got initiated. The whole society has gone against me, but I haven't minded. I left them also and gave my whole mind to you. And you say you won't give darshan? Then what have I come to Ananda Marga for? Better you strike my name off the register of Ananda Marga!"

Dasarath tried to calm her down but Baba put his hand on him to stop. "Mother, you are quite correct," he said, like a son being chastised by his mother. He sat down and gave darshan.

Some months later, she attended a darshan in the newly constructed Jamalpur jagriti. When she entered the room, Baba was sitting on the cot with his legs hanging over the side. Also entering the room was a poorly dressed man in his fifties from Darbanga who carried with him a pitcher of water that he had drawn from the well. A couple of Margis, including Bindeshvari, had asked him not to sit close to Baba. They were rather perturbed that someone who looked more like a beggar than a devotee was in the darshan hall at all. But the man did not pay them any heed. He managed to get a seat right in front. Once everyone was settled, he positioned his water pot and reached out with a pair of unsteady hands in an obvious effort to wash Baba's feet. As soon as he reached out his hands, Baba pulled up his feet and sat cross-legged.

When she saw this, Ramtanuka became incensed. "Baba, you put your feet back down right this minute!"

Bindeshvari immediately objected. "This man is a sinner," he told her.

"He may be," she said, "but if a poor sinner cannot get refuge at the Lord's feet, then where will he go for refuge? Baba, you put your feet down or else you might as well go back to the seventh heaven, or wherever it is you came from."

Baba put his feet down and the tearful devotee's wish was fulfilled. Afterward Bindeshvari tried to take her to task for scolding Baba. "You have no idea. This fellow was keeping marijuana in his blanket!"

"Baba may have given you the divine sight," she retorted, "but I only see one thing—the person's devotion for Baba."

One day Ramtanuka prepared a batch of *peras* for Baba, a milk-sweet that, legend has it, Krishna loved as a child. She brought them with her to the jagriti one Sunday and presented them to Baba after he had finished delivering his discourse. "Baba, today I have prepared a special dish; it's something I know you love. You will have to eat all of them. I won't allow you to go without finishing them."

"What have you brought for me, Mother?"

"*Pera*s, Baba."

"Oh, *pera*s. You are quite right. I love *pera*s. But not today, Mother. My mother will have my meal waiting for me when I get home. She would be upset if I spoiled my appetite. I will eat them another time, but not today."

Ramtanuka would not be dissuaded. "No, Baba. You must eat them today."

Finally, in the face of her insistence, Baba relented and accepted one *pera*. "How tasty!" he said with obvious relish. "I have never had a *pera* this tasty." Baba got up to go, but again Ramtanuka insisted he finish the rest of the plate before he leave. "No Mother, no more today," Baba told her, pointing to his stomach. But Ramtanuka would not listen. She continued to insist. "All right," he said, "but you must feed me from your own hand." Delighted by the offer, Ramtanuka took a *pera* and Baba opened his mouth. The *pera*, however, never made it to its destination. She froze in place, her hand still extended, and moments later fell to the ground in trance. Baba calmly got up from his cot and left for home.

When she came out of her trance, the other devotees asked her what had happened. "When Baba opened his mouth to eat the *pera*," she said, "I saw the whole universe—the sun, moon, stars, galaxies—I saw them all. The entire cosmos was dancing in his mouth."

After this experience, she would often lose herself in various states of *bhava* when she saw Baba, sometimes merely upon hearing Baba's name, a state of affairs that continued for months afterward.

Sarala Bihari arrived for her first darshan with Baba in a manner common to many of the female disciples: her husband brought her, and as a proper Hindu wife she could not refuse. She had taken initiation for the same reason a few months earlier in Jaipur, where her husband, Mangal Bihari, was the Deputy Secretary of Finance for the state government of Rajasthan. When it came time for them to take their next vacation, they decided to go to Puri, a popular beach resort on the east coast of India, and one of the important Hindu pilgrimage sites. There they would have an opportunity to perform their worship and enjoy the beaches at the same time. The vacation was planned for two weeks. When Mangal Bihari informed his acharya, Shankarananda, of their plans, Nityananda, who was on tour there, suggested that they stop along the way in Jamalpur and see their guru for the first time, an opportunity that Mangal Bihari was eager to take advantage of.

When the couple arrived in Jamalpur Station, tired after the long journey from Jaipur, they took a rickshaw to the jagriti. They were expecting to find a traditional Indian ashram, large and luxurious, full of flower-lined paths, shady trees, spreading lawns, marble floors, and comfortable accommodations for visiting devotees. What they found instead was a closed gate to what could only be described as a rather ramshackle property, seemingly still under construction, in a poorer section of town. No one was there to receive them or even open the gate. After knocking for a few minutes, one of the neighbors stuck her head out a door and volunteered the information that "they" were all in Monghyr for some program.

Sarala wanted to give up then and there. She suggested to her husband that they find someplace to take a shower and then catch the next train for Puri. But he convinced her that as long as they had taken the trouble to get down in Jamalpur, they might as well continue on to Monghyr. After all, it was only seven kilometers away. They returned to the station and caught a bus that turned out to be full of Margis heading for the DMC program. When they arrived at the DMC site, the first thing they did was to ask where they could find a bathroom to wash up after their long journey. They were directed to some portable bathrooms whose condition so shocked Sarala's sensibilities that she refused to use them. Her aristocratic husband, a bit shocked himself and concerned about his wife, went to talk to the acharyas about an alternative. One of them suggested they take a rickshaw to the nearby Ganges and bathe there. In the end, it seemed like the best solution possible.

When they went to catch a rickshaw, Sarala was startled to see that the rickshaw driver, a tall, dark, bare-chested man, seemed identical to the strange figure she had seen in a troubling dream just before leaving for Puri. When the driver told them he would wait for them while they bathed because they would have difficulties getting a rickshaw back, despite their insistence that it was not necessary, and then disappeared after dropping them off at the DMC site without even collecting his fare, her sense of foreboding increased exponentially.

That evening, Sarala sat in the ladies section for Baba's DMC discourse. The spectacle of so many women making strange noises, crying and weeping, some throwing up their hands, others falling over, made her think that she had landed in a lunatic asylum. But when Baba finally gave his talk, she was so impressed by the philosophy that she overcame her urge to flee the scene at the first opportunity. After the DMC, the acharyas arranged for her and her husband to make the short trip back to Jamalpur in Baba's car. Bindeshvari also went with them. When Bindeshvari leaned over and whispered to her that she was sitting with Shri Krishna, it reinforced her conviction that she was surrounded by madmen. As guests, they were to stay in the jagriti, but as soon as they arrived in Jamalpur, Sarala told her husband that she refused to stay there. She was afraid that if she did, she might go mad like the rest of these people obviously had. After talking to some Margis, Mangal Bihari was able to make arrangements for them to stay with Bindeshvari.

For the next seven days, Sarala refused to go to the jagriti to see Baba. She remained behind at Bindeshvari's house while her husband went on field walk each evening or had Baba's darshan at the jagriti. Each night he came back more and more inspired, and each morning she tried to convince him to leave the next day for Puri. He pleaded for one more day, and she relented, growing more and more annoyed with each passing moment. When the week was about to finish, her husband realized that he would have a domestic revolt on his hands if he put off their departure any longer, so he went to the station and was able to get reservations for Sunday night. The next morning, Sarala agreed to accompany him to the Sunday darshan, relieved that she was finally getting out of there, and they caught a rickshaw for the jagriti. Mangal Bihari was sad that this would be his last darshan for who knew how long, but Sarala was glad that her ordeal would soon be over.

When the rickshaw arrived at the jagriti gate, Mangal Bihari noticed Baba walking unaccompanied up the lane, holding his umbrella aloft to protect himself from the late morning sun. Hurriedly, he told his wife to go and touch Baba's feet while he paid the rickshaw driver. By the time he was done haggling over the price, he saw that Baba and his wife had already disappeared through the jagriti gate. He went in and was somehow able to squeeze into the room where Baba was sitting. Sarala remained with the women crowded outside in the next room, forced to watch Baba through the open door that connected the two rooms, in keeping with the mores of traditional Hindu society which would have mounted a social scandal had women and men been crowded together so tightly in the same room.[6]

It was a hot summer day. Baba's discourse went on for what seemed an eternity to Mangal Bihari, acutely aware of how uncomfortable his wife must be feeling in that heat, sandwiched among a crowd of devotionally maddened females. He knew that the more time that passed, the hotter the reception he would get when he had to face her. When Baba's talk was finally over and the master had passed through the crowd, he went to look for his wife, steeling himself to face her displeasure. Instead, he found her still sitting, her head slumped over and her eyes closed. Surprised, he called her name but didn't get any response. Then he saw the tears streaming silently down her cheeks. Gradually, it dawned on him that his wife was in some kind of a trance. Finally, she whispered that she did not want to open her eyes, the feeling was so sweet. He sat there patiently until she finally opened them. Then he told her softly that they could go now and get ready to leave for Puri. "We are not going anywhere," Sarala told him. "We are staying right here with Baba."

Afterward, Sarala recounted for her husband and others what had transpired when she went to do pranam to Baba outside the gate. After she touched Baba's feet and straightened up, she saw bright effulgence. Within that effulgence, she saw the image of Shiva that she worshipped at home every Sunday. Then the image metamorphosed back into Baba's form, and it seemed as if the entire world were contained within him. "Mother," she heard him say, "you must be feeling hot. Come under the umbrella with me." She ducked under the umbrella and accompanied Baba into the ashram. As they walked in, Baba smiled and told her, "Bindeshvari says that you have gotten your Krishna. Is it so?" Inside the gate, the Margis were waiting to garland Baba. One of them gave her a garland to place around Baba's neck. As she garlanded him, Baba said, "Mother, you have made me like the Shiva of your desires." Baba went into the room and sat on the cot. She took her seat among the women. When she looked at Baba, the room filled with that same bright effulgence until that was all she could see, and she remained in that state until she heard her husband calling her name.

After Sarala and Mangal Bihari returned to Jaipur, they convinced her uncle Tej Karan to take initiation and go to Jamalpur for Baba's darshan. Greatly inspired by their stories of Baba's divine presence and his many miracles, Tej Karan left immediately, after promising to write them every day with an account of his experiences. For nine days he wrote as promised, each letter more discouraged than the previous. He appreciated the spiritual teachings. He admired the rational, scientific bent of Baba's philosophy and enjoyed the cheerful company of the devotees. He described all of this amply in his letters. But he had not seen a single miracle. In the ninth letter, he wrote Mangal Bihari that he was going to give it one more day. If he did not see any miracle, then he would not accept Baba as a divine guru and would return to Jaipur.

That day in darshan Baba looked in his direction and said, "A few people are planning to leave today. Before they leave they want to see a miracle. However, in order to see a miracle, one has to become miraculous oneself." Baba fixed his gaze on Tej Karan. "Tej Karan, you have done nothing in your life to deserve seeing a miracle. Still, I am going to show you one. Come here." Tej Karan came to the front of the room and sat in front of Baba. Baba touched him between the eyebrows at the *ajina* chakra. Immediately he cried out, flung up his arms, and fell back in a state of trance. Baba instructed several acharyas to massage him and give him hot milk when he came out of samadhi. As they massaged him, Tej Karan writhed and wriggled like a snake. This made it difficult for them to grab hold of him. But as they continued the massage, the convulsions gradually abated and he finally became motionless. Afterward he described his experience:

> The moment Baba touched me, an immense light penetrated me and I fell flat. I was in extreme bliss and could feel the kundalini running from *muladhara* to *ajina* like an electric current. People told me that I was crying "Baba, Baba" loudly and throwing my arms and legs, and that he told three acharyas to massage me. I was in this state for about eight hours. It happened at eight in the morning and I remained like that until around five in the afternoon. I kept on singing and crying and feeling the current pass through me. It gradually decreased until I became normal. After that, I wrote to Mangal Bihari that I had

realized that Baba was the Supreme Consciousness. I wrote it on a postcard; it was my last letter. It was such an ineffable experience that I couldn't describe it.

It would take Tej Karan a full month before he would regain his normal consciousness.

In the winter of 1960, a college student by the name of Arun who was studying in Muzaffarpur arrived in Jamalpur for his first darshan.[7] He arrived at the ashram about eight in the evening and had his personal contact, an experience that he would not be willing to share. He would only say that it was the most cherished memory of his life. Afterward, Baba called everybody into the room for darshan. It was quite dark, nearing the time of new moon, and Baba was in a jovial mood. He asked Dasarath, "Do you want to see God?"
"Yes, Baba."
Baba pointed toward the open window and told Dasarath, "See Paramatma in the sky."[8]
"Yes, Baba, I see him," Dasarath replied.
Then Baba told him in succession to see Paramatma in the room, in his shoe, and in the glasses Arun was wearing. Each time, Dasarath replied that he saw the Divine Presence there. "Paramatma is everywhere and you have seen him," Baba said. "Some people think that Paramatma dwells in the seventh heaven. Now that you have seen him, you know that he dwells not only in the farthest sky but that he is everywhere and in everything. Now I will bring the nucleus of this cosmos to this room and you will hear the sound om resonating here."
After a short pause, Baba asked Dasarath if he were hearing the sound.
"Yes, Baba, it is very loud."
"You will continue to hear this sound all through the night," Baba said.
Then Baba pointed toward the open doorway. "Many *siddha*s have entered the room and are congregating there.[9] Look. Do you see them?"
"Yes, Baba. There are many of them."
Baba pointed to one Margi sitting to the side of his cot. "Gaze into his mental plate and see if there is any stain in his mind."
"Baba," Dasarath exclaimed, "his sadhana is so good that there is no stain at all in his mind."
Baba turned toward the Margi and said," Very good, very good, go ahead with your sadhana, with all sincerity and effort, and you will be successful."
For nearly two hours, Baba continued performing similar demonstrations. Finally, Arun was chosen along with Dasarath and several others to accompany Baba to his house. After Baba entered his gate, Arun went up to Dasarath, burning with curiosity, and asked him what he had seen during the demonstration.
Dasarath broke into a broad smile, like an innocent child. "Wherever Baba

pointed, I saw a soothing, milky-white light—in the sky, in Baba's shoe, in the room, in your glasses. I saw the entire world enveloped in that beautiful effulgence. It was everywhere."

At that time, the Jamalpur jagriti did not have a flush toilet but only a service toilet that required frequent cleaning.[10] Once, when the person who regularly cleaned it was absent for several days, it reached such a state that the devotees had to think twice about using it. Jaidhari Pandit, a young disciple from an upper-caste family who was visiting from Motihari, thought it deplorable that such a situation should exist in the place where his guru came every day to meet the devotees. Despite his caste prohibitions, he took it upon himself to clean the toilet.[11] Afterward, he took a bath at the well and changed his clothes, but he was unable to shake the conviction that the foul odor still clung to his body. He sniffed his right hand and then his left, distinctly uncomfortable, sure that he had not gotten rid of it.

At dusk, Baba showed up at the jagriti unexpected and unannounced. It was only when a couple of Margis saw him standing in the courtyard that anyone realized he was there. They started shouting, "Baba has come, Baba has come." This brought Madhav, the jagriti manager, running. After doing pranam, he told Baba that he would make immediate arrangements for General Darshan. "No," Baba told him. "I won't sit for darshan today. But please call Jaidhari and tell him I want to speak to him."

Jaidhari, who was meditating in Baba's room at the time, came running as soon as he was called. After accepting his pranam, Baba asked him to extend his hands. He took Jaidhari's hands in his own and started smelling them. "Jaidhari, what a beautiful fragrance is coming from your hands!" Jaidhari recoiled in embarrassment, thinking that Baba was teasing him for the bad smell, but Baba said, "No, no, it's true Jaidhari. Smell your right hand." Jaidhari smelled his right hand and was stunned to discover a wonderful fragrance coming from it. "Now smell your left hand." He smelled his left hand and discovered a different, indescribably beautiful fragrance. "In fact," Baba continued, "it seems that wonderful fragrances are coming from every part of your body." Jaidhari smelled other parts of his body and in each he discovered a different, beautiful fragrance. He felt exalted by a growing sense of ecstasy. Baba patted his cheek and said, "Good actions always bear good results." Then Baba left the jagriti for home to get ready for his normal field walk.

One of Baba's favorite passages from the Bhagavad Gita, one that he would often quote for the disciples, was, "This maya is insurmountable. But he who has taken shelter in me will surely go beyond the influence of this maya."[12] Many of the disciples took this teaching to heart and came to rely on Baba not only for their spiritual salvation but to rescue them from their mundane difficulties as well. Ram Bahadur Singh was one of these, a Deputy

Superintendent of Police in charge of highway vigilance in Barhi. His refusal to accept bribes or cooperate in any way with the criminal element in that town had made him many enemies, a fact which he would shrug off, saying, "Baba will take care."

In the summer of 1960, Ram Bahadur, who invariably spent his weekends and holidays in Jamalpur, began losing the sight in one eye. He took advantage of his proximity to Baba to request the master's help. "Ram Bahadur," Baba told him, "why are you asking me? You should see an eye specialist and get it properly treated."

Ram Bahadur caught hold of Baba's feet and repeated his request. "Baba, only you can help me. I don't have faith in any doctor."

"Ram Bahadur, stop pestering me. Go see an eye specialist."

This scene repeated itself a number of times as the summer progressed. Finally, when his sight had completely failed in that eye, he went and saw an eye specialist who told him that his problem was due to an untreatable degenerative condition. He caught the next train to Jamalpur. As soon as he had a chance to go into Baba's room, he caught Baba's feet and implored him to restore his eyesight.

"Baba, I saw the doctor just as you told me I should, but he said that he can't do anything for me. Only you can save me."

"Okay, Ram Bahadur. Do one thing. There is a plant growing in your courtyard. If you extract the juice from that plant and apply it to your eye, then you will recover your sight."

Baba explained to him how to recognize the plant and prepare and apply the extract, but Ram Bahadur was not satisfied. "Baba, you should cure me. If you wish it, you can cure me instantly."

An exasperated tone crept into Baba's voice. "I told you how to cure your eye."

"Baba, I will take the medicine, but it is only you who can cure me, not any medicine."

When Ram Bahadur returned home, he extracted the juice from the plant as instructed. After a few days, he started noticing some slight improvement. A couple of days later, Baba passed through Barhi on his way back from a DMC program. As soon as Ram Bahadur heard that Baba had reached, he hurried home from his office to give his pranam. He had already arranged a two-day leave so he could accompany Baba back to Jamalpur.

"Ram Bahadur," Baba asked, "how is your eye now?"

"Baba, it is improving. It is still swollen but I am starting to get some sight back."

"Very good. Then I want you to drive me to Jamalpur."

"But Baba, how can I drive you with my eye is in this condition?"

"Argh! You just sit in the driver's seat and drive." Baba reached out his hand and placed it over Ram Bahadur's eye. Ram Bahadur experienced bright effulgence in the affected eye. When the momentary radiance cleared, he found that his vision was completely restored.

A year or two later, Baba again passed through Barhi on his way back from Ranchi. Ram Bahadur was on duty at the time. When he saw Baba's car, he took advantage of his police authority to stop it and give Baba his pranam.

"How are you doing, Ram Bahadur?" Baba asked. "How is your health?"

"I am fine, Baba," he replied. But the very next day he fell seriously ill and was forced to go on medical leave. Over the next three weeks, he saw doctors in Berili, Kodarma, and Chaibasa, but his condition continued to worsen. Then his brother offered to bring him to Patna, where he would be assured to receive the best treatment possible. Ram Bahadur reluctantly accepted his brother's offer. His wife was afraid to be left alone with the children—Ram Bahadur had made powerful enemies among the local coal mafia, having made it impossible for them to transport stolen coal along the local highways—but he assured her that Baba would take care of them.

Ram Bahadur saw the doctors in Patna, but his condition worsened even further. He began to pray out loud to Baba to be merciful and let him leave his physical body rather than force him to undergo such suffering. His brother was horrified to hear this kind of prayer. "You have a wife and small children," he told him. "Who would look after them? How can you even think such a thing?" After he had calmed his brother down, Ram Bahadur decided to write a letter to Baba to explain his predicament and ask for his help.

A couple of days later, when Baba passed by the jagriti in the morning, he asked Pranay if he had received a letter from Ram Bahadur.

"Yes, Baba. A letter arrived just this morning."

"Read it out to me."

After listening to the letter, Baba dictated a reply in which he told Ram Bahadur that he would be all right. He should not worry. The only remedy he needed was to repeat his ista mantra while lying on his bed, especially at night. There was no need for him to sit up to repeat his mantra.

Ram Bahadur was overjoyed when he received Baba's reply. He started paying more attention to his mantra and from the following day his condition started to improve. When he was completely well again, he took a train back home, having been gone a total of forty days.

When his wife came to receive him at the station, she had a curious tale to tell. At nightfall on the day he'd left, two huge, ferocious-looking black dogs appeared in front of the property and started roaming around the house as if they were on guard duty. At the slightest sound they would begin growling and barking fiercely. This eased her apprehensions about being left alone there with the children. In the morning, she gave the dogs some milk and bread. After that, they never left the premises, not even for a moment.

Ram Bahadur didn't say anything, but he remained thoughtful. When they arrived at the house, she called for the dogs to show her husband but the dogs were no longer there. Ram Bahadur closed his eyes and folded his hands to his chest in a silent pranam. "Baba sent those dogs," he told her. "You see? Baba always takes care."

The dogs were never seen again.

One night, Ramchandra Paswan had to change trains at Barauni Junction, on the north side of the river Ganges. Unfortunately, his connection was not due in until the morning. He found an empty bench on the platform where he hoped to get some rest while he was waiting. It was a hot summer night, so he changed into a pair of shorts and a t-shirt and placed his folded pants and shirt on top of his suitcase below the bench. He wanted very much to be able to catch a few hours of sleep, so he decided to entrust his belongings to Baba. He told Baba mentally that he was too sleepy to stay awake; could he please watch over his luggage while he was taking rest? He closed his eyes and was soon fast asleep. When he woke up in the morning, however, his luggage and his clothes were gone—his money as well, since he had left his wallet inside the suitcase. In a fit of frustration he got angry at Baba. Baba, when I went to sleep, I left you in charge of my belongings. What were you doing? Were you also asleep? Everything I had is gone. How am I going to get home with only a pair of shorts and no money? He dropped his head into his hands, blaming Baba and wondering what he was going to do next. Just then, an elderly man stopped in front of the bench and addressed him. "Why are you blaming your guru for your own carelessness? That's not right. Anyhow, if you run now to the bus stand, you will find the man who has stolen your luggage." The man turned and walked away. Ramchandra jumped up and rushed to the bus stand. When he reached there, he saw a man carrying his suitcase. He started running after him, shouting. The thief ran away and managed to escape, but only after dropping the suitcase.

The next time Ramchandra went to Jamalpur for General Darshan, Baba started talking about how fond the disciples were of testing the guru. "They will go so far as to ask him to guard their luggage so that they can sleep on a railway platform." Looking at Ramchandra, he smiled and said, "If I would ever take a real test of my disciples, not very many would pass."

In one of his Sunday discourses, Baba talked about the five faces of Shiva. He explained the symbolism behind this concept of ancient Indian mythology. In the center is the eternally blissful face of Kalyana Sundaram, beyond thought, beyond manifestation, while the other four, two on each side, show varying degrees of sweetness and sternness, causing the devotee to shed either tears of joy and laughter, or tears of suffering, remorse, and pain. All four are aspects of Rudra, a name of Shiva that means "one who makes others shed tears." In Baba's General Darshans, the disciples experienced all five faces of Shiva and the tears that went with them, from the divine bliss of samadhi to the extreme discomfort of having their ego forcefully powdered down under the all-seeing glare of their guru's eyes. The face on the far left is known as Vama Deva, the fiercest face of Shiva, the one who metes out merciless punishment to the created beings when necessary for their correction. This was the face of Shiva that would make the devotees tremble when they saw it manifest in Baba, the one they did their best to avoid, though as Baba pointed out in his discourse, "the underlying purpose is to teach people, not to harm them."

One day Taraknath Ghosh, a police inspector, was sitting in darshan when Baba asked him if he were doing his meditation twice a day.

"Yes, Baba," Taraknath replied, "but occasionally I miss a session due to time pressure."

"Do you follow yama and niyama?" Baba asked.

"Yes, Baba."

"Is that so?" Suddenly Baba's tone became stern and his face grew menacing, as if a storm cloud had passed across the face of the sun. "Then why did you accept a bribe on such and such day from such and such person? Is this how you follow yama and niyama? Tell me?"

Taraknath started shivering. "I made a mistake, Baba."

"I see." Baba then asked a poor Margi from Bhagalpur to stand up. "Do you do your sadhana twice a day?" he asked.

"I try, Baba, but it is very difficult. During sadhana time I am busy tending my cattle."

"Then when do you do your sadhana?"

"Baba, when my cattle become tired and are resting or grazing nearby. Then I sit under a tree and do my meditation."

"We need people like you in Ananda Marga, not police officers who take bribes." Baba turned again to Taraknath. "Tarak Ghosh, as long as you continue with this filthy practice, don't come here to visit me. I don't want to see your face." Tarak started crying. He went out to the veranda and wept where everyone could hear him. In the meantime, Baba continued talking with the rest of the Margis with his usual serene expression on his face, as if nothing had happened.

On another occasion, Devi Chand stopped in Kiul to change trains on his way to Jamalpur from Ranchi. While in Kiul, a leper entered his third-class compartment and sat on the floor. Devi Chand started to rebuke him. "How dare you, a leper, enter this train!" Devi Chand got down and alerted the railway authorities that there was a leper in his compartment. The railway officials came and removed the leper. When Devi Chand arrived at the jagriti, Baba was sitting with the devotees. He went in front of Baba's cot and did sastaunga pranam. When he got up, he saw Baba glaring at him. "Devi Chand," Baba said, "this tendency you have of detesting other human beings has grown very powerful."

"Baba, I don't understand," he said, tears welling in his eyes in the face of Baba's displeasure.

"When you asked the leper in Kiul to leave your compartment, your mind was full of contempt. You caused him great pain. You are a sadhaka. You should never do such a thing. Such people deserve our mercy, not our contempt."

Devi Chand started crying openly. It was a lesson that he would remain acutely conscious of until the end of his life many years later.

Ratneshvar was the leader of the Yadavs, the dominant local caste, in his native village of Srinagar, not far from Arraha. For several years the Yadavs had been in conflict with the other main caste group of the village, sometimes leading to open fighting between the two. One evening, he was invited to attend a mediation session in a house on the other side of the village. While he was walking there, a snake crossed his path and lifted its body up to face him. He backed off and took another path, but the same snake appeared again to block his way. Again he backed off and chose another route, and again the snake appeared. This happened twice more. When the snake appeared for a fifth time, he was ready with a large stone. Just as he was readying the stone, the snake slithered into the brush and didn't appear again.

The next time Ratneshvar attended darshan in Jamalpur, Baba started scolding him. "Haven't I told you not to get involved in village politics and caste conflicts? You refuse to listen."

"Baba, it's not true. I stopped that."

"What are you saying? Then tell me, what was that meeting you attended the other night? Even when somebody comes and tries to stop you, you don't stop. Isn't it so? Didn't someone try to stop you, repeatedly?"

Ratneshvar bowed his head. "Yes, Baba, a snake tried to stop me."

"And you thought to kill it with a stone, didn't you? Is that how you follow yama and niyama?"

"No, Baba."

"And why didn't you kill the snake?"

"Because it disappeared, Baba."

"And how many times did it try to stop you?"

"Five times, Baba."

"And still you didn't pay heed. Are you ready to take punishment for your actions?"

Baba asked Ratneshvar to do forty tic-tics in front of the Margis.

Kuldip Narayana Dubey had become an acharya and was making fast progress in his sadhana, but he had also started developing some ego. He began thinking of himself as a great yogi with budding spiritual powers. He recalled in an interview how Baba put his pride to a fall:

> I went to see Baba in the ashram one winter night, but no one was there, not even the ashram manager. So I went to sleep. When I woke up early in the morning, I saw Baba through the window. He was coming in through the gate. I quickly threw on my clothes. By that time, Baba was standing on the veranda, reading the notice board. I did sastaunga pranam. As I was getting up, Baba touched my body and I fell down to the ground, unconscious. When I came to my senses, Baba was standing over me and smiling. I asked him what he had done to me, whether he wanted to kill me or not. Baba told me I had developed some pride in my spiritual power; he had come to put an end to that pride. I tried to get up, but my body was extremely sluggish; none of my limbs were working. There were only the two of us. Baba told me to try to get up. I tried several times but I couldn't do it. My body had become totally inactive. Baba then went into his room. I could hear him inside his room shouting for me to try and get up. I shouted back, "How can I get up in this condition?" He called out for me to keep trying. Finally, after many attempts, I was able to get up and go to his room. Baba asked me whether the pride of power in me was finished or not. I told him it was. He asked me whose power it was. I told him it was all his power.

This sterner side of Baba was not reserved for disciples alone. Ananda Prasad Thakur, who worked under Asthana in the Central Excise Department, remembered entering a train with Baba and sitting across from a group of teenagers, one boy and three girls.

> Baba asked the boy in a stern tone of voice who the girls were. It was a tone of voice I was quite familiar with. The boy replied that they were members of his family. Suddenly Baba started rebuking him. "You bastard, you liar." The boy was shocked. Baba started telling who the girls were and where they were from. The moment he began exposing the unsavory relations between the four of them, the teenagers fled the compartment. The rest of the passengers were astonished to see this.

Even the littlest deviation from Baba's teachings came under the microscope of his scrutiny. Once Rameshvar Baita, who by then had been transferred to the Danapur office of Customs and Central Excise, asked his secretary to type out his name and post it on the back of his office chair, as his fellow employees had taken to doing. The following Sunday, he went to Jamalpur for darshan. Baba gave a talk on the universe as the joint property of all. In the middle of the talk, he looked at Rameshvar and said, "Rameshvar, just because you paste your name on the back of your chair, it doesn't mean that it becomes your property." Then he continued with his discourse.

One hot summer afternoon in the jagriti, Acharya Dipnarayan and Harinarayana Sahu got involved in a heated discussion about casteism and the significance of racial differences. Dipnarayan argued the part of the philosophy, while Harinarayana stubbornly insisted that such differences would remain in everyday life, even if he accepted on principle what the acharya was saying. Suddenly, in the middle of their conversation, they were stunned to see Baba standing next to them. They had been so engrossed in their discussion that they had failed to see him enter the jagriti gate. Baba called them both into his room and started scolding them. "I was taking rest at home in this terrible afternoon heat when I overheard two sadhakas of the Marga discussing the caste system. One of them was trying to justify its existence. So I put on my shirt and my shoes and rushed over here. Now, what do you have to say for yourselves?" Both disciples kept quiet. Baba started explaining the evils of the caste system to Harinarayana; he did not stop until his wayward disciple had fully gotten the point.

One Margi from Trimohan, Surendra, remembered going home one day during this period when a poisonous snake crossed his path. Frightened, he called Baba's name and the snake turned away. Even then, Surendra took the bamboo staff he was carrying and killed it. A few days later, Baba came to Trimohan. When Baba was leaving, Surendra was one of a large number of Margis who went to the station to see him off. Baba called him over and started scolding him. "Surendra, why did you kill that snake when you were walking home the other day? You took my name and it turned away. Why did you have to be so cruel? By beating him, you were beating me. Just look." Baba lifted his shirt and exposed several welts on his back.

Early in 1960, a young student from Ranchi named Asim Kumar came to Jamalpur to enjoy Baba's darshan for a few days. One morning, he woke up somewhat late by ashram standards, just as Ananta Ram and his family were sitting down to a breakfast of fresh puris, yoghurt, beaten rice, *singharas*, and warm *jilebis*, a Bihari sweet especially popular on cold winter mornings. They invited Asim to come and join them for breakfast. When Asim protested that he hadn't meditated yet, Ananta Ram said, "It will be cold by then. Take some breakfast and then go and meditate." His advice seemed reasonable and the food very attractive, so Asim joined them for breakfast. When he was finished, he went to the well to wash his clothes and take a bath before sitting for meditation. Just then, Baba entered the jagriti gate in a lungi and t-shirt, rather than his usual dhoti and kurta, and an umbrella in his hand. It was not yet seven thirty, well before Baba's usual time to come to the jagriti.

As Baba passed by the well on the way to his room, Asim could see that he was in a serious mood. Baba called everyone who was staying in the jagriti to his room, some ten or fifteen people. Once they were gathered there, he asked them how they were, if they had meditated and taken breakfast. Some had eaten, some had not, but everyone had done their meditation—except one. Asim was sitting in a corner. Baba pointed to him without looking and said, "Ask this boy if he has done his meditation or not. He has not meditated, but he has already taken his breakfast." Then he looked at Asim. "Did I make this ashram for goats or for human beings? How is it you feel hungry so early in the morning, before you have even meditated?"

"Baba, I'm sorry. I will fast the whole day."

"No, no," Baba said, softening his tone. "You can't fast. If you don't eat then how can I eat?"

"Baba, please give me punishment."

"Very well. Rub your nose on the ground in front of everyone."

Asim rubbed his nose so hard it started bleeding.

"Why did you rub your nose so hard?" Baba asked. He told him to run into the garden and pick some leaves from a certain plant and press them to his nose. Asim did so and felt immediate relief from the pain. He returned to Baba's room and again insisted on fasting.

"Don't fast," Baba said, smiling now, "but promise me you won't ever do it again. Because of you, I wasn't able to finish my housework in peace. I had to run here at this early hour."

Whether their mistakes were large or small, the tears the Margis cried only served to bring them closer to the master whose reprimands they cherished almost as much as his affection. Their relationship, as Baba pointed out time and again, was purely personal. He was not only their teacher—he was their father, and as their father, he showered them with affection and took them to task for their mistakes, sometimes in a single breath. Even when they were singled out for punishment, either alone or in front of the Margis, they took it as a blessing. It meant they had Baba's attention, and his attention was the boat they were sure would see them across the ocean of maya. They could live with him rubbing their ego into the ground. What they could not live with was his indifference. And while Baba could be as stern as he was loving, he was never indifferent as long as the disciple was sincere, no matter how misguided or wayward that disciple might be. And so they came, ready for whatever face Baba chose to show them. Whatever face of Shiva they saw, it was, after all, Shiva's face they were seeing.

XXIV

The Tiger's Grave

There is spiritual potential in all people. Some people have harnessed it, and these people are able to help other people to arouse it. Some people will arouse it if they are in the company of those who have already awakened it; this is the importance of good company (satsaunga). Your duty is to awaken yourself and help others to awaken.[1]

During the century before Baba's birth, the area north of the Jamalpur railway station was a dense forest that included the Kharagpur Hills and the valley beyond, an area inhabited only by wild animals and an occasional Tantric yogi drawn by the impenetrable solitude. After the establishment of the railway workshop in 1862, the British gradually began cutting into the forest as they expanded their facilities and cleared expansive meadows for their recreational pursuits. By the time India gained its independence in 1947, the open areas between the railway institute and the Kharagpur Hills and Death Valley comprised hundreds of acres of spreading meadows, sprawling shade trees, a long curving reservoir, and numerous pathways that led up into the hills where one could find secluded vistas that afforded a spectacular view of the Monghyr valley all the way to the river Ganges. In the middle of the open meadows, about a twenty-minute walk from the main workshop, lay two graves spaced about twenty meters apart. In June 1864, a foreman from the railway workshop was out hunting when he ran into a tiger at the edge of the forest. He was able to get off a shot, but the tiger still mauled him. When his fellow workers sent out a search party the next morning, they found both him and the tiger dead. After the funeral services, they erected a small tomb for their fallen comrade at the spot of his death and buried the tiger nearby under an unmarked tomb.

The Kharagpur foothills and Death Valley had been Baba's private wilderness throughout his childhood. They provided him with the seclusion he needed for his spiritual pursuits. When he returned to Jamalpur after college to take a position in the railway workshop, he made it a habit to spend his evenings walking through the enchanted scenery of his younger days. He would cut across the meadows and fields toward the hills, then along the reservoir and past Death

Valley, before turning back and completing the circuit. Weather permitting, he would leave the house at seven or seven thirty and rarely returned home before ten. Occasionally, an office colleague or a friend from his earlier days would join him, something that became more frequent once Pranay and others took initiation, but in his first years back home he would often walk alone, sometimes disappearing into the forest as he had done when he was a boy. Typically, in the middle of his walk, Baba would stop and take rest on the tiger's grave, sitting and staring off into the vast night sky. Once he began gathering disciples around him, the mid-walk pause at the tiger's grave became a permanent fixture of his evenings. It was not uncommon for him to spend a couple of hours there sitting and chatting, telling stories, giving spiritual instruction and demonstrations, and even dictating books by candlelight.

When Mangal Bihari went on his first field walk, he was so overwhelmed by Baba's presence that he spent the entire time repeating silent prayers: O Baba, lead me to the right path; guide me to the light; help me to surrender. The next evening, when they were about to leave, Baba turned to him and said, "Mangal Bihari, don't be in a prayerful mood. Be natural." It was as if a spell had been broken. From that moment on, Mangal Bihari felt the way the rest of the Margis felt when they went on field walk with Baba to the tiger's grave. He felt as if there was no distance between them, as if he were walking and chatting under the open sky with his best friend and his father, enjoying the beauty of nature and the company of the one dearest to his heart. Baba would talk about everything the disciples could imagine, and many things they couldn't, and they would cherish those memories as the most intimate of their lives.

One evening Madhan and Harinder of Trimohan were alone with Baba on field walk. They were still teenagers at the time. Both of them had sneaked out of their houses to catch the train and come see Baba. While they were walking in the direction of the tiger's grave, Baba asked, "What would you do if a tiger jumped out now and attacked us? Would you run or would you fight?"

Madhan replied in a defiant tone, "Baba, I will fight the tiger and I will kill it. I am a very good fighter." (Years later, he would point out that he had been young and not very sensible at the time.)

"Okay," Baba said, "but what about Harinder?"

"Baba, we are best friends," Harinder said. "If he doesn't run, then how could I? We will give our lives to protect you. Only then could the tiger attack you."

Baba patted them both on the shoulder and said, "You are both very brave and I love you very much. In the future, Ananda Marga will need your bravery. You are both my Bhimas."[2]

Later, while they were sitting on the grave, Baba began discussing various aspects of astronomy. He pointed to one star and started describing both that star and the solar system it belonged to. As he was talking, they both stared wide-eyed as the sky gradually started descending lower and lower. When it reached the level of the palm trees, they became frightened and grabbed Baba. "Baba, get down, get down," they shouted. When Baba asked them what was going on, they said, "Baba, don't you see? The sky is falling. It will kill us."

Baba smiled. "Don't worry, nothing will happen." He pointed once again toward the sky and started tracing slow circles with his finger. Gradually, the sky retraced its course until it was once again back where it belonged. Baba got up and told them that it was time to go to the station and catch their train; otherwise, they might get a beating from their parents. When Madhan told him that it was already so late, they would surely get a beating, Baba assured them that everything would be okay. He accompanied them to the station and saw them off. When they got home, they were able to sneak back into their bedrooms without their parents ever knowing that they had been gone.

One day on field walk, Dr. Vishvanath Singh told Baba that the acharyas were having difficulties in prachar for two principle reasons: One was the rule that people had to follow yama and niyama; the other was that it was so difficult to have Baba's darshan. "First, people have to take initiation and then they have to practice sadhana for some time before they are allowed to see you. During DMC they have to have a gate pass. There are so many rules and regulations that many people are hesitant to take initiation, even though they are impressed with the ideology. Can't you relax these restrictions a little? If you did, then many more people would join Ananda Marga."

Baba laughed softly and said, "It's an interesting idea, Vishvanath. Let me think about it."

A few days later, Vishvanath was sitting on the tiger's grave with several other disciples when Baba brought up the subject.

"Vishvanath, the other day you said that there are two reasons why many people are not joining Ananda Marga: first, because they have to follow yama and niyama; and second, because there are so many rules and regulations they have to follow before they can see me. Is it not? Now I will give you your answer. As to the second question, there are reasons why I don't disclose myself in public. One reason is that if too many people know me for who I am, then it will make it difficult for me to do my work. Another is that when I appear as guru in DMC you people become abnormal. You know this. Why does it happen? Because when you come into contact with me your kundalini gets awakened. For sadhakas who are doing sadhana this is fine. There is no adverse reaction. But if people are not doing sadhana, it could cause them to become mentally imbalanced, or even physically ill. Would you be able to look after them if this happened and make them normal? Would it be proper for me to allow that to happen?

"As to your first question, removing the restriction of following yama and niyama—well, you see I am not a magician. At present, the greatest magician in India is P. C. Sorcar. It is his job to show magic. I am a normal human being.

The only magic I can perform is to turn bad people into good people, to make them walk the path of righteousness and make them human beings in the real sense. Would this be possible if people didn't follow yama and niyama? Ananda Marga is a man-making mission. If I removed yama and niyama, then millions of people in India might join, but what good would it do? I want to create human beings, not a religion. Do you know what happens to people when they don't follow yama and niyama?"

Baba touched Vishvanath between the eyebrows and asked him to describe what he was seeing.

"Baba, I see a market area, a road with shops on both sides."

"Look a little farther."

"Down the road I can see a temple."

"Look closer. Do you recognize the area?"

"Yes, now I recognize it. It is the Vishvanath temple in Varanasi."

"What else do you see?"

"Outside the temple there is a crowd of people standing in a line. They appear to be beggars."[3]

"Do you see two lepers sitting in the midst of them?"

"Yes, Baba."

"One was a foreigner in his previous life and the other was a commissioner. Do you know why they have become beggars in this life? . . . Because they didn't follow yama and niyama. Look again and describe what you see."

Again Baba pressed his thumb to Vishvanath's trikuti. Vishvanath started describing a well-dressed man in black robes and a powdered wig sitting in a courtroom during a trial.

"Yes, one of these lepers was a judge in England in his past life," Baba continued, "but he was a corrupt judge who accepted bribes and put innocent people in jail. Now he is a beggar and a leper as a consequence of his actions. So, do you still want me to relax the restrictions of yama and niyama? I want to create a sadvipra society, and that is impossible without yama and niyama. I put my emphasis on quality, not quantity. Don't worry, the work that needs to be done will be done, at the proper time."

A few months after the introduction of Prout, Vaedyanath was sitting on the tiger's grave with Baba and a few other Margis discussing the new philosophy. When he questioned Baba whether or not it would really be possible to establish a sadvipra society one day, Baba assured him it would, as long as he and his fellow Margis worked selflessly toward that end. Then he expressed another doubt that had been in his mind for some time.

"Baba, some people say that you rehearse with Dasarath before the demonstrations, that you go over what he will say and what you will say. They say he doesn't actually see anything."

"Why are you speaking such nonsense?"

"It is very easy to get angry, Baba. Very well then, I will keep quiet, but it doesn't change what some people are thinking or saying."

"Okay then, do you want to see a demonstration for yourself? I will do a demonstration on you."

Baba told Vaedyanath to sit directly in front of him and begin performing his meditation. Vaedyanath did as instructed, but he kept his hands on Baba's feet, worried that Baba might deceive him and leave while he had his eyes closed. After five minutes, Baba asked him to open his eyes. "Look at the moon and describe what you see."

"Baba, it is the sun," he exclaimed, astonished to see the sun blazing in the night sky.

"No, you are mistaken. Look again."

He looked again and saw the sun blazing even brighter, illuminating the sky as if it were midday instead of nearly ten at night.

"No," Baba insisted once again. "You are mistaking the moon for the sun. Here is the sun."

Baba raised his hand and Vaedyanath saw the sun shining in Baba's palm, even brighter than what he had seen in the sky. He began to lose consciousness of his surroundings. As he did, he saw the entire solar system revolving around the sun, planet by planet, with the universe as a backdrop. While he was lost in his ecstatic vision, he heard Baba's voice echoing through the heavens. "Do you know what will happen if I displace the sun? All the planets will crash and be destroyed. The balance of the universe will be lost. Do you want me to do that demonstration?"

"No, Baba, no," Vaedyanath cried, suddenly overcome by fear. At that moment the vision started to recede. When he regained consciousness of his surroundings, Baba put down his hand. The other Margis were looking on, speechless. That was the end of Vaedyanath's doubts about his guru. A few days later Baba initiated him into kapalik sadhana.

Once Chandrashekar, at that time a student of engineering, was sitting on the grave with Baba, massaging the master's feet and gazing up at his face. He was scarcely paying attention to the conversation going on between Baba and the other three disciples who were sitting there. Baba changed the subject to yoga therapy and began to describe a course of treatment for those who had problems passing urine or stool. Chandrashekar started paying closer attention, since he had been suffering from that same problem and had been reluctant to ask Baba about it. He did his best to memorize what Baba was saying. When Baba finished, he looked at Chandrashekar and told him that his mother was putting onion in his food without his knowledge. For this reason his spiritual practice was hampered. Then Baba laid his hand on Chandrashekar's head. "At that moment," Chandrashekar later recounted, "all tension went out of my mind. My mind became lighter and lighter and I started to feel blessed. Whatever feeling of distance I felt from Baba, either due to my samskara or for some other reason, disappeared."

Then Baba surprised him by saying, "Chandrashekar, I have visited your house. You should ask your mother about it. Now you are tired. Enough massage." Baba took Chandrashekar's hands in his and started massaging them until it was time for them to leave, inspiring ecstatic feelings in his speechless disciple.

The next morning Chandrashekar asked his mother if she had secretly been adding onion to his vegetables. At first she denied it. But after he pressed the point, she admitted that since he had refused to eat onions she had started making an onion paste and adding it to the vegetables so that he wouldn't notice.

"But how did you find out?" she asked.

"Baba told me last night on field walk. He also told me that he has visited our house and that I should ask you about it."

His mother appeared startled by the comment. "No, your Baba never came here." For a few moments she was silent. Something was obviously troubling her. Then she said, "Something strange happened last night. It was about eight or eight thirty in the evening. I was standing in the yard when I looked up and saw a man with spectacles standing on the roof. It was a shock. I ran across to the neighbor's house and shouted to ask them to check from the upper-story window to see who was on the roof. I thought it might be a thief. But by that time the man had vanished."

Chandrashekar went into his room and came back to the kitchen with a photograph of Baba in a standing pose. "Is this the person you saw on the roof?"

"Yes, that's the person I saw," his mother replied in a momentary state of confusion.

"This is my Baba, my Gurudeva. At the same time that he was sitting in the field with me and talking, he appeared to you on our roof."

His mother folded her hands to her chest and bowed before the photo. Shortly afterward, she took initiation and gave up eating onions herself.

Although field walks with Baba were among the most intimate moments that the disciples spent with him, there was no escape from the disciplinarian side of the Tantric guru. Surendra recalled sitting on the tiger's grave one evening with Baba. Among the disciples present was a university professor from Bhagalpur. During the course of the conversation, Baba asked them one by one how their meditation was going. When it came the professor's turn, he replied that it was going fine. Baba became furious. "You scoundrel! Do you think my eyes are limited only to Jamalpur? These eyes are behind every atom and every molecule of the universe. They are watching everything. Do you want me to tell these Margis here what you have done? Should I reveal the contents of the letter in your pocket? Should I tell them where you told your family you were going, and where you actually went, and what you did there?" The professor shuddered, visibly frightened. He began pleading with Baba to forgive him. "Are you ready to accept punishment then?" Baba asked him to lick the sandals of each Margi present and then rub his nose on the ground. The professor was still in a state of shock when Baba left for home with a separate group of disciples who were waiting to accompany him back.

On another occasion, a rich businessman from Gorakhpur named Hanuman Prasad went for his first walk with Baba; accompanying them was his acharya, Sachidananda, along with Ramakanta and a couple of other Margis. As they were entering the field, they came to a large puddle in the road several inches deep, left there by a recent downpour. Baba started to take off his shoes, preparing to wade across in his bare feet, but Hanuman Prasad insisted that Baba keep his shoes on. "Baba, I will carry you across," he said. And indeed, Hanuman was a strong, well-built man who looked as if he could carry several Babas on his broad shoulders. But Baba replied that it would not be necessary. "The water is not deep," he told him. "I won't have any problem crossing." But Hanuman continued to insist and finally Baba agreed. Hanuman squatted down and asked Baba to place a leg over his shoulder. Then he tried to straighten up and lift Baba onto his back, but try as he might he was unable to lift Baba even a single inch, much to his embarrassment. Later, he told the other Margis that he had felt as if he had almost died from the weight of Baba's leg, as if Baba had placed the weight of the three worlds on his back.

When the Margis reached the tiger's grave, Baba asked Hanuman where he was from and what he did. He told Baba that he worked for the Gita Press in Gorakhpur,[4] and that he hoped to use his ties with the Gita Press to help Ananda Marga, as well as to find the path to nirvikalpa samadhi. "It is good that you publish books that help people learn about dharma," Baba said, but as the conversation continued, Baba started asking more and more pointed questions as to whether he actually followed the tenets of the Gita, quoting one of the Gita's famous verses that referred to promoting the welfare of society and other living beings. As Hanuman grew more and more uncomfortable under Baba's scrutiny, Baba began to reveal examples of his misconduct, telling the date and place of his misdeeds for all to hear.

"You are an imposter," Baba said in a scathing tone. "You cheat people out of their money while you hide behind a veil of dharma. With such despicable conduct, nirvikalpa samadhi is far beyond your reach." Baba turned to Sachidananda. "You brought him here. You were thinking that if this man donated some of his wealth, it would benefit the mission, but I tell you, you should not mix business with spirituality. What can such a man give the mission when the elements provide everything it needs? Just look. Look at the hills."

Baba pointed to the eastern hills. The Margis turned in unison and saw the hills transformed into gold, shining brilliantly under the night sky. Baba started berating Hanuman in a loud voice. "Do you know whose hills these are? These are Baba's hills! Do you think you can purchase me with your money? Do you think you can purchase spirituality?"

Hanuman started weeping and begging Baba's forgiveness. Baba softened his tone. "Will you make me a promise that from now on you will follow the principles of yama and niyama with all strictness?"

"Yes, Baba."

"Very well then. Practice your sadhana sincerely and follow yama and niyama. If you can do that, you will get everything you are hoping for."

By 1960, the number of people wanting to go on field walk each day had increased to the point that they had to be divided into three groups, with a maximum of four in each group. One group would accompany Baba to the tiger's grave where a second group would be waiting for him. The third group would come later to accompany Baba back to his house. One evening, Asim was in the second group along with his friend Panna, Acharya Pashupati, and a young initiate of Pashupati's. After the first group had turned back, Baba sat on the tiger's grave with the four devotees and turned his attention to Pashupati's initiate.

"Do you repent for your wrong deeds?" he asked.

The boy insisted that he hadn't committed any misdeeds. Baba's mood turned grave. "Who has brought him here?" Pashupati folded his hands to his chest and said in a humble voice that he had brought him.

"Why did you bring him?" Baba asked. "What is the reason?"

Pashupati remained silent. Baba turned his attention back to the boy and started recounting his misdeeds, including the date, time, and place of each. After Baba had described four or five sordid incidents, the boy fell to the ground in front of Baba, begging Baba to save him. Baba was silent for a minute or two. Then he asked the boy to sit in front of him.

Baba extended his legs. "Press my feet against your chest."

The boy did so. After a few moments, Baba asked, "Is your chest pain gone?"

"Yes, Baba," the boy replied, tears streaming down his face.

Baba addressed the Margis. "Both of this boy's lungs were filled with water. He was in the third stage of tuberculosis and his doctors had given up hope. At this point he met his acharya, who told him that if he learned meditation and went to Baba, Baba could cure him. He has come here hoping to get his TB cured, but he has been trying to hide the fact from me." Baba looked at the boy. "Isn't it so?"

"Yes, Baba," the boy replied, sobbing even more loudly.

"How many chapattis did you eat the night before last? You have forgotten? Well, I remember. I know each and every pore of your body. Whatever happens in this world takes place in front of my eyes. And you are trying to hide from me?" The boy continued weeping. Baba softened his tone. "Now, now, don't cry.

Come and sit closer." The boy sat just beside Baba and Baba started patting him on his back. "Your TB is cured now. Tell your doctor that you don't have any more problems. From now on you are a new man. Forget the past; just look ahead. Promise me that from today on you will be a new and ideal person and serve the society." The boy promised and Baba blessed him. "No one should waste time thinking about the past. Look toward the Lord and move ahead. You will reach your goal."

When it was time for Baba to return back, he joined the third group, which was waiting a short distance away. As they started walking back toward town, Asim's group followed them, close enough to hear the conversation. One of the devotees in the third group was a police officer. At one point, he turned to Baba and said, "Baba, we must be strong moralists. The cardinal moral principles should be propagated everywhere."

"Yes, you are right," Baba said. The officer continued in the same vein for several minutes more. Asim was impressed. What a strong moralist he must be, he thought. Suddenly Baba stopped beneath a tree that was towering over the roadside and asked the officer if he knew the meaning of the word *asteya*.

"Yes, Baba," the officer replied, "it means not to steal from others."

"Tell me, is taking a bribe against *asteya*?"

"Yes, Baba, it is. We shouldn't take bribes."

Baba planted himself in front of him with both hands on his hips. "Bring out the sixty-two rupees you have in your back pocket. Bring them out!" The chagrined officer removed exactly sixty-two rupees from his back pocket. Baba turned to the rest of the Margis and said, "This man accepted a bribe of one hundred rupees this morning. From this money he took his meal and paid his train fare to come here. Now only sixty-two rupees are left. And he is talking of morality?" Baba turned back to the officer. "Spit on the ground and lick it with your tongue. Spit!" The man spit and began to bend over, but Baba stopped him before he could carry out his order. "Okay, okay," Baba said. "Promise me that you will return the money to the person who gave it to you and that you will never again accept a bribe."

The officer promised and Baba gave him his blessing. "You will never have problems providing food and clothes for your family," he told him. "If you ever find yourself in difficulty, come to me and I will help you." Baba started walking again toward his house, but he continued talking to the officer, who was crying openly by now. "Don't think about the past," he told him. "God has given you two eyes in the front of your head to look forward. Forget the past. You are a moralist now." Baba changed the subject and started inquiring about the welfare of his family, asking by name about his wife and each of his children.

In the winter of 1959, Ramasvarath decided to spend his Dipavali vacation in Jamalpur. As he was traveling there by train, he was thinking about the Margis' claim that Baba was *antaryami*—all-knowing and all-seeing. I won't believe it without proof, he thought. First I will have to put the master to the test. If he passes the test, then and only then will I accept him as *antaryami*. Knowing that the list for field walk was always full, he told Baba mentally that if he really were all-knowing, then he should invite him to go alone with him on field walk that evening.

When his train arrived, he went straight to Baba's quarters in Rampur colony. Several Margis were already waiting under the neem tree a short distance from Baba's house to go on field walk. A short while later, Baba came out. He spent a few minutes talking with the Margis; then, to Ramasvarath's stunned surprise, he announced that only Ramasvarath would accompany him on walk that evening.

As they began walking toward the field, Ramasvarath followed closely behind Baba, thrilled to be alone with his guru but angry with himself for having doubted him. It took several requests from Baba before he began walking side by side with him. They headed toward the main bridge, crossed the railway tracks, and soon reached the old church. At that moment a black dog appeared. "Ramasvarath," Baba said, "stay between me and the dog. Do not, under any circumstances, let him touch my body." Ramasvarath did as he was told, fending off the dog whenever he made an effort to approach the master. When they reached the tiger's grave, the dog jumped on the tomb with them. "Shoo it off," Baba said, motioning with his hand. Ramasvarath pushed it off the grave, and the dog sat on the ground, a few paces away.

"Do you know this dog?" Baba asked.

"No, Baba."

"He was a human being in his past life. He used to pose as a religious man, but actually he was a man of bad character. He committed some very serious misdeeds. This animal body is his punishment for those misdeeds. The reason I told you not to let him touch me is that if he were able to, then he would die immediately and get a human body in his next life. I can't allow that. He is still under punishment for four more years according to cosmic law."

A little while later Baba added, "Despite having a dog's body, he still has a human mind. That's how he was able to recognize me. He also recognized Dasarath since he was Dasarath's relative in that past life. Whenever Dasarath and I go out walking, he comes."

"But Dasarath is not with us," Ramasvarath pointed out.

"Go toward the road a little ways; you'll see Dasarath coming. Go and see. He won't move."

Ramasvarath got up and started walking toward the road. After a minute or two, he saw Dasarath approaching. As they walked back toward the grave, he asked Dasarath about the dog. Dasarath related that the dog had been following him and Baba for the past few days. Baba had told him to pet it but not to allow it to touch Baba's body; when he had asked why, Baba had told him who the dog had been in its past life.

A few days later the dog was again present at the tiger's grave with Baba, Dasarath, and several others. This time the Margis pleaded with Baba to release the dog from its bondage. Baba argued that it would not be proper, the dog had to undergo the reaction of its actions, yet after a short time Baba relented. He closed his eyes for a few moments. Suddenly the dog, which had been sitting nearby, stood up and then keeled over dead.

Professor Suresh Mandal's stomach problems had been disturbing his peace of mind for some time. Early in 1960, he finally consulted a doctor in Hazaribagh about it. The doctor, who happened to be a Margi, also named Suresh, told him that there was no use taking medicine. If he wanted to cure his stomach problems and find peace of mind, he would do better to adopt the meditation and yoga practices of Ananda Marga. The doctor referred him to Shiva Shankar Bannerjee, then living in Hazaribagh, and assured him he would find what he was looking for. Suresh was skeptical, but he was ready to take the chance that it might work. He took the precaution, however, of informing Shiva Shankar that he was a communist and a non-believer. "It doesn't matter," Shiva Shankar told him. "All that matters is whether or not you do the practice sincerely." Relieved that belief was not a prerequisite, Suresh did his practice sincerely; within a few months his stomach problems cleared up and he started finding the peace of mind he had been looking for. This induced him to begin reading Baba's books. He was greatly impressed by the philosophy, but when he asked Shiva Shankar about Baba's educational qualification, he was surprised to hear that Baba had only passed ISc and was working as an accountant in the Jamalpur railway workshop. Nevertheless, he became a willing traveler when Shiva Shankar told him that it was time for him to go to Jamalpur to have Baba's darshan.

When Suresh arrived in Jamalpur with his letter of introduction from Shiva Shankar, Pranay gave him permission to go to the field that evening, but only after answering three questions successfully: Did he keep the topknot? Did he wear the sacred thread? Did he believe in idol worship? Suresh, as a self-respecting communist, answered no to all three questions, thus successfully passing Pranay's exam. An acharya brought him to the tiger's grave, where Baba was sitting with a small group of disciples. After Suresh sat down, Baba asked him if he did his meditation twice a day regularly.

"Yes, Baba, I do, at least when I am in Hazaribagh. I find it difficult to do when I am out of town."

"Do you take your food regularly?" Baba asked in a trenchant tone. "Do you do your other necessary daily duties regularly? God has given you this human body to do sadhana. This is the main purpose of your life. You do all your other duties but you don't do the most important one? Do twenty-five tic-tics."

When Suresh had finished the tic-tics, Baba asked him to sit beside him. He patted him on the head and said some words of spiritual encouragement. Then he asked him to explain the meaning of *asteya*. Suresh could not. "Then tell me the meaning of *aparigraha*." Again Suresh didn't know. "What? You don't know the meaning of *aparigraha*? What is your educational qualification?"

"MSc."⁵

"MSc! You have such a big degree and you don't know the meaning of *asteya*? I have only an ISc."

The next morning was New Year's Day. Suresh was still smarting from the blow to his ego. When Baba came to the jagriti for General Darshan, he asked Dasarath to give a talk, but Dasarath begged to be excused. He requested Baba to give his usual discourse. "Okay," Baba said, "then let the topic be *asteya*, non-stealing. *Asteya* is of two types. One is physical *asteya*, where you physically steal some material object. This is visible to other people's eyes and if you get caught the law may punish you. The other type of stealing is mental stealing. The law cannot punish you for this." Baba turned his attention to Suresh, who was sitting in the front. "Am I right, Suresh? Suppose a person works in a government college, and in a warehouse under his supervision there is a stock of goods that has been sitting there for several years, seemingly forgotten. So he thinks to himself, better he sell those goods and pocket the money. No one will notice. If this idea comes into his mind, is it not mental stealing?"

Suresh hung his head. He had indeed been thinking to sell such a stock that had been lying in his warehouse for ages. After Baba left for his residence, Suresh sat by himself, thinking how fortunate he was to have found such a guru. A worldly father would have only scolded him had he actually done the deed, but his spiritual father had pointed out the error in his thoughts in order to guide him down the proper path. He thought about his communist beliefs and realized that only spirituality could make a true human being. If there could only be a blending between the ideals of communism and the spirituality of Ananda Marga, he thought. How nice it would be. It could lead to the formation of an ideal human society.

In the evening, Baba returned to the jagriti for General Darshan. During his discourse, Baba pointed to Suresh and said, "Professor Suresh of Hazaribagh has been sitting here thinking that a happy synchronization between communism and Ananda Marga would lead to the formation of an ideal human society, but I say that communism fosters the suppression of human thought and can only lead to disaster. Suppose a driver is driving on a road that is full of pits but he is unaware of them. Chances are, he will meet with an accident. But if he knows the road, then he will be conscious of the holes and he will avoid them. In Ananda Marga, the pitfalls in the road are well known, so such accidents can be avoided, but in communism the lack of understanding of the human being's spiritual nature is a recipe for disaster."

Baba went on to analyze some of the problems that Russian communism had faced during the time of Stalin due to inherent defects in the system. "Remember, Suresh," he said, "do not keep your feet in two different boats, otherwise you are sure to drown. If you struggle against injustice, and if at the same time you perform your sadhana and walk the path of morality, then you can be sure that I will always be with you. You will have my blessings and victory will be yours."

When Suresh returned to Hazaribagh, he informed the school administration of the neglected stock in the warehouse and it was soon disposed of. By then, he had been introduced to Prout, and his days as a communist were behind him.

When Rajnath Pandey,[6] then a college student, went on his first field walk, he was in the group selected to accompany Baba from his house to the tiger's grave. He followed Pranay's instructions and went to Baba's house where he found a group of government officers waiting for the master, a group that included Nagina and Ram Bahadur. When Baba came out and the Margis did pranam, they noticed a beautiful fragrance emanating from his body. Baba began walking with his habitual speed and the Margis had difficulty keeping up, sometimes losing sight of him in the dark. Whenever this happened, Baba would stop briefly and call out his location. When they approached the bridge, several of the Margis, including Rajnath, had fallen behind again. They began talking about the fragrance that was coming from Baba's body. When they caught up again, Baba said, "What conspiracy were you hatching back there?" They told him about the scent.

'I don't use any scent," Baba said. "It must be coming from you."

"No, Baba, it's coming from you."

"Okay then, tell me what kind of fragrance you smell."

Each of them ventured a guess, but no one could correctly identify the scent.

Baba pointed to Rajnath. " If you want to know what fragrance it is, then you have to ask the youngest member of the group." Rajnath stepped forward and Baba said, "I will put my finger on your crown chakra. After ten seconds you will see a bud, but you will not recognize the flower. After fifteen seconds it will begin to blossom, and after forty-five seconds you will be able to name it. As soon as you identify the flower, I will remove my finger. If I keep my finger there any longer, then your attention will be diverted, so I will only give you forty-five seconds."

By this time they were standing on the railway bridge. Baba put his finger on Rajnath's head; immediately Rajnath saw a bud appear. Gradually the bud started to blossom until it became a fully bloomed flower. When the stipulated time had passed, Baba asked him to name the flower.

"A lotus, Baba."

"What color?"

"White."

"Yes. I am very fond of the white lotus. The fragrance you smell is the scent of the white lotus when it is fully bloomed. I like it very much. When you learn the process of dhyana, then you will understand the significance of the white lotus." They resumed walking. Baba began talking about the botanical characteristics and history of the white lotus. The scent continued for the duration of the field walk, some two and a half hours.

It was not uncommon for new initiates to test Baba in order to see if he was the guru they were looking for and the realized soul that everyone claimed he was. One evening, Kamalakanta was sitting on the tiger's grave with two other disciples when Baba suddenly sent them both on errands: one to convey a message to Pranay; the other to fetch paper, pen, and a candle from the jagriti. Unexpectedly finding himself alone with Baba in that solitary setting, Kamalakanta thought that this would be the perfect time to test his guru. If he truly is a sadguru, he thought, then he should give me the realization of the presence of Paramatman. And if he is really omniscient, as everyone says he is, then there is no need for me to say anything. He should simply read my mind.

Both were silent for a minute or two. Then Baba closed his eyes. "Kamalakanta, what do you think would happen to a person who suddenly found himself with a *crore* of rupees in his hand?"

After a moment's thought, Kamalakanta said, "Baba, he would probably go mad or even possibly die from the shock."

"Do you think that if Paramatman were present, he might be worth even more than a *crore* of rupees?"

"Baba, he would be worth more than a thousand *crores* of rupees."

"I see. Now think about this: if an unprepared person suddenly got the realization of the presence of Paramatman, what would be his mental condition? He would become disturbed; he would go mad. I don't want anyone to go mad. Unless and until a person's reactive momenta are exhausted, he cannot achieve liberation. For this reason, I don't give that realization to sadhakas who are in the preliminary stages of their sadhana. Do more and more sadhana. Then you will have your realization."

Such tests were a favor Baba often returned. Once Baba was on field walk with Ram Naresh and several other Margis. Among them was a recent initiate who had come from Ranchi. Baba asked him where his hometown was (he was from Bagha, near Betia), and then remarked that he seemed to be having problems with his fear propensity.

"No, Baba," he replied. "There are only two things I am afraid of: snakes and mad dogs."

"Is that so? There is a Malwa tree over there. Go and touch it and then come back."

The new initiate began walking toward the tree. Before he had advanced ten paces a sudden storm arose. Lightning flashed, followed by loud peals of thunder. Within moments, it grew so dark that Ram Naresh could barely make out Baba, though he was standing right beside him. The boy who had gone to touch the tree ran back and fell on the ground, shouting and begging for Baba to please save his life, while the electric storm raged all around them. Suddenly the storm ended as abruptly as it had begun.

"What has happened to you?" Baba asked the disciple who was still whimpering on the ground. "Why are you whimpering like this? What did you see that scared you so?"

"Baba, as I was walking toward the tree, all of a sudden the tree disappeared and I was surrounded by a group of skeletons. It was terrifying."

"But you told me that you were only afraid of two things: snakes and mad dogs. There were neither snakes nor mad dogs. Then why did you get scared?"

The disciple kept silent.

"You should never boast. When you are asked something by your guru, answer simply and truthfully. You were proud. You should never allow pride to take root in your mind."

Om Prakash Goenka learned a similar lesson about pride when he went on his first field walk with Baba. A recent graduate in chemical engineering, Om Prakash had heard many stories about Baba from the other disciples in Madras; nevertheless, he harbored the conviction in his mind that at least in the area of chemistry he knew more than Baba.

As they sat on the tiger's grave, Baba asked him about the various Margis in Madras and how they were doing. When Baba asked him about his education, he felt a puff of pride as he told Baba about his degree.

"Is that so?" Baba said. "Very good. Then you should be able to teach me something about uranium isotopes?"

Om Prakash started explaining about the naturally occurring isotope, U-238.

"No, no, no," Baba said. "I want to know about the fissionable isotopes, U-233 and U-235."

Unfortunately, Om Prakash knew very little about these isotopes, and what little he did know only seemed to make Baba grow more and more disappointed.

"But I can get that from the books of Narasimham, Rakshit, and Kapoor. You have a degree in chemical engineering. I want to learn something that I can't get just as easily from reading a book. Can't you teach me anything that is not in those books?"

Om Prakash did not know what to say. He remained silent, wondering what knowledge, if any, he had that could not be gleaned from books.

"You disappoint me," Baba continued. "I thought you could teach me something."

Baba then began explaining about uranium as an energy source and its high value when compared to coal, petroleum, and natural gas. He went on to describe in detail the beneficial properties of these isotopes. "The fissionable rays of uranium can be used for constructive purposes as well as for destructive purposes," he said. "Since you are all Ananda Margis, you should only use them for constructive purposes."

Om Prakash assumed that Baba must have learned these details from some book that he had yet to read. In 1972, however, he was surprised to read in a newspaper article that some Canadian scientists had discovered some of the beneficial properties of the uranium isotopes that Baba had discussed nearly a decade earlier. It was only then that he realized that Baba could not have gotten that information from any book since it had not yet been discovered at the time.

XXV

Personal Contact

The secrets of Brahma, his macropsychic and cognitive secrets, are known only to him, and unless and until he expresses himself through some physical form, how can his secrets be known to others? And that is why it is said, Brahmaeva gurureka na pariah. That is, Brahma himself is the guru. There cannot be any second guru. His secret is known to him only, and he expresses himself through a framework, a form. Now generally people say that the form is the guru, but the form is not the guru. Guru is expressing himself through that form.[1]

WHEN BABA ANNOUNCED late in 1958 that each disciple would have the right to one Personal Contact, it seemed little more than a chance for the new initiates to be alone with Baba, a privilege the senior disciples had often enjoyed during the early days of Ananda Marga. But as the lines started forming during DMC, it gradually became clear that PC was not simply a chance for the new disciples to be alone in the room with the master and chat. The formality that began to accompany Baba's PC sessions was indicative of a deeper import: the landmark nature of this private contact between master and disciple.

A few years later, Kshitij accompanied Baba to Delhi for DMC as his attending secretary. One of his duties was managing Baba's PC schedule. The first session was fixed for after Baba's return from morning walk; however, it started late because the walk had been delayed by the passage of a long freight train at a crossing. When Kshitij stopped the PC at one thirty, the time fixed for Baba's midday bath and lunch, there were still four or five disciples in line. Kshitij informed Baba that it was time for his bath, but Baba told him to send the next person in. "Okay, Baba," Kshitij said, "but please finish the PC in two minutes; otherwise you'll be late for your lunch." Baba didn't reply, but the disciple didn't leave his room for half an hour. When he finally came out, Kshitij stopped the PC again and told the women in the kitchen to get Baba's lunch ready. Then he went in to inform Baba that PC was over.

"You know, Kshitij, there is a boy sitting outside, and he is praying to me to please give him PC. He has been waiting a long time. So kindly allow me to do one more, only one."

"Okay, Baba, but please finish in two minutes. It's getting late."

Baba told Kshitij to close the door and asked him to sit next to him on his cot. "You see, Kshitij, when a person comes to me for PC, I first have to clean his mental plate. In order to do that, I have to make him realize his mistakes. He may weep, he may resist, but one way or another I have to get him to repent for his misdeeds. After that I have to infuse more life into his ista mantra. Once I do this, the person develops a great interest in sadhana, so I have to take an oath to look into all his activities for the next six months. This is a technical process; even if I wanted to do it quickly, I could not. It cannot be done in two minutes."

"Okay, Baba, but please finish as soon as possible; otherwise you will have to take your lunch very late."

Baba took another half hour to complete the PC. When he finally sat down to lunch, it only lasted two minutes—a couple of mouthfuls of vegetables and a glass of milk.

During Baba's visit to Gorakhpur in 1960, he stayed in the house of Acharya Sachidananda. An indigent law student named Rajendra Pandey got permission for PC and remained in Baba's room for nearly forty minutes.[2] When he came out of the room he was crying. He went to the portico of the house and sat by himself, lost in his thoughts, the tears flowing profusely. One of his professors, Acharya Pratapaditya, who was employing him as a tutor for his children in order to help him out, grew concerned. He went and asked him what the matter was. "Acharyaji, please don't ask me anything now," Rajendra replied. "I am not in a state of mind to say anything. I will tell you everything later on. I can only say this much. Baba is not a human being. He is God Himself."

Rajendra later left without informing anyone. When Pratapaditya learned that he had gone, he became worried that he might have left out of reaction to some punishment Baba had given him. He went to the attending secretary and got permission to enter Baba's room.

"Baba, Rajendra was crying a lot after his PC. What was the matter?"

"The boy has committed a lot of sins in his life, so I gave him punishment."

"But Baba, is there a single human being on this planet that has not committed some sin or another? It is human nature to err."

"You are quite correct. It is perfectly natural for a human being to commit sins. But there are different gradations of misdeeds. Have you ever been to a post office?"

"Yes, Baba."

"Then you might have seen that there is a mail sorter who sorts the letters. He has a number of different bins in front of him and he drops the concerning letter in the appropriate bin. In the same way, I demarcate human beings into different categories and behave with them accordingly. Those who need to be punished, I punish. Those who don't need any punishment, I don't punish."

"But Baba, how could you know that he had committed so many sins?"

"Pratapaditya, if you make your conscious mind as subtle as your causal mind, then you can penetrate into the deepest recesses of anyone's psyche and uncover all the experiences undergone by that mind since its origin. Everything is stored in the causal mind. If you make your mind subtle enough, you can know everything."

The next day, Rajendra returned to Sachidananda's house to have Baba's darshan. Pratapaditya availed of the first opportunity he got to ask him about his PC. Rajendra narrated for him his experience:

> When I went inside the room, I did sastaunga pranam and then sat in front of Baba. As soon as I sat down, Baba said, "At such a young age, you have committed so many sins! Why did you do such things? Explain yourself." I thought this was something sadhus generally tell their disciples. I assumed Baba was doing the same thing, so I denied it; I told him I hadn't committed any sins. He told me to try to remember correctly; again I insisted that I had not done anything wrong. Baba became angry. "You still deny it? Look behind you!" I turned to look, and there on the wall behind me I saw one of my sinful actions being played out as if it were a movie reel. I turned away out of shame and hung my head. "Now do you remember?" "Yes, Baba," I said. "I remember." "This is not all, my boy," he said. "You have committed many sins far more serious than this." I thought then that Baba might have hypnotized me, so again I denied that I had committed any other sins. Baba commanded me to turn back and look at the wall again. I saw another sinful act from my life projected on the wall, just like before. Then Baba started to show me one shameful scene after another. They were incidents only I knew about. While I was watching them, Baba remained silent. I knew then that he had miraculous powers, but I thought it must have been because he was a powerful Tantric. Baba asked me if I understood. I told him I didn't understand. He asked me to sit in meditation. I meditated for a few minutes and then I heard him ask me to open my eyes. When I opened them, I could see neither Baba, nor the cot on which he was sitting, nor the walls, nor the room itself. All I could see was overpowering effulgence in all directions. Nothing else was visible. Then I became senseless. When I came to my senses, my head was on Baba's lap and he was patting me affectionately. He made me promise not to do such mistakes again, to be an ideal person and do only good work for the society. Then he blessed me and sent me out. There was no punishment or any mention of it. All I could feel as I left the room was a love that I cannot describe and tremendous bliss from the touch of his hand on my head. I thought that if even the persons closest to me like my parents came to know about even some of my black past,

they would hate me. But Baba, though he knew everything, gave me more love than I have ever experienced in my life. Only a God can love a sinner like me as much as Baba loves me.

By the time Baba started giving Personal Contact, his strictness with his disciples' faults and his readiness to punish them for their misdeeds was a frequent topic of discussion among the Margis, a fact Baba was well aware of. One Sunday morning, Baba was tending the small garden in his Rampur colony quarters, a regular part of his daily routine throughout the years he lived in Jamalpur. While he was clearing the soil for some new seedlings, a young man walking along the road stopped and asked him if he knew the way to the Ananda Marga ashram. Baba gave him directions and asked him why he wanted to go there. The young man explained that he was going to meet his guru. He politely invited Baba to come as well and take advantage of the opportunity to learn spiritual sadhana.

"Oh no," Baba said, "I would be afraid to go there. We've heard stories about Ananda Marga and its guru."

"What kind of stories?"

"We've heard that the guru punishes his disciples. I've heard from the neighbors that he can be very severe with them. I wouldn't have the courage to go in front of him."

"I'm sure he only punishes people who deserve it," the young man replied, signs of worry starting to creep into his face.

"Maybe. . . . Are you really sure you want to go there? There is still time to turn back."

"I'm sure."

The young man thanked him for the directions and headed down the route that Baba had pointed out. Later that day, the new initiate, who had yet to see a photo of Baba in keeping with the rules prevalent at the time, was ushered into Baba's room for PC. He was stunned to see the same person who had given him directions that morning. Baba, on the other hand, was laughing.

"You see? You are braver than I am. You came knowing that you might be punished, whereas I might not have come had I been in your shoes."

Early in 1961, Shiva Trivedi was accompanying Baba to the office when he noticed some swelling in Baba's hand. When he voiced his concern, Baba explained that he had had to punish a person in PC who had committed a murder. He had had no choice but to be very severe with that person. Then Shiva remembered one PC a couple of days earlier. Baba had dragged a young man out of the room by his hair and told him in front of the Margis that if he had been a judge, he would have sentenced him to hang. Shiva suggested to Baba that he use a stick for such people in order to save his hands. Baba approved his suggestion and a small stick was brought for that purpose. From then on, Baba kept the stick under his pillow whenever he gave PC. He would not discontinue using other forms of punishment, but the stick soon became his favorite medium for removing the samskaras of his more wayward disciples. Soon it would become so famous among the Margis that they even gave it a name—*dukhaharan*;[3] even Baba called it by that name on occasion.

Sometimes Baba would also bring out the stick during General Darshan. One time a new initiate, a rather fat gentleman from Bhagalpur, was in the audience. Baba asked Dasarath to see his mental plate. When Dasarath told Baba that it was blackish in color, Baba said that if he died he would take the body of a small animal in his next life. The man became frightened and started shouting, "Baba, Baba." Baba grabbed his ear and gave him several sharp thwacks on the thigh with the stick, which he had kept behind the bolster. Then Baba asked Dasarath to see the color of his mental plate again. This time it was much clearer. Baba scolded him for his mistakes and extracted a promise that he would rectify himself. He told him to forget his past, do his sadhana sincerely, and start a new life from that day forward.

In July of that year, a DMC was held in Betia during which Baba called attention to the punishments he was giving to some of the disciples in open assembly. "Some people commit great crimes while others only commit small mistakes; as per cosmic law, punishment has to be meted out accordingly. What is your opinion? Should I continue giving punishment as per cosmic law?" The hundreds of Margis present all agreed in unison and the stick became a permanent feature of Baba's rendering of divine justice.

Once the stick was securely under Baba's pillow, the particular disciple's samskaras would dictate whether it needed to put in an appearance or not. Ram Chandra had a close friend in Sahebganj, Ram Lakhan, who was a Brahmin and proud of his high caste. Ram Chandra tried to convince him to abandon his caste feelings but he met with little success. He did, however, convince him to take initiation. Soon afterward, Ram Lakhan told him, "I want to ask your Baba something. If he answers me correctly, then I will follow your Ananda Marga."

Ram Chandra laughed. "My Baba is more beautiful than you can imagine. Come, let us go to Jamalpur. You will get the answers to all your questions without even having to ask."

The following Sunday, they and one other friend boarded the early morning train for Jamalpur. As they were approaching Jamalpur Junction, Ram Lakhan's legs started to grow heavy. By the time they reached the station, he was unable to even get up from his seat. He became frightened. "I don't think I can get off the train," he said. "My legs won't move." Ram Chandra grabbed his shoulders and shook him. The strange sensation passed just as suddenly as it had come.

When they reached the jagriti, the three companions were the only candidates for PC. Ram Lakhan was the first to enter Baba's room. When he got up from sastaunga pranam, Baba asked him his name.

"Ah, so you are Ram Lakhan Mishra," Baba said. "You are not a good man. In fact, you are a great sinner. So, you have come to test me. Ask me what you want to ask."

Ram Lakhan was confused. Ram Chandra had been with him the whole time. He didn't understand how Baba could have known.

"Ask, you sinner. Ask what you came here to ask."

Ram Lakhan remained mute, unable to think properly. Baba pulled out his stick from beneath the pillow and gave him a good thwack on his side. "Look at the back wall," he commanded. Ram Lakhan turned and saw scenes of his misdeeds projected on the wall, one by one, while Baba provided the narration: "Alcohol at this place, robbery at that . . . What do you say now? Tell me, tell me!" Ram Lakhan was speechless. The tears started pouring down.

Baba's tone softened. "Okay, my boy. You are my son; you are my responsibility now." Baba continued speaking with such compassion that Ram Lakhan thought he must be dreaming or else in heaven. Then he lost consciousness and entered into trance. Baba had to call for his attendants to enter the room and carry him out.

When Ram Chandra saw the attendants carrying his friend out of Baba's room, he became frightened. He was afraid that Baba had hit Ram Lakhan so hard that he had killed him. What would he tell his children? When he stammered his concern to Baba's attendants, they smiled and told him not to worry. He was in a state of trance and would soon come back to his normal consciousness.

Then his other friend entered Baba's room. He came out soon afterward, red-faced and crying. Ram Chandra steeled himself, convinced that his position was indeed grave. Though he hadn't committed any mistakes that he could remember, he was sure that Baba would not spare him. He went in and did sastaunga pranam. When he got up, Baba was all smiles. "So Ram Chandra, you have come. How nice. You have been doing good work, I hope? How is your sadhana going? You have to improve your concentration. . . ." And so on.

When Ram Lakhan came back to normal consciousness, he recounted what had happened in his PC for his two companions. "He really is a God," he told them when he had finished telling the story. Shortly after that he left his job in Sahebganj to become a full-time volunteer worker for Ananda Marga, to the marked displeasure of his in-laws who would continue to hold Ram Chandra responsible until Ram Lakhan finally returned to Sahebganj where he became one of the pillars of the local Margi community.

Devi Chand was one of the most prominent and productive acharyas in Ananda Marga, a robust, energetic man, who, it was sometimes said, could do the work of three acharyas in half the time. He had been a freedom fighter during India's struggle for independence and commanded tremendous respect and reverence among the general public wherever he went. He did, however, have one bad habit: he used to falsify his travel allowance vouchers and pocket the extra money. In those days this was a common, even expected practice among government employees (and still is), but it was, nevertheless, an embarrassment for the other Margis who worked under him in the Department of Agriculture in Ranchi, especially Kshitij—for Devi Chand was not only his boss but also his acharya. Some of his co-workers would sometimes taunt him about it. "How can you teach morality when an acharya of Ananda Marga falsifies his TA vouchers?" There was nothing he could say to them. He sometimes prayed to Baba to remove his acharya's bad habit, but neither he nor the other Margis there dared say anything directly to Devi Chand due to the great respect they felt.

During one of Baba's visits to Ranchi, Kshitij served as the local attending secretary. During PC, he sent in a young initiate who worked as a clerk in his office. After a few minutes, he heard Baba calling his name. When he opened the door, he found Baba glaring at the boy.

"Kshitij, what kind of a scoundrel have you sent me! Did you know that this boy falsifies his TA vouchers and pockets the money?" Baba turned back to the boy and shouted, "Who is your acharya?" The frightened boy was unable to get the words out. "Kshitij, who is his acharya?"

"Baba, his acharya is Devi Chand."

"Bring him here, right now."

Kshitij bolted out of the room and returned a minute or two later with Devi Chand. "Devi Chand," Baba said as the acharya entered the room, "this boy is your initiate. Did you not look into his conduct before you initiated him? Did you know that he has been presenting false TA vouchers and pocketing the money? What punishment should I give him?"

Devi Chand kept silent.

"Okay then," Baba continued. "I am going to beat him for his crime unless and until you forgive him." Baba took out his stick and hit the boy on the side of his thigh. "Devi Chand, do you forgive him?"

Devi Chand's face became flushed, but he remained silent. Baba nodded and hit the boy a second time. "Devi Chand, do you forgive him now?" Devi Chand's face turned even redder, but he still didn't say anything. Baba continued to beat the boy, who by then was pleading with his acharya to forgive him.

Finally Devi Chand answered Baba in a weak voice. "Baba, I forgive him." Baba smiled and told the boy to beg forgiveness directly from his acharya. The boy touched Devi Chand's feet and asked his pardon. By this time, Devi Chand was visibly shaken; tears were streaming down his face. He stammered out his forgiveness. Baba consoled the boy and made him promise to become an ideal human being.

Once the boy had left the room, Baba turned his gaze on Devi Chand. "Devi Chand, a person has no right to forgive others if he is guilty of the same mistake. Do you understand?"

"Yes, Baba."

There was no more mention of the TA bills, but Devi Chand never presented another false voucher.

Occasionally, the work of cleaning a person's mental plate required extreme measures. One Sunday before General Darshan in Jamalpur, Baba was giving PC to Baleshvar's nephew, an officer in the BMP. After a few minutes the Margis heard Baba shouting inside the room. This was followed by the sound of him beating the officer with his stick. It was so loud that some of the Margis who were waiting for Baba's darshan flinched when they heard it. After a couple of minutes, Baba called out for another stick; he had broken the first one. Nagendra of Muzaffarpur, who was the attending secretary, cracked opened the door and handed Baba another stick. The beating resumed. A few minutes later the door burst open. The police officer, a burly hulk of a man, came running out, with Baba, all 5' 3" of him, chasing him from behind and scolding him mercilessly. While the officer cowered in one corner of the darshan room, Baba caught him by the ear and shouted, "Should I reveal to the authorities what you have done and have you executed? Better I kill you right here and now." The policeman, weeping loudly, begged Baba for mercy. "Beg pardon from each and every Margi in this room," Baba told him. "If even one Margi does not pardon you, then I will kill you here and now." One by one, he went to each of the Margis present and finally even to the volunteer who was serving as gatekeeper. No one knew what to think, but everyone pardoned the policeman of his unknown crime. Then Baba softened somewhat and took him back into his room to complete the PC.

A few days later, Nagendra had a chance to go on field walk with Baba. When they reached the neem tree, he got an opportunity to talk to Baba privately. He asked him why he had given that officer so much punishment and whether or not all his sins were gone. Baba told him in confidence that he had raped and murdered a young woman, the sister of one Margi, even though she had pleaded for mercy. "This is a social crime," Baba told him, "and social crimes cannot be pardoned without severe punishment.[1] I could have produced proofs of the crime, but he admitted it and accepted his punishment. Fifty percent of the samskara was removed by the beating, twenty-five percent by repentance and asking pardon, and the remaining twenty-five percent will be taken care of through sadhana."

A year later, Nagendra was again overseeing the personal contacts during one DMC. A lean, young man came up to him and requested permission to have PC with Baba. When he asked him who he was, the man replied, "Don't you recognize me? I'm Baleshvar's nephew. I begged you for pardon that day when I had PC with Baba." Nagendra was shocked to see how much he had changed. "I have suffered a lot since we last met," the young man said. "I lost my job, then I fell ill for a long time and lost a lot of weight. Now I'm working as a clerk. But no matter what happens, I will never leave my sadhana."

One day, Baba was giving PC in the Jamalpur jagriti to the last person on the list, Shiva Narayana. After half an hour, Baba opened the door and called Chandradeva, Dasarath, and another couple of Margis inside. They found Shiva Narayana sitting in lotus posture in front of Baba's cot, absorbed in samadhi. Baba sat back down and asked them to sit as well. "Dasarath," he said, "see this boy's previous life."

"Baba, that is not possible without your grace."

Baba leaned forward and touched Dasarath at the back of his head. He repeated his request. Dasarath described a person walking in a village.

"What is the name of the village?" Baba asked.

"Baba, I am going all over the village but I don't see any signboard."

"Then come back to the present, go to the nearest railway station, and read the sign there."

After Dasarath read out the name, Baba said, "The village you saw is four miles from the railway station. The boy's name in that life was Devanath Bannerjee. He was born four hundred years ago in that village. Now look again into his past life and see what he is doing."

"Baba, he is angling for fish in a nearby river."

"Yes, this was his main work. He was a fisherman."

When the demonstration was over, Chandradeva asked Baba a question. "Baba, you always show us everyone else's past lives, but you never tell us about yours."

Suddenly everyone became tense, except for Shiva Narayana, who was still in trance. They were afraid of how Baba might react to what was assuredly an inappropriate question. Chandradeva, who had realized his indiscretion the minute it came out of his mouth, felt a sinking feeling in the pit of his stomach. Baba closed his eyes for a few moments. When he opened them, they were noticeably red. The disciples grew even more anxious. But Baba smiled and said, "I am your slave from long, long ago." Baba looked at Dasarath. "Dasarath, say something about me. Who was I?"

"How can I do that, Baba?"

"Do dhyana." Baba reached out and touched him again. "What do you see now?"

"Baba, I see the currents of *saincara* and *pratisaincara*.[5] The entire universe is emanating from you. I see creatures that I have never seen before, such creatures as are not found on this earth."

"Yes, there are many different planets in this universe that contain life. The creatures found on other planets are different from the ones found here. Now what do you see?"

"I see that you are nourishing living creatures and then killing them."

Baba smiled. "No, no, no. How can I kill anyone? You should use a different word."

At this moment, Chandradeva shouted *Bhagawan Sri Krishnachandra ki jai,* victory to Lord Krishna; the other Margis followed suit. When they calmed down, Baba told them that Shri Krishna had shown the same scene to his disciple Arjuna.

"For many births you have been with me and worked with me. We have established dharma on many different planets, but you don't remember it. It is God's desire that dharma be established from one planet to another. You have all helped me in this work. Many times the immoralists have done you great harm, but you have always emerged victorious. We have also come to this planet for a special work, and after we finish it we will go elsewhere. Those children who need salvation will get it, and those who want to come to other planets with me will come."

Baba then walked out of the room and headed out the gate for his house. The Margis remained in his room, looking at each other, still overcome by the significance of what they had just seen and heard.

PART THREE

XXVI

Revolutionary Marriage

The people of Asia and America are touching each other's minds and have learned to accept each other sympathetically as their own. Europe, Africa, Australia, Mercury, Jupiter, the stars, the comets, the constellations—none of them is alien to the other, none is distant from another. Gradually everyone has begun to realize the vibration of the One Integral Mind. It is my firm conviction that the future of humanity is not dark. Every human being will attain that inextinguishable flame that is forever alight beyond the veil of the darkness of the present.[1]

AS THE NEW decade got underway, Baba began to rapidly expand and accelerate the activities of Ananda Marga, paving the way for the transition to what he had termed the "intellectual phase." His principle medium for this work was the rapidly growing number of acharyas. By 1960, he had created nearly one hundred acharyas. Within the next few years an even greater number would pass their acharya exam. More of Baba's time was now taken up with the training of these acharyas. He often held classes for them at the jagriti. After one such class in which he emphasized the importance of the work they were doing, he told them, "*Mukti* and *moksha* are in your folded fist.[2] Anytime you wish, you can open your hand and get them. But for me they are like a gold cot. I may take rest on it for a short while, but for endless time I have to return to this soil and serve the creation. Now, all of you, tell me, what do you want? Do you want liberation and salvation, or do you want to come with me, life after life, wherever I go, and serve the creation?" Every acharya present, many of them with tears in their eyes, replied that they wanted to come back with Baba to serve the creation.

Despite the necessity of passing the acharya course, Baba's training methods extended far beyond his formal classes. Once, while returning from a DMC, Baba was traveling by train with a small group of acharyas. He took the opportunity to give them a class on certain aspects of the spiritual philosophy. During the conversation, Balendu, a quiet, introverted man, complained to Baba that while he understood the philosophy, he still had trouble doing prachar. "I don't seem to be able to convince anyone to take initiation," he lamented. Baba nodded and agreed to give him some pointers. Moments later, the train pulled into a small station and a teenage boy entered the compartment. Baba called the boy over and asked him his name and where he was from.

"Your house faces east, does it not?" Baba said. "And if I am not mistaken, right beside it there is a football field and just behind the house there is a small temple."

The boy was understandably surprised. He nodded in agreement and then listened with even greater astonishment as Baba described in great detail his house and his neighborhood.

"But sir, how do you know my house and my neighborhood so well? I don't remember seeing you before. Did you use to live there?"

Baba smiled but didn't answer. Instead, he began quoting the names of the boy's relatives back to his great-great-grandparents, telling him facts about them that the boy had never heard before. When he was finished, Baba said, "Look here, I have told you many useful things about your family that you should know. Will you do one thing for me? These fellows here are acharyas of Ananda Marga. They teach meditation and yoga. Would you be willing to learn meditation and yogic practices from one of them? This will be for your welfare; it will help you in your studies also."

The boy agreed with alacrity. Baba instructed Kshitij to note down his contact information and arrange for his initiation as soon as possible. After the boy got down at the next station, Baba turned to Balendu. "You see how it is done, Balendu?"

Everyone laughed. "I'm sorry, Baba," Balendu said, " but only a God can do this. We are just human beings."

Baba was laughing as well. "Okay then. Have you ever attended a football match? If you watch carefully, you can easily see which people are really absorbed in the match. When someone makes a goal or a great play they automatically react to it; they may shout 'goal' or slap themselves on the thigh. Then you know that the person is really into the match. When you give a lecture, it's much the same. You should carefully scan the crowd to see who is really paying attention and responding to your talk. They'll nod their head when you make a point, or give some such telltale sign. After the lecture, go up and talk to those people. You will find it easy to convince them to take initiation."

Baba's acharya exams were also decidedly idiosyncratic. Though the new candidates would sometimes be sent to his room for a formal oral exam, Baba would often give the exam at the tiger's grave, sometimes without any prior warning. Thirty marks was the passing grade, but it was rare that anyone answered Baba's questions well enough to be able to pass the exam on the merit of their answers. If Baba was satisfied with their effort, he would give them "grace marks" to make up the difference. As might be expected, the exam was more a test of sincerity and surrender than of intellectual knowledge. It was not unheard of for a new acharya to pass his exam after receiving one mark for his answers and twenty-nine grace marks.

Mashin Bahadur, a member of the BMP, was the first Nepali acharya. He took his exam on the tiger's grave along with several others. Baba pointed to himself and told the candidates to imagine that he was a Muslim. Their task was to convince him to learn sadhana. Each took turns trying to convince Baba, but only Mashin Bahadur passed. A few months later, he recommended Giridhara Upadhyaya, a fellow Nepali officer, for acharya training, hoping to have another acharya in Nepal to help him with the work of Ananda Marga. Giridhara was an enthusiastic practitioner of sadhana, as well as a Brahmin and a reputed scholar. When Mashin Bahadur proposed his name to Baba, Baba told him to give him training in Nepal and bring him to Jamalpur for his exam. By that time, Giridhara had already mastered the philosophy and was proud of his accomplishment. He was sure that whatever question Baba asked, he would be able to answer it. Again the exam took place on the tiger's grave. Baba had only one question: "Giridhara, do you practice meditation regularly?"

"Yes, Baba, at least one hour in the morning and one hour at night."

"Then you must be able to remember your mantra?"

"Yes, Baba."

"Then tell me your mantra."

Try as he might, Giridhara was unable to answer. Baba turned to Mashin Bahadur and said, "It seems his training is not yet complete. Train him for a few days more."

Giridhara's ego was crushed. When they got back to the jagriti, he explained to Mashin Bahadur that his mind had gone totally blank the moment Baba asked him to tell him his mantra.

"It is your ego," Mashin Bahadur said. "Baba will not allow any expression of ego in his disciples. You have to learn to surrender; otherwise, you'll never pass. Tell him mentally to do whatever he wants—make me or break me, whatever be your wish."

Giridhara understood. He spent the next couple of days surrendering mentally to Baba. Then Mashin Bahadur sent him for field walk again, alone this time. As Baba saw him approaching, he shouted out, "Giridhara, go to the general secretary and collect your acharya certificate."

Visheshvar's acharya exam took place after he attended the first Prout training in Jamalpur in 1959. Pranay gave him his initial test after Baba had sent an order that he sit for the acharya exam. Pranay asked him one question: "Do you want to become an acharya?" Visheshvar, a teacher from Arraria, answered no. Pranay declared him passed and sent him on field walk for his final exam. When they reached the tiger's grave that night, Baba asked him several questions, none of which he could answer to Baba's satisfaction. The first question Baba asked was, "If a Muslim girl wants to marry a Hindu boy, what should you do?"

"I would give them permission," he answered.

"No. That is not the correct move. If they want to do a love marriage then first you should test the intensity of their love.³ You should tell the girl to ask the boy whether or not he would be willing to convert to Islam. If he shows his willingness, then it will prove he loves her. Tell Pranay that you failed the exam, but he can send you again tomorrow evening. You can repeat the exam then."

When they reached the tiger's grave the next evening, Visheshvar was thoroughly annoyed. He had already made up his mind to tell Baba that he didn't want to take the test, that it was too hard, that no one could pass such a test and hence he had decided not to become an acharya. Before he had a chance to say anything, however, Baba took an acharya certificate out of his pocket, wrote Visheshvar's name on it, signed it, and handed it to him without even mentioning the exam.

Pratapaditya's exam took place at the tiger's grave in the summer of 1960. By then, a Prout section had been added to the regular exam. Since Pratapaditya had a MA in Political Science, he was sure he could pass this portion of the exam at least without any difficulty. Baba's lone question was on an aspect of international politics he knew nothing about and was unable to answer. "Keep studying," Baba told him. After a couple of days, he was sent back on field walk to take the Prout exam again. By this time, he had realized that it was not possible to pass Baba's exam unless Baba willed it so, that it was not a matter of knowledge but of devotion. This time he did not even mention the exam. He was happy just to be sitting there with Baba. Someone else, however, mentioned it to Baba. Baba immediately asked him for his application, took out his flashlight and a pen, and wrote "passed" across the top without asking a single question.

Baban's acharya exam, which had taken place a few years earlier, had even less to do with philosophy. Gopen brought him to Baba's house for his exam, but instead, Baba took him to the field. They climbed up into the hills and Baba took a seat on a large stone. "Go to the top of that hillock and jump down," Baba told him. "Don't worry, you won't get hurt." Baban did as Baba asked, shouting Baba's name as he jumped. He landed in a small patch of mud; except for getting his clothes dirty, he was fine. As Baba was helping him to get unstuck, he said, "Your acharya exam is now over. You passed."

When Professor Indradev Gupta took his exam, he took the precaution of consulting with an authority on the subject before answering Baba's questions.

> Beloved Baba was giving darshan in Jamalpur. There were ten to twelve of us. Suddenly Baba said that he was going to conduct an examination for all the trainees. At the very outset, Baba put a question to me in English. The question was as follows: "The human body is endowed with living cells. Because these cells have life, they possess life force

as well as mind. Is the human mind, then, a conglomerate of all the minds of each of the cells?" Because the question was both difficult and in English, I didn't understand it. Since I didn't understand it, I remained silent. I kept gazing at Baba. "Why are you staring at me?" Baba said, half-annoyed, half smiling. "It's your examination! Answer me. Think carefully and answer the question." Baba's facial expression used to have a fascinating, double-edged charm to it. He could simultaneously express both annoyance and sweetness. It was almost as if he could scold with one eye and enchant with the other. Then I thought, since I don't know the reply, let me ask him. I asked him mentally and immediately received an answer in my mind. I merely parroted what I heard, which was, "The human mind is an independent mind. Those living cells, which had been referred to earlier, also have independent minds that hold the possibility of becoming human minds, but they are in an undeveloped stage. However, the human mind is not a composite mind but an independent entity."

When Baba heard my reply, he said, half-annoyed, half sweetly, "No one will consult anyone before answering. Answers will be given independently." No one understood what he meant, since I hadn't asked any of them for the answer. But I understood. Baba was telling me to think it through myself. Then he asked his second question: "Does the unit mind through the sensory organs enjoy the original object, or the shadow of the object, or its shadow's shadow. Explain it logically." Since I did not know the answer to this question either, I asked him internally again and received the answer. Then I repeated it orally: "The unit mind does not enjoy objects in their physical form. Through the sensory organs, the mind enjoys the *tanmatras* emanated by the physical world composed of the five fundamental factors.[4] So here the mind does not enjoy the original object, but rather its shadow, i.e. the *tanmatras* of the object. But this physical world itself is a shadow of the Cosmic Mind. So it can be said that the unit mind does not enjoy the original object, the Supreme Consciousness, or its shadow, the physical world, but the shadow of the shadow, i.e. the *tanmatras* emanated by the physical world."

The answer was correct. This time Baba was very upset. "I said there should be no cheating. No one should consult with anyone else before giving his answer." Again, everyone but me was confused by what Baba said. Then Baba asked a third question. "What is the difference between Purushottama and Nirguna Brahma from the point of view of philosophy?" I didn't feel confident enough to reply. Since Baba had scolded me quite soundly the last time around, this time I remained silent. When Baba persisted, I plucked up my courage and said, "Baba, it seems that the person I consulted doesn't know the answer." Baba burst into laughter. Then he gave detailed answers to all three questions. After giving the answer to the third question, he quietly asked me, "Did the person you consulted know the correct reply?" I laughed. Everyone else was scratching his head. The general secretary could not contain himself anymore. "Baba, whom was he consulting before giving his replies?" Baba cleared up the confusion. "He was answering all the questions by asking me." Then everyone broke into a chorus of laughter.

Asim Kumar Pathak took initiation from Acharya Kedarnath Sharma in Ranchi at the end of 1959, a few days before the first VSS camp that was held there at Birla Boarding. He was twenty at the time, a student and an ardent devotee of Krishna who had been fanatically practicing various yogic techniques from books for several years, adamant that he did not need or want a guru. While Baba was at Ranchi, Kedarnath brought Asim to a General Darshan, over the objections of Devi Chand Sharma, who insisted that the boy wait at least six months before seeing Baba, as per the rule. All Asim remembered from that first darshan was that it was so philosophical, he couldn't understand a single sentence. Afterward, he was convinced that Baba was a clever pundit who was able to befool those gullible, crying people with his high-sounding words.

About a half hour later, Kedarnath told Asim that Baba wanted to see him. "Baba said that you came late," Kedarnath told him. "He said that you should have come long before." These words made Asim even more suspicious. He accompanied Kedarnath to Baba's room where he found Baba eating his dinner. Before they went in, Kedarnath told him that he should do sastaunga pranam when he entered, but Asim was not about to do that. He gave Baba his namaskar, just as he would anyone else that he was meeting for the first time. Baba looked at him and asked, "What is the highest oxide of aluminum?" Asim was too surprised by the question to answer. "Aluminum tetroxide," Baba said. After a couple of similar questions that Asim found equally irrelevant, he was led out of Baba's room, his frustration mounting. Why did I come to these people? he fumed as he was going home. Why should I have to accept a guru? I don't want a guru. But as soon as he arrived home, he was overpowered by an inexplicable desire to see Baba again. It was a feeling of longing greater than anything he had ever experienced, a sensation that he could only describe as having been forcefully separated from the person dearest to him in his life. By then it was after midnight. He knew it would be futile to head back at that hour. After a fitful sleep, he got up at five, took a shower, and got on his bicycle to head back to the house where Baba was staying.

It was six o'clock when he arrived. Devi Chand Sharma was standing outside the gate. "Come, Baba is waiting for you," he said as Asim rode up.

"What do you mean, Baba is waiting for me? I didn't tell anybody that I was coming."

Devi Chand grabbed his hand and said in his normal gruff manner, "Come, you will understand everything." He led him into Baba's room where Baba was waiting to conduct PC, having informed Devi Chand earlier that Asim would be arriving at that time for Personal Contact.

This time Asim did sastaunga pranam when he entered the room. As soon as he sat up, Baba began recounting details and incidents from his life that no one could have possibly known, one after the other, until Asim was convinced that Baba was able to read his mind. Baba told him why some of the practices he had learned from books were misguided.

"Do you see now how much energy you have wasted by not having had proper guidance? Do you understand?"

"Yes, Baba."

"You know, if you write something on a piece of paper and put it under your pillow but don't follow it in your life, then it has no value."

I haven't put anything underneath my pillow, he thought. Perhaps Baba's power has reached its limit.

Baba looked him in the eyes and said, "Don't you remember?" Suddenly a forgotten memory flashed in his mind. Some months earlier, he had written some inspirational advice from Aurobindo and the Buddha on a piece of paper and put it under his pillow, thinking to read it each morning when he woke up. But he had forgotten about it and never read it again.

"Baba, how did you know that?"

"Your mind tells me."

Asim was not satisfied with the answer, since he himself had forgotten the incident. "Who are you?" he asked.

Baba smiled. "I am not your guru. I am your Baba."

Asim began to cry. Baba called him closer and touched his trikuti. He became lost in a blissful, effulgent light and entered into a state of trance. When he came out of his trance, Baba asked him to hold his feet and take an oath. The oath was in English, a language Asim didn't understand at the time. Asim repeated it and then asked Baba what it meant. Baba smiled and translated it into Hindi for him. Then he added, "You came very late. You should have come earlier."

After his PC, Asim found himself torn between his devotion to Krishna and his love for Baba. When Baba returned to Ranchi in April, Asim heard that he would be giving DMC in Saharsa in the middle of May to celebrate Ananda Purnima. He had no idea what DMC was, much less Ananda Purnima, but he was seized by a powerful desire to attend. When he told Baba of his desire, thinking that Baba might ask one of the older disciples to help him, Baba said, "Develop your willpower." After Baba left for Jamalpur, a sense of determination flared in Asim's mind. He started selling the few possessions he owned—a few books and some clothes—adamant that he would find a way to raise the money for the train ticket. But when Kshitij learned of what he was doing, he told him to stop. He would take him to Saharsa with him.

Thus, on May 14, Asim found himself traveling in the same first-class compartment as Baba. While Baba was talking with the other devotees in the compartment, Asim decided to test him. He had seen that Baba could look within his mind, but was it really true what the devotees said—that Baba resided within every mind, all the time? How could this be possible? If Baba really knows everything of everyone, all the time, he thought, he will look at me just now. At that moment, Baba turned and looked at him and then returned to his conversation.

Maybe it was a coincidence, Asim thought. Maybe he was thinking about me while he was talking to the other Margis. I'll let some time go by and try again. Fifteen or twenty minutes passed. Again he said to himself, If he is really within everyone's mind all the time, then he will look at me just now. Again Baba looked at him and smiled and then returned to his conversation. Still, Asim was not a hundred percent convinced. Maybe he was still paying attention to me somehow, he thought. But he can't possibly know what is going on inside my mind when his attention is occupied elsewhere.

Shortly afterward, the train pulled into the next station and a group of devotees entered and started talking with Baba. They brought him food and flowers and offered their pranams. Ah, Asim thought, now is the perfect opportunity, while Baba is busy with these Margis. If he knows everything of this world all the time, he will look at me just now. Baba looked at him and said, "My child, why are you thinking in this way?" Again Baba turned his attention back to the Margis. Asim was left to choke down his embarrassment.

Later in the trip, Asim had a chance to be alone with Baba in the compartment. Baba was reclining on his berth when he asked Asim to tell him three things he was proud of. "Baba, the first thing I'm proud of is my singing voice; the second is that I'm handsome; and the third is that I'm a good devotee."

"You know, when I was a child I used to study music with a teacher. He taught me some Rabindra Samgita.[5] Do you want to hear?"

"Yes, Baba, please sing."

Baba sang three songs: *kon alote praner pradiip jhaliye*; *sadha kabha premi kabha pago logo*; and *tumi kahar sandhane*. Asim was enthralled. It seemed as if he had never heard such a sweet voice in his life.

"Now you sing the same three songs," Baba said, "and I will listen."

Asim sang the first song, but after listening to Baba, his own voice sounded to him like a donkey's braying in the wake of a cuckoo's song. He was so embarrassed that when Baba asked him to sing the second song, he requested Baba to sing instead.

"No," Baba replied, "it is a little difficult to sing while lying down. I want to take rest for a while."

Some minutes later, the train pulled into the next station and Chandranath's son Amarnath entered Baba's compartment along with several other Margis. They all sat on the floor and started chatting merrily with Baba. Amarnath was sixteen at the time and extremely handsome. When Asim looked at Amarnath sitting in front of Baba, he felt ugly by comparison.

At the next station, Devi Chand Sharma entered Baba's compartment. "Devi Chand," Baba said, "tell me what you are proud of."

"Baba, I am only proud of one thing: I am your son."

When Asim heard this, he felt a sinking feeling. What kind of devotee am I by comparison? he thought. Only then did he suspect that Baba had been playing a game with him in order to deflate his ego.

When the train pulled into Saharsa, Asim was surprised to see that nearly a thousand Margis had gathered for the DMC. He had no idea that Ananda Marga was anything more than the guru and a handful of devotees. Baba was taken to the house of Bal Mukunda Rastogi, where a room had been prepared for him to stay during the program. It was breakfast time, but when Baba was brought his breakfast, he refused to eat. The Margis became worried that they had committed some mistake. Cautiously, they asked Baba if they had done anything wrong. "No," he told them, "you haven't done anything wrong, but someone else has." Baba told them to call a certain Margi to his room. They went out to the compound where the Margis had gathered to attend Baba's darshan and made an announcement by loudspeaker, but no one came forward. Knowing that Baba would not eat until they found him, they conducted a search and finally found the young man sleeping behind the stage. They brought him to Baba along with his acharya.

As soon as he was presented to Baba, Baba asked him how he came.

"By train, Baba."

"I know, but *how* did you come?"

"By train."

"That is not what I am asking. Did you purchase a ticket?"

"Yes, Baba."

"And where did you get the money for this ticket?"

This time the young man did not answer, but his fear was visible on his face.

"Nothing to say, huh? Then I will tell the story of how you got this money." Baba looked at the Margis and pointed to the young man. "This boy has committed a crime. He stole that money from the pocket of a carpenter—sixty-two rupees. It was the man's monthly earnings; he was on his way to purchase provisions for his family. After he noticed that the money was gone, he became so distraught, he began saying that there is no God in this universe, no divine justice, that he was going to commit suicide because he was a poor man and could not survive without that money. Now I am responsible, since it is my devotee who stole his money."

Baba called the young man's acharya and started scolding him for initiating the boy without having properly evaluated his conduct. Then he told the young man to touch the feet of everyone present and leave. When he was going out the door, Baba called him back.

"I want you to return that money to the person you stole it from."

The young man was crying now. "But Baba, how can I do that? I don't know who he is or where he lives."

"You will not get off so easily. Ask someone here to run to the post office and bring back a money order form."

A few minutes later, one Margi returned with the form. Baba took out his pen and wrote the name and address of the carpenter on it. He handed it to the boy. "Now go to the post office with your acharya and send the money. Write on the back of the money order that you have stolen this money from him and now you are returning it."

Baba told the young man's acharya to make sure that he followed his instructions. When they had gone, he told the Margis, "Actually, he is a sincere devotee. When I conducted his PC, I took an oath from him not to pick any more pockets. Up until a few days ago he had kept his oath, but when he heard that Baba was coming here, he decided to pick one last pocket so that he could have my darshan. So you see, it is my responsibility."

On the night of the DMC, Asim was seated near the front. During the guru-puja that followed Baba's discourse, he suddenly saw Baba disappear from the platform. In his place, he saw the figure of Krishna surrounded by bright blue effulgence. Within moments Asim lost consciousness of his surroundings; he started making a soft choking sound. Several minutes passed. When he opened his eyes again, he saw Baba standing in front of him, on his way out of the compound. "Bujhecho?" Baba asked in Bengali. Understood? Asim reached out and grabbed Baba. "Discipline, discipline," Baba ordered. Asim let go, but as soon as Baba left, he started crying and remained in that condition for the next seven or eight days.

By 1960, Baba had become an auditor in the accounts department with a reputation for strictness and thoroughness that was unmatched in the workplace. Even high-ranking officers used to become apprehensive when they heard that P. R. Sarkar was coming to inspect their office, and it was commonly whispered that if there were any irregularity in their accounts, P. R. Sarkar would be sure to find it.[6] His subordinates recalled that when they accompanied him on inspection, he would regularly direct them to the exact page of the exact ledger that contained bookkeeping errors, something they were used to from the accounts office where he would often call out across the room while they were working to alert them to an incorrect entry they had just made. Nor was it any secret that Baba vocally condemned some of the senior officers for the way they treated the people who worked for them.

In early summer, Baba went to inspect the books of Sarvananda, one of the supervisory officers. When Baba found evidence of corruption and misappropriation of funds, Sarvananda tried to convince him to hush it up. Baba not only made the matter public, he scolded him mercilessly in front of his subordinates.

Things soon became so uncomfortable for Sarvananda that within a matter of weeks he resigned from his job, but not before filing a report that eventually led to Baba being transferred. Part of the charges levied against him was that he was allegedly converting Muslims to Hinduism.

Shortly after Sarvananda's departure, notice arrived of Baba's transfer to Asansol, some 220 kilometers from Calcutta. A furor broke out among the local Margis, who were aghast at the thought of losing Baba to another city and worried about how they would be able to administer the organization without Baba's immediate physical guidance. Pranay called a meeting of all acharyas and senior Margis. They took a collective decision to ask Baba to resign from his service. Pledges were taken to provide Baba with the money he would need to maintain his family. Then they took the proposal to Baba in the form of a written letter.

Baba read the letter and wrote "rejected" at the top. "It is a good proposal," he said, "but it is not yet time for me to resign from my service, nor is there any reason to worry about my transfer. Let tomorrow take care of tomorrow. For now, I will go on leave. Let us see what happens."

Baba requested one month's leave for the stated purpose of putting his personal affairs in order. The day before he went on leave, Nilen Bose approached him during the lunch break to commiserate. "Now that you are leaving Jamalpur, what are we going to do without you?" he said. "Every day we listen to your stories and your advice. When will we ever get such a chance again?"

"Don't worry," Baba said. "I will not be transferred."

"But your transfer letter has come!"

"I assure you, after my leave is over, I will be sitting at this same desk doing the same work."

Baba did not, however, mention this to the Margis, nor did he make any plans or preparations, either personal or organizational. Instead, he went on tour to a number of different cities where Ananda Marga was active. Whenever Pranay or other Margis brought up his transfer, he told them that there was no need to be concerned. Time would take care of it.

At the end of June, while Baba was on leave, he developed a boil on his leg. Instead of taking rest, as Pranay insisted, he went to Muzaffarpur as scheduled and stayed there for eight days in the house of Acharya Sakaldev. The word spread quickly that Baba had come, and Sakaldev's house was soon turned into an ashram, with devotees constantly coming and going to see Baba and attend the morning and evening General Darshan. One day, Baba was sitting in his room with Acharya Gangasharan and his family. In the course of the conversation, Gangasharan asked his niece Indu in a playful way when she was going to get married. When she didn't reply, Baba answered for her. "Don't worry," he said, "the groom will appear on this very doorstep within a few days." Then Baba explained his concept of revolutionary marriage. "The easiest and best way to break down the barriers that separate different races and different cultures is through intercaste and intercultural marriage. Suppose a girl and a boy from different castes marry. It will help to dissolve their own caste feeling, and their children will have no caste. Suppose a boy of this land marries a girl from England. He would never like to see England ruined and vice versa. Nor will their children have anti-English or anti-Indian feelings. It is the easiest way to break down these barriers."

A couple of days later, Sujit was massaging Baba when Baba sent him home on the pretext that he wanted to do sadhana. Shortly after he left, Gangasharan arrived with his family and a number of other Margis, including Nagina and Shashi Rainjan. While Baba was conversing with them, he announced that he wanted a revolutionary marriage to be solemnized within the next twenty-four hours. Indu, if she agreed, would be the bride; Sujit would be the groom. Baba sent someone to bring Sujit, who was surprised that Baba would call him back so quickly. When Sujit entered the room and did pranam, Baba told him, "Sujit, if you agree and the girl agrees, then I want you to marry Indu." Baba called Indu into the room and repeated what he had told Sujit. The marriage was fixed for the following evening.

The sudden decision was a shock to both the bride and the groom, but they acceded to the wish of their guru, despite the fact that they not only came from different castes but lived in Bihar, the most caste-conscious region of India. In fact, it would be many years before either Sujit's parents or the other non-Margi members of his family would openly accept their marriage or offer any kind of support to the young couple.

The next morning in General Darshan, July 8, Gangasharan folded his hands in namaskar and invited everyone to the wedding. Then, getting slightly carried away, he invited all the subtler and subtlest entities of the universe, as well as all disciples of Baba, on this planet or any other. The marriage was celebrated that evening with a traditional wedding procession. Baba accompanied the groom's party halfway to Gangasharan's house, where the bridal party was waiting to receive them. Then he asked his driver to take him to Gangasharan's so he could welcome the groom's party as a member of the bridal party. On his arrival there, he politely requested everyone not to insult him since he was coming as a member of the bride's party, it being the custom in Bihar for the bride's party to welcome guests from the groom's side with colorful abusive epithets. The ceremony took place on the roof of Gangasharan's house, a spacious, flat surface that was able to accommodate the more than three hundred Margis and neighbors who attended. Many neighbors, unable to attend for lack of space, climbed into the nearby trees to watch. Devotional songs followed and Indu quickly became abnormal, carried away by her devotional fervor. Baba scolded her and warned her that if she didn't remain normal for her wedding he wouldn't stay. Then he joked that it was normal for Indu to become abnormal. During the reception afterward, it was her new husband's turn to become abnormal during the devotional singing.

That night, while Gangasharan was sleeping on the veranda, he had a dream that many saints and sages with white beards and beads entered the compound, paid their respects to the new couple, and went away. The next morning, when Baba was getting ready to leave for Jamalpur, Gangasharan asked him about his dream. "It was due to your invitation," Baba said. "Do you think that human beings were the only beings to attend?"

After the wedding, Indu and Sujit went to Jamalpur for what amounted to their honeymoon. They went on field walk with Baba on their first night there; the next day a telegram arrived from Pranay in Bolpur with the message that he needed an English-speaking acharya right away to deliver a lecture at Shantiniketan university. Baba asked Sujit to go. He selected a topic and gave him some suggestions on how to organize his talk. Then he called Sujit and Indu into his room to bless their marriage. That night, Sujit left for Shantiniketan and the honeymoon was over. Neither one complained. For both of them Baba's work came first, and this would continue to be the theme of their lives.

That same week a letter arrived from Baba's sister in Chinchura informing him that his son, Gautam, had been born on the ninth in Bandel at Uma Sarkar's parents' house, where she had gone for the last stage of her pregnancy and the birth of her first child, in keeping with a centuries-old Indian tradition. Baba noted down the date in his diary, but as usual there was nothing in his demeanor to show that anything had changed, even after Uma Devi returned to Jamalpur a few weeks later with the newborn child.

After Indu and Sujit's marriage, "revolutionary," or intercaste, intercultural marriages quickly became the norm in Ananda Marga. Instead of looking for suitable partners within their caste, a rigid practice in traditional Hindu society, or within their religion in the case of other religions, Margi families started making it known that any caste would be acceptable, except their own. The backlash from the non-Margi members of their families, as well as from neighbors and colleagues, was predictable and immediate in a country and at a time where it was not unheard of for intercaste couples to be physically attacked or even killed for breaking taboo. It was the norm, rather than the exception, for such couples to be ostracized by their family and community, especially in smaller towns and rural areas where such marriages were considered unthinkable. Each couple had their stories to tell of the trials they had to face, but they accepted them willingly and pointed to them as a badge of honor in their struggle to spread their guru's teachings. "Yours should be a pauseless struggle against corruption, hypocrisy, and animality," Baba had told them, and in January 1961 he gave them the message that would become the foremost creed of all Margis as the organization began to grow rapidly and meet the mounting opposition that Baba had warned them to expect: "Fight for your ideology. Be one with your ideology. Live for your ideology. Die for your ideology." Revolutionary

Marriage was simply another way to put their ideology into practice, one that would have far-reaching consequences, both for the couples that embraced it and for the society they lived in.

With the rapid implementation of intercaste marriage and the strict prohibition against accepting dowry, already long since established in the Ananda Marga community, only one social evil regarding marriage remained to be dealt with: the prohibition against widow remarriage. For several thousand years, there had existed a strict ban against widow remarriage in Hindu society. When a woman's husband died, she was expected to remain in chaste enclosure for the rest of her life, either in self-imposed exile in her husband's house, or in some cases banished to widows' ashrams. For centuries, a woman who immolated herself on her husband's funeral pyre, a practice known as *sati*, was considered the most virtuous of women and promised liberation by the scriptures. In fact, the word *sati* means "virtuous woman." Though the British had outlawed *sati* in the nineteenth century, the social taboos against widow remarriage still remained firmly in place. With the publication of *Caryacarya*, Baba removed that taboo within the community of his disciples. He declared that any man who married a widow, or a shelterless, fallen, or outcast woman, would be considered "Dharmamitram," a friend of dharma, and would be honored with that title within Ananda Marga. A few months after Sujit's marriage, Shambhunath Verma married a widow, the first example of such a marriage in Ananda Marga. He received Baba's outspoken praise and the title of Dharmamitram. In November, Baba went to Motihari to give his blessings to the newly married couple. He held a special DMC for them and the local Margis in Nagina's quarters. Thereafter, widow remarriage became a common occurrence in Ananda Marga.

After Sujit's marriage, Baba extended his leave by an additional month and continued touring various cities. During this time, he told the Margis that they should start making preparations for propagating the ideology outside India. Three acharyas, Asthana, Sarangi, and Srivastava, took the initiative to form a committee and proposed the name "foreign prachar committee" to Baba. "You can use this name for the time being," Baba told them, "but at some point it will have to be changed. No one is foreign to us."[7] He quoted a Sanskrit saying: *Hara me pita, gaori mata, svadesha bhuvantrayam*—the Lord is my father, Prakriti is my mother, and the universe is my homeland. He went on to explain why Ananda Marga would gain acceptance in other countries: "First, because neither capitalism nor communism can fulfill the needs of human life and hence have no future—only a spiritually based economy can succeed. Second, because people outside of India are hungry for spirituality, and those with a scientific or rational background will easily adopt our ideology." Baba then gave a long discourse about the different cultures of the world, their languages, religions, social customs, history, geography, and flora and fauna. One Margi asked Baba, "We see you all the time in Jamalpur; when did you visit those countries to be able to know them so well?" Baba laughed and said, "In the government, you have a system of special messengers to convey and collect messages and information. I also have my own courier system that brings everything to me at Jamalpur."

When his leave was about to finish, Baba returned to Jamalpur, to a group of concerned Margis who were wondering what action they should take now that his transfer could be put off no longer. But the next day a telegram arrived in the accounts department canceling the transfer. When an excited Pranay brought the telegram to Baba, he smiled and continued with what he was doing as if it were of no more importance than a passing breeze.

XXVII

A Monastic Order Begins

A sadhaka who views everything with equanimity, be it one's own home or the burial ground, gold or grass, one's own children or one's enemies, fire or water, one's own property or another's property, lives in the world as an avadhuta, as if he or she were the second manifestation of Shiva.[1]

ONE DAY IN the early spring of 1961, Baba asked Sushil Dhar, his customary lunch-hour stenographer, to bring a candle, a glass, some paper, and a pen to the tiger's grave that evening. He would be giving some dictation. When they arrived at the grave, Sushil put the glass over the candle, thus creating a small, makeshift lantern. Baba gathered the Margis around him and began explaining that a spiritual philosophy needed one book to serve as its fundamental text. Up until that point, *Idea and Ideology* had been serving that purpose, but now he intended to begin dictating the definitive text of Ananda Marga philosophy. It would be in the form of *sutras*,[2] or aphorisms, thus resuscitating the traditional form of Sanskrit philosophical discourse that had been in vogue for more than five millennia but which had been gradually dying out. The title of the new work, he said, would be *Ananda Sutram*.

Baba closed his eyes and chanted the first sutra—*Shivashaktyatmakam Brahma*—while pointing to the sky and tracing slow circles with his finger. Then he added a commentary in Bengali, which Sushil noted down. The first sutra was a definition of God, or Supreme Consciousness, as the composite of Shiva and Shakti, the witnessing consciousness and its operative principle or energy. It was the opening to the first chapter, which dealt with *brahmacakra*, the cycle of creation. After explaining that consciousness and its creative force, or energy, cannot be separated from each other, like the two sides of a piece of paper, he explained that there could be no substantiation of existence without the presence of the witnessing consciousness, thus making it the starting point of any philosophical enquiry.

> The physical sense of the body is telepathized on the mental plate. In other words, the physical sense is awakened in the mental plate due to the reflection that follows the impact of the crude physical

waves on the mental plate. Similarly, the sense of every crude object is awakened in the mental plate as soon as the reflection takes place following the impact of the waves of the object on the mental plate. Identical waves hit the soul entity, causing the reflection of those mental waves, and this awakens in the unit a sense of its indivisibility from the soul . . . All mundane objects, crude, subtle or causal, consist of mental waves or thought waves, and so in the fullest accord with reasoning and logic, we may call the Soul omni-telepathic. It is because of this omni-telepathic *atman* that the existence of all mundane objects, visible or invisible, large or small, finds its factual substantiation and recognition.[3]

After defining Shakti as the creative force of Shiva in a second sutra, and explaining the relationship between the two in his commentary, as well as differentiating between the instrumental, material, and efficient causes of creation, Baba gave a third sutra in which he asserted that the proof of the existence of God was to be found in saincara and pratisaincara, the introversive and extroversive phases of creation. In the short commentary that followed, he stated:

> The existence of any entity is known by the process of its activity, thought or witness-ship, of which witness-ship belongs to Purusha and the other two substantive factors primarily belong to Prakriti. And so the fact of Prakriti being the causal entity of the stream of action and thought will be recognized only when she completely identifies herself with objectivity. This appropriation of objectivity by Prakriti depends on her ever-increasing (Saincara) or decreasing (Pratisaincara) influence on Purusha. Prakriti's manifestation lies in these extrovertive (Saincara) and introvertive (Pratisaincara) processes.[4]

In the conversation that followed, Baba explained that a cause can be known by its effect. Just as a scientist is able to substantiate the existence of the electron by measuring its effect, the traces it leaves of its presence, the spiritually aware mind is able to intuit the existence of Shiva and Shakti by the traces they leave in the form of the endless cycle of creation. One Margi asked if the short explanation he dictated would be sufficient. "It will be sufficient for Margis and acharyas," he replied. "You will have to give a more detailed explanation for the general public in a language they can understand. The detailed explanation is in *Subhasita Samgraha*, but for many people the language there is too difficult. Nevertheless, the interpretation I have given will be enough to avoid others giving radically different interpretations in the future, as has happened with the Gita of Krishna and the Yoga Sutras of Patanjali." Baba then corrected the spelling of the Sanskrit words and the night's work was finished.

Over the next several months, Baba gave two or three sutras per night, several nights a week, always at the tiger's grave. The first twenty-five sutras were dedicated to the cycle of creation. They began with the involution of consciousness into matter and concluded with the evolution of consciousness out of matter, a process that reaches its culmination when the human being attains spiritual illumination, thus completing the cycle of creation. In the second chapter, he examined the spiritual nature of the living being and its relationship with the Cosmic Entity. He also refuted two religious beliefs from opposite ends of the globe, declaring in one sutra that there is no such thing as heaven or hell, and in another that Brahma is truth and the world is relative truth, a refutation of Shankaracharya's assertion that God is truth and the world is false or illusion.[5] In the third chapter, he dealt with the unit mind, samskara, death, and transmigration, and the path to liberation. He ended the chapter with a sutra citing prayer and ritualistic worship as sources of confusion rather than spiritual practices, and another defining devotion as ideation on God, rather than any kind of external worship or praise. The fourth chapter dealt with the origin of creation. In the sixteen sutras of the fifth chapter, he elucidated the fundamental principles of his social philosophy, Prout. He ended the book with an epigraph: *pragatishiila upayogatattvamidam sarvajanahitártham sarvajanasukhártham pracáritam*—this is the progressive utilization theory, propagated for the welfare and happiness of all.

On June 28, Baba dictated the last of the ninety-four sutras. The five chapters of *Ananda Sutram* were complete. On the previous day, he had begun giving a week-long series of Prout classes as part of the second annual Proutists conference, later compiled as the "Observer's Diary." In these classes, he used the sutras from the fifth chapter as a point of departure before launching into detailed discussions on a variety of topics, from land reform to the cultivation of a world language. From then on, *Ananda Sutram* would become the main text for the training of acharyas and volunteers. As in ancient times, candidates would be required to memorize the sutras and to be able to give a thorough exposition of each of them. Though Baba would be the author of over two hundred books by the end of his life, *Ananda Sutram* would be the crowning achievement of his philosophic and literary work, the foundation stone of his teachings.

Early the previous year, Baba had called Nityananda aside one day and told him that he wanted to give him an independent responsibility for prachar. "You see," he said, "the general secretary is not able to concentrate so much on prachar; he has severe time constraints. If things continue as they are, it will take hundreds of years for the ideology to spread throughout the world. I want you to start building up an independent structure. Concentrate on the young people and the students. Start your work from today and my blessings will be with you." Later that evening, Nityananda accompanied Baba to the tiger's grave, where a group of Margis was waiting. As they were passing the church, Baba stopped and said, "If I die today, how many people will have come to know our ideology?" Recognizing the import of Baba's words, Nityananda reaffirmed his promise to take responsibility for spreading the ideology as quickly and as widely as possible.

He began his work by organizing VSS camps at regular intervals. He designed a course in Ananda Marga spiritual and social philosophy based on *Idea and Ideology* and used it to train the participants in the philosophy, strengthen their spiritual practices, and instill in them a zeal for prachar and social service. As Baba advised, he concentrated on the youth and the students. In each camp, he kept his eye out for promising young men who could help him with his work. Soon the number of initiates started increasing rapidly, the majority of them college-age students. The addition of Prout training to the camps helped stoke the fervent idealism that the younger initiates brought with them. The independent structure that Baba had asked for gradually began to take shape. In fact, the work progressed so quickly that after a few months Nityananda petitioned Baba to allow him to renounce his job at the railway workshop and dedicate himself full-time to the organization. "The time has not yet come for you to leave your service," Baba told him. "I will let you know when that time comes." Instead, he started taking long leaves of absence, using that time to travel to different parts of India to conduct camps.

As the number of initiates continued to mount, so did the signs of opposition. After Visheshvar completed his acharya training, Pranay warned him that he would encounter severe opposition in his area when he began to propagate Ananda Marga there. The prediction was an accurate one. The leading capitalists, alarmed by the ideals of Prout, hired a group of thugs to drive Ananda Marga out of town, and one young Margi was killed in the attack. The Margis lodged a case and refused to leave. In the May 1961 DMC in Monghyr, Baba held a meeting for kapaliks and talked to them about the types of opposition they could expect to face in the future. He warned them that the time was not far off when the government would become their principle opposition. "If a time comes that you find yourself in prison," he told them, "you should know how to perform your kapalik sadhana under those conditions." Then he taught them the process for performing kapalik sadhana in jail. Afterward, some of the senior acharyas got together to discuss the unusual nature of those instructions. They agreed that when Baba said "if," he really meant "when." After the DMC, an all-India VSS camp was held in Hazipur. Hundreds of volunteers attended, a clear indication to all of how rapidly the organization was growing.

In the meantime, Nityananda had purchased a motorcycle and two jeeps for his fledgling organization. One of the young men who came to Jamalpur for training was Ram Tanuk, a lawyer from Beghuserai who had recently married Ram Khilavan's daughter Ahalya Devi. He and another volunteer, Lalan, took the jeeps out for driving practice to the ring road outside of town. Meanwhile, Baba was sitting on his cot in the jagriti talking to Haragovind Mandal and

Vivekananda Singh. Suddenly, in the middle of their conversation, Baba let out a grunt and some words that sounded to them like "be safe." When they asked him what had happened, he told them that there had just been an accident. Within half an hour, they got the news that Ram Tanuk had crashed his jeep into a tree and was now in the hospital in a coma. An old woman had attempted to cross the ring road without looking. In an effort to avoid her, Ram Tanuk had lost control of his vehicle. Lalan, who had been following behind him in the other jeep, had rushed him to the nearby hospital, where the doctors informed him that it would be touch and go whether or not Ram Tanuk survived.

Baba was about to give an acharya class when he got the news. He called Ramakanta aside and gave him instructions to go to the hospital and remain in Ram Tanuk's room round-the-clock and to send back regular reports of his condition. Nityananda accompanied him and did his best to console Ram Khilavan and his family, who beseeched him to bring Baba there. Nityananda conveyed their request to Baba and Baba sent him back with a message that if Ram Tanuk did not recover consciousness within seventy-two hours, then he would go himself.

On the third afternoon, Ramakanta was alone with Ram Tanuk when the doctor made his rounds and examined the patient. When he completed his examination, he informed Ramakanta that an accumulation of blood in the patient's brain had formed a large hematoma. If it were not drained within the next few hours, the patient would likely die. Unfortunately, they did not have the requisite facilities for such a procedure in that small Jamalpur hospital. He would have to be rushed to Patna. The doctor told him to inform the family so they could make immediate arrangements to move the patient.

Ramakanta became frightened. He was unsure what to do, so he ran as fast as he could to Baba's office, about ten minutes from the hospital. Baba listened quietly to the news and then told him to return to his vigil. "Whatever you do," he said, "don't allow them to move the patient. I will be there shortly."

Baba sent for Nityananda and together they walked over to the hospital. By that time, Ram Khilavan and the rest of Ram Tanuk's relatives had arrived. As soon as they saw Baba, they fell at his feet, crying and begging him to save Ram Tanuk's life. Baba walked over to the patient's bedside, touched him on the forehead, and said in a gentle voice, "Ram Tanuk, I have come."

Ram Tanuk's eyelids fluttered open and a sigh escaped his lips. He looked at Baba; then he lifted his hands and said, "Baba, what happened to me?"

Baba clasped the patient's hands and smiled. "Rest now. Everything will be fine." When he closed his eyes again, Baba told his relatives that there was nothing to worry about, but they should not allow the doctors to move him; nor should they talk to him until he was fully recovered. Baba embraced Ram Tanuk, then got up and left.

A short while later the doctor came back. Seeing that the patient was still there, he began shouting angrily, demanding to know why they had not moved him.

Ramakanta, following Baba's instructions, explained to him that the only place they could have taken him would have been Patna, nearly five hours journey. He would have died before they reached there. "Better for him to die here," he told the doctor, "in the presence of his family." The doctor thought about it for a moment and then calmed down. He began examining the patient. After a couple of minutes, he called for a nurse and asked her to begin removing the bandages, startled to see no sign of the hematoma and obvious improvement in his vital signs. As they were removing the bandages, Ram Tanuk opened his eyes again and began moving his hands and feet. The doctor told the family it was a miracle. If they wanted, they could give him a little soup in the evening. The next day he allowed him solid food, and a day later he released him from the hospital. Not long afterward, Ram Tanuk would take on the role of legal secretary for the organization, a post he would hold for the rest of his professional life.

For the Durga Puja holidays in mid-October, Baba scheduled a DMC tour to various cities in Bihar and Uttar Pradesh. Nityananda had been planning to take a holiday of his own, far from his organizational duties. For a long time he had been feeling a strong urge to spend some time in the Himalayas, meditating in the mountain solitudes and living the life of a solitary sannyasi, if only for a few days. He had not told Baba about it, suspecting that Baba might disapprove. His fears were soon confirmed. A day before the holidays began, he went to Baba's office during the lunch hour and found Baba in a grave mood.

"How are you planning to spend your holidays?" Baba asked.

Nityananda squirmed in his chair. "Baba, I was thinking to go to Rishikesh to meditate."

"I see," Baba said quietly. "You are thinking about your own liberation without paying any heed to the distressed and downtrodden people. How selfish!"

Tears welled in the corners of Nityananda's eyes. He grabbed a piece of paper and placed it in front of Baba. "Baba, kindly write out my tour program for me."

Baba took his pen and wrote out a program that began with the Lucknow DMC and included prachar visits to Allahabad, Raipur, Tata, and Calcutta before returning to Jamalpur. Nityananda followed the program that Baba had written out. He did prachar in each of those cities, but he still hoped that he might be able to visit Rishikesh for a day before proceeding from Lucknow to Allahabad. On that day, however, he came down with a fever and his wish for some taste of the sannyasi life went unfulfilled.

On October 30, a few days after they had returned from the holidays, Nityananda paid Baba a visit during the lunch hour. They were discussing spiritual matters when Baba said, "I am thinking of creating avadhutas. If you find anybody suitable, let me know."

"Baba, what is an avadhuta?"

"An avadhuta will have to follow certain rules and regulations. In the future they will lead the organization."

"What kind of rules?"

Baba picked up a piece of paper from his desk and passed it to Nityananda. "Note down." He dictated more than forty rules of conduct.

As he was noting down the rules, it suddenly dawned on Nityananda that Baba was talking about making an order of monks. This provoked an immediate reaction. "But Baba, I always thought you were against the idea of monastic orders. You've told us about the problems Buddhism had due to the creation of their monastic order. And now you want to create an order of your own? Were you just deceiving us when you said these things? Were you planning all along to create an order of renunciant disciples?"

"It is not like that," Baba said. "You see, the organization is beginning to grow very fast now. It won't be possible for family people to do the necessary work that will be required. I need some people who can dedicate themselves full-time—that's all. Now, if you find a suitable person who is ready to take avadhuta initiation, you should forward his name to me. That person should be unmarried, since this will be an order of celibate monks, but if he is married it may still be possible. In that case, he'll have to get permission from his wife and make arrangements for her financial security."

The next day, Nityananda brought the list of rules to Baba at lunchtime. "Baba, some of these rules are only suitable for monks who live in the forest or in seclusion. They are not for monks who will be serving the society or taking an active part in social construction, as you are proposing."

"Which rules are those?"

Nityananda made his case against several of the rules that Baba had included.

Baba nodded and said, "Okay, then strike them off the list."

Nityananda gathered his courage. "Baba, if you are going to go ahead with this plan of yours, then I want to be the first avadhuta."

Baba smiled. "Okay, if that is your wish. But first you will have to get permission from your wife."

All through the month of November, Nityananda struggled with his emotions. He had long dreamed about renouncing the world and leading the life of an ascetic, however the sannyasi order that Baba envisioned was not the life of sole dedication to spiritual practices that he associated with the traditional Indian monk. While the Ananda Marga monks, by rule, would be required to perform their spiritual practices four times a day, the rest of their time would be dedicated to the missionary work of the organization. He had seen the list of rules, and he knew it would not be easy for him.

In the last week of November, he took leave from the office and went to his native village of Amra to talk to his wife about his desire to become a sannyasi. To his great surprise, she gave him permission without any hesitation. If he wanted to dedicate himself to the great cause of Baba's work, she said, he had her full support. His parents and other relatives were less accommodating, but after a few days they also acquiesced. He made arrangements for his wife to remain in his father's house to raise their young child and named her as the legal heir to his family inheritance. The morning of his departure for Jamalpur, the entire village came to see him off. The village elders garlanded him and gave him their blessings—last of all, his father.

On December 10, he informed Baba that he had begun following the avadhuta rules. Thus began a one-year trial. If he were able to follow the rules to Baba's satisfaction, he would then become eligible for avadhuta initiation. When news leaked out of Baba's plans to create a monastic order with Nityananda as the first candidate, it brought mixed reactions. Pranay, especially, did not like the idea. He tried to dissuade Nityananda from his decision, but the die was cast.

That winter, a renowned astrologer from Muzaffarpur initiated a scare throughout India by publishing the news that a planetary conjunction of eight planets, forecast for February 3 to 5, 1962, would engender a disaster of biblical proportions, hailed afterward by the Indian media as the "end of the world." The news began dominating the headlines. Tales of panic became commonplace. A sacrificial fire on a scale never seen before was prepared in Deoghar to ward off the evil effects of the conjunction. Similar rituals were performed all over India, prompting Baba to say that instead of wasting so much ghee in the sacrificial fires, they should give it to the poor.

In the meantime, a month-long training session began in Jamalpur. Dasarath and Nityananda taught most of the classes, often in Baba's presence. One day, one of the trainees was taking a bath at the well when his watch was stolen from the pocket of his pants, which he had left hanging on a wall. It was the first time anything like that had happened at the jagriti. He reported it to the ashram manager, who in turn reported the matter to Baba. "What can I do?" Baba said. "You should inform the police." The idea of notifying the police, however, was repugnant to them. Seeing Baba's indifference to the matter, there was little more they could do.

That evening Dasarath gave a class in the jagriti courtyard. Baba sat beside him, interrupting from time to time to explain certain points. Suddenly Baba asked a heavyset young man to stand up. "What do you have in your left pocket?" he asked. The young man kept quiet. Baba called him over, reached into his pocket, and pulled out a watch. He held it up so everyone could see. "Is this the watch that was stolen?" Baba handed it back to its owner and turned his gaze once again on the thief. "Is this the first watch you have stolen?" Again the young man didn't reply. "It is not. In fact, it is the ninth watch you have stolen. Up until now you have been able to escape the consequences, but no more. If you steal one more time, I promise you, you will be caught by the police."

After the frightened young man sat down, Asthana asked Baba a question about the planetary alignment. Baba got up and went to the chalkboard, where he began drawing the zodiac, followed by a series of complicated mathematical formulas. With the aid of the diagrams and the equations, he explained how it would not be possible for these eight planets to come into an exact line. "Had they done so," he said, "it would have had an adverse affect on the earth, but this will not happen." Then he asked the Margis to print a leaflet on the subject and distribute it throughout Bihar. The text of the leaflet was subsequently printed in various regional newspapers. This helped to some extent to allay the fears of the general public. When the alignment passed without incident, the Ananda Marga office received words of thanks from different sectors for helping to calm the apprehensions of the public.

National elections in India took place in February of that year. Throughout the winter, the Proutists had been busy preparing to contest seats in Jamalpur and nearby areas. Lalan, a young intellectual and future professor who was serving as the Chief Secretary of the Universal Proutist Students Federation, proclaimed to the young Margis in his seminars that these elections would be a historic landmark in the history of Prout. He predicted that within ten years the Indian government would be in the hands of a Proutist party. Nityananda took offense at these words, which he considered unrealistic and irresponsible propaganda, but he could do nothing to dissuade Lalan from inflaming the hopes of the young volunteers.

The Proutist candidates were routed in the elections; some only received the votes of their fellow disciples and their families. Discouraged by this setback, many of the Prout volunteers left Jamalpur for their homes at the end of a winter of hard work and frustrated hopes.

One morning, a few days after the election, Baba arrived at the jagriti shortly after eight. Nityananda was staying there by himself at the time, still recuperating from a jeep accident that he had suffered during the VSS camp at the end of December. Baba asked him about the present condition of the organization he was building up, and Nityananda took the opportunity to express his frustration. Many of the volunteers who had been helping him had gone back to their homes after the elections; moreover, he was dissatisfied with the amount of cooperation he was getting from the general secretary. "Then what do you propose to do about it?" Baba asked. Nityananda's answer was to create a corps of whole-time workers, supported by organizational funds; he could then post these workers in different areas of the country to do full-time prachar; preferably, they would be young, single Margis who did not have a family to support. He asked permission to do a tour of Bihar and Uttar Pradesh for the purpose of recruiting workers. "Do whatever you think is needed for the welfare of the mission," Baba told him. "No need to consult me. Work fearlessly and the invisible power of the Lord will be with you."

The following week, Nityananda left on a long tour of Northern India. Soon scores of young Margis volunteered to work full-time for the organization. Once they completed their training and became acharyas, he began dispatching them to different parts of India with the help of donations from the householder disciples, mostly to places where Ananda Marga had not yet reached. The new "wholetimers," as they were called, were instructed to stay in the inexpensive railway retiring rooms at night and to spend their days doing prachar in whichever city they were posted. At the beginning of each month, Nityananda would send them their monthly allowance care of the local postmaster.

This allowance did not always prove sufficient. Ramasvarath and Ramesh Kumar were sent to South India. Once they were doing prachar in the state of Kerala when their money ran out. They decided to buy lemons with their last two rupees and fast on lemon water until the new month arrived and they could expect their monthly allowance. Meanwhile in Jamalpur, Baba suddenly stopped eating. He would not disclose the reason to Pranay or any other householder disciple. When Nityananda asked him about the matter, however, he told him. "Ramasvarath and Ramesh Kumar are fasting because their money has run out. How can I eat when my children are suffering? Do you think you could send them some money by telegraphic money order?" It was only after Baba got word that the two young men had received the money and eaten, that he broke his own fast.

Asim was assigned to the nearby areas of Bihar. Ananta Ram, a prominent Margi from Ranchi, took responsibility for paying his bus tickets. In an interview, Asim described what it was like for him to be a young wholetime worker:

> For meditation you would talk with your acharya. For work you had to talk to Nityananda. Baba would only talk to you about your personal affairs. It was father and son. If you had any complaint about work, you'd tell him. He would tell the in-charge and solve it. So you got a father who supported you, loved you, favored you, inspired you, took care of you. The acharya showed you your defects in meditation, Nityananda showed you the defects in your work, but Baba just took you on his lap. We were crazy to meet him . . . it was the same as going to Braj and seeing Krishna—always charming, loving, happy, full of flow. You are in a trance, you have no thought, no problem, just wait for Baba to come and go running to his room. He had a *choki*, a hard bed with a blanket. There was no cushion on his *choki*. Sometimes I have seen a pillow, sometimes not. There was no carpet on the floor where we sat. The ashram gate would be open. The cows would enter. There were a few flowers, a small well where we took bath, a toilet in the back—no comfort, no kitchen, no phone. There was a light but no fan. We fanned Baba by hand. Baba never paid any attention to external decorum or comfort. He

only cared about preparing us, one by one, like you make a doll by hand. The external surroundings were immaterial. When Baba came to the jagriti, he would wear slippers. Many times you would see that the slipper was finished; the sole would be worn through so that his heel touched the ground. Many times he would be working in the garden and you would see a hole in his t-shirt. That was the beginning of the Marga.

I was sent to do prachar in the surrounding areas. Go in the morning, come back in the evening and have his darshan. A charming life. You don't get any food. You have to arrange that yourself. You have to sleep on your blanket. All you get there is a place to lie down and water to drink. But we didn't care; all we cared about was the chance to be near him. Then he made it three days. I was only supposed to come back to Jamalpur after three days in the field, but I couldn't stand to go three days without seeing him. When Nityananda saw me, he said, "You know, when Baba becomes angry with somebody, he does not talk with him. You came back before the three days were up; Baba won't like that." I didn't care. I wanted to see him. But when Baba came to the jagriti, I saw that he was right. Baba wouldn't talk to me. So again I left to go do my work. A day or two later, Baba's train passed through the place where I was working. Everybody went to the platform to see him. I went also but I stayed in the back because Baba was unhappy with me. Why should I go in front and displease him? He started asking about people: Where is this person, where is that person? Then I heard, "Oh, there you are. I was looking for you." Just to make me happy, you see. Then he left.

When I came back to Jamalpur, I thought that since Baba was unhappy with me, I wouldn't eat. I'd just fast. Why should I live if he doesn't talk to me? That day Baba came to the jagriti from the office about twelve thirty. It was his lunch hour, but instead of taking lunch he came to the jagriti. I was alone there at the time. When I saw Baba coming, I went and hid in the room. Baba came and found me. He said, "How are you? I came to talk to you. But first you go and eat. I will wait for you." He waited in his room while I ran across the street—there was a Margi there who had a small café; he used to charge a half rupee for a meal. I broke my fast and ran back. Baba started talking about this and that, as if nothing had happened. He had come just to make me eat. The relationship was that deep; it was that close.

Once I went to give a talk in Bariapur, a town near Jamalpur, maybe forty-five minutes journey. It was the end of 1962 and I was maybe twenty-three then. There were about thirty-five or forty people in the room and nearly all were aged. I gave a talk on meditation and universal fraternity. They started quoting from the scriptures in support of the topknot and sacred thread and caste and creed. I replied as much as possible on scientific grounds, but they really had me cornered. They knew so many Sanskrit verses, one after the other, and I was only talking science and rationality. At the end, one boy stood up. He knew them; he knew their character. He said, "You people do this and that nonsense in your personal life, and yet you are talking in this way! Don't you see the glowing face of this young man? And such nice answers he gives, so scientific and rational." He really rebuked them. They became ashamed and left. Afterward, four or five people stayed and learned meditation. They gave me food and brought me to the train station and bought my ticket back. So I got food and my ticket and some people learned meditation. I did my job. But I didn't come back happy. I came back disturbed. When I entered the jagriti, Baba was just finishing his evening talk. I met him between the gate and the room.

The first thing I said to Baba was, "Until I get realization I will not be able to go out for prachar."

Baba said, "But did it not so happen that a young boy helped you in the meeting?"

"But Baba," I said, "I could not answer their questions. I embarrassed you in the field."

"Tell them as much as you know," he said. "When you pass high school, you can teach children. When you pass university, you can teach high school."

Then I said, "But Baba, I need to meditate and realize first before I can represent you."

And he said, "By the time you meditate and realize, many will die. Will you teach the ghosts?"

He is the master but just see the patience, talking to me as if I were his equal, his friend. Then I said, "Baba, I have so many weaknesses. How can I teach people unless I go and develop myself?"

"You are much better than the common mass," he said. "Do your work and you will be able to help. You know, what you can get in a whole life's meditation, I can give you in five minutes. I have come here to establish a mission. I need some medium to implement it. Do the work and you will see that everything is set right, as if you were just a medium being used to implement it. Go and do, and you will see, it will be possible. Remember one thing: costly things are not available cheap. If you give a very valuable thing to somebody at a cheap price, they will fail to respect it, and if you give a very costly thing to someone who does not deserve it, they will fail to maintain it. Now, tell me what I said."

I repeated what Baba said.

"Okay. Remember this: your duty is to do what I ask you to do; it is my headache to solve your problem. Are you ready?"

"Yes, Baba."

"You know a day will come when just by looking, you will know the nature, the mind, and the condition of a person."

I thought that he was just trying to inspire me, to lift my spirits, but today I see that everything he said that day has come true.[6]

Almost overnight, the new wholetimer system changed the character of the organization. Many of the young men who came forward had already been looking for a cause they could dedicate themselves to. Others saw the enthusiasm and fire of their comrades and found it contagious. Some were simply enamored with Baba and were ready to do anything to please him. When Master Dhiren first saw Baba in Barrackpur early that year,[7] he watched in amazement as Baba scolded his friends for faults no one could have known about. One boy had slept late and missed his Wednesday morning meditation; another had missed his Monday evening meditation because he had been chatting with friends; a third was guilty of smoking *bidi* cigarettes in secret and became red in the face when Baba pulled a pack from his pocket. Master Dhiren had been looking for a great guru with whom he could take shelter, and that was all he needed to see. When he went to Jamalpur a few weeks later, he met Baba at the gate of the Jagriti and told him that he had come to stay forever. Baba smiled and told him to attend the Prout camp then taking place in Bhagalpur and then come back to Jamalpur for training.

Another college student, Vishvabandhu, had his PC in the December 1961 DMC at Raipur. During his PC, Baba related to him three incidents from his childhood when he had almost died. The first was when he had fallen from a tree and lost consciousness. He had felt an invisible energy revive him and thrust him back into the world of the living. Baba described the incident in detail to the astonished young man and told him that he had actually died and been saved by a divine power. The second time was when he was about to be hit by a train and had felt a force throw him out of the way. The third time, he had gotten stuck in some railway tracks and had again felt an invisible force free him. After recounting these three incidents, Baba said, "So you see, this life is not yours; it is mine." Vishvabandhu started crying and embraced Baba. "You have great work to do for humanity," Baba said. "When the right time comes, I will call for you." With the creation of the wholetimer system, he would also come to Jamalpur, ready to volunteer.[8]

Though Pranay was uneasy about Baba's decision to make an order of sannyasis, he felt a deep affinity with the life of a renunciant and tried to follow that ideal in his personal life. Baba had, in fact, given him the name Sadhanananda several years earlier. Though Pranay was instructed not to use the name in public, he was proud of it and considered himself Baba's first and only avadhuta. Then, while his concern continued to mount over the prospect of Nityananda becoming an avadhuta and adopting the orange robes of a sannyasi, Baba gave him an order that shocked him and sent the course of his life in an unforeseen direction.

On April 14, a vivacious young woman from the Hooghly district of West Bengal named Pratima Roy arrived in Jamalpur to visit her sister Nilima and take part in a dance recital scheduled for the sixteenth. Her father, a film director and writer who had trained her in dance and music since her early childhood, accompanied her. On her arrival, she went to the house of Amar Sen,[9] a friend of her sister and brother-in-law, for the first rehearsal. While she was there, she was introduced to her host and his friend Prabhat Sarkar, who had dropped by to visit Amar and watch the rehearsal. All she remembered about Baba from that first glimpse was that he passed the time with his friend telling humorous stories and laughing.

After the rehearsal she returned to her sister's house. Shortly thereafter, a messenger arrived at the door bearing a message for her father. Though it was already late in the evening, her father left the house as soon as he read the note, taking her brother-in-law with him. Though nothing would be communicated to her, the content of the message was an invitation to discuss a marriage proposal for his daughter. The proposal originated from one Prabhat Sarkar through the offices of that friend of the family, Amar Sen. The name of the prospective groom was Pranay Kumar Chatterjee, a good friend of Pratima's brother-in-law.

For reasons Pratima could never discover or quite understand, her father agreed to the proposal after a short talk with Baba; he did not even take the time to consult with his wife or his mother, as one might have expected (neither of them had made the trip). The next day, after the morning rehearsal, Pranay's mother dropped by to see the girl that her guru had selected for her son to marry. She sat and talked with Pratima as if she had dropped by for a simple visit, never once mentioning the subject of marriage. She was impressed with what she saw. That evening, while Pratima and her sister were at the cinema, she returned and finalized the negotiations with Pratima's father. Afterward, they informed Baba that the negotiations had been successfully concluded. He, in turn, sent a message to Pranay, through Sukumar, that the time had come for his disciple to get married.

Pranay was shocked when he got the news. Disbelief soon turned to anger, but he realized there was nothing he could do. He could not and would not go against his guru's orders. At Sukumar's insistence, he went to Pratima's sister's house and met with her father. Pranay agreed to the proposal but he put one condition: the marriage would have to be celebrated within twenty-four hours; otherwise, the marriage was off. "I felt that no sensible person could agree to such a condition," Pranay later said, "and thus the marriage would be dismissed and

I would not be violating Gurudeva's order." Much to Pranay's dismay, however, Pratima's father agreed to his condition. When Pratima and her sister arrived home, her father requested her to sing a couple of bhajans for his guests. Pranay listened with his eyes closed. When he opened them again, they were red, as if he were drunk, an odd detail that Pratima found exceedingly strange. When the guests had left, her father gave her some Ananda Marga books to read in which he had marked specific passages. She found them interesting, but she still had no idea what fate held in store for her.

The next morning, a rickshaw rolled through the nearby streets with a drummer and a boy who was passing out leaflets. The leaflets announced that there would be a marriage that evening in the Ananda Marga jagriti. Everyone in the neighborhood was invited, Margis and non-Margis alike. It also mentioned that the jagriti would be open to the public throughout the day. When the rickshaw pulled up in front of Nilima's house, Pratima ran outside to see what was going on. When she read the leaflet, she asked her brother-in-law who was getting married and was stunned to find out that she was the bride. She could not quite believe it, but when her father came home in the afternoon, fresh from seeing to the marriage preparations, she dried her tears and accepted her fate, resigned to the hope that her father would not have done such a thing if it were not in her best interests.

Baba oversaw the preparations in the jagriti. He bought a new sari for Pratima and a new kurta for Pranay to wear during the ceremony and the reception. He also sent telegrams to invite the Margis living outside Jamalpur. Baba even let it be known that he would conduct the wedding. When the hour drew near, however, so many non-Margis crowded into the ashram to attend that Baba deputed Arun Mazumdar and Sukumar to conduct the ceremony on his behalf. He explained to them that if he presided over the wedding, the public would come to know that Prabhat Sarkar was the guru. Instead he remained in his room.

Pratima arrived at the jagriti shortly after seven, where she was welcomed with garlands and the trumpeting of conch shells. Uma Sarkar took her hands and led her to the tiger skin on which she was to sit during the ceremony and then sat down beside her as the wife of the guru. Pratima still did not know whom she was going to marry. The groom had to be pointed out to her. She was surprised to see the same man who had kept his eyes closed the previous evening when she had sung and had afterward avoided her.

As the final preparations were being made, Pranay looked at his watch and felt a slight glimmer of hope when he saw the minute hand reach seven thirty, the precise time that he had agreed to the wedding with Pratima's father and put his one condition. He went to Baba's room and told him that the twenty-four hours were up. Now he would not marry. Baba roared at him to go back and sit for his wedding, and his last glimmer of hope went out.

After the ceremony, the new couple went to Baba's room, placed garlands around his neck, and received his blessing. A reception followed, after which it was announced that the couple would conduct a Hindu ceremony in the traditional Bihari fashion in the house of Pratima's sister, followed by a British-style ceremony. All were invited and the festivities lasted well into the next day.

That evening, Pranay and Pratima went alone with Baba on field walk. When they reached the tiger's grave, Pranay's frustration spilled over. He fought with both Baba and his new bride. Baba defended Pratima, who said that she felt Baba's power for the first time that night, enveloping her on all sides. Pranay stormed off, leaving her there with Baba; he did not return to his house in Rampur Colony that night, the night of *phul-sajya*, when the groom traditionally decorates the bridal bed with flowers to welcome his new bride. Instead, he took the flowers to the empty jagriti and tearfully adorned Baba's cot. It was just before dawn when he finally arrived home. Pratima was asleep. A few minutes later there came a knock at the door. When he opened it, he was surprised to see Baba standing there. Bleary-eyed and still tearful, he touched Baba's feet and invited him in. "Pranay," Baba said, "I have come to initiate Pratima. Tell her to take a bath, put on clean clothes, and get ready."

When the initiation was over, Pratima requested Baba to give her a new name. "Why?" he asked.

"All my life people have been teasing me about my name, asking me what I am the image of."[10]

"But Pratima is such a beautiful name." Baba began reciting a poem of Dvijendra Lal, a mystic poet of Bengal:

> *How can I worship you with an image?*
> *Your image is this vast universe.*
> *How can I build a temple for you?*
> *The boundless sky is your temple.*
> *Your image is the planets, the stars and the sun,*
> *The oceans, the springs, the mountains and forests . . .*

Then he smiled and changed her name to Pramila.

A few days later, Baba returned to their house to give Pramila her second lesson, the guru mantra. When he asked her how she was finding her meditation, she said, "Baba, I don't understand this meditation. I am not used to sitting like this. Moreover, there is nothing in front of me—no idol or image. I don't know whom to worship. I am trying, but it is difficult. And I have to tell you, if I don't like it, then I am going to give it up, and I will tell everyone it's a fraud."

Baba smiled. "You don't see anything when you meditate?"

"No."

"I will show you then."

Baba reached out and touched her forehead. Pramila suddenly felt her body growing light. She lost consciousness and entered into a state of trance. Nearly two hours passed before she became aware again of who and where she was. She was still sitting in meditation posture, her mind inundated by bliss. Baba was still sitting in front of her.

"How do you feel now, Pramila?"

She smiled sheepishly. "Very nice, Baba. I think I will continue to do this sadhana."

Over the next few months, Baba gave her the rest of her lessons personally, and the following year he began teaching her the lessons of kapalik sadhana.

On the first of May, a Monday morning, two weeks after Pranay's marriage, Baba came to the jagriti accompanied by a couple of local acharyas. Nityananda met him near the gate. Baba's first words to him were, "Are you ready now?" Unable to understand what Baba was referring to, he kept silent. When Baba didn't say anything, he told him that he couldn't understand his question. "If I decide to make you avadhuta right now, are you ready?" Nityananda was taken by surprise. He had thought that he would have to follow the rules for one year first, as Baba had indicated. Barely five months had passed.

"Well, what do you think?" Baba asked.

"I am having some difficulty, Baba, with something."

"What is that?"

"It is a private matter."

"Then let us go to my room."

Once inside Baba's room, Nityananda explained that he was having difficulty with the rule that enjoined upon avadhutas to treat all women as mother. He would need more time before he could habituate himself to this way of thinking.

"Is this the only rule you have difficulty with?"

"Yes, Baba."

"Then I will take that responsibility."

Emboldened by Baba's promise, Nityananda agreed. Baba initiated him into the avadhuta order and gave him the monastic name Acharya Satyananda Avadhuta. "If, unknowingly or unwittingly, anyone calls you by your old name," Baba said, "tell him that you are now Acharya Satyananda Avadhuta." Baba explained to him that traditionally the guru hands the saffron dress to his disciple at the time of his initiation into the order of sannyasis; then the disciple puts it on for the first time. However, it was not yet decided what dress he would wear. Baba asked him to design a suitable dress and have it ready for Baba's birthday on the nineteenth of that month, ten days before the Ananda Purnima DMC in Monghyr.

Over the next couple of weeks, the newly christened Satyananda experimented with different modes of sannyasi dress: pants, dhoti, lungi, kurta, etc. Finally, he decided on the dress that would be used by Ananda Marga monks from then on: saffron lungi, tunic, turban, and waistband. On the nineteenth morning, while a crowd of devotees gathered outside Baba's room, he showed the dress to Baba, along with a necklace of rudraksha beads and vermillion paste to apply to his forehead. Baba approved the dress but told him that it would be better not to wear the rudraksha beads or the vermillion mark because it might create fear or mistrust among members of the general public.[11] Baba handed the dress to his disciple, who put it on and stood in front of him as his first sannyasi.

Satyananda was overcome by emotion. For a few minutes, he felt his sense of self-existence merging into that of his guru. When his mind returned to normal, he came out of the room and presented himself to the Margis. Some of them wept openly. Others touched his feet and then their foreheads, symbolically accepting the dust of his feet. Most embraced him. Ten days later, at the DMC, Satyananda sat in full dress by the side of Baba's cot in front of several thousand Margis while the devotees danced and sang and forgot themselves, despite the scorching summer heat. Many went into samadhi and fell to the ground in trance. One devotee recalled that there was not a single person present who was not dancing in devotion—man or woman.

After the DMC, Baba put Satyananda in charge of training the future avadhutas. He rented a small apartment not far from the jagriti to make it easier for the trainees to follow their rules of conduct. A number of the wholetime workers put in requests to be accepted for training. Many of them started facing pressure from their families to return home—their relatives became afraid that they might lose them to the new sannyasi order. Some parents traveled to where their sons were working to try to bring them back; others went directly to Satyananda to beg him not to take them. In response, Satyananda issued a circular saying that no one under twenty-one could become a sannyasi without the permission of his parents. This helped to calm the preoccupations of some of the families. But still the candidates appeared. Those who were accepted remained in Jamalpur to take training and begin their trial period.

On January 1, 1963, Baba initiated three more trainees into the avadhuta order. Two of them were young wholetimers: Ramesh Kumar and Asim Kumar.[12] The other was a married disciple, Ramasvarath, whose wife, an ardent devotee, had been happy to give him permission. While Ramasvarath was in Baba's room being initiated, Baba asked him what his mother tongue was.

"Hindi, Baba," he said, the normal reply for any Bihari.

"Hindi is your mother tongue?" Baba's mood became grave. "Suppose you meet your mother, what language will you speak?"

"Maithili."

"You and your mother speak in Maithili, you speak with the villagers in Maithili, so how can you say that Hindi is your mother tongue? You use Hindi to talk with outsiders. There is no region anywhere in India where the mother language is Hindi." Baba enumerated the mother tongue for every region in Bihar before continuing. "Now tell me, is there any place where Hindi is the mother tongue?"

Ramasvarath kept silent. Baba went on to explain that the British had cultivated Hindi during the colonial period as a medium for instruction and administration. Rather than being an indigenous spoken language, it had evolved out of certain dialects prevalent in and around Delhi.

"Where do you want to be sent for prachar?" Baba asked.

"Do you mean foreign countries, Baba?" Ramasvarath asked, aware of Baba's desire to see Ananda Marga spread throughout the world.

"What do you mean by 'foreign'? Tell me what the word 'foreign' means." Ramasvarath kept silent. "It means 'what is not your own.' If you have a wound filled with pus, then the doctor calls the pus 'foreign matter,' a substance that should not remain inside the body. Not a single person in this world is foreign. For an avadhuta, the entire creation is your own. There is no country that is not your country. Now tell me, which country is not your country?"

Again Ramasvarath remained silent.

"You are also kapalik, so you should remember your oath. If you say 'foreigner' then you will divide yourself. So from today onward you will say 'overseas,' those who live on the other side of the sea or outside India. They are not foreigners—they just live in a different place."

Baba completed the initiation and gave him the monastic name Acharya Shivananda Avadhuta. Shivananda informed the Margis what Baba had told him, and the recently formed committee for propagating the mission outside India dropped the word "foreign" and replaced it with "overseas." Before the organization could expand overseas, however, it would need trained, experienced representatives who would not have to leave a family behind. Those representatives were now on their way.

XXVIII

The Search for the City of Bliss

Anandanagar is the nucleus of this universe. It is not merely the physical Anandanagar; it is also the Anandanagar of our inner heart. We will have to build it in all possible ways; we will have to take all steps for its rapid development so that it can show light to the entire universe.[1]

DURING THE CONSTRUCTION of the Jamalpur jagriti in 1958, Baba alluded to a future project that he had long had in mind. While on field walk one night with Acharya Kuldip and several others, he said, "You are all working very hard for the jagriti construction, and it will serve a good purpose. People will be educated here. They will come here to learn spirituality. But in the future, you will have a much larger place where you will have to work much harder than you are working now. It will have many schools, a veterinary college, a university, a hospital, and different other facilities. People will come from all corners of the world to see it and to study there."

In early summer 1962, Baba called several senior Margis together in Jamalpur and told them that he wanted to make a model community where the world could see the ideology of Ananda Marga in practice. A tribal area would suit them best, he said, an impoverished, neglected area that would offer scope for numerous social service projects benefitting people who had no access to proper education, modern medical treatment, and so on. Furthermore, the organization was now growing rapidly, and a small town like Jamalpur would not do as the central headquarters of the global organization he had promised them Ananda Marga would soon become. Efforts immediately got underway to look for land that would fit his criteria. Pranay put ads in various newspapers and key Margis were alerted to be on the lookout. When Acharya Sarangi cautiously pointed out to Baba that they had no money to negotiate with anyone, should they find a suitable place, Baba asked him if he knew how Benares Hindu University and Vishvabharati had been built up.[2] "No great cause will suffer for want of money," Baba told him. "There are people who are eagerly waiting to donate land and money for such a cause."

In mid-May Baba paid a visit to Ranchi. On the way back to Jamalpur, his train passed through Purulia District. Baba pointed out the window toward the stark, arid rolling hills and started narrating its history for the acharyas who were accompanying him. "The ancient name for this area was Rarh, the land between the Kamsavati and Damodar rivers. It has a great spiritual and cultural heritage. For many, many centuries it was the meeting place for the three Tantras—Hindu, Buddhist, and Jain. Kapil Muni was born and raised here.[3] His ashram was situated on a hill just outside the town of Jhalda. Nowadays, however, Rarh, along with Magadha,[4] are the two areas most neglected by historians. If I find time, I will add a special chapter in Indology about these two."

Baba went on to describe how the inhabitants of Rarh had come to be among the poorest in India, mostly illiterate, the majority of them eking out a meager existence through subsistence farming. In recent years, it had suffered from extensive deforestation as the poor villagers found themselves forced to cut the few trees for fuel, further eroding the already rocky soil. "Yet despite all this," Baba said, "for many centuries this land has been home to some of India's greatest Tantrics. Many saints achieved liberation here, far from the eyes of so-called civilization. This would be the ideal place to build our model community and headquarters."

To the acharyas looking out the window, it seemed like a stony wilderness, hardly suited to be the headquarters of their rapidly growing organization, but they all knew that if Baba suggested they try there, chances were, their future would be tied to the seemingly inhospitable region they were passing through. Soon afterward, Pranay was informed that the previous raja of Garjaipur, Raghunandan Singh Deo, would be a good person to approach in that area about a possible donation of land.

Pranay, along with Sarangi and Kedarnath Sharma, went to visit the raja. They found him to be a poor but large-hearted man without sufficient funds to properly maintain his house but eager to do something for a good cause, exactly the kind of person they felt most comfortable with. The king introduced them to his wife, Prafulla Kumari Devi. He explained that they had some land in her name that they had been looking to donate to some spiritual group, but up until then they had not found one that seemed suitable. With the change in the zamandari laws, they had to donate the land or else the government would appropriate it, but they were not willing to give it to just anyone. Some days earlier, he had dreamed of sannyasis in orange robes that would come asking for the land. When the Margis explained to him who they were and what they wanted to do with it—to build children's homes, schools, a hospital, and other social service projects—the raja became convinced that these were the people he had been waiting for. Almost apologetically, he explained that the land had no commercial value. It was not near any township, nor was it rich agricultural land, but it was right in the midst of the people who most needed such humanitarian projects. Sarangi and Kedarnath went to see the land, and when they returned to Garjaipur they finalized the agreement. On August 23, the final papers went through. Pranay, who was in Garjaipur taking care of the final details, sent a telegram to Baba with the news that Ananda Marga was now the proud owner of five hundred acres adjoining the tiny village of Baglata in Garjaipur Thana.⁵ To the naked eye, it was five hundred acres of barren, rocky hills, but to the acharyas who found the place, it was the beginning of a dream that for the moment existed only in Baba's imagination. On August 31, Baba gave the new land its name: Anandanagar, the city of bliss.

On July 22, Chamaklal and several other Margis went to the jagriti for Baba's darshan. They found Baba in a pensive mood. For several minutes they remained silent. Then they asked Baba if anything was the matter. Baba nodded his head and said, "As we speak, Krishna Menon, India's Defense Minister, is making friends with the Chinese in Geneva. This will prove very harmful for India. Today's friendship will turn to enmity. Bad days are coming for India. In three months, China will attack and India will lose."

On several occasions, the Margis had heard Baba express his displeasure over the popular slogan proclaiming India's friendship with China—*Cini bhai bhai*, the Chinese are our brothers—and his disapproval of Nehru's talks with Chou En Lai. Only now did they know why.

That evening, Aniruddha Mukhya accompanied Baba to the tiger's grave. When they reached the street lamp at the edge of the field, Baba stopped and asked Aniruddha if he had a piece of paper. "Note down. Ninety days from today China will attack India. When you get home note it in your diary." Aniruddha scribbled the note but he told Baba that he didn't believe it. "Anandamurti says they will attack," Baba replied. "Believe it. Did you note down the date? Good."

When Aniruddha returned home, he wrote it in his diary as Baba had instructed, but he was not convinced. When he told his family what Baba had said, they told him that if Baba said it was true, it was true, but Aniruddha took exception to what he considered blind faith. "We are friends with the Chinese," he said. "It can't happen." A few days later, the newspapers came out in support of his argument. Chen Yi had given private assurances to Krishna Menon in Geneva during discussions over the periodic skirmishes then taking place on the disputed Himalayan border between India and China, part of tensions between the two countries that had flared up when India gave sanctuary to a fleeing Dalai Lama in 1959. "There may be skirmishes between the forces of the two countries," Chen Yi told Menon in the published reports, "but full-scale hostilities are unthinkable."

This assurance was enough for Nehru and Menon but not for Baba, who on several occasions reminded the Margis that bad times were coming. When they asked Baba why he didn't warn the government if he knew this was going to happen, Baba told them that a report on the Chinese preparations for war had been forwarded to Menon earlier in the year from the President, Rajendra

Prasad, and that the report had reached the Prime Minister's desk. But Nehru had written "impossible" on the file and sent it back. "Neither of them want to listen," he said, "so there is nothing more to be done other than to prepare oneself." Later in the conversation, Baba voiced his views on India's position: "Tibet should never have been lost to the Chinese in the first place. Nehru, in effect, handed Tibet over to the Chinese when it was not his to hand over. Rather, the Indian army should have taken offensive action on the Tibet-China border when it was still feasible. Their plan of action should have been offensive-defensive, knowing that China had designs on Tibet. Tibet would have then remained as the buffer state that the British had intended it to be."

On October 10, a small skirmish took place on the China-India border. Thereafter, Nehru uttered his infamous statement that the Chinese should be thrown out of Dho La, a statement that the Chinese would later use as support for their claim that India was planning to attack China and that they were acting out of self-defense. By this time, a skeptical public was beginning to brace for the possibility of war. In the meantime, the forewarned Margis were busy acting on Baba's suggestions to prepare themselves. Many Indians were now counting on rapid US help, should hostilities begin, but on the sixteenth of that month, the Cuban missile crisis broke out and American eyes quickly turned elsewhere.

On the nineteenth, Aniruddha was again in Jamalpur for field walk. "Where is your diary?" Baba asked him. When he told Baba that he had left it at home, Baba scolded him and told him to take out a piece of paper. "Note down. Tomorrow is the nineteith day; the Chinese will attack." Still somewhat skeptical, Aniruddha asked Baba if it were really possible.

"Wait until the morning. Then you will have your answer."

The next morning, when Aniruddha woke up, his family was listening to news of the attack on the radio. He hurried back to Jamalpur that evening to see Baba.

"Where is your newspaper?" Baba called out when he saw him. Aniruddha held it out to show Baba.

"Did they attack or not?"

"Yes, Baba."

"Did you check your diary? Was it the nineteith day or not?"

"Yes, Baba."

"Now do you have faith in Anandamurti? When I say something is going to happen, it will happen."

During the next few days, as the conflict heated up and the Indian army suffered demoralizing losses, Baba came to the jagriti each day and described what was happening on the battlefield, news which would only come on the radio or appear in the newspapers afterward. He drew a map and pointed out the areas the Chinese would attack and explained how they would conduct their operations, where they had their soldiers stationed, and in what numbers.

According to Baba, China's secret wish was to capture the land north of the Ganges, the fertile Gangetic plains, which they had long coveted due to China's overpopulation and relative lack of arable land. Their desired route would bring them all the way to Calcutta.

In a later field walk, Baba stopped under a shade tree near the tiger's grave due to a light shower. He asked Dasarath to sit in meditation posture and touched him at his *ajina* chakra. Then he asked him to go to Peking. Dasarath replied that he was seeing a signboard in Chinese.

"Now go to the house of Chou En Lai."

"I am in front of a large house guarded by security men."

"That is the house. Go inside and see what Chou En Lai is doing."

"Baba, Chou En Lai is sitting on a chair in front of a table. He is resting his head on his hand. There is a bottle of alcohol on the table and a world map on the wall behind him."

"Look at India on the map and see if you see anything special."

"Yes, Baba. There is a red line drawn on the map encircling the Gangetic area up to Calcutta."

"Now see what he has in his pocket."

"He has some papers in his pocket."

"Read them and tell us what they say."

Baba, they are written in Chinese. I cannot understand them."

"All right. I could convert them into cosmic language and then reconvert them into Angika so that you could read them, but it is not necessary. You can come back now."

On several occasions, Baba exhorted the Margis to create a second line of defense, should the Indian Army not hold. In response, the Margis organized two self-defense camps in Danapur, and Pranay sent messages to the different units to organize similar camps. "Do not expect any mercy from the Chinese soldiers," Baba told them. "They are capable of great acts of cruelty." He told the Margi women that they should be ready to self-immolate, if necessary, rather than let themselves be violated and killed by the Chinese soldiers. "Stand on your feet and guide the public," he exhorted them. "Give them training."

In one meeting Baba said, "If they approach Patna, the Indian army may have to blow up the Mokama Bridge; otherwise, there is the danger that China will overrun the entire country." But after a short pause, Baba assured the concerned Margis that this would not happen. "The Chinese will turn back. It is not the wish of Paramapurusha that the Indian spiritual tradition disappear from this planet."

Baba's assurances helped to calm the Margis, but the general tension in the country was heightened even more by the nuclear impasse that was taking place halfway around the globe. One evening, after returning from the tiger's grave, the Margis expressed their concerns about the possibility of a world war. When they reached Baba's house, they stopped under the tree opposite the gate. Baba told Dasarath to look at the sky and concentrate until he could see President Kennedy and Premier Khrushchev.

"Describe the color of their mental plates," he said. Dasarath peered into the sky and said that Kennedy's mental plate was white with black spots, while Khrushchev's was red with white and black spots. "Had Khrushchev's mental plate been totally red," Baba said, "then he would be ready for war, but as it is, there is no chance of war. Khrushchev wants to suppress the war, and so does Kennedy."

By mid-November, the Chinese forces had routed the Indian Fourth Division and no longer faced any organized resistance anywhere along the border, having advanced by then close to the outskirts of Tezpur in Assam. Then, suddenly, for reasons never publicly disclosed, the Chinese turned back. On November 21, they declared a unilateral ceasefire.

One morning, a few weeks after the ceasefire, Baba came to the jagriti and conducted General Darshan for a small group of seven or eight Margis. The discussion turned to the conflict with China and the Margis took advantage of the opportunity to ask Baba questions on the subject. One of them was a young Punjabi with a turban who was a supporter of Nehru at a time when Nehru was drawing heavy criticism in the Indian press for his perceived mismanagement of the recent crisis. After a few minutes, Baba turned to Dasarath and told him that he wanted to show him what two people were doing at that moment. One of the new wholetimers, Master Dhiren, recalled the scene:

> Baba said that he was taking Dasarath's mind to a far-off place on the other side of the border to show him someone he knew. Saying this, Baba touched the back part of his head, at the medulla oblongata. Dasarath's body became stiff and started to sway from side to side. Baba asked him to narrate what he saw. He said that he had reached Delhi. From there he continued on to Jammu. Then he crossed over to the other side of the Himalayas where he described some mountains covered with snow and then a snow-capped peak that was glittering in the sun. Then he described a small stream of water flowing down the mountain. Baba asked him to follow the stream. Dasarath described the stream becoming bigger and bigger, slowly becoming a river that continued to get wider. On both sides of the river there were Buddhist temples, and beside the temples, Buddhist Gompas. Baba asked him to cross that area and proceed further. He directed him to one of these Gompas and asked him to narrate what he saw. Dasarath said that it was very hazy and dark inside, but he could make out someone sitting there in meditation. The person's head was covered with a cloth and only the face was visible. When he saw his face, Dasarath told Baba that the person looked like Subhash Chandra

Bose. Baba asked him to enter his ectoplasmic cells and see what he was doing. Dasarath said that he was doing meditation. Baba asked Dasarath to enquire whether or not he was willing to return to India. Dasarath replied that he was shaking his head in negation.

Baba then asked him to come back by retracing the same path. When Dasarath reached Delhi again, Baba asked him to see what Pundit Nehru was doing in Teenmurti Bhavan. Dasarath saw Nehru sitting alone in a room in front of a desk with two drawers. Baba asked him to enter inside one of the drawers and see what he kept there. Dasarath saw three bottles and a glass. There was also a knife inside. Baba asked him what was in the bottles. Dasarath said that it was some kind of alcohol but he could not identify exactly what kind. Baba asked him what colors they were. As Dasarath described the color of each bottle, Baba said what it contained. They were whiskey, champagne, and brandy. Nehru started drinking from one of these bottles. Then Baba said, "Yes, his leadership has become compromised due to his habit of drinking alcohol. Now see the difference: In the morning, one man is absorbed in the meditation of God, while the other drowns himself in the intoxication of alcohol. They were working together for the independence of India. One is a symbol of extreme renunciation, and the other, of extreme indulgence." The Punjabi boy was shocked.

After the demonstration, I started wondering. I was convinced that Baba was capable of such clairvoyant powers, but was he indeed the same person that we thought him to be, the all-powerful and all-knowing perfect master. Baba stood up as if to leave. Abruptly he sat back down and asked Dasarath to see his own past life. Baba said that he was taking Dasarath's mind back seven thousand years. Dasarath's body started to shiver. Even the color of his face started to change. He started to perspire a lot. He started repeating, "Baba, Baba, Baba," and then he said that he saw a flood of effulgence. In the midst of that effulgence he saw Lord Shiva sitting in meditation. Baba said, "Is it so?" Then he asked Dasarath to move forward 3500 years and describe what he saw. Dasarath saw a charming personality with fair complexion wearing a crown. Baba then asked him to move forward in time and say what he saw. Dasarath replied that he was seeing Baba in a radiant form. Baba smiled and said, "See Dasarath, I was a king in my past life. Now I'm a poor man."

Just before the ceasefire, on November 17 and 18, Baba made a weekend excursion to Gazipur and Ara.[6] He conducted DMC in each place and arrived back in Jamalpur on Monday night, the nineteenth. On Sunday afternoon, while he was waiting in the Buxor Station waiting room to catch the train to Ara, a couple walked in with their little boy. Baba called the boy over and asked him his name but the boy remained silent. Again Baba affectionately repeated his question and again the boy didn't answer. Baba asked him several more questions, but the boy didn't reply to any of them. Finally, Baba turned to the mother, who by this time had tears in her eyes, and said, "What is the matter with your boy? Why is he not answering?"

"I'm sorry, Sir," the mother replied, "the boy has been dumb since birth. He is not able to speak."

Baba shook his head slowly. "No, no, this cannot be. Such a bright, good-looking child—how can it be? Surely he can speak." Baba reached out and gently touched the boy's throat, at the point of the vishuddha chakra. In a cajoling tone of voice, he said, "Now speak for me, speak. You are not dumb. You can speak, I know. Go ahead and say something for me." To everyone's surprise, the boy began talking. The parents began to cry and fell at Baba's feet. Baba gave them his blessing and then returned to his conversation with Pranay.

By this time, Pramila had completed her meditation lessons—all taught to her directly by Baba—but her family life was not what she had been brought up to expect. Her husband not only had a full-time job in the railway workshop, he spent virtually every free hour attending to his duties as the general secretary of Ananda Marga. He was in many ways more sannyasi than the monks in orange robes. As the months passed, Pramila began to despair that she would ever enjoy a normal family life with children, a nice house, and a husband with whom she could share her life and not simply a name.

One afternoon she was feeling very depressed. The thought crossed her mind that it might be better to end her life rather than continue childless and companionless for the rest of her days. She was thinking how she might go about doing this when there came a knock at her door. She went to open it and was stunned to find Baba standing there alone. Not knowing what to do, she invited Baba inside and hurried to the kitchen to get some water for the master. When she brought the water, she found Baba sitting at the table. She offered the water with both hands and then sat down herself at Baba's request.

"How are you, Pramila?" Baba asked.

Pramila started crying. She told Baba what she had been thinking and why—how difficult her life had become, always alone, without the hope of ever having children or a proper place to live.

"No, Pramila. You shouldn't think like this. Suicide is not the answer. You cannot run away from your samskaras. They will follow you into the next life, and the samskara you create by such an act is a terrible one. Anyhow, you have no reason to despair. You will have your children and a house and a wonderful family life." Baba began describing a charming two-story house with the front of the house to the north, facing a small residential street, and the back opening up to a lovely pond with flowers and shade trees. "You see, Pramila, when you want to look out at the world, you can go to the front of the house and see your neighbors walking by. But if you want to be alone, you can sit on your back veranda, look at the flowers and enjoy the solitude of nature. Don't you like flowers?"

As Baba talked, Pramila started seeing the house in front of her as if she were watching a movie. Without realizing it, her eyes closed and she slipped into trance. Baba started describing her children, two boys and a girl, and she saw them appear in front of her inner eye in the same house, enchanting her with their smiles as if they were waiting patiently for her to come.

How long she continued in that dreamlike trance, she didn't know. Her normal consciousness only returned when she heard Pranay calling her with obvious overtones of annoyance. "Pramila, what are you doing, asleep at the table at this hour? It's not even dark yet!" Pramila looked around for Baba and was startled to see that she was alone in the house with Pranay. The tears started to fall. She began telling Pranay how Baba had come and shown her their future house and their three children. Pranay was more than a bit skeptical. "Baba? Here? Visiting you alone in the middle of the afternoon? Please. You fell asleep and had a dream, that's all."

Pramila, however, was adamant that it had not been a dream. "It doesn't matter what you say. Gurudeva was here. We are going to have a two-story house with a pond in back and three children. Mark my words." Pramila got up and began preparing Pranay's dinner. The despair that had been growing over the past few months was gone and would never return. Gurudeva had revealed her future. For Pramila, it was not a matter of if, but only of when.

The following year, Baba started teaching Pramila the different lessons of kapalik sadhana. Before the year was over, she would become one of only three people, as far as is known, to whom Baba taught the fourth and final lesson, *shava* sadhana. One new moon night, Pranay informed Pramila that she should eat very little and be prepared, but he offered no explanation beyond that. Just after midnight, there was a knock at the door and Pranay admitted Baba into the house. Pranay asked if he should leave, but Baba instructed him to remain. Pranay spread a blanket for the three of them to sit, and Baba began questioning Pramila about her experience with the previous lesson of kapalik, whether or not she had perceived the concerning *shakti* and other questions to verify that she had successfully performed the sadhana. Then he informed her that she should prepare herself to receive the final lesson of that practice. At this point, Pranay objected. He began quarreling with Baba. Pramila did not quite understand what they were quarreling about; it was only afterward that she realized that Pranay had not wanted her to learn the lesson.

When Pranay finally relented, Baba explained to Pramila that the last lesson of kapalik was *shava* sadhana,[7] meditation performed while sitting on a corpse, a practice that was normally the exclusive domain of avidya Tantrics. After teaching her the process, he explained that he was going to withdraw Pranay's life force temporarily so that he could provide the corpse, an arrangement to which her husband reluctantly agreed. Pramila did not bat an eyelash. She had already known that the practice of *shava* sadhana existed. Moreover, she had implicit faith that if Baba removed her husband's life force, he would return it to him as well. Baba closed his eyes and started chanting some mantras. After a minute or two, Pranay lost consciousness and fell over. Baba examined him for vital signs. When he was satisfied that Pranay's life force had left him, he arranged the body in the corpse pose and left the room so that Pramila could perform the sadhana.

When she finished the practice, Baba returned and told her, "Now you will have to take an oath that you will never disclose this process to anyone." After she took the oath, he said, "The powers you will earn through this practice should never be misused. You will live like an ordinary person, but in secret you will do your kapalik practice. If you ever misuse these powers, then you will meet your downfall."

Baba started chanting mantras in order to bring Pranay's mind back to his body, but there was some problem. It seemed that for some reason the mind was not willing to come back. Baba raised his voice and ordered it to return, but it took some time before Pranay's heart started beating again. It was nearly dawn when Pranay finally revived.

In the late seventies, Pranay would take a job in the railway workshop at Lilluah, on the outskirts of Calcutta. When they moved there, Pramila insisted they buy a house, but Pranay balked at the idea. He pointed out that their financial position was too precarious to think about buying anything but a very small place. Pramila, however, continued to ask her friends and relatives to keep their eyes open. One day, her brother-in-law told her about a two-story residence for sale in the Calcutta suburb of Bali. The owners lived on the second floor and rented out the first floor. The moment she heard about the house, she felt a premonition. She told Pranay that she wanted to go and look at it, but Pranay objected. In the first place, he said, a two-story house would be way beyond their budget, and in the second place, with the tenancy laws in communist West Bengal being what they were, it was a hell to deal with renters once they were installed. There was no point in going, Pranay told her firmly, but he was no match for Pramila. She used the time-honored logic that it doesn't cost money to look. Before Pranay knew what was happening, they were on their way to look at the house. As they started walking down the street where the house was located, Pramila started feeling an unaccountable sense of familiarity. They entered the gate and started climbing the stairs to the second floor. When she reached the second-floor veranda and saw the pond in back, she remembered the vision she had had many years before. It was the exact scene that she had witnessed. She turned to Pranay and told him, "This is our house, Pranay. This is the house that Gurudeva showed me."

"You are a dwarf and you want to touch the moon," was Pranay's laconic reply.

"There is no way I can get together enough money for this house."

Pramila was undeterred. She continued to visit the house, made friends with the owners, the tenants and the neighbors, and eventually worked out a deal with the owners. She would have three children, just as Baba had said, two boys and a girl, and their faces would be the same that she had seen in her vision at the ages that Baba had shown them to her.

XXIX

Education, Relief, and Welfare

It must be borne in mind that as long as a magnificent, healthy and universalistic human society is not well established, humanity's entire culture and civilization, its sacrifice, service and spiritual endeavor will not be of any worth whatsoever.[1]

By January 1963, Baba's plans for a large-scale rural development project at Anandanagar were underway. Dr. Sachinandan Mandal shifted his medical clinic there from Kirnahar. Other volunteers soon followed. What they found when they arrived was part jungle, part stony hills, filled with snakes, scorpions, and unbroken solitude. Nothing was available in the local villages, other than eggplant and a poor grade of rice adulterated with stones. Supplies had to be brought from the nearest town in the one train a day that stopped at the local station, Pundag. If the volunteer missed the train back, he would have to wait in the station until the next day, or else undertake the ten-kilometer hike through the brush with the supplies on his back.

After several months of work, a small contingent from Anandanagar led by Sachinandan went to Jamalpur to see Baba. When they got an opportunity, they asked Baba what Anandanagar would be like in the future, unable to visualize that desolate area as the teeming development project and Ananda Marga headquarters that Baba had said it would become.

Baba called one young volunteer forward and asked him whether he would like to see London or Anandanagar. Much to Sachinandan's annoyance, he replied that he wanted to see London. Baba told him to close his eyes and concentrate. Then he touched him on his forehead and asked him to describe what he saw. He began describing the buildings of a huge city. After a few minutes, he asked Baba, "How can I know if this is London or not?"

"Foolish boy," Baba retorted, "can't you read the signboards?"

"Yes, Baba," the boy replied, with a sheepish smile. Finally he located a sign on one building that said London.

"Okay," Baba said. "Now you will see Anandanagar as it will be in the future." He began describing a busy place with numerous projects, beautiful gardens, and many buses and trains connecting it to the outside world. Sachinandan and his companions were satisfied that they wouldn't be stranded in the middle of the jungle forever.

Now that the development of Anandanagar was underway, Baba informed the Margis in the beginning of April that he was creating a new wing to oversee the social service projects; he called it ERAWS, the Education, Relief, and Welfare Section. He announced its formation during the Sunday darshan. Afterward, he called a meeting of the principal Margis, during which he elaborated in detail the work of the new wing.

"Ananda Marga education," he told them, "should focus on the all-around progress of the individual; its motto will be *sa vidyaya vimuktaye*—education is that which liberates. It should be as cheap as possible and extend to the village level so that the children will not have far to travel. No distinction will be made between rich and poor. The relief section will create a team to respond in times of natural and man-made disasters.[2] This team will pride itself on its rapid response to unexpected calamities and its ability to reach affected areas that other relief agencies do not reach. All medical professionals should be encouraged to be de facto members of this team. In times of disaster, all local Margis should consider themselves members of this section and be ready to volunteer. The welfare section will be responsible for establishing permanent welfare projects, such as children's homes, medical clinics, and so on."

When Baba finished detailing the activities of each section, he asked for secretaries to be nominated to oversee the work. Pranay nominated Asthana for education, Kedar for relief, and Dr. Ramesh for welfare.

In the weeks that followed, Baba met with each of the new in-charges and gave them guidelines for the development of their department. When he met with Dr. Ramesh, he asked him to establish a children's home as his first welfare project and gave him detailed instructions about the running of the home.

"The children will never be referred to as orphans," Baba told him, "and our homes will not be called orphanages, because no one in this world is an orphan. In other children's homes, they send the children out to beg. This will not happen in our homes. Our workers will beg, if necessary. They and the local Margis are responsible for meeting all the requirements of the children. The children's living standard should be the same as that of middle-class Margis and their children."

Within a short time, the first children's home opened in Patna under the supervision of Akhori Himachal Prasad, then Additional Superintendent of Police in Patna; Sambuddhananda, formerly Asim; and Dr. Ramesh from Ranchi. The second home opened at Anandanagar shortly afterward, and others soon followed.

Baba gave the same impetus to the establishment of the education wing. With the inauguration of ERAWS, the opening of schools became an organizational priority. Margi educators under Asthana's supervision began developing an Ananda Marga system of education and a curriculum for their schools. They met with Baba, who gave them guidelines, both for the running of the schools and for the educational methods they would use, just as he had done with the children's homes. As was to be expected, Baba emphasized the spiritual and ethical aspects of a child's education.

> In Prout's educational system, emphasis should be given to moral education and the inculcation of idealism—not only philosophy and traditions. The practice of morality should be the most important subject in the syllabus at all levels. The sense of universalism should also be awakened in the child. Etiquette and refined behavior are not enough. Real education leads to a pervasive sense of love and compassion for all creation.[3]

He used the letters of the word "education" to create an easily remembered reminder of some of the fundamental principles of Ananda Marga education: E—Enlargement of mind; D—DESMEP (D for Discipline, E for Etiquette, S for Smartness, M for Memory, E for English, P for Pronunciation); U—Universal Outlook; C—Character; A—Active habits; T—Trustworthiness; I—Ideation of the Great; O—Omniscient grace; N—Nice temperament.[4]

After this, Baba would make it a regular part of his program to visit the new schools and homes whenever he went out on DMC tour.

In the meantime, Baba continued his literary and philosophical work during his lunch-hour dictations. In May, the second volume of *Human Society* went to print. *Human Society, Part Two* was a book-length treatise on Baba's theory of the social cycle. It began with a philosophical analysis of the laws of social dynamics that had many of the disciples scratching their heads until Baba's abstract language descended to a plane they could understand. The opening pages began in this way:

> The existence of the relative factors of time, space and person is substantiated in the field of cognition and the cognizant bearing in its inertness is the highest stance of these factors. The inherent dynamicity of an entity, depending on the existential collaboration of another entity (or in certain cases, of other entities, in which case immobility becomes of indefinite character) is called its movement or *gati*, while that of an entity independent of other entities is called its immobility or *agati*. When this relative movement loses its adjustment with the temporal factor it may be called a state of pause—in a limited sense, staticity. The movement of an entity in relation to the witnessing faculty may be called its accelerated or retarded movement depending upon the degree of its actional expression.

The question of whether or not movement and inertness are absolute is a knotty problem for both science and philosophy. In fact, just as dynamicity is characterized by the stigma of relativity, by the same logic inertness is also characterized by the stigma of relativity. So from an absolute point of view, if the existence of movement is denied, the existence of inertness or existential faculty will also have to be denied. When the observable objects do not seem to change place judged by relative standards we call that state a state of inertness. But in such circumstances the movement of the observer and the observed entity within the Macrocosmic arena remains beyond the comprehension of our crude and subtle minds. That is why this so-called state of inertness cannot be called absolute inertness. In individual life the supreme stance is that state in which the causal mind or astral mind remains inactive. We cannot call the disembodied state of mind the supreme stance because in that case the seed of dynamicity is still active in the Cosmic Mind and the Cosmic Corpor with the help of the Cosmic Operative Principle. From this we can deduce that the supreme stance can be attained only when the seed of psychic functioning has been demolished . . .

Unit consciousness, when it is self-dependent (it is dependent on others also), views the transposition of objects, and only that part of movement actually comes under the category of motion. When the self-dependent movement (as also the dependent one), giving up its effort or failing in its effort to exert, surrenders to the state of motionlessness, such a condition indeed is called cessation. Apparently all kinds of movement in this expressed universe are linked with the state of pause. Thus, every action is systolic. The systalticity is an attempt to find stability in a state of pause. Pause is only a temporary state of inertness. Full expression occurs only after attaining momentum for movement from the state of inertness. No action is possible without momentum attained from the state of inertness, and thus every action (roughly it is also called movement) must be systolic or pulsative by nature. In the same way unhindered expansion or enhancement and unhindered contraction is impossible in the realm of mundanity. The manifestative bearing of action or movement is directly related to the relative factors of time, space and person, and the contractive bearing is an attempt at detachment from the temporal factor. As the state of contraction is entrenched in inertness, the unit entity loses its awareness of the temporal factor . . .[5]

After comparing systolic movement to a trek across a series of hills where the ascent brings one to the state of manifestative pause and the descent to systolic pause, Baba embarked on a lengthy discussion of the concepts of movement, momentum, and death, before finally showing how this same movement governs the birth and death of societies. He thus provided the philosophical underpinnings for his subsequent analysis of the social cycle in a manner that was characteristic of his love for pure philosophy.

One morning in early June, Baba arrived at the jagriti about nine o'clock to give a short class. With the help of a world map that was affixed to the wall, he started giving a historical overview of the global situation at that time, pointing to the different countries with his stick. When his stick fell on Canada, he stopped and asked Arun to go to the kitchen and fetch some drinking water.[6] As soon as Arun left the room, he asked Acharyas Suresh and Lalan if Arun had a brother in Canada.

"Yes, Baba," Lalan replied. "His brother is teaching in a medical college in Canada."

"Don't say anything to Arun when he comes back, but his brother has just this moment been involved in a terrible accident. The car that he was driving has just had a head-on collision with a truck. He is still alive, but he is badly injured. His ribs have been caved in and he has sustained a severe head injury."

As Baba said this, images of the accident flashed in the minds of those present. Lalan and Suresh, who were both close friends of Arun's other brother Sujit, cried out in dismay.

"Baba, please do something to save him, otherwise the family will suffer. Their brother is the family's only means of support. If he dies, they will be in great trouble."

For several long moments, Baba didn't say anything. His eyes appeared to be unfocused, as if he were still gazing at the scene of the accident more than seven thousand miles away. Finally he said, "Meet me at my house in the evening before field walk. I will tell you then. In the meantime, do not tell Arun what has happened."

That evening, Baba told them that there had been no use in saving him. "His skull was badly smashed and his brain was damaged. I could have saved his life, but his brain would not have been able to function properly. It was better he take a new body with new vigor and work for humanity. But don't worry about his family. They will not undergo undue hardship. I will see to that."

Baba then told Pranay to send a telegram to Sujit in South India, where he had been posted for prachar, informing him of the accident and asking him to come back to take care of his family.

The next morning, Baba returned to the jagriti and gave a talk on death. "Everyone who takes birth in this universe has to die," he said. "It is a perfectly natural process and there is no reason to be afraid of it." He asked Arun to stand up and repeat some of the salient points of his talk. Afterward, he called Arun to his room and broke the sad news. Later that day, a telegram arrived for Arun with the news of his brother's death.

Education, Relief, and Welfare 293

Late that summer, Baba overhauled the wholetimer system that Satyananda had begun. Wholetimer candidates would from then on be considered sannyasi trainees until they received their avadhuta initiation. By the fall, there was at least one wholetimer in every state, with Bengal and Bihar broken down into zones, each with their own wholetimer. Through these young monks the organization was in the process of spreading to every corner of India.

The rapid growth of the organization became a source of pride for the disciples, but not everyone was happy with the increasingly important role that the sannyasis were playing. Baba now began spending more and more time with his monastic disciples, encouraging and guiding them, and delegating to them much of the responsibility for implementing his many new plans and programs, a responsibility that had formerly rested with the householder disciples. Some of these, most notably Pranay, began to feel that their authority and prestige was being usurped by this band of young newcomers, despite the fact that the family people had been the ones to build up the organization.

One day, Pranay and Dasarath went to Baba to complain that Satyananda was abusing his authority by not informing the general secretary of his and the other wholetimers' activities, thus making it difficult for the family acharyas to do their work. The next morning Baba called Satyananda and informed him of the charges.

"We are going to have a meeting about it this evening. Come fully prepared. I am going to scold you in front of them."

That evening in the jagriti, Baba gave Satyananda a dressing-down in front of Pranay and a group of important family acharyas; this went a long way toward appeasing their hurt feelings. After the meeting, Baba called Satyananda to his room and told him not to worry. "Don't pay any attention to what anyone says. Your work is coming along nicely. Go ahead with full speed and don't look back."

A few days later, Baba called Chandranath and Ram Tanuk and asked them to work directly with Satyananda to help him established the new sannyasi structure.

Afterward, Pranay was more openly cordial to Satyananda, convinced that Baba had taken his point, but the rapid rise of the monastic structure continued unabated. The new cadre of wholetimers would be the key to spreading Baba's mission throughout the world in the years to come.

In mid-August Baba went to Ranchi to conduct a DMC. Unable to get time off work, Acharya Kamalakanta could not attend the program. His five-year-old daughter, Sujata, was sorely disappointed when she heard the news. She began pestering her father.

"Dad, if we can't go there, then please go and bring Baba back here. I want to see Baba."

Kamalakanta's wife tried to explain to her daughter that her father had important work to attend to. He could not bring Baba this time, but he surely would the next time. Sujata was not so easily pacified. "Why can't you bring Baba here? I want to see him now. Baba goes to everyone else's house. Why can't he come to ours?" Nothing they could say would console the determined child.

After the program was over, Baba returned to Jamalpur by car. During the trip, he kept asking repeatedly for water, far more than he normally did. Before long they ran out of drinking water, but Baba was still thirsty.

"Baba, there's no more water," Pranay said. "I'm sorry. As soon as we find a good place to stop, I will try to find some good drinking water."

They traveled a ways further without finding a suitable place to stop. Baba began to grow impatient. He insisted that Pranay stop the car at some Margi's house where he could get a drink. Pranay consulted with the other Margis in the car. At that moment, they were passing through Pakribarama, where Acharya Kamalakanta lived. One of them knew the address, so they turned off toward the house.

When the surprised acharya and his wife found Baba at their door, they asked him to take a seat. At Pranay's behest, they ran into the kitchen to bring a cool glass of water.

"No, no, not yet," Baba said, when they handed him the glass. "I will drink a little later. First I want to see Sujata." A few moments later, Sujata came running in to see Baba. Baba patted her on the head and said, "So, Sujata, are you happy now? Your Baba has come to see you."

On September 15, Baba held a DMC in Gorakhpur. Numerous well-known personalities from the upper social strata of the city attended the program, indicative of Ananda Marga's growing reputation in Northern India. The organization, which had begun with Baba's fellow railway employees and members of the BMP, was now seeing more and more lawyers, doctors, politicians, and wealthy businessmen enter through its doors. None of them, however, received any preferential treatment from Baba. As usual, Baba took advantage of the darshans, PCs, and field walks in Gorakhpur to point out the ethical shortcomings of his followers and provide them with suitable blows to their ego. When Acharya Pratapaditya saw Baba scolding several prestigious members of the community, some of them his initiates, he became concerned. He went to talk to Baba privately about it.

"Baba, if you punish all such highly placed, prestigious people in this way, who is going to stay in Ananda Marga?"

"I cannot discriminate between people on this basis," Baba said. "What this organization needs in order to grow successfully is purification. If the people I punish become strict about the ideology, then everyone is benefitted. But if they feel otherwise and leave, then that also benefits the organization."

Baba confided in him that hard times for the organization were coming in the not-too-distant future. Fair-weather disciples, those attracted by Baba's personality or the growing reputation of Ananda Marga but not firmly dedicated to the ideology, would not remain.

Back in Jamalpur, Akhori and Dr. Ramesh accompanied Baba on field walk, during which they briefed him on the progress of the children's home in Patna and on ERAWS in general. At one point Baba stopped and said, "The conflict between us and the dogmatic pundits will bring us hard times in the near future, but our last and greatest enemies will be the government and the communists. They will torture and beat our Margi brothers and sisters simply for being Margis. People will be afraid to admit they are Margis. If they do, they will be humiliated, threatened, and imprisoned. Will you stick by me when that happens?"

The Margis pledged that they would stand by Baba no matter what.

"Are you sure?" Baba asked again. "Hard times are coming soon, and a lot of work will need to be done in the meantime."

Again they reaffirmed their vow.

"The religion developed by the Brahmins is not true dharma," he went on to say. "It was developed by them to fulfill their own interests. It is based on selfishness and hence cannot give the people what they need. As regards communism, Marx was a good person, a thoughtful person, and a prophet for the poor." As Baba said this, he brought his folded palms to his chest. "But his theory is completely impractical, hence its downfall is certain. It will collapse in your lifetime. Capitalism makes people beggars, but communism makes them animals. It deprives them of their thinking capacity."

At the end of the conversation, Baba told them that when it came time for communism to collapse, he would also leave.

Shortly before the Gorakhpur DMC, Baba called Satyananda to his room and asked him to go to Behala, a suburb of Calcutta, to convey a message to Gopen. "Satyananda, make him understand this time. Let him know that this is his last chance."

The message was essentially the same as the one Baba had sent through Satyananda the previous year, when he had warned Gopen to stop misusing his powers and instead help the organization with its missionary work. At the time, Gopen had replied, "Satyananda, you know very well that Baba does not depend on anyone. He has come with a mission and he will get it done. If human beings don't help him, he will get the cows and goats to do it." Baba's brow had darkened when Satyananda told him of Gopen's response, but he had said nothing more at the time.

The problem had begun after Gopen's transfer to Patna in 1961. He collected a circle of followers there that included two family acharyas. They called their circle "Madhuchakra" to differentiate it from the Dharmachakra of Ananda Marga. With the powers that Gopen had gained through his sadhana and frequent samadhis, he would tell people's future, give solutions to their difficulties, and counsel them in their spiritual practices and family affairs. The Margis who encircled him became so enamored of his spiritual gifts and palpable charisma that they stopped going to see Baba in Jamalpur or participating in Ananda Marga activities.

In an interview, Acharya Kishori Devi recounted some of her experiences with Gopen in Patna in the early sixties:

> I took initiation in 1960 from Gopen-da, fifteen days after my husband. When he was giving me my first lesson, he went into trance and suddenly I saw Baba sitting in front of me. I did meditation for twenty minutes; when I opened my eyes, I saw that Baba was still sitting there. I prostrated before him.
> He said, "Mother, get up."
> I said, "Please, I am your daughter."
> He said, "Yes, you are my daughter, but I will call you mother."
> When Gopen-da and his wife moved to Patna, they stayed with us for a while. Gopen-da used to remain in trance all the time then. He used to dance on one foot and a sweet fragrance used to come from his body. His wife objected to his meditation. Margis used to come and garland him, touch his feet, and have his darshan. His wife complained that they were disturbing her husband and would break his heart. His face looked like Baba's at that time. While he was staying with us, I used to see divine light in my meditation and had many other experiences.
> I had two young daughters then, my first two children. Poonam was one and a half years old and the other was only a few months old. One day, during General Darshan in Patna, Poonam ran to the dais and touched Baba's feet. People shouted for me to control her. I went up and grabbed her, but I also touched Baba's feet and so did the daughter on my lap. Afterward, Gopen told me that since they were so young, they would either die or become great meditators. Fifteen days before they died, a saint came to my door. I told him to please wait; I would just go inside and bring something for him. He said, "No, I don't want anything. I have come to tell you that your daughters will die soon. You have a strong attachment to them, so they have to go." Some days later, they came down with smallpox. One day, while they were dying, they were sitting on Gopen-da's wife's lap. The window suddenly opened and a halo of light entered. It enveloped them and at that moment they died.

Satyananda left for Behala as instructed and attended the Sunday sitting of the Madhuchakra. Once the collective meditation concluded, he conveyed Baba's message. Gopen remained silent but the other members of the group started reviling Satyananda. Offended by their insults, he left and took the night train back to Jamalpur. He met Baba in the jagriti before office hours and described what had happened.

"Baba, I will not go back there, never again," he said, still offended by his ill treatment. Baba turned to Pranay and asked him to bring a piece of paper and a pen.

"Pranay, draft a telegram to Gopen and send it immediately. State in the telegram that his acharyaship is suspended from this day henceforth, and that I, Anandamurti, withdraw all his spiritual power from this very moment."

Not long afterward, the news started trickling back from Calcutta that Gopen had lost his abilities. His followers had begun deserting him, one by one. Soon he stopped attending the Behala meditation (which by then had dropped the name Madhuchakra), as well as all Ananda Marga activities and functions in the metropolitan area.

On December 12, Baba arrived in Calcutta for a DMC program, accompanied by Satyananda. He was brought to the residence of Manohar Lal Gupta, who would be his host during his stay. While a car was being readied to take Baba for his morning walk, he asked Satyananda if he knew Gopen's address.

"No, Baba."

"Then find out, and keep it in strictest confidence. I wish to see Gopen this morning, but no one should know that I am going there."

Manohar Lal Gupta knew the address. He accompanied Baba and Satyananda and gave directions to the driver as they made their way toward Behala. When they arrived at Gopen's residence, Baba and Manohar remained in the car while Satyananda climbed the stairs to Gopen's second-floor apartment. When he knocked at the door, Gopen opened it, dressed only in a towel, still wet from his morning bath. When Gopen heard the news that Baba was downstairs in the car, waiting to see him, he ran straight down the stairs without bothering to put on any clothes. He fell at Baba's feet, weeping. "Baba, please forgive me, please forgive me," he stammered, over and over again, while the passersby paused to gape at the odd sight.

Baba comforted him and Gopen quickly entered into a state of samadhi. He was still in samadhi when Satyananda carried him in his arms back up to his apartment as if he were carrying a sleeping child. Baba would have no more cause to complain about Gopen's behavior in the future.

One of the obstacles Baba had to face in his rapid push to accelerate the growth of the organization was the willingness of parents to use whatever means possible to prevent their children from becoming sannyasis. In one such case, the parents even went to the extreme of filing a case against Baba.

Amit was the son of wealthy parents. When he graduated from the Bihar Institute of Technology in the summer of 1962, his father, Sirdhan Singh, then Income Tax Commissioner at Calcutta, secured a position for him in a prestigious Calcutta firm. A few months later, however, he resigned his job and came to Jamalpur to be a wholetimer. His parents were mortified by his decision. They came to Jamalpur several times to try and convince him to come back with them. Satyananda, wary of the problems they could pose for the organization, cooperated with them. He even posted Amit in Jamalpur to facilitate their visits, but Amit was adamant about his intentions to become a monk. When he reached the age of twenty-one, he entered the training center. There was nothing more his parents could do.

Or so he thought.

At the beginning of December 1963, Sirdhan Singh filed kidnapping charges in Monghyr court against Baba and Pranay. By then Amit had taken avadhuta initiation and received the monastic name Amitananda. He was posted in the southern state of Kerala, though at the time that the charges were being processed, he was in Anandanagar preparing for the year-end VSS camp and the New Year DMC.

After the charges were processed, constables came to inform Baba and Pranay of the charges and require them to appear in court to give their bail plea. Pranay sent a messenger to Beghuserai to apprise Ram Tanuk and Vaedyanath Singh, both advocates, of the situation. Then he took Baba by car to Monghyr. Pranay asked Baba to wait outside in the shade of a towering mango tree while he went inside to inform the court that he and Baba had arrived. He was led into the courtroom of Bal Mukunda Rastogi, to whose court the case had been assigned. When Rastogi, a longtime Margi and staunch disciple, saw Pranay and had the papers handed to him by the bailiff, he was horrified.

"Where is Baba?" he asked Pranay, jumping up out of his seat. When Pranay informed him that Baba was waiting in the car under the mango tree, he hurried outside as fast as he could.

"What game are you playing with me, Baba?" he asked, "Why are you coming in front of your disciple as an accused? I cannot bear the thought of you having to stand in the witness box."

"Don't worry, Bal Mukunda," Baba said. "That won't happen. Everything will be fine, but you will have to be patient for two years."

Rastogi went back to his courtroom and signed the papers for Baba's bail. Baba was able to return to Jamalpur without having to set foot in the courthouse. Ram Tanuk and Vaedyanath arrived the next day. They met with Rastogi and began processing the paperwork for the case. After the New Year DMC, Amitananda filed a statement in the Monghyr court that he was not a minor and had become a monk of his own volition. The case, by then, had become headline news throughout the country. Amitananda accompanied Ram Tanuk to Delhi to meet the Home Minister. After their meeting, the charges were dismissed and Amitananda went back to his post in Kerala. As Baba had foreshadowed, Bal Mukunda Rastogi would face severe tribulations in his professional life over the next two years, in part due to his being the judge associated with the case. When the two years ended, so did his difficulties.

Shortly after the case was thrown out, Amitananda's father began printing anti-Ananda Marga leaflets and distributing them by sending them to legislative members in different parts of the country. The leaflets contained allegations that included mesmerism and kidnapping of minors. A superintendent in the District Attorney's office in Patna showed the leaflet to Rameshvar Baita, who brought it to Jamalpur to show to Baba. Baba laughed when he saw it. "The sun is yellow," he said. "Can anyone say that it is black? They may try and do so, but it doesn't make it any the less yellow."

A few months later, Baba was traveling by train with Devi Chand to attend a DMC program. While the train was stopped at a station along the way, a man appeared on the platform outside the window where Baba was sitting and pressed a loaded revolver to Baba's ear. Baba looked at the man impassively; Devi Chand remained frozen in his seat, unable to react. Suddenly Baba snatched the revolver from the man's hand and said, "This is the third time you have tried to harm me, and still you can do nothing. This gun belongs to your friend, a DSP (Deputy Superintendent of Police). If I turn the gun over to the IG (Inspector General of Police), what do you think will happen to you then?"

The shocked assailant was unable to say anything, but Devi Chand could see the fear on his face.

"I am going to let you go," Baba said, "because your son Amitananda is a sannyasi in my mission, but let this be the last time." Amitananda's father fled the scene and never troubled Baba again.

At the end of December, Baba sent word that he wanted the Anandanagar Primary School to open on the second of January. At that moment, hundreds of disciples were attending the year-end VSS camp in Anandanagar underneath a huge tent that had been erected as a temporary shelter. The local volunteers held an emergency meeting and decided to start classes in the tent immediately following the program. They also began construction of two buildings: a hostel and a school building.

In the meantime, back in Jamalpur, Baba began asking for daily progress reports. Money was scarce, however, and one day Abhedananda, who had recently become Baba's personal assistant, was forced to inform Baba that the work was delayed due to lack of funds. Baba glowered at him and said, "The work of Ananda Marga will never stop due to financial problems. Look there!" Baba pointed to a rack that moments before had been empty. Abhedananda and his three companions were startled to see the rack filled with precious jewels, gold, and silver. Abhedananda fell at Baba's feet. Again Baba repeated—this time in a softer tone of voice—that the work of Ananda Marga would never stop due to financial problems.

Under this constant pressure from Baba, the buildings were erected and made functional within one month. Margi families from Patna and other cities started sending their children to study there, alongside the village children who streamed in each day from the surrounding area. For most of the village children, it was their first opportunity to get an education. Classes began with grades one through four, and in late March, Sujit pushed through their application with the State Board of Education to extend the instruction up to grade eight.

Baba paid his first visit to Anandanagar on March 6 and stayed until the tenth. While he was there, he inspected the existing buildings and gave detailed plans for the future development of the project. He chose a spot for a hospital, whose construction began as soon as Baba left, and he laid the foundation stone for a technical college, which he christened AMIT, Ananda Marga Institute of Technology. He also chose the sites for a future liberal arts college, veterinary college, naturopathic and ayurvedic clinics, agricultural research center, various cottage industries, and offices for the different wings of Ananda Marga. He suggested to the volunteers that they use an inexpensive type of construction that would be good for at least eight to ten years, a foreshadowing of things to come.

Along with the detailed planning that Baba dictated as he walked, he kept up a ceaseless commentary on the natural and cultural history of the area, a practice that he continued during the morning darshans underneath a palash tree. He talked about Rarh,[7] which he considered the cradle of human civilization, and told the Margis that they would find many precious archeological artifacts on their land, including the remains of an indigenous Indian civilization much older than the Mohendaro and Harappa civilizations. He also said that they would find many fossils there, explaining that Anandanagar had long been an area of hot springs and mineral salts; for that reason it was an ideal environment for the preservation of fossils. "Just as human beings have common graveyards," he said, "so did the ancient dinosaurs and mammoths." Before he left, he took them to a hill that he revealed to be a huge fossilized mound of bones.

Above all, Baba paid special attention to the rich spiritual heritage of the region. He explained that the name of the nearby village of Chitmu was a corruption of the original Sanskrit *caitanya mukha*, meaning, "face toward consciousness." It was so named because this area was home to the earliest practitioners of spiritual meditation on the planet. In response to an unvoiced question of Sujit's, who had been wondering why Baba had chosen such a solitary place for his future headquarters, Baba explained that the entire area of Anandanagar was highly spiritually vibrated. In the distant past, it had been home to a great school of Jain Tantra whose center had been situated on the bank of the Kamsavati River, which wound through the center of Anandanagar; its influence had spread Tantra for a far distance on both banks of the river. Many sadhakas had attained liberation while meditating in these solitary wastelands, and the places they chose for their meditation had become *tantra pitha*s, seats of Tantra, coveted by yogis for their meditation, since it was well known that the vibrations left by a realized saint at the place of their practice would greatly benefit any yogi who meditated there, even centuries afterward. In fact, Baba told them, the entire Anandanagar area, framed by the Kamsavati and Suvarnarekha river basins, could itself be considered a *tantra pitha*. It was home to over seventy individual *tantra pitha*s where sadhakas of different traditions in different eras had achieved enlightenment.

While the volunteers who came to live and work in Anandanagar found it to be an ideal place to pursue their spiritual practices, it was also full of mundane challenges, among them the constant presence of scorpions and snakes, many of them poisonous. Baba assured Sujit that the scorpions would not bother them, and this proved true, but snakes were a bigger concern. One had to be constantly on the lookout, especially at night when the chances of stepping on a snake without seeing it would keep people from venturing out. Every year, several villagers in the surrounding areas would die from venomous snakebites. The workers found snakes in their beds when they retired for the night and on their mosquito nets when they woke up in the morning. Once the first students had been admitted into the newly constructed hostel, they became concerned that if any of the students were bitten, some of the guardians might withdraw their children and the schools would get a bad reputation.

One day, shortly after Baba's first visit, Acharya Svarupananda, then posted to Anandanagar as a teacher, went to Jamalpur to ask for Baba's help.

"All right," Baba said. "I will teach you a certain mantra. If there is any case of snakebite, use the mantra and no harm will come to the person. Come tomorrow night at ten or eleven and I will teach you. And come prepared."

Svarupananda had no idea what Baba meant by "prepared." The next night, when he came to Baba's room, Baba said, "Did you take a bath?"

"I took one at noon, Baba."

"No, you must take a bath before you come here. Take a bath, do sadhana, and then come to me. All right, come again tomorrow."

The next night, Svarupananda took a bath and went to Baba's room. "Did you take your guru mantra before sitting?" Baba asked.

"No, I forgot," Svarupananda replied.

"Well, then I can't teach you tonight."

For the next several nights, Baba put Svarupananda off with similar tests. Finally, one night he seemed ready to give him the mantra.

"Before I give you this mantra, there are some conditions."

"What are they, Baba?"

"They are very simple. The first is that if you come to know of any case of snakebite, you must rush immediately to that place and help the patient. The second is that if someone dies of snakebite, it will be your responsibility."

"Baba, how can I take such a big responsibility?"

"If I am to teach you this mantra, you must accept the responsibility."

Svarupananda thought about it for a few moments. He was about to agree when Baba said, "Rather than giving you a mantra, would it not be better if from now on the snakes at Anandanagar didn't bite anyone?"

"Yes, Baba. That would be best."

"Then go and tell everyone there that nobody will die of snakebite in Anandanagar. Only, do not harm them, or else they may bite. But even then, you will not die from it."

Svarupananda did as instructed. From that day on, there was no case of snakebite within the boundaries of Anandanagar, though the snakes continued to be their constant companions for some years more until the development of the project and the influx of people gradually convinced the creatures to migrate to less-populated areas.

There continued to be occasional cases of snakebite among the villagers, but they would bring the patient to the Anandanagar hospital and none of them died. A few years later, a police outpost was erected near the jagriti building, and the police began behaving badly with the sannyasis and the students. After two months, there were so many cases of snakebite in their camp that they packed up and left. Before they left, the local villagers pointed out to them that there were so many sannyasis and students of different ages at Ananda Nagar, yet none of them had ever been bitten by a snake. "You must have some bad intention," they said. "That is why God is punishing you."

XXX

Past Lives

All knowledge, one's entire past history and flashes of one's previous lives, remain stored in sequential order in the causal mind, just like a colorful panorama, one layer representing one life, followed by a gap, followed by another layer representing another life, and so on . . . Human beings, if they so want, may try to relive those experiences in their memories. This endeavor is called sadhana or spiritual practice. Sadhakas or spiritual aspirants, by dint of sadhana, suspend their crude mind in the subtle mind, and the subtle mind in the causal mind. They can then clearly visualize that panorama of sequential events in the causal mind. As they have full control over the time factor they can easily transcend the intervening gaps between two lives and establish a link between them. A series of lives slowly and gradually unfold themselves like a moving panorama before their eyes.[1]

IN LATE FEBRUARY 1964, Baba was traveling by car to Darbanga for a DMC. When the car passed through Laharia Sarai, Baba instructed the driver to turn west toward the station. When Jiteshananda, one of the new avadhutas, asked him why they were turning off from their route, Baba told him that he had some purpose and left it at that. Baba got out of the car when it reached the station without saying a word and walked toward the platform. The Margis in his entourage followed behind.

Inside the station, Haraprasad Haldar was on the platform waiting for a train. When he noticed Baba approaching, he tried to turn his face in the hope that Baba wouldn't notice him.

"Where are you going?" Baba asked as he caught up to him. "Are you trying to avoid me? Come with me."

Baba grabbed him by the elbow and escorted him out of the station and into the waiting car. When they arrived in Darbanga, Baba went straight to the room that had been prepared for him and brought Haraprasad with him.

When Haraprasad finally came out of Baba's room, the curious Margis who had been in the car crowded around him and asked him what was going on.

"For some time now," Haraprasad said, "I've been feeling a strange force attracting me toward the Himalayas. I felt a longing to go there and dedicate myself to meditation. It kept getting stronger and stronger, to the point that I just couldn't put it out of my mind any longer. Finally, I took the decision to abandon my worldly life and spend the rest of my days in solitary meditation. Once I made up my mind, I decided to go visit my closest friends one last time, since I knew I would likely never see them again. But I was sure that if I saw Baba, he wouldn't allow me to go. Since I knew that he was scheduled to be in Darbanga, I decided to catch a train for Gorakhpur in Laharia Sarai so I wouldn't have to pass through Darbanga. But as you saw, Baba caught me anyhow. When he took me into his room, he scolded me for entertaining thoughts of abandoning my family and service to the society. Then he gave me direct orders to desist from any thought of fleeing to the Himalayas, now or ever."

Later, the Margis got a chance to ask Baba about it as well, and he filled in some of the missing details.

"In Haraprasad's last life, he was a yogi who lived in a cave in the Himalayas. He was the disciple of a Himalayan master. One day he went to the river to bring water and he drowned. Though that was many years ago, his guru is still alive, and he still keeps Haraprasad's meditation seat and his water pot from that life. This is the source of the great attraction he feels toward those mountains. In fact, he actually started for the Himalayas on an earlier occasion, but he came back. Now I have forbidden him to make any further attempts. It would not be good for his spiritual progress."

Another curious incident occurred during the Darbanga DMC. An unknown woman approached the Margis in front of the house where Baba was staying and said she wanted to meet Baba. They informed her politely that Baba did not meet non-Margis, but, if she wished, she could see him from a distance when he went for his customary walk. They thought nothing more of it, until Baba sent word that there was a non-Margi woman outside the gate matching her description who should be sent away. They went outside and found her still sitting there, waiting for Baba to come out. They tried to get her to leave, as Baba had requested, but the woman would not budge. Finally, they gave up, unwilling to go against the mores of Indian culture, which demand that a high level of respect be shown toward women and the elderly.

Some time later Baba came out. As he was getting into the car that would take him to the area chosen for his evening walk, the lady approached him.

"What do you want, Mother?" Baba asked.

"Baba, I have brought this flower for you."

Baba accepted the flower and got into the car. When the person sitting next to him in the back seat offered to hold the flower for him, Baba warned him and everyone else not to touch it. When they got out of the car for their walk, Baba was still holding the flower. Their route took them over a stream. As they were crossing the bridge, Baba stopped and explained to everyone that the lady who had given him the flower was an avidya Tantric.

"She has infused this flower with a certain power so that anyone who willingly accepts it will come under her control. This power is called *sammohani vidya*. After she gave it to me, she realized that her power had no effect over me, but if any of you touch it, you may be affected."

Saying this, Baba dropped the flower off the bridge and into the flowing water. He then explained that this would nullify its effect.

On March 4, just prior to his first visit to Anandanagar, Baba arrived in Dhanbad for a DMC program. Vishvanath acted as his local attendant.[2] Baba arrived in the evening from Asansol in Kedarnath's car and was brought to the house of Sachidananda, where a room had been prepared for him. As he stepped onto the veranda, the Margi women welcomed him with lighted lamps and washed his feet with scented water in the Bihari tradition. Sachidananda was lying on the veranda with a high fever, wrapped in a blanket, but he got up to garland Baba; instead of Baba inclining his head to receive the garland and then giving namaskar as he usually did, Baba slapped him on his cheek hard enough that he lost his balance and fell. When he got up, the fever and pains were gone and would not return.

The number of Margis who assembled the next day for DMC far exceeded expectations, and the organizers grew worried when it became obvious that the hall they had rented for the occasion would not hold everyone, no matter how tightly they packed it. While they were discussing what to do, a rich businessman pulled up in a new Mercedes and asked to speak to the organizers.

"I have heard that you are religious people," he said, "and that you are planning a big function here in Dhanbad. I have a large building with all the facilities you need that I'd like to offer for your program, if you'd be willing to oblige me. I also have a new car that you can use."

Surprised by this unexpected offer, the Margis went with him to inspect the building and found that it was exactly what they needed. They quickly arranged to move the DMC program there. Later on, they heard from the neighbors that the building was supposedly haunted and that the man who owned it was afraid to enter. He had been counting on the bhajans and kirtan to drive away the evil spirits.

After the DMC was over, Vishvanath and Gurugopal went into Baba's room to massage him. When Vishvanath began massaging Baba's head, he started to cry, overcome by the sad realization that Baba was leaving the next day for Anandanagar.

"Don't cry," Baba told him. "Haven't you all promised that you will follow me wherever I go? You know, you have followed me here to this planet, and wherever I go next, you will be with me."

The next morning, before Baba was scheduled to leave, Vishvanath was fanning him in his room. On Vishvanath's urging, Pranay informed Baba that Vishvanath was going to have his exams the following week. Baba looked at Vishvanath, but didn't say anything at that moment. A few minutes later, however, while washing his hands, Baba instructed Vishvanath not to forget to repeat his second lesson mantra before beginning his exams. Then Baba went out to the car that was waiting to take him to the station. The businessman who had offered his building was waiting by the side of the car along with the Margis and Baba gave him his blessing, which was unusual since he was not initiated. The local Margis heard later from him that his wife, who had been childless for many years, had gotten pregnant after the DMC. This had been his unspoken wish when he saw Baba off.

Vishvanath repeated his second lesson mantra before sitting for his exam, but when the results were posted, he was disappointed to learn that he had failed. Vexed with Baba, he borrowed some money and went to Jamalpur. In the evening, while sitting on the tiger's grave, he voiced his complaint.

"Baba, you told me to do my second lesson before my exam, and I did but I still failed."

"Vishvanath, you failed because you are not sincere in your studies, and because you worship the goddess Sarasvati and ask for her help,[3] which you know you should not do."

Baba resumed talking with the other Margis, but a few minutes later he turned back to Vishvanath and said, "There was a tabulation error in your workshop management paper. Go to the board and they will correct it."

Vishvanath went to the board. After reviewing the paper, they found that one question had been tabulated incorrectly. They changed it and he passed—though just barely.

In late March, Baba surprised the Margis by deciding to hold a DMC in the small village of Ambagan in the northeastern state of Assam. On the afternoon of the DMC, Baba asked his attending secretary, Acharya Sambuddhananda, to take him to the Lau Khowa reserve forest, an elephant corridor and rhinoceros preserve about eight kilometers outside the village. Sambuddhananda arranged for a car and set off with Baba and three local Margis: Indra Talukdar, Yogeshvar Barua, and Umesh.

As they neared the forest, Sambuddhananda started to turn onto an outlying route that would take them along the outskirts of the reserve, but Baba told him to take the road that passed through the middle of the jungle. That road soon turned into a narrow dirt path that wound its way through the densest part of the forest. The three Margis started to grow apprehensive, uncomfortably aware of the possible consequences of running into an adult elephant or rhinoceros in the middle of the wilderness. As the twilight shadows deepened, they quietly suggested to Sambuddhananda that he turn back. Sambuddhananda paid no attention to them. He knew better than to suggest such a thing to Baba after having received direct instructions. A little farther on, the Margi's fears were confirmed. One of them spotted a rhinoceros with her calf about a hundred meters up the road. He cried out a warning. Sambuddhananda looked back at Baba. Seeing Baba smile, he continued onward at a careful pace, while the three Margis grew increasingly tense, aware of the danger that the rhinoceros might attack them in order to protect her calf.

When they were about ten to fifteen meters away from the rhinoceros and her calf, Baba called out for Sambuddhananda to stop the car. Baba got out and started walking toward the animals, with Sambuddhananda trailing close behind. One by one, the other disciples, struggling to master their fear, stepped cautiously out of the car and followed as well. Baba walked up to the mother rhinoceros and started stroking her callused back while her confused calf moved from one side of her to the other. After a minute or two, he began stroking the calf. The calf's mother looked on silently without making the slightest movement. Finally, Baba began to whisper something in the mother rhino's ear in a language none of the Margis could understand. Emboldened by Baba's example and the seeming tameness of this otherwise imposing animal, the four disciples also patted her and her calf. By this time, it was starting to grow quite dark. Baba asked Sambuddhananda to turn the car around so they could leave. As he was doing so, the headlights fell on the rhinoceros. The Margis were astonished to see tears falling from her eyes.

On the way back to Ambagan, Yogeshvar asked Baba why the mother rhinoceros had acted so docilely in his presence. "You are little children," Baba said. "You will understand it when you grow up."

Umesh mentioned the rhinoceros's tears and asked why she had seemed to be crying. "She was crying because she was remembering her past life," Baba said. "In her past life she was a human being. She was my friend."

Some time later, Baba was traveling to Calcutta for a program. On the way, his train passed through Sahebganj. As usual, a great throng of Margis came to the station to have his darshan while the train was stopped at the platform. Among them was a newly initiated couple, Ramchandra Gope and his wife, Chandravati. Like many Indian wives, she had taken initiation because her husband had done so, but within a few days she had second thoughts about the wisdom of her decision.

For one thing, she had been a devout devotee of Krishna since childhood. She had long since grown attached to the idol of Krishna that she kept on her altar and the comfort of her daily ritual worship. In her initiation, she was given a mantra designed to cultivate a sense of identity with the Supreme Consciousness. This didn't seem right to her. How can God and I be one? she thought, as she looked at Krishna on her altar. He is there, wherever he is, and I am here. It not only seemed absurd; it seemed downright blasphemous.

And then there was another thing: Her acharya was her sister's husband. With the intimacy born of close family ties, he had assured her and her husband that Anandamurti was a living God. This didn't seem right either. How could any human being be a living God?

When she heard of Baba's forthcoming visit, she decided that she would put the master to the test and resolve her doubts, once and for all. If he passed the test, then she would continue her meditation, but if he failed, then she would give it up and go back to her worship of Krishna.

The test Chandravati devised was a simple one. She had heard how people would bring garlands and place them around the guru's neck as a sign of reverence. Due to the great number of devotees, it was not an easy thing to be able to garland the guru personally. Normally, he would accept one or two and the rest would be handed to his personal assistant for him to bless. She decided to bring a garland with her to the station, but she would not make any effort to offer it to the master. If he were really the living God that her brother-in-law said he was, then he would know her mind and would ask her for the garland personally. If he did not, then she would know that he was not what they said he was, and she could go back happily to her traditional worship.

When Baba's train pulled in, several hundred devotees were there to receive him, many of them with garlands of their own. Chandravati hung near the back, waiting to see if Baba would call for her, until finally the whistle sounded and the train started to pull away. She had been hoping for just that outcome, anxious to be able to give up her meditation and return to her traditional worship. But when she saw the train pulling out, she felt a pang of disappointment, as if deep within she had been hoping that he really could be a living God. Moments later, her husband caught up to her, his enthusiasm bubbling over, and told her that they would have another chance in a few days to see the master, when his train passed back through Sahebganj on the return trip.

Chandravati thought about it for a moment. As long as I take care of the garland, she thought, keep it in a box, and sprinkle some water over it at intervals, it can last for a few days. I suppose I can give him one more chance.

Without saying anything to her husband, she carefully kept the garland as fresh as she could and returned to the station with him a few days later. Again she remained at the back of the crowd while her husband pressed forward, eager to get as close to Baba as he could. She kept her head down and waited while everyone brought their garlands to Baba. A couple of women urged her to go forward and give Baba her namaskar and her garland, but she replied politely that it wasn't necessary.

Finally, the guard waved the green flag and the whistle sounded. This time her disappointment turned to anger. She pictured herself running forward and throwing her garland at Baba. She started rehearsing in her mind the scolding she would give her acharya at the first opportunity. But for some reason the train did not move. Several Margis went to inquire about the problem. They came back and informed Baba that the station officials did not know what was wrong. Everything seemed to be in working order, but for some unknown reason the train was not moving. Suddenly, Chandravati was jolted out of her angry reverie. Anxious voices informed her that Baba was calling for her. She inched forward toward the open window of Baba's compartment. Baba requested everyone else to stand aside and make room for her.

"Mother," Baba said, when she reached his compartment, "have you not brought a garland for me? You know, this train will not move until you have given me your garland."

Chandravati brushed aside her tears and placed the garland over Baba's neck. Baba gave her his namaskar. At that moment the whistle sounded again and the train started to move.

Baba paid his second visit to Anandanagar in April of that year. The wholetimer training center had been shifted there from Jamalpur late the previous year, and one of the trainees was a former deputy personnel manager in the Ranchi firm of Usha Martin Black. In those days, Kedarnath and Kshitij used to search Ranchi and its vicinity for spiritually minded persons whom they could convince to take initiation into Ananda Marga. In late 1963, they heard about a certain Vijay Kumar Mishra, a respected, well-educated young man in his late twenties from a well-known family who was considered by many to be an elevated soul. People claimed that he kept total fast during Durga Puja. During his fast, the goddess Durga would appear before him in white robes and give him instructions that he would follow for the rest of the year.

They got his home address and went there one afternoon to talk to him. Vijay received them in a cordial manner and listened attentively while the two acharyas talked about Ananda Marga practices and ideology. After they had been talking for a few minutes, a couple of visitors appeared in the doorway. Vijay excused himself and said, "There is an important matter that I have to discuss with these gentlemen; I won't be long." He stepped out onto the veranda. From inside the sitting room, Kedarnath and Kshitij could hear him scolding the two men. "Why do you persist in bothering me about getting married? I told you yesterday that I don't intend to get married. Just give it up." When Vijay came back in, he apologized for the interruption, lit up a cigarette, and explained that the two men were relatives who were continually bothering him with marriage proposals.

"Why don't you want to get married?" Kshitij inquired politely.

"Well, that's a long story. In brief, however, my mother was childless for a long time. She didn't think she could ever have a child. Then one night she dreamed that she saw a great yogi sitting in a shrine. When she approached the yogi, he blessed her and offered her a coconut. He told her that after she ate the coconut, she would conceive a child and her child would become a great saint. Just after she had the dream, my mother got pregnant. So she had this conviction that her baby would become a saint. My father was an astrologer and something of a fortune-teller. When I was born, he cast my horoscope, and he also predicted that I would become a saint. Some friends of his who were also astrologers came to the same conclusion. And ever since I was a young child,

I've been devoted to spiritual life and spiritual practices. If I were to marry, the girl would have to face great hardship, so it's better I don't marry."

"But even after marriage a person can practice yoga and achieve liberation," Kedar interjected.

"Be that as it may, I still think it better that I not marry."

The two acharyas continued talking about Ananda Marga while Vijay smoked one cigarette after another and listened with obvious interest. Finally, they asked him if he were interested in taking initiation.

"I will take initiation when I find the right guru."

"In the meantime," Kshitij, said, "there is no harm in learning the technique and trying it for some time."

Vijay agreed and took initiation from Kshitij. Four or five days later, he showed up at Kshitij's house complaining that he was facing a certain problem in his meditation.

"Every time I meditate I have the same vision. A beautiful, olive-skinned hand appears wearing a gold ring with a pearl inset on the middle finger. The hand is holding a lighted cigarette, which it brings to my mouth, but when I try to take a puff, the hand vanishes. Then it appears again, several times in succession. Every time I meditate, the same vision disturbs me. Since it began, I've started developing an aversion to smoking. Can you explain this?"

"Do you think you would be able to recognize this hand if you saw it in real life, especially if it had the same ring on it?" Kshitij asked, sure that the hand Vijay had seen was Baba's.

"Certainly. I've seen it so many times by now."

"If you want to see that hand, then you must go to Jamalpur and visit our ashram there."

"Okay," Vijay answered, without any hesitation. "I'm ready to do that if it will solve this mystery. How many days leave will I need to take?"

"You should take four or five days. Your work will be done in one day, but you will need that much time to be able to process your experience and understand it. I know you have a very high position with heavy responsibility in your firm. Do you think you will be able to get that much time off, or will it create problems for your business?"

"It will be difficult but I will manage somehow."

Kshitij gave him the address. A few days later, Vijay informed him that he had gotten four days leave and had booked a reservation for Jamalpur for the following day. Kshitij informed Kedarnath of the news, and they were both anxious to hear what Vijay would say when he came back. But the time for his return came and went and Vijay didn't show up. Two weeks passed and still there was no word from him. Vijay's relatives came to Kshitij, anxious to find out what had happened to him. Kshitij gave them the address in Jamalpur, but there was little else he could do since he was unable to go himself at that time. It was a full month before Vijay returned. When he did, he went straight to

Kshitij's house. The elegantly dressed personnel officer, who generally wore the finest-tailored suits, was now dressed in a simple white cotton kurta and pajama pants.[4] His proud demeanor had been replaced by a humble expression. He appeared to be on the verge of weeping. Vijay bent over and touched Kshitij's feet.

"Acharyaji, you have changed my life. The day you came to my house was the turning point in my life. Because of your help, I have found the right path. I have decided to leave everything and dedicate my life to Baba."

The next day, Vijay arrived at Kshitij's house with two trucks loaded with his belongings. Now that he was going to become a wholetimer, he wanted to donate everything to Ananda Marga. He even took off his watch and handed it to Kshitij, but Kshitij told him to keep it. "You will need it," he said, "because as a wholetimer you will have to properly utilize every second of your life."

On April 9, Baba arrived for his second visit to Anandanagar. Kshitij and Kedar made the short trip from Ranchi along with many other Margis to attend the program. When they went looking for Vijay, they were surprised to find him working in the kitchen, washing pots and pans with his lungi doubled up above his knees. When Kshitij asked him why he was working in the kitchen, he told them in a humble voice that some Margis had had to catch the train, so they had made rice pudding for them and he was doing the washing up. Kshitij felt proud that his initiate was such a good soul, glad to see that this man who had had servants his entire life to do his menial work was now happy to be a humble servant to his brother disciples.

Kshitij and Kedarnath went up to Baba's room. When they entered, Baba asked them where Vijay was.

"He's washing pots, Baba," Kshitij answered.

"Call him. I'm going to catch his thread."[5]

Kshitij smiled and ran back to the kitchen. When Vijay protested that he was dirty and would have to take a bath first, Kshitij said, "What are you saying? There's no time for that. When Baba calls you, you don't keep him waiting. Just wash your hands and feet quickly and come."

Vijay washed his hands and feet, let down his lungi, and followed his acharya to Baba's room. When they got there, Kshitij started massaging Baba's feet and asked Vijay to massage his back, which he did after some slight hesitation. Baba was quiet but hunched his shoulders once or twice, as if it felt uncomfortable. Then he told them to sit down. He was going to tell them a story.

"Three hundred years ago," Baba began, "on the outskirts of Rewa, there was a great yogi, a realized soul, who lived in an ashram with his disciples. One of his disciples was a young man from a wealthy royal family who had come to the ashram at an early age, leaving behind his comfortable life to dedicate himself to the spiritual path. This boy was a highly elevated soul with a pure mind who had almost no material desires other than a weakness for sweet fruits. One day, the guru called him to his room to tell him that he would be out of the ashram for a few days and that he was leaving him in charge. His one admonishment was not to violate any of the ashram rules while he was gone. The boy promised and the master left for his trip.

"While he was gone, the queen of Rewa paid a visit to the ashram, as was the habit in those days among royal families. During her visit, she was attracted by the spiritual aura of the boy. Being childless herself, she conceived a desire to adopt him and make him her heir. When she conveyed her feelings to the boy, he disappointed her by replying, 'Mother, I was born into a royal family. I have left everything behind to come and learn meditation at the feet of my guru. As he is happy with me, he is teaching me. Please, don't ask me to go back to what I have left behind. It cannot be.'

"The queen was saddened by his answer, but she accepted his decision. As a parting gift, she offered him some gold and silver ornaments for the support of the ashram. It was a strict rule, however, that the disciples could not accept anything from outside without the permission of the guru. He explained to her why he could not accept her offer. 'You see,' she said, after listening to his explanation, 'I am like a mother to you. If your mother offers you something, you should accept it. If you cannot accept the ornaments, then at least accept a coconut from me.' The boy didn't want to offend her any more than he already had; furthermore, he had a weakness for coconuts. It is only a coconut, he thought; surely this much will be okay. So he accepted. The queen cut the coconut up into pieces and offered it to the boy, who ate some and saved the rest, thinking to offer it to his guru, who was due back at any time. Then the queen took her leave.

"The next day the guru returned. As soon as he entered the ashram, he called his disciple to his room. In an angry tone of voice he told him, 'It is a rule in this ashram that no disciple can accept anything without my permission. And you have violated this rule, just for the sake of a coconut? How can you think you are fit to learn yoga from me if you cannot follow these simple rules?'

"The boy left his master feeling distraught and depressed. For a long time, the thought of his mistake haunted his mind. He died shortly thereafter. Due to his mistake and the force of this thought in his mind, he had to take birth in his next life as a coconut palm, and he remained in that body for nearly three hundred years."[6]

By this time Vijay was crying silently. Baba looked at him and said, "Now tell me, Vijay, is there any connection between your birth and a coconut?"

"Yes, Baba."

Kshitij and Kedar also had tears in their eyes. By now they had realized that the story was about Vijay. Kshitij noticed that Baba was lying back on his cot in *aparchakra mudra*, a posture that signifies that if the guru tells the disciple to ask for something and the disciple expresses his desire, then that wish will be fulfilled.

Again Baba looked at Vijay and said, "Tell me, Vijay, what do you want?"

Vijay kept silent. Again Baba asked him. This time Vijay did sastaunga pranam. Crying softly, he said, "Baba, I don't want anything. Just give me the strength to serve your mission until I die. I don't want anything else."

Baba sat up, leaned over, and touched Vijay on his *ajina* chakra. Vijay fell backward in samadhi. Then Baba excused himself and said that he needed to use the bathroom. When he came back, he told the two family acharyas to cover Vijay with a blanket and not disturb him since he was in intense bliss. A little while later, he asked them to move the still-unconscious Vijay to Pranay's room.

Kshitij took the opportunity to question Baba about the story. "Why," he asked, "did the disciple have to suffer such a great punishment for such a little offense?"

"For him, it was not a little offense," Baba said. "The higher one climbs on the ladder of spirituality, the greater the repercussions for any fault. If an acharya and a general Margi commit the same mistake, the acharya's punishment will be greater, because he has been given the greater responsibility. That disciple was a great yogi who went against the instructions of his guru, so accordingly he was given a severe punishment. This is the *lila* of Paramapurusha."[7]

One evening in early April in Muzaffarpur, Shashi Rainjan's teenage son Kartik Rainjan started feeling stiffness in his neck and back. When Guddu, as he was better known to family and friends, woke up in the morning, it had gotten worse, so he went to a hakim, who adjusted his spine, but he left the hakim's office feeling even worse. The following morning, it got so bad that he found it difficult to move. He was unable to do anything without help from the family servant. His father, then a prominent MP in the Congress party, became alarmed. Being a man of means, he was able to take his son to several of the best specialists in the Bihar capital of Patna, but none of them could give him a firm diagnosis. The nerves on the left side of the body appeared to be damaged, but they had no idea of the cause. They recommended immobilizing the patient for an extended period of time and prescribed painkillers.

Guddu was put into a body cast, but several weeks went by with no improvement in his condition. His father arranged for several other specialists to see him, hoping that one of them could make an appropriate diagnosis and suggest a better course of treatment, but they could do no better than the previous doctors. In late April, Baba's tour program took him through Delhi on his way to Jammu for a DMC. During the one-day layover, he was scheduled to give General Darshan and go on field walk with the local Margis. The Margis, aware of Guddu's condition, suggested to Shashi Rainjan, now back in Delhi, that he ask Baba for his help, but Shashi Rainjan was hesitant to do so.

"Baba knows everything," he said. "There is no need to tell him. Baba knows what's best for Guddu." But they repeated their suggestions and he reluctantly agreed.

Baba arrived on the afternoon of the twenty-fourth, by plane from Varanasi. In the early evening, the Margis gathered for field walk and General Darshan at Shashi Rainjan's 93 North Avenue quarters where Baba was staying. As usual, the Margis lined up near Baba's car and began singing devotional songs. When Baba came out, he greeted everyone with namaskar and chatted with the Margis for a few minutes, inquiring about their health and welfare. Quietly, the Margis urged Shashi Rainjan to speak to Baba about Guddu, but now that Shashi Rainjan was in the master's presence, he found that he couldn't go through with it. All he could do was pray silently to Baba to do whatever he felt best.

As Baba passed by Shashi Rainjan on the way to his car, he stopped and asked him how he was. "And how is Guddu?" he said. That simple question was enough. Overcome by emotion, Shashi Rainjan told Baba in a halting voice what had happened.

Baba nodded his head slowly. "Don't worry," he said. "Note down this address." Baba gave him the name and address of a doctor in Burdwan. "Take Guddu to see him. He should be able to help."

Shashi Rainjan was elated. As soon as Baba left Delhi, he returned to Muzaffarpur and made travel arrangements for Burdwan. A couple of days later, he and Guddu were installed in a Burdwan hotel with Guddu's medicines and his wheelchair. Shashi Rainjan hired a rickshaw and asked the driver to take him to the address Baba had written, the medical clinic of Dr. Shailen Mukherjee. He assumed that Dr. Mukherjee would be a specialist in neurology or perhaps orthopedic medicine, but as the rickshaw wound its way into one of the poorer sections of town, Shashi Rainjan began to wonder what kind of specialist would have his offices in such a humble area. He asked the rickshaw driver if he was sure he had the right address, but the driver simply nodded and kept on pedaling.

Finally, they pulled up in front of a somewhat dilapidated, one-story bungalow. As Shashi Rainjan paid the rickshaw driver his fare, he saw the small signboard with faded letters hanging to the right of the wooden door: Shailen Mukherjee, MBBS.[8] It was the right place, undoubtedly, but the MBBS next to his name made it clear that Dr. Mukherjee was no specialist. He began to feel uneasy, but he tried to stifle his worry. If Baba had sent him here, he thought, there had to be a reason. He took his guru mantra, put his faith in Baba, and went and knocked on the door. A man wearing a lungi and a stained t-shirt opened it. His mouth was bright red from chewing on a betel-nut preparation.

"Yes?" the man asked.

"I'm looking for Dr. Shailen Mukherjee."

"How can I help you?"

"Are you Dr. Mukherjee?" Shashi asked, momentarily surprised.

"Yes."

Shashi Rainjan took a deep breath. "My son is very ill. My guru gave me your address and told me to send him here for treatment."

The doctor looked surprised. "Your guru? What is his name?"

"Shrii Shrii Anandamurti, or Prabhat Rainjan Sarkar."

"I'm sorry, but I don't know your guru. I've never heard of him. How is it he sent you to me?"

"I can't say, but if he sent me here there has to be a reason."

The doctor invited him in and listened patiently while he described Guddu's symptoms and the diagnosis and treatment prescribed by the different specialists in Patna.

"To be honest," the doctor said, "I don't know what I can do for your son that the specialists you consulted couldn't do. I am a simple MBBS. I give some basic allopathic treatment and occasionally some homeopathic remedies to the people of this area. If they can pay me a few rupees, I'm happy. However, you've come all this way and your guru gave you my address. If you want to bring your son here, I will try and do my best. I can't promise anything more than that."

Shashi Rainjan was not very hopeful, especially when he learned after some inquiries that the doctor had a drinking problem and had been divorced and remarried to one of his patients, but he was determined to follow Baba's instructions. The next day, he arranged for a car to bring Guddu to Dr. Mukherjee's clinic. The doctor examined him. After informing Shashi Rainjan that he had nothing more to tell him about the disease, other than what he already knew, he gave Guddu a cortisone shot, some massage, and a homeopathic remedy. He told him to bring him back the next day.

The following morning, Guddu felt slightly better. Or at least it seemed so, and this gave Shashi Rainjan some encouragement. He continued bringing him to the clinic each day, and each day Guddu responded with some slight improvement. The doctor wasn't sure what was working, or why, but he was happy to see the improvement. He enjoyed the young man's company and continued to give him massages and homeopathic remedies.

Shashi Rainjan and Guddu remained there for twenty days, by the end of which Guddu was about eighty percent recovered. He could walk, though he walked with a limp and needed to use a cane. The pain was mostly gone, except when he remained sitting or standing for too long in one position, or when he got up in the morning. At the end of the twenty days, Shashi Rainjan thanked Dr. Mukherjee and took Guddu back to Muzaffarpur, hopeful that with the medicines the doctor sent with him, he would soon be entirely well. Once Guddu was back in Muzaffarpur, however, there was no further improvement.

Some time afterward in Jamalpur, Sujit, who was also from Muzaffarpur and well known to the family, asked Baba why Dr. Mukherjee had been able to help Guddu when a number of renowned specialists in Patna had failed.

Baba smiled. "The medicines had nothing to do with it, Sujit. It was a matter of samskara. You see, Guddu's disease was due to a very old samskara. Around nine hundred years ago, Guddu was born as a wealthy landowner's son in the Jalpaiguri district of North Bengal. As he was growing up, the boy developed an unsavory character. As a teenager, he would squander his father's wealth carousing with his friends and engaging in all sorts of bad behavior. His father was a pious man, an honest man. He did his best to try to reform his son, but the boy only despised him all the more for it. This greatly distressed his father. When the boy came of age, the father decided to forcibly curtail his spending. He informed his son that he was going to withhold from him his inheritance, unless and until he reformed his character.

"The boy became incensed. One day, he approached his father in an inebriated state and demanded his inheritance. The father tried to reason with him. He told him he could consider releasing his inheritance once the boy reformed his character, but his son didn't want to hear this. Finally, the father refused and the boy lost his temper. He grabbed a heavy cane that was lying nearby and started beating his father out of anger. A couple of blows landed on the man's head and left him bleeding. He fell to the ground, senseless, and died some days later from the injury.

"Now those samskaras have ripened and Guddu is paying the price for his actions in the form of this disease. There was nothing any medicine could do for him. The samskara had to be exhausted. However, I saw that the boy's father from that life had also incarnated at this time. He was living as a doctor in Burdwan. I knew that if some attachment could develop between the two, then this would help to exhaust the samskara. So I asked Shashi Rainjan to bring Guddu there. While he was there, the doctor developed a strong sense of affection for Guddu, as did Guddu for the doctor. The doctor was sorry to see such a nice young man suffering in this way; he started to develop a strong desire to see him get well. It wasn't the doctor's medicines or his treatments that helped, but rather this desire and the compassion he felt."

For the next eight years, Guddu was able to lead a normal life, but he had to learn to live with some measure of pain and a constant limp that forced him to carry a walking stick. Near the end of 1971, Baba was admitted into Patna Medical Hospital for tests. A group of Margis was accompanying him down the hallway to a room where some tests were scheduled. Guddu, who was there with Shashi Rainjan, quietly asked the Margi pushing Baba's wheelchair to allow him to do it. When they reached the doorway, Baba asked who was wheeling the chair.

"Baba, it's me, Guddu."

"Oh, it is you, Guddu. Were you pushing my chair? But are you not unwell? Come, let me see you."

Guddu moved forward and did pranam.

"Tell me, Guddu, where exactly do you feel the pain?"

Guddu told him. Baba reached out his hand and touched those areas. "Now you will not die from the disease," he said.

As Baba touched him, Guddu felt a shock run through him like an electric current. He felt as if he had just been relieved of a heavy load. The pain was gone. For the first time in nearly eight years, he could straighten up without discomfort and throw away his cane.

After spending most of March and April on tour, Baba was back in the office for the summer. On Wednesday, May 27, Baba unexpectedly came to the jagriti during the day. As he entered the gate, Dasarath saw him and did namaskar. Baba asked him if he were able to see any bodiless mind. Dasarath concentrated for a moment and noticed the presence of a bodiless mind. "Whose bodiless mind is this?" Baba asked. Dasarath concentrated for some moments more and then said in a shocked tone of voice, "Baba, it is the bodiless mind of Jawarhalal Nehru."

"Yes," Baba replied. "He left his body a short while ago. The news has not yet been announced."

Though Baba had been an outspoken critic of Nehru's foreign policy, especially his part in the debacle with China two years earlier, and had pointed out certain faults in his character, he also had many positive things to say about Nehru's role in India's independence and the formation of the new nation. As the Margis followed him into his room, he described how Nehru's bodiless mind was searching for a new body as they spoke. He talked for a long time about his life and even described his past life in which he had been a sadhu who had conceived a strong desire for power, creating a samskara that had led him to great political power in this life. Finally, he asked them, one by one, to sing bhajans in their mother tongues to commemorate his passing.

That summer, Ashish Kumar Pandey, a resident of nearby Trimohan, paid his first visit to Jamalpur. He had been initiated early in the year and had first seen Baba at the end of March when Baba's train halted at Bhagalpur Junction. He had not been impressed at the time. Baba had been seated by the window; four sannyasis stood close by. He asked a nearby Margi which one was Baba and was disappointed to find out that he was the clean-shaven gentleman in the white clothes. Thinking back to the stories he had heard—that Baba knew everything, that he would punish his disciples for mistakes in their past that even they had forgotten—he dismissed them as pure propaganda. But at the end of May, with his health worsening, he decided to go to Jamalpur to have PC in the hope that it might help. He got written permission from his acharya, Baldeva, and took along his friend Niwas Chandra Saha, a confirmed reveler who would only refrain from drinking one day a week—Tuesday, Dharmachakra day.

They arrived in the ashram about eight in the morning. When Baba arrived, Ashish was surprised to see how different he looked up close. He became aware of an aura of great power that emanated from him. For the first time, he began to feel afraid of getting punished.

When the line formed for PC, Ashish was first and Niwas right behind him. Ashish entered Baba's room and prostrated in front of him as instructed. Baba asked him his name and where he lived, and then began describing his house and his neighborhood and the route that he would take home each day, as well as other details that he couldn't possibly have known.

Ashish was surprised and curious. Baba asked him to admit his wrong deeds and prepare himself to accept punishment for them. When Ashish denied that he had done anything wrong, Baba caught him by the ear and started scolding him. For the next twenty to thirty minutes, Baba described a long litany of his misdeeds, beginning with his childhood and continuing up to only a few days before. Ashish perspired more and more profusely. He wondered how Baba could have possibly known these things.

"You thought that nobody was seeing you but the darkness," Baba said, "but the entity in your heart was witnessing everything."

When he was done pointing out his mistakes, Baba asked him if everything he had said was correct.

"Yes, Baba."

"Then what kind of punishment do you want: natural or social? Or should I punish you?"

"It is better if you do it, Baba," Ashish replied.

Baba brought out his stick from behind him on the cot and started beating Ashish on his back. After a few good thwacks, Ashish grabbed Baba's hand. "Baba, this is not the way to beat me. You should beat me in different spots, not at one spot."

As Ashish was saying this, he was surprised by the strength in Baba's arm. Ashish was a strong man, a wrestler, but he instinctively felt that he couldn't maintain his grip on Baba's wrist with one hand, so he grabbed it with both hands. Baba flicked his wrist and Ashish was thrown to the floor. Realizing that it was futile to use physical force with Baba, he got up and requested Baba politely to beat him in different places, not at one spot.

"Come here," Baba ordered him in a grave voice. Ashish approached the cot once again and Baba beat him until he fell unconscious. Then Baba pressed his thumb to his forehead and he regained consciousness.

As soon as he was conscious again, Ashish cried out, "Please Baba, I can't tolerate any more." The thought crossed his mind that he wouldn't be able to lie down for months.

"Okay, come here. I won't beat you anymore."

Baba started caressing his back. Ashish felt a cooling sensation as the bruised skin healed itself and the pain disappeared.

"Baba, how did you know all those things?" he asked.

"Paramashiva told me." Baba made him promise to do only good deeds from then on and serve the suffering humanity.

When Ashish finally came out from Baba's room, his friend Niwas Chandra was shaking with fear. "What happened to you will certainly happen to me," he said. "I have never done a good deed in my life."

When the acharya in charge of PC called out Niwas's name, he fell to the ground, shivering with fear. It took a concerted effort from Ashish and several others to finally convince him to go into Baba's room. He came out five minutes later saying that he was saved. Baba had told him that he would not beat him, but he had had to promise to do good deeds from then on and lead a sober and pious life.

True to his word, Niwas Chandra gave up drinking and became a good Margi. He would claim ever afterward that Baba had given him a new life.

As usual, Baba continued to give regular demonstrations that summer. One evening in General Darshan he called Shyama Sundar Goenka to the front and asked him to tell him his permanent address.[9] Shyama Sundar, a young businessman from a wealthy Bombay family who was there with his wife, recited the street address of his house. Baba told Dasarath to gaze into his mental plate and see where he had been fifty years back. Dasarath concentrated for a few moments and then said that he was working in an office in Colombo. He described a scene in which he was asleep at his desk when his boss came in and started scolding him.

"No, he was not sleeping," Baba said. "He was doing meditation. He was a sadhaka in his past life. Now, go further back and see where he was 125 years ago."

This time Dasarath said that he was living in a Portuguese colony in Africa at that time.

Baba turned to Sudarshan, who was sitting nearby, and asked him where his permanent address was. "My permanent address is Paramapurusha," Sudarshan replied.

"Yes, you have given the correct answer. In this entire creation there is only one permanent address, one destination, and that is Paramapurusha."

On another occasion, Satchidadananda Srivastava brought his son from Gorakhpur to see Baba. His son was quite ill at the time. When Baba came to the jagriti and saw the boy's condition, he started scolding Satchidadananda for not bringing his son to a doctor when the disease was still in its beginning stages. "Now the disease has become fatal," he said, shaking his head. Baba called Dasarath over and asked him to see how long the boy would survive.

"Not long," Dasarath said, after closing his eyes and concentrating for some moments.

"Very well then. Gather round. I am going to do a demonstration about death."

Baba asked the boy to sit in meditation posture and concentrate his mind. As he had done nearly ten years earlier, Baba ordered the vayus to leave the body, one by one. The boy fell over unconscious. Baba asked a doctor who was present to examine the boy for signs of life. There were none. The boy was not breathing, nor did he have a pulse.

"Yes," Baba said, "according to your medical science he is dead, but actually there is still life in the body. He can be revived by divine power as long as he does not remain in this state for more than half an hour or so."

Baba explained the process of dying for some minutes more. Then he revived the boy. He told Satchidadananda to give him lemon water with salt, morning and evening, until he was totally cured. He gave him some other instructions as well. Within two weeks his son was fully recovered.

In another General Darshan, a Margi gentleman came to Baba complaining of severe stomach pains. He had been to the doctor and taken the prescribed medicines, but had failed to get any relief. Baba called Dasarath and asked him to concentrate his mind.

"Look into his stomach and tell me what you see." Dasarath began describing a round, black, tumor-like ulcer.

"Yes, he has had a chronic gastric problem for some years now that has gone untreated. In time it became a peptic ulcer, and now it has entered into the first stages of cancer. As his condition stands, he cannot survive much longer."

Baba took his stick and began drawing circles on his stomach with the tip.

"Now, Dasarath, look again and describe his condition."

"Baba, the area is no longer black. I cannot see any tumor now."

Baba gave the Margi instructions to abstain from certain types of foods and to work sincerely for the mission. "Do this and everything will be all right. Seventy-five percent, I have cured. The rest you will have to do yourself."

Afterward, the Margi told everyone that when Baba touched him with his stick, he felt a painful burning sensation for a few moments and then nothing. The pain he had been suffering from was completely gone.

That summer, Baba gave Pranay instructions to prepare to shift his office to Anandanagar. "You are not doing anything without my pressure," Baba said, "so now I am going to give you pressure to shift your office. Go there and build up the ashram."

Pranay did not warm up to the idea. He did not see the logic behind locating the global headquarters of the organization in such a desolate, isolated place. His previous visits had convinced him that Anandanagar was unsafe as well as uncomfortable, but Baba left him no choice. Later in the year, he resigned from his job at the railway workshop, and he and Pramila made preparations to move to Anandanagar to set up the central office and oversee the construction of the various projects. His wife would enjoy the adventure and the camaraderie with the young workers posted there, but her husband would never completely adjust.

In November, Baba conducted a DMC in Ranchi. One morning, Acharya Sarangi arrived at Kshitij's house, where Baba was staying, just as Baba was getting ready to shave. Sarangi arranged a table, a chair, a mirror, and a basin of water for him. As Baba was sitting on the chair shaving, Sarangi asked him a question.

"Baba, you tell us often of Ananda Parivara, of establishing a brotherhood among all the people of the world. Will it really be possible to do that, in reality?"

Baba kept silent for a few moments, staring into the mirror as he shaved. Then he looked at Sarangi and asked, "Have you read the Mahabharata?"

"Very little. I haven't gone through it in detail."

"Are you are aware that there was a battle on the field of Kurukshetra?"

"Yes."

"Do you also know that the battle took place between the Pandavas and Kaoravas?"

"Yes, Baba."

"Then you must also know that the Pandavas won the battle."

"Yes."

"I see. Do you know that there were only five Pandava brothers, whereas there were one hundred Kaorava brothers?"

"Yes, I know."

"Then why did you tell me that you knew hardly anything about the Mahabharata?"

Sarangi smiled, but he didn't say anything.

"So, what is the lesson that the Mahabharata teaches?"

Again Sarangi remained silent.

"The moral of the Mahabharata is that five percent moralists can conquer one hundred percent immoralists; that is, if five percent of the society becomes moralist, then a strong moralist society can be created. That is your mission. Make five percent of the society moralist."

"Baba, that is an impossible task."

"Then make three percent."

"But Baba," Sarangi objected, "the mission of Ananda Marga is so difficult. What to speak of three percent—even three-hundredths of a percent is near impossible."

Baba paused for a few moments. "Then do one thing," he said. "Let the world know that there is an organization named Ananda Marga. Let them know what it stands for. That's all. If you can do this, then our purpose will be served, and the goal will be achieved."

XXXI

In the Office

Retreating to the jungle is not a way to obtain relief from the trials and worries of the world. There is yet another great advantage in living a worldly life. It provides one with the opportunity to serve humanity, an important aspect of intuitional practice.[1]

WHEN PULAK RAY arrived for his first day of work at the Jamalpur railway workshop on May 12, 1964, the administrative officer in charge of his orientation, Vinay Ghosh, took him through the necessary paperwork and then gave him a brief tour of the facilities. Before bringing him to the accounts section, where he would be working, the officer gave Pulak one last piece of advice: "The man under whom you are being posted is an extraordinary personality; you should consider yourself extremely fortunate to be able to work for such a man. However, you should watch your conduct and not engage in any kind of immoral activity. This man will not tolerate such things."

After the officer had brought him to Baba's desk and introduced them, Baba asked Pulak to pull up a chair. He reached out and caught the tip of Pulak's right index finger. "You have four brothers," Baba said, "Dipak Ray, Alok Ray, Kirat Ray, Kanak Ray, and one sister, Reena Ray. Your mother's name is Srimati Gita Ray." Baba smiled as a look of bewilderment spread over his new subordinate's face. "Your sister-in-law's name is Purnima Ray, is it not?"

"Yes, that's right," Pulak replied.

"She has fair complexion and is quite pretty."

"That's true."

"But let me say one thing. You don't get along with her very well, do you?"

"How do you know that?" Pulak exclaimed.

"You told me," Baba answered with a smile.

"But I've never spoken to you before," Pulak protested. "This is the first time we've met."

"The thing is, you should be careful about her."

"Why?"

"You see, women with her looks can be somewhat arrogant sometimes; in her case, she is especially so. You had best be careful."[2]

As the conversation continued, Baba began to tell Pulak about his forefathers and the village in East Pakistan from where they had emigrated. Each time Pulak asked him how he knew these things, Baba gave the same reply: "You told me." Finally, Pulak asked him why he had caught his finger. "No special reason," Baba said.

Later that morning, while Baba was away from his desk, Shiva Shankar Mukherjee and several of his co-workers, all posted directly under Baba, pulled Pulak aside and said, "We are not going to tell you anything about him. We will let you discover that for yourself. We will only tell you this much: he is a great *vibhuti*, a divine personality; he has no parallel in this world."

The faith and reverence that Shiva Shankar and his co-workers felt for Baba had little or nothing to do with his growing reputation outside the Jamalpur workshop as a spiritual master. As would be the case with Pulak Ray, who soon joined their circle of admirers, they had fallen under the influence of Baba's personality and begun to seek out his guidance long before they became aware that their colleague in the accounts section was also known to the outside world as Shrii Shrii Anandamurti, the spiritual guru of Ananda Marga.

Baba himself did everything possible not to allow that reputation to enter the office. He guided those of his colleagues and subordinates who looked to him for guidance, but he did it in the role of colleague or friend or boss. Initiated disciples were under strict instructions not to act in any manner that might call attention to him while on the workshop premises. Still, it was inevitable that his colleagues became aware of his growing fame, no matter what precautions Baba adopted, and Pulak Ray was no exception. While he was still fairly new in the office, the young clerk noticed that mail was coming to Baba's desk addressed to Anandamurti. He asked his supervisor about it.

"Prabhat-da, who is this Anandamurti? It's you, isn't it?"

"No, no," Baba said. "He is the guru of Ananda Marga. He stays near Purulia. I go there from time to time to have his darshan."

Pulak was not so easily duped. "If the guru really stays near Purulia, then bring me a photo of him."

"Okay, I will bring one tomorrow." But the next day, Baba told Pulak that he had forgotten. For the next several days, he put his subordinate off with different excuses, until Pulak made it clear that he couldn't be fooled any longer. After that, whenever he asked Baba about being the guru, Baba just smiled and either changed the subject or ignored the question.

The circle of Baba's non-Margi admirers in the office, to which Pulak now belonged, included Shiva Shankar Mukherjee, Vimal Chandra Mitra, N. C. Gangully, Nilen Bose (Gokul), and a number of others. Most of them accepted Baba as their spiritual guide, even though they were not disciples in the formal sense or initiates of Ananda Marga. Whenever they had any important decision in their life to make, they would seek Baba's counsel and follow his instructions. Since most of them were practicing Hindus, Baba guided them in their Hindu practices. He would always tell them that the spiritual path they chose was a personal matter but that everyone should follow some spiritual ideal in his life.

As a simple guide to leading a proper life, he used to tell them to remember the word *bhavisca*, "future." "*Bha*," he explained, "stands for *Bhagawan*, God; have faith in the Supreme Lord and attribute your existence and everything else to him. *Vi* stands for *vinay*, modesty and kindheartedness; one's actions should always be full of modesty and kindness toward all living beings. *Sa* stands for *samyam*, self-control; one must always exercise self-control in every walk of life. *Ca* stands for *charitra*, character; one's character should be stainless and of the highest order. If you keep these things in mind, you will overcome whatever problems you may face in your life, and you will grow spiritually."

One day, Shiva Shankar, perhaps Baba's closest friend in the office, asked him for initiation into Ananda Marga. "For you it is not necessary," Baba said. "You will get initiation elsewhere when the time is right." Shiva Shankar was disappointed but he did not argue with Baba. Some years later, he would take initiation from the Ramakrishna mission, but he would always consider Baba his guru. As an old man, reflecting on Baba's answer to his request, he said that he believed that had he taken initiation, it would have changed the character of their friendship to a relationship of guru and disciple, something Baba evidently did not want. Indeed, Baba's relationship with his non-Margi friends and admirers in the office was quite different from his relationship with his disciples, and the Margis in the workshop made conscious efforts not to interfere in that relationship or to bring organizational matters to the office, except when Baba specifically called for it, such as his lunch-hour dictations.

By the mid-sixties, Baba had developed the custom of giving a short talk for his colleagues when he entered the office at ten o'clock. As soon as he took his seat, he would drink a glass of water and then begin. Typically, thirty to forty persons would crowd into the space in front of his desk, a sort of natural cubicle formed by the large filing cabinets that bordered either side. Most of the participants were from Baba's section, but occasionally visitors came from other departments as well. They would listen for forty-five minutes to an hour while Baba discoursed on diverse subjects, from spirituality to science, most often in Hindi but at times in Bengali, English, Angika, or Bhojpuri. On a couple of occasions, he even began his talk in Sanskrit, until one of his colleagues complained that he couldn't understand him, whereupon Baba smiled and changed to Hindi.

Once, one of the accountants in the office complained to a senior officer that Baba was doing something with the accounts staff each morning that was hampering the office work. When that officer went to Baba to question him about it, Baba told him that he was giving them moral instruction and philosophical lessons. Rather than hampering the work, such instruction was inspiring the workers to work with more dedication and helping them to increase their capacity and efficiency. The officer was satisfied with his explanation.

On a later occasion, however, a Punjabi officer, R. M. Arora, was making his rounds when he noticed the empty chairs at a number of desks and the crowd gathered at Baba's cubicle. He came over and started scolding Baba for taking office time for non-office matters. If Baba wanted to talk about spirituality or such things, he should do it on his own time and outside the office premises. Baba's colleagues were offended by the outburst, but no one said anything. After they had returned to their desks, Baba called Gunadhar Patra and asked him to convey some instructions to Arora's orderly.

"But Prabhat-da," Gunadhar protested, "why should you have anything to do with him after he upbraided you over such a simple matter?"

"You see, his son is sick; he will need my help."

When the officer received the message, he rushed home, worried, and found that his son was vomiting blood. He called a doctor but the treatment didn't help. Arora became convinced that it was his own fault for having scolded Baba. That night he sent a messenger to request Baba to come to his East Colony quarters. Baba did not go, but he sent some simple instructions with the messenger, along with assurances that the boy would be all right. Arora followed his instructions and the boy made a rapid recovery. The next day, Arora came to the accounts office and apologized to Baba with folded hands for the injustice he had done him. He assured him that he was welcome to give talks for his colleagues whenever he saw fit.

Though Baba used these talks to teach and guide his colleagues, he never hesitated to give them personal advice when they came to him with their problems or questions, or to call them aside when he felt that they were deviating from the proper path. One evening, a disturbance arose in Pulak Ray's boarding house. Pulak asked one of his roommates to vacate the premises and find another place to live because of the problems he was creating for the rest of the residents. A heated argument ensued that almost led to fisticuffs. When Baba arrived at the office the next morning, he drank his glass of water and gave his customary talk. As soon as the talk was over, he called Pulak aside and told him to sit down next to him.

"I told you to avoid quarreling," Baba said. "Why did you quarrel yesterday evening in your boarding house?"

Pulak became flustered. He tried to explain, knowing Baba well enough by then not to bother asking how he had known about the quarrel. "I am the boarding house in-charge," he said. "If somebody is creating problems, the matter comes to me. I voiced my objections but he wouldn't listen. What was I supposed to do? Should I have just kept quiet?"

"No. First you try to make him understand, calmly and rationally. If he still doesn't understand or doesn't listen, then make arrangements to remove him from the boarding house, but don't ever resort to physical violence. You must have control over your anger."

"Was I wrong to object then?"

"I'm not saying that you were wrong. *Hati cale bazaar, kuttha boke hazaar.*³ When the elephant walks through the market, the dogs come out and bark, but does the elephant care for it?"

"But he'll never learn like this. Please, Prabhat-da, you talk to him; make him understand."

Baba agreed to his proposal. That evening after work Pulak told the offender, P. K. Ghosh, that Prabhat Sarkar wanted to talk to him about the matter.

"So you want me to get scolded by Prabhat-da?" P. K. replied. "Forget it."

When Pulak informed Baba of his reaction, Baba told him to tell the boy that he wouldn't scold him. Still, P. K. refused to come and talk to Baba. Thereafter, whenever he crossed paths with Baba in the workshop he would avoid him and head the other way. If he needed to talk to Pulak about something, he would send his orderly to call him to his section. After that, he slowly rectified his behavior and there were no more problems in the boarding house.

It was the same way whenever we made any mistake. He would call us aside at the next available opportunity and make us understand that it was wrong to do such things. One evening I smoked a cigarette. The next morning, as soon as I reached the office, he called me over. He asked me, "Pulak, where were you last evening?" I told him that a football team had come from the Eastern Railway. We had played a match against them and afterward there was a party. Then he said, "I am not asking about that. What was the need for you to smoke there?" I tried to hide it a little bit. But when he repeated the question, I admitted my mistake. He told me that smoking spoils the lungs and the liver. He said, "In the future, I don't want to hear that you have smoked or chewed pan (betel nut). This is my strict order to you." I never smoked again after that. Whenever I felt like smoking or chewing pan, I used to remember that I had given him my promise.

I knew that he was always with me and that he was watching all my actions. Anytime I felt a desire to do something bad, I would get afraid. I knew that if I committed any mistake, I would get a scolding the next morning. That fear used to keep me from doing it. His graveness deterred one and all. He would point out even small mistakes. The next morning he would say, "You said such-and-such thing to such-and-such person. It was not proper on your part." If I tried to justify what I did in any way, he would ask me to sit near him and then make me understand why I was wrong. This happened every time I made a mistake, no matter if I was out with my friends or at home or in the office. Sometimes he would say that so-and-so was committing a certain mistake at that moment. Then he would say, "Make sure you never do such a thing."

He used to admonish all of us in this way—Vimal Kumar, Gaur, Shiva Shankar, Ganesh Jha, Pakira, Vyomkesh Mitra—everyone who was close to him. But he never scolded us in the presence of others. He would always call us aside and talk to us separately. He would talk in a very low voice, so that those at the nearby desks could not overhear. One of the most remarkable things about him was the way he scolded us. The way he dealt with us was so attractive and his manner so touching that sometimes it would go on for an hour or more and we would find it a very pleasant experience. If anyone interrupted, he would tell him to come back a little later.

Even those whom he did not admonish for their mistakes would not dare to commit any wrong or indulge in indecent talks around him or anywhere in the vicinity. In the hall where our office was situated, people used to maintain silent respect whenever they were anywhere near Prabhat-da. Nobody would ever smoke when he was there, or anywhere else where he was present. He seldom got up from his seat, except to attend nature's call. Even senior-ranking officers would rarely call for him if they had any important matter to discuss. Usually they would come to him instead and seek his advice. No one ever behaved in any way that might attract his disapproval. But he always dealt with others with a smiling face. When the atmosphere was very serious, he would lighten the mood by telling humorous stories and making everyone laugh.

One of the aspects of Baba's personality that fascinated his colleagues was the way knowledge seemed to pour forth from him in an inexhaustible stream, from subjects as diverse as philosophy or history to the intimate details of a person's life. Vimal Chandra Mitra had been a playmate of Baba's during his childhood. He drew close to him again as an adult when he joined the railway accounts office shortly after Baba did.

> From then onward, I felt hesitant to meet him, because I felt I could very easily lose myself in him. My head would automatically bow before his profound, serene personality. If anyone asked him any question on any subject, he would answer it thoroughly, as if he were an authority on the subject. This amazed all his office colleagues. Often we would read the newspaper together. He would finish reading the entire newspaper while I was still reading the headlines. Then he would tell me the important news items so that it would not be necessary for me to read them, or else he would direct me to read certain important items. Then, after a few days, he would ask me about them, but by then I had already forgotten. "If you touch my toe, you will remember everything," he would tell me. I would touch his

toe and immediately all that forgotten information would reappear in my memory in a flash. I could retell it all verbatim. He explained once that all such phenomena were based on a definite theory, but I forget that theory now. While he was elucidating it, he also said that all people in the world are linked together.

One time we started discussing a certain topic. The discussion ended but some questions remained in my mind. When we were about to separate, Bubu-da suddenly asked me if I still had some remaining doubts, some questions that had gone unanswered. We resumed our discussion and he answered all my unspoken questions without my asking. Then he left. This happened innumerable times. On occasion, I would feel an urge to ask him about something that was on my mind, but I lacked the courage to approach him. He would come to me and ask me if there wasn't something I wanted to ask him. My colleagues and I all had the same experience: we saw that our thought-waves were reflected on his mind like a picture on a cinema screen.

One Monday morning, Gokul asked him how he was able to know what was in everyone's mind. "There is a certain technique, a certain science behind it," Baba said, "but this science is not known to anyone." Baba explained to him how it worked, but his explanation was too subtle for Gokul to follow. Then Baba reached out and grabbed Gokul's finger. "Now, tell me, what were you doing yesterday afternoon in Monghyr, wandering along the bank of the river?" Normally Gokul spent his Sunday afternoons playing football, but that Sunday afternoon he had gone to the river instead of the football ground. When he asked Baba how he knew, Baba said, "It is as I explained. You told me."

Baba's theory also accounted for his knowledge of future events. N. C. Gangully, who used to love to talk philosophy with Baba, discussed communism with him on several occasions, and Baba never failed to comment how harmful the communist philosophy was for human society. One day in 1952, during the lunch break, he asked Baba about the future of communism.

"Prabhat-da, to what extent will communism be able to spread through the world?"

"The communist philosophy is unrealistic; it goes against the human spirit. Before long, you will see this theory become completely irrelevant in society."

Niren and several others were sitting there also. Niren asked Baba if they would see this with their own eyes.

"Yes, you shall see it in your lifetime. Toward the end of the century, you will see the Soviet Union break into pieces, but I shall see only the beginning of this process, not the end."[4]

Once, in the early sixties, Baba was talking with Gokul about the same subject. While he was explaining the defects of Russia's social theories, he said, "They are going in the wrong direction; before long communism will no longer exist there. I have written a social theory and one day that theory will be adopted by the world, even in Russia. You see, those who do not follow dharma can never be truly happy in this world. They may achieve everything else—economic success, name and fame—but without dharma they will never be satisfied. I have not passed a single day in my life without first completing my meditation before taking breakfast, at least one hour or one and a half hours. Meditation is essential. One must remember God and try to think that God is everywhere."

One day in late 1964, Baba called out from his desk to Vyomkesh Mitra, who worked in a different section of the accounts office, and asked him to come over. He had something he wanted to tell him.

"Listen, Vyomkesh, do you have a maternal uncle in the Andaman-Nicobar islands?"

"Yes. Why do you ask?"

"I want you to go and place a trunk call to see if he is okay."

Vyomkesh immediately became worried. "Prabhat-da, what is it? Has something happened to him?"

"Don't waste any time. Go now, this very minute, and place the trunk call."

Vyomkesh hurriedly informed his supervisor that he had a family emergency to attend to and rushed out of the office. As soon as he had left, Baba's staff members, including Pulak Ray, Taradas Gangully, and Gokul, gathered round him to find out why he had asked Vyomkesh to place the call.

"His uncle is an officer there. Today he went to the beach with his family for a picnic. His wife went for a swim but she was overcome by the current and was starting to drown. I could see him trying to save her, but while saving her he was caught by the waves and pulled under. I sent Vyomkesh to place the call when I saw him being swallowed up by the waves. After he makes the call, we'll know if he survived or if he drowned, but I have a feeling he won't survive."

"What about his wife?" they asked.

"She and the children are okay."

Later in the day, Vyomkesh returned to the office in tears and told Baba that his uncle had suffered an accident at the beach and was feared drowned. He begged Baba to save his life. "It is too late now," Baba said. "Even his dead body won't be recovered." He consoled Vyomkesh for some time and then asked him to go home and be with his family. That day Baba would not eat the lunch he had brought with him in his tiffin box. He told his colleagues that after seeing the accident occur before his eyes, he was not in a mood to eat. Instead, he asked them to give his food to anyone who might want it.

Later, news of Vyomkesh's uncle's death and the unsuccessful efforts to recover his body were published in the workshop newspaper, along with expressions of condolences. What was not published, but what was even bigger news in the accounts office, was the role that Baba had played in the drama by informing

Vyomkesh about the incident as it was taking place more than a thousand miles away.

A similar incident occurred with Hamsi, another colleague from the accounts office. During a tea break in the canteen, Baba told him that his uncle in Karachi had met with a jeep accident and was dying. Hamsi did not believe him. "My uncle is in Pakistan and you are sitting here in Jamalpur. How can you possibly know if something has happened to him?"

Baba lowered his voice. "Your uncle is dying. Prepare yourself and your family to receive the news."

Three days later, a telegram arrived for Hamsi with the news of his uncle's death.

Many of Baba's office colleagues were awed by such happenings and spoke in hushed tones about Prabhat's great powers, but there were some who had quite the opposite reaction. When Rasamay joined the accounts office in 1947, for example, he was warned to avoid Baba because he was a Tantric and would "eat his brain." All of Baba's admirers heard such whisperings from time to time. But whenever they informed him about it, he would laugh and tell them not to pay any attention. "Be like the lotus," he told them, "where the water simply rolls off."

The strict disciplinarian side of the Tantric guru was also evident in his relationship with his colleagues. In 1964, about 230 employees worked in the accounts office. The majority of them knew that if there were any fault in their conduct, Baba would learn of it and take them to task. For this reason, it was rarely necessary for Baba to discipline anyone. The only time Pulak ever saw Baba severely scold someone in the office involved one of his fellow clerks, S. P. Pakira.

One day, Baba gave some official work to Pakira, but Pakira told him that he wouldn't be able to do it because he had to leave at three that day in order to catch a train to Calcutta. Baba's eyes began to blaze. "Pakira, what did you say?"

"Prabhat-da, it will be hard for me to complete this work. I have to leave the office early to prepare for my journey."

Baba raised his voice and a hush fell over the office. "Pakira, beware! Do you know that in a moment you may be dead? You may die this very instant. You may cease to exist. Do you realize that?"

Pakira started to cry, shivering with fear. Pulak and several others crowded around Baba and begged him to cool down, afraid that something serious might happen to their colleague.

Baba listened to their entreaties. In a stern tone of voice, he said, "He should complete his assigned work and only then should he leave."

They turned to Pakira. "Pakira," they said, "you should never have refused Prabhat-da. You have to complete your work before you can think of leaving. But don't worry, we will help you with it."

Pakira bent down and touched Baba's feet. "Please accept my apology, Prabhat-da. I said it without thinking. I should never have refused to do the work. I am your younger brother. I won't leave this spot until you say that you forgive me."

"Pakira, until today no one has ever refused to obey any of my instructions. There has never been a reason for that to happen. I have never once given improper instructions. This was your job. I asked you to do it and you refused. You could have come to me, told me you had to leave at three, and asked for advice on how to complete the work. I would have managed it for you. But instead you refused."

"I'm sorry, Prabhat-da. I realize my mistake. It will never happen again. Please forgive me."

Baba forgave him, told him to see that it didn't happen again, and gave him his blessings. It was a lesson for everyone else as well. Thereafter, everyone in the office was careful never to show the slightest hint of insubordination or improper conduct of any kind in Baba's presence, not that anyone would have dared do so before then.

Fortunately such incidents were rarely necessary. Despite Baba's strictness, they were all deeply aware of the great affection he held for them, an affection that shone through in his constant concern for their welfare, his exhortations for them to be ideal human beings, and in his subtle, but ever-present sense of humor.

One day, he called Pulak to his desk and said, "Pulak, you are good at football, and you also exercise regularly. You must be quite strong. Let us arm-wrestle and see if you can press my hand to the table."

Pulak happily faced off with Baba and started to apply his youthful strength. But struggle as he might, he could not budge Baba's arm even a single centimeter. "Press harder," Baba told him, but it was like trying to arm wrestle with a stone wall. Then Pulak asked Baba to try to pin him so he could see if he could hold him off. Baba smiled and Pulak's arm slowly bent back until it was pinned to the table.

"Let me go, Prabhat-da, it hurts."

"What!" Baba said, as he released him. "You are as strong as a wrestler and you can't take even this much?"

"Prabhat-da, you must do a lot of exercise to be so strong," Pulak said, as he rubbed his hand and wrist.

"I do regular pranayama and asanas every morning and evening. It is the regular practice of pranayama that gives me so much energy."

Pulak asked the names of the asanas he practiced. Among others, Baba named *sarvaungasana, mayurasana,* and *matysendrasana*.[5]

By the mid-sixties, Baba's reputation in the office had grown to the point that it was not uncommon for railway officials from other cities to invent excuses to come and meet him, sometimes waiting patiently for hours for a chance to talk with Baba. Once an official from Bhagalpur came by the office while Baba was out and left a single rose on his desk. When Vimal Chandra asked Baba about it, Baba said, "He is a clever man. He does not disclose his intention, but he cherishes a secret desire that one day Prabhat Babu will grant his prayers." Vimal Chandra also recalled periodic visits by intelligence officers from the central government deputed to gather information on Baba's activities. He described how some of them became so impressed by Baba's personality that they ended up taking initiation into Ananda Marga.

By 1965, Baba was often out of the office on sanctioned leave, sometimes for a few days, sometimes longer, as the activities of Ananda Marga and the number of DMCs increased. Each time he took leave, he would inform his fellow workers where he was going—though he would never tell them the reason for his trip—and make whatever arrangements were necessary for the work in his section to continue smoothly while he was gone. When he came back, he would invariably bring small presents for his co-workers, often fruits or sweets typical of the regions he had visited, such as apples and raisins from Kashmir or a special type of cake from South India. Taradas Gangully, fascinated by these exotic regions that he had never had a chance to see, would ask Baba about those places and Baba would describe for him the culture and the people. On one of these occasions, Baba told him that he had toured all over India and wherever he went people were the same: "They love their life and they love their food."

Before one of these leaves, when he was scheduled to be out of the office for ten days, he called Vimal Khor and Pulak and gave them detailed instructions for the time that he would be gone. When they asked him where he was going, Baba informed them that he was catching a train to Calcutta, and from there, a flight to somewhere else. Baba invited them to come to the station to see him off. When they went to the station, they were astonished to see the huge crowd that had gathered.

> An enormous crowd had come to see him off with garlands and flowers, including many monks. We were really surprised. Seeing the crowd, we kept in the back. While we were standing there, two avadhutas came up to us and asked if we were Pulak Ray and Vimal Khor. They told us that Baba had sent them to fetch us. We went to the compartment with them. It wasn't easy to get through the crowd; the people wouldn't make way, but Prabhat-da told them to let those boys through. He made us sit next to him. He said, "What type of young men are you that you couldn't get through the crowd? In life you have to fight to get anywhere. If you stand still, you won't achieve anything. It is only by struggle that you will gain something." He told us to work properly over the next ten days in the office and not to

do anything amiss. We asked for his blessings, and he put his hands on both our heads and blessed us. He said that after these ten days, he would return and see how we had used our time.

Baba had been sought after in the office since the 1940s for his counsel—partly due to his early renown as a palmist—and for his help in times of emergency when no other recourse would do. This would continue to be a part of his office life until the day he resigned.

Once, one of Baba's office colleagues, Shankar Bannerjee, was deeply disturbed by the plight of his brother who was suffering from eczema. N.C. Gangully advised him to bring his problem to Baba. When an opportune moment arose, Shankar approached Baba, who told him to bring his brother to the office when he got a chance. A few days later, he brought his brother to see Baba. Baba asked him about the history of his disease and what treatment he had received. Then he asked him to lift his shirt and show him the affected areas. Baba's colleagues gathered round to watch. As he passed his hand lightly over those areas, they saw with amazement that the eczema cleared up almost instantaneously.

Those who were closest to Baba often found themselves thrust into the role of intermediary when one of their colleagues wished to request Baba's help. Shiva Shankar Mukherjee was the person people most often approached, and he himself was always advising people to talk to Baba if they had any problems. Once a friend of his, Tapan Chatterjee, was suffering from severe stomach problems. He had been to several doctors in Jamalpur, but their treatment had not given him much relief. Finally, Tapan and his friend Sushil Ghosh went to see a doctor in his hometown of Burdwan. While they were in Burdwan, Shiva Shankar approached Baba, explained the situation, and requested his help.

Baba closed his eyes for a moment. When he opened them, he said, "Shiva Shankar, your friend is suffering from intestinal tuberculosis. He will not survive long."

"Prabhat-da, please do something. Help him. He has a wife and children. If he dies, what will become of them?"

Baba appeared unmoved. "His disease is too far gone," he said. "There is nothing I can do for him."

In the meantime, the doctor in Burdwan made the same diagnosis. He told Tapan that his only hope was an operation, but he warned him that it was unlikely he would survive it. Tapan told him to schedule the operation.

When they returned to Jamalpur, Shiva Shankar asked Sushil about their visit. Sushil told him that Tapan had an appointment with a surgeon for an operation, but he refused to disclose the nature of the disease. Shiva Shankar came straight to the point.

"Sushil, I know that Tapan has intestinal tuberculosis. Prabhat-da told me while you were gone. And I know how far gone he is. We must ask Prabhat-da for his help. It is his only hope."

Again Shiva Shankar went to Baba to plead Tapan's case. "Look, Shiva Shankar," Baba said, "I know Tapan. He is a communist. He has no faith in me, so whatever help I give him won't bear any fruit." Shiva Shankar would not back down. After repeated requests, Baba finally acquiesced. He told Shiva Shankar to bring him a certain red flower. When he brought the flower, Baba touched it and handed it back to him. "Give it to Tapan's wife and tell her that a monk gave you the flower. Under no circumstances allow them to know it came from me. If Tapan hears my name, he will have an adverse reaction and it won't work."

Shiva Shankar brought the flower to Tapan's wife, and she tied it to Tapan's wrist. The operation was successful and there was no reoccurrence of the disease. Neither Tapan nor his wife ever learned the identity of the monk who had given them the flower.

In the early sixties, Shiva Shankar's nephew Badal Chatterjee was transferred from the Calcutta railway offices to the Jamalpur workshop accounts section. When Badal first arrived, his uncle's close association with Baba annoyed him, but his attitude eventually underwent a drastic change. One Saturday morning, Badal came running to Shiva Shankar and told him that his son had been up all night crying. The boy had dreamed that his father had been in the hospital and had died. Shaken by the boy's story, Badal's wife asked him to go to his uncle and request him to ask Baba about the meaning of the dream. Badal was not happy with the idea. He was still uneasy about Baba's reputation and his uncle's unabashed devotion, but he did as his wife requested.

On Monday morning, the two men approached Baba at his desk during the lunch hour. Shiva Shankar explained briefly the problem. Baba asked Badal to hold the little finger of his right hand, whereupon Baba started describing the boy. Then he asked Badal several questions: "Does the boy often rub his legs together? When he was an infant, did you use to put him on a cot during the day in Krishnagar with a photo of Vivekananda near his head? Did he use to stare at the photo? Was the boy's nickname 'Bile'?"

When Badal answered yes to all these questions, Baba said, "Whenever anybody touches the little finger of my right hand, I see the facts as if I were watching a movie; if they touch my right toe, I see them in the form of separate pictures. In his last life, your boy was the son of a Christian priest. He was at his father's bedside in the hospital when his father died. The boy later died at the age of eighteen and took birth in your family. What he saw in the dream were images from his previous life that have crystallized in his subconscious mind.[6] There is nothing to worry about. You and your wife will have no problems. The boy has good samskaras."

Badal didn't know what to make of what Baba said, but he felt relieved nonetheless, and over time his colleagues noticed a remarkable change in him. His character improved considerably, and he soon became one of Baba's faithful admirers. When he was later transferred out of Jamalpur, a farewell party was organized for him in the office. One of his colleagues brought a beautiful garland for him, but when he was about to be garlanded, he refused to accept it. "I have already mentally offered this garland to Prabhat-da," he said, "so I cannot wear it in front of him." He then requested that the garland be offered to Baba, who accepted it and then handed it to Badal.

"Keep this garland in your house," Baba said, "and treat it with respect. Whenever you go to work, look at it before you leave."

Badal took the garland home and kept it in a box wrapped in a red silk cloth. In the coming years, he would look at it every day before leaving for work, and he would attribute his good fortune in life to Baba's blessing.

Each of Baba's colleagues in the office had his own stories to tell, great or small, about instances when Baba had rescued him or his family and friends from their difficulties. One day, for instance, Taradas Gangully came into the office feeling disturbed because a neighbor's servant was very sick and was expected to die at any time. When Baba saw the concerned expression on his face, he asked him what the matter was. After listening to Taradas, Baba handed him a twenty-rupee note and told him to go to the pharmacy after work and purchase a certain medicine. Baba assured him the man would soon be cured, and such was the case.

On another occasion, a workshop employee named Vinay Singh approached Vimal Chandra and requested him to ask Baba if he would read his palm. "I don't know palmistry," was Baba's brief reply when Vimal approached him. "Ask him to go see Vishvanath." (Vishvanath was one of the people in the office to whom Baba had taught the science of palmistry.) When Vishvanath saw Vinay's palm, he started chiding him. "Are you not ashamed to show your palm to me." Then he sent him away. Vimal reported this to Baba and Baba said, "All right, bring him to me tomorrow." When Vinay was brought before Baba, Baba told him that he had called him there because he wanted to disclose his crimes in front of everyone in the office so that he could then reap the consequences of those bad actions. Vinay was shocked by Baba's words. He pleaded for Baba's help, and over time Baba helped him to reform his character.

One of the most well-known stories, one always mentioned by his colleagues in the office, was the story of Lakshmikant Singh, the brother of Kamalapati Singh, one of the senior supervisors in the accounts section, and Sanjay Singh, who also worked in the same office. Lakshmikant worked in a different area of the workshop, but he knew who Baba was. At home, his brothers would often tell stories about their experiences with Baba in the office.

One day, a local thug with a reputation as a smuggler and a black marketeer was found by the side of a lonely street lying in a pool of blood. He was still alive when the police arrived on the scene, and before he died, he named Lakshmikant Singh as his assailant. On the strength of the dying man's accusation, Lakshmikant was arrested and prosecuted by the Monghyr District Court for first-degree murder.

Kamalapati was hesitant to bring the matter to Baba, so Gokul and Shiva Shankar went to talk to Baba on his behalf. They protested Lakshmikant's innocence and requested his help. Baba told them to fight the case and assured them that everything would turn out okay. The verdict, however, came back guilty and the district court sentenced Lakshmikant to hang.

When Baba's distraught colleagues informed him of the verdict, Baba said, "I can see that he is destined to live a long life. He will not die. Tell them to file an appeal with the High Court."

The case went to the High Court, but the High Court upheld the verdict and the sentence of death by hanging. This time Kamalapati came personally to Baba, accompanied by his colleagues, and begged for his help.

"I said before that Lakshmikant is destined to live a long life," Baba told him. "I know his future. He will not die. Now, come with me."

Baba took Kamalapati and Gokul over to the technical school. Along the way, he picked a flower from one of the flowerbeds lining the pathway. When they reached the technical school, he picked up a small copper ring from a workbench and made an amulet to which he fixed the flower. When he was done, he held the amulet in his hands, closed his eyes, and concentrated. Then he handed it to Kamalapati.

"Bring this to your brother and tell him to wear it on his body. Make it clear to him that he must not take it off until he has been freed."

The next day, Gokul and Kamalapati caught a train for Bhagalpur and went to the central jail where Lakshmikant was interned, bringing with them the amulet. Kamalapati told his brother not to take it off under any circumstances, not even while bathing. When his brother asked why, Kamalapati said, "Prabhat-da made this amulet. That means you are under his protection now. If you value your life, you won't take it off under any circumstances."

Lakshmikant did not hesitate. "If Prabhat-da sent this amulet," he told them, "then you can rest assured that I won't take it off."

Lakshmikant fixed the amulet to his upper left arm and it would remain there long after the copper had turned to black. When Kamalapati returned to the office the next day, he informed Baba that his brother was wearing the amulet. Baba asked him to sit down and wrote out some instructions on a piece of paper. "Take this to your lawyers. Tell them to appeal the case to the Supreme Court. When they prepare their case, they will prepare to argue on the basis of these five points." Baba explained to him in detail the legal strategy he had outlined for the lawyers. Kamalapati took the paper to his advocates. They raised a few eyebrows but agreed to follow the strategy Baba had proposed. After a few months, the case was argued before the Supreme Court. In a landmark verdict, the decision was overturned on the basis of a legal technicality pointed out by Baba.

When Lakshmikant was freed and returned to work for the first time in nearly a year, Kamalapati, Shiva Shankar, and others welcomed him back and told him that before doing anything else, he had to go to the accounts office and pay his respects to Prabhat-da. "You know, you owe him your life," they reminded him.[7]

"I know," Lakshmikant said, "but I don't dare face him. He is like a lion. I don't dare look him in the eyes." It was at that moment that Shiva Shankar realized that Lakshmikant had indeed committed the crime.

After repeated requests, they convinced Lakshmikant to go to Baba and thank him. When he did, Baba was very gracious. He blessed him and told him to be an ideal person from then on. Later, Baba explained in private that Lakshmikant was a good man at heart. The two men had gotten into an altercation and he had stabbed his victim in self-defense. If he had not killed him, he would have been killed himself.

Most of Baba's non-Margi followers and admirers in the office never thought to take initiation into Ananda Marga or, in a few cases, like that of Shiva Shankar, were discouraged by Baba from doing so. There were, however, a few exceptions. One young man from the accounts office used to go for a walk near the hills each evening and drink mineral water from the spring. Once, while returning home, he was startled to see an effulgent form gliding along some distance away. When he got closer, he was surprised to discover that it was Baba, out for his evening walk. Then, in the office, something even more curious happened. At times, he would sit at his desk and chant Krishna's name under his breath. One day, he heard a soft voice asking him what he was doing. When he opened his eyes, he saw Krishna standing in front of him, smiling. Taken aback, he closed his eyes, still seeing Krishna's form in his mind. When he opened them again, he saw Baba standing in front of his desk. This happened more than once before he was transferred to Asansol. After his transfer, he met an acharya and took initiation into Ananda Marga, never having forgotten his strange experiences with Baba from his days in the Jamalpur office.

By and large, Baba's office colleagues knew little about Ananda Marga, apart from the stories that circulated in Jamalpur and, as time went on, what they read in the newspapers. Baba never talked about the organization with them, and when he met Margis in the office for some work, such as dictation, they were careful not to bother him. Though they didn't talk about it with Baba, they were justifiably proud of his accomplishments and the fact that people would come from all over India to see their colleague, and soon from all over the world. Those who had been with Baba in the office since the early forties, such as N. C. Gangully and Vimal Chandra Mitra, remembered that in those days Baba would sometimes mention his aspirations to open schools, children's homes, hospitals, and other welfare projects for the poor and underprivileged. When they saw this come to pass during Baba's last years in the office and afterward, it gave them great satisfaction.

Once Baba left the office, most of his colleagues continued to follow his career through the press and word-of-mouth. Many of them, such as Pulak Ray, Shiva Shankar, Kamalapati Singh, and Vimal Chandra, visited Baba on occasion and were always received graciously as a special guest, without any of the protocol that his Margi disciples had to pass through. Baba would chat with them about Jamalpur and ask how their mutual acquaintances were doing, renewing instantly the affectionate intimacy that he had shared with them in the office. That special relationship was what prompted Kamalapati to tell us proudly when we went to interview him at his house in 1999, "I know your Baba better than you!"

XXXII

Last Years in Jamalpur

The devotee will not only sing spiritual songs and chant. Those spiritual aspirants who move speedily on the path of evolution toward the Supreme Consciousness can never be blind to the sufferings of countless people around them due to the lack of a solid social system, solid economic system and human feeling. If anyone is blind to the ill-management of the social system, they have not been able to understand the Supreme Consciousness fully... Hence the devotee must be ready to serve humanity. The spiritual aspirants who do not render social service do not have real devotion. In their devotion lies selfishness. Devotees who are selfish do not attain God. Devotees are workers. They will never be afraid of work. They will do maximum work.[1]

NINETEEN SIXTY-FIVE WAS a busy year for Baba. The organization was growing rapidly and his DMC tours provided much of the impetus for that growth. Wherever he went, people thronged to see him. When he traveled by train, the platforms in stations along the way filled up with Margis eager to have the darshan of their guru. In many places, the PC lines were longer than Baba had time to attend to and a selection process had to be introduced. Ananda Marga was quickly gaining recognition as the fastest-growing spiritual organization in India. The contrast between that and Baba's simple job as a section head in the Jamalpur accounts workshop led Shiva Shankar Mukherjee to ask Baba one day why he continued to remain there. Baba replied, "I am working in order to show people that one can lead a life of devotion and spiritual practice without giving up one's normal lifestyle." Periodically, Margis and wholetimers would request Baba to retire from his job, but he continued to tell them that it was not yet time. Nevertheless, the growing amount of time that Baba spent away from the office on leave gave every indication that that time was not far off.

In February, Baba made the first of two trips that year to the northeastern states of Assam and Tripura, where several years earlier Rasamay had begun the prachar efforts after borrowing money to travel there and create a presence for Ananda Marga. On the morning of the Karimganj DMC, Baba expressed a desire to visit Rasamay's native village of Sadarasi. Though not a scheduled part of Baba's program, the local Margis made hasty arrangements and took

Baba to the remote village for a surprise visit. It was not, however, quite the surprise they had imagined. When they arrived at the outskirts of the village, they found the local Margis and villagers lining both sides of the road to receive them. They found out afterward that one Margi from the village had dreamed the previous night that Baba would be arriving there around eight in the morning. At dawn, he had begun going around the village spreading the news that Baba would be arriving at that time. The Margis erected a shamiana and the entire village turned out to hear Baba give a talk.[2] Baba also paid a visit to the house of Rasamay's maternal uncle, the house in which Rasamay had been raised, thus fulfilling a secret desire of his faithful disciple. Though Rasamay was not physically present, it would remain one of the most cherished memories of his life.

When the DMC program was over, several busloads of Margis accompanied Baba to the airport to see him off. When Baba passed through security, he was frisked by a local sub-inspector—there were no metal detectors in those days. After emptying Baba's pockets, the sub-inspector put Baba's keys back in his right pocket and his handkerchief in the left, precisely opposite to where Baba normally kept them. As Baba was leaving the security area, he checked his pockets. When he found that his things were misplaced, he started scolding the sub-inspector. The superintendent of police, who was standing nearby, came over to see what was going on. "Look here," Baba said, "your officer has disturbed the system that I have been following for more than thirty years. My keys go in my left pocket and my handkerchief in my right. He has displaced and misplaced them." The SP apologized and Baba smiled. The monks who were accompanying him did their best to suppress their laughter.

Back in Jamalpur, the number of devotees visiting the jagriti continued to increase. Many of these were young people who became inspired to dedicate their lives as wholetimers, numbering in the hundreds by the end of 1966. One of them was Lakshmi Prasad Nayak, who had his PC in early 1965 in the Jamalpur jagriti. Recently initiated, he had heard many stories about Baba from the devotees. While he found them inspiring, he also felt uncomfortable with the unfeigned adulation he saw. Hence, when he entered Baba's room, he did not do sastaunga pranam, both because he could not accept Baba as a God, as many devotees were fond of saying, and because he was wearing a brand new pair of pants and did not want to mess up the crease. Instead, he did namaskar, sat down in front of Baba's cot, and asked, "Baba, people are saying that you are a God, but how can that be? I think you are a guru."

"Right you are," Baba replied. "But tell me, do you accept the existence of God?"

"Yes, Baba."

"Very good. Now I want you to admit all your sins and misdeeds, one by one."

"I have committed some, it is true."

"No, no, tell me them, one by one."

Lakshmi Prasad thought for a moment, trying to decide which one he should tell. Then he remembered the time in the tenth grade when he and two friends had been kicked out of school for stealing a carom board. In order to get reinstated, they had to admit in front of the entire school assembly that they had stolen it and then beg everyone's pardon.

"One time I stole something from school, Baba."

"Be specific."

Lakshmi Prasad was uncomfortable about revealing the details of what he still remembered as a shameful incident. Despite the fact that he had been the ringleader, he said, "But it wasn't really my fault. My two friends pushed me into it."

"What are you saying? You stole the carom board. You misguided your friends and goaded them into helping you. I was not present, but Paramatma was watching everything. Don't try to hide from him. I don't want to have to ask you again. Tell me your crimes, one by one—in detail."

Lakshmi Prasad's cheeks began to burn. He realized, to his extreme discomfort, that he could not hide anything from Baba. One by one, he recounted the details of whatever misdeeds he could remember, save one, a heinous crime that he had committed when he was eleven and which he had tried to hide ever since, even from himself.

"There is one more crime that you have not admitted," Baba said, after the list had grown rather long.

Lakshmi Prasad was too ashamed to continue. Finally, after a short silence, Baba started narrating the details of that incident. "Do you accept it?" he asked.

Lakshmi Prasad broke down and started crying. Baba embraced him and said, "Human beings commit crimes. You have accepted it; that is your punishment. From this moment on, you will not think about it any more, nor will you ever tell anyone. Rather, you will think that you have not committed this crime. Your life begins from today."

Lakshmi Prasad embraced Baba with his head in Baba's lap and unburdened himself. He told Baba about his father's grinding poverty and the great struggle his family was facing. Baba assured him that he had nothing to worry about. Paramatma would take care of everything.

"Do you remember when you were a child, you were riding in the back of a truck with some friends on the way to the market? You climbed up on top of the cab and turned around to tell your friends, Vaekuntha and Shankar Saha, to climb up with you. Just as you leaned down to lend a hand to Vaekuntha, the truck passed under the overhanging branches of a mango tree. One thick branch passed just over your head at that precise instant, not two feet above the cab. When you saw the branch after it went by, you realized that if you had not leaned over at that moment, you would have been killed. Do you remember?"

"Yes, Baba," Lakshmi Prasad replied, reliving once again the trauma of that day. Painful images flooded back into his mind as Baba spoke the names of his childhood friends, long since forgotten.

"You were so afraid that day that you remembered God with great intensity and thanked him for saving your life. Then you went home and cried to your mother and she forbade you to ever ride on trucks again."

Lakshmi Prasad clung to Baba even more tightly and continued to cry, the emotions pouring out of him like a river. "You see," Baba said, "Paramatma is always with you. He has been watching over you since your childhood. Rest assured, whatever is necessary to promote your welfare, Paramatma will take care of it. You shouldn't worry about it. Great persons do not worry about worldly matters. They trust in the will of Paramapurusha. Now tell me, to whom does your body belong? Your legs, your hands, your eyes?"

"To Paramapurusha."

"Yes. And since they all belong to him, you won't hesitate to offer them to him, will you?"

"No, Baba, I won't hesitate. I promise."

"Good. You have a great power sleeping within you. Use it for the service of Paramapurusha. Paramapurusha has given you your life. Use it to serve the creation."

Lakshmi Prasad Nayak's PC lasted forty-five minutes. When he came out of Baba's room, he went straight to Abhedananda, Baba's personal assistant, and told him that he wanted to become a wholetimer. Abhedananda told him that he would have to wait until he turned eighteen, still several months away; otherwise, his parents could file a case against the organization. In the meantime, Baba arranged for Acharya Pashupati to sponsor his studies in Bhagalpur. Once he passed his eighteenth birthday and graduated from high school, he left for the training center in Varanasi.

Another young disciple had his PC around the same time and had a very similar experience. Baba reminded him about a couple of childhood incidents in which he had almost died. He, too, had thanked God for saving his life. In contrast to Lakshmi Prasad, he asked Baba directly in PC whether or not he should become a monk. In reply, Baba said, "Look, during your past several lifetimes you have been quite happy; you've enjoyed a lot. You can endure some hardship for one lifetime for a great cause, can you not?" The next day, he caught a train from Jamalpur to Varanasi and entered the wholetimer training center.

One evening that spring, Harinder was walking with Baba toward the tiger's grave. By now, he had graduated and taken a job with the government in the electricity office. As they were walking, Baba turned to him and said, "Now you have also started taking bribes?"

Harinder was startled. "But Baba, I don't remember ever taking any bribe, ever."

Baba smiled. "The person who was able to resist a bribe of two hundred rupees accepted two chum chums (an Indian milk sweet), which is four annas, and a cup of tea, which is two annas—in total six annas."

Suddenly the scene flashed in Harinder's mind. The previous year, a businessman who owned a successful t-shirt factory had come to his office with an application for a fifty-horsepower connection for a rice mill that he was constructing. The businessman had offered him a two-hundred-rupee bribe to speed up the approval process and Harinder had sent him away with a severe scolding for attempting to bribe a government official. Just two weeks before his field walk, Harinder was returning to work after his lunch break when he passed the same businessman standing in front of his newly opened mill. The man invited him inside to see the mill, and Harinder, remembering the scolding he had given him and feeling some sympathy for that reason, agreed to go inside and have a quick look at the setup. When he was leaving the factory, the man's mother offered him a couple of chum chums and a cup of tea. Initially he refused, protesting that he had just finished his lunch, but the woman insisted and finally Harinder relented.

When he told Baba that he remembered the incident, Baba said, "It was also a kind of bribe, Harinder. The sweets and the tea should have been given to some beggar, or to a leper struggling to pass the cold winter in the street.[3] His mother addressed you as 'son' and practically forced the sweets on you, I know, but do you know what that businessman was thinking in the meantime? He was thinking that this man did not accept my two-hundred-rupee bribe but he has taken some sweets from my mother; this will make him better disposed toward me in the future. I will always have some work or other with the electric office, and he may help me when I need him."

Kiran and Kishan were the closest of friends, so much so that their friendship had become a topic of conversation among the other wholetimers. Both had been initiated at the same time in Jammu. Both had decided to go to training at the same time, and when they finished training they requested Baba to post them in the same place. Baba, as one might have expected, posted them in different areas, but whenever they returned to Jamalpur for reporting sessions,[4] they would spend all their free time together.

One day in General Darshan, Baba touched Dasarath on the back of his head and asked him to see Kiran and Kishan's past lives.

Dasarath closed his eyes and concentrated for a few moments.

"Baba, I see two corpses on a pyre in a burning ghat on the banks of the river Padma in East Bengal.

"Whose bodies are they?"

"They are the bodies of two handsome young men."

"And who were these young men?"

"Baba, they were brothers. They died together."

"How did they die?"

"They went to bathe in the river. One of them ventured out too far and got caught by the current. He began to drown. His brother attempted to save him, but he was also caught by the current and both of them drowned. They were well loved in their community, and there was a great outpouring of grief when the news became known."

"Yes," Baba said, "in that life they were born into a prosperous family of East Bengal. Due to their unfulfilled samskaras, the two of them have met again and become inseparable friends. Even though they have become wholetimers, they still long for each other's affection, just as they did in their previous life, right up until their final breath."

One day, Acharya Sambuddhananda, then posted in the northeast states, came to Jamalpur for reporting. While he was presenting his report to Baba, Baba inquired about the welfare of different Margis and workers in his region.

"And how is Paresh in Guwahati doing?" Baba asked.

"Baba, he is doing fine."

"Fine, you say! Don't you know that he has come down with malaria? Don't you know how serious his condition is? The local Margis are not taking proper care of him and he is blaming me mentally. He is complaining to me that even *I* don't look after him. Return immediately to Guwahati and make proper arrangements for his treatment. Tell the local Margis there that Baba is displeased that they were indifferent to the health of their worker. As soon as you have done that, go straight to Karimganj. Don't waste even a single second. On your way to Karimganj, get down at Badarpur station. When you get down, you will see a train standing on the opposite platform, the Barrack Valley Express. It will be going in the opposite direction. On that train you will find your initiate, Dr. Anukul Ray. You will take him off that train immediately and bring him along with you to Karimganj."

Baba gave his instructions with such firmness that Sambuddhananda did not dare ask any questions. He left immediately for the railway station and took the first train out that had connections for Guwahati. It was a long trip, nearly two days, and while he was traveling he thought back to the day, nearly three years earlier, when he had first heard the name of Dr. Anukul Ray. On that day he had also been in Jamalpur for a reporting session. Baba had called him aside and said, "Asim, when you go to Karimganj there is a certain person there whom I want you to initiate. His name is Dr. Anukul Ray. He is a good man. He has been searching for a guru for a long time, but he hasn't yet found a suitable master. This is his address. Go to his house. He will have four questions. Answer these four questions to his satisfaction and he will agree to take initiation. Now, note down the questions and the answers. . . ."

Dr. Anukul had indeed been eager to find a sadguru. Years earlier, he had visited a number of different masters in his search. The first of these was Ram

Thakur, who told him that he could not initiate him because his guru was already decided; Ram Thakur also told him that his guru would be a very great master. Later, he went to visit Swami Svarupananda, from whom he also requested initiation, but only if he would answer four questions. The swami, unhappy with his lack of humility, refused to initiate him. Finally, he went to the ashram of Anukul Thakur in Deoghar, another well-known guru. Anukul Thakur also declined to initiate him, but he told him that there was no need to keep searching. He would soon be initiated by a guru of the highest order. Anukul Thakur would not disclose that guru's name, but after repeated requests he gave him a hint. He said his name would start with "Shrii Shrii A."

Dr. Ray returned home to Karimganj, disappointed, but hopeful that the guru he had long been waiting for would soon find him, but years passed and still there was no sign of his guru. One morning, he was sitting at home in a contemplative mood when there was a knock at his door. He opened it to find a young man dressed in white. Without introducing himself, the young man asked him if he were Dr. Anukul Ray. When he answered yes, the youth said with an air of authority, "Please, take a quick bath and then come."

"I don't understand," the doctor said, taken aback by the young man's temerity. "Who are you?"

"My name is Asim. I'm a teacher of meditation and yoga; I've come to initiate you."

Dr. Anukul was startled by his answer. "I see. Please, come in and sit. Can I bring you something—some tea or other refreshment?"

"Actually, I have some pressing work waiting for me," Asim said, with an air of impatience. "I will initiate you, but then I must be going."

"May I ask why you are so eager to initiate me? I haven't asked for initiation."

"These are my guru's instructions."

"Your guru?" Anukul asked, suddenly hopeful.

"Yes, my guru. Oh yes, he told me you would have four questions that I would need to answer."

Asim repeated the four questions Dr. Anukul had posed to Swami Svarupananda, along with the answers Baba had dictated. "What is your guru's name?" Dr. Anukul asked in amazement. When he heard the name "Shrii Shrii Anandamurti," his heart leapt and he gave his silent thanks to the guru he had not yet seen.

When Sambuddhananda arrived in Guwahati, he found that Paresh had indeed come down with malaria and was in bad shape. He called an immediate meeting of the local Margis and informed them of Baba's displeasure. Duly chastised, the Margis arranged for Paresh to be hospitalized and made a list of who would take turns remaining in the hospital with him. As soon as that was taken care of, Sambuddhananda set off for Karimganj, despite going nearly two days without sleep, having traveled from Jamalpur in the unreserved compartment.

When the train reached Badarpur Station, he got down and found the Barrack Valley Express standing on the opposite platform, just as Baba had said it would be. Hurriedly, he entered the train and quickly went from one end to the other and back again without finding his initiate. Finally, on the third pass, he heard a familiar voice call out to him, "Dada,[5] what are you doing here?"

"Anukul-da, there you are! Come on. Get down from the train. You have to come with me to Karimganj right this moment."

"Karimganj? What are you talking about? I have some important work to take care of. I can't go to Karimganj now."

"Don't argue with me. I'll answer your questions later. Right now we have to get off this train and get on the train for Karimganj. Where is your luggage?"

When Dr. Anukul motioned toward his bag, Sambuddhananda grabbed it and summarily tossed it out onto the platform. He grabbed the uncomprehending doctor and escorted him off the train, much to the latter's silent annoyance. Once they were safely on their way to Karimganj, Sambuddhananda related Baba's instructions to him. It wasn't much of an explanation, but the doctor realized that if Baba had given an order, it was best not to question it. The next morning, the daily papers supplied the reason. The train that Dr. Anukul had been on had suffered a derailment soon after leaving Badarpur Station. It had fallen into a gorge and a large number of passengers had been killed, including most of the people in his coach.

On May 22, Baba gave his semi-annual RU address in Patna, a talk entitled, "Science, Civilization and Spiritual Progress." The next day he gave his Ananda Purnima DMC address, and that morning in front of the gathering he announced the formation of WWD, the Women's Welfare Department of Ananda Marga. Preparations for creating the women's wing were already underway, though they had not been without opposition from within the organization. Baba had been creating female acharyas since the founding of the organization, but up until that point there had been no hint that he would create an order of female sannyasis. Earlier that year, however, Vimala Vishishta, then district secretary for Ananda Marga in Bombay, had expressed to Baba her desire to dedicate herself to the mission, just as the avadhutas were doing. Baba then disclosed to her his plans for the creation of WWD and an order of female sannyasis.

Vimala was fifty-two at the time, a well-educated, sophisticated, and talented woman from the upper circles of Bombay society who had been married off at the age of fifteen by her family to a wealthy and materialistic businessman. Her maturity, intelligence, and many talents made her the perfect person to become Baba's first female sannyasi and head of the women's wing.

Vimala had been leading a spiritual life since her childhood. Once her three children were married and settled down, she left her home in Bombay and went to live in the Kerala ashram of her guru, Swami Ramdas, where she built a house. After Ramdas died in 1963, however, she felt the need for a living guru.

With that in mind, she went to Rishikesh to meet Anandamayi Ma, who told her that there was no need for her to go anywhere to take initiation. Her guru would come to her, and very soon now.

Trusting in the saint's words, she left Rishikesh for Udaipur to visit her daughter and son-in-law. While she was there, Mangal Bihari, a friend of the family, heard about her avid interest in spiritual matters and invited her to a spiritual gathering at his house. That night, Vimala had a dream in which she saw a sannyasi clothed in orange robes and a turban. Voices urged her to touch the sannyasi's feet. As she did, she saw the sannyasi turn into the figure of her departed guru, Swami Ramdas, smiling bounteously at her. Then the figure of Ramdas changed into that of an unknown man wearing eyeglasses and a white dhoti and kurta. With her hands still touching his feet, she heard a voice resounding all around her: "You are touching the divine light." Then she woke up. Her entire body was vibrated with feelings of bliss. It was already early morning, so she took a bath and got ready to go to Mangal Bihari's house. When she entered his house, she saw the same sannyasi she had seen in her dream, an avadhuta of Ananda Marga. She took initiation, and later that day Mangal Bihari showed her the letters that Tej Karan had written during his first visit to Jamalpur. Deeply inspired by the letters, she asked to see Baba's picture. As she suspected, it was the same person who had appeared to her in her dream.

On Baba's instructions, Pranay called her to Varanasi in April to take training. In the first week of May, she arrived in Jamalpur to take her final acharya classes and sit for the acharya exam. Joining her was Acharya Kailas Balla's nineteen-year-old daughter Pramila, who had been pestering Baba for the past couple of years to allow her to dedicate herself full-time to the mission. Baba made his plans public in a meeting in his room with Satyananda, Pranay, and several others while the two prospective female monks waited outside. A heated discussion ensued, loud enough for the two women to know that Baba's plans were not entirely well received. Satyananda, in particular, was strongly opposed to the idea. He tried to argue with Baba that one of the main factors that had led to the decline of Buddhism in India had been Buddha's controversial decision to create female sannyasis, but Baba would not hear of it. "Like a bird, an organization needs two wings to be able to fly," he said, a comment he would often repeat in the future. Nor would he listen to any of the other traditional arguments against the inclusion of women voiced by the other men in the room. Vimala received her avadhutika initiation in October and was given the monastic name Ananda Bharati. Pramila received her initiation a few months later and was given the name Ananda Gita. Together, they set up the WWD headquarters in Varanasi and the training center for female wholetimers.

On June 8, two weeks after the Ananda Purnima DMC, Narasingh, an elderly devotee from nearby Trimohan, came to Jamalpur to see Baba. When Baba reached the jagriti in the late afternoon, Narasingh informed the master that it was time for him to leave his body. Baba reached out and took his disciple's hand.

"Narasingh, why are you talking like this? You should not think such thoughts."

"You can't cheat me, Baba," Narasingh replied. "I know that my time has come."

Baba remained silent for a moment. Then he said softly, "Do you want me to extend your life?"

"No, Baba. I want your promise that I will be reborn into a family of Margis and become an avadhuta in my next life."

"How can I promise you that? It is my wish that you merge into the Supreme Consciousness when you leave this body and attain *mahamriytu*, the great death."

Narasingh would not be deterred. He continued to insist. Finally Baba relented. "*Tatastu*," he said, so be it. A few minutes later, Baba called two disciples into his room, Chirainjivi and Karmeshvar Lal. He told them that Narasingh was not well and asked them to accompany him back to his house in Trimohan that night. He also asked them to convey a message to Narasingh's eldest son, Aniruddha, that he should not leave his father alone the next day.

In the evening, when Baba went out for field walk, he asked Pranay why Narasingh was not there. When Pranay explained that he had given his place to a South Indian Margi because he had come from such a long distance, Baba rebuked him. "What! Go and bring Narasingh immediately. I have urgent work with him." It was to be Narasingh's last darshan and the culmination of an old story.

Narasingh had been a devout Hindu his entire life. When his eldest son, Aniruddha, took initiation in 1956, he was happy to see the unexpected change in his character, but he was equally disturbed to see him abandon idol worship and other traditions of his Hindu faith. This led to arguments between the two that were compounded when his second son, Harinder, took initiation shortly afterward at the insistence of his brother. One day in mid-1957, while visiting Aniruddha in Bhagalpur, Narasingh got into yet another argument with his eldest son over Ananda Marga. This time his son was uncompromising. "You are a great devotee, I know, but now it is time for you to join Ananda Marga."

"I will not join the religion of sinners," Narasingh bellowed, but a week later, he came to Aniruddha in an apologetic mood and asked him who his acharya was.

"Unless you are ready to take initiation, I am not prepared to talk to you."

"Bring me to your acharya then. I am ready."

Surprised at this unexpected and unexplained change of heart, Aniruddha brought his father to his acharya, Chandranath. During his initiation, Narasingh went into trance and remained in that state for several hours. When he regained his normal consciousness, he lamented that he had come so late. He insisted on being brought to see Baba. They told him that new initiates were required to practice meditation for six months before they were allowed to meet the guru, but Narasingh would not be put off. Finally, after five days of entreaties, they brought him to Jamalpur. When Baba saw him for the first time, he said, "Narasingh, you have come very late. I have been waiting for you for three years. Go and ask Mahadeva. Three years ago I told him, 'There is a great devotee in Trimohan by the name of Narasingh; go and bring him to me,' but he didn't do it."

That evening on field walk, Narasingh told Baba that no son had ever repaid his debt to his father, but his son had done so. "No, Narasingh," Baba said, "Aniruddha has done you a great service, no doubt, but that debt is not yet paid. Something more is left."

A few days later, Narasingh brought a basket of ripe mangos from his orchard to offer to Baba. Baba scowled and scolded him. "Don't you know that Baba does not accept offerings from anyone? Take them back!"

That night Narasingh had a chance to talk to Baba alone at the gate of Baba's house after returning from field walk. "Baba, why did you scold me today?" he asked. "The orchard that I brought the mangos from is your orchard; the mangos are your mangos." Baba smiled and invited him to sit on the veranda with him. Baba went inside the house and brought out two cups of tea. They sat and chatted for some time. Thereafter, Baba gave orders that any offerings from Narasingh would be accepted, but from no one else. The story circulated among the Margis. From then on, he became known as "Pera Baba," because he never came to Baba empty-handed. He always brought some sweets, such as *pera*, or some fruits. From that day until his death, Narasingh would not miss a single DMC, prompting Baba to once remark, "No one has been present at every DMC, except Narasingh and myself."

A few years later, Narasingh asked Baba to teach him how to extend his lifespan. "Why do you want to learn that?" Baba inquired.

"Baba, I am very old. I came very late to your mission. I want to be able to complete my sadhana properly, but I have very few years left."

"This is possible, but it is not recommended. After a person passes eighty years of age, the glands lose their vitality and sadhana becomes more difficult. Even asanas don't have much effect any longer. For this reason, Providence has decreed that a person's lifespan should not much exceed this age. It is better to take rebirth and start fresh with a new body. You will pick up your sadhana where you left off in the last life but with a body that is young and strong. It is better this way."

Narasingh accepted Baba's advice and did not repeat his request.

On another occasion, Baba told him, "If a person is very attached to his family, and if his family members are present when he dies, then it will become an obstacle for his spiritual advancement. It may even cause him to take rebirth in that same family."

"Baba, then I want to die either in your presence or when I am alone."

"Yes. It would be best that way."

Now, on this summer night in 1965, after what would be his last darshan, Narasingh took the late train back to Bhagalpur, accompanied by the two Margis. When they reached Bhagalpur Junction in the early morning hours, he insisted on going the rest of the way to Trimohan by himself. Despite Baba's instructions, Chirainjivi and Karmeshvar let him have his wish. They turned back for Jamalpur and thus did not have a chance to give Baba's message to Aniruddha.

Narasingh arrived home around three thirty in the morning. He did his morning spiritual practices and then collapsed on his bed in a weakened state, while the ladies of the house did their best to take care of him. Later in the morning, Aniruddha stopped by. By this time, Narasingh was feeling somewhat better. He told his son that he had an appointment in Bhagalpur and had to leave. Aniruddha did not want to let him go, but Narasingh insisted. He had given his word, he said. He had to go and he wanted to go alone. Aniruddha tried to convince his father to allow him to send someone with him, but he eventually gave up. He dropped him off at the station, but afterward he instructed his household servant, Safijan, to follow the old man secretly and keep an eye on him, just in case. Once in the station, Narasingh boarded the local train for Bhagalpur, which was standing empty on the platform. He found an upper berth in a vacant compartment and sat for meditation. Fifteen minutes later, he shouted in a loud voice, "Baba." Safijan, who was keeping out of sight nearby, peeked in and saw Narasingh slumped against the wall of the compartment in meditation posture. Alarmed, he entered the compartment and found that Narasingh was dead.

Narasingh's funeral rites were performed in Trimohan according to the Ananda Marga system, despite the virulent objections of the villagers. It was the first funeral ever conducted according to the system Baba had given in *Caryacarya*. Though Baba did not attend, he sent a special message: "His death was not *mrityu* but *mahamriytu*.[6] He is the only person in the organization who was chanting his ista mantra continuously up until his last breath."

On August 15, the increasingly frequent skirmishes between India and Pakistan in the Kashmir region broke out into full-scale hostilities when the Indian Army crossed the international border into Pakistani Kashmir, in response to what it termed as massive armed infiltration by Pakistani saboteurs into Indian Kashmir. Baba was on his way to the jagriti when the news broke that the Indian army had crossed the border. Though Pakistan claimed that the attack was unprovoked, Baba did not agree. He supported Prime Minister Lal Bahadur Shastri's decision to go on the offensive. That evening, he gave the Margis a history lesson on the conflict and analyzed the mistakes made by Nehru, the previous Prime Minister, which had left India in a tenuous position along the Kashmir border.

As he had done during the Chinese conflict, Baba kept up a running commentary on the war each day thereafter for the Margis. In the meantime, the upcoming two-week DMC tour, scheduled for Srinagar, the capital of Kashmir, along with Agartala, Chandigarh, Jammu, and Simla, had to be altered. The Srinagar DMC was cancelled and Jaipur was added to the program.

Baba arrived in Agartala, the capital of Tripura, on the nineteenth, his second visit to the northeast that year. Sambuddhananda, who was in charge of prachar in the states of Assam and Tripura, brought him by car to the house where he would be staying. There he was met by Gopiballah, the district secretary for Ananda Marga in Agartala and Baba's designated local guardian during the DMC. As per tradition, Gopiballah garlanded Baba and received his namaskar. As they were walking into the house, Baba asked him how he was doing.

"I am fine, Baba," he said.

Baba stopped in the hallway. "I can see that you have gout in your knees; they give you a great deal of pain in the night, do they not?"

Gopiballah folded his hands to his chest and confirmed with a nod what Baba had said. Baba prescribed for him a diet to help him with his disease. Then he bent over and pressed both of Gopiballah's knees with his hands.

"Go now," he said, "It is all cured."

Gopiballah prostrated in front of Baba and protested, aghast that he had allowed Baba to reverse the Indian tradition of showing respect to one's elders by touching their feet.

"Baba, why did you touch my legs?"

"Your entire body is an expression of Brahma," Baba replied.

While on field walk in Simla, Baba talked about Tantra and the special significance it held in Himachal Pradesh. "Sadashiva lit the lamps of Tantra in each and every corner of this area, but nowadays very few people in India have any real understanding of Tantra. Most of the available texts exist only in distorted form, and the original texts are very difficult to find. One of the few people who understand something about Tantra is the scholar Gopinath Kabiraj,[7] a disciple of Anandamayi Ma. Now you Ananda Margis should revitalize Tantra in each and every part of Himachal Pradesh."

The next day in Jammu, Baba continued his discussions on Tantra. He urged the local Margis to try to collect the ancient Tantric texts, many of which were in the possession of local pundits, though many others had been burned by Muslims. In his discourse, he gave a long account of the history of Kashmir, detailing the origins of its name and pointing out that due to certain philosophical confusion the Indian people had developed an apathy toward history; as a result much valuable historical information had been lost or was never recorded. He also talked about the war raging not far away and told the Margis that Kashmir's future was very dark. "Great struggles lie ahead," he said. "In the meantime, you should make every effort to preserve Kashmir's culture; if not, many things will be lost." While on field walk, he told the Margis that there would come a time when Pakistan would cease to exist. "First, East Pakistan will separate from Pakistan and become an independent country. Eventually, both Pakistan and this new country will once again become part of India. Thus both Bengals, both Kashmirs, and both Punjabs will be reunited and the name Pakistan will be forgotten by all but students of history."[8]

After Baba returned to Jamalpur, he continued his analysis of the war on field walk and in the jagriti. As the Indian army was losing ground in Kashmir, Baba told the Margis that if the army would attack near the Ichhogil Canal, it would divert Pakistan's attention toward the defense of Lahore. Two days later, on September 6, the Indian Army did exactly that, crossing the canal near the village of Barki. Within a short time, they came within range of the Lahore airport, which forced the US to request a temporary ceasefire to allow it to evacuate its citizens. The battle in the Lahore sector raged until the UN mandated a ceasefire on the twenty-second. Afterward, Baba praised the actions of the Prime Minister, not only the astuteness of his strategy but more importantly the fact that he was a moral man who acted with moral courage.

Lal Bahadur Shastri died less than four months later, on January 11. Baba asked Vijayananda to prepare a condolence message to be printed in the organization's magazines. The draft he showed to Baba for his approval contained the following sentence: "Mr. Lal Bahadur Shastri, the honorable Prime Minister of India, died in harness." After a few moments pause, Baba told Vijayananda, "My philosophy is a little different. It is certainly laudable to die while working. In philosophical parlance, this is called karma sadhana. But it is even better to work while dying. This is called karma yoga. I want people to follow the path of karma yoga, not karma sadhana."

"It is good to die while working; it is better to work while dying" was a phrase that would be oft repeated by Baba in the years to come. It would, for many of his disciples, sum up the spirit of their missionary endeavors.

In 1966, Baba's pace became even more hectic. He spent more time away from the office, giving thirty-nine DMCs during the calendar year, and continued to increase the pressure on the wholetimers and Margis for social service projects and prachar. By now, this pressure was becoming a fundamental characteristic of the guru-disciple relationship. The carefree beginnings of Ananda Marga, when the entire office fit in a shopping bag dangling from the handle of Pranay's bicycle, had become a thing of the past, and often the older disciples would wax nostalgic about the "early days." For the young monks, raised in an atmosphere of dedication to an idealistic mission, Baba's pressure to materialize his plans and programs was as natural as the air they breathed, but for some of the older disciples it was a difficult adjustment. Some were not able to keep pace, among them Pranay.

By the end of 1964, the pressures of being the general secretary, directly responsible to Baba for the growth of the mission, had taken its toll on Pranay.

He had already begun to think seriously about leaving the organization, a thought that had first entered his mind the previous year when he saw the leadership of the mission gradually passing to the sannyasis, leaving him uncertain about his own place in the organization. Life in Anandanagar was like a microcosm of Ananda Marga's growth elsewhere in India. In only a couple of years, the project had grown to include a primary school, high school, degree college, technical college, hospital, children's home, students home, invalids home, leper asylum, academy for the handicapped, printing press, the central offices of Ananda Marga, and extensive agricultural projects. Living conditions, however, were still difficult. Nearly every day, it seemed, Baba was adding to the projects he wanted established and the programs he wanted carried out. He wanted regular progress reports on everything, and even when some of his programs seemed beyond the disciples' capacity to materialize them, no one would dare to tell him that they couldn't be done. Financial shortfalls were a daily reality, but the dire lack of funds was not an excuse that Baba was willing to entertain. Furthermore, Pranay had to deal with constant complaints and pressure from parents whose young sons or daughters had left home to become Ananda Marga monks and nuns. In some cases, he advised trainees to return to their parents or discouraged candidates from going to the wholetimer training center, actions which brought him into conflict with Satyananda. For Pranay, all of this had become a source of increasing anxiety and stress.

It would, however, take Pranay more than a year to follow through on what was for him a very painful decision. In late January 1966, Baba sent word to Anandanagar for Pranay to transfer Sarveshvarananda, then a teacher in the technical college, to Orissa with instructions to start a school there, and for Pranay to make arrangements for another teacher to take his place. This set Pranay off. He had already been at odds with some of Baba's decisions; this one seemed to have no logic behind it. Why transfer his only available Bengali-speaking teacher in the technical college and send him to a part of Orissa where there were no Margis to support him, where he didn't even speak the local language, and ask him to start a school? Pranay sat down and wrote a long letter to Baba in which he complained that he was giving them voluminous works to carry out with no money in their coffers and creating even more difficulties with such transfers. "You are the guru and the president," he wrote, "but I am the general secretary. As the general secretary, I am countermanding this order."

When Baba received the letter in Jamalpur, he declared that he was relieving Pranay of his post as general secretary and posting Prashantananda in his place, a young monk still in his mid-twenties. He called four acharyas, including the stalwart ex-policeman Kedarnath Sharma, and sent them to Anandanagar to relieve Pranay of his duties and accompany him back to Jamalpur.

When the four acharyas arrived in Anandanagar with news of Baba's decision, it sent shock waves throughout the rapidly growing settlement. It was a natural reaction—Pranay was the first Margi and the only general secretary they had ever known—but everyone knew that Baba was implacable in matters of organizational discipline. Pranay dutifully handed over the accounts and other records to Prashantananda and went to the station with the four acharyas, accompanied by the rest of the Margis and wholetimers from Anandanagar, some of them crying openly. Pranay told them not to cry. "I am not leaving Anandamurti," he said. "He wanted me to work for this length of time and now it is finished. Now it is your turn to work for Ananda Marga and establish Baba's mission."

Instead of going straight to Jamalpur, as Baba had ordered, Pranay broke his journey in Kiul, where they were to change trains. He spent a day there at a friend's house to prepare himself for his encounter with Baba. Pranay reached Jamalpur the following evening, walked to Baba's house, and knocked on his door. When Baba opened the door, Pranay told him that he was leaving the organization and handed him the diaries in which he had handwritten Baba's instructions for performing the various lessons of *vishesh* yoga and kapalik sadhana.⁹ Baba accepted the diaries and gave Pranay his namaskar, but other than that he remained silent. It was the last time that disciple and master would meet face to face. In the months that followed, Pranay would go half-mad and complain that he was seeing Baba wherever he looked. Baba asked Chandranath and others to take care of him. Slowly he regained his mental balance, but he would remain estranged from the organization until after Baba's death, though he remained devoted to Baba as his guru and continued to perform his spiritual practices with strict regularity.¹⁰

In January 1965, at the Ara DMC, Dr. Ramesh and Shashi Rainjan went on field walk with Baba near the aerodrome. During that walk, Baba stopped and pointed to an irregular mosaic of cracks in the earth. After explaining how these cracks were different from the usual summer cracks, he said, "Such a pattern of cracks presages the immanent possibility of a severe famine; if the shortage of water continues for one or two more years, then this famine is sure to occur."

A year and a half later, a terrible famine broke out in Southern Bihar due to a prolonged drought. As news of the famine began to circulate, Dr. Ramesh and Shashi Rainjan, both working for the relief section of ERAWS, came to Jamalpur and requested Baba's PA, Abhedananda, for permission to go on field walk. As soon as Baba came out of his house, he started speaking about the drought.

"Those of you who wish to serve humanity now have your chance. I would like you all to cooperate in this effort and form a committee to help you carry out your plans."

As they walked toward the tiger's grave, he discussed with them how to get the work off the ground. Ramesh asked him what they should name the committee. "In Ananda Marga," Baba said, "we should not name anything after individuals. In our organization, everything should carry the name Ananda Marga. In the future, you shouldn't need to ask such a question."

Last Years in Jamalpur

They discussed it for a few minutes and then named it the Ananda Marga Drought Relief Committee. Baba instructed them to find out which areas were most badly affected, especially those that were not receiving relief aid from the government or other agencies, and to start working in those areas as soon as possible. When Dr. Ramesh suggested that they should first collect sufficient funds, at least a few hundred thousand rupees, along with supplies like food and clothes, Baba said, "That is precisely what you should *not* do. First start the relief work. Money and supplies will follow. Send a team to the worst-affected areas without any delay. You should be the first to arrive."

After receiving instructions from Baba on everything from how to collect materials and funds to how to organize and carry out their fieldwork, Dr. Ramesh returned to Ranchi and started putting together his relief team. Shashi Rainjan set up a relief office in Patna to administer the fundraising efforts, and Acharya Sarangi, the government's subdivisional officer for Aurangabad, arranged jeeps for the volunteers.

The first volunteers were six young Margi students from the Birla Institute of Technology and Science in Pilani, Rajasthan—among them, Mangal Bihari's eldest son, Ananda—who arrived unannounced with over eight thousand rupees and bundles of clothes. As soon as they heard of the drought, they started collecting money and supplies from the public, but rather than hand over what they had collected to some relief agency, they had decided to take it to Bihar and distribute it themselves. Dr. Ramesh sent them to the Nawada area of Gaya District, an extremely poor area that was one of the hardest hit by the famine. What they found when they arrived was more shocking than they had imagined. The government had yet to begin relief efforts there and local officials were at a loss what to do. Everywhere the boys looked, the ground was rent with fissures up to a foot deep and several inches wide. The land looked as if it had been scorched by fire; not a single patch of green was visible in any direction.

They loaded their jeeps with corn, the cheapest grain available on the market, and started going village to village, door to door, covering more than fifty remote villages in several days. Most of the people they met had not eaten for many days; many of them had not even seen food for days. The people were so poor that the boys rarely saw a cooking pot or a metal utensil, only some simple earthen vessels; nor did anyone even have salt in their house. It pained them to see how the villagers would scramble on the ground if a few grains of corn fell out of their jeep.

Money started pouring in from Margis all over the country, and numerous volunteers arrived. Dr. Ramesh formed them into teams and sent them to nearby blocks. Baba sent a message to all the volunteers: "Do not forget that the quantity of materials you bring does not matter as much as the solace the people feel from seeing you come to their aid. Even people who would have died otherwise can be saved by the happiness and satisfaction they feel when they see you."

When Dr. Ramesh went to Jamalpur to give his report and handed to Baba a bank statement for the account that he had set up for the relief work, Baba's mood turned grave. "I have not established this relief committee for depositing funds in a bank account. Remember, if even a single person starves to death in your jurisdiction, and there is even a single rupee in that bank account, then you will be held responsible."

After that, whatever funds or materials they received were immediately forwarded to the respective relief centers. Baba also insisted that they conduct regular audits of the accounts. A copy of the audited statements was to be sent to all donors, and if a donor specified that the donation should be used for a certain purpose, then a separate statement was to be sent to that person showing how their donation was utilized.

The relief efforts quickly expanded to cover all the affected areas of Bihar. Committee members started attending meetings of the government's Bihar Relief Committee, chaired by Jaya Prakash Narayana, which had been established to coordinate the work of the different relief agencies. Jaya Prakash was so impressed by the Margi's efforts that he started taking the report of the Ananda Marga committee first. He also helped them to secure government funding. In one meeting, he said that his workers went out for relief work shabbily dressed and came back with new clothes and new watches, but this never happened with the Margis. He also singled out Sarangi for praise for his efforts coordinating the work in the Aurangabad area and said that what the government workers did with twelve rupees, the Margis did with four. These remarks received considerable press in Delhi and Patna and helped greatly to buoy the fundraising efforts.

The relief efforts continued into 1967, and Baba continued to add new programs. The next was free kitchens, which were set up all over Bihar, then cheap kitchens. He created a program for building dams, wells, reservoirs, and access roads, part of the emphasis on solving the water crisis, all under the banner of "work for food." These programs became very popular in the villages. They gave the local people a sense that it was by the sweat of their own labor that they were overcoming the crisis. These programs were soon copied by other aid agencies.

During the Ananda Purnima DMC in May 1966, Baba announced that for the first time an avadhuta, Atmananda, had been posted overseas, to Kenya. He explained that he had chosen Africa because it was the most exploited and neglected continent, and thus the place where Ananda Marga was most needed.

In July, Baba went on a DMC tour to Western and Northern India. In Kota he held a ladies meeting, during which Savita asked, "Baba, why don't you give individual PC to ladies?[11] We have also heard that you keep a stick that you use in PC to give punishment."

Baba smiled. "Do you want to see the stick?" Baba pulled it out from underneath his pillow and showed it to them. "Why do you want to have PC like the men? Don't ladies already get enough trouble from their husbands and their fathers? That's why I give them PC, so they can get what's coming to them."

In the evening, the Margis gathered on the roof of the house where Baba was staying and sang devotional songs. The devotional mood became so intense that Baba called everyone to come closer and they started jumping on him, trying to embrace him, men, women, and children. When the wholetimers tried unsuccessfully to restrain them, he said, "Let them be. This is the land of Mira,[12] and I am in the mood of Mira."

The next day, Baba did a demonstration he would repeat often in the coming years with different variations. After talking about the roles the glands play in differentiating one type of bodily structure from another, he called an avadhuta to the front, touched him with his stick, and said that his glands were now being converted into those of a monkey. The avadhuta started grunting and jumping up and down frenetically. While he was doing so, Baba told the astonished Margis that if he left him in that state for six hours, he would start to grow monkey hair and show other structural changes. Baba touched him again and his strange behavior ceased. Then he asked someone to give him a cup of warm milk.

From Kota, Baba went to Delhi by train. The next morning, he boarded a plane for Patna, along with Kshitij and Asthana. During the stopover in Varanasi, it was announced that the plane had mechanical problems and was delayed indefinitely. Baba asked Kshitij to see about arranging a car to Patna, a five-to-six hour ride. Kshitij suggested that there might be another flight available, and with a nod from Baba he went to check. In the meantime, Asthana took Baba to the waiting room where the local Margis had gathered to receive him during his stopover. While Baba was chatting with the Margis and enjoying the devotional songs, Kshitij returned and informed him that there was another flight, but the airline could not guarantee when it would leave. "Don't waste any more time," Baba told him. "I have to give evening General Darshan in Patna. Arrange for the car immediately." Kshitij hired a private taxi and packed the food that the Margis had brought for Baba. When everything was ready, he informed Baba. "Are you sure the driver knows the way?" Baba asked. Kshitij assured him that he did and they set off.

As they were leaving the outskirts of Varanasi, they encountered a detour. Despite Kshitij's previous assurances, neither he nor the driver was sure they were on the right road. Kshitij asked the driver to stop for a moment so he could get out and ask someone for directions. When he returned with confirmation that they were on the right road, Baba pointed out that he had not thanked the person who gave him directions. Kshitij apologized to Baba and they set off again. Some time later they met with another detour. Again Kshitij got out to verify the directions, and again Baba brought it to his attention that he had forgotten to thank the person. When they reached the Ara-Patna turning, they came to an unmarked fork in the road. Kshitij started to get out to ask for directions but Baba stopped him.

"Twice you've asked for directions and twice you've neglected to show the common courtesy of saying thank you to the person who helped you. This time I will ask for directions myself."

Baba told the driver to pull up to the curb where an old man was sitting. He asked him in Bhojpuri if this was the way to Patna. The old man jumped to his feet holding a garland in his hands. "Yes, Baba, this is the way to Patna." He placed the garland around Baba's neck.

Baba patted the old man affectionately on the cheek, asked him how he was doing, and gave him his blessing. "Now you should go and eat something; you haven't eaten all day."

"Yes, Baba. Had you not come, I would have been here until night without eating anything. I knew you would come. I've been waiting here to give you this garland."

Once they were back in the car, Baba told his curious disciples that the old man's name was Sarju Pahadi, a Bhojpuri-speaking Margi from a village in Ara District. "He is a good devotee, but he is very poor. For this reason, he has found it very difficult to attend darshan. He had a dream that I would be passing this way by car on my way from Varanasi, so he left his house early this morning and walked several hours to reach this place. He did not want to take food before he saw me."

By this time, Kshitij was annoyed that Baba had put his physical body to so much trouble just to take this man's garland. As they were heading out of Ara, Asthana smiled and said softly to Baba, "Baba, you did all this just to grace this old man."

"It's okay," Baba replied. Though it was late in the afternoon, Baba still had not eaten. In the end, they arrived in Patna just in time for the scheduled program. Baba's packed lunch went unopened.

In the second week of September, Baba left Jamalpur for a DMC tour that took him to seven different cities in different parts of India. Before leaving for the tour, Baba informed the Margis and workers in Gujarat that the DMC in Surat would be cancelled unless the school that he had earlier asked them to open was up and running by the time he reached there. With less than a month remaining before his visit, Baba's ultimatum provided the necessary impetus for the local Margis to find a building and open the school. Baba arrived in Surat on the twenty-sixth and was brought to the house of Kanchanlal Seth, a multimillionaire businessman who had recently taken initiation.

Kanchanlal's house was a spacious three-story mansion located in an upper-class neighborhood. In preparation for Baba's three-day stay, he had recarpeted the entire first floor with white velvet carpets. By the time Baba arrived, the house was full of Margis and wholetimers who had gathered to receive him. The moment Baba sat down on the bed in his room, however, he started acting uncomfortable. "Where have you brought me?" he asked. "What kind of a place is this? Who has arranged for me to stay here? Call the district secretary! I cannot stay in this place!" Acharya Keshavananda offered Baba some water, but he refused to drink it. "I do not want to take even a single drop of water in this place! Turn off the fan! I don't want to use even a single penny of electricity from this house!"

Everyone was stunned. Lakshmi Chand Ananda, who had accompanied Baba on the train from Bombay, tried to placate him. "Baba, it is much too hot in this room without a fan. It's nearly forty degrees." But Baba would not relent. Then Lakshmi Chand brought out a thermos of *musambi* juice and offered to pour him a glass. "Baba this is not from this house; I brought it with me from Bombay."

"I cannot drink it here," Baba said. "Save it for me."

Keshavananda went out to talk to the Margis and explain the situation. V.J. Jani immediately offered his house for Baba to stay. When Keshavananda brought him to Baba, Baba asked, "My son, do you have a little room in your house where your Baba can stay?"

"Baba, my house is very simple," he replied, "but it is yours. The Dadas thought it would be better if you stayed here."

"I would much rather stay in a simple person's house."

V.J. and Sambuddhananda rushed over to Jani's house to prepare a room for Baba, though there was little they could do other than put a clean sheet over the bed and set up a partition. Once they brought Baba there, however, he was happy. An old lady, who had tried to offer him something to drink at Kanchanlal's house, offered him a glass of water. This time he accepted, draining the glass in one go. Shankarananda started massaging Baba's hand and Baba said to him, "Look, before taking food in someone's house, you should inquire what sort of food it is, whether it is worthy to be eaten or not. And if it is not worthy to be eaten, then a spiritual monk should starve rather than eat that food. But I have made householders exempt from this rule; if they are in danger of starvation, then they can eat it in order to survive."

Baba remained in Jani's house for the next three days and gave darshan in the nearby Regional Institute of Technology, where Jani was the principal. In the meantime, Kanchanlal made repeated requests to meet Baba, but the dadas would not let him. The next day, while giving PC at the school, Baba asked the unit secretary, Mahendra Bhai Joshi, how Kanchanlal was doing.

"Baba, he is very distraught that you refused to stay in his house."

"What could I do? I am bound by the laws of dharma."

When he left Baba's room, Mahendra phoned Kanchanlal and informed him that Baba had been asking about him. Kanchanlal started for Jani's residence and was stopped at the gate by Madhavananda, who refused to let him in. When

Kanchanlal told him that Baba was calling for him, Madhavananda went to check with Baba. This time Baba softened his stance. "I have not called for him, but you can send him in once I have finished giving PC."

When Kanchanlal entered the room, he did full prostration and knelt in front of Baba's cot with his hands folded to his chest.

"Do you do your sadhana twice a day?" Baba asked.

Kanchanlal remained silent.

"You don't, do you?" Baba asked. Kanchanlal nodded in agreement.

"Do you follow the principles of yama and niyama?

Once again he remained silent.

"The answer is no," Baba said, and again Kanchanlal agreed.

"Do you realize that you have accumulated your wealth by exploiting thousands of innocent people?"

"Yes, Baba," he replied, his head bowed.

"Was that not wrong of you?"

"Yes, Baba."

"If I stay in your house, will people not say that Baba supports this sin?"

"Yes, Baba."

"Do you want Baba to be blamed for that?"

"No, Baba."

"Whatever may be, you are my son. I want you to take an oath that you will not perform any more dishonest deeds and that you will try your best to follow yama and niyama from now on. Do this and then I will come to your house."

Kanchanlal gave his promise and left Baba's room with a lightened heart, but afterward Baba said to Sambuddhananda, "The man will never change his habits, because if he did, he would lose his wealth. So I will never be able to stay in his house."

After Surat, Baba went to Bombay for the final DMC of the tour and from there back to Jamalpur. It was the end of one era and the beginning of another. Ananda Marga had begun as a small circle of devotees gathered around a spiritual master who hid his greatness behind the unassuming guise of a simple railway clerk in a small Indian town. The circle continued to widen, soon at a dizzying pace that even his disciples found difficult to comprehend. Along the way, the character of their lives began to change as they imbibed the teachings of their guru that theirs should be a pauseless struggle against injustice and exploitation, a continuous effort for the upliftment and enlightenment of society in all arenas of human endeavor. They watched him as he built an organization and became the sternest of taskmasters, directing that organization like a driver tugging at the reins of a team of horses and urging it toward an ideal that seemed beyond their reach, if not for his assurances that their efforts would one day be crowned with victory. All that was left now to bring this era to a close was his departure from Jamalpur, an eventuality that could no longer be delayed.

XXXIII

Departure

No power in heaven and earth can separate me from my children. Even if this universe comes to an end, I will be with them in the expressionless Cosmos. My children—be they gentle, be they naughty—they are mine.[1]

At the end of September, Baba informed the Margis that it was now time for him to leave his job at the railway office and dedicate all his time to the work of the mission. It was something they had been hoping to hear for a number of years. The following day, Baba applied for an extended leave in preparation for his departure. He was granted three months leave, until the end of December. In the middle of October, he declared his intentions to shift to Anandanagar. Then he left Jamalpur to go on tour, and he remained on tour until the end of the year.

The ten-week tour, which covered all of India, would be the longest and most extensive of Baba's life, a preview of the years to come. It was witness to the first two films ever taken of him, both silent films, one of the DMC in Madras and another of a field walk to the Elephanta caves near Bombay. People flocked to see him wherever he went, and the increased exposure and added press thrust him even more prominently into the public eye. Thousands were curious to see the guru of Ananda Marga, if only from a distance, and a number of social dignitaries and intellectuals made requests to meet him, all turned down due to Baba's policy of only meeting initiated disciples.

On more than one occasion, fundamentalist Hindu groups took advantage of Baba's increased exposure to publicly voice their displeasure with his teachings. When Baba was leaving Gorakhpur on the twelfth of December, the mahant from the famous Gorakhnath temple arrived at the station with a large crowd of followers carrying anti-Ananda Marga banners and shouting slogans. Baba was sitting with a group of devotees in Acharya Shyama Narayana Srivastava's private coach,[2] awaiting his departure for Muzaffarpur, which would eventually be delayed by a couple of hours. As he looked out the window at the demonstrators, he asked the name of the mahant.

"Baba, his name is Mahant Digvijayanath," someone said.

"Ah yes, Digvijayanath. He is a great sinner. He is a drunkard and misuses the money of the common people. He keeps many different kinds of alcohol in his room. What I would like to ask him, and people like him in these rich temples, is, How are you using your great wealth to help the common people? People fight to become the mahant of these temples, but of what use is their wealth to the people who are suffering in this country? They have a storeroom filled with gold bars in the Gorakhnath temple. Let them explain to me what good their hoard of gold is doing the people outside their doors who have difficulty feeding their children."

After continuing in this vein for several minutes, Baba mentioned that there was one good man in the Gorakhnath temple, Akshaya Kumar Bandopadhyaya, who was a true scholar, a spiritual aspirant, and a man of philosophical nature whom the temple authorities employed to answer their letters. Then he changed the subject and paid no more attention to the demonstration taking place outside his window.

Although the annual year-end DMC was held in Gazipur on the twenty-sixth, a special DMC was scheduled for the thirtieth at Jamalpur. Devotees came from all over the country to attend the event that would commemorate Baba's departure from the place where both he and his mission had taken birth. A couple of days before the DMC, Baba took a few monks and some Margis to visit the places of his childhood. One of the Margis brought along a film camera and recorded parts of the walk. Baba showed them where he had studied, the temple where he had recited the dhyana mantra of Shiva, and the mosque of Jamal Mina, the Muslim saint from whom Jamalpur got its name. Then he led them toward the hills and showed them the different spots near Kalipahar where he used to sit and meditate. He pointed out the hill to the west of Death Valley where he used to play the flute, and walked out onto the pier overlooking the reservoir where he would sometimes meditate when he was done playing.

As they walked, he told stories of his childhood, some that people had never heard before, such as the time in the seventh grade when he had been meditating and a sadhu had jumped out of a tree, grabbed his hand, and took him to another secluded spot to meditate together. After ascending Kalipahar, he pointed out a mountain in the distance and told the Margis that Shiva used to meditate there. It was a very old hill, he said, where many ancient, invaluable artifacts were lying buried, waiting to be unearthed. He even allowed the Margis to take snapshots of him meditating in lotus posture on one of his old spots, facing the forested valley of the Kharagpur Hills, still an untamed wilderness. Finally, Baba led them back down to the field and to the three palm trees where he told the history of that *tantra pitha* after insisting that everyone remove their shoes before they enter. The walk ended, as usual, at the tiger's grave.

In the meantime, a huge tent had been erected in the jagriti courtyard, and it was soon filled to overflowing. Despite the poignant sadness and the pangs of separation felt by the Jamalpur Margis, the atmosphere was alive with the devotional fervor of the disciples, a scene as intense as any that had gone before it in the nine years of the jagriti's existence. In every corner of the grounds, people were dancing and singing, falling to the ground in trance or crying loudly with tears of bliss. People would splash water in their face or massage them or give them something to drink. Then they would get up and start dancing again. Others were crying and praying for Baba not to go. Many of the local Margis, such as Ram Khilavan's wife and daughters, refused to return home at night. Baba spent several hours each day at the jagriti, sitting on a wooden cot on the veranda, but until the night of the DMC, he did not say much when he sat there. He just closed his eyes while the devotees danced and sang around him.

On the afternoon of the thirtieth, Baba visited the accounts office for the last time. There he and his co-workers said their goodbyes, many of them with tears in their eyes. He asked everyone to excuse him if any of his expressions had ever wounded anyone; then he gave away the personal items that he had left there. To Shiva Shankar Mukherjee, he gave the glass that he had used for so many years. Then he embraced him and said, "Shiva Shankar, though I am leaving physically, we will never be separated. Whenever you need me, wherever you might be, don't hesitate to come to me."

In the evening, Baba gave his DMC discourse on *bhágavad dharma*, the spiritual nature of the human being. He emphasized once again the guiding principle with which he had begun his formal teachings twelve years earlier: "Internal service, *atmamokshártham*, leads to fulfillment and immortality; external service, *jagaddhitáya*, leads to universal welfare. . . . When spiritual aspirants establish themselves in *bhágavata dharma*, by virtue of *vistara, rasa* and *seva*, their journey comes to an end. They become one with the nucleus, one with the Supreme Consciousness. At that stage, they realize the secret of the divine sport of the Supreme Consciousness. This is the true dharma of human beings, *bhágavata dharma*."[3]

After the discourse and the collective gurupuja, Baba gave everyone his blessing and a long *varabhaya mudra* that left the devotees reeling in bliss. Then he left for home with the promise of one last darshan the next morning.

Baba and Uma Devi spent the night packing and spending some last moments with Baba's family, especially Baba's mother who found the coming separation from her eldest son difficult to face, though she did her best to keep her composure. A few hundred kilometers away in Chinchura, at the home of Baba's sister, Hiraprabha, final preparations were underway for the marriage of Hiraprabha's youngest daughter, Ruby, thus fulfilling a promise Baba had made to his mother years earlier. Abharani had told her son, "Look Bubu, I know that one day you will leave home to work for the Marga. I have two requests before you do. First, you are the eldest son of our family and Ruby is the Hiraprabha's youngest daughter. You must not leave until Ruby gets married. Second, do not resign your job in haste." Baba agreed to his mother's requests. He and his brothers had taken care of Hiraprabha and her family since the death of her husband in 1950. He did not resign from his job,[1] but instead went on extended leave, and the date of Ruby's marriage also marked the date of his departure from Jamalpur.

On the morning of the thirty-first, Baba said his last goodbyes to his family and then went by car to the jagriti. A crowd of Margis was waiting outside his house. They accompanied his car as it wound slowly through the narrow streets of Jamalpur. When he reached the jagriti, he sat on his cot for a few minutes while Natkat Kedar sang a devotional song that brought tears to the eyes of everybody who was not already crying. He gave one final talk, exhorting the Margis to work to establish the mission, like a commander exhorting his troops to battle. Then he took a collective promise from everyone to fulfill the ideology that he had come to establish.

After the Margis had voiced their promise, Baba stepped down from the cot and took leave of everyone. He told them that he would always be with them, whenever and wherever they looked for him. As he moved toward his car, the Margis began weeping loudly. Many of them pleaded with him not to go. The volunteers had to struggle to open up a path for him. When Baba was about to get in the car, he turned to the Margis and promised that he would be back. One Margi in the crowd shouted out, "Krishna never returned to Vrindavan after he left." Baba smiled solemnly. "This is the starting point of my *lila*; I will be back." Then he turned and got in the car. The Margis surrounded the car and refused to let it move. It was only with great difficulty that the volunteers were finally able to clear the road. As the car started moving, hundreds of Margis ran after it. Many of them followed it all the way to the outskirts of Jamalpur. There they watched as the car stopped and Baba got out and gave one long last namaskar to the town that had sheltered him for the first forty-four years of his life.

It would be thirteen years before Baba would return to Jamalpur to give one final DMC. In those thirteen years, the city he left would remain much the same—a little more rundown, a little more crowded, but still the same sleepy, provincial town. The biggest change would be his absence, but the mission he had founded there would be changed almost beyond recognition.

Epilogue

When one sets out to complete a great task, innumerable difficulties must be confronted. The greater the task, the mightier the obstacles. That is why the person who wants to perform noble deeds must be ready to face opposition from the very outset. [1]

IN THE YEARS after Baba left Jamalpur, he spent most of his time with the wholetimers and volunteers, guiding them in their work, directing and reviewing the activities of the organization, conceiving and implementing newer and newer programs. The road was now open for Ananda Marga to become a powerful influence in Indian society, but as Baba had forewarned the Margis years earlier, the ideals he preached, especially the radical social ideals of Prout, would generate a growing firestorm of opposition from various vested interest groups, especially the state and national governments, who soon came to perceive the rapidly growing organization as a threat to their power.

This opposition did not take long to materialize. Within weeks of Baba's arrival in Anandanagar, the local communist leaders, alarmed by the sudden acceleration of Ananda Marga activities in the area, began spreading rumors that the Ananda Margis had plans to steal the villagers' land. Playing upon the fears of these simple tribal folk, they organized a mob attack on the morning of March 5, 1967. Several thousand villagers armed with clubs, spears, and bows and arrows descended on the small enclave of unarmed volunteers. Five monks were killed in the initial minutes of the attack. When the mob neared Baba's house, shouting "death to the sadhus," Baba came out of the gate to face them. For reasons no one could ever explain, the attackers began to flee as soon as they saw Baba, leaving the five dead bodies behind them. The Margis filed a case and eventually the block development officer, Ashok Chakravarty, and eight other communist party members were convicted of conspiracy to commit murder for their part in organizing the massacre. The court also issued a scathing denunciation of the government for its efforts to cover up the complicity of the police in allowing the attack to take place. As tragic as the event was, however, it was but an augury of things to come.

After the attack, Baba moved the Ananda Marga headquarters to Ranchi. During the next five years, the organization grew so rapidly that in a special report commissioned by the Indira Gandhi government in 1971, it was estimated that Ananda Marga contained seven million members; the report also claimed that every major train in India had at least one Ananda Marga monk traveling on it as the orange-robed wholetimers crisscrossed the country to propagate their mission. The numbers were a gross exaggeration, but they reflected the growing concern of the Prime Minister over the alarming growth of an organization whose social teachings were in direct conflict with the capitalist philosophy and growing dictatorial tendencies of her government. By this time, Baba had earned the double distinction of being the most well-known and the most controversial spiritual figure in India.

In the summer of 1971, Baba shifted his headquarters to Patna. In December, while leaving in his car for a field walk with Acharya Vijayananda, he pointed out some men on the street who appeared to be watching them. Baba told him that they had been tracking his movements for more than a month. "In 1967," he said, "the West Bengal communists made our headquarters at Anandanagar their target. They thought that if they could destroy our headquarters and beat a few of our workers, the whole organization would collapse. They committed murder, what to speak of destruction, yet since then the mission has grown manyfold. A few Congress Party politicians who have close ties to Moscow have studied the matter thoroughly with the help of the CBI. They have discovered that the actual headquarters of Ananda Marga is not situated at Anandanagar but in the brain of Anandamurti. Now they have made me their target."

Ten days later, he summoned his personal assistant and the general secretary and pointed to a suitcase. "You see this suitcase?" he told them. "It contains my clothes and other daily necessities. I have not told you yet, but the CBI, under pressure from the KGB, has been plotting against us. They will come to arrest me any day now. When they come, don't leave this suitcase behind. When they arrest me, they won't spare the general secretary, either, so you should also get ready." Baba smiled at the shocked looks on their faces. "Don't worry. This time, the fight between virtue and vice will be something to behold, but in time you will see that all their plots and intrigues will be thwarted. As you watch the drama play itself out, keep in mind that the workings of dharma are very subtle. They will do their best to stop us, but nobody can stop the progress of Ananda Marga."

Baba was arrested on conspiracy charges on December 28, 1971, at five in the morning. When the CBI arrived at his house, he was ready and waiting with his suitcase in his hands. It would take the government more than four years to begin their trial, during which time they conducted a public smear campaign against Anandamurti and Ananda Marga, accusing both the organization and its leader of everything from homosexuality to murder, without producing any evidence to substantiate their claims. It was a trial they had hoped would never begin. On February 12, 1973, under secret orders from the CBI, the prison physician, Dr. Rahamatulla, administered what should have been a lethal overdose of barbiturates on the pretext that it was a medicine prescribed by the Patna Civil Surgeon.[2] Baba went into convulsions and remained in a coma. Contrary to expectations, however, he did not die. As soon as he regained consciousness, he filed a complaint against the prison doctor and informed his disciples, who then alerted the press. Thereafter, he refused to take any food supplied by the prison. On the first of April, he began a protest fast that he would not break until his release from prison—five years, four months, and two days later. Throughout that time, his only nourishment would be two cups of liquid per day, supplied by his personal assistant.[3]

In January 1975, Baba instructed Acharya Keshavananda to inform all Margis in India that they should store a two-year supply of rice, dal, and salt for their families; he also instructed the wholetimers that they should not do so. On June 12, the High Court of Allahabad found Indira Gandhi guilty of two counts of election fraud stemming from her 1971 election. The decision, if upheld by the Supreme Court, would require her resignation as Prime Minister. Widespread unrest erupted throughout the country, as both the public and opposition leaders called for her immediate resignation. On the twenty-sixth, before the Supreme Court had a chance to meet and confirm the ruling, she declared a state of emergency. Under the sweeping powers granted her by the state of emergency, she proceeded to imprison virtually all prominent political opposition leaders; she also took advantage of the opportunity to ban Ananda Marga and imprison all those monks of Ananda Marga who were not able to go into hiding before they were arrested, as well as a number of prominent family Margis. Fortunately, due to Baba's previous instructions, those families did not suffer undue hardship during the twenty-one months that the state of emergency lasted.

In was in this context that Baba was finally brought to trial in 1976. His conviction under those circumstances was a foregone conclusion; he and his four co-accused were sentenced to life imprisonment on November 29. Though he had no witnesses to speak on his behalf, the courtroom was far from empty. Representatives of Amnesty International, the International Commission of Jurists, and the International League for Human Rights were on hand to observe the trial. In August of that year, Mr. Claude-Armand Sheppard of the Canadian Bar, in a report commissioned by the International Commission of Jurists and the International League for Human Rights, had this to say about the proceedings:

> The political connotations of this trial are inescapable. They are apparent in the testimony of some witnesses whose evidence appears to be designed more to discredit Ananda Marga than to implicate the accused in the commission of a criminal offence. They are also evident in the manner in which the Indian authorities make use of the trial to attack at every opportunity the motivations and conduct of Ananda Marga and of P.R. Sarkar.
>
> Reading the Indian press and official comments about Ananda Marga, as well as listening to some of the witnesses called by the

prosecution, one cannot avoid the conclusion that a governmental witchhunt has been instituted against anyone associated with Ananda Marga. Nothing favourable to Ananda Marga seems to be permitted to appear in the press.

... in the authoritarian climate of India today it is virtually impossible to find witnesses willing to brave the authorities by testifying on behalf of the accused. Indeed, many Margis are either in detention, or in hiding. Even if they could be found, such witnesses are said to be utterly afraid to come forward. Their testimony would expose them almost certainly to arrest. In other words, the accused not only have arrayed against them the entire power of the Indian police establishment, but even if they had all the funds necessary to prepare an adequate defense, it is highly unlikely that they could find, or if they found them, could produce, witnesses willing to testify on their behalf. Fair trials in a dictatorial framework are difficult to conceive and probably impossible to achieve.[4]

Though from the outside the situation appeared hopeless, Baba continued to assure his disciples and his fellow prisoners, including members of the political opposition, that dharma would prevail. One day, the assistant jailor, Bharat Singh, was accompanying Baba on his regular evening walk near the wall of the prison compound. Bharat, who looked upon Baba as a great guru, had a question on his mind. "The people say you are God. If you are really God, then why do you allow yourself to remain in prison? Why don't you use your divine powers to take yourself out of here?"

"I have never said that I am God," Baba told him. "But I tell you—I am here because I choose to be here. If I did not wish to be here, then no one could hold me against my will. The day I choose to come out, I will walk out of here a free man."

"That is easy to say, Baba, but how can I know that it's true?"

"Close your eyes."

The assistant jailor closed his eyes. When he opened them a few seconds later on Baba's command, he was astonished and frightened to see that they were now standing in a field outside the prison.

"Baba, what have you done! If you escape like this, not only will I lose my job, they will throw me in prison for having helped you to escape! No one will believe me if I tell them how you did this. Please, have mercy, bring us back inside."

"I have no intentions of escaping, Bharat. The day I come out of this jail, it will be due to an honorable acquittal. I only wanted to show you that no one can hold me against my will. Now, close your eyes."

When Bharat opened them again, they were back inside the prison.

Bharat was one of a circle of admirers inside the prison who felt blessed to be so close to Baba, despite the unusual circumstances. Another of these was Dr. Dharma Das Kalwar, the jail physician who had replaced Dr. Rahamatulla. Among the many stories he told of his time with Baba in the prison was the following experience:[5]

> In those days, there was a rule that the jail physician had to live within a certain distance of the jail, so that if there were any emergency he could go there immediately. One evening, shortly after I'd gone home for the day, an officer from the jail knocked on my door in a state of agitation and told me that there was an emergency, I had to come immediately. When I asked him what the matter was, he told me that Baba had escaped. I was dumbfounded. I had just seen Baba a short while earlier. How could that possibly be! I hurried to the jail with him. When I approached the gate to the courtyard where Baba's cell was, I saw the superintendent and assistant superintendent standing there. They were both very afraid of Baba. They considered him a great Tantric and would never approach him if I was not there, or one of the other officials who were close to Baba. When I reached there, they told me that Baba was not in his cell. Actually, they had not approached the doorway to verify the fact. They were too afraid. That is why they called me. They wanted me to go in and check if Baba was there. You see, from the gate you can see in through the open doorway of Baba's cell; you can see his cot, but there are blind spots. I passed the gate, and as I approached the doorway I saw a soft light coming from the room. When I looked in, I saw that Baba was floating in the air near the ceiling in meditation. The light was coming from his body. I was so astonished, I didn't know what to think. I must have blinked my eyes, for in the next moment Baba was back on his cot, still in meditation posture. I blurted out something like, "Baba, what was that!" "Be quiet!" he told me. I went back to the superintendent and said, "Why did you call me here? Baba is sitting on his cot, meditating."

In 1977, with international pressure mounting,[6] Indira Gandhi agreed to hold free elections, for which she was forced to let the opposition leaders out of jail. In her arrogance, she misjudged the acumen of her opponents and the level of public mistrust of her administration. Rather than rejoin their different parties—always numerous in the Indian political system—they banded together and contested the elections from a single platform, which they named the Janta Party, the people's party. Gandhi lost the election, the state of emergency was lifted, and the thousands of Ananda Marga monks and family people who had been detained for nearly two years were released, many having been severely tortured during their incarceration. The judgment against Baba was overturned on appeal and he was declared innocent of all charges—as he had promised everyone he would be.

On the day of his release, more than fifty thousand devotees showed up to receive him. The police blocked off traffic from the train station to the Bankipur Jail gate, a distance of approximately three hundred meters. Some of the incoming trains were so crowded with devotees that some of them had to ride on top of the trains because they could not fit into the compartments. In some cases, whole villages made the trip. That night, on the veranda of his house, Baba reminded the devotees of what he had said at the time of his arrest: In the end, dharma always prevails.

In the years that followed, the opposition to Baba and Ananda Marga gradually died down, especially as the scope of the many service projects continued to expand and attract nationwide, and sometimes worldwide, attention. The last major incident occurred in April 1982, when a group of seventeen young monks and nuns, all of them teachers in Ananda Marga schools attending an education conference in Calcutta, were brutally murdered in broad daylight in front of hundreds of witnesses. Once again, the culprits were local communist leaders who had whipped up mob sentiment by accusing the Ananda Marga sannyasis of kidnapping young children. The brutal murders, in which the monks and nuns were attacked with clubs and knives and then set on fire, were widely condemned in the Indian press and occasioned a wave of public sympathy for the much-maligned organization.

The last years of Baba's life were spent in Calcutta, though he periodically toured India to conduct DMC programs. As always, he was extremely busy overseeing the work of his organization, which by now had spread to nearly every country of the world. His lectures and dictations during this time were compiled into numerous books, including the *Liberation of Intellect: Neohumanism* and *Microvita*, both of which began to attract attention in academic circles. In September 1982, he began composing devotional songs. Over the next eight years, he would compose 5018 songs, which collectively became known as "Prabhat Samgita."

In 1990, he began to undergo health problems stemming from the aftereffects of his poisoning, including diabetes and high blood pressure. His personal assistant, Acharya Keshavananda, described his final hours and the days leading up to them:

> Since August, he was clearly in a hurry. He spent very little time alone; instead, he was calling frequent group and individual meetings. Over the last weeks, many times in the wee hours of the morning, say at three or at four, he would wake me and instruct me to call certain wholetimers. The first time it happened, I told him it was three o'clock, they would surely be sleeping. He became angry and said that if those wholetimers were not here within ten minutes, then he

would not have a chance to give them the program that was in his mind. Of course, I got them. We all became exhausted by his speed, but instead of slowing down, he accelerated. Sometimes we talked among ourselves, wondering about the cause of his haste. No one, however, came close to imagining that he was busy putting the final touches to his life's work.

One week before his departure, Baba gave kapalik initiation to the largest number of wholetimers ever. He requested one hundred. Because he had always been very selective in approving wholetimers for this purpose, we were not prepared and could only round up seventy-nine. He always rejected more applicants than he approved, but this time, without even asking any questions, he approved them all. We were bewildered by his behavior.

Immediately after the initiations, Baba became sick. This, at least, was normal. After taking on many persons' samskaras, he usually became sick. And this was by far the greatest number that he had ever initiated.

On the last day, October 21, his health actually improved. It was better than it had been in a long time. The morning was normal. He was working with the same tremendous speed that he had shown during these last months. Though he had composed the final two Prabhat Samgitas (numbers 5017 and 5018) late the previous night, he rose at three o'clock as usual to perform his spiritual practices. Later, he reviewed the work of various departments and gave instructions while shaving; even this was a usual part of his hectic schedule. He always told us, "You should not only be prepared to die while working; you should also work while dying." These words he clearly practiced.

Shortly before two in the afternoon, he said to me, "I want to think." As I shut the door, I thought to myself that he had never said such a thing before. After a few minutes, he called me. I believe it was during those minutes that he carefully reviewed all his plans and confirmed that nothing remained to be done. He asked me to send one of the new avadhutas in to see him. He spent one hour alone with that Dada. That was the last work of Baba's life, personal attention given to a young wholetimer. After that, he told me, "I want to rest now." These words also he had never spoken before. About five minutes later, he rang the call-bell; when I came, he pointed to his chest and said, "Heart." I ran to bring the doctors. They came quickly and began massaging Baba. But when they felt for his pulse, their faces turned ashen. His life force was gone.

Shrii Shrii Anandamurti left behind him a list of accomplishments that defies the imagination: hundreds of thousands of devoted disciples; a global organization with centers and service projects in virtually every country of the world; a comprehensive spiritual and social philosophy; more than two hundred books covering diverse topics from linguistic studies to children's stories to philosophy; over five thousand devotional songs. But for many people, the stories of his life and his love for his devotees are the sweetest and most satisfying part of his legacy. They are stories we can come back to over and over again when we are in need of inspiration, stories that can move us to laughter and to tears, stories that can give birth within us to the greatest of all human emotions: devotion for God. They are stories that can sometimes even save us when it appears that nothing else can.

Early in 2004, Acharya Akshayananda was diagnosed with cancer of the liver, stomach, and bone marrow. He was given chemotherapy, but the doctors held out little hope for his survival. In the first week of June, shortly before his third chemo treatment, Acharya Pranavatmakananda approached him and requested him to tell his Baba stories so that he could record them for posterity. For the past week, Akshayananda had been suffering from terrible stomach pains, and for months he had had a burning sensation in his liver. Wishing only to be left alone with his pain, Akshayananda became angry and shouted for him to leave the room. All these years, he thought, and he never once came to record my Baba stories; and now that I am dying, he comes like a vulture waiting to pick my bones. Yet, despite the verbal abuse, Pranavatmakananda would not desist. He continued to press Akshayananda, until finally the ailing monk agreed to talk for five minutes. Those five minutes, however, turned into three hours. By the time Pranavatmakananda asked him to stop, concerned about the strain on his health, Akshayananda was feeling better than he had in months. His stomach pains had quieted down for the first time in a week, and the burning sensation in his liver, which had persisted for months, had completely disappeared. The next day, he asked Pranavatmakananda to come and record some more stories. When Akshayananda told him that the symptoms he had been suffering for the past few months were gone, Pranavatmakananda assumed that the Baba stories had helped him to temporarily forget his pains, but when the doctors examined him a few days later, they found that the cancer was gone—as of the writing of this epilogue, more than five years later, it has not returned.

Whatever power these stories have—the power to heal, the power to instruct, the power to lift our spirits—I hope we may all feel it; and as we do, may we be aware of the boundless love from which it springs, the love that prompts the devotees to sing:

I do not know you, but still I am in love with you.

— Prabhat Samgita, # 3207

Selected Bibliography

Dhruvananda, Acarya. *Baba Loves All*. 2nd ed. Calcutta: Ananda Marga Publications, 1992.

Hamrahi. *Namami Kalyanasundaram, Part 1*. Calcutta: Ananda Marga Publications.

Hamrahi. *Namami Kalyanasundaram, Part 2*. Calcutta: Ananda Marga Publications.

Krpananda, Acarya. *My Master, The Supreme Guide*. New Delhi: Proutist Universal, 2003.

Nagina, Acarya. *Ananda Katha*

Sarveshvarananda, Acarya. *My Days With Baba*. Calcutta: Ananda Marga Publications, 1995.

Traveller, *I Meet My Beloved*. Philippines: N. A. Cantara, 1985.

Vijayananda, Acarya. *Anandamurti as I Knew Him*. Calcutta: Ananda Marga Publications, 1994.

Vijayananda, Acarya. *The Life and Times of Shrii Shrii Anandamurti*. Calcutta: Ananda Marga Publications, 1994.

Glossary

Ananda Marga: The path of bliss; the organization Baba founded to disseminate his teachings.
Acharya: Spiritual teacher; literally, "one who teaches by example."
Ajina: The sixth chakra, controlling point of the mind, located in the center of the brain at the level of the eyebrows, sometimes referred to as the "third eye"; it is pronounced "ah-gya."
AMPS: Ananda Marga Pracarika Samgha, the society for the propagation of Ananda Marga.
Anahata: The fourth chakra; the spiritual heart.
Ananda Purnima: The full moon in the month of Vaishak (mid-April to mid-May), celebrated as the birthday of Baba, as well as the birthday of Buddha.
Anna: One-sixteenth of a rupee. The anna was discontinued in 1957 when India adopted the metric system for its currency.
Arati: A Hindu ritual in praise of the divine.
Asana: Yoga posture.
Atman: Unit consciousness or soul.
Avadhuta: A monastic disciple in the order of Avadhuta.
Avidya: Ignorance.
Avidya Tantra: The branch of Tantra that concentrates on developing occult powers; for this reason it bears some similarities with black magic. It is also known as the "left-hand path."
BMP: Bihar Military Police.
Brahma: Supreme Consciousness; God.
Brahma Chakra: The cycle of creation.
Bubu: Baba's *dak nam*, or nickname, used by family and close friends.
Chakra: Psychic energy center. There are seven main centers located along the spinal column.
Crore: Ten million.
Dada: Literally, "elder brother." It is used in Bengal as a respectful form of address. It is commonly used in Ananda Marga to address male monks.
Darshan: Literally, "sight;" seeing the guru physically, or being in his presence; also used to refer to his talks.
Devayoni: A luminous being whose body only contains three fundamental factors: luminous, aerial, and ethereal.
Dharma: Characteristic property; spirituality; the path of righteousness in social affairs.

Glossary

Dhoti: A long piece of white cloth, several meters in length, which is worn as the traditional Indian male dress, in lieu of pants.
Dhyana: Literally, "meditation." Often used in Ananda Marga to refer to the sixth lesson of Ananda Marga meditation.
DMC: Dharmamahachakra—a program where Baba would give discourse twice a day for one to three days.
ERAWS: Education, Relief, and Welfare Section of Ananda Marga.
General Darshan: A semi-formal program where Baba would sit with his disciples and deliver a discourse.
Guru Mantra: The second lesson of Ananda Marga meditation.
Ista: One's personal conception of the goal; the personal God.
Ista Mantra: One's personal mantra.
Ishvara Pranidhana: The first lesson of Ananda Marga meditation, involving the use of mantra.
Kapalik: Literally, "one who has taken a vow to serve the creation." Here it refers to a technique of Tantric meditation that Baba taught to selected disciples. Also, one who practices kapalik meditation.
Kirtan: Devotional chanting of mantras.
Kshattriya: The warrior- or military-class mentality.
Kundalini, Kulakundalini: Latent spiritual energy of the human being, said to be lying coiled at the base of the spine like a serpent.
Kurta: A traditional Indian long-sleeved shirt.
Lila: Divine play.
Lungi: A length of fabric wrapped around the waist and worn as a kilt by men; Indian equivalent of the sarong.
Jagriti: Spiritual meeting place or center; ashram.
Margi: One who follows Ananda Marga ideology and practices Ananda Marga meditation.
MP: Member of Parliament.
Omkara: The sound om; the sound of the first vibration of creation.
Moksha: Salvation.
Mudra: Gesture.
Mukti: Liberation.
Narayana: A name for God or Supreme Consciousness.
Paramapurusha: Supreme Consciousness.
Paramatma. Supreme Soul.
PA: Baba's personal assistant.
Pasha: Fetter. The *asthapasha* are the eight mental fetters: hatred, doubt, fear, shyness, hypocrisy, vanity of lineage, vanity of culture, and sense of prestige or self-importance.
PC: Personal contact with the guru.
Prachar: Literally, "propagation." Here it refers to efforts to disseminate the teachings.

Prakriti: The Cosmic Operative Principle. In colloquial language, it means "nature."
Pranam: To bow, to greet with respect; often done by touching the feet of the person you are greeting or else by bringing the folded hands to one's heart.
Pranayama: Yogic technique of breath control.
Prout: Progressive Utilization Theory. The social philosophy propounded by Shrii Shrii Anandamurti.
Reactive Momenta: The as-yet-unrequited reaction to any action; samskara.
Ripu: Enemy. The *satripu* are the six mental enemies: blind attachment, anger, avarice, infatuation, vanity, and jealousy.
Rudraksha: A tree whose dried, corrugated seeds are used as prayer beads.
Sadguru: A true or perfect guru.
Sadhaka: Spiritual aspirant or practitioner.
Sadhana: Spiritual practice or meditation. Literally, "effort to complete."
Samadhi: Yogic trance; merger of the individual mind or individual consciousness with the Cosmic Mind or Cosmic Consciousness.
Samaj Chakra: The social cycle.
Samskara: Reactive momenta, the as-yet-unrequited reaction to any action.
Sannyasi: The word *sannyasa* in Sanskrit means "renunciation." A sannyasi is a renunciant monk. Many of the sannyasis in India are wandering mendicants. Most, however, belong to formal monastic orders.
Sastaunga Pranam: Full prostration before the guru as a sign of surrender.
Shudra: The working-class mentality.
Sutra: Aphorism.
Tantra: The indigenous philosophy of India, from which we get the science of yoga and meditation.
Tantra Pitha: A site where a yogi has achieved liberation.
Tic-tics: Deep knee bends with the hands clutching the opposite ears.
Trikuti: The spot between the eyebrows, sometimes called the "third eye" in occult sciences. It is considered by yogis to be the seat of the sixth chakra, the controlling point of the mind.
Vaeshya: The capitalist- or acquisitor-class mentality.
Varabhaya mudra: A gesture Baba would adopt to bestow his blessings and emanate spiritual power.
Vayu: Literally, "vital air." The vital energy of the human being is divided into ten different vayus.
Vipra: The intellectual-class mentality.
VSS: Volunteer Social Service; a wing of Ananda Marga that provided security for Baba and participants in Ananda Marga functions, as well as providing volunteers for service and relief activities.
Wholetimer: A dedicated monk or nun who works full-time for Ananda Marga. Also called "wholetime worker."
Yama and Niyama: The ten principles of yoga ethics.

Notes

Source Notes

Unless otherwise indicated, the sources for the material in each chapter belong to the Ananda Marga Archives in Kolkata, India, with a branch office in Warren, Vermont. The archive material consists primarily of recorded interviews conducted by Acharya Pranavatmakananda Avadhuta, as well as magazine articles and books published by AMPS, video footage, photos, and artifacts. These interviews or oral histories were recorded in Hindi, Bengali, and English. The Hindi and Bengali interviews were then translated and transcribed into English by various persons and made available to the author. In addition, the author also conducted his own interviews with many of the persons who appear in this book. Whenever more than one account appears of any incident, every effort was made to examine any discrepancies and arrive at appropriate conclusions. For example, more than ten people were interviewed who were present at the death demonstration in November 1954. Their oral accounts of that incident were then compared to the written accounts that appeared in old magazine articles present in the archives. Where there was disagreement over certain details, clarification was sought from those who had been interviewed. Finally, those details that appear in only one person's reminiscences were discarded and those details that were agreed upon by a number of participants were retained.

Preface

1 **Baba:** In Sanskrit, the word *guru* literally means "dispeller of darkness"; while it can be used as a generic word for "teacher" or "master," it carries with it an inherent spiritual implication. The literal meaning of the word "Baba" is "most beloved entity." Its colloquial meaning is "father." In India, as in the West, it is used to refer to one's biological father, one's spiritual teacher or priest, and God, the Divine Father. As an expression of reverence and affection, spiritual disciples in India generally refer to their guru as "Baba" if he is male, and as "Ma" or "Mata" or "Amma" (different words for "mother") if she is female.

I: An Old Soul

1 Anandamurti, *A Few Problems Solved, Part 1*, (Calcutta: Ananda Marga Publications, 1987), 54.
2 **Birth date:** The date of Anandamurti's birth, as confirmed by his brothers, was in

1922 on the full moon in the month of Vaishak, the first month of the Bengali lunar calendar. In the early publications of Ananda Marga, it was mistakenly listed as 1921. When this was eventually brought to Anandamurti's attention some years later, he joked that they should leave it—it would make him look older. To further compound the confusion, the date listed in his grade-school enrollment form, the only surviving document listing his birth date, is 1923. His brothers explained that when his father brought him for enrollment, he could not remember the correct date. The birth certificate for Anandamurti's brother Sudanshu, one and a half years younger, still survives. Sudanshu was born December 22, 1923.

3 **Vaishak:** The first month in the Bengali calendar and the second month in the Indian civil calendar (roughly mid-April to mid-May). Since these are lunisolar calendars, birthdays and most holidays are celebrated on the lunar day, which varies from year to year. In 1922, the full moon of Vaishak fell on May 11.

4 **Prabhat Rainjan:** The word *prabhat* means "dawn." The word *rainjan* means "dyeing" or "coloring."

5 **Bubu:** In most Bengali families, a child is given their legal name, or *bhalo nam*, at birth (the name used on legal documents and in formal situations), and a *dak nam*, or nickname, which is the name that family and friends use. Bubu was Prabhat's *dak nam*.

6 **Shiva lingam:** (also, *linga*) An ancient Tantric symbol, phallic in shape, which is said to represent the formless divine consciousness.

7 Anandamurti, *Namah Shiva Shantaya*, 2nd ed. (Calcutta: Ananda Marga Publications, 1985), 238.

8 **Dhyana mantra:** Mantras used to either invoke a particular deity or to meditate on that particular conceptual aspect of the Divine. In Anandamurti's book on Shiva, *Namah Shiva Shantaya*, he dedicates a chapter to the subtle mystical symbolism behind this mantra.

II: School Days

1 Sarkar, P. R., *The Thoughts of P. R. Sarkar* (Calcutta: Ananda Marga Publications, 1981), 144.

2 **Provident fund:** A compulsory contributory fund that provides for the future of an employee after his retirement, or for his dependents in case of his early death.

III: Kalikananda

1 Anandamurti, *A Few Problems Solved, Part 5* (Calcutta: Ananda Marga Publications, 1988), 21.

2 **M. N. Roy:** Manavendranath Roy's real name was Narendranath Bhattacarya. He was forced to change his name for fear of being caught by British spies. Roy played a leading role in revolutionary movements in Mexico, the Middle East, the Soviet Union, Indonesia, and China, before he broke with the communist party in 1929 and devoted himself full-time to the cause of Indian independence. On one of his visits to M. N.

Roy, Prabhat brought his brother Himanshu; he remembered Prabhat being closeted with Roy for a private discussion of over three hours while Roy's attractive German wife, Ellen, entertained him.

3 **Pen names:** Prabhat wrote under various pen names, among them Rangadadu and Priyadarshi. He used the pen name Afatab Uddin (Rising Sun) for his contributions to the Urdu paper *Ittafaq*, published in Dacca.

4 **Shravan:** The fourth month of the Bengali calendar, falling in July-August.

5 **Bhang:** A mildly intoxicating beverage prepared from the leaves of the cannabis plant.

6 **ISc:** Intermediate in Science degree. It requires two years of college-level studies and is equivalent to an Associate of Science degree in the US.

IV: Accounts Department: 1941-1947

1 Sarkar, P. R., *The Thoughts of P. R. Sarkar*, 116.

2 **Palmistry:** Palmistry, which originated in India thousands of years ago, is a branch of Indian or Hindu astrology (*jyotish*). The first book on palmistry, written by the Indian sage Valmiki, is reputed to be five thousand years old. The art of astrology includes analysis of a person's *samskaras*—or karma, as it is better known in the West; a prognostication of how those samskaras will impact on a person's current life (in other words, their fate); and aids or indications on how to alter those samskaras. Despite his reputation as an accomplished astrologer, Anandamurti taught his disciples not to depend on astrological prognostication. A person's destiny depends on their actions, he explained, and pointed out that the lines in a person's palm may change over time as a result of their actions or by the grace of God or guru. In 1982, Prabhat told Dada Chandranath that his samskara was to live until the age of sixty-four. Dada was approaching sixty-four at the time. Then Prabhat told him not to worry, he would extend his life. After that, Dada noticed that his lifeline, originally rather short, started growing. He would not die until 2007 at the age of eighty-nine.

3 **Natural remedies:** In his interviews, Gunadhar left a detailed record of the treatments and natural remedies Prabhat taught him, enough to fill a small book.

4 **Dada:** The word "Dada" in Bengali means "elder brother." It is not only used for one's older brothers, as in this case, but also as a common form of respectful address.

5 **Indian Territorial Army:** The ITA is comprised of volunteers who receive military training for a few days a year so that in case of an emergency they can be mobilized for the defense of the country. It is equivalent to the US National Guard.

6 **Anna:** A unit of currency formerly in use in India, equal to one-sixteenth of a rupee. Though the government abandoned the anna in 1957, replacing it with the metric system (one hundred paisa to the rupee), people still use the word *anna* in colloquial speech. Eight annas, for example, is fifty paisa.

7 **Partition of India:** In later years, Anandamurti would explain in fascinating detail for his disciples what went on behind the scenes during the partition of India, some of which he had put into his letters to Shyamaprasad Mukherjee. These details included how the Muslim League in Bengal presented false maps to Sir Radcliffe so that the Meherpur and Gangni thanas of Meherkis subdivision and Chuadanga, Alamdanga,

Damurhuda, and Jivannagar thanas of Chuadanga subdivision, which should have gone to India, were awarded to Pakistan instead. Similar deception took place with parts of Jessore and Khulna, and other areas as well. Other injustices were allowed to take place at this time so that certain political figures could save face, including Nehru. Shyamaprasad brought up some of these points in Parliament. In 1950, he resigned from Nehru's cabinet over differences in Kashmir and East Pakistan.

8 **Visits from political figures:** Gauripada Mukherjee, an office colleague of Prabhat at the time, noted that other political figures also paid visits to Prabhat during office hours. "We got our freedom in 1947, and then the election would be held to select the different ministers and all. Bihar always had a chaos of caste and creed. At that time, Jagjivan Ram wished to stand in the election, but the Thakur, Harijan, and lower-caste communities had great differences with him. At that time, it was the custom and tendency to go to a temple or see a guru or such persons and take their blessing before contesting the election. Prabhat-da used to remain in the office up until four p.m. After that he was not available, therefore most of the people used to come to see him during the daytime in the office. One day, I found Krishnaballabh Sahay and Jagjivan Ram both entering the office at the same time to pay him a visit." Jagjivan Ram was a former freedom fighter and social reformer who in 1946 became the youngest minister in Nehru's provisional government; after Independence, he became Labor Minister in the Nehru cabinet. K. B. Sahay later became Chief Minister of Bihar.

9 **Indira Gandhi:** During her first few years as Prime Minister, Indira Gandhi was quite favorable towards Anandamurti and Ananda Marga. During the North Bengal floods in 1969, she visited the afflicted area at the behest of the state governor. When she appeared at a public gathering, the crowds became unruly and Acharya Ramananda, who was leading the Ananda Marga relief activities, stepped in and restrained the crowd with the help of some of his fellow disciples. Afterward, Indira inquired from Shashi Rainjan, a devoted disciple of Baba and a friend of the Nehru family, about the young monk who had leapt to her and the governor's defense. A few days later, Ramananda received sizable checks from both Indira and the governor that greatly facilitated his relief efforts. A year later, however, when Baba asked Shashi Rainjan to resign from the central government and help establish the Proutist Bloc of India with a view to begin contesting elections, Indira's opinion of Anandamurti began to change.

10 Sarkar, P. R., *Prout in a Nutshell, Part 18* (Calcutta: Ananda Marga Publications, 1988), 60.

V: The Early Disciples

1 Anandamurti, *Baba's Grace* (Los Altos Hills: Ananda Marga Publications, 1973), 171.
2 **Sadhu:** The Sanskrit word *sadhu* literally means "honest." It is commonly used in India to refer to a wandering renunciant, or to any monk or sannyasi or swami.
3 **Trikuti:** The spot between the eyebrows is known in Sanskrit as *trikuti*, sometimes called the "third eye" in occult sciences. It is considered by yogis to be the seat of the sixth chakra, the controlling point of the mind. The word *trikuti* (three curvatures) refers to the confluence of the three principle psychic nerves in the human body, the *ida*, *pingala*, and *shushumna*, which meet at the sixth chakra.

4 **Yama and Niyama:** The ten principles of yoga ethics. The five principles of *yama* are: non-injury, truthfulness, non-stealing, avoiding over-consumption, and seeing everything as an expression of God. The five principles of *niyama* are: physical and mental cleanliness, contentment, service, spiritual study, and meditation on the Supreme. These principles form the first two limbs of Patanjali's Ashtaunga Yoga and are considered the foundation of yogic practice. In *A Guide to Human Conduct*, Anandamurti's book on yama and niyama, he says, "The spiritual aspirant starts spiritual practices with the principles of morality, of not indulging in theft or falsehood. The aim of such morality is the attainment of such a state of oneness with Brahma where no desire is left for theft, and all tendencies of falsehood disappear. In the sadhana [spiritual practice] of Ananda Marga, moral education is imparted with this ideal of oneness with Brahma, because sadhana is not possible without such a moral ideation. Sadhana devoid of morality will divert people again towards material enjoyments and at any moment they may use their mental power, acquired with much hardship, to quench their thirst for meager physical objects.... It must, therefore, be emphasized that even before beginning sadhana, one must follow moral principles strictly. Those who do not follow these principles should not follow the path of sadhana; otherwise they will bring about their own harm and that of others."

5 **Guru mantra:** The second lesson of Ananda Marga meditation. It is a mantra that the practitioner recites before starting any action or dealing with any object. The purpose of the mantra is to remind the practitioner that that action or that object or person is an expression of the Divine Consciousness. Thus, the practitioner imposes the idea of divinity on all actions and entities.

6 **Nath yogi:** The Nath tradition is Tantric in origin and traces itself back to Gorakhnath, a yogic master believed to have lived in the ninth or tenth century.
Tantra Pitha: A *tantra pitha* (literally "seat of Tantra") is a spot where a great yogi has attained liberation after practicing meditation there for many years. In ancient times, Tantric yogis would consecrate a spot that they had chosen for their daily meditation by performing certain rituals. The principle ritual included planting a circle of five trees—bel, silk cotton, banyan, neem, and Indian gooseberry—and beneath them five skulls—tiger, male cat, monkey, king cobra, and human. This ritual was supposed to empower the spot and facilitate concentration. The yogi would then do his daily meditation within that circle; if he attained illumination there, it would then attain the status of a *tantra pitha*. These ancient *tantra pitha*s are favorite spots for yogis to meditate. It is said that if one meditates in a true *tantra pitha*, then it greatly facilitates one's concentration and accelerates one's spiritual progress. Out of respect for the sacred history of that particular *tantra pitha*, Prabhat would always remove his shoes before entering.

7 **Sacred thread:** A thin circular cord (tied end to end) consisting of three strands that is worn over the left shoulder and under the right arm. Young Hindu males are invested with the thread around the age of seven as a rite-of-passage ritual in traditional orthodox Hinduism. In his article, "The Psychology behind the Creation of the Vedic Gods and Goddesses," Anandamurti explained that the sacred thread (*upaviita* in Sanskrit) was originally a deerskin that used to be worn over the shoulder during the performance of ritual sacrifices. The word *upaviita* means "hide," more specifically "deerskin."

8 **Pranayama:** Yogic respiratory exercise, an essential part of yogic practice and the fourth limb of Patanjali's Ashtaunga Yoga. Some pranayama techniques are primarily used for facilitating meditation and others, such as the one Prabhat taught Shiva Shankar, are used as treatments in yoga therapy.

9 **BMP:** The armed police of Bihar. Most Indian states have a separate armed police force. The civil police are unarmed. They staff police stations, conduct investigations, answer routine complaints, perform traffic duties, and patrol the streets. They usually carry *lathis*, bamboo staffs weighted or tipped with iron. The military or armed police are organized along the lines of an army infantry battalion. They are assigned to police stations, perform guard and escort duties, and are responsible for riot control. They also serve as a reserve strike force for emergencies.

10 **Brahma:** One of the most common Sanskrit words for God or Supreme Consciousness. Its etymological derivation means "one who is great and makes others great."

11 **Maya:** Often popularly translated as "illusion." Literally, *maya* means "covered" or "imbued with." In spiritual philosophy, it refers to the cosmic causal force that transforms pure consciousness into the expressed universe, thus "covering" consciousness with a mantle of matter and hiding spirit from view. In this sense, it creates the illusion that matter is different from spirit, when in fact matter is merely a transformed state of consciousness.

12 **Dhoti, kurta:** A dhoti is a long piece of white cloth, several meters in length, which is wrapped around the waist, passed through the legs, and tucked in at the back. A kurta is a long-sleeved shirt that generally hangs well below the waist. Together with the dhoti, they form the traditional men's dress in most parts of India.

13 **Sadhana:** Literally, "effort to complete." It is commonly used to refer to spiritual practices in general, and more specifically to meditation.

VI: The Death of Stalin

1 Sarkar, P. R., *Prout in a Nutshell, Part 15*, 2nd ed. (Calcutta: Ananda Marga Publications, 1992), 56.

2 **Chakra:** Literally, "wheel." In yoga philosophy and practice, the word *chakra* refers to the seven psychic centers that control the mind, the flow of vital energy, and, indirectly, the physical body. Each of these seven centers is connected with certain endocrine glands and nerve ganglia (plexuses). The seven chakras are located within the spinal column, the lowermost at the base of the spine and the highest at the crown of the head, and they are used in different meditation techniques as focal points of concentration. The Sanskrit names and locations for the seven chakras are as follows: *muladhara*, at the base of the spine; *svadhisthana*, two fingers above *muladhara*; *manipura*, at the umbilical level or solar plexus; *anahata*, at the heart; *vishuddha*, at the throat; *ajina*, at the level of the third eye; and *sahasrara*, at the crown of the head.

3 **Death demonstration:** This was not the first time that Baba had asked a disciple if he would like to experience death. A year earlier, he was sitting on the tiger's grave with Pranay when he posed the same question. "Will you bring me back?" Pranay asked. "Certainly, don't worry," Baba replied. Pranay agreed. Baba then commanded the *vayus* [vital airs or vital energy] to leave his body one by one. As he did, Pranay felt his life force slipping away. His breathing began to labor. He lost consciousness and had no further experience until Baba brought him back. "It was not much different," he later recalled, "than falling into a deep sleep. I felt a sense of happiness when I recovered my consciousness, though not spiritual happiness. And it was not painful at all, even the death rattle, which I asked him about afterwards."

4 **Mudra:** The Sanskrit word *mudra* literally means "gesture." In yogic science these gestures are used to symbolize certain spiritual concepts. It is also taught that each specific *mudra* generates a specific type of energy or feeling. Spiritual masters are known to adopt specific *mudras* when they emit certain flows of energy.

5 **Bodiless mind:** A mind that has left its body upon death; *videhi manas* in Sanskrit. It is then propelled by *prakriti*, the Cosmic Operative Principle, to search for a new body.

VII: The First Gathering

1 Anandamurti, *Subhasita Samgraha, Part 2*, 2nd ed. (Calcutta: Ananda Marga Publications, 1992), 53.

2 **Bhava:** One meaning is "ideation." Through concentrated spiritual ideation, an aspirant may enter into a type of trance known as *bhava samadhi*, a state of intense bliss wherein the aspirant remains absorbed in the ideation of his beloved, his chosen ideal of God. There are many types of *bhava samadhi*. While duality between the aspirant and his object of ideation still remains in this state—unlike in the two highest states of *savikalpa* and *nirvikalpa samadhi*, described in endnote eight—they are states of great spiritual intoxication.

3 **Railway colony:** The Indian Railways built railway colonies for the residential needs of their employees. As the residences were built, they were allotted to employees depending on their position and length of service. In Jamalpur, some were allotted to families and some served as boarding houses for unmarried employees.

4 **Eight-fold path:** About 2900 years ago, a great yogi was born in Bengal by the name of Patanjali. After spending a lifetime studying the different branches and schools of yoga, he systematized what was by then a myriad of different practices and approaches into a single, unitary discipline, which he then outlined in his book *Patanjali Yoga Darshan* (Patanjali's philosophy of yoga), more commonly known as the "Yoga Sutras," since it was written in the form of *sutras*, or aphorisms. He called his system *ashtaunga* yoga, or the eight-fold path (literally, "eight limbs"). The eight steps of *ashtaunga* yoga are: yama, niyama, asana, pranayama, *pratyahara* (sensory withdrawal), *dharana* (concentration), *dhyana* (meditation), and *samadhi*; each of these steps lead the aspirant progressively higher and higher until he or she achieves union with the Supreme, or *samadhi*.

5 **Ista chakra:** In the first lesson of Ananda Marga meditation, the initiate is assigned a specific chakra at which to concentrate during the repetition of his or her mantra. This chakra varies from person to person and is called *ista chakra*.

6 **Kundalini or kulakundalini:** Literally, "coiled serpentine force." The kundalini represents the latent spiritual force of the human being and is said to be lying in a dormant state in the *muladhara chakra* at the base of the spine, coiled like a serpent. Under the stimulation of yogic practice, the kundalini awakens and rises up the spinal cord passing through the various chakras until it reaches the seventh chakra, wherein the aspirant experiences the highest state of spiritual trance, union with the Divine.

This is believed to be the first time that the disciples had heard the name Anandamurti, which literally means "embodiment of bliss."

7 **Ajina:** Pronounced "ah-gya." The sixth chakra, sometimes referred to in the West as the "third eye"; it is the controlling point of the mind.

8 **Savikalpa samadhi:** There are two principle types of Samadhi, or spiritual trance: *savikalpa*, or the trance of determinate absorption, achieved when the kundalini reaches the sixth chakra; and *nirvikalpa*, the trance of indeterminate absorption, when the kundalini reaches the seventh chakra. The first is the merger of the aspirant's mind into the Cosmic Mind, and the latter is his or her merger into pure consciousness beyond all manifestation.

VIII: Death Demonstration

1 Anandamurti, *Ananda Marga Ideology and Way of Life in a Nutshell, Parts 5-8* (Calcutta: Ananda Marga Publications, 1988), 404.
2 **Darshan:** Literally, "sight." The sight of a spiritual master is considered to be auspicious for the disciple, conferring on him or her an instant blessing, thus this word is commonly used in the yogic tradition for any opportunity the disciple has to meet with or see the master. When a guru gives a talk or imparts spiritual instruction to his disciples, it is also called darshan.
3 **Prana:** Generally translated as either "energy" or "vital energy." It can refer to either the vital energy of a particular living body or to the universal energy that animates the cosmos (being the cosmic source from which all forms of energy, such as mechanical or electromagnetic, are derived). There is however a slight difference in the Sanskrit spelling that does not usually show up in the transliteration. The same word is also used to refer to the vayu that controls the chest area and respiration.
4 **Indian saint:** Two of the disciples present remembered that the bodiless mind gave his name as that of a nineteenth-century Indian saint.
5 **Widows:** At the time that this demonstration took place, the condition of widows in Hindu society was still quite deplorable, despite government legislation to the contrary. This social discrimination against widows was primarily based on certain passages in the *Manu Samhita*, the Hindu social code, and went to the extent of extolling the virtue of wives who immolate themselves on the funeral pyres of their husbands. Now, more than fifty years later, significant progress has been made in Indian society towards alleviating this discrimination, and widow remarriage is becoming increasingly common (though still relatively rare); however, life for widows in India is still difficult.

IX: Now Many People Will Come

1 Baba's message to the Margis, January 1975. Anandamurti, *Ananda Vanii Samgraha*, 2nd ed. (Calcutta: Ananda Marga Publications, 1990), 24.
2 **Pranam:** Literally, "reverent salutations"; the traditional form of greeting in India. There are three types of pranam. One may touch the folded palms to the chest and say *namaskar* or *namaste* [I bow in salutation]; this is the most common form. One may bend down and touch the feet of the person; this is reserved for one's elders and highly respected persons. Or else one may prostrate on the ground in front of the person; this is known as *sastaunga pranam*. Sastaunga pranam is only done before one's spiritual master or guru.

3 **Varabhaya:** The word *vara* means "blessing" and the word *abhaya* means "fearlessness." In this *mudra* or gesture, performed while sitting cross-legged, the right hand is raised upward with the palm facing outward, a *mudra* which signifies the bestowing of blessings, and the left hand is placed on the left portion of the lap, palm up, a *mudra* which signifies fearlessness. Ancient statues of Buddha have been found in this *mudra*, and it is assumed that he used to adopt this pose in the presence of his disciples in order to confer on them his blessings. Baba also used to adopt this *mudra*, through which he emanated his blessings, at the close of certain gatherings with the disciples, most especially at the end of Dharmamahachakra, a collective function described in the next chapter. Many disciples used to experience various states of ecstasy when Baba gave this *mudra*; due to this, many shouts and cries were heard at that moment.

4 **Touching the feet:** In the spiritual traditions of India, it is considered a great blessing and a privilege to be able to touch the guru's feet. Sometimes Baba would allow one or another of his disciples to massage his feet. This was a privilege much coveted among the disciples.

5 **Gurupuja:** Literally, "adoration of the guru"; a ritual wherein one offers one's desires and attachments to God or to the spiritual master in the form of mental flowers of whatever color and form one finds most attractive at the moment while simultaneously reciting certain verses taken from the *Guru Gita*. It is a practice Baba taught his disciples to help them develop detachment and surrender, two essential qualities for spiritual advancement. The verses used for gurupuja are: *Akhanía manìalákáram Vyáptam yena carácaram Tatpadam darshitam yena Tasmae shrii gurave namah/Ajinana timirándhasya Jinánáinjaná shalákayá Cakshurun miliitam yena Tasmae shrii gurave namah/Gurur brahmá gurur vishnu Gurur devo maheshvarah Gurueva parama brahma Tasmae shrii gurave namah/Taváravyyam jagatguroh Túbhyameva samárpayet*. [I bow to the Divine Guru, who reveals to one the Divine Being that encircles and permeates the moving and non-moving/I bow to the Divine Guru who by the application of the ointment of knowledge opens the eyes of one blinded by the darkness of ignorance/ The Guru is none other than Brahma, the Creator. The Guru is none other than Vishnu, the Preserver. The Guru is none other than Shiva, the Destroyer. The Guru is verily Brahma, Itself. To that Divine Guru I bow/All is your wealth, Guru of the Universe, unto you only I surrender.]

6 **Acharya:** The word *acharya* literally means "one who teaches by example." It is commonly used in India as a title for spiritual teachers.

7 **Quinquelemental:** The word appears to have been coined by Baba. It is derived from the Latin words *quinque*, meaning "five," and *elementum*. It refers to the yogic concept of the expressed universe being composed of five elements or factors: ethereal, aerial, luminous, liquid, and solid.

8 Anandamurti, *Subhasita Samgraha, Part 1*, 3rd ed. (Calcutta: Ananda Marga Publications, 1992), 6.

X: Bindeshvari's New Lease On Life

1 Anandamurti, *Subhasita Samgraha, Part 2*, 2nd ed. (Calcutta: Ananda Marga Publications, 1992), 93.

2 **Prakriti:** The creative principle of the Cosmic Consciousness, composed of three binding forces: *sattvaguna*, the sentient force; *rajaguna*, the mutative force; and *tamaguna*, the static force. According to Tantra, it is the interplay between these three forces that qualifies or conditions pure consciousness and thus gives rise to the manifest universe.

3 Anandamurti, *Subhasita Samgraha*, Part 1, 14.

4 **Prasad:** An offering of food to a Hindu deity or to a guru that is later shared among the devotees.

5 **Hari bol:** A Sanskrit mantra often used for chanting. *Hari* is a common Sanskrit name for God, usually translated into English as "Lord." Its literal meaning is "one who steals sins." *Bol* means "sing." Thus *Hari bol* means "sing the name of the Lord."

6 **Ji:** An honorific attached to the end of the name. It denotes respect, somewhat similar to Mr. or Ms. in English. It is also used to denote affection.

7 **Samskaras:** The as-yet-unrequited reactions of one's actions and the cause of rebirth. In order to achieve liberation or illumination, a yogi must exhaust his or her accumulated samskaras. At the same time, he or she must learn how to act in an egoless or surrendered state and thus not create new samskaras. The spiritual technique of acting without creating new samskaras is termed *madhuvidya*, or "honey knowledge." It is done by imposing the thought of divine authorship on any action, thus inculcating the feeling that the subject, the object, and the action are all expressions of the one Divine Consciousness. When speaking in English, Baba often used the words "reactive momenta" as the English equivalent for samskara.

8 Final breath: Tantra and yoga both teach that the final thought determines the next life. If a yogi is able to keep his or her mind fixed on God at the time of death, then he or she merges into Supreme Consciousness and attains liberation, thus escaping from the cycle of birth and death. This can be achieved by mastering the practice of mantra. The final breath is always an exhalation, and the second syllable of the mantra, repeated mentally during the exhalation, represents the infinite Supreme Consciousness. By concentrating on the mantra at the moment of death, the yogi's mind remains absorbed in the thought of God.

75 XI: A Philosophy Takes Shape

1 Anandamurti, *Subhasita Samgraha*, Part 2, 43.

2 **Guni:** The adjective form of the noun *guna* (binding force). See endnote 2, chapter 10. *Tamaguni* is generally translated as "static," *rajaguni* as "mutative," and *sattvaguni* as "sentient."

3 **Sankhya:** Philosophy propounded by the yogi saint Kapil approximately five thousand years ago in Western Rarh (modern-day Jhalda in West Bengal), a few kilometers from Anandanagar, the international headquarters of Ananda Marga. It served as the philosophical predecessor of Patanjali's philosophy of yoga, which borrows many of its ideas from Sankhya. The six recognized classical schools or systems of Indian philosophy are: Sankhya, Yoga, Vedanta, Vaisheshika, Nyaya, and Mimasa.

4 **Dharma:** Literally, "nature." It is the dharma or nature of fire to burn. It is used colloquially to mean either "spirituality" or "religion."

5 Anandamurti, *Elementary Philosophy*, 2nd ed. (Calcutta: Ananda Marga Publications, 1992), 1.
6 *Ibid.*, 4.
7 *Ibid.*, 8.
8 *Ibid.*, 99.
9 Anandamurti, *Subhasita Samgraha, Part 1*, 105.
10 **Religious beliefs:** In *Caryacarya*, Baba took measures to ensure that the new community would not fall prey to the evils of sectarianism. "Never attack the religious beliefs of anyone . . . If you attack a person's religious beliefs, it means you have attacked Ananda Marga." [Anandamurti, *Caryacarya, Part 1*, 5th ed. (Calcutta: Ananda Marga Publications, 1998), 17.] This echoes in part statements from the edicts of Ashok, made some twenty-two centuries earlier: "For he who does reverence to his own sect while disparaging the sects of others wholly from attachment to his own sect, in reality inflicts, by such conduct, the severest injury on his own sect."

XII: Samkalpa

1 Anandamurti, *Subhasita Samgraha, Part 19* (Calcutta: Ananda Marga Publications, 1992), 18.
2 **Shanti:** Peace.
3 **Samkalpa:** "Resolution," "determination," or "vow." Without samskara a human being cannot remain in a physical body. When spiritual aspirants exhaust their final samskaras, equivalent to the state of attaining spiritual illumination or liberation, they must then create a new samskara if they wish to retain their physical structure rather than leave their body and merge into the Cosmic Consciousness. This generally takes the form of a vow to remain on the earth and serve the creation by working for the welfare and liberation of other living beings. It is said that the great spiritual masters were liberated or realized beings who took a samkalpa to reincarnate on this earth for a certain period of time and guide others to the path of liberation.
4 **Ista mantra:** *Ista* means "one's personal conception of God or the spiritual goal." The ista mantra is the mantra that is given to the disciple in the first lesson of Ananda Marga yoga to use in their meditation. It is called "ista mantra" because it creates a link between the devotee and his or her personal conception of the spiritual goal. The ista mantra is a personal mantra, in the sense that different mantras are given according to the particular psychological makeup of the aspirant. The word *mantra*, sometimes translated by "incantation," literally means "that which liberates the mind."
5 **Vishvanath:** For decades afterwards, Vishvanath would enjoy the unique grace of being able to see Baba's image and converse with him whenever he wished, no matter where he or Baba was at the time.
6 **Maithili:** A language spoken in Northern Bihar; the language of the ancient kingdom of Mithila.
7 **Janusparsha mudra:** A posture in which the guru has his legs crossed and his hands on both knees, palms up. *Janusparsha* means "touching the knees."
8 **Sadhaka:** Literally, "spiritual aspirant," i.e. one who performs spiritual practices. It was a word that Baba commonly used, even when speaking English.

9 **Fifty Years:** Shortly after Baba's release from jail in 1978, he held a meeting with his monastic disciples and told them that the mission of Ananda Marga was well ahead of schedule. Acharya Ananda Bratati, who was present at that meeting, remembers that when Baba said this she immediately became worried that he would not stay until 2005, as she had long assumed he would. Not long afterward, Baba told a couple of senior monastic disciples that Ananda Marga was fifteen years ahead of schedule. Though this statement was much discussed among the disciples at the time, no one other than Ananda Bratati seemed to realize that it might be a veiled hint that Baba would leave his body ahead of "schedule." I was one of those who discussed this statement at the time. I felt proud of Ananda Marga's rapid progress but never connected what Baba said to the possibility that he might be planning to leave the earth well ahead of the time we were expecting him to leave. I even had plans to move to wherever Baba would be living after the turn of the century, so that I could be physically close to him during his last few years. I was not alone; many others were making similar plans. When Baba died in 1990, it came as a shock to everyone. We had all been expecting him to live until the year 2005. Such was the influence that Nagina's experience that April night at the tiger's grave had over the collective psychology of Ananda Marga. At that time we were unaware that Baba had given clear hints to his colleagues in the accounts office of when he would leave his body (see his conversation with Niren and N. C. Gangully in chapter 31 and endnote 4 from the same chapter). Nagina was as shocked as anyone else by Baba's unexpected departure. Once he got over his shock, he went back to his original diaries from the years 1955-1957—it was from these diaries that he wrote his book, *Ananda Katha*—and looked again at Baba's words, as he had recorded them. He realized then that they might have been more ambiguous than he had originally thought. It did not take long for some disciples to realize that this entire drama might have been staged by Baba for the sole purpose of planting in the minds of his disciples the idea that he would leave much later than he was actually planning, so that he could do his work unimpeded in his final years, free from the multitudes of disciples, such as myself, who would have surrounded him had we suspected that he might be entering the final phase of his earthly incarnation—especially when he began to suffer from serious health problems in early 1990. Whatever the explanation, this is a story that significantly influenced the generation of Margis that accompanied Baba on his sojourn through our planet.

XIII: Prachar

1 Baba's message to the Margis, January 1969. Anandamurti, *Ananda Vanii Samgraha*, 15.
2 **Prachar:** Literally, "propagation." *Samgha* means "society."
3 **Tattva:** The Sanskrit word *tattva* has a number of different meanings, including "fundamental truth," "theory," "principle," etc. *Sabha* means "congregation" or "meeting."
4 **Shikha:** A tuft of hair that orthodox Hindu men keep unshorn at the top of the head. Some Hindus believe that it allows God to easily pull them to paradise at the time of death.
5 **Oil mill:** In the traditional village oil mill of India, a bullock is tied to a pole connected

to the shaft of the mill. As the bullock walks in circles around the mill, the oil is pressed out of the grain. It is a common metaphor in India for repetitive or meaningless actions.

6 **Satripu and ashtapasha:** *Satripu* means "the six enemies." They are: blind attachment, anger, avarice, infatuation, vanity, and jealousy. *Ashtapasha* means "the eight fetters." They are: hatred, doubt, fear, shyness, hypocrisy, vanity of lineage, vanity of culture, and sense of prestige or self-importance. In *Subhasita Samgraha*, Baba says, "*Prakriti* exercises her influence on the human mind in fourteen ways. Some of these bondages are related to the external world and the rest are related to the internal world, the psychic world ... While moving towards the cosmic goal, while moving towards the Cosmic Cognitive Faculty, one must continue to fight against one's internal and external bondages. These external bondages, that is, imposed bondages, imposed from outside, are known as *pasha* ... And then there are six *ripu*. *Ripu* means 'internal enemies' ... So one should wage war against these eight external bondages and six internal enemies. This fight is with the left hand. And with the right hand, what should one do? One should serve the entire universe without any restriction of caste, creed, or nationality, and with the sentiment, the feeling, the knowledge, of Neohumanism: 'This universe is mine; all living beings are mine. I must serve them, I must help them. If I don't serve them, if I don't help them, then who else will?' If, in this way, you are fighting those inner and outer bondages with one hand and serving the universe with the other, what will happen? Your existence will become blissful in each and every field of movement." (Anandamurti, *Subhasita Samgraha, Part 17*)

7 **South India:** This was a common ploy used by the Margis in those early days in order to keep Baba's identity secret. Names that end in *murti* are common in South India and rare in North India, thus their claim aroused little suspicion.

8 **Samsara:** The world of relativity; it is often compared to a tempestuous ocean that one must cross in order to reach the divine empyrean at the far shore.

9 **Ista devata:** A person's personal deity in orthodox Hinduism.

10 **Mahabharata:** A great civil war engulfed most of India approximately 3500 years ago. This war was chronicled in the epic entitled *Mahabharata*. *Mahabharata* means "great India." The Bhagavad Gita, a central yogic text revered by orthodox Hindus as sacred scripture, is said to be an account of conversations between Krishna and his disciple Arjuna on the eve of the final and deciding battle. It forms one chapter in one of the nineteen books that comprise the *Mahabharata*.

11 Anandamurti, *Subhasita Samgraha, Part 1*, 52.

12 **Crore:** Ten million years; 3500 crore years is 3.5 billion years.

13 **Dvapara Yuga:** In Hindu cosmology, human society passes through four different eras in an ever-revolving cycle: the Satya Yuga (*yuga* means "era"; *satya* means "eternal truth"), or the golden age, the age of maximum spiritual awareness; Treta Yuga (*treta* means "third"), an age of partial spiritual decline, sometimes translated as the silver age; Dvapara Yuga (*dvapara* means "second"), an age of increased spiritual decline, sometimes translated as the iron age; and the Kali Yuga (*kala* means "dark"), the age of spiritual darkness and materialism. It is generally thought that we are now in the Kali Yuga.

XIV: The Circle Widens

1 **Hari kirtan:** (or *harinam kirtan* or simply *kirtan*) The practice of chanting the names of God. This practice develops devotion in the aspirant and is an excellent preparation for meditation. "Intelligent people should do kirtan as much as possible. When people, due to psychic complexities, cannot find the solution to their difficulties and they are at a loss what to do, if they sit together at any place and do kirtan wholeheartedly for a while, their psychic complexities will be removed and they will easily seize upon the solution to their problems." Anandamurti, *Ananda Vacamrtam, Part 22* (unpublished in English)
2 Anandamurti, *Ananda Vacamrtam, Part 7* (Calcutta: Ananda Marga Publications, 1987), 96.
3 **Dr. Bidhan Chandra Roy:** At this time Dr. Roy was Chief Minister of Bengal. He continued to see cases in his off-hours.
4 **Raghuvir Prasad:** There was a strong history of spirituality in Raghuvir Prasad's family. His father, Dwarka Prasad, was Paramahansa Yogananda's childhood friend and appears in a couple of early chapters in Yogananda's spiritual classic, *Autobiography of a Yogi*. His father was fond of telling stories of Yogananda while Raghuvir was growing up. According to Dwarka, Yogananda had several early samadhi experiences while meditating under a tree in the courtyard of the Prasad residence in Bareilly. The family always treated that spot with great reverence.
5 **Cikitsa:** Literally, "treatment." In 1957, Baba began dictating a book to Sukumar Bose during his lunch hour, *Yaogika Cikitsa o Dravyaguna* [Yogic Treatments and Natural Remedies]; it would be published in May 1958. The book contained a yogic analysis of the etiology of numerous common diseases and a course of yogic treatment for each that included dietary restrictions, asanas, mudras, naturopathic treatments, and natural remedies. During the course of the dictation, Baba mentioned to Sukumar that Kalikananda aided him in his research by gathering the plants he needed and trying the remedies out on himself.
In the preface to the book, dated the full moon of Karttiki (November 7), 1957, Baba writes: "The object of the art of healing is to cure a patient, both physically and mentally. So the main question is not to uphold any particular school of medical science; rather, the key task is the welfare of the patient. Just as diseased body organs can be restored to normal by administering medicines internally or externally, they can also be healed, more safely and more perfectly, with the help of Yaogika Asanas and Mudras. The aim of this book, therefore, is to make the general public aware of the Yaogika methods of treating the various illnesses.
My purpose is to let people cure themselves by practicing the Asanas and Mudras described in this book. People are requested not to take the risk of practicing Asanas and Mudras by themselves, but rather to do so under the guidance of an experienced Acharya (spiritual teacher). Ananda Marga Acharyas will always be ready to help without any remuneration. Detailed instructions for practicing the Asanas and Mudras, for bathing, etc. have been given in Part Three of *Ananda Marga Caryacarya*. If necessary, the reader may consult that book.
Along with the Asanas and Mudras, a list of some free or inexpensive and easily available, but proven and useful, medical remedies, as well as the methods of their application, has been given in this book. The public can make use of these applications by themselves,

or, if needed, may consult experienced Acharyas in this respect also." Anandamurti, *Yogic Treatments and Natural Remedies*, 3rd ed. (Calcutta: Ananda Marga Publications, 1993), i.

XV: Demonstration Year

1 Anandamurti, *Ananda Marga Philosophy in a Nutshell, Parts 1-4* (Calcutta: Ananda Marga Publications, 1988), 248.

2 **Baba's sandals:** In 1966, when Baba was in Raipur to conduct a DMC, Acharya Kailas Balla noticed that the sandals Baba was wearing had been repaired numerous times with small nails; some of the nails were partially protruding. Pained at seeing this, Kailas bought a new pair of sandals for Baba. At first, Baba told him he did not need a new pair—he hardly felt the nails. But after much persuasion, he agreed to accept the new sandals. Kailas kept the old sandals for many years as his most treasured possession. They are now in the museum at Tiljala that houses many of Baba's personal effects.

3 **Aparigraha:** One of the ten ethical principles of yama and niyama. It means "non-accumulation" and implies that a spiritual aspirant should avoid unnecessary possessions. The proper observance of this principle fosters simplicity in one's life, so important for mental peace. It is also an ecological principle implying the proper use of all natural and manmade resources without unnecessary wastage. While Baba praised austerity and was exceedingly austere in his personal life, he always made it clear that austerity was only an intelligent effort not to let unnecessary indulgences become an obstacle to the attainment of inner contentment and spiritual elevation.

4 **Master Sahib:** Dasarath recalled how one time he began his morning meditation with his usual sastaunga pranam before Baba's photo and somehow fell asleep in that position. He was awakened a few minutes later by the sound of Baba's voice calling him from within: "master sahib, master sahib, master sahib." Three times he heard Baba's voice calling him jocularly, each time sweeter than the previous. The third time he heard the voice so clearly that he went to his door and opened it, but no one was there. Then he sat and started his sadhana. When he saw Baba that evening, the first thing Baba said was, "So master sahib, how did you enjoy your sadhana this morning?"

5 **Amit:** Later he would become a monastic disciple, Acharya Amitananda Avadhuta.

6 **Luminous body:** *Devayoni* in Sanskrit. Luminous bodies are composed of only three fundamental factors: ethereal, aerial, and luminous. The solid and liquid factors are absent. According to yogic philosophy, a human mind can sometimes inhabit such a body for short periods of time due to certain attachments developed during one's lifetime. Luminous bodies cannot act upon the physical world in the absence of the solid factor, nor can they meditate in the absence of a brain. Once the samskara that caused them to take that body is exhausted, they leave and take another human body. They can occasionally be perceived by advanced sadhakas under appropriate conditions. There are seven types of luminous bodies.

7 **Lungi:** A single piece of cloth worn by men as a type of male kilt, the Indian version of the sarong. It is generally worn in the house under informal conditions and sometimes in public by poor people who cannot afford a dhoti or pants. It is also part of the traditional sannyasi dress.

8 **Manohar Lal Gupta:** He later translated most of Baba's early books from Bengali into English.
9 **Reactive Momenta:** A term Baba often used as the English equivalent for *samskara*.
10 **General Darshan:** Both Baba and his Margi disciples referred to Baba's discourses as "General Darshan," except for his DMC and RU discourses.

XVI: Divine Madness

1 Anandamurti, *Ananda Marga Ideology and Way of Life, part 9* (Calcutta: Ananda Marga Publications, 1988), 630.
2 **Taking on samskaras:** In the yogic tradition, it is said that a realized master can take upon himself the samskaras of a disciple if he so desires: for example, enduring an illness so that the disciple does not have to. Once, Dasarath asked Baba during a field walk what happened to the samskaras that he absorbed from his disciples. Baba replied that those samskaras could be neutralized. He could exhaust them through his own body, but they did a lot of damage to his body.
3 **Ishvara Pranidhana:** Literally, "running after God." Here it refers to the first lesson of Ananda Marga Sahaj Yoga. Dhyana literally means "meditation." Here it refers specifically to the sixth lesson of Ananda Marga Sahaj Yoga.

XVII: Problem Of The Day

1 Anandamurti, *Ananda Vanii Samgraha*, 3. This was Baba's message to the Margis on the occasion of the Shravani Purnima DMC, August 1957. In 1956, Baba had begun giving a twice-yearly message to the disciples, called Ananda Vanii, on the occasion of the New Year's DMC and the Ananda Purnima DMC, a practice he would continue for the rest of his life. In 1957 and 1958, he gave a third Ananda Vanii during the Shravani Purnima DMC.
2 Sarkar. P. R., *Problem of the Day*, 4th ed. (Calcutta: Ananda Marga Publications, 1993), 1.
3 Ibid., 3.
4 Ibid., 4.
5 Ibid., 6.
6 Ibid., 4.
7 **Ahimsa:** The first of the ten principles of the yogic code of ethics (yama and niyama). It means "non-injury to any living being through thought, word, or deed." Mohandas Gandhi used the word *ahimsa* for his principle of non-violence upon which his Satyagraha movement was based. While Baba paid great respect to Gandhi as a person and a social crusader, he disagreed strongly with his interpretation of this ancient yogic concept and considered Gandhism a "defective" philosophy that "instead of guaranteeing liberation from exploitation, favors the interests of the exploiters." In *A Guide to Human Conduct*, Baba discussed this interpretation of ahimsa: "The champions of non-violence (so-called

ahimsa) have, therefore, to adopt hypocrisy and falsehood whenever they seek to use this so-called ahimsa for their purposes. If the people of one country conquer another country by brute force, the people of the defeated nation must use force to regain their freedom. Such a use of force may be crude or subtle, and as a result, both the body and mind of the conquerors may be hurt. When there is any application of force, it cannot be called non-violence. Is it not violence if you hurt a person not by your hands but by some other indirect means? Is the boycott movement against a particular nation not violence? Therefore I say that those who interpret non-violence and ahimsa to be synonymous have to repeatedly resort to hypocrisy to justify their actions. The army or police are necessary for the administration of a country. If these organizations do not use force even in case of necessity, their existence will be of no meaning. The mark of so-called ahimsa or non-violence on a bullet does not make the bullet non-violent.

"Those who are not adequately equipped to oppose an evildoer should make every endeavor to gain power and then make the proper use of this power. In the absence of the ability to resist evil, and in the absence of even an effort to acquire such ability, declaring oneself to be non-violent in order to hide one's weaknesses before the opponent may serve a political end, but it will not protect the sanctity of righteousness." (Anandamurti, *A Guide to Human Conduct*, 7th ed. (Calcutta: Ananda Marga Publications, 1985), 6.

8 Sarkar, P. R., *Problem of the Day*, 4.
9 Ibid., 19.
10 Ibid., 24.
11 Ibid., 26.
12 **Ananda Parivara:** Literally, "blissful family."
13 Sarkar, P. R., *Problem of the Day*, 38.
14 **Democracy:** It was Baba's contention that democracy cannot promote the well-being of society unless the people are well-educated, moralist, and socially, economically and politically aware. "Otherwise," he said, "government 'of the people, by the people and for the people' will only mean a government of the fools, by the fools and for the fools." Sarkar. P. R., *Abhimata, Part 1* (Calcutta: Ananda Marga Publications, 1987), 12.
15 Sarkar, P. R., *Problem of the Day*, 40.
16 Ibid., 48.
17 Ibid., 49. In a later discourse, Baba said that he created Prout "to represent the spirit of *Samgacchadvam*." (Anandamurti, *Ananda Vacamrtam, Part 3*, 50.)
18 **Economic policy:** Section 1.27 of *Caryacarya* is entitled "Economic Policy": "You shall utilize unitedly the entire property of the universe considering yourselves members of a joint family. Remember, you are responsible directly for every child and every human being of the society. Do not strive to keep yourself aloof from them. Those who do not make use of this wealth, or misuse it, violate the orders of the Father of the Universe, because they want to deprive his other children, i.e. their own brothers and sisters, of their just share. In fact, such persons are suffering from mental disease. Make efforts to bring all such exploiters of society to the right path by means of mental and spiritual education; should you fail in this attempt, you shall create circumstances to compel them to follow the path of virtue and shall show them the path of spiritual practices for permanently eradicating their mental disease. But always bear in mind that this reform can be materialized only if you have true love for humanity." Anandamurti, *Caryacarya, Part 1*, 53.
19 **Bengali:** Almost all of the early DMC discourses were delivered in Hindi, the lingua

franca of Northern India. When a DMC was held in Bengal or Assam, Baba would speak in Bengali. In South India or overseas he would talk in English.
20 Sarkar, P. R., *Human Society, Part 1*, 4th ed. (Calcutta: Ananda Marga Publications, 1998), 9.

XVIII: Tantric Guru

1 Anandamurti, *Discourses on Tantra, volume two* (Calcutta: Ananda Marga Publications, 1994), 26.
2 **Kapalik:** Literally, "one who has taken a vow to serve the creation." In *Discourses on Tantra*, Baba states, "The entity that preserves this objectivated world is *ka*. Human beings who have taken the responsibility, the moral responsibility, of serving this *ka*, that is, of serving this objectivated world, are called *kápálika*." (Anandamurti, *Discourses on Tantra, volume two*, 72) It was the word Baba used to refer to the Tantric meditation he taught to his monks and selected family disciples, as well as to the practitioners of that meditation.
3 **Fear complex:** "The very first night that a Tantric goes to the burial ground he is stricken with fear; there is horripilation all over the body. But when he returns home after finishing sadhana, the mind is much lighter than before. When he goes out for sadhana the next night, he is much less fearful. And thus the Tantric steadily and slowly overcomes fear." (*Ibid.*, 133)
4 **Harinder:** This is not the Harinder mentioned earlier. When necessary, this Harinder will be referred to as Harinder of Trimohan in order to differentiate the two.
5 **Avidya:** Vidya literally means "knowledge"; avidya means "not-knowledge." The two words are commonly used in spiritual philosophy to denote the force that propels one towards consciousness (*vidya maya*) and the force that leads away from consciousness, towards matter (*avidya maya*). "In Tantra the endeavor to establish control over matter or over external forces is called avidya sadhana. And the practice which leads to self-realization is called vidya sadhana . . . To become one with Brahma, they [spiritual aspirants] must practice Vidya Tantra, and not Avidya Tantra. Of course, through either kind of sadhana, sadhakas gain freedom from the páshas and ripus. But the difference between the two sadhanas is that the practitioners of Vidya Tantra channelize their spiritual powers towards the attainment of Paramátmá [Supreme Soul], whereas the practitioners of Avidya Tantra utilize their acquired powers for mundane benefits." (Anandamurti, *Discourses on Tantra, volume two*, 63)
6 Anandamurti, *Discourses on Tantra, volume one*, 2nd ed. (Calcutta: Ananda Marga Publications, 1997), 161.
7 **Adrajji:** An insult for acharyaji.
8 **Murgi:** Literally, "hen"; thus Anandamurgi is a slur for Anandamurti.
9 **Kishun:** A direct initiate of Baba's, an acharya, and a founding member of the organization. He was quite curious about avidya practice and had many long discussions with Baba on the subject during which Baba not only explained in detail the history of avidya but also revealed to him some of their techniques.
10 **Marpa and Milarepa:** Both belonged to the Kargü lineage of Tibet, a branch of Buddhist Tantra. When Milarepa was a young man, he learned certain avidya Tantra

practices in order to take revenge on an evil uncle and aunt who usurped his family's land after his father's death and virtually enslaved him and his mother. Through the use of secret mantras and Tantric rites, he killed most of his uncle's family. Afterwards, ashamed of his actions and afraid of the heavy karma he had accrued, he resolved to seek out a spiritual master and dedicate himself to the attainment of spiritual enlightenment. This led him to Marpa. Marpa agreed to accept Milarepa as his disciple, but with one condition: he must build him a stone house. Milarepa agreed and set to work. When it was nearly finished, Marpa shocked Milarepa by telling him to tear the house down and build a different one on the opposite ridge. This scene repeated itself five more times, each time under a different pretence. Finally, Milarepa, his body nearly broken down from several years of backbreaking work, despaired of ever receiving initiation. He decided to leave and look for initiation elsewhere. After an unsuccessful attempt, Marpa's wife interceded on his behalf and convinced her husband to initiate him. After the initiation, Marpa explained that he had put him through such severe tests in order to exhaust the heavy karma he had accrued through his evil deeds. Had he completed the final house, he would have exhausted the last of those samskaras and thus would have attained liberation very quickly. Since he hadn't, he would have to spend many years meditating in order to reach the goal.

11 Anandamurti, *Discourses on Tantra, volume two*, 40.

12 **Sadguru:** Literally, "true guru." While the word *guru* can refer to spiritual teachers of varying levels of realization, *sadguru* means a fully realized or perfect master.

13 **Kamadal:** A traditional pot carried by wandering monks in India; it is used for begging alms, drinking water, and cooking food.

XIX: A Place Of Awakening

1 Anandamurti, *Ananda Vacamrtam, Part 34* (Calcutta: Ananda Marga Publications, 2000), 17.

2 **Ramnagar:** Kaoshala Devi recalled an interesting incident from the Ramnagar DMC in her interview: "Baba was staying in Sakaldev's place and we had all planned to go to the DMC. Suddenly my father got a serious stomachache. Since we were in Jamalpur, we thought that now we couldn't go to the DMC. So we went to sleep. Suddenly my kids shouted that Baba had come and rushed to the door. Baba came in and asked for my father. He touched his stomach for ten minutes. Then he said that he had a stone in his stomach but he was now cured. So we were able to attend the DMC after all. My father's problem never returned. Baba said that a red snake had bitten him in his childhood and this problem had arisen as a result."

3 **Kirtan:** This practice originated in the Rarh region of India in ancient times, but Chaitanya was instrumental in giving it the wide popularity it now enjoys. He also popularized singing kirtan while performing the *lalita marmika* dance, which is done with the hands raised overhead to symbolize both surrender to the Divine and opening oneself to receive the divine energy. Kirtan can also be done while sitting. The kirtan mantra that Chaitanya used was the ever-popular "Hare Rama Hare Krishna."

4 **Bhajan:** Devotional song. "He [Mahaprabhu] said that the lyrics of the song should directly reflect Parama Purusha himself. And this category of song, directly reflecting

Paramapurusha, is known as kirtan. The other category of song that also reflects Paramapurusha, but which expresses many tangential ideas before returning to the one central idea of Paramapurusha, is called bhajan. This is the basic difference between bhajan and kirtan." Anandamurti, *A Few Problems Solved, Part 3* (Calcutta: Ananda Marga Publications, 1988), 10.

5 **... ki jai:** A popular Indian slogan that literally means "victory to..." It is sometimes translated as "long live..."

6 **Bujali:** A type of short sword similar to a machete.

7 **Stamban kriya:** *Stamban* means "stopping," "retention," or "stupefaction." *Kriya* means "action." *Stamban kriya* is a type of psychic power whereby one person can induce a temporary paralysis in another person.

XX: A Civil Ceremony

1 Anandamurti, *Discourses on Tantra*, volume two, 41.

2 **Marriage procession:** In traditional wedding processions in India, the groom rides the lead elephant and a band brings up the rear.

3 **Arati:** A traditional Hindu ritual that includes the chanting of the arati mantras and the waving of incense and lamps in a prescribed manner in front of an image of the deity. It has also become part of the Indian spiritual tradition for devotees to perform arati in front of their guru. While Baba generally discouraged such practices, he always made a point of respecting local traditions.

4 **Bhagavad Gita:** In later years, Baba pointed out in private that since the Sanskrit language of the Bhagavad Gita is the language of 1200 years ago, it shows that the Gita was rewritten at this time by the Vaishnavites. Baba said that at that time the Vaishnavites were in conflict with the Shaivites, so they added a number of new chapters in order to bolster their arguments. He mentioned that the original Gita ended when Krishna showed his universal form to Arjuna, making the point that after going into trance, Arjuna would have been in no condition to continue the conversation.

5 **Marga Mata:** *Mata* means "mother" in Sanskrit, thus "mother of the Marga."

XXI: For The Welfare And Happiness Of All

1 Anandamurti, *Idea and Ideology*, 7th ed. (Calcutta: Ananda Marga Publications, 1993), 75.

2 **Avatar:** The concept of avatar or incarnation has a strong hold in Indian culture and spiritual writings. It is generally accepted that the great masters of the past were incarnations of God. Baba, however, did not support this theory. "Incarnation is an illogical hypothesis. The whole universe being created out of him and by him is his incarnation. The term *avatara* means a 'derivation,' and the application of this term to individual units who are far advanced in the process of *pratisaincara* [evolution] is a misleading misnomer. It is illogical to consider that the Macrocosm metamorphosed himself directly into some unit structure, in most cases a human being. Human beings are the most

evolved individual units as a class in his creation, and every stage of the elevated psychic Mahápurusha [great soul] is the result of *saincara* [involution] and then pratisaincara. It is a gradual elevation and not an abrupt descent or occurrence. Logically speaking, therefore, it will be correct to designate any unit consciousness as an incarnation of God or to say that the Messenger of God traverses the path of saincara, goes through a process of evolution, and through psychic dilation in the process of pratisaincara reaches different stages of elevation. The incarnation theory, or *avatáraváda*, however, hypothesizes that the incarnated being is the direct descent of the Almighty, the rest of his creation remaining unexplained as to its source of origin." (*Ibid.*, 43)

3 *Ibid.*, 63.

4 **Crude, subtle and causal:** Baba generally employed the terms "crude," "subtle" and "causal" mind as the English equivalents for the corresponding Sanskrit terms, rather than the more popular "conscious," "subconscious," and "unconscious," because he considered the latter two terms too imprecise or misleading.

5 **Ectoplasm:** The word Baba commonly employed to refer to mind as a psychic substance. He also used the word "mindstuff," which was his English equivalent for the Sanskrit word *citta*.

6 Anandamurti, *Idea and Ideology*, 11.

7 **Varna:** The word that Baba used for "dominant psychology"; *varna*, literally means "color." It refers to a person's psychic color. The four *varnas* are symbolized by the colors black, red, white, and yellow. Interestingly, the words that Baba used for the four *varnas* are the same words used in Hinduism to denote the four major castes, suggesting that the idea of the four castes may have evolved in ancient India due to an awareness of the four psychological types, later degenerating into the dogmatic, hereditary divisions that we are familiar with today, and which Baba so vehemently opposed.

8 Anandamurti, *Idea and Ideology*, 67.

9 *Ibid.*, 68.

10 *Ibid.*

11 **Sadvipra:** "Sadvipras, or spiritual revolutionaries, will inspire and mobilize the crusading human spirit against barbarity, injustice and rapacity, and help accelerate the speed of antithetical social movement. Afterwards, during the stage of synthesis, they will take the leadership of society into their own hands. If proper adjustments are maintained with time, space and person, the sadvipra-inspired synthetic age will be permanent. In a society governed and administered by these sadvipras, the synthetic structure of society will remain intact, although different eras may come and go. The Shudra era will come but there will be no exploitation by the Shudras. The Kshattriya era will come, but exploitation by the Kshattriyas will not be possible because of the synthetic order prevailing in society. Only sadvipras can constantly maintain proper adjustment with time, space and person. Those who propagate materialist philosophies, but are not morally and spiritually conscious, are quite incapable of constantly maintaining such proper adjustments, for all changes take place within the purview of relativity. Those who have accepted the Supreme Entity as their goal, those who really believe in universal humanism and reflect universalism in the fullest measure, are alone capable of constantly maintaining proper adjustment, for under the influence of a spiritual ideal their temperaments become great and benevolent. Due to their benevolent idealism and mental development they naturally look upon all with love and affection. They can never do any injustice in any particular era or to a particular individual. Sadvipra

society is both the aspiration and demand of the oppressed humanity." Anandamurti, *A Few Problems Solved, Part 2*, 9.
12 Anandamurti, *Idea and Ideology*, 80.
13 *Ibid.*, 81.
14 *Ibid.*
15 **Five fundamental principles of Prout:** "(1) No individual should be allowed to accumulate any physical wealth without the clear permission or approval of the collective body. (2) There should be maximum utilization and rational distribution of all mundane, supramundane and spiritual potentialities of the universe. (3) There should be maximum utilization of physical, metaphysical and spiritual potentialities of the unit and collective bodies of the human society. (4) There should be a proper adjustment amongst these physical, metaphysical, mundane, supra-mundane and spiritual utilizations. (5) The method of utilization should vary in accordance with the changes in time, space and person and the utilization should be of a progressive nature." (*Ibid.*, 81)

XXII: To The Patriots

1 Baba's message to the Margis, May 1956. Anandamurti, *Ananda Vanii Samgraha*, 1.
2 **Zamindar:** The zamindar or zamindari system was created by the Mughals to collect taxes from the peasants. In time it became a generic term to refer to landed interests.
3 **Vira bhava:** Literally, "ideation of courage."
4 Sarkar, P. R., *To the Patriots*, 4th ed. (Calcutta: Ananda Marga Publications, 1993), 14.
5 *Ibid.*, 18.
6 *Ibid.*, 25.
7 *Ibid.*, 31.

XXIII: A Family Relationship

1 Anandamurti, *Baba in Fiesch* (Rungsted Kyst: Proutist Universal, 1979), 41.
2 **Lost discourses:** The organization first purchased a tape recorder in late 1960 or early 1961, but in the early and mid-sixties it was only used to record Baba's DMC and RU talks. In general, it was difficult for the Margis at that time to get Baba's permission to record his talks. Indeed, they could not even take notes without his permission. Occasionally, he asked for certain talks to be noted down, those he wished to be preserved, but he made it clear that some of what he said was directed to certain individuals only and was thus personal, and certain discussions concerned sensitive matters that were not for public consumption. By the late 1960s, however, he began to relax his restrictions. These recordings have been published in the series entitled *Ananda Vacamrtam*.
3 **Cosmic sound:** As the kundalini rises in the process of spiritual elevation, the meditator, as he or she enters deeper and deeper into trance, hears the cosmic sound generated by the Supreme Consciousness in the never-ending process of creation; this sound is known as the *omkara* or simply om. When the kundalini crosses the first chakra, the *muladhara*, the sound resembles the drone of crickets. When it crosses the second

chakra, the *svadhisthana*, it resembles the sound of ankle bells. When it crosses the third chakra, the *manipura*, it resembles a sweet flute sound. Crossing the fourth chakra, the *anahata*, it resembles something between the sound of the sea and the sound of a deep gong. At the fifth chakra, the sound becomes clearly discernible as om. Reaching the sixth chakra, the sound disappears as the unit mind merges into the Cosmic Mind in the state of savikalpa samadhi.

4 **Baba's toe:** His toe was not abnormally large, but he made it appear so in this instance in order to satisfy Gwarda's desire.

5 **Tic-tics:** One of Baba's favorite forms of punishment. They are done by grabbing one's ears with the opposite hand and doing deep knee bends. Public tic-tics, Baba once said, are good for diminishing one's ego. They have also been shown to be beneficial for the brain and have recently been popularized under the name "superbrain yoga."

6 **Women's seating:** This would happen when there was a large crowd. Normally the women would sit on one side of the room or at the back.

7 **Arun:** He would later become the monastic disciple Acharya Cidghananda Avadhuta.

8 **Paramatma:** Literally, "Supreme Soul."

9 **Siddha:** A class of *devayoni* or luminous body. In *Yoga Psychology*, Baba says: "Wherever there is any spiritual gathering, siddhas come. And during a musical function, whenever the mind of a particular artist becomes concentrated, they will see the luminous bodies of gandharvas. Similarly, during meditation, or particularly during kirtan, when a spiritual aspirant's mind becomes concentrated, they will feel the existence of those siddhas. In Jamalpur, in the area of the tiger's grave, there were assemblages of large numbers of siddhas. One of our senior family acharyas used to see them." Anandamurti, *Yoga Psychology* (Calcutta: Ananda Marga Publications, 1987), 18.

10 **Service toilet:** An outdoor toilet with a chamber-pot system; a type of outhouse.

11 **Toilet cleaners**: This work was done by one of the lower castes; they were considered untouchables before independence and were later included among the scheduled castes. It was unthinkable for a Brahmin, such as Jaidhari, to do such work.

12 **Original verse:** *Daevii hyeshá gunamayii mama máyá duratyayá; mámeva ye prapadyante máyámetám taranti te.*

XXIV: The Tiger's Grave

1 Anandamurti, *Ananda Vacamrtam, Part 31* (Calcutta: Ananda Marga Publications, 1997), 68.

2 **Bhima:** One of the heroes of the Mahabharata, renowned for his strength and his bravery. He was the second of the five Pandava brothers and a disciple of Krishna.

3 **Beggars:** During his childhood, Vishvanath's grandmother used to take him to the Vishvanath temple, where he would watch the beggars while she did her worship.

4 **Gita Press:** One of the foremost publishers of religious books in India. It advertises itself with the following words: "The institution's main objective is to promote and spread the principles of Sanatana Dharma, the Hindu religion, among the general public by publishing the Gita, Ramayana, Upanishads, Puranas, discourses of eminent Saints and other character-building books & magazines and marketing them at highly subsidized

prices. The institution strives for the betterment of life and the well-being of all. It aims to promote the art of living as propounded in the Gita for peace & happiness and the ultimate upliftment of mankind." Gita means "song." When people say "the Gita," they are referring to the Bhagavad Gita.
5 **MSc:** Master in Science degree.
6 **Rajnath:** He would later become the monastic disciple Acharya Ramananda Avadhuta.

XXV: Personal Contact

1 Anandamurti, *Ananda Vacamrtam, Part 3*, 2nd ed. (Calcutta: Ananda Marga Publications, 1986), 11.
2 **Rajendra Pandey:** He would later become a leading advocate in Akbarpur, U.P.
3 **Dukhaharan:** Literally, "stealer of pain." It was so called because by removing the disciples' samskaras, Baba was saving them from a far greater suffering.
4 **Punishment:** In later years, when faced with particularly serious misdeeds or crimes on the part of his disciples, Baba would sometimes ask them if they wanted punishment from him or from nature (sometimes he would say "Yamaraja," the god of death). He told the disciples on occasion that had such people received punishment directly from nature, it would have been much more severe. On these occasions, Baba took the greater portion of the samskaras on himself. As mentioned earlier, he once told Dasarath that by personally taking on those samskaras, he could thereby neutralize them. Sometimes these samskaras were so severe, he said, that had he transferred them to a rock, the rock would have been reduced to ashes. It was thus that this disciple could get off with such a light punishment, considering the magnitude of his crime.
5 **Saincara and Pratisaincara:** *Saincara* is the process of involution wherein the pure, undifferentiated Supreme Consciousness gradually passes through successive stages of crudification under the influence of Prakriti. First, it metamorphoses itself into the different layers of the Cosmic Mind and then into the different layers of the material universe. *Pratisaincara* is the process of evolution wherein consciousness, within the arena of the living being, gradually evolves out of matter, where it had been lying dormant. In this process, it retraces its steps back to its original state, which is realized when the human being, as the most evolved living being, attains God-realization. Together *saincara* and *pratisaincara* form the *brahmachakra*, the cycle of creation. Both processes are described in great detail in *Idea and Ideology*.

XXVI: Revolutionary Marriage

1 Anandamurti, *A Few Problems Solved, Part 1*, 54.
2 **Mukti and moksha:** Mukti is often translated as "liberation" and moksha as "salvation." Technically, mukti means merging the unit mind into the Cosmic Mind at the time of death, equivalent to the state of savikalpa samadhi. Moksha means merging the

unit consciousness into the Cosmic Consciousness at death, equivalent to the state of nirvikalpa samadhi. Moksha is the culminating point of the spiritual journey.

3 **Love marriage:** In traditional Indian society, as in many traditional societies, marriages were generally arranged by the families. The parents would choose a suitable bride or groom for their child and then enter into negotiations with the other family. It was generally accepted that the parents, with the wisdom afforded by their years, were best able to select a suitable match for their child. While this practice still continues today, especially in rural areas and in more orthodox families, there is a greater and greater incidence of young people falling in love and deciding to get married, due to the increasing influence of other cultures and the natural tide of social change. Such a marriage is commonly called a "love marriage" in India to differentiate it from an arranged marriage.

4 **Tanmatra:** Literally, "that minutest portion." In Ananda Marga philosophy, *tanmatra* refers to the emanations of the five fundamental factors through which the process of perception is activated. In *Idea and Ideology*, Baba explains: "Every *bhuta* [fundamental factor] from the ethereal to the solid is in an eternal flow. The very existence of *bhutatattva* is just a pattern of waves, a microscopic fraction of waves taken in a collective form by the sensory organs-cum-Citta. These microscopic fractions carried through waves are called *tanmatras*. Hence tanmatras are nothing but the waves produced by the objects concerned as a result of reflection of the subtler bhuta on the cruder ones. Tanmatras in the mathematical sense are not something homogeneous. They are heterogeneous in character and their heterogeneity gives rise to the varieties in the perceptible external world. The heterogeneity is specialized by the difference in wavelengths amongst different tanmatras within or without the scope of any particular bhuta." (Anandamurti, *Idea and Ideology*, 20)

5 **Rabindra Samgita:** The songs composed by Rabindranath Tagore. *Samgita* means "song." It is tradition in India to refer to the body of songs composed by an Indian composer with their first name followed by *Samgita*.

6 **Baba's inspections:** While Baba's inspections were rightly feared by those who had discrepancies or shortages to hide, he never neglected the welfare of the offending parties. On one occasion, he was sent to inspect the accounts of an officer who was suspected of illegitimate dealings. When the officer learned of the pending inspection, he went to Baba, confessed to the irregularities, and begged him not to expose him, since he had a large family to feed and could not afford to lose his job. Baba told him that he could not consider his request since he was bound to do his duty properly. He did the inspection, handed in his report, and the man lost his job. Once he was dismissed, however, Baba gave him money out of his own pocket, enough to support his family for a week, and before the week was up, he secured a position for him in a private firm.

7 **Foreign:** The name was later changed to "overseas."

XXVII: A Monastic Order Begins

1 Anandamurti, *Ananda Marga Ideology and Way of Life, Part 9*, 648.
2 **Sutra:** The word *sutra* literally means "thread." However, in this case it can best be translated by the English word "aphorism," the expression of an idea or constellation of ideas in the most succinct manner possible. By analogy, a sutra connects a group

of ideas around a central key concept, just as a thread can be interwoven with many other strands. Historically, the tradition of writing sutras developed in the time before the invention of written script. In those days, a text needed to be memorized in order to be passed on. Thus, in order to facilitate the memorization of difficult philosophical teachings, the tradition developed of summarizing an argument or nexus of ideas in one succinct phrase that could be easily committed to memory. A teacher would customarily give a class or a discourse on a certain sutra. Once the disciple understood the argument and its supporting ideas, he or she could then recall them by remembering the sutra. By committing to memory the body of sutras (texts rarely consisted of much more than a hundred sutras), disciples would then have the entire philosophy at their fingertips. There have been many important texts written in the form of sutras, not only spiritual texts but other types of treatises as well. However, the most famous of these is *Patanjali Yoga Darshan* (Patanjali's philosophy of yoga), more popularly known as the Yoga Sutras. It serves as the fundamental text for most modern schools of yoga. It contains what is arguably the most famous sutra of all time: *yogash cittavrittinirodha*—yoga is the cessation of the thought waves of the mind.

3 Anandamurti, *Ananda Sutram*, 2nd ed. (Calcutta: Ananda Marga Publications, 1996), 1.

4 *Ibid.*, 4.

5 **Two refutations:** While predominantly a concept of Western theistic religions, the belief in heaven and hell is also found in certain Eastern theistic sects. Baba's sutra on truth, *brahma samyam jagadapi satyámaekshikam*, deliberately echoes Shankaracharya's famous sutra, *Brahma samyam jagat mithya* (Brahma is truth, the world is false), a concept that has dominated Indian spiritual thought for centuries.

6 **Asim's powers:** In later years, Asim, by then the monastic disciple Sambuddhananda, would become well-known for his ability to diagnose the hidden causes of people's maladies just by looking at them, including the antecedents that had led to the development of those maladies. He became an adept in curing such people through the practice of yoga therapy, whose principles and treatments Baba had taught him.

7 **Master Dhiren:** At that time, there were two young disciples named Dhiren who both became wholetimers and later avadhutas. In order to differentiate them, Baba called one Master Dhiren, since he was a teacher. His name later became Acharya Vijayananda Avadhuta. The other Dhiren became Acharya Nirmalananda Avadhuta.

8 **Vishvabandhu:** He would later become a monastic disciple, Acharya Vandanananda Avadhuta.

9 **Amar Sen:** He was Baba's childhood friend and co-worker in the railway workshop. He also did military service together with Baba and had a number of interesting stories to tell from those days, such as the time he and Baba were out on patrol in the wilds of Assam and came upon a Bengal tiger coming down from the hills. Amar was terrified but Baba maintained his usual calm. He looked at the tiger and the tiger at him. Both were motionless for a minute or so; then the tiger bowed his head and ambled off into the brush.

10 **Pratima:** Literally, "image."

11 **Rudraksha beads and vermillion paste:** Many people in India associate these two things with avidya Tantrics.

12 **Ramesh and Asim:** They were given the monastic names Acharya Pranavananda Avadhuta and Acharya Sambuddhananda Avadhuta.

XXVIII: The Search For The City Of Bliss

1 Anandamurti, *A Few Problems Solved, Part 4* (Calcutta: Ananda Marga Publications, 1988), 38.

2 **Benares Hindu University and Vishvabharati:** Benares Hindu University is Asia's largest residential university. It began as an idealistic proposal on the part of Mrs. Annie Besant, head of the Theosophical Society, and Pundit Madan Mohan Malaviya, who then organized the fundraising work that would turn their dream into a reality. Vishvabharati is the renowned university established by Rabindranath Tagore. After using the money he received from the Nobel Prize in 1912 to start the project, he went on numerous fundraising tours to finance its development.

3 **Kapil:** He lived approximately five thousand years ago. He was the propounder of the world's oldest philosophy, Sankhya, the first of the six Indian systems of philosophy and the philosophical basis for Patanjali's system of yoga. Kapil was the first known philosopher to propound the theory of cause and effect and is generally considered to be the world's first true philosopher.

4 **Magadha:** The ancient kingdom of Magadha covered most of Southern Bihar and extended into parts of Uttar Pradesh and Bengal. Both Buddhism and Jainism originated in Magadha. Rarh extends from the western plateau to the Ganges Delta of modern-day West Bengal.

5 **Thana:** A police station. It also refers to the area under the jurisdiction of that police station, i.e. a subdivision of a municipality. Anandanagar would soon grow to over three thousand acres as the organization continued to purchase the surrounding lands.

6 **Ara DMC:** Baba was welcomed at the station by a huge procession of Margis; the procession included a special elephant with a maharaja's throne atop it that had been hired to carry Baba through the streets of Ara. Midway through the procession, Baba had to jump down from the elephant into a makeshift net—four Margis holding tight to a folded dhoti—because a live electric wire was strung low across the road and the mahout was unable to get the elephant to stop. Baba later wrote a detailed account of this incident in his series on linguistics, *Sabda Cayanika*. "I looked behind me and saw that the accident had been avoided. The elephant was sitting down, but his trunk was now dancing to the same beat that his feet had been dancing to before. The members of the procession had formed a circle around him, all of them dancing to that same beat. Their joyful sound, their booming 'Jaya,' and the stanzas of their song, were reverberating throughout the atmosphere—*Ánhár bhaila dúr ráh bancke cable ho; kekar gahab ho málik kekar gahab ho* (Darkness is over, behold the proper path and proceed; say, O my master, whose glory can I sing). How they danced around the elephant that day!" (author's translation)

7 **Shava sadhana:** In this rare and misunderstood practice, the sadhaka animates the dead body by supplying it with vital energy through a specific technique, thereby activating the lower five chakras. The body does not have a mind, only the physical expression of energy. The sadhaka then, through a type of struggle, removes that vital energy, returning the body to its original inert state. As with other forms of kapalik sadhana, one of the principle objectives is to overcome the fear propensity.

XXIX: Education, Relief, And Welfare

1 Baba's message to the Margis, January 1973. Anandamurti, *Ananda Vanii Samgraha*, 21.
2 **Relief team:** This team was formally registered in 1970 as AMURT, the Ananda Marga Universal Relief Team. AMURT is an NGO and has received commendations from governments and private organizations for its work in different parts of the globe, in both disaster relief and long-term relief projects. It is the first international relief organization to be founded in a so-called Third World country.
3 Sarkar, P. R., *Prout in a Nutshell, Part 18*, 38.
4 *Ibid.*
5 Sarkar, P. R., *Human Society, Part Two*, 1.
6 **Arun:** Soon afterwards, Arun became the monastic disciple Acharya Svarupananda Avadhuta.
7 **Rarh:** In 1981, Baba dictated a book on the history of Rarh entitled *Rarh: The Cradle of Civilization*.

XXX: Past Lives

1 Anandamurti, *Yoga Psychology*, 7.
2 **Vishvanath:** This is not Acharya Vishvanath Singh, who appears elsewhere in this book. This Vishvanath is an engineer from Danapur.
3 **Sarasvati:** The goddess of knowledge. It is tradition in India for Hindu students to worship Sarasvati and make an offering to her before any important exam.
4 **Pajama:** Thin, baggy pants, sometimes called "yogi pants" in the US. They are one of the traditional garments of India, serving as an alternative to the dhoti, which is considered more formal wear. It is from Hindi that the word "pajamas" entered the English language.
5 **Catch his thread:** A Hindi expression that means to show the link between the past and the present: *Mai usko rasi pagra deta hun*.
6 **Past life:** Baba also showed this past life of Vijay, by then named Acharya Parashivananda Avadhuta, during a demonstration in Ranchi in 1969.
7 **Lila:** Literally, "divine play" or "divine sport"; that action which is beyond cause and effect. It carries the implication that the mystery of God's desire as he plays with his creation is beyond explanation. "If human beings try to trace the cause behind this divine *liilá* or sport, they will never succeed, because the Cosmic Mind is the source of all causes, the source of all the unit minds. Now if the unit minds want to know the cause, they will have to go back to the Supreme Source; but it is impossible for them to do this. If they ideate on the Supreme, then one day all their thoughts will be suspended in Parama Purusha, and they will no longer be able to think—their minds will stop functioning. In that state of mindlessness, there remains only the Soul or Self (Átman). So if you really want to reach the source of your life you will have to lose your mind, and when your mind is non-existent, how can you run after that Supreme Entity? In logic this is called the fallacy of infinite regress: your mind cannot make any statement

about an entity whose origin must remain forever unknown." Anandamurti, *Subhasita Samgraha*, Part 18 (Calcutta: Ananda Marga Publications, 1992), 27.
8 **MBBS:** Bachelor of Medicine, Bachelor of Surgery. It requires five years of study and is the minimum degree for practicing allopathic medicine in India.
9 **Goenka:** Shyama Sundara is the brother of S. N. Goenka, the world-renowned teacher of Vipassana meditation. Though they have their philosophical differences when it comes to spirituality, each has great respect for the other's practice.

XXXI: In The Office

1 Anandamurti, *Elementary Philosophy*, 5nd ed., 128.
2 **Prediction:** This prediction would prove perfectly accurate. Pulak continued to have problems with his sister-in-law and credited Baba's advice with having saved him from a number of embarrassing situations.
3 **Hati cale . . . :** A Hindi saying that means, "the elephant walks through the market; thousands of dogs bark."
4 **Breakup of Soviet Union:** On another occasion, Baba told Gokul that the men in his family were generally short-lived, so he did not expect to cross seventy. He died at the age of sixty-eight, two weeks before the Berlin wall came down.
5 **Asanas:** These three yoga postures are generally known in English as the shoulder-stand, the peacock, and the twist.
6 **Past-life memories:** In his book *Yoga Psychology*, Baba discussed in detail the phenomena of young children remembering incidents from their past lives: "The memory of its past life remains awake for approximately the first five years of its new life. Although the child remains in a new physical environment, mentally it continues to live the joys and sorrows of its previous life. That is why children sometimes laugh and cry in their sleep, and their mothers often think they are talking with God. In colloquial Bengali this is called *deola kátá*. In actual fact, this laughter and crying is nothing but the reappearance of past memories. To re-experience past events one does not need the cooperation of the old brain. The newly born mind has not yet had time to build a close relationship with the new brain. The revival of past experiences is what we call 'extracerebral memory,' and is the principal task of the causal mind. The experiences of a crude mind cannot be reflected in a subtle mind. In the case of a child, since the crude experiences are relatively few, the subtle mind remains tranquil. Thus the waves of the causal mind easily surface in the child's subtle mind. As a result, the accumulated experiences of the child's previous life can easily be recollected. As the child's crude mind is not yet mature enough to work externally, the dream experiences are not expressed in the wakeful state. This extra-cerebral memory begins to fade after five years . . . Sometimes children can remember their past life even after the age of five. In this case the mind of the new body remains free from environmental influences. That is, the waves of the external world are unable to influence the mind. Such people are called *jatismara*, or one who remembers one's past lives. Normally, the extra-cerebral memory of such people remains active up to the age of twelve. If one still remembers one's past life after that it becomes difficult to survive, because two minds will try to function in one body—the mind of this life and that of the previous one. A single body cannot tolerate the clashes of two minds,

hence psycho-physical parallelism is lost leading to eventual death. Forgetfulness is a providential decree . . . The problems of one life alone are enough to make people restless. If they had to face the problems of several lives, they would be unable to lead a natural life." (Anandamurti, *Yoga Psychology*, 6)
7 **Meeting Lakshmikant:** In 1999, Acharya Pranavatmakananda and I met Kamalapati Singh, who had just turned eighty, at his home in Monghyr. When he first saw us in front of his gate, he said, "I know your Baba better than you!" He took us up to the roof and told us stories about his long association with Baba (he joined the accounts office in 1943), among them this story, which we had already heard from Shiva Shankar, N. C. Gangully, and others. Throughout the conversation, he continually expressed his devotion for Baba, whom he considered to be his guru and his guide, though he was not a disciple of Ananda Marga. Near the end of the interview, we discovered that he was living there with his two brothers, Lakshmikant and Sanjay, although neither was at home at the time. Afterward, when we were going out the gate to the street, we saw an old man walking toward us accompanied by a couple of teenage boys. As he approached, I noticed a beatific smile on his face and an aura of saintliness. We both wondered if this could be Lakshmikant. When we asked him if he was, the old man gave us his namaskar and nodded. Then Acharya Pranavatmakananda turned on the video camera and asked him if he could say something about his experience with Baba. With a radiant smile Lakshmikant said, "What can I say? I owe him my life. My life belongs to him." Dada asked him the same question several times, but the only reply we got was, "What is there to say? He gave me my life. My life belongs to him."

XXXII: Last Years In Jamalpur

1 Sarkar, P. R., *The Thoughts of P. R. Sarkar*, 81.
2 **Shamiana:** A decorative, circus-style tent generally used for hosting outdoor events.
3 **Deoghar:** This temple town has many beggars.
4 **Reporting session:** As the monastic order became established, Baba started conducting periodic reporting and planning sessions with the wholetimers. He would take reports on various organizational activities in their respective areas or departments, analyze the problems, and propose solutions, in addition to planning how to expand the organization in those areas. Eventually these meetings were given the name RDS, an abbreviation for "review, defect, solution."
5 **Dada:** The word "Dada" (elder brother) is commonly used in Ananda Marga as a respectful form of address for male sannyasis.
6 **Mahamriytu:** *Mrityu* means "death"; *mahamrityu* means "great death." It is synonymous with liberation.
7 **Gopinath Kabiraj:** Stimulated by Baba's remarks, both Satyananda and Nirmohananda would later visit Gopinath and hold discussions with him about Tantra and Baba, with whose work Gopinath was well acquainted.
8 **Reunification:** On an earlier field walk in Jamalpur, Baba told Harinder of Trimohan that in the future both Germanys, both Vietnams, both Bengals, both Kashmirs, both

Punjabs, and all such divided societies would become one again. They were artificially divided and it was God's will that they become reunited.

9 **Vishesh yoga:** An advanced meditation practice consisting of numerous lessons that Baba taught to certain selected disciples. The word *vishesh* means "special."

10 **Pranay's departure:** Before Pranay left, he developed a theory that as Anandamurti, the guru, Baba was divine and infallible, but as P. R. Sarkar, the president of the organization, he was human and therefore fallible. On one of my visits to him to collect material for this book, he repeated his theory to me once again. His wife Pramila was also present. She remarked that it was this kind of thinking that had been the cause of his downfall. Pranay laughed. Then he said, "You know, there is no separation between myself and Gurudeva. No disciple is closer to Baba than I am—then or now." Then Pramila started telling a fascinating story of a basket of mangos that Baba sent Pranay shortly before Baba left his body, while Pranay nodded and added a few proud, smiling comments. But that is a story that will only appear in a later volume.

11 **PC for ladies:** In India, it would have generated a tremendous scandal had Baba given individual personal contact to women, since it would have involved being alone in the same room with a female for a period of time, something that was completely unacceptable in Indian society. After Baba's marriage, he began receiving small groups of women in the presence of his wife, especially the female wholetimers. After Baba's first visit to the West, he started giving personal contact to small groups of female devotees, but always in the presence of a female sannyasi.

12 **Mirabai:** (Mira for short) A sixteenth-century Rajput princess from Rajasthan who became famous as both a poet and a saint. She was renowned for her burning devotion to Krishna and the many mystical and devotional songs she composed, which are still immensely popular throughout India. There are many inspiring stories of Mirabai's life that have passed into popular lore. For example, when Mirabai approached the famous saint Ravidas for initiation, she was told by one of his disciples that the master did not meet or initiate women. She asked that disciple to convey a message to the master— "Tell me, who is a second *purush* in this world?"—thus implying that all human beings are female before the Lord. (The word *purush* means both "Divine Consciousness" and "man.") When the master heard the message, he realized that the person who sent it was a great devotee. He came out to meet her and agreed to give her initiation. Baba once did a demonstration in which he asked Dasarath to concentrate in sadhana and describe what he heard. He described a beautiful female voice singing a devotional song in a language he couldn't completely understand, but which seemed to be a dialect of Marathi. Baba said that it was the Braj language and explained that he was hearing Mirabai singing one of her songs some four hundred years earlier. He said that the sound was still traveling in the cosmos and that one day scientists would develop instruments that would be able to record such phenomena.

XXXIII: Departure

1 Sarkar, P. R., *The Thoughts of P. R. Sarkar*, 53.
2 **Private coach:** Shyama Narayan Srivastava was the Divisional Traffic Superintendent of Gorakhpur Division at that time, which is why he had a private coach.

3 Anandamurti, *Ananda Marga Ideology and Way of Life*, part 10 (Calcutta: Ananda Marga Publications, 1988), 712.
4 **Resignation:** Baba never did resign, nor did he ever withdraw his provident fund.

Epilogue

1 Anandamurti, *Namami Krsnasundaram*, 2nd ed. (Calcutta: Ananda Marga Publications, 1997), 9.
2 **Poisoning:** In late 1974, an inquiry commission concluded that Baba had been deliberately administered an overdose of barbiturates by the jail doctor; in addition, the Civil Surgeon went on record as saying that he had not been consulted on the prescription.
3 **Liquid:** For a time, Baba was taking two cups of yoghurt water; later he took water mixed with Horlicks.
4 Schneider, Vimala, *The Politics of Prejudice* (Denver: Ananda Marga Publications, 1983), 10.
5 **Jail Doctor:** The doctor told me this story in August 1977, shortly before I entered Baba's cell to see him for the first time.
6 **Elections:** Another reason why she allowed the elections was that she received an intelligence report assuring her that she would easily win.

About The Author

Devashish holds an MFA in fiction from San Diego State University. He divides his time between Ananda Kirtana, a spiritual community in the Brazilian countryside, and his farm in Puerto Rico, where he has a yoga center and a tropical-fruit plantation.

CPSIA information can be obtained at www.ICGtesting.com
Printed in the USA
BVOW05s2119310314

349350BV00001B/15/P